complete

Tort Law

Text, Cases, and Materials

D1341663

complete

Tort Law

Text, Cases, and Materials

S. I. Strong

Liz Williams

OXFORD

UNIVERSITY PRESS

Great Clarendon Street, Oxford OX2 6DP

Oxford University Press is a department of the University of Oxford.
It furthers the University's objective of excellence in research, scholarship,
and education by publishing worldwide in

Oxford New York

Auckland Cape Town Dar es Salaam Hong Kong Karachi
Kuala Lumpur Madrid Melbourne Mexico City Nairobi
New Delhi Shanghai Taipei Toronto

With offices in

Argentina Austria Brazil Chile Czech Republic France Greece
Guatemala Hungary Italy Japan Poland Portugal Singapore
South Korea Switzerland Thailand Turkey Ukraine Vietnam

Oxford is a registered trade mark of Oxford University Press
in the UK and in certain other countries

Published in the United States
by Oxford University Press Inc., New York

British Library Cataloguing in Publication Data

Data available

Library of Congress Cataloging in Publication Data

Data available

Typeset by Newgen Imaging Systems (P) Ltd, Chennai, India
Printed in Great Britain
on acid-free paper by
Ashford Colour Press Ltd, Gosport, Hampshire

ISBN 978–0–19–929224–0

10 9 8 7 6 5 4 3 2 1

Dedication

Dedicated to Peter and Zachary—not that they will necessarily grow up to be lawyers, but that they will grow up to be whatever they want and do whatever they set their minds to do.

S.I. Strong

Dedicated to the memory of my grandparents and aunt—Tom, Isa, Jack and Elma—in gratitude for their love and encouragement.

Liz Williams

Guide to using the book

Complete Tort Law: Text, Cases, and Materials is complemented by a number of features which are designed to enrich your learning and provide additional support as you progress through your tort law module. This guide highlights the various features to help you to get the most out of your textbook.

> ● John H. Wigmore, *'The Tripartite Division of Torts'*, 8 Harvard Law Review 200
>
> If we are ever to have, as Sir Frederick Pollock puts it, not books about specif
> books about Tort in general, some further examination of fundamental ideas
> One might proceed with such a general analysis without regard to the definiti
> or—what is much the same thing—without setting forth one's view as to th
> ation of Tort-relations from others in the general classification of private law.
> sake of clearness, the latter task will here be briefly attempted…
> Private law, then, deals with the relations between members of the comm

Cases and materials

Cases play a pivotal role in shaping tort law, so it is important to read first-hand reports in order to fully understand the subject. This text includes extracts from a wide range of cases, legislation, and academic material which complement and illustrate the text.

> **think point**
> *Signs in restaurants and car parks often include disclaimers. What other disclaimers have you seen in your daily life?*
>
> must have taken reasonable steps to draw it to the c
> took place. The court will take into account factors su
> how obvious it was, how easy it was to see and read, a
> worded and not ambiguous. If the exclusion is part
> of contract law that the court has to consider in or
> exclusion is effective. These issues may include wheth
> incorporated into the contract, whether it is sufficientl
> to the contract has misled the other party as to wha

Think points

Why was a particular decision reached in a certain case? What everyday examples of torts might you already be familiar with? Thinking points throughout the text draw out these issues and encourage you to stop and reflect on some of the key issues.

> **TIP** Start keeping a running list of the torts you have studied, their defi-nitions and their elements. You will need this infor-mation for your examinations, par-ticularly problem questions.
>
> ally has two sub-elements: causation and remote
> must show that, had it not been for the breach, the
> Remoteness means that the claimant has to show th
> not so improbable that the defendant should not be
> these elements in turn. This chapter focuses on the
>
> In practice, judges often analyse facts in a way that
> various elements of negligence. The extent to whi
> be separated is a common essay question. For now
> possible in your own mind. Later, you can come ba

Tips

Helpful pieces of advice for learning and understanding specific aspects of tort law are designed to help make your studying easier and more efficient.

> **EXAM TIP** Because awards in respect of personal injury and death are so common, you can expect your examiners to test you on this. Be prepared!
>
> of civil actions that are started in the courts in the
> how to calculate these sorts of damages, one needs
> what a claimant can recover. The answers to these
> on whether death or simply personal injury occurred
>
> **Damages recoverable after death**
>
> When death occurs as a result of a tortious action,
> (1) the decedent in his or her own right (represented

Exam tips

These tips are focused particularly on helping you to maximize your performance in exams.

> **Exercise**
>
> You can find duties everywhere in your life—just think of all the situations in
> you have a responsibility to take care not to injure someone. For example, if
> you have a responsibility to other drivers and pedestrians to drive carefully
> share a duty not to injure you. For example, if you ride a bus, the driver has
> not to injure you. Make a list of everyday situations where you have a respon
> and where others have a responsibility to you. As you read, look out for princ
> you to work out whether each of those responsibilities is recognized as a le

Exercises

Practical tasks encourage you to engage with the material and practise applying your knowledge to check your understanding.

Notes

negligence on his part whereby she might suffer r
Asquith J., however, continued, at p. 518:

'There may be cases in which the drunkenness of t
extreme and so glaring that to accept a lift from H
ally and obviously dangerous occupation, intermed
walking on the edge of an unfenced cliff. It is not n
a case the maxim 'volenti non fit injuria' would app
fact that the driver's degree of intoxication fell shor

The question before us, I think, is whether, as a ma
Asquith J. refers to and, if so, whether this prese

These useful notes clarify and emphasize particular facts or points of law to help you in your studies.

Compare features

compare
A no-fault com-
pensation scheme
has, in fact, been
adopted in New
Zealand.

of an emotional nature, e.g., that these boys by
happened to do no harm to anyone but themselv
happened to think that the plaintiff should be comp
think that the deceased driver of the motor cycle, ha
ought to be compensated, and that leads into the n
ought to be a universal scheme for compensation
regard to fault.

Beyond that, appeal to the public conscience wou
galities according to moral turpitude, and I am imp
in *Jackson v Harrison*, 138 C.L.R. 438, 455: 'ther

Although tort law covers a wide range of very different top-ics, there are some common elements that span the entire course. The compare features highlight those elements to help you see how the various strands of tort law relate.

Cross reference notes

cross reference
Nettleship v Weston
[1971] 2 QB 691
involved learner
drivers and was dis-
cussed in chapter 3.

Nettleship v Weston [1971] 2 QB 691 by Lord Den

Knowledge of the risk of injury is not enough. N
of injury. Nothing will suffice short of an agreem
gence. The plaintiff must agree, expressly or im
injury that may befall him due to the lack of reas
more accurately, due to the failure of the defenda
of care that the law requires of him.

Another important principle is that consent which

These helpful notes make navigation quick and easy by pointing you to a different section or chapter where a topic is discussed in more detail.

Vocabulary

VOCABULARY
A 'dependent' is
someone financially
dependent on the
decedent and linked
by legal or familial
ties—a child, a
parent, a spouse,
etc.

For many years, the common law did not allow dep
a tortfeasor for losses the dependants suffered as a
the tortious act. An exception was made by statute,
in 1846 to allow the families of victims of railway ac
The initial legislation was gradually expanded over t
common law rule and allowing recovery in all type
The current statute, known as the Fatal Accidents
proper category of defendants, stating that:

Key terms are highlighted in colour when they first appear and are clearly and concisely explained in definition boxes. These terms are collected in a glossary which can be found on the Online Resource Centre that accompanies this book.

Examples

Courts also must decide which statute applies. For example, in *Shine v L*
of Tower Hamlets [2006] EWCA Civ 852, a boy hurt himself trying to lea
which turned out to be loose. The court found that he could not claim
from the council for breach of its statutory duty to maintain the highwa
bollard was not part of the highway—it was an article placed on the high
purposes, which meant it fell under a different statutory provision that d
a duty.

Because of the need to look closely at what the defendant is required to d
for the defendant to be liable in negligence without also being liable for h

Real life examples illustrate the law and help to bring the subject to life.

Revision tasks

revision
task

If, pursuant to an agreement, I spend time and money build
point where only the tyres and internal trim have to be adde
to say that our partly executed agreement has not formed
because we did not specify the types of tyres or trim). The co
not claim the price from you even though I had virtually buil
tual right to enforce the agreement I am asking for my barg
the courts leave me with an almost finished car but no mor
and have wasted expenses.

Each chapter ends with some revision tasks which recap the topic covered and encourage you to test your understanding of the law and apply your knowledge to different scenarios.

Guide to the Online Resource Centre

The Online Resource Centre that accompanies this book provides students and lecturers with ready to use teaching and learning resources. They are free of charge and are designed to maximize the learning and teaching experience.

www.oxfordtextbooks.co.uk/orc/strong_complete

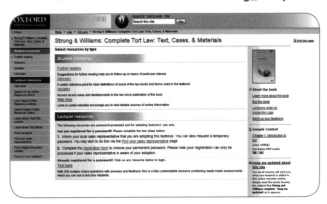

For students
These resources are accessible to all, enabling students to get the most from the textbook; no registration or password is required.

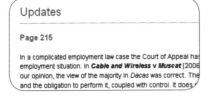

Regular updates

An indispensable resource providing access to recent cases and developments in the law that have occurred since publication of the book. These updates are accompanied by page references to the textbook, so you can see how the new developments relate to the existing case law.

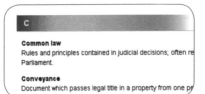

Glossary

A useful reference point for clear definitions of some of the key words and terms used in the textbook.

Web links

Law Society:
http://www.lawsociety.org.uk/home.law

Bar Council:
http://www.barcouncil.org.uk/

Legal Executives:

Web links

Links to useful websites encourage you to visit reliable sources of online information and direct your online study in order to work efficiently and effectively.

Chapter 08

On private nuisance:
G. Cross, 'Does Only the Careless Polluter Pay? A Fresh Ex

On nuisance and other torts:
C. Gearty, 'The Place of Nuisance in a Modern Law of Torts'

On private nuisance:

Further reading

Suggestions for further reading help you to follow up on topics of particular interest and highlight relevant established and recent texts, articles, and comments on many areas of tort law.

For lecturers

Password protected to ensure only lecturers can access the resource; each registration is personally checked to ensure the security of the site.

Registering is easy: click on 'Lecturer Resources' on the Online Resource Centre, complete a simple registration form which allows you to choose your own username and password, and access will be granted within 48 hours (subject to verification).

Which of these is **not** one of the three key questions you been a breach?

◉ What standard of care applies?
◉ How does the defendant's conduct compare to the sta
◉ Has the defendant's conduct caused any damage?
◉ How can I prove that there has been a breach?

1 out of 1

Test bank

Comprising 200 multiple choice questions with answers and feedback, this is a fully customizable resource containing ready-made assessments which you can use to test your students.

Preface

The books in this series reflect a new method of presenting legal materials to law students. Rather than presenting summaries of the law as it currently stands, this text and its companion editions utilize the casebook method, which provides readers with the judicial opinions and statutes as they appear in the original. Although some extracts are run into the text, the larger blocks of quoted materials are offset in different type for ease of identification. Although the materials in this book have been heavily edited, they will help students become familiar with the types of materials that they will encounter later in their careers. At the same time, the brevity of the excerpts will keep students from becoming discouraged, since many statutes and judicial decisions can be heavy going, even for experienced practitioners.

Even with new presentation methods, student legal texts can be quite dense. We have attempted to address some of these issues through the use of 'tip boxes' in the margins. These boxes include vocabulary, cross references, and additional ideas for consideration, as well as the occasional exam tip. Readers should not ignore the material in these boxes simply because it is offset from the main text—the information contained in the boxes is still useful and important.

Revision skills constitute an important part of any course of study, particularly in law, where both the materials and the concepts are very different from the subjects that are commonly studied at school. Therefore, we recommend that students read both chapter 1—which includes a number of suggestions on how to approach a course in law, in addition to an outline and guide to this particular text—and chapter 18—which addresses revision skills. A separate list of revision suggestions appears at the end of each substantive chapter. Students would be well advised to take heed of all of those items.

Finally, this series has taken the study of law into the twenty-first century by providing a wealth of additional information on the Oxford University Press website. The site for this particular book is found at www.oxfordtextbooks.co.uk/orc/strong_complete/. Not only will the online resource centre contain additional revision suggestions and material, it will contain a question bank that students can use to test themselves in the various areas of tort law.

The law is stated as we believe it to be on 31 August 2007.

S.I.S.

L.W.

Acknowledgements

The books in this series reflect a new method of presenting legal materials to law students. Rather than presenting summaries of the law as it currently stands, this text and its companion editions provide readers with the judicial opinions and statutes as they originally appear, albeit with considerable editing. The hope is that students will gain an increased familiarity with the materials that they will be working with later in their careers by working with them from the very beginning of their legal studies. Thus, the authors and series editors would like to thank the publishers for their support in making the project a reality.

No book can be created out of whole cloth. Although two names appear on the front cover, the expertise embodied in this book goes much deeper. In particular, Dr Strong would like to thank the following people for their personal and professional contributions to this text: colleagues and students, both past and present, at the University of Cambridge, the University of Oxford, and the University of Missouri; the many fine lawyers at Baker & McKenzie (London and Chicago offices) who supported this project; Dr Rosy Thornton of the University of Cambridge, for the first opportunity to teach tort, way back when; Sarah Hyland and Rachael Willis at OUP; and Liz Williams, without whom the book could not have been written.

Liz Williams would like to join Dr Strong in thanking Sarah and Rachael, and also to thank Dr Strong for the invitation to work on this project; Peter Schwartz and John Leadley for making it possible for her to accept; Lucinda Davies, Henry Garfield, Tristran Grimmer, Kathy Hall, Greg Lovell, Hajra Maka, Geoff Martin, Nicola Mead, Jennice Ng and Stefanie Worden of Baker & McKenzie (London) for invaluable help in editing the manuscript; her family, especially David, Giles, Ryan, Simon, Ben, Chris and Ros, for their forbearance; Ani, Anne, Dave, George, Marcus, Tat and many other friends for moral support and reassurance on the writing process; and finally, Katy, for knowing exactly when to provide cake.

Professor S.I. Strong

Liz Williams

Contents

Part 10: Revising for a Tort Exam

Chapter 18: Revising for a tort exam

Table of Cases

Table of Statutes

Table of Statutory Instruments

Part 1

Introduction to Tort

1 Introduction to tort

 ## 1.1 Introduction

Studying law opens doors in ways that other courses quite simply do not. While many people may single out the power and prestige of lawyers as the two most compelling reasons to read law, the truth is that knowledge of the law provides other benefits, even to those who will not eventually practice law or work in government. First, reading law teaches precision, both as a matter of analysis and as a matter of communication. Those who have graduated with a degree in law have learned to choose their words carefully and to look very closely at any piece of writing that is given to them. While these skills are obviously important to barristers and solicitors, they are also incredibly useful to people in business or public service. Second, those who have read law realize that it is a multi-faceted thing—criminal law, for example, is different from employment law, which is different from international law. Every area of specialization has its own quirks, so much so that questions about 'the law' usually lead practising lawyers to counter with 'what kind of law do you mean?'

Thus, student lawyers learn, from day one, that broad, sweeping generalizations about 'the law' are problematic. Instead, students are introduced to different areas of study, such as property law, contract law, and constitutional law, all of which makes intuitive sense. Property law deals with real property, i.e. land. Contract law deals with contract, meaning business agreements (students quickly learn that a contract need not be commercial in nature, but at least the concept of a contract is familiar). Constitutional law deals with overarching rights against the state and how the government conducts itself. Tort law, on the other hand, does not provide an easy or familiar way in, and few new students even know what a tort is before their first day of class. However, understanding tort is easier when you have a basic understanding of the social context in which this area of law is set. Therefore, this chapter will proceed as follows:

- Defining tort;
- Characteristics of a tort;
- The purpose of tort law;

- Principles of tort law;
- Policy and procedure;
- Factors affecting liability in tort;
- Motive and intent;
- Analysing torts; and
- Structure of the current text.

We will take each issue in turn.

1.2 Defining tort

Tort is a relatively young area of law and has only been in existence as a distinct area of study in the United Kingdom since 1860, when C.G. Addison's *Wrongs and Their Remedies: Being a Treatise on the Law of Torts* appeared on the bookshelves for the first time. However, the idea that tort law existed as a cohesive body of law was not readily adopted, and scepticism about the validity of tort as a separate branch of law continued for quite some time. In fact, one of the leading commentators of the day had problems even defining the term 50 years after *Addison on Torts* was originally published.

compare

The first treatise on tort in the English language was published by Francis Hilliard in the United States in 1859.

● Sir John C. Miles, et al., ***Digest of English Civil Law***, Book II (1910)

> No such definition of a tort can be offered. A tort, in English law, can only be defined in terms which really tell us nothing. A tort is a breach of a duty (other than a contractual or quasi-contractual duty) which gives rise to an action for damages. That is, obviously, a merely procedural definition of no value to the layman. The latter wants to know the nature of those breaches of duty which give rise to an action for damages. And the only that can be given to him is: 'Read this and the preceding volume.' To put it briefly, there is no English Law of Tort; there is merely an English Law of Torts, i.e., a list of acts and omissions which, in certain conditions, are actionable. Any attempt to generalize further, however interesting from a speculative standpoint, would be profoundly unsafe as a practical guide.

Experts in other common law jurisdictions had similar difficulties in classifying the types of wrongs that fell under the heading of tort.

● R.W. Lee, **'Torts and Delicts'**, 27 Yale Law Journal 721 (1918)

> The definition of a tort may be said to have baffled the text-book writers not so much on account of the inherent difficulty of the conception as because of the implication of the conception in questions of jurisdiction. It is a creation of the common law, a fact which rules out on the one side personal rights created by equity, and on the other, rights created by ecclesiastical or admiralty law. Further, it is usual to exclude from the definition most if not all of the rights and duties arising out of the family relation—that is, as regards the

> immediate parties. Again, a tort is usually defined negatively in such terms as to distinguish it from breach of contract, and sometimes also from the breach of duties, vaguely described as quasi-contractual. Perhaps none of the text-books succeeds in introducing all of these limitations into its definition.

As it turns out, the word 'tort' derives from the Latin 'tortus' or 'twisted', and was once in common usage in English as a general synonym for 'wrong'. Nowadays, the term exists only as a legal term meaning a civil wrong, other than a contractual wrong, for which an action in damages exist. Although the acts or omissions giving rise to certain torts—most obviously assault and battery—can resemble behaviour that leads to criminal charges being brought, the nature of the two cases are different. A civil action—including an action in tort—addresses the alleged wrongs visited upon one private individual or legal entity, such as a company, by another private individual or legal entity. Public entities—such as a local council or the BBC—can also be subject to an action in tort. A criminal action, on the other hand, arises when the state, in the form of the Crown Prosecution Service, identifies an individual who has violated a provision of the criminal code. Criminal cases always involve the Crown against an individual defendant. If the Crown prevails, the defendant faces imprisonment or a fine payable to the state. In civil cases, a losing defendant never faces imprisonment and will pay any award of damages to the other party, not to the state.

NOTE Those who act wrongly can face several different types of actions simultaneously. For example, if Joe slaps Sheila across the face, Joe can be brought up on criminal charges by the state and can also face an action in tort, if Sheila decides to sue him for damages associated with his actions. Thus Joe could end up in gaol and could also have to pay Sheila for the harm that he has done her. The bringing of a criminal action by the Crown does not deprive a private individual of an action in tort.

Most definitions of tort stemming from common law jurisdictions distinguish a tort from contract actions, although this is not the case everywhere. As you will learn (or have learned) in your contract course, an action in contract is based on obligations that are set forth in an enforceable agreement between two parties. Causes of action in tort, on the other hand, often arise in the absence of any such agreement. Instead, obligations in tort are imposed on every person as a matter of law, whether or not that person agrees to adopt that code of conduct. In other words, actions in tort impose a certain standard of behaviour which is necessary for people to live in an efficient, harmonious, and civilized manner. Although a violation of this standard of behaviour will not result in a criminal action—since the acts constituting a tort do not threaten the fabric of social order in the same way that a criminal act does—those who have committed torts are still considered to have acted wrongfully. As a result, the state gives the injured party the right to pursue individual compensation in the courts. Doing so encourages civilized behaviour—since, by giving injured parties access to monetary damages, the state limits the likelihood of lawless self-help of the 'eye for an eye' variety—without involving the

NOTE Every so often the question 'is there a law of tort or only a law of torts?' has been known to pop up on exams, so the issue is still alive and testable.

cross reference

For more on the reinvigoration of *Rylands v Fletcher*, see chapter 9.

cross reference

For more on *Khorasandjian v Bush [1993] WLR 476*, see chapter 8 and chapter 17.

cross reference

For more on the judicial test for when a novel cause of action should arise, see chapter 2.

cross reference

For more on negligence and *Donoghue v Stevenson [1932] AC 562*, see chapter 2. For more on the changes in the law relating to psychiatric harm arising out of the Hillsborough disaster, see *Alcock v Chief Constable of South Yorkshire [1992] 1 AC 310* and *White v Chief Constable of South Yorkshire [1999] 1 All ER 1* in chapter 12.

state in numerous, potentially petty lawsuits. Allowing the wronged parties to decide for themselves whether to pursue a case provides a useful gate keeping function, since private citizens and entities are perfectly capable of evaluating whether their cases are (a) strong enough as a matter of law, and (b) important enough to them personally to incur the risk and potential cost of litigation.

One of the reasons why courts and commentators have had difficulty in describing tort law in any coherent manner is because the types of wrongs that fall under this heading are incredibly diverse. Some involve harms purposefully visited upon others (such as in assault and battery) while others involve unfortunate outcomes that the defendant may not have ever intended (as in negligence or products liability). Some torts protect interests in land (for example, trespass and nuisance), whereas others protect interests in a person's social standing or commercial endeavours (as with defamation). The wide range of issues and concerns that fall within the field of tort have led no less eminent a commentator than Sir John Salmond to claim that there is no such thing as the law of tort but only a law of individual, unconnected torts. While academics may debate the theoretical underpinnings and proper nomenclature for this field of law, practitioners and students must ultimately focus on recognizing what falls into the realm of redressable wrongs and what does not.

Because tort is primarily a creature of the common law, it is particularly amenable to change, and courts are constantly expanding and contracting the boundaries of tort. For example, few parties had based their claims on the principle espoused in *Rylands v Fletcher* for many years, leading some commentators to argue that that the tort had disappeared as a separate cause of action. However, *LMS International Ltd v Styrene Packaging and Insulation* [2005] EWHC 2065 (TCC) put the lie to the naysayers and demonstrated that the doctrine was still alive and well. Similarly, new causes of action are constantly being considered. For example, in *Khorasandjian v Bush* [1993] WLR 476, the Court of Appeal found that a woman who was subjected to numerous harassing phone calls from a former boyfriend could recover for the injury done to her, despite the fact that there was no statutory or common law action providing damages for harassment until that point. Although the point was overruled by a higher court in an unrelated case, Parliament stepped in and enacted the Protection from Harassment Act 1997 to address the kind of harm in *Khorasandjian v Bush* [1993] WLR 476. Courts are also at liberty to expand the categories of persons who can recover damages. Often these shifts will be in response to certain social changes (such as the Industrial Revolution, which led to the rise of actions in negligence, starting with groundbreaking cases concerning the liability of railways in the 1800s and taking a quantum leap forward with *Donoghue v Stevenson* [1932] AC 562), whereas others will be in response to a single event, such as the Hillsborough Stadium disaster. While change in the common law often comes at an incremental pace, under extraordinary circumstances, the courts will respond with a more radical leap. Parliament can also step in to provide a remedy for future claimants, either by reinforcing the common law's position or by creating a cause of action out of whole cloth after the courts have considered themselves unable to act.

1.3 Characteristics of a tort

Although the word 'tort' has resisted simple definition, the cause of action known as a tort displays several characteristics, regardless of its precise subject matter. First, a wrongful action can typically be considered a tort only if the injury which has resulted—or which may result—can be cured by monetary damages, although in some cases an additional remedy may also be available. Furthermore, a tort arises when one party breaches a duty imposed on it toward another party as a matter of law, regardless of whether the defendant agreed to take on that duty. In some cases (those involving strict or absolute liability), it will not even matter that the defendant took all reasonable or even all possible measures to avoid causing injury to others.

There is also no need for the defendant to know consciously that a duty exists. For example, many tort textbooks illustrate the duty/breach of duty scenario by referring to the duty incumbent on the driver of a car to avoid injuring others. As you know, a driver must take all reasonable actions to avoid damaging other vehicles, other road users (such as pedestrians) and property alongside the road (such as fences and street lamps). If the driver acts without using reasonable care and injures someone else's person or property, a tort has likely occurred. As useful as this example is, it can be misleading because anyone who drives a car is required to pass an examination on the rules of the road and the proper standards of behaviour. Guidebooks are available that describe, in great detail, what drivers must do in any given situation. Therefore, this illustration suggests that torts can only arise in situations that are heavily regulated by the state or in situations where someone either knows or should know precisely what is expected of him or her. In fact, a tort can arise even in situations where there is little state involvement and the defendant has not been specifically briefed on the existence of a duty, let alone the exact details of that duty, as is true with the car example. For example, Cynthia may inherit some land from her grandfather, not knowing that the property contains a reservoir that was dug in the 1800s. If that reservoir bursts its bounds the day after Cynthia inherits the property, flooding the neighbouring yard, Cynthia will be liable under *Rylands v Fletcher* for the escape of a non-naturally occurring thing (the accumulated water) that caused harm to the property of another. Cynthia is liable for the resulting damages even though she did not know about the reservoir, did not put it on the land, did not do anything affirmative to acquire the property, did not have time to inspect the property prior to the accidental release of the water, and did not have time to research any legal obligations associated with the property. She is still responsible to her neighbour for the damage to that neighbour's yard.

There is a difference between being instructed as to the existence and extent of a legal duty (as is the case with the driver of an automobile) and being able to discover the existence and extent of a legal duty. The principle known as 'the rule of law' demands that any person must be able to know, in advance, what the law requires of him or her. In other words, the legal rules and principles must be published and available for inspection prior to any person's being charged with a legal duty. In this second example, Cynthia has not been told that a duty to take reasonable care exists and what must be done to discharge that duty, but she could have conducted legal research to learn whether the action (in this case, owning the property) could carry the risk of liability in tort. Indeed, that is precisely what businesses often do. Newspapers, for example, routinely consult with a solicitor or barrister in advance of publishing potentially defamatory material to make sure that they do not commit a tort by publishing the information. The fact that Cynthia did not have time to conduct any research is irrelevant—it is enough that the law regarding liability under *Rylands v Fletcher* existed prior to the act that resulted in Cynthia's liability.

Another characteristic of tort is the imposition of duties towards people generally. Contract law imposes obligations between those who are parties to the contract; the duties are specific to certain individuals, rather than to society as a whole. In tort, a defendant will likely not know all the people to whom a duty is owed—certainly the driver of a car cannot name each and every person who is on or near the road every time the driver goes out for a spin, yet the driver owes a duty to each of these unnamed persons. So long as a potential claimant and defendant are in the proper sort of relationship—driver to passenger, landowner to neighbour, etc—that is sufficient for potential liability to arise in tort.

For the most part, tort law addresses past wrongs, since the existence and quantum (amount) of damages will not be known with certainty until after the injury has occurred. However, there are times when a party can seek the assistance of the court in prohibiting an activity that is likely to lead to grave or irreparable future injury. A common example would be a newspaper that was intending to print an article or photograph that would injure someone's reputation. In that case, the court might stop the publication from being distributed, at least until the court had the opportunity to consider whether damage would result. Alternatively, a factory owner might be ordered to cease plans to manufacture a product that would cause poisonous waste to be expelled into the environment.

1.4 The purpose of tort law

When considering the purpose of tort law, it is again helpful to distinguish its function from that of contract law. The sole aim of contract law is to enforce the promises of others; any other interest—commercial stability, moral claims, etc—is subsumed within this single goal. Similarly, criminal law has as its purpose the protection of public interests, meaning those interests that are shared by everyone within society. Those interests are so important and so general that the state—in the form of the Crown Prosecution Service—steps in to act as the enforcement mechanism. The remaining body of law of civil wrongs—which focuses on the compensation of individuals for the infringement of individual interests—constitutes tort. Indeed, one commentator has focused on the concept of private compensation as perhaps the primary hallmark of tort law.

● Cecil A. Wright, *'Introduction to the Law of Torts'*, 8 Cambridge Law Journal 238 (1944)

While no definition of a 'tort' has yet been made that affords any satisfactory assistance in the solution of the problems we shall encounter, the purpose, of function, of the law of torts can be stated fairly simply. Arising out of the various and ever-increasing clashes of the activities of persons living in a common society, carrying on business in competition with fellow members of that society, owning property which may in any of a thousand ways affect the persons or property of others—in short, doing all the things that constitute modern living—there must of necessity be losses, and to afford compensation for injuries sustained by one person as the result of the conduct of another. The purpose of the law of torts is to adjust these losses and to afford compensation for injuries sustained by one person as the result of the conduct of another...

The study of the law of torts is therefore a study of the extent to which the law will shift the losses sustained in modern society from the person affected to the shoulders of him who caused the loss. It is obvious that no system of law will ever attempt to compensate persons for *all* losses...Actuated by some such view of social policy the law, about three hundred years ago, began to take into consideration, in imposing liability, something akin to 'moral blameworthiness.' Was the defendant in 'fault' in causing the plaintiff's loss? Did he act 'wrongfully'?

1.5 Principles of tort law

As the preceding excerpt suggests, fault and blameworthiness are central features of tort law, and ones to which we shall return. However, an even more fundamental principle of tort law is that liability results when the defendant's conduct is socially unreasonable. In some cases, the decision about what is unreasonable is decided in great detail ahead of time—thus, the driver of a car in Britain knows that driving on the right hand side of the road is unreasonable in British society and doing so will result in liability in tort, barring unusual circumstances such as a broken steering mechanism. In other instances, neither the court nor Parliament nor any of the state's regulating bodies have considered the particular circumstances that have occurred in advance of the event, at least in any great detail. In those cases, the court must weigh the various countervailing issues to decide whether the conduct is unreasonable. Often, the court considers things such as (1) what it would cost (in terms of time and money) the defendant to act differently; (2) who is most able to bear the loss; (3) who is most able to protect against loss (through its actions or through the purchase of insurance cover); (4) the social value of the activity that caused the injury; (5) the social value of the interest which has been infringed upon, etc. While the court will have some guidelines to help it in making a decision, the outcome of many cases will depend on the particular facts, requiring the court to make an independent judgment about whether the activity was socially unreasonable. Finally, in a small group of cases—those known as strict liability cases—the court will not look at any facts other than whether the defendant in question was responsible for the act in question. There, it does not matter what the defendant did or did not do to protect

think point
The attention paid to individual characteristics is one of the hallmarks of tort law. Does this increase or decrease the predictability and 'justness' of the law?

against the harm; society, in the form of Parliament, has decided that the behaviour is so risky that any error will be considered socially unreasonable and the actor will be liable for any harm that results. The entire issue of whether the actor was reasonable has been taken out of the court's hands altogether.

Obviously, what is socially unreasonable differs according to one's point of view. A smoker may believe that lighting up in a public place is entirely reasonable, but a non-smoker may disagree. Though society—again, in the form of Parliament—for many years sided with the smokers, the tide has turned and society has now decided that it is unreasonable to allow people to smoke in public places. Similarly, one person may believe that it is entirely reasonable to crank up the stereo at 2 am, whereas another will disagree. Since the law must balance the interests of many different people, it cannot consider all perspectives equally valid and reasonable. It must decide which behaviours to allow and which to limit.

While some people might argue that the court should always look at the question of reasonableness from the point of view of the defendant—since the defendant is the person who will be liable for damages—that approach causes considerable problems. First, it may be difficult to figure out what the defendant was thinking at the time of the tort. Few defendants will admit to believing that they knew they were acting unreasonably at the time the accident occurred. Second, that kind of standard might unduly benefit reckless people, since the only people who could be held liable would be those who admit that they knew—or could be shown to have known—that they were behaving unreasonably at the time of the incident. Reckless people would never know they were behaving unreasonably and thus would be able to injure numerous people without ever having to pay the price associated with their conduct. Instead, innocent victims would have to pay the cost of the reckless person's choices. Since it doesn't seem fair to force victims to suffer loss, the courts decided to impose an objective standard of reasonableness, often referred to as the hypothetical 'reasonable man'. This objective standard may conclude that, while the actor's behaviour was reasonable from the perspective of the person in the actor's position (i.e. the **subjective** position), the common consensus would be that the action was unreasonable and that the actor should pay for the harm to the injured party. Thus, a trespasser who intrudes on another's property, thinking the owner won't object, may still be required to compensate the owner for the infringement of the property interest. Similarly, the person whose compost heap smells so strongly that it offends the neighbours may still be required to pay damages and cease composting, no matter how reasonable and beneficial composting is to the environment and society at large.

VOCABULARY
'Subjective' standards look at the issue from the defendant's point of view. 'Objective' standards look at the issue from the point of view of the hypothetical 'reasonable person'.

think point
Feminist commentators have argued that formulating the standard as that of the 'reasonable man' reinforces certain invisible biases that can be detrimental to women. For example, tort law permits a defendant to use reasonable force to repel an attack. If person A attacks person B with fists and person B responds by grabbing a knife and slashing person A, the claim of self-defence may not exist under the objective, reasonable man standard. If, however, person A is a six-foot, four-inch tall man and person B is a five-foot tall woman, using a knife in self-defence seems slightly more reasonable.

1.6 Policy and procedure

Because of its reliance on the reasonable man (or reasonable person) standard, tort law has become something of a proving ground for issues of social theory. Although tort law is a form of private law, in the sense that its focus is on compensating injured individuals for harms brought about by the acts or omissions of other individuals, the reality is that public interests are often at stake, even in so-called private disputes. For example, two neighbours may appear to be fighting over a smelly compost heap, but the court is likely to consider issues of public policy when it is determining what is reasonable (and thus what actions are permissible). One place where you can see the relationship between public policy and tort law particularly well is when established precedent is overturned or modified. For the most part, courts respect decisions that have been handed down in the past and try to issue judgments that are in accordance with those principles. One of the few things that will allow a change in the law is a change in the social circumstances on which the law is built. Similarly, courts explicitly consider issues of public policy when they are deciding a case of first impression, since there will be no legal precedent that is squarely on point and public policy at least provides a useful and principled grounds for decision-making. Although there may be good arguments made by both sides, courts will ultimately choose that which is deemed better for society as a whole.

TIP Lawyers often use the phrase 'public policy' to describe the general principles or rationales that underlie more specific rules about particular conduct. What law students often fail to recognize is that public policy arguments always exist on both sides of a dispute. Therefore, it does not advance an argument one whit to say that 'public policy suggests that X should prevail.' When setting out a position, be explicit about what the public policy at issue is, whether it's the need to preserve public resources, the desire to make the party who is most able to obtain insurance liable for losses, the need to protect the rights of private property owners, or something else. Describing competing policy considerations will often earn you extra points, though you should recall that public policy arguments are secondary to arguments based on specific laws.

Thus, tort law addresses the needs of both the individual and society at large. Individuals who come to court seek redress for a variety of wrongs and protection for a variety of rights and interests. On the one hand, these people want to enhance their personal security and be free from personal assaults. On the other hand, these people want to protect their livelihoods, their personal property, their real property and their ability to enjoy the fruits of their labour. Individuals also want to ensure that their workplaces are safe and free from unnecessary risks. The list of individual rights, wants, and desires protected by tort law could go on and on, just as the list of public concerns could.

Although the individuals involved in a dispute obviously have a great deal at stake, society also has at least two interests in the outcome of a tort case. First, society at large benefits from the just and efficient resolution of private disputes. In the absence of a workable legal system, the fabric of society begins to fray as individuals seek to resolve their differences through self-help. While a return to 'an eye for an eye' seems unlikely, anyone who has seen adjoining property owners argue about an unsightly fence or a constantly barking dog can imagine any number of problematic outcomes (torn down fences, poisoned dogs, blaring music or light late at night to 'punish' the wrongdoer) if people do not believe that they can get justice in court. Second, society has an interest in tort disputes because the common law relies on precedent that has evolved in both a principled and systematic manner. Since a decision laid down today will affect the resolution of future disputes, it stands to reason that society will want courts to adopt rules that achieve desirable long-term social ends.

Inevitably, there will be times when public and private interests collide. Courts will have to consider whether to adopt a strategy that will promote the greatest good for the greatest number of people (often described as a utilitarian model of justice) or give certain rights and interests, including private rights, an enhanced status that will trump other countervailing interests. Although every area of law undertakes this sort of balancing analysis to some extent, the law of tort can be said to do so to a larger degree, precisely because of the diversity of rights and interests—both public and private—that are at stake in this area of law. For example, courts might be asked to consider whether there should be a right to privacy that trumps property rights, as in the well-known case involving illicitly obtained photographs of the wedding of Michael Douglas and Catherine Zeta-Jones in *Douglas v Hello! Ltd* [2001] QB 967. Alternatively, courts could have to decide whether the right to personal safety and security is more important than the right to be secure in one's own home, as was necessary in *Revill v Newbery* [1996] QB 567, wherein a homeowner shot a burglar and was subsequently sued for assault.

cross reference

Douglas v Hello! Ltd [2001] QB 967 is discussed in more detail in chapter 14.

cross reference

Revill v Newbery [1996] QB 567 is discussed in more detail in chapter 17.

1.7 Factors affecting liability in tort

Liability in tort depends on certain bedrock principles. First among these is the idea that the primary aim of tort law is compensation for losses. This compensatory principle differs radically from the criminal law's goal of deterrence and punishment of wrongdoers and contract law's goal of enforcing the performance of promises. In tort, the defendant is liable to the claimant for the damages caused, but no more than that. This approach is different from that used in some legal systems, where tort law can include punitive as well as compensatory damages.

Another fundamental principle affecting tort liability involves the moral culpability of the defendant's conduct. Although a few areas of tort law impose liability regardless of the defendant's mental state, typically a defendant in tort must have acted in a blameworthy way, either through an affirmative action or through an omission. The necessary mental element will depend on the tort alleged. Some torts, such as battery, assault, and false imprisonment, require a specific intent to carry out the tortious act. Others indicate that a tort exists if the defendant either knows or should have known an injury could arise as a result of the defendant's actions. Because tort relies heavily on the standard of reasonable behaviour exemplified by the reasonable person, the law of tort tends to

cross reference

Moral culpability in tort was mentioned in Cecil Wright's article, which is excerpted above.

reflect popularly held ideas of morality. When tort law was in its youth, most people believed that a person who hurt another, either intentionally or even through pure but foreseeable accident, should be required to make good the losses of the injured party. Those sentiments about who should properly bear the loss still hold true today, which is why tort law has continued and grown as it has.

When considering whether a defendant's behaviour is blameworthy enough to require him or her to pay compensation, courts distinguish between legal fault and moral fault. The law is not and never has been entirely consistent with the moral code held by society, so courts cannot be used to address purely immoral behaviour. True, tort law finds 'fault' in the failure to live up to an ideal standard of conduct which may be beyond the knowledge or capabilities of any particular individual, but that ideal standard is based on acts which are normal and usual in society as it currently stands. Because tort law imposes liability even in instances where the **tortfeasor** has acted innocently or even in good faith, there is not the same kind of moral reproach attached to a claim in tort as there is, for example, in criminal law, which penalizes acts that society deems both blameworthy and morally reprehensible. Thus, tort law fails to address some acts which some people may find immoral while simultaneously providing compensation for harm which has been innocently (i.e. non-intentionally) caused. Furthermore, tort law does not encourage affirmative acts of morality; there is no mechanism in tort for encouraging wealthy people to share their riches with the poor or for requiring passers-by to come to the aid of an ailing stranger on the roadside. Finally, tort addresses behaviour rather than belief. Therefore, tort law does not act as a purely moral code of conduct.

The key to understanding the terms 'fault' and 'blameworthiness' in tort is to see that in all cases, tort law is attributing some element of volition to the actor—even when the injury is caused by an innocent mistake, tort law takes the so-called 'moral' view that the actor still could have done something to take more care to avoid the accident. Alternatively, one can take the view that fault or blameworthiness in tort law is synonymous with anti-social behaviour, meaning acts or omissions that injure society (often personified by one individual claimant) in some way. In this second approach, the defendant incurs 'blame' by failing to live up to the standard of behaviour required for the reasonable protection of others.

The concept of fault or blameworthiness can apply even in situations involving strict liability. For example, even though the defendant in those cases may have taken all reasonable and unreasonable efforts to avoid harm, one could say that society has deemed the activity so dangerous or tangential to the social good that, by deciding to undertake the act in the first place (thus meeting the volition test of fault or blameworthiness), the defendant has breached the standard of normal or usual social behaviour and thus must pay compensation for any harm that results. Alternatively, one could say that deciding to undertake an act that has dubious social value means that any injury that occurs violates the requirement that everyone act for the mutual protection of others. Tort law's emphasis on the protection of others becomes readily apparent when one considers that strict liability in tort attaches most readily in cases involving product liability. Here, manufacturers gain a great deal of profit as a result of developing and marketing new products. Although the creation of new products for sale—including medicines and

VOCABULARY

A 'tortfeasor' is a person who has committed a tort.

machinery—is socially valuable, society wants to ensure that no corners are cut and no products are sent to market before all the flaws have been discovered and cured. Therefore, the law supports the creation of new products by allowing production to continue, but puts a high price on the activity by holding manufacturers strictly liable should anything go wrong. In this system, manufacturers know that it is in their own best financial interests to test their products rigorously before sending them to market, lest all their profits disappear in tort compensation awards. Society benefits from the development of new products, but is also protected from harm to the highest degree possible.

A third element affecting liability in tort involves the historical context of the law of tort. First, as a primarily common law remedy, tort is strongly affected by precedent. While some common law torts have now been superseded by statute and a few torts have been initially created by statute, the vast majority of actions have developed through the common law. Thus, anyone considering bringing a claim in tort must consider the historical antecedents of the modern cause of action, since the courts will consider the origins of the action when deciding whether to expand the law in any particular direction. For example, when considering whether to require an element of foreseeability in a claim based on *Rylands v Fletcher*, a land-based tort, the Court of Appeal in *Cambridge Water Co Ltd v Eastern Counties Leather plc* [1994] 2 AC 264 investigated the extent to which *Rylands v Fletcher* was historically based on an action in nuisance, another land-based tort. Second, tort is strongly influenced not only by social mores (which change with the times) but by other historical movements. Thus, the Industrial Revolution led to certain developments in the law of tort, just as the rise of the electronic age in more recent years has done. Understanding the social, economic, and political climate in existence at the time any particular case was decided provides a useful framework for analysis. Changes in social and political realities will often lead to changes in the law. Furthermore, knowing the environment in which a case was brought helps lawyers and courts faced with a new dispute decide whether an opinion can and should still be considered good precedent. While historical arguments will not trump good legal precedent, they—like good public policy arguments—can be persuasive, so long as they are adequately explained and analysed.

A fourth element affecting liability in tort involves the limited resources of the courts. Some behaviour—though blameworthy in the normal tort sense—will not be deemed actionable in courts because the conduct is so common that allowing a cause of action would lead to a massive influx of similar claims, swamping the courts. For example, the law at one time did not allow recovery for damages to feelings or for psychiatric harm unassociated with physical harm, allegedly on the grounds that such claims could not be adequately quantified or proven, but really based on the fear that recognizing these types of injuries would lead to a huge increase in the number of cases brought each year, thus putting a huge amount of administrative pressure on the judicial system. When the courts finally did allow recovery for these sorts of losses, they set strict guidelines on who could recover and under what circumstances, thus restricting the number of claimants who could obtain damages for these sorts of injury. Similarly, in the years

cross reference
For more on liability under Rylands v Fletcher and Cambridge Water Co Ltd v Eastern Counties Leather plc [1994] 2 AC 264, see chapter 9.

cross reference
For more on psychiatric harm, see chapter 12.

cross reference

For more on the nascent right to privacy, see chapter 14.

. . . .

VOCABULARY

Concerns about limited judicial resources are often referred to as 'floodgate arguments', suggesting that allowing such causes of action would open the floodgates of litigation, swamping the courts.

. . . .

cross reference

For more on contributory negligence and contribution as a means of distributing loss among different parties, see chapter 4.

leading up to the adoption of the Human Rights Act 1998, courts and commentators both feared that allowing litigants to rely on the European Convention on Human Rights in domestic actions would open up wide vistas of tort liability. In actuality, that has not been the case. For example, one area where a new cause of action seems to have been established as a result of the 1998 Act—the right to privacy—has not seen rampant litigation, but has instead been growing in small, measured steps. Overall, cases have been brought slowly and conservatively, allowing the law to grow modestly and ensuring that the courts have not been overwhelmed in the process.

The fifth factor that courts consider when deciding whether to establish liability in tort is the parties' ability to bear financial loss or distribute it among other entities. For the most part, litigation is a zero-sum equation, meaning that the losses associated with an injury fall entirely on one or another of the parties. Although there are mechanisms for attributing fault among the various parties and thus placing financial loss on more than one party in individual cases, as a general matter tort takes very much into account the ability to bear or anticipate a risk of loss. The analysis does not look so much at the relative wealth of the parties but rather at the ability to avoid the loss entirely (through preventative measures or insurance) or absorb the loss (either because of financial resources gained over time or by passing the loss on to others in smaller portions, such as through raised prices).

This analysis is particularly useful when the defendant is in a position to anticipate and possibly protect itself from loss through the adjustment of prices, rates, taxes, or insurance, as is the case when the defendant is a private or public corporation, a commercial enterprise, a car owner, a property owner, etc. Tort law tends to take the view that such persons or entities are more able and more likely to protect themselves from loss than a private individual going about his or her business—walking down the street, shopping in the grocery store, riding on a train—would be. While private individuals can take out what is called first-party insurance—where the individual insures him or herself from unknown dangers and injuries caused by others—such cover is difficult to find and expensive to obtain. Furthermore, a private individual—who tends not to have the same resources as a commercial enterprise or insurer—is more likely to be ruined by a single catastrophic event than these other parties. It is much easier and more cost-efficient for those in the first group—the corporations, car and property owners, etc—to find and purchase insurance to cover risks associated with their activities. Thus, as a matter of economics, courts prefer to place the loss on those who can ensure or guard against it in the easiest and least expensive manner.

However, courts will not always force industry to bear the risk of loss, since to do so could force businesses out of the market, with a detrimental effect to society as a whole. Tort law is particularly cautious about requiring businesses to bear liability that extends to an unlimited number of unknown persons or liability that cannot be estimated or insured against in advance. Courts may also tend to protect new or growing industries, at least in their early years, since to do otherwise might thwart a socially valuable activity.

Finally, when imposing liability in tort, courts will consider the extent to which the allocation of loss will serve as a preventative measure. Courts may even view allocation of loss

cross reference

For more on punitive and other types of damage awards, see chapter 11.

as taking on a slightly punitive function. Although these concerns are often considered to be at the forefront of criminal law, tort law also wants to make sure that wrongdoers do not repeat their antisocial behaviour. Having to pay damages is a strong incentive for everyone, from the private individual to the publicly held company, not to undertake tortious conduct. Even though a tort award only compensates the claimant for the injury suffered, tortfeasors still suffer a loss when ordered to pay damages, and that can have a punitive effect. Furthermore, once the judicial decisions become public, the case will also hopefully prevent other potential defendants from acting wrongfully by showing them they will have to pay damages.

1.8 Motive and intent

Motive and intent play a different role in different types of legal action. Most crime dramas suggest that the defendant's motive is a key part of criminal law (whether this is actually true or not is something to discuss in your criminal law course). Certainly intent is vitally important in criminal law. On the other hand, the defendant's mental state—whether it is defined as motive or intent—is virtually irrelevant in contract and property cases, which primarily focus on outcomes alone. Tort law lies somewhere between these two extremes, although it is closer to criminal law than to the other types of law mentioned, since a defendant's mental state often has some bearing on whether a tort has occurred. In particular, tort law takes a great deal of interest in the intent of an actor, meaning an inquiry into the actions the person intended to take (i.e. to throw a ball, drive a car, make a certain statement). Tort law considers the motive of an actor, meaning the results the person hoped would occur following the act (i.e. to hit a certain person with the thrown ball, to injure a pedestrian while driving a car, to damage another person's reputation by making a certain statement), to a much lesser extent, since motive relates to a more distant event or effect, whereas intent focuses on the immediate act.

In many cases, motive is irrelevant to a determination of tort liability. For example, a person may eject one trespasser, while allowing another to remain on the property, based on all sorts of improper (and, in other contexts, potentially illegal) rationales, such as gender, race, ethnic or national heritage, religion and sexual orientation, as well as simple personal taste. So long as the ejectment of the trespasser is carried out with no more than reasonable force, however, the landowner will not be liable in tort. Similarly, a person may say the nastiest, most harmful thing in the world about another person, with the end goal of ruining that person's personal and professional life, but will not be liable in tort if one of the defences to defamation—such as truth—exists. In these cases, the courts may look at intent—meaning whether the defendant undertook the ejectment or the statement voluntarily, recklessly, negligently, or in any other way that is relevant to a tort analysis—but will not look at the motivation behind the act. In such cases, malevolence, vindictiveness, and ill will are all permissible as a matter of law.

In other cases, however, tort law will consider the motive underlying a particular act. For example, in the tort of nuisance, the court can and will look at whether a fence between two neighbouring properties was built simply out of spite. On the whole, however, tort law is much more concerned with intent, rather than motive, and the inquiry is much more likely to focus on whether the act was done negligently (which would be contrary to what the reasonable person would do in like circumstances) or intentionally than whether it was done maliciously or spitefully.

A very few torts result in strict liability. In those cases, the defendant's mental state is not at issue at all, since it does not matter how careful or well-intentioned a defendant may have been when the action took place. If the defendant undertook the act (such as putting a particular product into the line of commerce), then the defendant is liable for any and all injuries that result. In such instances, both motive and intent are immaterial.

TIP Beginning law students often have trouble when they run into a defendant who has acted cruelly or maliciously and/or a claimant who is particularly sympathetic. Although tort law often reflects popular conceptions about morality, it does so on a global scale. It does not provide for damages simply because one party appears to be more deserving than the other. Focus on intent rather than motive to reach the proper conclusions.

1.9 Analysing torts

Previously in this chapter, we mentioned that some commentators believe that the diversity of actions in this area of law means that there is a law of torts, but not a law of tort. Indeed, the wide variation in the types of interests protected by different torts, as well as the range of elements that must be considered to prove an individual tort, can disguise the many similarities between the individual torts. In fact, all torts—both modern and ancient—can be analysed using a simple three-step procedure first advocated by John Henry Wigmore, one of the pre-eminent scholars on the early development of tort law.

· ·

● John H. Wigmore, *'The Tripartite Division of Torts'*, 8 Harvard Law Review 200 (1894)

> If we are ever to have, as Sir Frederick Pollock puts it, not books about specific Torts, but books about Tort in general, some further examination of fundamental ideas is desirable.
>
> One might proceed with such a general analysis without regard to the definition of a Tort, or—what is much the same thing—without setting forth one's view as to the differentiation of Tort-relations from others in the general classification of private law. But, for the sake of clearness, the latter task will here be briefly attempted...
>
> Private law, then, deals with the relations between members of the community regarded as being ultimately enforceable by the political power. Such a single relation may be termed a Nexus; it has a double aspect, for it is a Right at one end, and a Duty or Obligation at the other; every such relation or Nexus necessarily having both these aspects. In classifying them, we may of course rest the division on the nature of either the Rights involved or the

NOTE Wigmore was writing at the end of the nineteenth century, when capitalization of common nouns was apparently proper. Do not emulate him in this!

NOTE Wigmore's first category basically describes the principle of strict liability.

Duties involved. For the first and broadest division it seems best to take the latter point of view, and to distinguish according as the Duty has inhered in the Obligor (1) without reference to his wish or assent, or (2) in consequence of some volition or intention of his to be clothed with it. The former we may term Irrecusable,—having reference to the immateriality of the attitude of the obligor in respect to consent or refusal; the latter, Recusable,—for the same reason.... The former includes Torts.... Dividing further the former sort, we find (*a*) many imposed universally, *i.e.* on all other members of the community in favor of myself; and (*b*) a few imposed on particular classes of persons by reason of special circumstances... [T]he natural terms of distinctions are, for the one Universal Irrecusable Nexus; for the other, Particular Irrecusable Nexus. The subject of Tort, then, deals with the large group of relations here termed Universal Irrecusable Nexus...

The next question is, What is the content of the rights and duties included under this head?... The general character, then, of these nexus will be that of relations fundamentally necessary to civilized social intercourse—the minimum number of universal nexus without which... the community cannot get along... Furthermore,... these Universal Irrecusable Nexus are all negative, not affirmative; *i.e.*, the line is drawn at requiring others not to be the means of harm to me; our law has not yet gone so far, in Universal duties, as to impose any affirmative duty, as between one man and another, to take action to confer a good.

But,... we easily see, on examination, certain generic component elements in every relation of the sort we are considering. *First*, there are the specified sorts of harm which the obligor has a claim to be free from... *Second*, there must be something to connect the obligor with this harm,—that is, we must specify what is the sort of causality-connection, or the like, between the obligor and the harm in question for which he will be held responsible... *Third*,... there are numerous cases of circumstances to be specified in which the nexus fails, and is without application,—that is, although harm is done, and although there is no question as to a particular person's responsibility for it...

There are, therefore, three distinct classes of limitations... The first class deals with the sort of harm to be recognized as the basis of the right; this may be called the Damage element. The second class deals with the circumstances fixing the connection of the obligor with this forbidden harm; this we may call the Responsibility element. The third class deals with the circumstances in which, assuming both the Damage and the Responsibility elements to be present, the nexus still has no validity,—in other words, the considerations which allow the harm to be inflicted with impunity; this way may term the Excuse or Justification element. This analysis results in a tripartite division of the Tort-nexus...

I. *The Damage Element.*—The question is here, what sorts of harm is it that the law recognizes as the subject of a claim for its protection?...

NOTE Wigmore here discusses recovery in tort for psychiatric harm—a concept that was not recognized in the United Kingdom until approximately 100 years later.

Under the Damage element, of course, are to be considered physical injuries,—what sort of physical or corporal harm may be the subject of a claim. Mere touching of the person may be, while mere touching of personal property once was not. Physical illness of course is. Whether nervous derangement may be, when not brought about through corporal violence, may be, is still the subject of discussion. Forms of annoyance, such as disagreeable odors, sights, and sounds, are usually said to be the subject of recovery only in connection with the ownership of real property. There must in all such cases be a degree of inconvenience worth taking systematic notice of... The social relations must be enumerated with which interference is forbidden, and the words known as Libel and the words deemed slanderous *per se* are to be discussed. The...matters as to which we have a 'right to privacy,' and several other modes of harm, involve also some statement of the Damage element...

II. *The Responsibility Element.*—...[W]e have next to consider those limitations of the nexus which determine the nature of the Responsibility element, by defining what connection must exist between the obligor and the harm done, in order to bring him within the scope of the nexus....

The doctrine of 'acting at peril,' the phrasing and application of the tests of 'proximate cause,' 'reasonable and probable consequences,'—these, with their attendant refinements and exceptions, form the substance of the general topic. But the important circumstance to call attention to is that this topic has an application in the domain of each one of the common so-called Torts...Speaking roughly, a man may be made responsible for a given harm by initiatory action of one of three sorts: by acting (1) designedly, with reference to the harm; (2) negligently, with reference to it; (3) at peril, in putting his hand to some nearly related deed or some unlawful act...

The question is constantly likely to arise whether the consequences of certain conduct were such as a person of ordinary prudence ought to have foreseen...

III. *The Excuse or Justification Element.*—Assuming that the various sorts of harm have been specified, and that the conditions and tests of Responsibility for them have been determined, the general limitations under which the nexus exists still call for treatment. Perhaps the simplest illustration, if any is needed, is the excuse of Self-defence...

One or two general implications of the recognition of this tripartite division of Tort may now be pointed out...

A more important consequence of the recognition of the tripartite division is the helpful results to be reached by studying the different solutions of the same problems and the applications of the same principles in different torts. Clearer understanding of a general principle and its differing aspects in application, keener appreciation of its worth or perhaps of its incongruities, greater readiness for new developments already pressing upon us,—these are the benefits of such a recognition.

As you can see, Wigmore not only described a useful means of viewing a variety of existing actions through a single lens, he also foresaw the direction in which the law of tort would generally develop. The beauty of the Wigmore analytical model is that it reinforces the similarities between different torts and gives a simple method of organizing the constituent elements of each tort, particularly for students who are responsible for learning and memorizing a vast amount of information. However, there are other ways of breaking down this area of law, particularly as a conceptual matter. For example, Sir Frederick Pollock, who wrote one of the earliest textbooks on the subject, classified tort into personal wrongs; wrongs to property and possession; and wrongs to persons, estates and property generally. While this approach is still workable, the evolution of tort law, particularly in the areas of negligence and strict liability, means that there are times when a particular tort—such as negligence—will cross over into more than one category.

1.10 Structure of the current text

The current text is organized in a way that is intended both to help readers see how various torts interrelate and to track how most lecturers proceed through the course. That having been said, there is a great deal of variation in how instructors teach their courses. Some lecturers begin with negligence, since it often takes up the most time and includes a number of important elements, such as causation, that will be repeated throughout the course. Other people prefer to begin with the intentional torts, since their familiarity provides an easy entry into the study of law. Still others may start with another tort.

Most instructors appear to begin with negligence, so this text will do the same. The structure of the book is as follows:

- Negligence;
- Breach of statutory duty;
- Torts involving land;
- Damages and other remedies;
- Special kinds of harm;
- Product liability;
- Liability for the torts of others; and
- Torts against the person.

The final chapter will include tips on revising for your examination.

1.10.1 Negligence

Negligence is a tort of relatively recent origin, owing its genesis to the economic, social, and moral realities of the Industrial Revolution. It has become something of a catch-all tort, encompassing harms to an individual (including both personal injury and death); to real property (meaning land); to personal property (such as cars, clothes, jewellery, or furniture—basically anything that can be owned, other than real property); and even to intangible interests such as economic interests. Because the harms are so diverse, so, too, are the causes, which can range from a reckless driver to street vandals to the escape of water from one property to another. Although the breadth and scope of actions in negligence can lead to the tort seeming nebulous at first, its boundaries quickly become discernable as the basic elements of the tort become more familiar. This section includes four separate chapters, each dealing with one of the basic elements of negligence. The first chapter, duty, describes what has become known as the 'neighbour principle', which identifies the realm of persons to whom a duty of care is owed. The first chapter in this section also discusses some of the different types of harm that can arise in negligence cases.

The second chapter in this section involves **breach** of the duty of care. This discussion revolves around the amount and type of care that must be taken in any particular situation (often called the standard of care). Special circumstances exist with respect to professionals and employers, who are often held to a different standard of behaviour. This chapter also describes some of the procedural problems that are associated with proving negligence, as well as legal doctrines such as *res ipsa loquitur* (Latin for 'the thing speaks for itself') that can be used to overcome these problems.

The third chapter in this section deals with causation, a concern that exists in virtually any tort. Because tort law is based on a concept of fault, it is vitally necessary that the court be satisfied that the defendant is the person who is responsible for the action that led to the harm. However, causation in negligence—and indeed in other torts—exists in two forms—the 'but for' test and remoteness. The 'but for' test notes that, but for this defendant's action, the claimant would not have suffered injury. However, relying solely on the 'but for' test can lead to ludicrous results. For example, imagine that Ahmed is about to drive to the local market to do his weekly shopping—something that he does at the same time every week. This week, he is delayed for ten minutes because his next door neighbour, Sheila, comes over to discuss repairs on their common fence. When Ahmed finally drives to the market to do his shopping, he gets into a car accident, injuring another person. Under the 'but for' test, Sheila could be said to be liable for the accident victim, since she was a factual cause of the accident, since Ahmed would not have been on the road at that time 'but for' her delaying him. However, it seems wrong to hold Sheila responsible for the accident—she had no way of controlling Ahmed's actions or of foreseeing that he would be in a position to injure someone on the roadway in the near future. In fact, Sheila's liability is limited by the rules relating to the principle of remoteness. This chapter discusses these and related topics in more detail.

The final chapter in the first section covers defences. While the discussion devotes itself to the various ways in which a defendant can limit or escape liability in negligence, many of the subjects covered here apply equally to other torts. Contributory negligence, for example, can reduce a defendant's liability not only in negligence cases but also in other torts where the claimant's own wrongdoing has contributed to the harm suffered. For instance, say Patricia was injured when Gordon hit her with his car. Gordon was acting negligently because he was simultaneously talking on his cell phone and trying to read a map while driving. Normally, Gordon would be entirely liable for the injury he caused. However, if Patricia was also acting negligently—say, by failing to look in the proper direction when stepping into the street—then the amount that Gordon has to pay will be reduced by a sum proportional to the extent to which Patricia was at fault (i.e. was negligent). The same principle holds true if Patricia is injured whilst walking across a wooden bridge that the property owner knew was in disrepair—if she was acting negligently, as by jumping up and down on it or driving over it in a car when it was obviously meant to be nothing more than a footbridge, then the property owner's liability may be reduced. These and other defences are covered in detail in this chapter.

1.10.2 **Breach of statutory duty**

Negligence is almost entirely a common law tort, meaning that the elements of the cause of action and the defences to it are found in judicial opinions, as opposed to legislation. The emphasis on cases in tort courses can lead students to downplay the importance of statutory law. Therefore, the second section in this text brings statutory interpretation immediately to the fore by discussing breach of statutory **duty**. As discussed in this chapter, certain duties arise not as a result of a determination of what the hypothetical 'reasonable person' would do in any given circumstance, but as a result of a determination by Parliament that certain standards of behaviour must be met. These are known as statutory duties, since they are imposed by statute rather than by common law. When these duties are not met, an individual may bring a civil action for damages relating to the breach of the statutory duty. What is unusual about the tort of breach of statutory duty is that most of the statutes involved do not expressly impose civil liability in tort. Therefore, this chapter not only introduces some of the legislation that is commonly used as basis for tort liability, but also discusses how to go about interpreting statutory language and gleaning Parliamentary intent from potentially vague legislation. The chapter concludes with information on the defences that are available to this particular tort.

1.10.3 **Torts involving land**

When analysing problems in tort, it is important to learn how different causes of action interrelate and overlap. While there are times when a claimant will only have one cause of action, it is equally likely that a claimant will be able to proceed with several different claims arising out of a single series of events. It is to the claimant's benefit to consider bringing as many different claims as possible, since there is no guarantee of recovery with any single head of liability and different torts carry different types of awards and remedies. This section considers four different types of land-based liability which should typically be considered together, since they overlap significantly. Furthermore, when analysing an injury that arises out of the use, ownership, or occupation of land, a claimant should also consider whether negligence exists, since negligence addresses injuries to persons and property arising through any means.

The first chapter in this section addresses occupiers' liability, a statutory-based tort that outlines liability that can result from the occupation of premises. The chapter looks at the Occupiers' Liability Act 1957 and the Occupiers' Liability Act 1984 in great detail, as well as the cases that construe those statutes. The discussion also includes liability of non-occupiers and defences that arise under the statutory and common law.

The second chapter in this section discusses the law of nuisance, both public and private, while the third chapter covers liability under *Rylands v Fletcher*, a tort that is very similar to nuisance. Both causes of action relate to injuries that arise on one landowner's property as a result of another landowner's use, occupation, or ownership of property. Some of these injuries can be intangible in nature, such as when an offensive odour wafts from one place to another or a particularly loud noise can be heard by others. While these sorts of harms can be difficult to quantify, they are real and recoverable under tort law. Other types of injuries are much easier to understand as compensable harms since they involve destruction of property, either real (such as land contaminated by chemicals) or personal (such as a damaged vehicle that was sitting on the property). What is unusual about these torts is their links to the land—typically, both the defendant and the claimant must have some ties to the property in question. While this is also true with occupiers' liability, at least on the defendant's side (the claimant in those cases also has a tie to the land, but it is much more fleeting, since the claimant can be nothing more than a visitor or even a trespasser to the premises), both nuisance and liability under *Rylands v Fletcher* are the quintessential land-based torts.

The fourth and final chapter in this section covers the most commonly known land-based tort, trespass to land. In many ways, this chapter is the odd one out in this section, because the liability here is on the part of the person who does not own the land, which is the reverse of the other three torts. With trespass to land, the claimant is the landowner; in occupiers' liability, nuisance, and *Rylands v Fletcher* cases, the defendant is always a landowner. However, since in two of the other torts in this section—nuisance and *Rylands v Fletcher*—the claimant will also be a landowner (those two torts are always between two landowners or occupiers), it makes sense to consider trespass to land here. Many—though by no means all—of the actions that will lead to a claim in nuisance or in *Rylands v Fletcher* will also support a claim in trespass to land. Therefore, many injured parties will bring three separate causes of action for injuries to their land. It should be noted, however, that many textbook writers and lecturers include trespass to land with torts such as assault, battery, and false imprisonment, which are also known as trespass to the person. Together, trespass to land and trespass to the person constitute the intentional torts, since liability will not be imposed unless the defendant acted intentionally (as opposed to negligently). Therefore, it makes sense to cover the various sorts of **trespass** together, since there are theoretical and analytical similarities.

VOCABULARY

Although laypeople use 'trespass' to refer to 'trespass to land', the word actually is more properly defined as 'an infringement on the rights of'.

1.10.4 **Damages and other remedies**

In some cases (most notably, negligence), a claimant must prove the existence of damage as a required part of the tort. In other cases, damage is presumed as soon as the claimant proves the other required elements of the tort. However, most claimants will want to enter evidence of the type and extent of injury suffered, even when damage is presumed, since it will likely increase the amount of money they can recover.

This chapter discusses the various types of damages awards that a court can issue, depending on the type and scope of injury suffered. These awards can range from a single pound sterling—occasionally issued when the court recognizes that a tort has occurred but wants to signal its displeasure that a case was brought for such a trivial injury—to millions of pounds. In addition to listing the various categories of damages, this chapter discusses how damages are calculated in cases involving personal injury and death. While examiners seldom expect to see actual figures given in response to a question from an examiner, students will often be asked to show the type of calculations that a court must make when determining a damages award for personal injury or death. The analysis combines both case law and statutes, and can be somewhat detail-oriented, although there is little that is conceptually difficult about the analysis.

This chapter also covers non-monetary remedies such as injunctions. An injunction is not available in all cases, but can at times be more useful to a claimant than money damages. Injunctions forbid a defendant from undertaking a certain act going forward in the future, although in rare cases the court will order a defendant to take certain affirmative actions to cure an ongoing tortious circumstance. Thus, for example, one injunction may prohibit a factory from emitting noxious fumes that spread across the adjoining neighbourhood, while another injunction (the rarer type, which requires a particular action to be taken) might require a defendant to build a fence between two properties.

NOTE An injunction takes the form of a court order, which is nothing more than a piece of paper outlining what a party is to do or not do. Although this does not seem to be a very useful remedy, a party who fails to comply with the terms of an injunction may be brought into court by whoever was supposed to benefit from the order. The non-compliant party will be asked to show cause why the terms of the injunction were violated. Failing a very good reason, the non-compliant party will be held in contempt of court and will be required to pay a fine into the court and, in some cases, to the party who was injured as a result of the failure to comply with the terms of the injunction.

1.10.5 Special kinds of harm

Although it makes sense, in many ways, to begin a tort course with a discussion on negligence, there are numerous special cases that can confuse those who are new to the subject. The two most commonly studied special cases in negligence involve psychiatric damage and economic loss, which are covered in two separate chapters in this section. Psychiatric damage, as discussed in the first chapter in this section, is more than hurt feelings, although some torts do allow recovery for pain and emotional suffering associated with personal injuries. Psychiatric damage, as the term is used here, relates to mental trauma that arises as a result of a tortious event even when the claimant has not suffered any physical harm. For example, a person who, while standing in the front yard, witnessed the death of a loved one after a car ran up on the pavement may recover for shock and trauma, even if the claimant was in another part of the front yard and was not injured when the accident occurred. For many years, tort law did not award damages for this type of injury, since courts were concerned about matters of evidence (how does one prove mental trauma?) as well as matters of public policy (if we allow recovery in these types of cases, will the number of claims increase so radically that they flood the courts?). As a result, the rules about who can recover and when are somewhat complex and severely limit the number of situations in which damages are allowed.

Economic loss—also known as 'pure economic loss' to distinguish it from economic loss associated with other types of damage—is another area where courts have hesitated to allow recovery. In this case, the major concern was that the losses involved were too speculative. Pure economic loss can be difficult to quantify, since it's hard in many cases to know what kind of profits a business will make in the future. Furthermore, it might be difficult to say for certain that the defendant should be liable for such losses since, even if future profits could be quantified, there is nothing to say that some other catastrophic event wouldn't arise. Finally, courts are hesitant to hold defendants responsible for losses that they could not possibly foresee or guard against. As time passed, however, courts began to identify ways to restrict recovery in inappropriate cases but allow it in a tightly circumscribed set of circumstances. The second chapter in this section also discusses the development of the law on recovery for economic loss.

The third chapter in this section covers the law of defamation and the emerging law of privacy. Defamation is one of the torts protecting intangible interests, in this case the reputation of the claimant. Like it or not, people are social creatures who value the opinions of friends, family members, and business associates. Circulating falsehoods about someone's personal or professional characteristics can cause both emotional suffering and financial loss. For example, a wife might leave her husband if she is told that he has a mistress. A businesswoman might lose her job if her supervisor is told that she takes drugs and embezzled money from her last place of employment. A father might have his children put into state care if social services is told that he beats or neglects them. Lies and half-truths that injure a person's reputation can have severe consequences, and that is the interest that defamation protects. This chapter discusses the elements required to establish defamation as well as the special defences and remedies associated with this tort.

cross reference

The case involving this fact scenario, Douglas v Hello! Ltd [2001] QB 967, is discussed in chapter 14.

The chapter includes a short subsection on the developing law of privacy, which is related to defamation in that it also protects certain intangible values associated with an individual. However, the law of privacy does not protect against falsehoods, as defamation does; instead, it protects those parts of a person's life that can and should remain outside the public sphere. Thus, two movie stars can bring a suit to prohibit publication of certain photographs of their private wedding, even though the photographs are true and accurate depictions of the events, simply because the publication of the photographs would infringe on their private lives.

1.10.6 Product liability

The next chapter returns to an area of law that is largely controlled by statute: product liability, which involves injuries to persons and property that arise as a result of an item that has been produced for public consumption. Because personal safety is a major public policy concern, Parliament has a strong interest in protecting consumers from unsafe products and ensuring that the risk of harm falls on the appropriate party. As a result, Parliament has enacted legislation that addresses who will be liable for any losses associated with unsafe products. In fact, this is one of the areas where Parliament has used tort law as a means of moulding the behaviour of big business. Because consumer protection is so important, Parliament has made product liability a strict liability tort, meaning that it does not matter how careful the manufacturer was in researching, designing, and producing the item—if an injury occurs, then the manufacturer will be held liable for all losses suffered. This mechanism provides industry with a large incentive for ensuring that all products that reach the market are safe for use, since a rash of injuries would not only harm a company's reputation, it could result in a series of large damages awards that could bankrupt the company. This chapter discusses the relevant legislation, as well as the key cases construing that legislation, and provides a background on the development of strict liability in tort.

1.10.7 Liability for the torts of others

Although many people think of tort law as involving two private individuals—as is true in property disputes between neighbours, for example, or in cases involving auto accidents or other instances of negligence—tort law also governs relationships involving businesses. One way that a company or corporation might become involved in tort litigation is through the sale of its products, as discussed in the chapter on product liability. A commercial enterprise might also become subject to a claim in tort as a result of the actions of its employees or other hired help. This chapter addresses **liability for the torts of others**, including both employees and independent contractors. The discussion devotes considerable attention to the question of whether a person is an employee working for the company or an independent contractor working for him or herself, since liability often hinges on that distinction, as well as the question of whether an employee was working within the course of his or her duties at the time the injury arose.

1.10.8 Torts against the person

Following the discussion of intentional torts is a conclusory chapter that includes guidance on how to revise for a tort examination, including step-by-step revision techniques and sample revision plans. Although this chapter comes at the end of the text, you might want to glance at it now or at some other point well before your revision period, since it includes a number of suggestions that will help you understand and organize your materials as you go through your course. Furthermore, with all the things that must be done at the end of a course, it is easy to skip the last bit of reading. If you make a good start now, you can simply skim it later.

The substantive portion of the text will conclude with a chapter on torts against the person—assault, battery, and false imprisonment. Some lecturers choose to use these torts—which were amongst the first civil actions to be recognized as providing individual recovery for injuries suffered at the hands of another—as an introduction to the law of tort, whereas others choose to omit them altogether. Certainly the three torts are analytically different from other causes of action discussed in this book (with the exception of trespass to land), since they all require the tortfeasor to act with intent, rather than with some lesser mental state. This chapter will outline the necessary elements of each of the three torts and discuss the defences unique to these actions.

1.10.9 Revising for a tort exam

A few final points; first, you may notice that older cases include the term 'plaintiff' to refer to the person who filed the claim in court. This is typically the injured person. Recent reforms in the civil procedure rules have changed the term 'plaintiff' to 'claimant' to help de-mystify law. Be aware that the older terms will be used for older cases, whereas the new term will be used from the time of the change in the courts. The term 'defendant'—meaning the person against whom the case is brought—has stayed the same.

Second, the text is scattered with 'tip boxes' which show in the margins. These boxes include vocabulary, cross-references, and additional ideas for consideration, as well as the occasional exam tip. Sometimes the information in the tip boxes is not found in the main text, so you should be sure to read these tip boxes in addition to the body of the text.

Third, this series has taken the study of law into the twenty-first century by providing a wealth of additional information on the Oxford University Press website. If you go to www. oxfordtextbooks.co.uk/orc/strong_complete/, you will find additional revision suggestions and material, as well as a question bank that you can use to test yourself on the subjects contained in this book.

Fourth, a number of the case extracts use the new neutral citation system, introduced in 2001. In these extracts, the paragraph numbers from the neutral citation system have been omitted for easier reading. Should you go into legal practice professionally, you should be sure to use the paragraph numbers as indicated by the relevant practice directions. Furthermore, this text has adopted the convention of using the full case name and citation in the vast majority of references to cases. This way, you don't have to search for a full citation if your instructor only assigns parts of chapters or if you do your reading in short spurts and can't remember where the first case reference shows. By using this method, this text also underscores the importance of explicitly relying on legal authority in all of your work. However, you should be aware that your instructor may allow you to 'short cite' cases in your papers and examinations, and you should follow whatever conventions your examiner recommends.

You are now ready to begin reading about the first tort on your course. Enjoy your foray into what many people think is one of the most interesting areas of legal study!

 For more revision tips, including self-test questions and suggestions for further reading, see the Online Resource Centre at www.oxfordtextbooks.co.uk/orc/strong_complete/.

revision tasks

The most accurate and helpful revision is done while you are going through the course. There will not be time to do a proper job of revision if you wait until the conclusion of your lectures. Consider the following tips to help you organize your thoughts and your materials as you begin your course.

- Start a vocabulary list with all the terms—procedural and substantive—that you don't know and keep adding to it throughout your course. Using the right terms is half the battle on an examination, and knowing the terms in advance will make your weekly reading much easier.

- Browse through chapter 18 on revising for a tort examination now and identify which revision techniques work best for you. Although student lawyers must learn new analytical and revision techniques if they are to learn how to (a) remember and (b) manipulate the masses of information they will be given, there is no need to abandon all the revision techniques that have worked for you in the past. Be wise in what habits you prune, while also being open to new ideas.

- Your understanding of written material is best right after you have read it. Begin to organize the cases and statutes the minute you finish your reading. While you may want to do additional cross-referencing later, law does not build up on prior learning the same way that other courses do. You will be learning something new and different all the time. Don't make the mistake of thinking you should wait to do your organization later, when you understand the material better—make your start now.

TIP Don't wait until the end of term to begin revising. Start outlining from your very first week of lectures and reading. Organize it as you go for best results!

Chapter 1 Introduction to tort

28

Part 2
Negligence

Negligence: Duty

 2.1 ## Introduction: the importance of negligence

Negligence appears in four different chapters in this book, dealing with these topics:

- duty;

- breach;

- causation and remoteness; and

- defences.

Negligence also features heavily in the chapters on psychiatric damage, economic loss, damages, product liability and liability for the torts of others. Most other torts get only one chapter, or even part of a chapter, each. That is because negligence has become perhaps the most important and wide-reaching tort available.

Though negligence is now central to the law of tort, it is of relatively recent origin. Although different commentators trace its roots to the thirteenth, seventeenth, eighteenth or nineteenth centuries, its general principles did not begin to be established until 1932, when the House of Lords decided the case of *Donoghue v Stevenson* [1932] AC 562. Yet most tort textbooks are built around the tort of negligence, not just in the United Kingdom, but in other common law jurisdictions as well. Thus the question—why is negligence so special?

One answer is that, since 1932, negligence has rapidly developed into the cornerstone of our system for compensating people for accidental damage and injuries. This is because it allows the courts to award damages in tort in some circumstances where it is not possible to do so in contract. It has also been used creatively to compensate people for financial losses in business contexts where no other remedy was available. Another reason is that the development of negligence has had a knock-on effect on other torts. The existence of negligence as a civil remedy has changed the scope of other torts since 1932. Finally, many of the ingredients that are characteristic of negligence also feature in other torts, though often in a less 'pure' form. Thus, negligence is a good place to begin your study of tort law, because it will provide you with a mental framework that you can apply throughout your tort course.

This chapter proceeds as follows:

- The elements of negligence;
- The neighbour principle;
- Established duty situations;
- When to go back to first principles;
- What are the principles?;
- Acts and omissions;
- Duties to avoid particular kinds of damage.

 2.2 # The elements of negligence

Negligence can be defined as a breach of a legal duty to take care that results in damage to the claimant. When lawyers analyse a negligence case, they typically break it down into three elements: duty, breach and damage. Each of these elements must be satisfied for a claimant to establish liability on the part of the defendant. In other words, the defendant must owe the claimant a duty; the defendant must have breached that duty; and that breach must have caused some damage to the claimant. Damage usually has two sub-elements: causation and remoteness. Causation means the claimant must show that, had it not been for the breach, the damage would not have happened. Remoteness means that the claimant has to show that the damage which occurred was not so improbable that the defendant should not be liable for it. We will look at each of these elements in turn. This chapter focuses on the first element: duty.

In practice, judges often analyse facts in a way that creates some overlap between the various elements of negligence. The extent to which the different elements can really be separated is a common essay question. For now, keep the elements as separate as possible in your own mind. Later, you can come back to the question of overlap with less risk of becoming confused.

TIP Negligence is based on concepts of fault; specifically, on an allegation that the defendant should have taken care to avoid harming the claimant. Some other jurisdictions have 'no-fault' compensation systems.

TIP Start keeping a running list of the torts you have studied, their definitions and their elements. You will need this information for your examinations, particularly problem questions.

> **Exercise**
> . . . .
> You can find duties everywhere in your life—just think of all the situations in daily life where you have a responsibility to take care not to injure someone. For example, if you drive a car, you have a responsibility to other drivers and pedestrians to drive carefully. Other people share a duty not to injure you. For example, if you ride a bus, the driver has a responsibility not to injure you. Make a list of everyday situations where you have a responsibility to others and where others have a responsibility to you. As you read, look out for principles that enable you to work out whether each of those responsibilities is recognized as a legal duty.

The neighbour principle

2.3

As we have already mentioned, the development of general principles of negligence is usually traced to the leading case of *Donoghue v Stevenson* [1932] AC 562. The facts are simple. Mrs Donoghue went into a café with a friend, who bought her a bottle of ginger beer. Mrs Donoghue poured some of the ginger beer into a glass and drank it, but when she poured out the rest, a decomposing snail fell out. Mrs Donoghue later became ill as a result of drinking the contaminated ginger beer. Because Mrs Donoghue's friend was the one who actually bought the ginger beer, Mrs Donoghue had no contract with the owner of the café or with the manufacturer. She therefore had to turn to tort law, rather than contract law, to seek a remedy. She successfully sued the manufacturer in negligence. As you read the case extract below, look out for the general principle that Lord Atkin lays down as a rule of law.

· ·

● ***Donoghue v Stevenson*** [1932] AC 562

33

Lord Atkin: The question is whether the manufacturer of an article of drink sold by him to a distributor in circumstances which prevent the distributor or the ultimate purchaser or consumer from discovering by inspection any defect is under any legal duty to the ultimate purchaser or consumer to take reasonable care that the article is free from defect likely to cause injury to health. I do not think a more important problem has occupied your Lordships in your judicial capacity, important both because of its bearing on public health and because of the practical test which it applies to the system of law under which it arises. . . . I speak with little authority on this point, but my own research, such as it is, satisfies me that the principles of the law of Scotland on such a question as the present are identical with those of English law, and I discuss the issue on that footing.

The law of both countries appears to be that in order to support an action for damages for negligence the complainant has to show that he has been injured by the breach of a duty owed to him in the circumstances by the defendant to take reasonable care to avoid such injury. In the present case we are not concerned with the breach of the duty; if a duty exists, that would be a question of fact which . . . for the present purposes must be assumed. We are solely concerned with the question whether as a matter of law in the circumstances alleged the defender owed any duty to the pursuer to take care. It is remarkable how difficult it is to find in the English authorities statements of general application defining the relations between parties that give rise to the duty.

At present I content myself with pointing out that in English law there must be and is some general conception of relations giving rise to a duty of care, of which the particular cases found in the books are but instances. The liability for negligence . . . is no doubt based upon a general public sentiment of moral wrongdoing for which the offender must pay. But acts or omissions which any moral code would censure cannot in a practical world be treated so as to give a right to every person injured by them to demand relief. In this way rules of law arise which limit the range of complainants and the extent of their remedy. The rule that you are to love your neighbour becomes in law: You must not injure your neighbour, and the lawyers' question: Who is my neighbour? receives a restricted reply.

'The rule that you are to love your neighbour' and the question 'Who is my neighbour' refer to a story in Christian scripture in which Jesus answers a similar question.

This sentence is one of the most famous in all of the common law of tort.

You must take reasonable care to avoid acts or omissions which you can reasonably fore-see would be likely to injure your neighbour. Who then, in law, is my neighbour? The answer seems to be persons who are so closely and directly affected by my act that I ought reasonably to have them in contemplation as being so affected when I am directing my mind to the acts or omissions which are called in question.

This appears to me to be the doctrine of Heaven v Pender [[1881–1885] All ER Rep 35]…as laid down by LORD ESHER when it is limited by the notion of proximity introduced by LORD ESHER himself and AL SMITH, LJ, in Le Lievre and another v Gould [[1893] 1 QB 491]…:

'The decision of Heaven v Pender was founded upon the principle that a duty to take due care did arise when the person or property of one was in such proximity to the person or property of another that, if due care was not taken damage might be done by the one to the other.'

I think that this sufficiently states the truth if proximity be not confined to mere physical proximity, but be used, as I think it was intended, to extend to such close and direct rela-tions that the act complained of directly affects a person whom the person alleged to be bound to take care would know would be directly affected by his careless act.…

Proximity will be discussed further in 2.6 and chapters 12 and 13.

I draw particular attention to the fact that LORD ESHER emphasises the necessity of goods having to be 'used immediately' and 'used at once before a reasonable opportunity of inspection.'

This is obviously to exclude the possibility of goods having their condition altered by lapse of time, and to call attention to the proximate relationship, which may be too remote where inspection even by the person using, certainly by an intermediate person, may reasonably be interposed. With this necessary qualification of proximate relationship, as explained in Le Lievre and another v Gould…I think the judgment of LORD ESHER expresses the law…

Donoghue was a Scottish case that came to the House of Lords on appeal. Scottish law refers to 'pursuer' and 'defender' rather than 'claimant' and 'defendant'. Some other case extracts will refer to 'plaintiffs' rather than 'claimants'—this was the English terminology until 1999, when the Civil Procedure Rules replaced the old Rules of the Supreme Court.

The 'goods' in *Donoghue v Stevenson* [1932] AC 562, that is the ginger beer, could not be inspected either by Mrs Donoghue or by the café owner because it was in an opaque brown bottle.

The outcome was that the manufacturer owed a duty to Mrs Donoghue. Since this case, the courts have applied the principles laid down by Lord Atkin to many other situations. We will look at some of these in the next section.

2.4 Established duty situations

VOCABULARY

A 'precedent' is a decision that is suffi-ciently similar to the facts of the dispute at hand that the judge is obliged to follow it.

It is not always necessary to go back to first principles (such as those laid down in *Donoghue v Stevenson* [1932] AC 562) to decide whether a defendant owed a duty to a claimant. Instead, lawyers start by asking whether there is an established **precedent** which shows that there is a duty. This should also be your first step when you answer a problem question. In this section, we look at some of these 'established duty situations'. Some of the most straightforward are the following:

- Any road user owes a duty to any other road user to exercise due care and attention. 'Road user' includes not just drivers, but pedestrians, cyclists and even passengers.

- Employers have a duty to take reasonable care for the safety of their employees.

- Just as employers owe a duty to their employees, employees also owe a duty to one another to take reasonable care for each other's safety.

- Teachers, and anyone else left in charge of children, owe a duty to the children to take reasonable care for their safety. Note, though, that adults in general do not owe a duty to children just because the children happen to be nearby. The adult must be in charge of the child.

- Parents (including foster parents) also owe a duty to their own children to take reasonable care for their safety.

Each of these examples is relatively straight forward and easy to understand. Some situations require a more detailed analysis.

2.4.1 Mothers and third parties/unborn children

In general, mothers do not owe any duty to their unborn children. However, there is one significant exception to this, under the following statute:

35

● **Congenital Disabilities (Civil Liability) Act 1976**

1 Civil liability to child born disabled

(1) If a child is born disabled as the result of such an occurrence before its birth as is mentioned in subsection (2) below, and a person (other than the child's own mother) is under this section answerable to the child in respect of the occurrence, the child's disabilities are to be regarded as damage resulting from the wrongful act of that person and actionable accordingly at the suit of the child.

(2) An occurrence to which this section applies is one which—
   (a) affected either parent of the child in his or her ability to have a normal, healthy child; or
   (b) affected the mother during her pregnancy, or affected her or the child in the course of its birth, so that the child is born with disabilities which would not otherwise have been present.

(3) Subject to the following subsections, a person (here referred to as 'the defendant') is answerable to the child if he was liable in tort to the parent or would, if sued in due time, have been so; and it is no answer that there could not have been such liability because the parent suffered no actionable injury, if there was a breach of legal duty which, accompanied by injury, would have given rise to the liability...

Recall
The duty owed by the defendant always refers to the particular claimant who is suing. Claimants can't recover for a wrong which has been done to someone else.

think point

- *When can the child sue the mother for something that happened before birth?*

- *Why was this particular exception made?*

- *Who else can the unborn child potentially sue?*

(5) The defendant is not answerable to the child, for anything he did or omitted to do when responsible in a professional capacity for treating or advising the parent, if he took reasonable care having due regard to then received professional opinion applicable to the particular class of case; but this does not mean that he is answerable only because he departed from received opinion.

As a matter of public policy, a claimant whose disabilities were not correctly diagnosed before birth cannot sue for 'wrongful birth' on the basis that the mother would have had an abortion had the diagnosis been correct. However, parents may have a claim for the costs of raising the child and the distress caused to them by the disability, although this is an open question. Such a claim failed in *Rance v Mid-Down Health Authority* [1991] 1 QB 587, where a child was born with severe birth defects. There, the parents claimed that if the ultrasound had been done properly at 26 weeks, they would have found out about the congenital condition and had an abortion. In the end, the claim failed, but primarily because abortion would have been illegal in those circumstances.

● **Congenital Disabilities (Civil Liability) Act 1976**

2 Liability of woman driving when pregnant

A woman driving a motor vehicle when she knows (or ought reasonably to know) herself to be pregnant is to be regarded as being under the same duty to take care for the safety of her unborn child as the law imposes on her with respect to the safety of other people; and if in consequence of her breach of that duty her child is born with disabilities which would not otherwise have been present, those disabilities are to be regarded as damage resulting from her wrongful act and actionable accordingly at the suit of the child.

2.4.2 Professionals and other service providers/clients

Anyone providing a service—from physical services such as plumbing, building or medical care to more abstract ones such as private tuition, legal or financial advice—owes a duty to the recipient of the service to exercise reasonable care and skill in carrying out the service. We will consider some special cases of this type of duty below.

This is one of the areas where tort law and contract law overlap. Contract law also imposes duties of skill and care in the provision of services, as with the implied term under section 13 of the Supply of Goods and Services Act 1982. Such contractual duties exist concurrently with duties in negligence, so a claimant may sometimes be able to claim in both tort and contract. Claimants cannot recover damages twice (since to do so would violate the rule against 'double recovery'), but they can choose whichever action is most advantageous for them or bring both actions as alternatives.

Each type of action has its advantages and disadvantages. For instance, the measure of damages and the limitation period are calculated differently in tort and contract, and the available defences are different. We will discuss these factors in later chapters.

2.4.3 The courtroom

Advocates (both barristers and solicitor-advocates) used to enjoy immunity from negligence actions over the way in which they presented arguments in court and over preparatory decisions made before trial if those decisions affected the presentation of the case. However, in *Hall v Simons* [2000] 3 WLR 543, the House of Lords unanimously said that this immunity should be abolished for civil cases. A majority of four to three said immunity should also be abolished in criminal cases. Strictly, this decision was *obiter*, but because of the high respect accorded to the House of Lords, it will inevitably be followed in the lower courts. Advocates can therefore be sued for breach of their duty of care in providing legal services to their clients, just as other professionals can be sued. If advocates are sued by a client they defended unsuccessfully in a criminal claim, however, the claim will usually be struck out unless the client successfully overturned the conviction on appeal. Claims relating to civil cases can also be struck out if they amount to an attempt to re-litigate an issue that has already been decided against the claimant, rather than a genuine complaint against the advocate.

Judges continue to enjoy immunity from negligence claims. Therefore, an unsuccessful litigant cannot sue a judge for deciding a case without due care. Similarly, a litigant cannot sue witnesses for the way in which they give evidence, even if they perjure themselves or act with malice towards the litigant. This immunity includes preparatory activities such as investigating the matters the witness is to give evidence on, preparing a witness statement and so on.

> **Exercise**
>
> Look back at the list of situations you made earlier where you may have taken on a responsibility or where someone else may have had a responsibility to you. Which of them were established duty situations? Now make a note of any that are left, and as you read the next section, see how you think the principles will apply to them.

2.5 When to go back to first principles

Established duty situations do not (and cannot) cover every situation that may arise. It would be too difficult for judges to interpret each and every possible situation that could arise, and judges can only address the facts that are in front of them, anyway—they can't just make up rules of law based on hypothetical situations. You therefore need to be familiar with the principles that the courts apply when they are faced with a novel negligence claim. To put these principles in context and understand how to apply them, you need to know a sequence of cases. The first is *Anns v London Borough of Merton* [1978] AC 728, which involved a claim by tenants against a housing authority. We will consider other aspects of this case in chapter 7.

● *Anns v London Borough of Merton* [1978] AC 728

> Lord Wilberforce: [T]he position has now been reached that in order to establish that a duty of care arises in a particular situation, it is not necessary to bring the facts of that situation within those of previous situations in which a duty of care has been held to exist. Rather the question has to be approached in two stages. First one has to ask whether, as between the alleged wrongdoer and the person who has suffered damage there is a sufficient relationship of proximity or neighbourhood such that, in the reasonable contemplation of the former, carelessness on his part may be likely to cause damage to the latter, in which case a prima facie duty of care arises. Secondly, if the first question is answered affirmatively, it is necessary to consider whether there are any considerations which ought to negative, or to reduce or limit the scope of the duty or the class of person to whom it is owed or the damages to which a breach of it may give rise...

Lord Wilberforce's opinion gave the courts a great deal of freedom in deciding negligence cases, and the courts and commentators were concerned that the law of negligence would become too free-form and would not grow in accordance with established principles and case law. Less than ten years later, in the case of *Leigh v Sillivan Ltd v Aliakmon Shipping Co Ltd* [1986] AC 786, the Court of Appeal and the House of Lords expressed contrasting views on the meaning of this statement by Lord Wilberforce and on the role which precedent should play in determining whether there is a duty of care. This case involved a claim for goods that had been damaged by being stored incorrectly during a voyage.

● *Leigh v Sullivan Ltd v Aliakmon Shipping Co Ltd* [1985] QB 350 (in the Court of Appeal)

> Lord Donaldson MR: I must therefore move on to the second stage of the test, reminding myself that the first test only threw up a prima facie duty of care. For this purpose I have to ask myself whether there are any considerations which ought to negative, or to reduce or limit the scope of the duty or the class of person to whom it is owed and/or the damages to which a breach of it may give rise.
>
> Mr. Sumption for the shipowners had put forward three such considerations. The first is: 'In a trade governed by elaborate insurance arrangements based on a long-standing view of the incidence of liability, consistently sanctioned by the courts in the past, it would be wrong to disturb that view without compelling reasons based on the circumstances of the trade itself.'
>
> I am unimpressed by this argument. It is that which was condemned by Lord Wilberforce in the Anns case [1978] A.C. 728, when he said, at p. 751: 'in order to establish that a duty of care arises in a particular situation, it is not necessary to bring the facts of that situation within those of previous situations in which a duty of care has been held to exist.'

● *Leigh v Sullivan Ltd v Aliakmon Shipping Co Ltd* [1986] AC 786 (in the House of Lords)

> Lord Brandon: I now return to consider Mr. Clarke's submissions based on what Lord Wilberforce said in Anns' case [1978] A.C. 728. There are two preliminary observations

which I think that it is necessary to make with regard to the passage in Lord Wilberforce's speech on which counsel relies. The first observation which I would make is that that passage does not provide, and cannot in my view have been intended by Lord Wilberforce to provide, a universally applicable test of the existence and scope of a duty of care in the law of negligence. In this connection I would draw attention to a passage in the speech of my noble and learned friend, Lord Keith of Kinkel, in Governors of the Peabody Donation Fund v Sir Lindsay Parkinson & Co. Ltd. [1985] A.C. 210. After citing a passage from Lord Reid's speech in Dorset Yacht Co. Ltd. v Home Office [1970] A.C. 1004, 1027 and then the passage from Lord Wilberforce's speech in Anns' case [1978] A.C. 728, 751–752 now under discussion, he said, at p. 240: 'There has been a tendency in some recent cases to treat these passages as being themselves of a definitive character. This is a temptation which should be resisted.'

The second observation which I would make is that Lord Wilberforce was dealing, as is clear from what he said, with the approach to the questions of the existence and scope of a duty of care in a novel type of factual situation which was not analogous to any factual situation in which the existence of such a duty had already been held to exist. He was not, as I understand the passage, suggesting that the same approach should be adopted to the existence of a duty of care in a factual situation in which the existence of such a duty had repeatedly been held not to exist.

After *Leigh v Sullivan Ltd v Aliakmon Shipping Co Ltd* [1986] AC 786, further criticisms of Lord Wilberforce's approach in *Anns v London Borough of Merton* [1978] AC 728 arose. For example, in *Yuen Kun Yeu v Attorney-General for Hong Kong* [1988] AC 175, Lord Keith of Kinkel quoted with approval the statement of the Australian judge Brennan J that it was preferable that the law should develop novel categories of negligence incrementally and by analogy with established categories, rather than by a massive extension of a prima facie duty of care restrained only by indefinable 'considerations which ought to negative, or to reduce or limit the scope of the duty or the class of person to whom it is owed'. Lord Keith believed the purpose of the 'second stage' of the test in *Anns* was simply to allow for public policy considerations to be taken into account in rare cases.

Similarly, in *Curran v Northern Ireland Co-Ownership Housing Association Ltd* [1987] AC 718, Lord Bridge famously described *Anns v London Borough of Merton* [1978] AC 728 as:

> the high water mark of a trend in the development of the law of negligence by your Lordships' House towards the elevation of the 'neighbourhood' principle derived from the speech of Lord Atkin in Donoghue v Stevenson [1932] A.C. 562 into one of general application from which a duty of care may always be derived unless there are clear countervailing considerations to exclude it.

The suggestion of the Australian judge that new categories of duty should be developed incrementally and by analogy to existing ones was approved by the House of Lords in *Caparo Industries plc v Dickman* [1990] 2 AC 605, which is now the leading case on the principles which apply to duties of care in negligence. In that case, the House of Lords warned against trying to establish a single test for the existence of a duty of care. However, it agreed there is a clear need for some sort of guidelines which can be used when a case does not fall squarely within the existing precedents. In the next section, we look at some guidelines which have been derived from this seminal case.

2.6 General principles relating to a duty of care

Caparo v Dickman [1990] 2 AC 605 involved an allegation of negligence against accountants. It is famous for identifying three factors that the court should take into account in deciding whether or not there is a duty of care.

● ***Caparo Industries plc v Dickman*** [1990] 2 AC 605

Lord Oliver of Aylmerton: [I]t is now clear from a series of decisions in this House that, at least so far as concerns the law of the United Kingdom, the duty of care in tort depends not solely upon the existence of the essential ingredient of the foreseeability of damage to the plaintiff but upon its coincidence with a further ingredient to which has been attached the label 'proximity' and which was described by Lord Atkin in the course of his speech in Donoghue v Stevenson [1932] A.C. 562, 581 as: 'such close and direct relations that the act complained of directly affects a person whom the person alleged to be bound to take care would know would be directly affected by his careless act.'

It must be remembered, however, that Lord Atkin was using these words in the context of loss caused by physical damage where the existence of the nexus between the careless defendant and the injured plaintiff can rarely give rise to any difficulty. To adopt the words of Bingham L.J. in the instant case [1989] Q.B. 653, 686: 'It is enough that the plaintiff chances to be (out of the whole world) the person with whom the defendant collided or who purchased the offending ginger beer.'

The extension of the concept of negligence since the decision of this House in Hedley Byrne & Co. Ltd. v Heller & Partners Ltd. [1964] A.C. 465 to cover cases of pure economic loss not resulting from physical damage has given rise to a considerable and as yet unsolved difficulty of definition.

NOTE We discuss pure economic loss in chapter 13. For now, all you need to appreciate is that the courts have found it more difficult to define what degree of proximity is required when the claimant's loss is purely financial than when it includes some physical injury or damage. In *Caparo Industries plc v Dickman* [1990] 2 AC 605, investors lost money when they relied on a statement by an auditor which turned out not to be accurate.

The opportunities for the infliction of pecuniary loss from the imperfect performance of everyday tasks upon the proper performance of which people rely for regulating their affairs are illimitable and the effects are far reaching. A defective bottle of ginger beer may injure a single consumer but the damage stops there. A single statement may be repeated endlessly with or without the permission of its author and may be relied upon in a different way by many different people. Thus the postulate of a simple duty to avoid any harm that is, with hindsight, reasonably capable of being foreseen becomes untenable without the imposition of some intelligible limits to keep the law of negligence within the bounds of common sense and practicality. Those limits have been found by the requirement of what has been called a 'relationship of proximity' between plaintiff and defendant and by the imposition of a further requirement that the attachment of liability for harm which has occurred be 'just and reasonable.' But although the cases in which the courts have imposed or withheld liability are capable of an approximate categorisation, one looks in vain for some common denominator by which the existence of the essential relationship can be tested. Indeed it is difficult to resist a conclusion that what have been treated as three separate requirements are, at least in most cases, in fact merely facets of the same thing, for in some cases the degree of foreseeability is such that it is from that alone that the requisite proximity can be deduced, whilst in others the absence of that essential relationship can most rationally be attributed simply to the court's view that it would not be fair and reasonable to hold the defendant responsible. 'Proximity' is, no doubt, a convenient expression so long as it is realised that it is no more than a label which embraces not a definable concept but merely a description of circumstances from which, pragmatically, the courts conclude that a duty of care exists.

Despite these cautionary words of Lord Oliver's, lawyers usually treat *Caparo v Dickman* [1990] 2 AC 605 as establishing a threefold test for the existence of a duty of care. This test consists of three questions, which must all be answered in the affirmative in order to establish a duty:

- Is there sufficient proximity between the claimant and the defendant?
- Was it foreseeable that the defendant's action would cause loss or damage to someone in the claimant's position?
- Is it fair, just and reasonable to impose a duty on the defendant in the circumstances?

The extract also shows that the threefold test needs to be treated with caution. Just as duty, breach and damage often seem to overlap in the courts' analysis, so too do the three limbs of the *Caparo* test. However, as with the three elements of negligence, the threefold test can make a useful way of organising your thoughts—whether for studying and assessment purposes, or for a submission to a court—and it is the approach which practitioners typically use to estimate whether a court is likely to decide that there is a duty in a new situation. We will now look at each of the elements in turn.

2.6.1 Proximity

The requirement of proximity broadly corresponds to the second limb of Lord Atkin's neighbour principle in *Donoghue v Stevenson* [1932] AC 562, which asks whether the claimants are 'so closely and directly affected by [the defendant's] act that [the defendant] ought reasonably to have them in . . . contemplation as being so affected'. It is not possible to give a single definition of what proximity means. There are a number of ways for a claimant to establish that there was proximity in a given situation, for instance, by showing:

- that the defendant was close to the claimant in terms of place—for instance, that they were owner-occupiers of adjacent buildings;

- that the defendant and the claimant had a close family relationship—for instance, parents have duties to their children;

- that the defendant and the claimant had a contractual relationship;

- that the claimant relied on special skills which the defendant had undertaken to use for the claimant's benefit; or

- that the defendant's actions made the claimant's physical safety dependent on the defendant.

Another example of proximity is between the police and a police informant, as in *Swinney v Chief Constable of Northumbria*, The Times, 25 May 1999, where Mrs Swinney reported a criminal to the police in confidence and was later harassed by vandals after the police negligently allowed her name to leak out to the criminal concerned.

However, as a general rule there is no proximity between the police and individual members of the public as a matter of law. For instance, in *Hill v Constable of West Yorkshire* [1989] AC 53, the mother of one of the women killed by Peter Sutcliffe (the 'Yorkshire Ripper') sued the police for failing to prevent her daughter's death. The court found that there was no proximity between the police and the daughter, because before the murder took place, there was nothing to suggest that she was more at risk than any other woman. The court was also concerned that imposing a duty in this case might interfere excessively with police operational decisions and make it more difficult for police to investigate crimes effectively. Similarly, in *Palmer v Tees Health Authority* [1999] Lloyd's Rep Med 351, a mother sued the health authority for failing to prevent a mentally-ill man from murdering her daughter. Again, the court held that there was no duty to the daughter because she was not at special risk prior to the attack. However, if there is some indication of special risk—as in the case of Mrs Swinney, who was an informant—then there can be a duty. In *Palmer v Tees Health Authority* [1999] Lloyd's Rep Med 351, for instance, the court suggested that the authority might have a duty to a child in the household of a mentally-ill abuser.

The degree of proximity the claimant needs to show will depend on what the claimant says the defendant had a duty to do. It is more difficult to prove a duty to do something than a duty to refrain from doing something, as you will see later. The more decisions you read, the more you will develop a sense of the kinds of cases in which the courts will find that there is proximity. The following case provides a good explanation of the pragmatic considerations of proximity.

● *Watson v British Boxing Board of Control Limited* [2001] QB 1134

Lord Phillips of Worth Matravers: On 21 September 1991 Michael Watson fought Chris Eubank for the World Boxing Organisation super-middleweight title at Tottenham Hotspur Football Club in London. The referee stopped the fight in the final round when Watson appeared to be unable to defend himself. He had in fact sustained a brain haemorrhage and, after returning to his corner, he lapsed into unconsciousness on his stool. There was chaos in and outside the ring and seven minutes elapsed before he was examined by one of the doctors who were in attendance. He was taken on a stretcher to an ambulance which was standing by which took him to North Middlesex Hospital. Nearly half an hour elapsed between the end of the fight and the time that he got there. At the North Middlesex Hospital he was intubated, that is an endotracheal tube was inserted, and he was given oxygen. He was also given an injection of mannitol, a diuretic that can have the effect of reducing swelling of the brain. The North Middlesex Hospital had no neuro-surgical department, so Mr Watson was transferred by ambulance, still unconscious, to St Bartholomew's Hospital. There an operation was carried out to evacuate a subdural haematoma. By this time, however, he had sustained serious brain damage. This has left him paralysed down the left side and with other physical and mental disabilities.

The fight had taken place in accordance with the rules of the British Boxing Board of Control Ltd ('the board'). These rules included provisions for medical inspection of boxers and for the attendance of two doctors at a fight. In fact the board had required a third doctor to be present and that an ambulance should be in attendance.

Mr Watson brought an action against the board. He claimed that the board had been under a duty of care to see that all reasonable steps were taken to ensure that he received immediate and effective medical attention and treatment should he sustain injury in the fight. . . .

Some significant features of the present case . . . place it outside any established category of duty of care in negligence. These make it necessary: (i) to identify the principles which are relied upon as giving rise to a duty of care in this case; (ii) to identify any categories of cases in which these principles have given rise to a duty of care, or conversely where they have not done so; (iii) to decide whether these principles should be applied so as to give rise to a duty of care in the present case . . .

The conduct of the activity of professional boxing carries with it, for the small body of men that take part in it, the need for the provision of medical assistance to treat the injuries that they sustain and minimise their adverse consequences. It seems to me that, but for the intervention of the board, the promoter would probably owe a common law duty to the boxer to make reasonable provision for the immediate treatment of his injuries. An analogy can be drawn with the duty of an employer, whose activities involve a particular health risk, to make provision for its employees to receive appropriate medical attention: see *Stokes v Guest Keen & Nettlefold (Bolts and Nuts) Ltd* [1968] 1 WLR 1776.

The board, however, arrogates to itself the task of determining what medical facilities will be provided at a contest by (i) requiring the boxer and the promoter to contract on terms under which the board's rules will apply and (ii) making provision in those rules for the medical facilities and assistance to be provided to care for the boxer in the event of injury. In this way the board reduces this aspect of the promoter's responsibility to the boxer to the contractual obligation to comply with the requirements of the board's rules in relation to the provision of medical facilities and assistance. The board assumes the responsibility of determining the nature of the medical facilities and assistance to be provided.

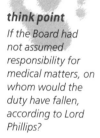

These facts bring the board into close proximity with each individual boxer who contracts with a promoter to fight under the board's rules . . .

Had the board simply given advice to all involved in professional boxing as to appropriate medical precautions, it would be strongly arguable that there was insufficient proximity between the board and individual boxers to give rise to a duty of care. The board, however, went far beyond this. It made provision in its rules for the medical precautions to be employed and made compliance with these rules mandatory. As Mr Morris accepted, by reason of its control over boxing the board was in a position to determine, and did in fact

> determine, the measures that were taken in boxing to protect and promote the health and safety of boxers.
>
> These facts produced a relationship of close proximity between the board and those of its members who were professional boxers.

This is an example of a case where the court imposed a duty because the plaintiff's (Watson's) safety was dependent on the defendant (the Board), as a result of the Board's actions in taking responsibility for medical precautions away from the promoters and making rules that promoters and boxers had to follow. Arguments based on the concept of assuming responsibility are quite common in negligence claims, particularly where the damage is financial, rather than physical as it was in this case. We will look at this in more detail in chapter 13 on economic loss.

2.6.2 Foreseeability

NOTE Foreseeability plays a role in the other elements of negligence, too. As you read the next two chapters, make a note of where else it appears.

The requirement of foreseeability in *Caparo v Dickman* [1990] 2 AC 605 corresponds to the first limb of the neighbour principle, which asks whether the defendant could 'reasonably foresee' that a given act or omission 'would be likely to injure [his or her] neighbour'.

2.6.3 Justice and reasonableness of imposing a duty

This is the only limb of the *Caparo* test that does not have an obvious equivalent in Lord Atkin's speech. Lord Atkins does suggest that the law of negligence reflects a 'general public sentiment of moral wrongdoing', but this is not quite the same as the mature judicial consideration that *Caparo v Dickman* [1990] 2 AC 605 seems to demand. However, it is probably better to regard this limb simply as (a) articulating the general principle that English judges always retain the right to take public policy considerations into account and (b) clarifying how it applies to negligence, rather than seeing it as introducing a completely new hurdle for claimants to satisfy.

2.7 Acts and omissions

compare
Other countries take a different approach to emergency situations. In many civil law jurisdictions there is a duty to help. Failing to do so may even be a crime.

There is an important distinction in negligence between acts and omissions. Generally, people only owe a duty under the neighbour principle to avoid harming each other by the things they do, not by the things they fail to do. For instance, in English law there is no general duty to help in emergencies: if you happen to come across a car accident, in most cases you have no duty to stop and help, and the accident victims cannot sue you if your failure to help makes their injuries worse. However, there are some exceptions, and we consider these in the following sections. Most of the exceptions can be understood as situations where there is a higher than normal degree of proximity, and therefore there is more reason to impose a duty. Even if the issue is something other than proximity, it is important to realize that the judges in these cases are applying the same *Caparo* principles that we have already looked at. The cases on omissions are not applying special rules; they are applying the ordinary rules to a special situation.

2.7.1 Ignoring instructions

If an employee is instructed to do something to protect the safety of a co-worker, then the employee has a legal duty to the co-worker to carry out that instruction and can be sued in negligence for failing to do so. A striking example of this is *Costello v Chief Constable of the Northumbria Police* [1999] 1 All ER 550, where a police officer stood by while another officer was attacked by a prisoner, without making any attempt to help her. May LJ, suggested in his judgment in that case that the same principle would apply if one worker were hypothetically instructed to hold a ladder for another worker and failed to do so.

In another case involving the police, *Kirkham v Chief Constable of the Greater Manchester Police* [1990] 2 QB 283, officers taking a prisoner from the police station to prison knew that he was a suicide risk, but failed to fill in the prescribed form to alert the prison authorities. The Court of Appeal found that they owed him a duty.

NOTE We will consider other aspects of *Reeves*, which were appealed, in chapter 4. The liability of chief constables (as opposed to individual officers) is considered in the next section.

A similar example is *Reeves v Commissioner of Police of the Metropolis* [2000] 1 AC 360, where officers ignored a standing order not to leave cell door hatches open because prisoners might be able to use the open hatch to hang themselves. A prisoner did so, and his partner sued. The judge at first instance found that 'having regard to the fact that the police knew that [the prisoner] was a suicide risk, they owed him a duty to take reasonable care to prevent him from committing suicide while being held in custody'. This finding, which is clearly in line with *Kirkham v Chief Constable of the Greater Manchester Police* [1990] 2 QB 283, was not appealed.

Notably, the prison officer's duty to prevent a prisoner from committing suicide only applies to prisoners who are known to be suicide risks, as the court indicated in *Orange v Chief Constable of West Yorkshire Police* [2001] EWCA Civ 611. The court decided there was no duty because there was nothing to indicate that the prisoner was at risk.

A rather different case, where the court also decided that no duty existed, was *Mulcahy v Ministry of Defence* [1996] QB 732. Mulcahy was a soldier serving in Iraq who was injured when his superior, a gun commander, gave an order to fire a gun which Mulcahy had been cleaning. The applicable gun drill required the commander to wait for Mulcahy to return to a position of safety before giving this order, but he failed to do so. The court decided that soldiers in battlefield conditions do not owe one another a duty of care. There was sufficient proximity and foreseeability, but it was not just or reasonable under *Caparo v Dickman* [1990] 2 AC 605 to impose a duty, because it would make battlefield operations impractical.

2.7.2 Control

Duties owed to third parties

Anyone who has control over the actions of another person has a duty to exercise that control in such a way as to prevent harm to others. Failing to do so can lead to liability in tort. The classic example of this is *Dorset Yacht Co Ltd v Home Office* [1970] AC 1004. In this case, some boys from a borstal (an old term for a young offenders' institution) were taken camping on an island. They escaped from the camp and tried to use some yachts in a nearby harbour to get off the island, damaging the yachts in the process. The court decided that, because the borstal officers were in a position to control the boys, and because it was foreseeable that they would be particularly attracted to the yachts if they escaped, the officers owed a duty of care to the yacht owners.

Duties owed to the person being controlled

Someone who has control over another person may have a duty to take care of that person's safety, in addition to any duty to third parties of the kind that existed in *Dorset Yacht Co. Ltd. v Home Office* [1970] AC 1004. For instance, in *Barrett v Ministry of Defence* [1995] 1 WLR 1217, a Navy officer came across a Navy pilot who had passed out after drinking too much. The officer arranged for the pilot to be returned to his room, but gave no instructions for anyone to watch him or take precautions in case he vomited. During the night, he choked on his own vomit and died. His widow sued for negligence. The court found that by taking control of the situation and ordering the pilot to be taken to his room, the officer had assumed responsibility for his safety and had a duty of care towards him.

The cases we have already looked at relating to suicides in police custody are another example of a duty toward a person under another's control. Both the individual police officers and the chief constable with overall responsibility for the relevant police force may owe a duty to a prisoner to prevent him or her from committing suicide. In *Orange v Chief Constable of West Yorkshire Police* [2001] EWCA Civ 611, the Court of Appeal held that this duty only applies to prisoners who are known to be a suicide risk. However, there are other duties which apply to all prisoners—for instance, duties to ensure that prisoners have adequate food and water, that they are not placed in dangerous buildings and so on—as suggested in *Vellino v Chief Constable of Greater Manchester* [2001] EWCA Civ 1249, which is described below. These duties are based on the police force's control over the prisoner rather than on any breach of instruction, so the claimant does not have to find any instruction or guidance which the chief constable has failed to follow.

Vellino v Chief Constable of Greater Manchester [2001] EWCA Civ 1249 demonstrates how courts formulate these duties. Vellino was a notorious local criminal who had been arrested on many occasions and had a reputation with the police and his neighbours for trying to escape by jumping out of the nearest window. One night, two police officers were called to his second-floor flat to deal with a noisy party, and they decided to take the opportunity to carry out an existing arrest warrant. After the arrest, both officers at first kept hold of Vellino, who was very drunk. However, one of the other party guests punched one of the officers, who let go of Vellino in order to defend himself. Vellino took advantage of this to escape from the other officer. He went into a bedroom, and the officers followed him, but apparently did not take any steps to stop him jumping out of the window. He did so and was so badly injured that he was paralysed. He remembered nothing of these events, but sued the officers for failing to prevent him from jumping out of the window.

· ·

● *Vellino v Chief Constable of Greater Manchester* [2001] EWCA Civ 1249

Schiemann LJ: It is common ground that under our law two persons can stand aside and watch a third jump to his death: there is no legal duty to rescue. Not all legal systems adopt that as their approach but for better or for worse that is the established position in English law. It is common ground that, prior to uttering the words 'I arrest you', the police owed him no duty to prevent him hurting himself while trying to escape.

How then is the position of the police in the present case to be distinguished from that of the ordinary citizen? The submission is that by arresting the claimant they notionally took him into their care and owed him a duty of care . . .

For my part I am content to assume, without so deciding, that when a police officer arrests a citizen the police officer puts himself in a relationship with that prisoner which can involve the police officer in having some duties for the breach of which the prisoner can sue. But in every case one has to identify the particular duty which it is that has allegedly been broken.

For instance if the officer detains the citizen then I would accept that he must take reasonable care that the citizen is not injured by lack of water. The officer might, if the roof showed signs of collapsing, be under a duty to take or let the citizen out of the flat where he was arrested. The fact that the citizen would never have been detained had he not previously committed a crime would not prevent an action from succeeding. The reasoning behind that approach is that by the fact of detention the man is prevented from getting his own water or escaping danger. It is not the arrest which gives rise to the duty of care to the man. It is his detention. That is also why there is a duty to try and prevent known suicide risks in prison from committing suicide.

However, where a man breaks away from the arresting officer the position is manifestly different. By so doing the man commits a crime and he is no longer in the immediate power of the officer.

Mr Stockdale, who appeared for the claimant had a difficult case and had some difficulty in formulating his propositions as to the nature of the duty of care which was allegedly broken . . .

I understood him to submit that the police are under a duty owed to the claimant to prevent him from sustaining foreseeable injury whilst foreseeably attempting to escape from custody. This, with respect, seems to me equally untenable: it would require the police to hold him in the loosest of grasps so that there was no danger of him wrenching his shoulder as he struggled to break free. Again no policy reason has been suggested for declaring this to be the law.

Moreover, even this formulation does not cover the present case. The claimant injured himself after he had escaped from custody, if by that one means containment by the police in some physical sense rather some jurisprudential concept.

Chapter 2 Negligence: Duty

47

cross reference

The first factor (criminality) will also be important when we look at defences in chapter 5.

There were two reasons for finding that there was no duty in this case: firstly, the prisoner was committing a crime when he was injured, and second, he was no longer in the control of the police.

2.7.3 Creating a risk

People may have a duty to act in such a way as to avoid creating risks for others or at least deal with the risk if it does occur. An example is *Stansbie v Troman* [1948] 2 KB 48, where the plaintiff's house was burgled because her decorator forgot to lock up when he had finished work. The decorator's omission created a risk of burglary and thus led to liability in negligence.

However, on the whole, courts are reluctant to make defendants responsible for the behaviour of others. Judges have used each of the three *Caparo* elements to avoid this result. Sometimes, two judges considering the same case have used different elements to explain the decision.

For instance, in *P Perl (Exporters) Ltd v Camden Borough Council* [1984] QB 342, the council owned two neighbouring properties. One was let to the plaintiff, and the other was unoccupied and was left unlocked. Burglars got into the unlocked property and drilled through a wall to enter the plaintiff's basement and steal some clothing. The court decided that there was no duty in this case, despite the landlord-tenant relationship and despite the holding in *Stansbie v Troman* [1948] 2 KB 48. The reason seems to have been that the court was reluctant to interfere with the freedom of owner-occupiers by requiring them to take specific steps to protect tenants. In *Stansbie v Troman* [1948] 2 KB 48, the decorator had no similar freedom to decide for himself what steps to take to protect the landowner. Lord Wilberforce suggested later in *Smith v Littlewoods Organisation Ltd* [1987] AC 241 that the real distinction between the two cases was that the burglars' route of entry in *Stansbie* was more foreseeable than in *Perl*, but the judgments in *Perl* do not appear to bear this out.

Smith v Littlewoods [1987] AC 241 was another case where the court refused to make an occupier responsible for acts carried out by others, even though the occupier had arguably created a risk. In this case, some developers purchased a cinema with the intention of turning it into a supermarket. They began to do some work on the site, but then left the premises empty and unattended for a number of months. The building attracted vandals, who started a fire on the property that spread to surrounding buildings and damaged them. The House of Lords held that the developers owed no duty to the owner-occupiers of the surrounding buildings to prevent this, relying again on *Caparo v Dickman* [1990] 2 AC 605.

● *Smith v Littlewoods Organisation Ltd* [1987] AC 241

Lord Brandon of Oakbrook: The particular facts of the present case appear to me to raise two, and only two, questions, on the answers to which the determination of the appeals depends.

The first question is what was the general duty owed by Littlewoods, as owners and occupiers of the disused cinema, to the appellants, as owners or occupiers of other buildings near to the cinema. The answer to that question is, in my view, that Littlewoods owed to the appellants a duty to exercise reasonable care to ensure that the cinema was not, and did not become, a source of danger to neighbouring buildings owned or occupied by the appellants.

The second question is whether that general duty encompassed a specific duty to exercise reasonable care to prevent young persons obtaining unlawful access to the cinema, and, having done so, unlawfully setting it on fire. The answer to that question, in accordance with general principles governing alike the law of delict in Scotland and the law of negligence in England, must depend on whether the occurrence of such behaviour was reasonably foreseeable by Littlewoods. It should have been reasonably foreseeable by Littlewoods if they had known of the activities of young persons observed by certain individuals in the locality. But they did not know of such activities because the individuals concerned did not inform either Littlewoods or the police of them, nor did the police themselves observe them. In the absence of information about such activities, either from the individuals referred to or from the police, I am of opinion that the occurrence of the behaviour in question was not reasonably foreseeable by Littlewoods. I conclude, therefore, that the general duty of care owed by Littlewoods to the appellants did not encompass the specific duty referred to above.

In another case, *Clark Fixing Ltd v Dudley Metropolitan Borough Council* [2001] EWCA Civ 1898, a council was found to have a duty to remove combustible materials from a site where trespassers frequently started fires. As Henry, LJ, stated:

> The council had both the knowledge and the means of knowledge of intruders creating fires on its property, the Need Steels building. It had the knowledge or the means of knowledge of that risk. Knowing that, it should have investigated and removed all readily moveable combustible material. The timber sectional building clearly fell within that definition. It could have been easily removed at trifling expense.

The difference between *Smith v Littlewoods Organisation Ltd* [1987] AC 241 and *Clark Fixing Ltd v Dudley Metropolitan Borough Council* [2001] EWCA Civ 1898 is that the judges in the earlier case did not think the owners knew or should have known about the criminal activities that were going on, whereas in the latter case, the court did think the council knew or should have known what was happening.

2.7.4 **Rescuers**

We saw earlier that in English law, there is usually no duty to help someone in an emergency. There are some exceptions to this rule, however, and the courts have considered the scope of the exceptions on many occasions. These cases are often referred to as 'rescuer cases'. We will look at some examples below.

Bystanders

In principle, bystanders who simply happen to witness an emergency have no duty to get involved. As the court observed in *Marc Rich & Co AG v Bishop Rock Marine Co Ltd (The 'Nicholas H')* [1994] 3 All ER 686, in which a ship sank after a classification society had deemed certain repairs sufficient to make it seaworthy, and the court considered whether the classification society had a duty to the cargo owners: 'Walking down the street I see a blind person about to cross the road in front of a vehicle. It is foreseeable that he will be injured. I am under no legal duty to take care to save him from danger'. Often, of course, people in such a situation try to help anyway. If they do so, they are probably not liable for any carelessness they may show in the heat of the moment, unless it is so serious as to make the original danger worse and cause more serious injury than if they had done nothing at all.

NOTE The conclusion in *Marc Rich* is supported by *East Suffolk Rivers Catchment Board v Kent* [1941] AC 74, a case on the duties of public authorities: see chapter 6.

Professionals

As we have seen, a mere bystander has no duty to help in an emergency. However, someone whose professional relationship with the victim results in some control over that person may be liable for failing to help. For instance, a lifeguard who sees someone drowning has a duty to try to rescue that person, and a driving instructor has a duty to try to intervene if the learner is about to cause an accident. This is because the relationship creates greater proximity between the professional and the victim.

Emergency services

You may be surprised to learn that the courts have generally treated emergency services in the same way as bystanders. In particular, the police, fire brigade and coastguard owe a duty to the public as a whole, but not usually to specific individuals. Therefore, these services have no duty to individuals to respond to a particular emergency call, nor to take any particular action if they do turn up. In *Alexandrou v Oxford* [1993] 4 All ER 328, the plaintiff's burglar alarm went off, and police officers went to investigate, but failed to inspect the back of the premises as well as the front. The premises were burgled shortly after the alarm stopped, with the burglars getting in through the back of the premises. The court held that there was no duty to respond, and therefore there should be no duty to inspect the back of the premises once the police did respond. To hold otherwise would create an incentive for the police to ignore emergency calls.

In *Alexandrou v Oxford* [1993] 4 All ER 328, the police had left before the offence took place. However, even if police are on the scene at the time, they have no duty to individual members of the public to prevent an offence from being committed. In *OLL Ltd v Secretary of State for Transport* [1997] 3 All ER 897, which involved the deaths of several children after errors were made during a rescue at sea, the court reached a similar conclusion about the coastguard, indicating it has no duty to respond to emergency calls, nor to pass on information to other emergency services. In *John Munroe (Acrylics) Ltd v London Fire and Civil Defence Authority* and *Church of Jesus Christ of Latter-Day Saints (Great Britain) v West Yorkshire Fire and Civil Defence Authority* (both reported at [1997]

QB 1004), the court decided that the fire service had no duty to property owners to inspect premises next door to a fire to check for smouldering debris, nor to maintain fire hydrants so that they would have enough water to fight fires.

However, emergency services may have a duty not to take positive steps that increase the damage beyond what would have happened if they had not intervened. For instance, in *Capital & Counties plc v Hampshire County Council* [1997] QB 1004, the fire brigade increased the damage by turning off a sprinkler system. The court held that the fire brigade had a duty to avoid creating risks in this way. In *Rigby v Chief Constable of Northamptonshire* [1985] 2 All ER 985, the court came to the same conclusion where the police created a danger by using CS gas. This gas is known to be flammable, and therefore the police had a duty to make sure that fire-fighting equipment was available before they used it.

The courts take a different approach to the ambulance service than to the other emergency services, however. In *Kent v Griffiths* [2000] 2 All ER 474, a GP called an ambulance for a patient who was having an asthma attack. The ambulance took far longer to arrive than it should have done, and the doctor gave evidence that if she had known how long the ambulance would take, she would have arranged for the patient's husband to drive her to the hospital. The patient's asthma was made considerably worse by the delay. The court decided that the ambulance service was more similar to other parts of the NHS, such as hospitals, than to the fire brigade or police. Since it is generally accepted that hospitals owe duties to individual patients, so should the ambulance service. There is a greater proximity between medical professionals and patients than there is between the police or fire brigade and members of the public. The court did allow for the possibility, however, that there might not be a duty to individuals if the failure to send an ambulance in time was due to a lack of resources rather than to carelessness. That was not true in this case.

Even if there is no duty in negligence, there may be other ways of holding the police accountable. For instance, a police officer who wilfully fails to carry out a statutory duty can be guilty of a criminal offence, as in *R v Dytham* [1979] QB 722, where a constable was convicted of wilful neglect of duty because he failed to intervene in a violent assault. However, criminal liabilities are beyond the scope of this book.

2.7.5 Public authorities

Public authorities are in a different legal position than emergency service providers. It can be difficult to bring a claim against a public authority. For example:

- Proximity may be a problem, since it may be difficult to show that the public authority owes you a duty as an individual, rather than just a general duty to the public as a whole.

- The court may decide that it is not just and reasonable to impose a duty on the public authority because the threat of being sued would make it too difficult for the authority to carry out its public functions.

- The court may be concerned that the factors a public authority needs to consider when it makes its decisions—particularly policy decisions, as opposed to operational decisions in particular cases—are so varied and complex and require such a degree of expertise that the court should not interfere. This is sometimes referred to as the issue of 'justiciability' and demonstrates how unwilling courts are to intervene in matters best left to another branch of government.

The approach the courts have taken in response to these difficulties varies depending on the nature of the duty that the public authority is supposed to have. If it is an ordinary duty of the same kind that a private citizen might have, then the authority may be sued in the usual way. If it is a duty that could never exist at all if it weren't for the authority's public functions, then a claimant has additional hurdles to overcome before a claim can be successful.

Private duties

Sometimes a public authority's duty may be equivalent to that of a private individual, as in the case of *Beasley v Buckinghamshire County Council* [1997] PIQR P473. In this case, the claimant was a foster parent to a disabled child. She injured her back on several occasions while catching or lifting the child. After the fifth occasion, she sued the local authority (who had placed the child with her) for failing to provide her with suitable training and a hoist for lifting him. The local authority said that it was against public policy to impose a duty of care on it in these circumstances.

think point

What are some of the duties that public authorities might share with private citizens?

· ·

● *Beasley v Buckinghamshire County Council* [1997] PIQR P473

Harris, J: If this is true it does put foster parents into a most vulnerable and unusual situation, and it is difficult, in my view, to see any very obvious public policy justification for it. Quite the reverse in fact since it is very much in the public interest to be able to call on a supply of altruistic and selfless people to look after unfortunate children with no satisfactory parents of their own. If such people are to have no redress if their employing authority is careless towards them and causes them harm, then this may very well inhibit the supply of suitable people...Furthermore, this is not a case involving anything in the way of policy, nor anything much in the way of delicate discretionary decisions or the balancing of conflicting interests. No doubt it was in one sense a discretionary decision to utilise the plaintiff's services, but that is more akin to choosing a nanny, a builder, a plumber or a doctor than the sort of discretion involved in deciding whether a parent's treatment of a child is such that it is proper to put it into care.

In short, in my view, the circumstances of the instant case are some considerable distance from the [public function] cases and much closer to normal employment situations.

At first blush, and indeed rather beyond that, it would seem odd if the foster parent cannot sue when a nurse, if hurt through having to lift a heavy patient in a hospital can sue the health authority, which is, after all, itself only carrying out its own statutory duties in accordance with policies it has reached and discretionary decisions it has made.

The judge mentions the decision to put a child into care because that is the situation that has most often been involved in cases about an authority's public functions. We will come to examples of these cases later.

In this case, the public authority was effectively acting as an employer and could have the same duties as ordinary employers. A public authority might also have a duty as an occupier of a building, as in the case of *Clark Fixing Ltd v Dudley Metropolitan Borough Council* [2001] EWCA Civ 1898 considered above. Similarly, a public authority's employees might have duties as road users, and the authority could then be liable for breaches. You may be able to think of other examples.

Public functions

Courts tend to be reluctant to impose a duty in negligence on public authorities in connection with their public functions. This is partly because of a concern that the decisions the authorities make are not 'justiciable', and partly because the functions are often laid down by statute. Courts therefore conclude that it is up to Parliament to provide remedies for individuals if it wanted to. If Parliament provides a remedy, the claimants should use it rather than coming to the courts. If Parliament does not provide a remedy, the courts ask whether it is consistent with Parliament's intention for them to provide one.

In *Harris v Evans* [1998] 1 WLR 1285, the court held that there was no duty in negligence because Parliament had provided another remedy. The Health and Safety Executive had decided Harris's crane was in breach of the Health and Safety at Work Act 1974, when in fact it was not. The court decided that his only remedies were prescribed in the Act, which included an appeals process. Similarly, in *Stovin v Wise* [1996] AC 923 there was no duty because it would not be consistent with Parliament's intention. The case questioned whether a local authority owed a duty to road users to clear obstructions from the roads. Parliament had given local authorities a statutory power to maintain the highways, but not a duty. The court held that to impose such a duty would interfere with the authority's discretion as to how to spend its budget, which would be inconsistent with Parliament's decision to create a power rather than a duty. However, if a public authority creates a danger on the highways, it may have a duty to remove it. In *Rowley v Secretary of State for Work and Pensions* [2007] EWCA Civ 598, the Court of Appeal held that the Secretary of State did not owe a duty in negligence to a child support claimant, because Parliament had created a complete statutory scheme for child support, which included substantial remedies for incorrect child support assessments. Therefore, the court thought that Parliament had not intended there to be an additional civil remedy. This contrasts with another recent case, *B v A County Council* [2006] EWCA Civ 1388, where adoptive parents sued the local authority, alleging that they had suffered harassment from the child's birth family after the authority told the birth family who the new parents were. In this case, the court found that the statutory adoption scheme was not comprehensive enough to exclude a civil remedy. However, on the particular facts of the case, the court did not accept that the adoptive parents had suffered any damage.

'Justiciability' cases often involve an authority's duty towards children. In 1996, the House of Lords considered a number of cases of this kind and decided on them together. These cases are reported as *X (Minors) v Bedfordshire County Council* [1995] 2 AC 633. Some of the cases involved the prevention of child abuse, while others dealt with the provision of education for children with special needs. The House of Lords said it was arguable that there was a duty in some of the education cases, but not in the child protection cases. The five cases were as follows:

- A claim by a child who had been wrongly taken into care because a local authority psychiatrist thought she had identified her stepfather as an abuser when in fact she meant her cousin, who did not live in her home;

- A claim by children whose health had suffered after social workers failed to remove them from a home where they were being neglected;

- Three separate claims by children whose learning difficulties were not accurately diagnosed or provided for by their education authority.

As you read the extracts below, make a note of (a) the hurdles a claimant needs to clear to prove that a public authority owes a duty to the claimant for negligence in the way it has carried out a public function, and (b) how a claimant may be able to avoid these hurdles by bringing a different kind of claim.

● *X (Minors) v Bedfordshire County Council* [1995] 2 AC 633

Lord Browne-Wilkinson: (a) Discretion

Most statutes which impose a statutory duty on local authorities confer on the authority a discretion as to the extent to which, and the methods by which, such statutory duty is to be performed. It is clear both in principle and from the decided cases that the local authority cannot be liable in damages for doing that which Parliament has authorised. Therefore if the decisions complained of fall within the ambit of such statutory discretion they cannot be actionable in common law. However if the decision complained of is so unreasonable that it falls outside the ambit of the discretion conferred upon the local authority, there is no **a priori** reason for excluding all common law liability...

It follows that in seeking to establish that a local authority is liable at common law for negligence in the exercise of a discretion conferred by statute, the first requirement is to show that the decision was outside the ambit of the discretion altogether: if it was not, a local authority cannot itself be in breach of any duty of care owed to the plaintiff.

In deciding whether or not this requirement is satisfied, the court has to assess the relevant factors taken into account by the authority in exercising the discretion. Since what are under consideration are discretionary powers conferred on public bodies for public purposes the relevant factors will often include policy matters, for example social policy, the allocation of finite financial resources between the different calls made upon them or (as in *Dorset Yacht*) the balance between pursuing desirable social aims as against the risk to the public inherent in so doing. It is established that the courts cannot enter upon the assessment of such 'policy' matters. The difficulty is to identify in any particular case whether or not the decision in question is a 'policy' decision.

(b) Justiciability and the Policy/Operational Dichotomy

In English law the first attempt to lay down the principles applicable in deciding whether or not a decision was one of policy was made by Lord Wilberforce in *Anns v Merton London Borough Council* [1978] A.C. 728, 754: 'Most, indeed probably all, statutes relating to public authorities or public bodies, contain in them a large area of policy. The courts call this discretion meaning that the decision is one for the authority or body to make, and not for the courts. Many statutes also prescribe or at least presuppose the practical execution of policy decisions: a convenient description of this is to say that in addition to the area of policy or discretion, there is an operational area. Although this distinction between the policy area and the operational area is convenient, and illuminating, it is probably a distinction of degree; many operational powers or duties have in them some element of discretion. It can safely be said that the more operational a power or duty may be, the easier it is to superimpose upon it a common law duty of care.'...

From these authorities I understand the applicable principles to be as follows. Where Parliament has conferred a statutory discretion on a public authority, it is for that authority, not for the courts, to exercise the discretion: nothing which the authority does within the ambit of the discretion can be actionable at common law. If the decision complained of falls outside the statutory discretion, it *can* (but not necessarily will) give rise to common law liability. However, if the factors relevant to the exercise of the discretion include matters of policy, the court cannot adjudicate on such policy matters and therefore cannot reach the conclusion that the decision was outside the ambit of the statutory discretion. Therefore a common law duty of care in relation to the taking of decisions involving policy matters cannot exist.

3. If justiciable, the ordinary principles of negligence apply

If the plaintiff's complaint alleges carelessness, not in the taking of a discretionary decision to do some act, but in the practical manner in which that act has been performed (e.g. the running of a school) the question whether or not there is a common law duty of care falls to be decided by applying the usual principles i.e. those laid down in Caparo Industries Plc. v Dickman...

[I]n my judgment a common law duty of care cannot be imposed on a statutory duty if the observance of such common law duty of care would be inconsistent with, or have a tendency to discourage, the due performance by the local authority of its statutory duties....

The Abuse Cases

...

The first question is whether the determination by the court of the question whether there has been a breach of that duty will involve unjusticiable policy questions. The alleged breaches of that duty relate for the most part to the failure to take reasonable practical steps, e.g. to remove the children, to allocate a suitable social worker or to make proper investigations. The assessment by the court of such allegations would not require the court to consider policy matters which are not justiciable. They do not necessarily involve any question of the allocation of resources or the determination of general policy...

Next, do the allegations of breach of duty in the operational field all relate to decisions the power to make which Parliament has conferred on the local authority, i.e. are they all decisions within the ambit of the local authority's statutory discretion? I strongly suspect that, if the case were to go to trial, it would eventually fail on this ground since, in essence, the complaint is that the local authority failed to take steps to remove the children from the care of their mother, i.e. negligently failed properly to exercise a discretion which Parliament has conferred on the local authority. But again, it would not be right to strike out the claim on this ground because it is possible that the plaintiffs might be able to

NOTE Elsewhere Lord Browne-Wilkinson says that the decision whether to build a school is a policy decision, but decisions on how to run it once it is built are operational.

NOTE The authority had said the claims should not go to trial because there was no duty. The court was not making a final decision on the claims.

demonstrate at trial that the decisions of the local authority were so unreasonable that no reasonable local authority could have reached them and therefore, for the reasons given by Lord Reid in the *Dorset Yacht case* [1970] A.C. 1004, 1031 fall outside the ambit of the discretion conferred by Parliament.

I turn then to consider whether, in accordance with the ordinary principles laid down in the Caparo case [1990] 2 A.C. 605, the local authority in the Bedfordshire case owed a direct duty of care to the plaintiffs. The local authority accepts that they could foresee damage to the plaintiffs if they carried out their statutory duties negligently and that the relationship between the authority and the plaintiffs is sufficiently proximate...

Is it, then, just and reasonable to superimpose a common law duty of care on the local authority in relation to the performance of its statutory duties to protect children? In my judgment it is not...

First, in my judgment a common law duty of care would cut across the whole statutory system set up for the protection of children at risk. As a result of the ministerial directions contained in 'Working Together' the protection of such children is not the exclusive territory of the local authority's social services. The system is inter-disciplinary, involving the participation of the police, educational bodies, doctors and others... To introduce into such a system a common law duty of care enforceable against only one of the participant bodies would be manifestly unfair. To impose such liability on all the participant bodies would lead to almost impossible problems of disentangling as between the respective bodies the liability, both primary and by way of contribution, of each for reaching a decision found to be negligent.

Second, the task of the local authority and its servants in dealing with children at risk is extraordinarily delicate...

Next, if a liability in damages were to be imposed, it might well be that local authorities would adopt a more cautious and defensive approach to their duties... If the authority is to be made liable in damages for a negligent decision to remove a child (such negligence lying in the failure properly first to investigate the allegations) there would be a substantial temptation to postpone making such a decision until further inquiries have been made in the hope of getting more concrete facts. Not only would the child in fact being abused be prejudiced by such delay: the increased workload inherent in making such investigations would reduce the time available to deal with other cases and other children.

The Education Cases

...

[T]he plaintiff is alleging that the defendant authority is itself under two direct duties of care. The first...is to perform carefully the statutory duties imposed on them by the [Education] Act of 1981. The second... arises from the provision by the authority of a psychology service and the negligent advice given by that service.

As to the claim based on the negligent failure to comply with the statutory requirements of the Act of 1981, it is in essence a claim that the authority was negligent in the exercise of the statutory discretions conferred on the defendant authority by the Act of 1981. The claim cannot be struck out as being not justiciable. Although it is very improbable, it may be that the exercise of the statutory discretions involved in operating the special needs machinery of the Act of 1981 involved policy decisions [but] it is impossible to be certain until all the facts are known. Therefore the claim cannot be struck out at this stage on the grounds that it is not justiciable or the acts complained of fell within the statutory discretion.

The question, then, is whether it is right to superimpose on the statutory machinery for the investigation and treatment of the plaintiff's special educational needs a duty of care to exercise the statutory discretions carefully? . . .

The parents are themselves involved in the process of decision making and can appeal against decisions which they think to be erroneous . . . [T]here is a very real risk that many hopeless (and possibly vexatious) cases will be brought, thereby exposing the authority to great expenditure of time and money in their defence . . . In my judgment, as in the child abuse cases, the courts should hesitate long before imposing a common law duty of care in the exercise of discretionary powers or duties conferred by Parliament for social welfare purposes . . . For these reasons I reach the conclusion that an education authority owes no common law duty of care in the exercise of the powers and discretions relating to children with special educational needs specifically conferred on them by the Act of 1981.

I turn then to the other duty of care which, it is alleged, the defendant authority owes directly to the plaintiff. There the position is wholly different. The claim is based on the fact that the authority is offering a service (psychological advice) to the public. True it is that, in the absence of a statutory power or duty, the authority could not offer such a service. But once the decision is taken to offer such a service, a statutory body is in general in the same position as any private individual or organisation holding itself out as offering such a service. By opening its doors to others to take advantage of the service offered, it comes under a duty of care to those using the service to exercise care in its conduct. The position is directly analogous with a hospital conducted, formerly by a local authority now by a health authority, in exercise of statutory powers. In such a case the authority running the hospital is under a duty to those whom it admits to exercise reasonable care in the way it runs it . . .

For these reasons, I can see no ground on which it can be said at this stage that the defendant authority, in providing a psychology service, could not have come under a duty of care to the plaintiff who, through his parents, took advantage of that service.

According to this case, the hurdles a claimant needs to clear to bring a negligence claim against a public authority for the way it has exercised a statutory function are:

- The acts which give rise to the claim must be so unreasonable as to be beyond the scope of the authority's discretion;

- The factors the authority took into account in exercising its discretion must not be policy considerations, because if they are, then the claim is not justiciable;

- The usual *Caparo* elements must be present, including the 'justice and reasonableness' element; and

- The duty must not be one that would prevent or discourage the authority from carrying out its statutory functions, because it is not just and reasonable for the court to impose such a duty.

think point

Do you think the distinction between the two kinds of claim is as clear as Lord Browne-Wilkinson suggests? What larger policy issue might be at work here?

However, some claimants can avoid these hurdles by showing that the public authority was not just exercising a statutory function, but was offering the claimant a service. In *X v Bedfordshire* [1995] 2 AC 633, which you have just read, Lord Browne-Wilkinson said that psychological counselling fell into this category. In that case, the claimant only needs to prove the usual *Caparo* elements.

In subsequent cases, courts have tended to stress the need for a case-by-case decision based on all the facts, rather than assuming that certain classes of decision—such as decisions on where to place a child for fostering—attract blanket immunity. In *W v Essex County Council* [2000] 2 All ER 237, the House of Lords refused to strike out a claim by foster parents whose foster-child had sexually abused their daughter. The parents had been given a specific assurance by the local authority that no child who was a known or suspected child-abuser would be placed with them. The Court of Appeal decided that there was an arguable case that the placement had been outside the scope of the authority's discretion. The Court of Appeal was also influenced by the fact that the previous case law had not considered the question of a duty to children who were not themselves in care. The court also considered the assurances which were given to the parents, which at least one judge saw as creating a situation similar to that in *Swinney v Chief Constable of Northumbria,* The Times, 25 May 1999 (mentioned above), where the police were responsible for the safety of an informant. The House of Lords did not deal with this question in detail, but said that a full investigation of the facts was required before it could be determined whether the case was justiciable, and that was best left to a full trial. In the event, the case settled before that trial could take place. In *Lawrence v Pembrokeshire County Council* [2007] EWCA Civ 446, a mother sued the local authority for damages for a psychiatric illness that she suffered after the authority wrongly placed her children on the child protection register. The Court of Appeal balanced her right to respect for her private life against the public policy of putting the welfare of children first, and held that the authority did not owe her a duty of care.

In these cases, the courts may have been influenced by *Osman v UK* [1999] 1 FLR 193. In this case, a mother sued the police for failing to protect her child from an abusive teacher. The Court of Appeal ordered the case to be struck out on the basis that the police had immunity. The case then went to the European Court of Human Rights, which disapproved of the use of blanket immunities without any real attempt to balance competing policy questions. Later, in *Z v UK* [2001] 2 FCR 612, some children sued a local authority for failing to take them into care. Again, the House of Lords struck out the claim. In this case, the European Court of Human Rights said that it was acceptable for the necessary balancing exercise to be carried out by the court at the striking-out stage. Despite this case, judges are still likely to exercise caution on the basis of *Osman v UK* [1999] 1 FLR 193. The law in this area is not yet fully settled.

2.8 Duties to avoid particular kinds of damage

Often, negligence cases do not turn simply on whether or not a duty exists, but on whether or not the duty extends to the type of damage that has actually been suffered. The two types of damage that cause the most difficulty are economic loss and psychiatric damage. The ability to recover for psychiatric and economic damages is discussed in chapter 12. Chapter 11 considers how damages are calculated.

For more revision tips, including self-test questions and suggestions for further reading, see the Online Resource Centre at www.oxfordtextbooks.co.uk/orc/strong_complete/.

revision tasks

Revision is most effective when you do the work yourself, rather than have someone do it for you. Here are four tasks to help you organize the materials discussed in this chapter.

- Create a running list of the torts you have studied, along with their definitions and their elements, giving negligence its own section.

- List the most important cases and statutes discussed in this chapter and work out how they flesh out the law of negligence so that you can use those materials in an exam situation. To work out which are the key cases, ask whether it:
  - establishes a fundamental principle (the most important category of cases to know);
  - expands significantly on an existing principle by showing how it can be applied to new situations (also important to know);
  - adds detail to an existing principle (worth learning if you have time); or
  - provides an additional example to illustrate an existing principle (the least important type of case to know).

  Categorize the cases in this chapter now while they are fresh in your mind.

- Create case summaries of the key decisions with the case name and year, a short summary of the facts (no more than two sentences) and the legal proposition(s) which the case establishes. Include no more than one or two sentences for each proposition. This will make revising for the exam much easier.

- Design a flowchart showing each of the questions you should ask yourself when considering whether a duty exists.

Chapter 2 Negligence: Duty

59

3 Negligence: Breach of duty

Introduction

As discussed in the last chapter, negligence is usually broken down into three elements: duty, breach, and damage. This chapter considers how a court establishes that a defendant has breached a duty. Again, the analysis is broken into three steps: deciding what standard of care applies in the circumstances, assessing whether or not the defendant has met that standard, and considering how to prove that there has been a breach. We will deal with each of these in turn. This chapter therefore proceeds as follows:

- Deciding on the standard of care;
- Assessing the defendant's conduct against the standard of care; and
- Proving breach.

Deciding on the standard of care

3.2.1 The general standard

Duties of care in negligence (that is, the kinds of duties we discussed in chapter 2) are not absolute. No one is expected to guarantee that others will be completely safe or that they will suffer no loss under any circumstances—people are only expected to meet a certain minimum standard of behaviour. In *Blyth v Birmingham Waterworks* [1843–60] All ER 47, the court defined the general standard in the context of the failure of certain valves that had been properly installed and fitted onto fire-plugs. However, an unusually sharp freeze caused the valves to fail, leading to the flooding of the plaintiff's house.

● **Blyth v Birmingham Waterworks** [1843–60] All ER 47

> Alderson B: Negligence is the omission to do something which a reasonable man, guided upon those considerations which ordinarily regulate the conduct of human affairs, would do, or doing something which a prudent and reasonable man would not do. The defendants might have been liable for negligence, if, unintentionally, they omitted to do that which a reasonable person would have done, or did that which a person taking reasonable precautions would not have done. The defendants might have been liable for negligence, if, unintentionally, they omitted to do that which a reasonable person would have done, or did that which a person taking reasonable precautions would not have done. A reasonable man would act with reference to the average circumstances of the temperature in ordinary years. The defendants had provided against such frosts as experience would have led men, acting prudently, to provide against; and they are not guilty of negligence, because their precautions proved insufficient against the effects of the extreme severity of the frost of 1856, which penetrated to a greater depth than any which ordinarily occurs south of the polar regions. Such a state of circumstances constitutes a contingency against which no reasonable man can provide. The result was an accident, for which the defendants cannot be held liable.

NOTE The judgment uses the word 'unintentionally' here because negligence is always about damage that is not deliberate or intentional. We consider intentional torts in chapter 17.

think point
Do you believe the term 'reasonable', as used in this decision and others, means 'perfectly rational'?

This is known as the 'reasonable person test'. However, applying such a vague test can be difficult, so courts have had to define the standard more stringently.

Another interesting case is *Hall v Brooklands Auto-Racing Club* [1933] 1 KB 205, which involved a car that swerved, touching the hubcap of another car during a race. This was enough to send the first car flying through the air over the trackside railings and into the crowd, injuring the plaintiff. No car had ever crossed the railings before. The case was brought in contract because the plaintiff had bought a ticket to the event, but judges have referred to Greer LJ's description of the 'reasonable member of the public' in many later tort cases.

61

● **Hall v Brooklands Auto-Racing Club** [1933] 1 KB 205

> Greer LJ: I do not think it can be said that the content of the contract made with every person who takes a ticket is different. I think it must be the same, and it must be judged by what any reasonable member of the public must have intended should be the term of the contract. The person concerned is sometimes described as 'the man in the street,' or 'the man in the Clapham omnibus,' or, as I recently read in an American author, 'the man who takes the magazines at home, and in the evening pushes the lawn mower in his shirt sleeves.' Such a man taking a ticket to see a cricket match at Lord's would know quite well that he was not going to be encased in a steel frame which would protect him from the one in a million chance of a cricket ball dropping on his head. In the same way, the same man taking a ticket to see the Derby would know quite well that there would be no provision to prevent a horse which got out of hand from getting amongst the spectators, and would quite understand that he was himself bearing the risk of any such possible but improbable accident happening to himself. In my opinion, in the same way such a man taking a ticket to see motor races would know quite well that no barrier would be provided which would be sufficient to protect him in the possible but highly improbable event of a car charging the barrier and getting through to the spectators. The risk of such an event would be so remote that he would quite understand that no provision would be made to prevent it happening, and that he would take the risk of any such accident.

These cases show that the law does not require perfection, but simply ordinary carefulness. This is an objective standard, though: what counts is what the court thinks a reasonable person would do, not what the individual defendant thinks is reasonable. In *Vaughan v Menlove* [1835–1842] All ER 156, a farmer was involved in discussions with his neighbours about what precautions should be taken to prevent fire in a haystack. Different people took different views, and the farmer took precautions that seemed adequate to him, but which turned out to be insufficient (and indeed may have ended up increasing the risk of injury). The court decided against the farmer, saying that '[i]nstead...of saying that the liability for negligence should be co-extensive with the judgment of each individual, which would be as variable as the length of the foot of each individual, we ought rather to adhere to the rule which requires in all cases a regard to caution such as a man of ordinary prudence would observe'.

There is no breach if a reasonable person would not have foreseen any danger. In *Glasgow Corporation v Muir* [1943] AC 448, a tea shop provided an urn of hot tea for a picnic. Two of the men attending the picnic were carrying the urn through the shop when one of them lost his grip. Some of the tea spilled and scalded some children who were standing at the shop counter. The manageress was sued for allowing the men to carry the urn through the shop when the children were present. The House of Lords decided that she was not liable because it was not reasonable to expect her to anticipate the danger. Similarly, in *Etheridge v Kitson* (1999) Ed C R 550, the court found that it was unreasonable to expect a school to foresee that allowing basketballs to be carried through a school might lead to injury. In that case, a teacher was struck when a student tossed the ball in a stairwell.

> **NOTE** Here foreseeability is an element in analysing whether or not there is a breach. Remember that foreseeability is also an element in analysing whether or not a duty exists.

3.2.2 Lower standards

Some special situations require courts to apply a different standard of care than is usually the case. For instance, courts will judge children by the standard of a reasonable child of the same age, not by the standard of a reasonable adult. In *Mullins v Richards* [1998] 1 All ER 920, two 15-year-old schoolgirls were play-fighting with rulers when one of the rulers snapped. A fragment of plastic from the ruler hit one of the girls in the face and blinded her in one eye. The Court of Appeal decided that it was not reasonable to expect a young person of 15 to foresee any injury from fighting with rulers.

> ***think point***
> *There are not many other cases where children are sued for negligence. Why might that be?*

Another possible area where courts may apply a different standard involves defendants with an illness or disability. Not many cases address this question, and those that do exist appear to conflict. For example, *Mansfield v Weetabix* [1998] 1 WLR 1263 involved a driver who caused an accident because he suddenly suffered an episode of low blood sugar that caused him to lose consciousness and crash his car, injuring the plaintiff. The drop was caused by a disease called malignant insulinoma, which the driver did not know he had. The Court of Appeal said that the standard of care should be that of the reasonable person who was not aware that he or she was about to have an episode of low blood sugar. However, a slightly older case—*Roberts v Ramsbottom* [1980] 1 All ER 7—held a driver who also lost consciousness and caused an accident to the same standard as a healthy person even though he had suffered a stroke just before getting into the car. Again, the driver did not realize he was ill. The Court of Appeal in *Mansfield v Weetabix* [1998] 1 WLR 1263 said that *Roberts v Ramsbottom* [1980] 1 All ER 7 was wrongly decided, so it seems that drivers who cause an accident because of an illness they do not know about will not be liable in negligence.

Different standards also apply to sporting events, with accidents between fellow competitors being treated differently than spectator-competitor accidents. For example, *Wooldridge v Sumner* [1963] 2 QB 63 involved injuries to spectators at a racecourse as a rider tried to return his horse to the racecourse after overshooting a corner.

● *Wooldridge v Sumner* [1963] 2 QB 63

Diplock LJ: The law of negligence has always recognised that the standard of care which a reasonable man will exercise depends on the conditions under which the decision to avoid the act or omission relied on as negligence has to be taken. The case of the workman engaged on repetitive work in the noise and bustle of the factory is a familiar example . . . [A] participant in a game or competition gets into the circumstances in which he has no time or very little time to think by his decision to take part in the game or competition at all. It cannot be suggested that the participant, at any rate if he has some modicum of skill, is by the mere act of participating in breach of his duty of care to a spectator who is present for the very purpose of watching him do so. If, therefore, in the course of the game or competition at a moment when he really has not time to think, a participant by mistake takes a wrong measure, he is not, in my view, to be held guilty of any negligence.

Furthermore, the duty which he owes is a duty of care, not a duty of skill. Save where a consensual relationship exists between a plaintiff and a defendant by which the defendant impliedly warrants his skill, a man owes no duty to his neighbour to exercise any special skill beyond that which an ordinary reasonable man would acquire before indulging in the activity in which he is engaged at the relevant time. It may well be that a participant in a game or competition would be guilty of negligence to a spectator if he took part in it when he knew or ought to have known that his lack of skill was such that, even if he exerted it to the utmost, he was likely to cause injury to a spectator watching him. No question of this arises in the present case. It was common ground that Mr. Holladay was an exceptionally skilful and experienced horseman.

The practical result of this analysis of the application of the common law of negligence to participant and spectator would, I think, be expressed by the common man in some such terms as these: 'A person attending a game or competition takes the risk of any damage caused to him by any act of a participant done in the course of and for the purposes of the game or competition, notwithstanding that such act may involve an error of judgment or a lapse of skill, unless the participant's conduct is such as to evince a reckless disregard of the spectator's safety'.

Thus, a spectator attends an event at his or her own risk, so long as the competitor is acting in the spirit and heat of the moment. Still, there are limits to what one may do in the context of athletic activity, even when bodily contact is anticipated, as *Condon v Basi* [1985] 2 All ER 453 demonstrates.

● ***Condon v Basi*** [1985] 2 All ER 453

Sir John Donaldson MR: This is an appeal from a decision of his Honour Judge Wooton in the Warwick County Court given in March 1984. It arose out of a football match played on a Sunday between Whittle Wanderers and Khalso Football Club... Most unfortunately, during the game the defendant tackled the plaintiff in such a manner as to lead to the plaintiff breaking his leg. The county court judge found that he had been negligent, and awarded a sum of £4,900 in damages.

It is said that there is no authority as to what is the standard of care which governs the conduct of players in competitive sports generally and, above all, in a competitive sport whose rules and general background contemplate that there will be physical contact between the players, but that appears to be the position. This is somewhat surprising, but appears to be correct. For my part I would completely accept the decision of the High Court of Australia in Rootes v Shelton [1968] ALR 33. I think it suffices, in order to see the law which has to be applied, to quote briefly from the judgment of Barwick CJ and from the judgment of Kitto J. Barwick CJ said, at p.34:

'By engaging in a sport or pastime the participants may be held to have accepted risks which are inherent in that sport or pastime: the tribunal of fact can make its own assessment of what the accepted risks are: but this does not eliminate all duty of care of the one participant to the other. Whether or not such a duty arises, and, if it does, its extent, must necessarily depend in each case upon its own circumstances. In this connexion, the rules of the sport or game may constitute one of those circumstances: but, in my opinion, they are neither definitive of the existence nor of the extent of the duty nor does their breach or non-observance necessarily constitute a breach of any duty found to exist.'

Kitto J said at p.37:

'... in a case such as the present, it must always be a question of fact, what exoneration from a duty of care otherwise incumbent upon the defendant was implied by the act of the plaintiff joining in the activity. Unless the activity partakes of the nature of a war or of something else in which all is notoriously fair, the conclusion to be reached must necessarily depend, according to the concepts of the common law, upon the reasonableness, in relation to the special circumstances, of the conduct which caused the plaintiff's injury. That does not necessarily mean the compliance of that conduct with the rules, conventions or customs (if there are any) by which the correctness of conduct for the purposes of the carrying on of the activity as an organized affair is judged for the tribunal of fact may think that in the situation in which the plaintiff's injury was caused a participant might do what the defendant did and still not be acting unreasonably, even though he infringed the "rules of the game". Non-compliance with such rules, conventions or customs (where they exist) is necessarily one consideration to be attended to upon the question of reasonableness but it is only one, and it may be of much or little or even no weight in the circumstances.'

I have cited from those two judgments because they show two different approaches which, as I see it, produce precisely the same result. One is to take a more generalised duty of care and to modify it on the basis that the participants in the sport or pastime impliedly consent to taking risks which otherwise would be a breach of the duty of care. That seems to be the approach of Barwick CJ. The other is exemplified by the judgment of Kitto J, where he is saying, in effect, that there is a general standard of care, namely the Lord Atkin approach in Donoghue v. Stevenson [1932] A.C. 562 that you are under a duty to take all reasonable care taking account of the circumstances in which You are placed, which, in a game of football, are quite different from those which affect You when You are going for a walk in the countryside.

For my part I would prefer the approach of Kitto J, but I do not think it makes the slightest difference in the end if it is found by the tribunal of fact that the defendant failed to exercise that degree of care which was appropriate in all the circumstances, or that he acted in a way to which the plaintiff cannot be expected to have consented. In either event, there is liability.

The defendant in *Condon v Basi* [1985] 2 All ER 453 was held liable for the plaintiff's injury because there was evidence that he had committed a blatant foul with reckless disregard for the safety of the other player. If he had simply been careless in the heat of the moment, the court might well have considered the injury reasonable in the circumstances. These cases suggest that there is a lower standard of care between spectators and competitors than there is in ordinary life, but that the usual standard of care applies between competitors themselves. However, the usual standard of care requires courts to take all the circumstances into account, and this means that they must also consider that the parties were playing a competitive sport when establishing the standard of care. The end result is likely to be much the same as it would be if the standard of care were lower in such cases.

Although the law has routinely set these sorts of special standards in cases involving children and competitors, courts are constantly being faced with novel situations. The following extract deals with another situation where the defendant claimed a lower standard of care should apply. In this case, Mr Nettleship was teaching his neighbour, Mrs Weston, to drive. During the lesson, she panicked and caused an accident in which Mr Nettleship was injured. The extracts are in a slightly different order than they appear in the original, to help you analyse the case more easily.

● *Nettleship v Weston* [1971] 2 QB 691

Lord Denning MR: The special factor in this case is that Mr. Nettleship was not a mere passenger in the car. He was an instructor teaching Mrs. Weston to drive.

Seeing that the law lays down, for all drivers of motor cars, a standard of care to which all must conform, I think that even a learner driver, so long as he is the sole driver, must attain the same standard towards all passengers in the car, including an instructor. But the instructor may be debarred from claiming for a reason peculiar to himself. He may be debarred because he has voluntarily agreed to waive any claim for any injury that may befall him. Otherwise he is not debarred. He may, of course, be guilty of contributory negligence and have his damages reduced on that account. He may, for instance, have let the learner take control too soon, he may not have been quick enough to correct his errors, or he may have participated in the negligent act himself...But, apart from contributory negligence, he is not excluded unless it be that he has voluntarily agreed to incur the risk...[I]t is clear that Mr. Nettleship did not agree to waive any claim for injury that might befall him. Quite the contrary. He inquired about the insurance policy so as to make sure that he was covered. If and in so far as Mrs. Weston fell short of the standard of care which the law required of her, he has a cause of action. But his claim may be reduced in so far as he was at fault himself—as in letting her take control too soon or in not being quick enough to correct her error.

I do not say that the professional instructor—who agrees to teach for reward—can likewise sue. There may well be implied in the contract an agreement by him to waive any claim for injury. He ought to insure himself, and may do so, for aught I know. But the instructor who is just a friend helping to teach never does insure himself. He should, therefore, be allowed to sue.

Salmon LJ: Mr. Nettleship when he gave evidence was asked:

Q. Was there any mention made of what the position would be if you were involved in an accident?

'A. I had checked with Mr. and Mrs. Weston regarding insurance, and I was assured that they had fully comprehensive insurance which covered me as a passenger in the event of an accident.'

Mrs. Weston agreed, when she gave evidence, that this assurance had been given before Mr. Nettleship undertook to teach her...[T]his assurance seems to me to be an integral part of the relationship between the parties. In Hedley Byrne & Co. Ltd. v. Heller & Partners Ltd. [1964] A.C. 465, the House of Lords decided that the relationship which there existed between the parties would have imposed a duty of care upon the defendants in giving the plaintiffs information but for the fact that the defendants gave the information 'without responsibility.' This disclaimer of responsibility was held to colour the whole relationship between the parties by negativing any duty of care on the part of the defendants.

Much the same result followed when a passenger accepted a lift in a car which exhibited a notice stating: 'Warning. Passengers travelling in this vehicle do so at their own risk.': Bennett v. Tugwell [1971] 2 W.L.R. 847. The present case is perhaps the converse of the cases of Hedley Byrne and Bennett v. Tugwell.

On the whole, I consider, although with some doubt, that the assurance given to Mr. Nettleship altered the nature of the relationship which would have existed between the parties but for the assurance. The assurance resulted in a relationship under which Mrs. Weston accepted responsibility for any injury which Mr. Nettleship might suffer as a result of any failure on her part to exercise the ordinary driver's standards of reasonable care and skill.

Megaw LJ: I have no doubt that the proper inference of fact to be drawn from the care which Mr. Nettleship took to investigate the comprehensiveness of Mr. Weston's insurance policy is that he would have declined to undertake the task of teaching Mrs. Weston if he had been told: 'If you are injured as a result of Mrs. Weston's lack of skill or experience, you will have to bear your loss without remedy against anyone.'

think point
Which of the approaches from Condon and Wooldridge did the judges use? What might the outcome have been if Mr Nettleship had been a professional driving instructor?

These extracts show that all three judges believed that Mr Nettleship's behaviour suggested he had not consented to the risk of being injured. This pointed towards applying the same standard of care to Mrs Weston as to a qualified driver, rather than the lower standard which might have applied if Mr Nettleship had consented to the risk (as occurred with the spectators in the sporting examples). This approach relied on the fact that Mr Nettleship had happened to enquire about insurance. Further discussion of the case continues below.

Lord Denning MR: I take it to be clear that if a driver has a passenger in the car he owes a duty of care to him. But what is the standard of care required of the driver? Is it a lower standard than he or she owes towards a pedestrian on the pavement? I should have thought not. But, suppose that the driver has never driven a car before, or has taken too much to drink, or has poor eyesight or hearing: and, furthermore, that the passenger knows it and yet accepts a lift from him. Does that make any difference? Dixon J. thought it did. In The Insurance Commissioner v. Joyce (1948) 77 C.L.R. 39. 56, he said:

> 'If a man accepts a lift from a car driver whom he knows to have lost a limb or an eye or to be deaf, he cannot complain if he does not exhibit the skill and competence of a driver who suffers from no defect . . . If he knowingly accepts the voluntary services of a driver affected by drink, he cannot complain of improper driving caused by his condition, because it involves no breach of duty.' . . .

We have all the greatest respect for Sir Owen Dixon, but for once I cannot agree with him. The driver owes a duty of care to every passenger in the car, just as he does to every pedestrian on the road: and he must attain the same standard of care in respect of each. If the driver were to be excused according to the knowledge of the passenger, it would result in endless confusion and injustice. One of the passengers may know that the learner driver is a mere novice. Another passenger may believe him to be entirely competent. One of the passengers may believe the driver to have had only two drinks. Another passenger may know that he has had a dozen. Is the one passenger to recover and the other not? Rather than embark on such inquiries, the law holds that the driver must attain the same standard of care for passengers as for pedestrians. The knowledge of the passenger may go to show that he was guilty of contributory negligence in ever accepting the lift—and thus reduce his damages—but it does not take away the duty of care, nor does it diminish the standard of care which the law requires of the driver.

Megaw LJ: As I see it, if this doctrine of varying standards were to be accepted as part of the law on these facts, it could not logically be confined to the duty of care owed by learner drivers. There is no reason in logic why it should not operate in a much wider sphere. The disadvantages of the resulting unpredictability, uncertainty and, indeed, impossibility of arriving at fair and consistent decisions outweigh the advantages. The certainty of a general standard is preferable to the vagaries of a fluctuating standard.

As a first example of what is involved, consider the converse case: the standard of care (including skill) owed, not by the driver to the passenger, but by the passenger instructor to the learner driver. Surely the same principle of varying standards, if it is a good principle, must be available also to the instructor, if he is sued by the driver for alleged breach of the duty of care in supervising the learner driver. On this doctrine, the standard of care, or skill, owed by the instructor, vis-à-vis the driver, may vary according to the knowledge which the learner driver had, at some moment of time, as to the skill and experience of the particular instructor. Indeed, if logic is to prevail, it would not necessarily be the knowledge of the driver which would be the criterion. It would be the expectation which the driver reasonably entertained of the instructor's skill and experience, if that reasonable expectation were greater than the actuality. Thus, if the learner driver knew that the instructor had never tried his hand previously even at amateur instructing, or if, as may be the present case, the driver knew that the instructor's experience was confined to two cases of amateur instructing some years previously, there would, under this doctrine, surely be a lower standard than if the driver knew or reasonably supposed that the instructor was a professional or that he had had substantial experience in the recent past. But what that standard would be, and how it would or should be assessed, I know not. For one has thus cut oneself adrift from the standard of the competent and experienced instructor, which up to now the law has required without regard to the particular personal skill, experience, physical characteristics or temperament of the individual instructor, and without regard to a third party's knowledge or assessment of those qualities or characteristics.

Again, when one considers the requisite standard of care of the learner driver, if this doctrine were to apply, would not logic irresistibly demand that there should be something more than a mere, single, conventional, standard applicable to anyone who falls into the category of learner driver: that is, of anyone who has not yet qualified for (or perhaps obtained) a full licence? That standard itself would necessarily vary over a wide range, not merely with the actual progress of the learner, but also with the passenger's knowledge of that progress: or, rather, if the passenger has in fact over-estimated the driver's progress, it would vary with the passenger's reasonable assessment of that progress at the relevant time. The relevant time would not necessarily be the moment of the accident.

The question, what is the relevant time, would itself have to be resolved by reference to some principle. The instructor's reasonable assessment of the skill and competence of the driver (and also the driver's assessment of the instructor's skill and competence) might alter drastically between the start of the first lesson and the start of a later lesson, or even in the course of one particular spell of driving. I suppose the principle would have to be that the relevant time is the last moment when the plaintiff (whether instructor or driver) could reasonably have refused to continue as passenger or driver in the light of his then knowledge. That factor in itself would introduce yet another element of difficulty, uncertainty and, I believe, serious anomaly.

I, for my part, with all respect, do not think that our legal process could successfully or satisfactorily cope with the task of fairly assessing or applying to the facts of a particular case such varying standards, depending on such complex and elusive factors, including the assessment by the court, not merely of a particular person's actual skill or experience, but also of another person's knowledge or assessment of that skill or experience at a particular moment of time.

Again, if the principle of varying standards is to be accepted, why should it operate, in the field of driving motor vehicles, only up to the stage of the driver qualifying for a full licence? And why should it be limited to the quality of inexperience? If the passenger knows that his driver suffers from some relevant defect, physical or temperamental, which could reasonably be expected to affect the quality of his driving, why should not the same doctrine of varying standards apply? . . . Logically there can be no distinction. If the passenger knows that his driver, though holding a full driving licence, is blind in one eye or has the habit of taking corners too fast, and if an accident happens which is attributable wholly or partly to that physical or that temperamental defect, why should not some lower standard apply, vis-à-vis the fully informed passenger, if standards are to vary?

Why should the doctrine, if it be part of the law, be limited to cases involving the driving of motor cars? Suppose that to the knowledge of the patient a young surgeon, whom the patient has chosen to operate on him, has only just qualified. If the operation goes wrong because of the surgeon's inexperience, is there a defence on the basis that the standard of

NOTE We will look at the duties of surgeons and other professionals later in this chapter.

skill and care is lower than the standard of a competent and experienced surgeon? Does the young, newly qualified, solicitor owe a lower standard of skill and care, when the client chooses to instruct him with the knowledge of his inexperience?

You can see from these extracts that the court decided by a majority of two to one that learner drivers have to meet the same standard of care as experienced drivers (Salmon LJ did not directly address this question, as he concluded there was no duty between Mrs Weston and Mr Nettleship in the first place, which meant that the question of the standard of care did not arise for him). Therefore, even if Mr Nettleship had not enquired about the insurance, it seems that he could still have sued Mrs Weston successfully. The reason for the decision appears to have been a pragmatic one. So many road traffic accidents happen each year that, if differing standards had to be applied to each one depending on the circumstances, the courts would quickly become swamped. As long as the rules are relatively clear-cut, the parties' insurers can settle most cases without too much difficulty.

VOCABULARY

Comments that are made *obiter*—which is short for the Latin phrase *obiter dictum*—are considered non-binding on later courts, because the comments were not essential to the decision.

We saw earlier that *Mansfield v Weetabix* [1998] 1 WLR 1263 decided that a driver who causes an accident because of an illness he does not know about is not liable in negligence. Thus, the comments in *Nettleship v Weston* [1971] 2 QB 691 should probably be read as applying only to drivers who are aware of their disability. In any event, the comments are, strictly speaking, **obiter**, since Mrs Weston was not disabled. However, it is likely that these comments will be followed if the question of a disabled person who knows of his or her disability comes before the courts, at least in road traffic accident cases. In other contexts, there may be scope for argument that disabled people should not be held to the same standard as those who are not disabled. For instance, W.V.H. Rogers states in *Winfield & Jolowicz on Tort* (7th edn, 2006) at 247 that 'some allowance is also probably to be made for physical disability, for example in judging whether a blind person took reasonable care as a pedestrian where a driver was injured trying to avoid him'.

3.2.3 **Higher standards**

cross reference

The phrase 'the man on the Clapham omnibus' was used in Hall v Brooklands Auto-Racing Club [1933] 1 KB 205, discussed earlier in this chapter.

People who hold themselves out as having a special skill are not judged by the standard of the 'reasonable person on the Clapham omnibus', because the average person will not have that same special skill. Instead, those who present themselves to others as having a special skill are judged by the standard of the reasonable person who has that skill. The courts first decided this concept in relation to doctors, in *Bolam v Friern Hospital Management Committee* [1957] 2 All ER 118, after a mental patient experienced bone fractures during the allegedly negligent administration of electro-convulsive therapy, but it applies to professionals in general. However, the question is whether a professional must be held to the standard of a perfect practitioner or whether—as with ordinary people—perfection is not required.

69

● *Bolam v Friern Hospital Management Committee* [1957] 2 All ER 118

McNair J: Counsel for the plaintiff put it in this way, that in the case of a medical man neg-ligence means failure to act in accordance with the standards of reasonably competent medical men at the time. That is a perfectly accurate statement, as long as it is remem-bered that there may be one or more perfectly proper standards; and if a medical man conforms with one of those proper standards then he is not negligent...I myself would prefer to put it this way: A doctor is not guilty of negligence if he has acted in accordance with a practice accepted as proper by a responsible body of medical men skilled in that particular art...Putting it the other way round, a doctor is not negligent, if he is acting in accordance with such a practice, merely because there is a body of opinion that takes a contrary view. At the same time, that does not mean that a medical man can obstinately and pig-headedly carry on with some old technique if it has been proved to be contrary to what is really substantially the whole of informed medical opinion. Otherwise you might get men today saying: 'I don't believe in anaesthetics. I don't believe in antiseptics. I am going to continue to do my surgery in the way it was done in the eighteenth century'. That clearly would be wrong.

The test described here involving a 'responsible body of experts' was used for several decades until it became apparent that a defendant could claim that any practice was legitimate, so long as it was followed by even a small segment of the professional popu-lation. The issue was decided in *Bolitho v City and Hackney Health Authority* [1998] AC 232, which involved a 2 year-old child who suffered brain damage after two instances of severe respiratory distress while in hospital. Although the doctor on call advised the nurses how to proceed by phone, she did not attend, which was itself considered negli-gent. The parties were in dispute as to whether the doctor would have and should have inserted a breathing tube after the first incident, based on commonly accepted medical principles.

● *Bolitho v City and Hackney Health Authority* [1998] AC 232

Lord Browne-Wilkinson: [T]he court is not bound to hold that a defendant doctor escapes liability for negligent treatment or diagnosis just because he leads evidence from a num-ber of medical experts who are genuinely of opinion that the defendant's treatment or diagnosis accorded with sound medical practice. In the Bolam case itself, McNair J. [1957] 1 W.L.R. 583, 587 stated that the defendant had to have acted in accordance with the practice accepted as proper by a 'responsible body of medical men.' Later, at p. 588, he referred to 'a standard of practice recognised as proper by a competent reasonable body of opinion.' Again, in the passage which I have cited from Maynard's case [1984] 1 W.L.R. 634, 639, Lord Scarman refers to a 'respectable' body of professional opinion. The use of these adjectives—responsible, reasonable and respectable—all show that the court has to be satisfied that the exponents of the body of opinion relied upon can demonstrate that such opinion has a logical basis. In particular in cases involving, as they so often do, the weighing of risks against benefits, the judge before accepting a body of opinion as being responsible, reasonable or respectable, will need to be satisfied that, in forming their views, the experts have directed their minds to the question of comparative risks and benefits and have reached a defensible conclusion on the matter.

There are decisions which demonstrate that the judge is entitled to approach expert professional opinion on this basis. For example, in Hucks v. Cole [1993] 4 Med.L.R. 393 (a case from 1968), a doctor failed to treat with penicillin a patient who was suffering from septic spots on her skin though he knew them to contain organisms capable of leading to puerperal fever. A number of distinguished doctors gave evidence that they would not, in the circumstances, have treated with penicillin. The Court of Appeal found the defendant to have been negligent. Sachs L.J. said, at p. 397:

> When the evidence shows that a lacuna in professional practice exists by which risks of grave danger are knowingly taken, then, however small the risk, the court must anxiously examine that **lacuna**—particularly if the risk can be easily and inexpensively avoided. If the court finds, on an analysis of the reasons given for not taking those precautions that, in the light of current professional knowledge, there is no proper basis for the lacuna, and that it is definitely not reasonable that those risks should have been taken, its function is to state that fact and where necessary to state that it constitutes negligence. In such a case the practice will no doubt thereafter be altered to the benefit of patients. On such occasions the fact that other practitioners would have done the same thing as the defendant practitioner is a very weighty matter to be put on the scales on his behalf; but it is not…conclusive. The court must be vigilant to see whether the reasons given for putting a patient at risk are valid in the light of any well-known advance in medical knowledge, or whether they stem from a residual adherence to out-of-date ideas.

....
VOCABULARY
'Lacuna' is a Latin word meaning a gap or blank.
....

As a result of this decision, professionals now must exercise the skill and care which is appropriate to a reasonable person in the post that they hold. As with drivers, this standard does not take account of individual inexperience. The law does recognize, however, that some posts are more specialized than others. For instance, according to *Balamoan v Holden & Co* 149 NLJ 898, a generalist solicitor in a country town may not have to show the same expertise in large, complicated claims as a specialist litigation lawyer from a city practice would have to show. The relevant time for judging what is the appropriate level of expertise is the date when the professional took the action that the claimant complains about, rather than the date of the trial, since there may have been developments in the state of knowledge in the expert's field between the time of the behaviour and the actual litigation. Thus, the law does not hold defendants liable for the risk of subsequent change, since requiring such foresight would be akin to forcing professionals to predict future events.

Someone who carries out a task which is often done by professionals but is not a professional him or herself does not need not show the same competence as a paid professional. Instead, the general standard of care applies to non-professionals acting in a professional capacity. *Cattley v St. John's Ambulance Brigade* 87 NJ 1140 confirmed this approach for volunteer first aiders. In this case, a boy was injured during a motorcycle race, and a first aider moved him without using a backboard to protect his spine. This action made his injuries worse, but the court found that the first aider was not liable. In *Wells v Cooper* [1958] 2 QB 265, a DIY carpenter used the wrong screws to fix a door handle, and a visitor to the premises was injured. Again, the court found that the carpenter was not liable because he was not a professional.

Even though the 'reasonable body of experts' test described in *Bolam v Friern Hospital Management Committee* [1957] 2 All ER 118 initially applied to professionals, it can be applied where non-experts make a controversial decision and responsible bodies of experts disagree on what the correct course of action would have been. For instance, in *Adams v Rhymney Valley District Council* [2000] Lloyd's Rep PN 777 a local council had to decide what type of window lock to use in its residential flats. One type was easier to open quickly in an emergency, but the other was more secure from burglars. The council chose the second type and was sued by a family whose children died in a house fire. At trial, the court heard from six experts, three of whom would have chosen the first type of lock and three the second. The court decided that in these circumstances, the 'reasonable body of experts' test applied and the council therefore had not breached its duty of care.

3.3 Assessing the defendant's conduct against the standard of care

Having decided what standard of care to apply, the court has to determine whether the defendant has met that standard. In doing so, the court can take into account all the circumstances of the case. However, the most common factors it will consider are:

- The general practice in the relevant field;
- Whether the damage was foreseeable;
- How serious the damage was likely to be;
- The defendant's objective;
- The knowledge available to the defendant; and
- The practicality of precautions.

We will consider each in more detail below.

3.3.1 General practice

If the defendant has complied with the common practice in the relevant trade or profession, the courts will treat that as strong evidence (but not conclusive proof) that the defendant was not negligent. For instance, a surgical operation carries many risks ranging from common complications to freakish accidents. Surgeons have to decide where to draw the line as to which risks to warn the patient about before the operation. A court will not usually interfere with that decision if it is in line with general practice in the field. The 'reasonable body of experts' test laid out in *Bolam v Friern Hospital Management Committee* [1957] 2 All ER 118 applies here just as it does to the decision to recommend the operation in the first place. However, as *Bolitho v City and Hackney Health Authority* [1998] AC 232 showed, the court may sometimes decide that the common practice itself is negligent, in which case the defendant will typically be held liable. An example is *Re*

cross reference
Bolitho v City and Hackney Health Authority [1998] AC 232 was excerpted above.

Herald of Free Enterprise, The Independent, 18 December 1987, where a ferry captain was found to be negligent for failing to check that his officers had secured the ferry's bow doors before sailing, even though the general practice was not to check.

3.3.2 Foreseeable likelihood of damage

The more likely it is that someone will be harmed by your actions, the more care the law will expect you to take. As the following extracts show, the activity itself is not determinative, since both cases involved damage caused by stray cricket balls. Instead, other factors come into play.

. . . .

● *Bolton v Stone* [1951] AC 850

> Lord Oaksey: Cricket has been played for about ninety years on the ground in question and no ball has been proved to have struck anyone on the highways near the ground until the respondent was struck, nor has there been any complaint to the appellants. In such circumstances was it the duty of the appellants, who are the committee of the club, to take some special precautions other than those they did take to prevent such an accident as happened? The standard of care in the law of negligence is the standard of an ordinarily careful man, but in my opinion an ordinarily careful man does not take precautions against every foreseeable risk. He can, of course, foresee the possibility of many risks, but life would be almost impossible if he were to attempt to take precautions against every risk which he can foresee. He takes precautions against risks which are reasonably likely to happen. Many foreseeable risks are extremely unlikely to happen and cannot be guarded against except by almost complete isolation. The ordinarily prudent owner of a dog does not keep his dog always on a lead on a country highway for fear it may cause injury to a passing motor cyclist, nor does the ordinarily prudent pedestrian avoid the use of the highway for fear of skidding motor cars. It may very well be that after this accident the ordinarily prudent committee man of a similar cricket ground would take some further precaution, but that is not to say that he would have taken a similar precaution before the accident...
>
> There are many footpaths and highways adjacent to cricket grounds and golf courses on to which cricket and golf balls are occasionally driven, but such risks are habitually treated both by the owners and committees of such cricket and golf courses and by the pedestrians who use the adjacent footpaths and highways as negligible and it is not, in my opinion, actionable negligence not to take precautions to avoid such risks.

. . . .

● *Miller v Jackson* [1977] QB 966

> Geoffrey Lane LJ: The judge accepted the plaintiffs' evidence that on a number of occasions cricket balls have been struck into their garden or against their house. Some chipped the brickwork: some damaged the roof. In particular in 1972 three caused damage. In 1974 several balls came over—one of which caused damage.
>
> The plaintiffs complained...In 1975 nine balls hit the fence and six went over it. In the 1976 season four hit the fence and eight or nine went over it, three on one single day—August 21. According to the plaintiffs, five of the 1975 ones landed in their garden and

two of those in 1976. On July 26, 1975, one just missed breaking the window of a room in which their son was seated. He was then about 11 or 12...The club officials who gave evidence were refreshingly candid and forthright. Mr. Jackson, the chairman of the club, freely conceded that there was no way in which they could stop balls going into the premises in Brackenridge from time to time; that the plaintiffs were likely to suffer in the future as they had done in the past from broken tiles and so on; that something like an average of eight balls a year were going to land in the vicinity of the plaintiffs' house. Mr. Nevins, the captain of the first team, agreed that when these homes were first built it was obvious that there was going to be trouble from balls driven over the bowler's head into the gardens.

I have dealt with the evidence at some length because in the end the outcome of the case may depend upon a decision as to the degree of potential or actual danger to person or property...In the present case, so far from being one incident of an unprecedented nature about which complaint is being made, this is a series of incidents, or perhaps a continuing failure to prevent incidents from happening, coupled with the certainty that they are going to happen again. The risk of injury to person and property is so great that on each occasion when a ball comes over the fence and causes damage to the plaintiffs, the defendants are guilty of negligence.

cross reference
Reasonable foresee-ability is discussed at length in chapter 4.

Thus, the defendants in *Miller* were found liable in negligence, while the defendants in *Bolton* were not. It was not the act as such that the courts found negligent, but the act viewed in context. In *Miller* injury was reasonably foreseeable. In *Bolton*, it was not. When the court assesses the likelihood of damage, it will also take into account special characteristics of the claimant, if the defendant either knows about them or should anticipate them. For instance, in *Haley v London Electricity Board* [1965] AC 778, a blind plaintiff succeeded because the electricity board had taken sufficient precautions to prevent sighted people from falling into a trench, but these precautions were not sufficient for a blind person. The court held that there are sufficient blind pedestrians in the general population that the board should have anticipated the risk. However, the court does not normally take into account the drunkenness of a claimant. For example, a taxi driver has a duty to stop in a place where it is reasonably safe for customers to leave the car, but does not normally have to choose the spot more carefully for a drunken customer. The case which decided this point, *Griffiths v Brown*, The Times, 23 October 1998, commented that the position might be different if the driver were expressly hired to make sure someone got home safely. Defendants who encourage others to get drunk may also be expected to take extra precautions, as in the case of *Brannan v Airtours plc*, The Times, 1 February 1999, where a holiday company which had encouraged holidaymakers to drink by offering unlimited free wine and had placed tables in such a way that guests who had drunk only a little too much were likely to injure themselves on nearby fans was found liable to an injured patron.

3.3.3 **Seriousness of likely damage**

Another factor the court takes into account is how serious any damage or injury is likely to be if it does happen. Again, the claimant's disability may be relevant here, provided the defendant either knows about it or should anticipate it. For instance, in *Paris v Stepney*

Borough Council [1951] AC 367, the court decided that an employer has to take additional precautions to protect the eyesight of a worker who, to the employer's knowledge, is already partially-sighted. In this case, the employee had lost an eye during the Second World War, but his employer did not provide him with goggles for his job as a garage mechanic. As he was removing a rusty bolt, a piece flew off and hit him in his remaining eye. The court held that the employer had been negligent, given the circumstances.

3.3.4 Defendant's objective

If the defendant's actions are intended to have some benefit to the public, the court is less likely to find that there has been a breach of the duty of care. A good example is *Watt v Hertfordshire County Council* [1984] 2 All ER 368, where London Transport had loaned a jack to the fire brigade. The jack was extremely heavy, and only one of the fire brigade's trucks was equipped to carry it. While that truck was out dealing with an emergency, the fire brigade were called to an accident where a woman was trapped under a heavy vehicle just two or three hundred yards from the fire station. There was only one other truck available which was strong enough to carry the jack, and the officer in charge decided to use it even though it was not fitted with the proper restraints to hold the jack in place. On the way to the scene, the driver had to stop suddenly, and the jack moved and injured one of the fire-fighters. The court decided that the officer in charge had not been negligent. Denning LJ stated:

> [I]n measuring due care...[o]ne must balance the risk against the end to be achieved. If this accident had occurred in a commercial enterprise without any emergency, there could be no doubt that the servant would succeed. But the commercial end to make profit is very different from the human end to save life or limb. The saving of life or limb justifies taking considerable risk, and I am glad to say there have never been wanting in this country men of courage ready to take those risks, notably in the fire service.

> In this case the risk involved in sending out the lorry was not so great as to prohibit the attempt to save life. I quite agree that fire engines, ambulances and doctors' cars should not shoot past the traffic lights when they show a red light. That is because the risk is too great to warrant the incurring of the danger. It is always a question of balancing the risk against the end.

3.3.5 Knowledge available at the time

The earlier discussion regarding professional duties noted that courts judge the conduct of professionals based on the state of knowledge in their field at the time the act leading to the injury occurred. The same applies to any other business that requires particular knowledge. For example, a manufacturer may create a product that later turns out to be dangerous to consumers' health. However, a manufacturer cannot simply turn a blind eye to a risk in the hope that injury never occurs. Once a manufacturer has reason to suspect that a product may be harmful, failure to investigate may constitute negligence. For instance, in *The Creutzfeldt-Jakob Disease Litigation, Plaintiffs v United Kingdom Medical Research Council* 54 BMLR 8, a large number of children were treated with human growth hormone that turned out to be contaminated and caused the children to become ill with Creutzfeldt-Jakob Disease. The court found that by 1976, the defendants had sufficient knowledge of the risk of contamination that they should have investigated further and were negligent in failing to do so.

Where the defendant is an organization, the court will assess what knowledge the organization had, considering the organization as a whole rather than the specific knowledge of the individuals who directly caused the damage. For example, in *Sandhu Menswear Company Ltd v Woolworths plc* [2006] EWHC 1299 (TCC), the claimant and defendant occupied adjacent premises on an industrial estate. Woolworths had a fire prevention manual which highlighted the risk of arson on premises of this type and gave advice on how to reduce this risk. However, the employees on the ground were unaware of the document and did not implement its advice. Arsonists started a fire in some rubbish which the employees had left behind, and the fire spread to the claimant's premises. The court judged the conduct of Woolworths by reference to the knowledge in the manual and gave judgment for the claimant.

3.3.6 **Practicality of precautions**

In deciding what precautions a defendant should have taken, the courts will consider how practical the precautions were, what they would have cost and to what extent they would have reduced the risk of injury. For instance, in *Latimer v AEC Ltd* [1953] AC 643, the Court of Appeal decided that an employer did not have to shut down an entire factory overnight simply because part of the floor had become slippery as a result of the escape of some cooling mixture. However, although the courts take the cost of the precautions into account, judges do not usually consider what financial resources the defendant has to meet that cost.

In some unusual instances, the court will take the defendant's finances into account. For example, in *Knight v Home Office* [1990] 3 All ER 237, a prisoner committed suicide in a prison hospital while waiting to be moved to a specialist psychiatric unit. The prison hospital did not have the resources to provide staff to watch him continuously, although staff had been checking on him every 15 minutes.

think point

Which policy rationales support the decision not to take the defendant's resources into account when deciding the practicality of precautions? Which suggest courts should undertake a means-based analysis?

· ·

● ***Knight v Home Office*** [1990] 3 All ER 237

> Pill LJ: It is for the court to consider what standard of care is appropriate to the particular relationship and in the particular situation. It is not a complete defence for a government department any more than it would be for a private individual or organisation to say that no funds are available for additional safety measures.
>
> I cannot accept what was at one time submitted by counsel for the defendants that the plaintiffs' only remedy would be a political one. To take an extreme example, if the evidence was that no funds were available to provide any medical facilities in a large prison there would be a failure to achieve the standard of care appropriate for prisoners. In a

different context, lack of funds would not excuse a public body which operated its vehicles on the public roads without any system of maintenance for the vehicles if an accident occurred because of lack of maintenance. The law would require a higher standard of care towards other road users.

In making the decision as to the standard to be demanded the court must, however, bear in mind as one factor that resources available for the public service are limited and that the allocation of resources is a matter for Parliament.

In the end, the court held that, given the circumstances, it was not negligent for the prison hospital to have checked on the inmate every fifteen minutes.

Precautions which have been found adequate in one case will not necessarily be adequate in another. Instead, the court must consider all the circumstances in each case. In *Daw v Intel Corporation (UK)* [2007] EWCA Civ 70, the Court of Appeal considered a case where an employee suffered from stress at work. The judge at first instance had noted that there was a previous precedent where an employer had been found not liable because stress counselling was available to employees. Intel had also provided such counselling, but the judge found that it was not sufficient to prevent stress in the specific circumstances of the case, and held that Intel was liable for the claimant's injury. The Court of Appeal upheld the decision, saying that the existence of a previous case could not excuse the judge from a full investigation of the case before him or her.

3.3.7 Proposals for clarification

The government recently proposed a new bill to clarify the standard of care in this area of law, in particular for public sector workers. The article below explains the proposal and comments on it critically.

● Kevin Williams, *'Legislating in the echo chamber?'*, 155 New Law Journal 1938

In spring 2005, Prime Minister Tony Blair said that too many public servants, particularly teachers and healthcare workers, were worried they might be subject to unfair legal action. He promised that ways would be found to 'protect' them from what he called this 'real problem'. Within eight months, the Department for Constitutional Affairs produced a Bill to address this...

Clarifying fault

Part 1 of the Bill, published in November, consists of a single clause, designed to clarify the law of negligence. As presently drafted it provides:

'1. Deterrent effect of potential liability. A court considering a claim in negligence may, in determining whether the defendant should have taken particular steps to meet the standard of care (whether by taking precautions against a risk or otherwise), have regard to whether a requirement to take those steps might— (a) prevent a desirable activity from being undertaken at all, to a particular extent or in a particular way, or (b) discourage persons from undertaking functions in connection with a desirable activity.'

The wording may seem uncontroversial. The explanatory notes accompanying the Bill tersely comment that the clause does no more than 'reflect the existing law'. How this will give effect to Mr Blair's wish to see defendants, particularly from the public sector, *better* protected from unfair litigation and judgments is, however, obscure. Will they feel reassured when told the clause is merely declaratory of the current situation?

Question of breach, not duty

Clause 1 is expressly confined to questions of *breach*—and how the standard of care is to be applied—rather than with *duty*. Judges will, therefore, continue to be free to recognise—in the now conventional, post-*Caparo Industries plc v Dickman* [1990] 2 AC 605, [1990] 1 All ER 568 incremental manner—new responsibilities in negligence, which may not be quite so welcome to defendants facing recently contrived causes of action, such as complaints of educational neglect, child protection failures or workplace stress. Clause 1 is side-noted 'Deterrent effect of potential liability', an effect which courts sometimes assume exists, but which is commonly questioned by academic commentators…

Creating defensive professions?

A good example is the often unsubstantiated claims by doctors that malpractice litigation leads to 'defensive medicine'. What we *do* know is that the medical profession has a strong tendency to exaggerate its exposure to the risk of being sued; a misperception that teachers seem equally keen to share. If attitudes such as these are thought to be a, or perhaps *the*, problem, clause 1 seems a poor solution. Given the paucity of demonstrable connections between the threat of liability and the quality of service provision, instructing judges to consider whether a 'desirable activity' may be 'prevented' or 'discouraged', and to what extent, seems a potentially fraught exercise. Moreover, uncertainty over what activities may count as 'desirable' may provide more rather than less scope for litigation. So far the government has merely said that courts will be able to 'consider the wider social context of the activity' (DCA Ministerial statement 2 November 2005).

Unnecessary solution

By offering a statutory steer to the courts, cl 1 purports to improve the lot of defendants while simultaneously allowing judges to continue to act as they always have done. This looks like an unnecessary solution to a non-existent problem. More to the point, it seems unlikely the clause will reduce fear of unfair litigation, risk averse behaviour, or the number of allegedly frivolous claims.

The bill discussed in this article became law in 2006. Clause 1—now section 1—was unchanged. It is clearly designed to prevent litigation from causing 'chilling effects' where people avoid activities that may lead to being sued. It is questionable, however, whether people who are affected by fear of litigation will be aware of the new statute.

 ## 3.4 Proving breach

Proving the breach of a duty has its own legal issues. The rest of this chapter focuses on that topic.

Exercise

· ·

Before reading on, think about what 'proof' means to you. How certain would you have to be about something before you would accept it as 'proved'? Does the amount of proof necessary increase proportionally to what is at stake?

3.4.1 The burden of proof and the standard of proof

As a general rule, it is up to claimants to prove the essential ingredients of whatever tort they allege. Negligence is no different. Claimants must prove that the defendant owed them a duty, that the duty was breached and that the breach caused them some sort of damage. This does not mean that claimants have to show that their version of events is the only possible one or absolutely rule out all other possible interpretations of what happened. Because torts are civil wrongs and not crimes, the standard of proof which claimants must meet is that of the 'balance of probabilities'. Generally, this means that it must be more likely than not that the claimant's version of events is correct. This may not necessarily mean that it is enough to show a 51 per cent likelihood that the claimant's version is the right one, however. The more serious the allegations, the higher the degree of certainty the court will require. If the claimant alleges something that is a crime as well as a tort, then, out of fairness to the defendant, the court will apply something very close to the criminal standard, even if the claimant only claims in tort. As you probably know, in criminal cases the standard of proof is 'beyond reasonable doubt'. In this section, we will look at some rules that can help a claimant to prove breach.

3.4.2 *Res ipsa loquitur*

Usually, claimants prove a breach of a duty of care by identifying an act of the defendant which caused them to suffer damage and then arguing that this act fell short of the required standard of care (which was discussed in detail in previous sections of this chapter). However, claimants sometimes have clearly suffered damage but have no way of pinpointing exactly what the defendant did to cause that damage. This makes it impossible to prove breach in the usual way. All of the critical knowledge lies with the defendant. This problem is particularly common in product liability claims and traffic accidents. For example, in *Carmarthenshire County Council v Lewis* [1955] AC 649, a four-year-old child caused a fatal road accident after somehow escaping from school premises. The education authority was found liable because it could not prove that the school was not at fault. In such cases, the claimant may simply put the facts before the court and ask the court to infer that 'the thing speaks for itself'. This means that circumstances strongly suggest that the defendant must have been in breach of the legal duty, because it is so unlikely that the accident could have happened in the absence of a breach of duty. Under this principle, the defendant should be held liable in tort, unless—as shall be seen—the defendant can demonstrate that he or she was not responsible for the injury. This argument is usually referred to as *res ipsa loquitur*, which is simply the Latin for 'the thing speaks for itself'. The principle was first established in *Scott v London & St*

Katherine Docks Co [1861–1873] All ER 246, where six sacks of sugar fell onto a work-man in a dockyard. The court found that the occupiers of the docks were liable for the injury to the workman. The short judgment stresses that the defendant's control over the thing causing the accident is a key factor.

....
● *Scott v London & St. Katherine Docks Co* [1861–1873] All ER 246

> Erle CJ: [W]here the thing is shown to be under the management of the defendant, or his servants, and the accident is such as, in the ordinary course of things, does not happen if those who have the management of the machinery use proper care, it affords reasonable evidence, in the absence of explanation by the defendant, that the accident arose from want of care.

Ratcliffe v Plymouth & Torbay Health Authority [1998] Lloyd's Rep Med 168 is a more modern case with a useful summary of how *res ipsa loquitur* works and a discussion of how a defendant can respond when the principle is used. In this case, the plaintiff lost sensation in his legs and genitals after a spinal injection, and he argued that *res ipsa loquitur* applied. However, the defendant produced a contemporary record of the treatment, which showed that the injection had been carried out correctly. The court accepted this evidence and dismissed the claim.

....
● *Ratcliffe v Plymouth & Torbay Health Authority* [1998] Lloyd's Rep Med 168

> Hobhouse LJ: The essential role of the doctrine of res ipsa loquitur is to enable the plain-tiff who is not in possession of all the material facts to be able to plead an allegation of negligence in an acceptable form and to force the defendant to respond to it at the peril of having a finding of negligence made against the defendant if the defendant does not make an adequate response. But, once the defendant has responded, then the question for the court is whether, in the light of that response, that is to say upon all the evidence that has been placed before it at the trial, both by the plaintiff and by the defendant, the court is satisfied that the defendant has been negligent and that his negligence caused the plaintiff's injury.
>
> The accepted categories of response that can be made to a case based upon res ipsa loqui-tur, that is to say, upon an inference of negligence, support this analysis. The defendant can displace the inference by showing, by reference to a closer examination of the plain-tiff's evidence or by reference to evidence adduced by the defendant, that the inference that on the balance of probabilities there was negligence is not justified. The plaintiff's case then fails unless a more specific case has been made out. Alternatively, the defendant can accept that there is a legitimate basis for the implication, but say that in the particular case the defendant in fact exercised reasonable care, notwithstanding the outcome and the inability fully to explain how the plaintiff's injury came about.

NOTE Exclusivity of control is a particularly important element, since it minimizes the possibility a defendant will wrongfully be found liable for an injury.

These cases show that claimants who want to rely on *res ipsa loquitur* have to establish the following:

- That the damage was caused by something over which the defendant (or someone for whom the defendant was responsible) had exclusive control;

- That the precise cause of the damage is unknown;
- That an accident of that type would not normally happen unless the defendant was in breach of duty.

Establishing liability using *res ipsa loquitur* is not the end of the matter. Even if the claimant makes a good case, the defendant can counter by putting forward a plausible explanation for the accident that does not involve negligence on the part of the defendant. Alternatively, the defendant may give evidence to show that he or she took adequate precautions. The following case extracts are examples in which *res ipsa loquitur* did not succeed. In the first case, *Easson v LNE Railway* [1944] 2 KB 421, a child fell through a door in the corridor of a train while the train was moving and was injured. There was no evidence as to how the door came to be open.

. . . .

● *Easson v LNE Railway* [1944] 2 KB 421

> Goddard LJ: Counsel for the plaintiffs has contended that, once it is established that the accident happened through the boy falling through the open door on the off-side of this corridor train, the burden of proof is on the railway company to explain how that door came to be open. That contention is based on the doctrine of res ipsa loquitur, which applies when the operation of 'the thing' which caused the accident is at the material time wholly under the control of the defendant. The classic case is Scott v. London and St. Katherine Docks Co...where bags of sugar fell from a warehouse occupied by the defendants on a passer by. The defendants were called on to explain how it came about that the bags so fell because 'the thing' which caused the accident was entirely under their control. Likewise, when a collision happens on the railway, since the railway system and the trains thereon are entirely under the control of the railway company, it is for the company to explain, if they can, how the accident happened and to show that it occurred without fault on their part...Can that doctrine apply in a case where the door of a railway carriage comes open? In some cases the plaintiff may be able to show a state of facts which **prima facie**, at any rate, establishes a case of negligence. Such was Gee v. Metropolitan Ry Co...None of the reported cases, however, really laid down any principle of law. They only show that in the circumstances of the case there was evidence on which the jury could find a verdict for the plaintiff. In Gee v. Metropolitan Ry Co...a train on the Metropolitan Railway started from Westminster station. At Victoria station, which is two stations west of Westminster, the plaintiff got into an empty compartment. Before the train had reached Sloane Square, the next station, the plaintiff leant lightly against the off-side door of the carriage. The door flew open and he fell on to the line. It is the duty of a railway company to have their train in a proper and fit condition with the doors properly fastened when it starts on its journey, and the obvious inference was that the railway company had not performed their duty and seen that the train was in a safe condition when it left Westminster station on its journey. In Burns v. North British Ry Co...a woman was walking along a platform at a station in Glasgow when she was struck from behind by the open door of a carriage of a train which was running into the station. That train had been stopping at various stations, and the inference was that at the last stopping place the door had not been properly closed, so that there was a prima facie case of negligence. The accident in Inglis v. London, Midland and Scottish Ry Co...was not unlike that in the present case, except that the fall of the boy, who was aged eight, was through the

door of a compartment of a carriage on the train. At the trial before the sheriff-substitute evidence was given by all the people in the carriage to negative the fact that they had in any way interfered with the lock of the carriage-door. Their evidence being accepted, the inference was that the door had not been properly closed by the railway company's servants when the train left the station, and, therefore, there was a case for the railway company to answer. Lord Moncrieff, to whose judgment I especially refer, said . . . : 'When the door which opens has in fact remained under the sole control of the company or its servants up to the moment of opening'—which was the case in Gee v. Metropolitan Ry Co . . . —the single fact of its unexplained opening may thus per se be relevant to infer negligence against them: and so to operate in a manner analogous to cases of res ipsa loquitur by itself transferring the onus of proof. Even in such a case, however, there will be at most an analogy with, and not a proper example of, an application of the maxim. In the present case, on the other hand, there is found to have been no continuity of any single control of the door. Control by the defenders must be taken to have ended at latest on the conclusion of the last inspection at St. Enoch's.' [sic]

In the present case it seems to me it is impossible to say that the doors of an express corridor train travelling from Edinburgh to London are continuously under the sole control of the railway company in the sense in which it is necessary that they should be for the doctrine of res ipsa loquitur, or a doctrine analogous to it, to apply. Passengers are walking up and down the corridors during the journey and get in and out at stopping places. I do not want it to be thought that I am minimizing the duty of the company. Before a train leaves a station the company must see that the carriage doors are closed. They are not under an obligation to inspect the off-side doors of the carriages at every stop. There must be reasonable inspection, and they must do the best they can.

Here the determinative factor appears to be that the railway company could reasonably show that it was not the only actor involved—any of the passengers could have unlatched the door. Now consider a more recent case involving spilled liquid.

● *Bell v Department of Health and Social Security*, *The Times*, 13 June 1989

Drake J: At about ten past three on the afternoon of 30th July 1984 [the plaintiff] went from her office along the corridor on the same floor to the ladies' lavatory. On her return to her office, as she was passing the doors of a lift, she slipped on some liquid and fell. As she fell she lunged forward to try to grab the handle on the door or gate of the lift to break her fall, but instead she landed on her hands. In doing this she did break the fall but as she landed she twisted over and fell on her bottom. She pulled herself together and got to her feet but she had hurt her chest in the fall. Subsequently she suffered lasting pain in the chest area and also pain to her back and her coccyx. She has continued to suffer pain up to the present time . . . Mrs Clark, who gave evidence for the Defendants, said she saw the scene of the fall some 10 minutes after it happened. She saw a little skid mark on the floor but there was hardly any liquid—she estimated no more than a dessertspoonful—and she was amazed that such a tiny drop could cause an accident. She thought the liquid was water.

Mrs Clark got the accident book and wrote in it details of the accident, which in my judgment do not differ materially if at all from the Plaintiff's account given to me in evidence. Mrs Clark shortly afterwards, but not in the presence of the Plaintiff, completed an

'Accident on Duty Report' in similar terms. Each of these two entries refers to slipping on 'liquid' but at the end of the 'Accident on Duty Report' Mrs Clark stated, and I quote: 'The accident was purely accidental. Water had been spilled on the floor and not been wiped up by whoever was guilty of the spillage'.

Mrs Clark agreed that the liquid whether tea, coffee or water was probably spilled by someone who had fetched water or tea or coffee and brought it downstairs by lift.

There is little dispute about any of this evidence, and all the witnesses without exception were clearly honest and doing their best to recall events which are by now very stale since the accident occurred almost five years ago. So far as it is necessary to make any findings of fact I accept Mrs Clark's evidence that the quantity of liquid was very small but I find it to have been rather more than her estimate of being only about a dessertspoonful. It does not seem to me to be material whether it was tea, coffee or water. On a balance of probabilities I find it was spilled by someone who had brought it down in a cup or mug from the fourth floor by the manually-operated lift.

There is little if any evidence which helps to determine how long the liquid had been there.... It was also submitted on behalf of the Plaintiff that the facts arising in the instant case are covered by the decision in Ward v Tesco Stores Limited [1976] 1 All ER 219, [1976] 1 WLR 810. In that case the Court of Appeal (Megaw and Lawton, LJJ, with Ormrod, LJ dissenting) held that where the Plaintiff slipped on a spillage in a supermarket and there was no evidence as to how long the spillage had been there the Defendants had failed to show that they had taken reasonable care to clear it up, and as the burden of proving they had taken such care was on them, the Plaintiff succeeded. On the basis of that case, Mr McMullen, for the Plaintiff, submits that the present facts are such that res ipsa loquitur. In my judgment the situation in a supermarket is clearly different from that in an office block. I think that Ward v Tesco Stores depends very much on the facts of that particular case and I reject the submission made on behalf of the Plaintiff in the present case that this is a case in which the facts speak for themselves to entitle the Plaintiff to judgment.

It is not clear why the court felt that *res ipsa loquitur* is more applicable in a supermarket than in an office block, but it may have been influenced by the fact that the office block had a system of regular health and safety inspections. Despite rejecting the *res ipsa loquitur* argument, the court went on to give judgment for the plaintiff, because the only other precaution the employer had taken was to give warnings to the staff about carrying drinks without using a tray or a saucer, and the court considered this procedure inadequate.

3.4.3 Criminal convictions

We mentioned earlier that in cases where the defendant's alleged act would be a crime as well as a tort, the court will apply something close to the criminal standard of proof. But what if the defendant has already been convicted of a crime? The Civil Evidence Act 1968 may be used to help claimants in certain circumstances.

● **Civil Evidence Act 1968**

> **11 Convictions as evidence in civil proceedings**
>
> (1) In any civil proceedings the fact that a person has been convicted of an offence by or before any court in the United Kingdom or by a court-martial there or elsewhere shall (subject to subsection (3) below) be admissible in evidence for the purpose of proving, where to do so is relevant to any issue in those proceedings, that he committed that offence, whether he was so convicted upon a plea of guilty or otherwise and whether or not he is a party to the civil proceedings; but no conviction other than a subsisting one shall be admissible in evidence by virtue of this section.
>
> (2) In any civil proceedings in which by virtue of this section a person is proved to have been convicted of an offence by or before any court in the United Kingdom or by a court-martial there or elsewhere—
>
> (a) he shall be taken to have committed that offence unless the contrary is proved; and
>
> (b) without prejudice to the reception of any other admissible evidence for the purpose of identifying the facts on which the conviction was based, the contents of any document which is admissible as evidence of the conviction, and the contents of the information, complaint, indictment or charge-sheet on which the person in question was convicted, shall be admissible in evidence for that purpose.
>
> (3) Nothing in this section shall prejudice the operation of section 13 of this Act of any other enactment whereby a conviction or a finding of fact in any criminal proceedings is for the purposes of any other proceedings made conclusive evidence of any fact.

think point

Does section 11 of the 1968 Act apply only to negligence claims?

NOTE Section 13 of the 1968 Act deals with the use of convictions as evidence in defamation proceedings (i.e. libel and slander). Those torts are covered in chapter 17.

The 1968 Act does not explain precisely what weight the court should give to convictions that are admitted under section 11. Certainly it is open to judges to decide that, despite the conviction, they believe it is proved that the individual in question did not commit the crime. However, courts will be extremely reluctant to make a finding which is inconsistent with the verdict of a criminal court, particularly when a jury has given it or the Court of Appeal has confirmed it. This is for reasons of both principle and pragmatism. For example:

- It is a basic principle of the English judicial system that decisions about a person's guilt or innocence in serious criminal matters should be made by their fellow laypeople and not by lawyers. This is an important protection for defendants. Thus, judges in civil matters should defer to the lay jury's conclusions.

- The criminal trial may have taken place several years before the civil one and witnesses' memories may have deteriorated in the meantime.

- Inconsistent decisions by civil and criminal courts can lead to confusion and a loss of public confidence in the legal system.

- If civil judges were perceived to be too ready to decide that someone who had been convicted was not in fact guilty, people who felt they had been wrongly convicted might be tempted to abuse the civil system by bringing ill-founded claims in an effort to clear their name.

You may be able to think of other reasons why judges in civil claims should defer to the decisions of criminal courts. In practice they almost always do so, which means that section 11 of the 1968 Act can be a useful way for claimants to support their case, reducing the risk of losing and perhaps also decreasing the number of witnesses and experts they need to call, thus shortening trial times and increasing judicial efficiency.

 For more revision tips, including self-test questions and suggestions for further reading, see the Online Resource Centre at www.oxfordtextbooks.co.uk/orc/strong_complete/.

revision tasks

Remember, your revision will be most effective if you do the work yourself! Here are some tasks to help you revise this chapter.

- List the different situations in which defendants' state of knowledge may affect whether or not they have breached their duty of care.

- Remind yourself of how foreseeability is relevant to whether or not there is a duty of care (i.e. the topic discussed in chapter 2.) Then describe the role foreseeability plays in assessing whether or not a duty has been breached.

- Summarize in no more than one page the law on breach of the duty of care at sporting events.

- Make a table outlining the law on breach of a driver's duty of care.

4 Negligence: Damage: Causation and remoteness

4.1 Introduction

NOTE Some authors prefer to say that there are four elements of negligence: duty, breach, causation and remoteness. Both approaches will give you the same result if you apply them properly.

We have now seen that in order for a claimant to sue successfully in negligence, the defendant must:

- owe the claimant a duty; and

- breach that duty.

There is one more element of negligence which has to be present for a successful claim, and that is damage. A claimant who has not suffered any damage has no claim. We will look briefly at what constitutes damage in the following section. Chapter 5 considers the remedies that a claimant may be able to obtain for such damage. Once the court is satisfied that the claimant has suffered some damage, it will consider two further requirements which are part of the concept of damage: firstly, the claimant has to show that it was the defendant's breach (and not some other occurrence) that caused the damage. Second, the claimant has to show that the damage was not too remote. This chapter looks at each of these concepts in detail.

Remember, 'causation' means that the claimant must show that, had it not been for the breach, the damage would not have happened. 'Remoteness', on the other hand, means that the claimant has to show that the damage which occurred was not so improbable that the defendant should not be liable for it.

cross reference
We briefly introduced causation and remoteness in chapter 2.

This chapter proceeds as follows:

- Types of damage;

- Causation;

- Remoteness.

4.2 Types of damage

Proving that there has been some damage is usually straightforward. The most common types of damage are personal injury, damage to property or financial loss. Usually, these are easily recognized (although financial loss can give rise to some special difficulties, which we will discuss in chapter 13). Sometimes, though, it is not easy to decide whether or not the law should recognize particular kinds of damage. For instance, in *Grieves v FT Edwards & Sons Ltd* [2006] EWCA Civ 27, the Court of Appeal had to consider whether or not claimants could sue for changes in their lungs (called 'pleural plaques') which were caused by exposure to asbestos. These changes do not cause any symptoms of illness, but increase the risk of becoming ill in future, which in turn understandably causes the patient to suffer anxiety. However, the Court of Appeal decided that this was not a form of damage that the law would recognize.

NOTE The residents also sued in the tort of nuisance, which is discussed in chapter 8.

Another example of the law struggling to decide whether certain types of damage should be recognized is seen in *Hunter v Canary Wharf Ltd* [1997] AC 665. In this case, the construction of a link road to serve the new Canary Wharf development in London's Docklands created large volumes of dust, which affected local residents. They sued for damages. The Court of Appeal held that the dust was not 'damage' for the purposes of a negligence claim.

The rule that a claimant in negligence must suffer damage has also featured in a number of controversial cases regarding the birth of children, usually in circumstances where one of the parents has undergone an unsuccessful sterilization operation and then sues for the costs of raising a child. Prior to 1985, judges were divided as to whether, on public policy grounds, the birth of a healthy child could be described as 'damage'. There were a number of contradictory decisions at first instance before the Court of Appeal considered the issue in *Emeh v Kensington and Chelsea and Westminster Area Health Authority* [1985] QB 1012. Here, the mother became pregnant within a few months of the sterilization operation. She claimed damages for the pregnancy and the costs of bringing up the child. The Court of Appeal decided that there was no public policy reason why these damages could not be awarded. Although the decision was followed in several later cases, defendants in cases such as the 1997 decision in *Roy v Croydon Health Authority* (1998) 40 BMLR 40 continued to argue that *Emeh v Kensington and Chelsea and Westminster Area Health Authority* [1985] QB 1012 should not be followed. The 1997 decision involved a woman who had applied for employment with the appellant health authority. In October 1988, prior to beginning work, she was required to undergo a medical examination, including a chest x-ray. The radiologist failed to advise the plaintiff that she had an untreatable lung condition, known as primary pulmonary hypertension or PPH, that would reduce her life expectancy if she became pregnant. Four months later, the plaintiff became pregnant and was eventually diagnosed with PPH. The legal aspects of the decision are discussed below.

think point
What is the key difference between *Roy v Croydon* and *Emeh v Kensington*? Did the court recognize the cost of bringing up the child in this case as damage?

87

● *Roy v Croydon Health Authority* [1998] 40 BMLR 40

> Kennedy LJ: [W]hen the mother wants both the pregnancy and the healthy child, there is simply no loss which can give rise to a claim for damages in respect of either the normal expenses and trauma of pregnancy or the costs of bringing up the child. There may be…other related disadvantages which a plaintiff suffers, as in this case the pulmonary embolism and the reactive depression, which can properly be regarded as losses flowing from the admitted breach of duty, but that cannot possibly be said in relation to a wanted child.
>
> Mr Robin Stewart QC, for the plaintiff, sought to overcome that difficulty by submitting that, if the plaintiff had known what she should have known about her own condition, including in particular the risks of pregnancy and the limitations upon her own ability to fulfil the role of a mother as she would have wished, she would not have had the child, and therefore the child should be regarded as an 'unwanted child' from the outset. I disagree. I accept that, subject to questions of remoteness of damage and scope of duty, to which I will turn in a moment, Mrs R may be able to claim, as flowing from the admitted breach of duty, her loss of the opportunity properly to evaluate the arguments for and against pregnancy, but that would hardly be a significant head of damages when, in the result, the hazards of pregnancy are negotiated without disaster, and she gives birth to a healthy and much loved child.

After *Emeh v Kensington and Chelsea and Westminster Area Health Authority* [1985] QB 1012 and *Roy v Croydon* (1998) 40 BMLR 40, it seemed that parents would be allowed to recover damages for the costs of raising a child where the pregnancy was not wanted at all, but not where they wanted the pregnancy and simply did not have full information about its dangers. However, while these developments were taking place in the English courts, a contrary line of authority was developing in Scotland, where judges were less inclined to award damages in such cases. In 2000, one of these Scottish cases—*McFarlane v Tayside Health Board* [2000] 2 AC 59, involving an unsuccessful vasectomy—reached the House of Lords for the first time. This gave the House of Lords its first opportunity to consider the issue for both Scotland and England, and, although this was a Scottish case, their Lordships commented (*obiter*) that the law should be taken to be the same in England. In the event, the House of Lords unanimously disapproved the decision in *Emeh v Kensington and Chelsea and Westminster Area Health Authority* [1985] QB 1012, but was divided as to why. Slynn LJ and Hope LJ decided that there was no duty on the part of the surgeon to prevent the parents from incurring maintenance costs, while Steyn LJ and Millett LJ took the view that the birth of a healthy child could not be considered as damage. This suggested that the birth of a healthy child was not 'damage' in English law, whether the pregnancy was wanted or not.

The emphasis in these cases on the fact that the children in question had been born healthy raises the question of whether the birth of a disabled child should be treated differently. The Court of Appeal considered this question in *Parkinson v St. James and Seacroft University Hospital* [2001] EWCA Civ 530, where the mother gave birth to an autistic child following a failed sterilization. The autism was not related to the negligence that caused the sterilization to fail. The Court of Appeal held that although the mother was not entitled to the basic maintenance costs of bringing up a child, she could claim the additional costs of raising a child with autism. In *Rees v Darlington Memorial Hospital NHS Trust* [2003] UKHL 52, the Court of Appeal initially extended this principle to cover cases where the additional costs were caused because the mother and not the child was disabled. However, the House of Lords overruled this decision and, perhaps in an attempt to settle the issue once and for all, held by a majority of 4–3 that all future cases involving the birth of a child after a failed sterilization should attract a 'flat-rate' award of £15,000, regardless of the circumstances of the child or the parent. This decision has yet to be considered in any subsequent cases—such as, for example, cases of failed vasectomies or negligent advice about the risks of pregnancy—but it is to be expected that a similar line will be taken in all cases involving a so-called 'wrongful birth' and that the law will no longer distinguish between wanted and unwanted children, or between disabled and non-disabled parents and children.

think point

What policy considerations support the courts' decision not to distinguish between the costs of maintaining children in different circumstances? What considerations point to the opposite conclusion?

(4.3) **Causation**

4.3.1 The 'but for' test

think point

Do you think the 'but for' test calls for a legal analysis or a factual enquiry? Based on your answer, what kind of person would you need to get evidence from in order to satisfy the test?

The basic test that courts use to decide whether or not the claimant has established causation is known as the 'but for' test. The court asks itself, 'But for the defendant's breach, would the claimant have suffered this damage?' If the claim is to succeed, the answer has to be 'yes'. If the answer is 'no'—in other words, if the damage would have happened anyway—the claim must fail, even if the defendant has breached a duty to the claimant. Lawyers often talk of an event or characteristic 'breaking the chain of causation'. If this sort of interference occurs, the claimant cannot proceed because the end result cannot be traced back to the defendant as a matter of law. We discuss this principle below in section 4.3. For instance, in the case of *McWilliams v Sir William Arrol & Co Ltd* [1962] 1 WLR 295, an employee died after a fall which could have been prevented if he had worn a safety harness. The employer had failed to supply a harness. However, the employee's workmates said that he would not have used it even if it had been provided. This meant that the employer's breach did not cause the fall, thus breaking the chain of causation and resulting in non-recovery by the employee's estate.

The classic case which established the 'but for' test is *Barnett v Chelsea & Kensington Hospital* [1969] 1 QB 428. The case involved three night watchmen who drank some tea. Soon afterwards, all three men started vomiting and went to the casualty department of the defendants' hospital. The nurse telephoned the casualty officer, a doctor, and explained the men's complaint. The casualty officer did not come to examine the patients, but said that they should go home and call in their own doctors. The men left the hospital, and one of them died some hours later from arsenic poisoning. Because very few people are poisoned by arsenic, there was little or no chance that the only effective antidote could have been administered to him in time, even if he had been examined and admitted to the hospital. However, the plaintiff sued the defendant hospital management committee for damages in negligence.

● *Barnett v Chelsea & Kensington Hospital* [1969] 1 QB 428

Nield J: My conclusions are: that the plaintiff, Mrs. Bessie Irene Barnett, has failed to establish, on the balance of probabilities, that the death of the deceased, William Patrick Barnett, resulted from the negligence of the defendants, the Chelsea and Kensington Hospital Management Committee, my view being that had all care been taken, still the deceased must have died. But my further conclusions are that the defendants' casualty officer was negligent in failing to see and examine the deceased, and that, had he done so, his duty would have been to admit the deceased to the ward and to have treated him or caused him to be treated...

There are two main questions here: Has the plaintiff established, on the balance of probabilities, (1) that the medical casualty officer was negligent, and, if so, (2) that such negligence caused the death of the deceased?...[T]he defendants were negligent and in breach of their duty in that they or their servants or agents did not see and did not examine and did not admit and did not treat the deceased.

It remains to consider whether it is shown that the deceased's death was caused by that negligence or whether, as the defendants have said, the deceased must have died in any event. In his concluding submission Mr. Pain submitted that the casualty officer should have examined the deceased and had he done so he would have caused tests to be made which would have indicated the treatment required and that, since the defendants were at fault in these respects, therefore the onus of proof passed to the defendants to show that the appropriate treatment would have failed, and authorities were cited to me. I find myself unable to accept that argument...There has been put before me a timetable which I think is of much importance. The deceased attended at the casualty department at five or 10 minutes past eight in the morning. If the casualty officer had got up and dressed and come to see the three men and examined them and decided to admit them, the deceased (and Dr. Lockett agreed with this) could not have been in bed in a ward before 11 a.m....an intravenous drip would not have been set up before 12 noon...Dr. Lockett, dealing with this, said: 'If this man had not been treated until after 12 noon the chances of survival were not good.'...

For those reasons, I find that the plaintiff has failed to establish, on the balance of probabilities, that the defendants' negligence caused the death of the deceased. *Judgment for the defendants*.

4.3.2 Problems in proving causation

In general, the 'but for' test is relatively easy to apply. It usually does not require any additional evidence, other than a witness of fact who can describe the circumstances of the damage. The court can then decide based on common sense whether or not the breach caused the damage. Some situations, though, can be more complicated. For instance, the cause of the damage may be something that only an expert can discover. In that case, the claimant will commission a report, and possibly oral testimony, from an expert in the relevant technical field. The defendants will usually commission a report from another expert in response. It is possible for the court to order a single joint expert, but in practice this is rare, especially where the damage is very serious. This need for expert evidence is one of the factors that can make civil litigation very expensive. There can

Recall

Because tort claims are civil matters, the claimant only has to prove causation 'on a balance of probabilities'. The cause of the injury does not have to be 100% certain.

also be other factors that make it difficult to decide the issue of causation. This section considers some of these factors.

Medical negligence claims

Causation is often particularly controversial in claims against medical professionals and hospitals (often referred to as medical negligence claims or clinical negligence claims). It is generally difficult for claimants to succeed in such cases because of the complex technical issues involved and the difficulty of proving causation. In the next case, the plaintiff was a child born prematurely and placed in a special unit at the defendant's hospital. He needed extra oxygen, and to ensure the administration of the correct amount, it was necessary to insert a catheter into an umbilical artery so that his oxygen levels could be accurately read on an electronic monitor. A doctor mistakenly inserted the catheter into a vein instead of an artery, with the result that the monitor gave a lower reading. Other doctors caught the error, but it took two more tries to insert the catheter properly. The plaintiff developed retrolental fibroplasia, a condition of the eyes often caused by excess oxygen, resulting in blindness.

· ·

● ***Wilsher v Essex Area Health Authority*** [1988] AC 1074

Lord Bridge of Harwich: In addition to the evidence of the medical and nursing staff at the hospital, the judge heard expert evidence from two paediatricians and two ophthalmologists called for the plaintiff and from three paediatricians and one ophthalmologist called for the [defendant hospital] authority. All were highly qualified and distinguished experts in their respective fields. In addition, no less than 24 articles from medical journals about RLF covering 129 foolscap pages of print were put in evidence...There was in the voluminous expert evidence given at the trial an irreconcilable conflict of opinion as to the cause of Martin's RLF. It was common ground that a sufficiently high level of [oxygen] in the arterial blood of a very premature baby, if maintained for a sufficiently long period of time, can have a toxic effect on the immature blood vessels in the retina leading to a condition which may either regress or develop into RLF. It was equally common ground, however, that RLF may occur in premature babies who have survived without any artificial administration of oxygen and that there is evidence to indicate a correlation between RLF and a number of other conditions from which premature babies commonly suffer...[T]here was not only a profound difference of view about the aetiology and causation of RLF in general but also a substantial difference as to the inferences which were to be drawn from the primary facts, as ascertained from the clinical notes about Martin's condition and treatment at the material time and amplified by the oral evidence of Dr. Wiles, the senior house officer in charge, as to what the actual levels of [oxygen] in Martin's arterial blood were likely to have been during a critical period...

Having found the authority negligent in relation to the five periods when the [oxygen] level was unduly high, the judge added: 'There is no dispute that this materially increased the risk of RLF.'

This statement, it is now accepted, was a misunderstanding of the evidence. Whilst it was common ground that one of the objects of monitoring and controlling the [oxygen] level in the arterial blood of a premature baby in 1978 was to avoid or reduce the risk of RLF, it was certainly not accepted by the defence that any of the levels to which Martin was subjected were sufficient in degree or duration to have involved any material increase in that risk. This misunderstanding was one of the factors which led the judge to the conclusion that Martin had established a prima facie case on the issues of causation. He then said: 'But it is open to the defendants on the facts of this case to show that they are not liable for this negligence because on the balance of probability this exposure did not cause Martin's RLF.'

In saying this, the judge effectively reversed the burden of proof, and the House of Lords found that this was unacceptable. The plaintiff had to prove that, on the balance of probabilities, the exposure to high levels of oxygen was at least a 'material cause' of the blindness. The outcome was that the House of Lords referred the case back to the first instance to re-consider the question of causation.

Some of the difficulties demonstrated in this case are:

- In cases of medical negligence, there are often a number of possible causes for the claimant's injury, and the defendant may not be responsible for all of those causes.

- Even very highly qualified experts may disagree about which of the possible causes actually led to the injury.

- It can be difficult for judges to understand the complex medical evidence which experts present to them.

- All of these factors make it very difficult for claimants to satisfy the burden of proof, even on the civil standard.

- The same factors make it difficult for claimants to assess the likely outcome of their cases and decide whether or not to pursue them, thus reducing the likelihood of pre-trial settlement.

There is a further difficulty in many clinical negligence cases, which is that they often require judges to make speculative decisions about what would have happened if medical help had been summoned earlier or if different treatment had been given. Sometimes, the judge must even go a step further and decide whether the treatment that would have been offered in the hypothetical situation might itself have been negligent. This difficulty was highlighted in the case of *Bolitho v City and Hackney Health Authority* [1998] AC 232, which involved a two-year-old child who suffered brain damage after two instances of severe respiratory distress while in hospital. Although the doctor on call advised the nurses how to proceed by phone, she did not attend, which was itself considered negligent. The parties were in dispute as to whether the doctor would have and should have inserted a breathing tube after the first incident, based on commonly accepted medical principles.

cross reference

Bolitho v City and Hackney Health Authority [1998] AC 232 was discussed at length in chapter 3 on breach.

● ***Bolitho v City and Hackney Health Authority*** [1998] AC 232

Lord Browne-Wilkinson: In all cases the primary question is one of fact: did the wrongful act cause the injury? But in cases where the breach of duty consists of an omission to do an act which ought to be done (e.g. the failure by a doctor to attend) that factual inquiry is, by definition, in the realms of hypothesis. The question is what would have happened if an event which by definition did not occur had occurred. In a case of non-attendance by a doctor, there may be cases in which there is a doubt as to which doctor would have attended if the duty had been fulfilled. But in this case there was no doubt: if the duty had been carried out it would have either been Dr. Horn or Dr. Rodger, the only two doctors at St. Bartholomew's who had responsibility for Patrick and were on duty. Therefore in the present case, the first relevant question is 'What would Dr. Horn or Dr. Rodger have done if they had attended?' As to Dr. Horn, the judge accepted her evidence that she would not have intubated. By inference, although not expressly, the judge must have accepted that Dr. Rodger also would not have intubated: as a senior house officer she would not have intubated without the approval of her senior registrar, Dr. Horn...However in the present case the answer to the question 'What would have happened?' is not determinative of the issue of causation...Dr. Horn could not escape liability by proving that she would have failed to take the course which any competent doctor would have adopted. A defend-ant cannot escape liability by saying that the damage would have occurred in any event because he would have committed some other breach of duty thereafter.

NOTE In *Bolitho* the potential actions being considered were defendant's. Where the question is what a third party would have done, the courts have taken a different approach, which we will consider later in this chapter.

cross reference

XYZ v Schering Health Care Ltd [2002] EWHC 1420 (QB) is also discussed in chapter 15.

Deciding questions of causation in medical cases may also involve judges in complex statistical analysis. *XYZ v Schering Health Care Ltd* [2002] EWHC 1420 (QB) is a good example. In this case, a large group of women claimed that they had suffered cardio-vascular disease as a result of taking the so-called 'third generation' combined contra-ceptive pill.

● ***XYZ v Schering Health Care Ltd*** [2002] EWHC 1420 (QB)

Mackay J: Have the Claimants proved that [the pills] carry a true excess risk of [cardiovas-cular injuries] which is more than twice that carried by [earlier generations of pills]? [A]ll agree that if the Claimants fail to prove this the action should go no further as it could not succeed...The reason why the Claimants accept through Lord Brennan QC that this first issue is capable of disposing of the claims should be set out. It is not because an increase of less than 2 would fail to render the product defective within the meaning of the Act, though the Defendants would so argue if they had to. It is for reasons of causation that he accepts this burden, correctly in my view. If factor X increases the risk of condition Y by more than 2 when compared with factor Z it can then be said, of a group of say 100 with both exposure to factor X and the condition, that as a matter of probability more than 50 would not have suffered Y without being exposed to X. If medical science cannot identify the members of the group who would and who would not have suffered Y, it can never-theless be said of each member that she was more likely than not to have avoided Y had she not been exposed to X. There is a statistical formula which expresses this concept, but in this case I intend to resort to words where I can, both from a preference for language over symbols and because I am conscious that this judgment should be accessible, above all to the women who bring these claims.

In order to decide whether the excess risk was less or more than twice that of the previ-ous generations of pills, the court heard evidence for 42 days, including expert evidence from no less than 15 experts. Of the claimants' experts, one put the increased risk factor at 2.2, another at 2.1 and a third at 1.9. This illustrates the fineness of the distinctions which judges may be asked to draw. The court also had to consider in some detail the

think point

Do you think these problems are limited to clinical negligence cases, or could they arise in other technical areas?

think point

Do you think this is really a test of causation, or does it simply collapse the issues of causation and duty?

cross reference

The case of Wilsher v Essex Area Health Authority [1988] 1 All ER 871, excerpted above, involved multiple potential causes of injury.

statistical reliability and compatibility of the various studies underlying the expert evidence and form judgments the statistical methods used by the various experts. The resolution of this single issue of causation required a 96-page judgment, in which Mackay J eventually concluded that there was either no elevated risk at all, or at best a risk factor of 1.7. The claims therefore failed.

One problem that is probably unique to medical negligence concerns the issue of informed consent. Doctors have a duty to take reasonable steps to inform patients of the risks of any procedure they are considering. If a doctor breaches this duty and the patient goes on to suffer an injury, it can be difficult to analyse whether or not the failure to inform has caused the injury. For instance, in *Chester v Afshar* [2004] UKHL 41 a patient was considering an operation for back pain. This operation occasionally causes a rare kind of paralysis. This paralysis occurs at random, regardless of how carefully the operation is performed. The patient's doctor failed to warn her about this risk. She went forward with the operation and did develop the paralysis. However, the evidence was that if she had been given the warning, she would have looked for alternatives to the operation, but would not have been able to find any better way of dealing with her pain. She would therefore have had the operation eventually, and would have been exposed to the same risk of paralysis. Of course there was no way of knowing whether or not she would actually have developed it if the operation had taken place at that later stage. The House of Lords acknowledged that these circumstances did not satisfy the 'but for' test. However, their Lordships were keen to protect a patient's right to informed consent. As a result, they held (by a majority of 3–2) that the claim should succeed. They reached this conclusion by replacing the traditional 'but for' test with a modified test: was the risk which led to the injury one which the doctor had a duty to warn the patient against? If so, according to the House of Lords in this case, the modified causation test is satisfied. This rule probably does not apply outside the medical field.

Multiple causes and material contribution

As the medical negligence claims show, courts sometimes have to deal with situations where the injury causing the damage is caused by several different factors also known as multiple causation. This problem can manifest in other areas as well and can take at least three distinct forms:

- First, there may be multiple potential causes of the damage—in other words, there is more than one possible explanation (cause) of the damage, and it is not certain which one actually caused the damage. It is difficult to apply the 'but for' test in these situations because the answer to the question 'But for the breach, would the damage have occurred?' is not clear.

- Second, there may be concurrent causes of the injury. This means that several different acts or omissions have joined together to cause the damage—critically, however, any one of the acts or omissions taken alone would have been enough to cause the damage. One example of this kind of case might be a shooting accident where two hunters simultaneously fire their guns and both hit a bystander. If the 'but for' test is applied to this situation in the usual way, then causation will not be established because if any one of the causes had been removed from the scenario, the damage would still have occurred due to the other causes. If that were true, then the claimant could not sue the people responsible for any of the causes, even though each of the causes alone would have been enough to cause the damage. This is patently unfair to claimants. Therefore, the law has devised a way around the problem, discussed below.

- Third, there may be several consecutive causes. These involve situations where several different causes operate one after the other, each of which contributes to the damage. For instance, a pedestrian might be hit by one car and then shortly afterwards be hit by a second vehicle whose driver failed to respond quickly enough to the first accident.

It is important here to understand that in the first type of case, the true cause of the damage is unknown. In the other two types of case, the causes *are* known, but there are several of them, and the question is how the court should allocate fault, and thus the amount of damages payable to the claimant.

In the case of multiple possible causes where the true cause is not known for certain, the claimant must prove on the balance of probabilities that the defendant was responsible for at least one cause that materially contributed to the damage. If the claimant succeeds in proving this, then the defendant is liable for the entire loss. For example, in *Hotson v East Berkshire Health Authority* [1987] AC 750, a boy suffered a hip injury after falling from a tree. Doctors diagnosed him incorrectly at first, and he developed a joint problem, which led to a disability. It was not clear whether the disability was due to the fall or the incorrect diagnosis. Experts estimated that there was a 25 per cent chance that the misdiagnosis had caused the disability. At first instance, the court awarded him damages for 25 per cent of his loss. This may seem like an attractive and pragmatic solution, but the Court of Appeal reversed the decision and held that damages could not be divided up to reflect the relative likelihood of different causes. The court must decide one way or the other whether or not the breach materially contributed to the damage, on a balance of probabilities, and must then make a corresponding award on an all-or-nothing basis. The House of Lords agreed.

NOTE A defendant who thinks another party is liable to the claimant may seek a 'contribution' from that party (chapter 9). Where one of the causes is negligence by the claimant, the defence of 'contributory negligence' may apply (chapter 5).

A similar approach is taken in the second category of cases, involving concurrent causes of injury. However, the third category, successive causes, is treated rather differently, because in these cases it is often (but not always) possible to distinguish between the damage caused by one act or omission and the damage caused by the next.

Some examples of situations involving successive causes of injury help to illustrate the courts' thinking. In the case of *Jobling v Associated Dairies* [1982] AC 794, for instance, the plaintiff had an injury at work which reduced his earning capacity by 50 per cent. His employers were liable for this injury. However, three years later he developed a spinal disease that left him totally unable to work. The employers argued that they should only be liable for damages for loss of earnings up to the point where the disease developed, because after that point he would have been unable to earn in any case. The House of Lords agreed.

This contrasts with *Baker v Willoughby* [1969] All ER 1528, where the defendant knocked the plaintiff down at a pedestrian crossing and injured his leg. Again, his earning capacity was reduced. Some time later, the plaintiff was shot in that leg by someone who was demanding money from him, and the leg had to be amputated. In this case, the House of Lords held that the defendant should continue to be liable for loss of earnings after the amputation, because the amputation did not cause any further reduction in his earning capacity. The gunman would in theory be liable for other forms of damages arising out of the amputation, such as compensation for the additional pain and suffering. In practice, however, the gunman was never traced, and this may have influenced the House of Lords to some extent, since it was clearly very unlikely that the plaintiff would ever recover any loss of earnings from the gunman.

The basic reasoning in both of these cases was followed by the Court of Appeal in *Murrell v Healy* [2001] EWCA Civ 486, where a claimant was injured in two different car accidents. The first accident prevented him from doing heavy work, and the second prevented him from being able to work at all. However, by the time of the trial, the claimant was also suffering from an unrelated illness that would have prevented him from working in any case. The court held that (a) the second driver was only liable for the additional injuries he caused; (b) the first driver's liability did not reduce after the second accident; and (c) the claimant was not entitled to any further compensation for loss of earnings after the date of the trial.

Similarly, in *Heil v Rankin*, The Times, 20 June 2000, a police dog handler, Mr Heil, suffered from post-traumatic stress syndrome as the result of two incidents—a shooting incident in 1987 and a car accident in 1993 caused by Mr Rankin. The 1987 incident left Mr Heil able to work, but the 1993 incident required him to take early retirement. The Court of Appeal found that the car accident had caused the exacerbation in Mr Heil's condition, but that after the 1987 incident, there had already been a 50 per cent risk that Mr Heil would have to retire early. Therefore, Mr Rankin was only liable for 50 per cent of Mr Heil's loss of earnings. Note that the outcome in this case is different from that in *Hotson v East Berkshire Health Authority* [1987] AC 750, the case where the boy fell from the tree, because here there were successive, but known causes, whereas in the boy's case the true cause of injury was not known.

Long-term causes

A related type of situation in which causation can be problematic is where a claimant has been exposed to a potential cause of damage over a long period of time rather than on a single occasion. Many of the cases in this area have concerned asbestos-related illness or other industrial diseases. An example of three different types of injury is given below, and then the outcome of each category of injury is explained.

- First, a defendant may have exposed the claimant to the same cause of injury in a range of different situations, some of which were justifiable on the part of the defendant and others of which were not. In the case of *McGhee v National Coal Board* [1972] 3 All ER 1008, the plaintiff's husband was exposed to brick dust at work over many years and developed a skin condition. The employers could not reasonably prevent this exposure while he was carrying out his duties, but they could have reduced the

think point

Which decision was the Court of Appeal following in each of (a), (b), and (c)?

length of his exposure each day by providing showers so that he could wash the dust off before returning home. There was no way of knowing whether or not this would have prevented him from developing the skin condition. The defence argued that the plaintiff could not prove that the employer's breach had materially contributed to her husband's illness, but only that it had materially increased the *risk* of becoming ill.

- Second, different defendants may have exposed the claimant to the same cause of injury at different times, but the effect may be 'one-off' in nature—in other words, once the disease has begun, it is not aggravated by future exposures. An example of this is an asbestos-related illness, mesothelioma, which is a form of tumour on the lung or peritoneum (the thin membrane around the abdomen). Mesothelioma can be caused by inhaling just a single asbestos fibre. Where claimants have been exposed to asbestos over long periods by different defendants, it is not possible to determine when they inhaled the particular fibre that was responsible for their disease. Nor does inhaling fibres over a longer period make the disease worse. At the same time, it is clear that the longer the exposure continues, the more opportunities there are for a fibre to enter a claimant's lung and cause the illness, so in that sense, the risk does increase with exposure. This type of situation was considered by the House of Lords in *Fairchild v Glenhaven Funeral Services* [2002] UKHL 22, where Mrs Fairchild's husband had been exposed to asbestos by a series of different employers over the course of his career before eventually dying of mesothelioma. It was impossible to prove which employer he was working for when he inhaled the 'fatal fibre'.

- Third, different defendants may have exposed the claimant to the same cause at different times, but the exposures may have had a cumulative effect—in other words, the later exposure aggravates the damage from the original exposure, and the longer the exposure continues, the worse the disease becomes. This is often the case where workers develop asbestosis, a different asbestos-related condition where the lungs are damaged by inhaling large quantities of asbestos dust rather than a single fibre. An example of this was the case of *Holtby v Brigham & Cowan* [2000] 3 All ER 421, where Mr Holtby contracted asbestosis after being exposed to asbestos for 24 years in a variety of different jobs.

In the first two of these cases, *McGhee v National Coal Board* [1972] 3 All ER 1008 and *Fairchild v Glenhaven Funeral Services* [2002] UKHL 22, the House of Lords decided that if the breach had materially increased the risk, that was sufficient to establish causation and allow the plaintiffs to recover compensation for 100 per cent of their losses. Therefore, Mrs McGhee recovered her full loss from her husband's employer even though some of the exposures by the employer were not negligent, and Mrs Fairchild recovered all of her losses from a single employer, even though other employers had also exposed her husband to asbestos. In *McGhee v National Coal Board* [1972] 3 All ER 1008 and several cases which followed it, the outcome was explained by saying that there was no difference between materially contributing to the damage and materially increasing the risk of the damage. However, by the time of *Fairchild v Glenhaven Funeral Services* [2002] UKHL 22, the House of Lords was willing to acknowledge that what is happening in these cases is that the courts are using a modified test of causation which is less stringent than the usual 'but for' test.

In *Holtby v Brigham & Cowan* [2000] 3 All ER 421, the Court of Appeal reached a different result. In this instance, the damage was cumulative. There was evidence that in asbestosis cases, the damage gets worse steadily on what is known as a 'straight-line basis', which broadly means that twice the exposure leads to twice the severity of illness, three times the exposure leads to three times the severity of illness and so on. The Court of Appeal said that damage of this kind was 'separable'—in other words, it could be separated into distinct amounts of damage caused by each employer. The Court of Appeal therefore apportioned the claimant's entitlement to compensation between the employers on a percentage basis based on the length of time he had been employed by each of them. As the claimant had only sued one of the employers (probably because the others were no longer in existence or no longer solvent), this meant that he was only able to recover 75 per cent of his loss.

It is worth pausing here to consider a 'snapshot' of the position the law in this area had reached after these three cases. The outcome of these decisions was that, if claimants became ill as a result of a series of long-term exposures to a harmful substance, they could recover compensation even if they could not prove which exposure caused the illness. However, whether they could recover all of their losses from a single defendant or had to sue everyone who was responsible for any of the exposures depended on the precise nature of the illness they developed. If they suffered from asbestosis or another disease which gets worse on a 'straight-line basis', then there had to be an apportionment between all the people who exposed the claimant to the risk, as in *Holtby v Brigham & Cowan* [2000] 3 All ER 421. If the disease was mesothelioma or another disease that can be caused by a single exposure, then the claimant could recover the full amount of the loss from any defendant who was responsible for any of the exposures. The reason for this was partly that the employer in *Fairchild v Glenhaven Funeral Services* [2002] UKHL 22 did not ask the court to apportion any of the damage to other employers, for reasons which are unknown. Because of *McGhee v National Coal Board* [1972] 3 All ER 1008, there was no apportionment between exposures which were a breach of duty and those that were not.

Unsurprisingly, employers and their insurers argued that *Fairchild v Glenhaven Funeral Services* [2002] UKHL 22 was unfair and made it difficult for insurance premiums to be properly assessed. Not all legal scholars agreed with the courts' reasoning, either. Here is an article which criticizes aspects of the state of the law on this issue.

● Colin McCaul, *'Holtby and the End Game'*, JPI Law 2006, 1 (footnotes omitted)

Introduction

A defendant is only liable for such damage as his tort has caused. If damage sustained by a claimant is divisible to the extent that one can isolate and identify the damage caused by a particular tortfeasor, then the latter is only liable for that identified damage and no more. There is nothing startling in such a proposition. It accords with common law principles amassed over the centuries and, better still, it accords with common sense (the two concepts not always being synonymous).

What does give rise to concern is a creeping tendency to use the concept of separable damage as a means of apportioning liability in cases where the principle should apply either not at all or only to a limited extent. This article looks at three areas of concern.

First area of concern

One can trace an increasing willingness by the courts to apply the principle of separable damage whenever the facts of a particular case can be made to fit it.

Mustill J. needed a broad brush in order to separate out hearing loss caused in Thompson v Smiths Shiprepairers Ltd, justifying apportionment on the basis that 'the whole exercise of assessing damages is shot through with imprecision'. Hence each claimant's hearing loss could be separated into three categories: that which would have visited him in any event as he aged, that which he suffered non-negligently at the hands of his employer and that which he sustained by reason of that employer's negligence. The defendant employer only stood to compensate the claimant in respect of the hearing loss that came within the third of those categories.

The principle of separable damage was again invoked in Holtby v Brigham Cowan (Hull) Ltd. The claimant there suffered from asbestosis, contracted as a result of working as a marine fitter in a number of employments stretching over some 42 years. For some 21 years, i.e. half of the total period, Mr Holtby was employed by the defendant. The Court of Appeal pointed out that the difficulties that had existed in Thompson (where the noise induced deafness caused greater handicap than that caused by the natural ageing process) did not exist in asbestosis cases because the progression of the disease is linear depending on the amount of dust inhaled. Conveniently, the facts as found in Holtby were that the claimant had been doing similar work in similar conditions whilst working for all the other employers, so it was easy to calculate the extent of his disability caused by the defendant's tort...

It is apt to recall a comment made by Professor Weir in the course of an excellent article he wrote on consecutive torts: 'the claimant is not half-mad because of what the first defendant did and half-mad because of what the second defendant did, he is as mad as he is because of what both of them did.'

Many saw the comments by Lords Bingham and Hutton in Fairchild v Glenhaven Funeral Services Ltd as an open invitation to defendants in mesothelioma cases to argue apportionment. The words used by the latter, in particular, are worth examining:

> 'I observe that no argument was addressed to the House that in the event of the claimants succeeding there should be an apportionment of damages because the breaches of duty of a number of employers had contributed to cause the disease and therefore the damages awarded against a defendant should be a proportion of the full sum of damages which the claimant would have recovered if he (or the claimant's husband) had been employed by only one employer for the whole of his working life. Therefore each defendant is liable in full for a claimant's damages, although a defendant can seek contribution against another employer liable for causing the disease.'

It is impossible to understand this observation in the light of legal principles as they currently stand. Apportionment of damage does not arise because there has been a breach of duty by a number of different defendants. To adopt such an approach is to look at the problem from the wrong end of the telescope. It is necessary to look at the damage, not the breach, in order to see whether apportionment is appropriate. If the damage is indivisible, then it matters not how many defendants' breaches of duty have caused it.

Nevertheless, their Lordships' invitation was accepted by the defendants in Barker v Saint Gobain Pipelines plc. The defendant's argument ran principally along the lines that, if it required a legal fiction to enable a mesothelioma sufferer to win on liability, then the Courts should be prepared to depart from the well-established script relating to indivisible injury when it came to assessing damages. In other words, that an indivisible injury should be divided up. Neither Moses J. at first instance nor the Court of Appeal was impressed and ruled that the indivisibility of mesothelioma prevented apportionment.

The House of Lords is due to hear Saint Gobain's appeal on March 13, 2006. The outcome is awaited with no little interest. Yet, whatever the outcome, most of us can live with the concept of dividing up a cumulative physical injury sustained as a result of two or more separate incidents or exposures, of which at least one has been tortious. The dividing up of damages for pain, suffering and loss of amenity in Thompson and in Holtby brought a just result... What is unjust is the approach that Courts tend to show to other heads of damage.

Second area of concern

The error into which the courts seem so readily to fall is to look no further than the severability of a physical (or psychiatric) injury. If the answer to the question, 'Is that injury severable?' lies in the affirmative, then the courts' knee jerk reaction appears to be to proceed to apportion all heads of damage sustained. Thus in Holtby, items of special damage such as inability to do DIY jobs, additional transport costs, care and attendance and extra heating were reduced by the same percentage as damages for pain, suffering and loss of amenity as part of the apportionment exercise. But a moment's thought leads one to question whether this was the correct way of disposing of the point. Without the negligence of the defendant employer in Holtby, the claimant would only have had half the amount of disability. It is entirely probable that such reduced disability would have brought the claimant up short of the point when he would have needed to incur any additional transport costs, care and attendance and the like. In such circumstances does the law demand that only Brigham Cowan (Hull) Ltd be liable for those extra costs? ... It is clear that the defendant in that case should have been found liable in full for the extra transport costs, care and the like (always assuming that such outgoings would not have arisen at all absent the defendant's negligence). The earlier tortious employers would likewise have been liable in full for those expenses, their negligence having been part of the cause of the physical state which the claimant had reached so as to necessitate such outlay...

The correct and simple legal principle is simply this. If what has sometimes been termed, 'the end game' is a state of affairs that only came about because of input from a number of sources, then all of the tortious sources will be liable in full for that end game. The reason for such liability is that the damage in question (the end-game) is inseparable.

The distinction between separable damage and inseparable cumulative damage was well illustrated by Devlin L.J. in Dingle v Associated Newspapers Ltd:

> 'If four men, acting severally and not in concert, strike the plaintiff one after another and as a result of his injuries he suffers shock and is detained in hospital and loses a month's wages, each wrongdoer is liable to compensate for the whole loss of earnings. If there were four distinct physical injuries, each man would be liable only for the consequences peculiar to the injury he inflicted, but in the example I have given the loss of earnings in one injury caused in part by all four defendants. It is essential for this purpose that the loss should be one and indivisible; whether it is so or not is a matter of fact and not a matter of law.'

cross reference
The House of Lords decision in Barker v Corus [2006] UKHL 20 is discussed later in this section.

The example is an apt one because it illustrates very well the point that one has to look at heads of damage individually and ask of each such head of loss, 'Was this indivisible damage?' The answer to each such question may not always be the same, as Devlin L.J.'s example shows.

Third area of concern

In Rahman v Arearose Ltd the Court of Appeal did manage to distinguish between various heads of damage when considering whether and when to apportion damage. The court was faced with a case which was highly unusual on its facts. The claimant worked as the manager of a fast food chain owned by the first defendant (D1). He was seriously assaulted at work by reason, as the judge at first instance found, of D1's negligence. One of his injures was a fracture to the orbital wall of his right eye. He was taken to the hospital of the second defendant (D2) where, through negligence, a bone graft impinged on the optic nerve, blinding him in his right eye. He developed four psychiatric disorders. The expert psychiatrists were asked whether they could attribute such disorders to either of the torts. They agreed that:

(1) The PTSD was largely a reaction to the assault but some symptoms related to the operation.

(2) The severe depressive disorder was largely a psychological reaction to the loss of the eye (D2).

(3) A specific phobia of black people was attributed to the assault and related incidents such as the ensuing court appearances in relation to the same (D1).

(4) The enduring personality change was due to the synergistic effect of the depression and the PTSD but probably would not have developed if the claimant had not lost his vision in one eye.

The experts further agreed that without the eye injury, the claimant would still have developed PTSD, the symptoms of which would have endured for three years and would have kept him out of work for that time. The prognosis held out by two of the experts was that the claimant would never return to work.

The Court of Appeal agreed with the trial judge that D1 could not avoid liability for all damage sustained as a result of loss of they eye. At para.34 of his judgment, Laws L.J. stated: 'there is nothing in the way of a sensible finding that while D2 obviously (and exclusively) caused the right-eye blindness, thereafter each tort had its part to play in the claimant's suffering'.

So far no-one could seriously disagree with the court's approach. But the Court of Appeal went on to say that the judge had been correct in weighing up the 'causative potency' of the acts of D1 and D2 as 25 per cent and 75 per cent respectively. Such apportionment was to apply to all heads of loss that had not been caused exclusively by one defendant. Thus damages for pain, suffering and loss of amenity were to be carved up in those proportions, as were future removal expenses! The first three years of loss of earnings were to be borne by D1 alone because the claimant would have suffered such loss even without the negligence of D2. Loss of earnings for year four onwards were to be divided up 25/75 per cent.

Whilst full liability of D1 for the first three years loss of earnings is unobjectionable, the apportionment of the years thereafter is unsustainable. The view of the experts and of the judge at first instance was that the enduring personality change was due to the synergistic effect of the depression (D2) and the PTSD (D1). The fact that the depression was a necessary trigger to bring about the enduring personality change cannot be used to disguise the fact PTSD was also an effective ingredient. The loss of earnings beyond year three was a classical case of inseparable damage for which both defendants should have been found fully liable . . .

Conclusion

No-one should dispute that there is a place for apportionment of damages where damage is truly separable. Indeed, justice to both parties may mean the use of a fairly wide brush when deciding whether particular physical injury is or is not separable.

However, the prevailing enthusiasm for apportionment of damage must not be allowed to ride roughshod over well-founded legal principles. This article has looked at three creeping tendencies that need to be curbed. First, injury or damage being divided up in a way that is wholly artificial (the half-mad man). Secondly, separating all heads of loss simply because a physical injury has been found to be separable (the Holtby approach). Thirdly, dividing up inseparable damage using 'causative potency' as the measure (the Rahman factor) . . .

think point

Do you agree with Colin McCaul's criticisms of the law on apportionment? Are there any other criticisms you would make?

The article refers to the House of Lords decision in *Barker v Saint Gobain Pipelines*, which was then still awaited. It was eventually handed down in May 2006, by which time some of the parties had reached a settlement and dropped out of the case, so the judgment was given under the name *Barker v Corus UK Ltd* [2006] UKHL 20. The claimant's husband, who died of mesothelioma, had been exposed to asbestos during three periods—once while working for the defendant, once while working for another company which had since become insolvent, and finally while self-employed. The judge at first instance found that the claimant could sue the one remaining employer for the full amount of her losses, and the Court of Appeal agreed. However, the House of Lords overturned this decision, saying that fault should be allocated according to the defendant's relative degree of contribution to the risk, and each defendant should only be liable for that contribution. Defendants should not be liable for the contributions of other parties (such as insolvent employers or self-employed claimants). Their Lordships thought that a defendant's contribution should probably be measured by the duration and intensity of the exposure involved.

However, this decision was widely seen as unfair to claimants, and Parliament was put under pressure to overturn it by statute. This led to a provision on mesothelioma being inserted in the Compensation Act 2006, which became law in July 2006, very shortly after the decision in the House of Lords. Section 3 of the 2006 Act provides as follows:

. . . .

● **Compensation Act 2006**

3 Mesothelioma: damages

(1) This section applies where—
    (a) a person ('the responsible person') has negligently or in breach of statutory duty caused or permitted another person ('the victim') to be exposed to asbestos,
    (b) the victim has contracted mesothelioma as a result of exposure to asbestos,

(c) because of the nature of mesothelioma and the state of medical science, it is not possible to determine with certainty whether it was the exposure mentioned in paragraph (a) or another exposure which caused the victim to become ill, and

(d) the responsible person is liable in tort, by virtue of the exposure mentioned in paragraph (a), in connection with damage caused to the victim by the disease (whether by reason of having materially increased a risk or for any other reason).

(2) The responsible person shall be liable—

(a) in respect of the whole of the damage caused to the victim by the disease (irrespective of whether the victim was also exposed to asbestos—

(i) other than by the responsible person, whether or not in circumstances in which another person has liability in tort, or

(ii) by the responsible person in circumstances in which he has no liability in tort), and

(b) jointly and severally with any other responsible person.

(3) Subsection (2) does not prevent—

(a) one responsible person from claiming a contribution from another, or

(b) a finding of contributory negligence.

(4) In determining the extent of contributions of different responsible persons in accordance with subsection (3)(a), a court shall have regard to the relative lengths of the periods of exposure for which each was responsible; but this subsection shall not apply—

(a) if or to the extent that responsible persons agree to apportion responsibility amongst themselves on some other basis, or

(b) if or to the extent that the court thinks that another basis for determining contributions is more appropriate in the circumstances of a particular case.

(5) In subsection (1) the reference to causing or permitting a person to be exposed to asbestos includes a reference to failing to protect a person from exposure to asbestos.

The effect of this legislative change is that, in mesothelioma cases, claimants can choose to sue any of the people who have exposed them to asbestos (usually employers), or any of those people's insurers. All of these are defined as 'responsible persons' under the 2006 Act. Any 'responsible person' who is found liable by the courts must pay the claimant's losses in full, but can then try to recover a contribution from other 'responsible persons'. Note, however, that this only applies to mesothelioma cases. If the claimant's losses were caused by some other illness, even one which is related to asbestos, then the applicable law is still as stated in the case law. As a result, whether claimants can recover all of their losses from a single defendant still depends depended on the nature of their illness. If it was mesothelioma, then the claimant can recover the full amount of the loss from any 'responsible person' under the Compensation Act 2006, and that person can then seek a contribution from any other 'responsible person'. If the disease was some other condition that can be caused by a single exposure, or if it was a disease such as asbestosis which gets worse on a 'straight-line basis', then there has to be an apportionment between all the people who exposed the claimant to the risk, as per the case law. There is no apportionment between exposures which were breaches of duty and those which were not. It seems somewhat unfair that claimants should be treated differently if they have mesothelioma than if they have some other 'single exposure' disease; this may

cross reference
For more on contribution, see chapter 16.

be a result of hasty drafting following the decision in *Barker v Corus UK Ltd* [2006] UKHL 20. It will be interesting to see whether the House of Lords will now be prepared to over-rule its previous decision in relation to other diseases, in order to bring the position more into line with the treatment of mesothelioma under the Compensation Act 2006.

Interrupted chains of causation

Sometimes a defendant breaches a duty, but then some other event happens before the damage occurs, and the courts have to decide whether the defendant is still responsible for the damage or whether the new event breaks the 'chain of causation'. If the chain of causation is broken, the defendant is not liable. This is known as the principle of *novus actus interveniens*, which is Latin for 'a new act intervening'. In such cases, the claimant may be able to sue the person who was responsible for the new event that broke the chain.

One of the best-known cases on *novus actus interveniens* is *Knightley v Johns* [1982] 1 All ER 851. In this case, a driver negligently caused an accident just outside the exit of a tunnel. The police inspector in charge of the accident scene ordered two other offic-ers to ride back through the tunnel on motorbikes and close the tunnel to oncoming traffic. Towards the other end of the tunnel, one of the police officers collided with an oncoming driver (who was not driving negligently) and was injured. He sued both the first driver and the inspector. The inspector conceded that he had been negligent in ordering the motorcyclists to ride into oncoming traffic, but the Court of Appeal had to decide whether the driver was also liable for causing the accident that led the inspector to give that order. The driver argued that *novus actus interveniens* applied. The following excerpt considers whether that defence should prevail.

● *Knightley v Johns* [1982] 1 All ER 851

Stephenson LJ: [T]he original tortfeasor, whose negligence created the danger which invites rescuers, will be responsible for injury and damage which are the natural and prob-able results of the wrongful act, and...those results include injury and damage from accidents of a kind or class which might normally be foreseen or contemplated, though the particular accidents could not be expected. There is no difference between what is natural and probable and what is reasonably foreseeable either in the act of rescue or in the steps taken to accomplish it. If it is natural and probable that someone will come to the rescue it is also foreseeable; if it is foreseeable that in doing so he may take a particular kind of risk or cope with the emergency in ways not precisely foreseeable, his acts will be natural and probable consequences of the wrongful act which created the emergency.

[In this case it was] natural and probable and foreseeable that some steps would be taken in controlling the traffic and clearing the tunnel and some things be done that might be more courageous than sensible. The reasonable hypothetical observer would anticipate some human errors, some forms of what might be called folly, perhaps even from trained police officers, and some unusual and unexpected accidents in the course of their rescue duties. But would he anticipate such a result as this from so many errors as these, so many departures from the common sense procedure prescribed by the standing orders for just such an emergency as this?...I would for these reasons allow the appeal, set aside the judgment for the plaintiff against the [driver]...and give judgment for the plaintiff against the [inspector]...on the basis of full liability.

compare

Novus actus interveniens exists as a concept in criminal law as well as tort law, but in general it is more often successful as an argument in tort cases than in criminal ones.

It therefore seems that the test of whether an event breaks the chain of causation is whether that event was itself a foreseeable consequence of the defendant's breach. Furthermore, Stephenson LJ said that it is helpful to distinguish positive acts from omissions and innocent conduct from negligent conduct. Negligence is more likely to break the chain of causation than an innocent mistake, and positive acts are more likely to break the chain of causation than omissions. Part of the reasoning here was probably that positive negligent acts are more likely to provide the claimant with an alternative defendant, so that the claimant is not left without a remedy.

In all the cases we have looked at so far, the new act was either the act of a third party or an illness that was beyond anyone's control. Sometimes, though, the act in question is something the claimant has done. Whether or not such an act will interrupt the chain of causation depends on whether or not the claimant was acting reasonably. For instance, in *McKew v Holland* [1969] 3 All 621, the plaintiff was injured at work, and one of the consequences was that his left leg sometimes gave way beneath him. A few days after the injury, he was going down a steep, narrow staircase when he felt his leg give way. He chose to throw himself down the stairs rather than fall naturally, apparently because he believed this would prevent him from landing on his head. In fact, he landed on his feet, and he suffered further injuries to his leg. The House of Lords found that throwing himself down the stairs was so unreasonable that the employers could not have foreseen it, and therefore the chain of causation was broken.

compare

Here we are talking about acts by the claimant that break the chain of causation. Cases where the claimant's actions help cause the damage are considered in chapter 5.

The courts have also considered whether or not suicide breaks the chain of causation. For example, *Reeves v Commissioner of Police of the Metropolis* [2000] 1 AC 360 involved a situation where police failed to prevent a prisoner from committing suicide. *Novus actus interveniens* was raised by the defendant in this case. However, the House of Lords held that the chain of causation could not be broken by an act which the defendant had a duty to guard against. The police had a duty to take reasonable care to prevent the prisoner from committing suicide, so they could not rely on that very suicide to avoid liability. This is not really surprising, since allowing them to do so would make the duty meaningless.

cross reference

Reeves v Commissioner of Police of the Metropolis [2000] 1 AC 360 is discussed in chapter 2.

Hypothetical outcomes

As the section above on medical negligence claims shows, sometimes the court has to consider hypothetical situations. For example, in *Bolitho v City and Hackney Health Authority* [1998] AC 232, the judge had to determine what treatment the defendant would have provided to the plaintiff if a doctor had arrived earlier. The court decided that the defendant could not escape liability by saying that it would have acted negligently in the hypothetical situation. However, this sort of judicial hypothesizing is not limited to medical negligence cases. Courts in other sorts of situations have also had to consider what a third party might have done in a hypothetical situation. For instance:

- In *Stovold v Barlows*, The Times, 30 October 1995, a house purchase fell through when the seller's solicitor sent some papers to the wrong address. The buyer bought a different house instead. The seller sued his solicitor, who argued that the buyer might have decided to change his mind and buy a different house even if the papers had arrived on time. The court awarded the seller 50 per cent of his losses.

- In *Allied Maples Group v Simmons & Simmons* [1995] 4 All ER 907, a firm of solicitors failed to advise their client that a takeover deal would leave the client with certain property liabilities. The court had to assess whether the other party to the deal would have agreed to give the claimant contractual protection against these liabilities if the defendant's solicitors had pointed the potential liabilities out. In the end, the court awarded him 66 per cent of his losses.

- In *First Interstate Bank of California v Cohen Arnold & Co*, The Times, 11 December 1995, a bank had lent money to a property developer. The bank had security over one of the developer's properties, which meant the bank was entitled to force a sale of the property to repay the loan. When the loan was due to expire, the developer asked the bank to extend the term of the loan. The bank was reluctant to do so, but agreed after getting a statement from the developer's accountants that he had personal wealth of over £45 million. This turned out to be incorrect, and the bank arranged for the property to be sold for £1.4 million. The court had to consider how much the bank would have been able to get for the property if it had insisted on selling when the loan initially expired. It decided the bank would have had a two-thirds chance of selling the property for £3 million. They were therefore entitled to £0.6 million in damages (two-thirds of £3 million, less the £1.4 m they actually got from the sale.)

EXAM TIP Don't assume a hypothetical outcome too often in your answers! 'Lost chance' cases are rare and tend to turn on a clear legal, business or medical decision.

As these cases show, the court decided that the correct approach when dealing with hypothetical situations is to estimate the percentage likelihood of the relevant event occurring and award damages accordingly. These types of cases are often known as 'lost chance' cases, because the claimant has lost a chance of recovery.

States of affairs

An existing state of affairs, as opposed to a single discrete event, will not break the chain of causation, as shown in *The Sivand* [1998] 2 Lloyd's Rep 97. In this case, the defendants' tanker collided with the plaintiffs' wharf. The plaintiffs hired contractors to repair the wharf, who did so with a barge supported on jacks. The seabed was unable to support the weight of the jacks, and the barge sank. The plaintiffs had to pay the contractors for the loss of the barge and wanted to recover this amount from the defendants along with the other costs of the repairs. No contractor could have foreseen the condition of the seabed, so the contractor was not negligent. The Court of Appeal held that the state of the seabed was a state of affairs which did not interrupt the chain of causation. Therefore, the defendants were liable for the loss of the barge as a natural consequence of the defendants' negligent collision.

4.4 Remoteness

Even after a claim has passed the **causation** test, it will not necessarily succeed. The court may still decide that the damage is too 'remote' from the breach. This broadly means that, although the defendant has in fact caused the damage, the causation mechanism was so convoluted or unlikely that it would be unfair to make the defendant

VOCABULARY

Some authors refer to remoteness as 'causation in law'. They usually also refer to 'causation in fact', rather than just 'causation', when they are discussing the 'but for' test.

liable for the resulting damage. In this section, we consider the tests that the courts use to determine whether or not the damage is too remote.

4.4.1 Two tests?

The key case on remoteness is *Overseas Tankship (UK) Ltd v Morts Dock and Engineering Co Ltd, The Wagon Mound* [1961] AC 388. This Australian case concerned a fire which destroyed the plaintiff's wharf. The plaintiff's workmen were carrying out some welding, and during this process some molten metal fell from the wharf and set fire to some cotton that was floating in the water. There was also oil in the water, which had escaped several days before from a ship that had been chartered by the defendant. The oil caught fire, leading to the destruction of the wharf. The Privy Council found that the defendant could not have foreseen the chain of events leading to the fire and should not therefore be liable for it.

Overseas Tankship (UK) v Miller Steamship Co (The Wagon Mound No.2) [1967] 1 AC 617 involved the same incident, but the parties there relied on slightly different evidence. The first-instance judge in the second case found that the fire *was* foreseeable, and the Privy Council found that on the new evidence, he was entitled to reach that conclusion. The Privy Councillors clarified that a risk could be foreseeable even if it was improbable.

In reaching this decision, the Privy Council was departing from an earlier Court of Appeal decision in *Re Polemis and Furness, Withy & Co Ltd* [1921] All ER 40, where a different test was laid down. In that case, the defendant's employees were unloading a ship when a wooden plank fell into its hold. The plank caused a spark which set fire to petrol vapours in the hold, and the fire destroyed the ship. The Court of Appeal found that, although the defendant could not have anticipated the fire, it was liable for all the direct consequences of dropping the plank, whether it could foresee them or not. The next extract explains why the Privy Council departed from this precedent.

● *Overseas Tankship (UK) Ltd v Morts Dock and Engineering Co Ltd, The Wagon Mound* [1961] AC 388

Viscount Simonds LJ: There can be no doubt that the decision of the Court of Appeal in Polemis plainly asserts that, if the defendant is guilty of negligence, he is responsible for all the consequences whether reasonably foreseeable or not. The generality of the proposition is perhaps qualified by the fact that each of the Lords Justices refers to the outbreak of fire as the direct result of the negligent act. There is thus introduced the conception that the negligent actor is not responsible for consequences which are not 'direct,' whatever that may mean . . . In their Lordships' opinion it should no longer be regarded as good law. It is not probable that many cases will for that reason have a different result, though it is hoped that the law will be thereby simplified, and that in some cases, at least, palpable injustice will be avoided. For it does not seem consonant with current ideas of justice or morality that for an act of negligence, however slight or venial, which results in some trivial foreseeable damage the actor should be liable for all consequences however unforeseeable and however grave, so long as they can be said to be 'direct.' It is a principle of civil liability, subject only to qualifications which have no present relevance, that a man must be considered to be responsible for the probable consequences of his act. To demand more of him is too harsh a rule, to demand less is to ignore that civilised order requires the observance of a minimum standard of behaviour... For, if it is asked why a man should be responsible for the natural or necessary or probable consequences of his act (or any other similar description of them) the answer is that it is not because they are natural or necessary or probable, but because, since they have this quality, it is judged by the standard of the reasonable man that he ought to have foreseen them... Their Lordships conclude this part of the case with some general observations. They have been concerned primarily to displace the proposition that unforeseeability is irrelevant if damage is 'direct.' In doing so they have inevitably insisted that the essential factor in determining liability is whether the damage is of such a kind as the reasonable man should have foreseen. This accords with the general view thus stated by Lord Atkin in Donoghue v. Stevenson: 'The liability for negligence... is no doubt based upon a general public sentiment of moral wrongdoing for which the offender must pay.' It is a departure from this sovereign principle if liability is made to depend solely on the damage being the 'direct' or 'natural' consequence of the precedent act. Who knows or can be assumed to know all the processes of nature? But if it would be wrong that a man should be held liable for damage unpredictable by a reasonable man because it was 'direct' or 'natural', equally it would be wrong that he should escape liability, however 'indirect' the damage, if he foresaw or could reasonably foresee the intervening events which led to its being done.... Thus foreseeability becomes the effective test. In reasserting this principle their Lordships conceive that they do not depart from, but follow and develop, the law of negligence as laid down by Baron Alderson in Blyth v. Birmingham Waterworks Co.

Because *Overseas Tankship (UK) Ltd v Morts Dock and Engineering Co Ltd, The Wagon Mound* [1961] AC 388 was a Privy Council decision, it was not binding on judges in the Court of Appeal, who could choose whether to follow it or continue to apply Re *Polemis and Furness, Withy & Co Ltd* [1921] All ER 40. Both cases are theoretically good law. However, in practice the Court of Appeal rapidly began to follow the Privy Council decision, as therefore did the lower courts, and the *Wagon Mound* test became the primary standard for analysis of remoteness issues.

EXAM TIP In essay questions on remoteness in negligence, you will almost always need to mention both *Overseas Tankship (UK) Ltd v Morts Dock and Engineering Co Ltd, The Wagon Mound* [1961] AC 388 and *Re Polemis and Furness, Withy & Co Ltd* [1921] All ER 40. In problem questions, unless the facts are identical to *Polemis*, you should apply *Wagon Mound*, but be guided by the word limit or the time available. A brief mention of *Polemis* may be appropriate.

4.4.2 Application of the *Wagon Mound* test

Type of damage

As we have seen, the key factor according to *Overseas Tankship (UK) Ltd v Morts Dock and Engineering Co Ltd, The Wagon Mound* [1961] AC 388 is whether the damage the claimant has suffered is of a kind which a reasonable person should have foreseen. The courts have had some difficulty in determining where to draw the lines between different 'kinds' or types of damage. In the case itself, the Privy Council found it relatively easy to determine that, although the defendant was not liable for the fire damage, it was never-theless liable for damage to the slipway caused when the oil first escaped. That type of damage was foreseeable, whereas damage by fire was not. *Hughes v Lord Advocate* [1963] AC 837 raised a slightly trickier question. Some Post Office employees were work-ing inside an open manhole, and when they finished work for the day, they covered the manhole with a canvas tent and surrounded it with paraffin lamps to warn passers-by. An eight-year-old boy picked up one of the lamps and took it into the tent to play. He accidentally knocked the lamp down the hole, where it ignited some petrol vapours and caused an explosion. The boy suffered burns. The Post Office argued that the explosion was unforeseeable. The House of Lords held that this did not matter; it was foreseeable that people might suffer burns, and that being the case, it did not matter if the burns came about by an unforeseeable route. The relevant 'type' of damage was the burn and not the explosion.

The following year, however, the issue was somewhat complicated by the decision of the Court of Appeal in *Doughty v Turner Manufacturing Co* [1964] 1 QB 518. In that case, the defendant's factory had some cauldrons that were used to hold molten metal. Each cauldron had an asbestos lid. One of the lids fell into a cauldron, which unexpectedly caused the molten metal to erupt, burning the plaintiff. The plaintiff argued that it was foreseeable that if something fell into the cauldron, metal would splash out. However, the Court of Appeal held that splashing was a different type of damage from the erup-tion that actually took place. Such an eruption was not foreseeable, and therefore the defendant was not liable. At first blush, this decision is difficult to reconcile with *Hughes v Lord Advocate* [1963] AC 837. The judges put forward an interesting explanation as to why they were not obliged to follow that case.

. . . .

● *Doughty v Turner Manufacturing Co* [1964] 1 QB 518

Pearce LJ: Mr. James has further argued that . . . the defendants are liable on grounds simi-lar to those on which the House of Lords . . . upheld a judgment for the infant plaintiff in Hughes v. Lord Advocate . . . See Lord Reid's speech . . . He concluded with these words: 'This accident was caused by a known source of danger, but caused in a way which could not have been foreseen, and, in my judgment, that affords no defence'.

In the present case the potential eruptive qualities of the covers when immersed in great heat were not suspected and they were not a known source of danger, but Mr. James argues that the cause of injury was the escape of the hot liquid from the bath, and that injury through the escape of liquid from the bath by splashing was foreseeable . . . It is clear, however, both by inference and by one explicit observation, that the judge regarded splashes as being in quite a different category. Moreover, according to the evidence, it seems that the cover never did create a splash: it appears to have slid into the liquid at an angle of some 45 degrees and dived obliquely downwards…On broader grounds, however, it would be quite unrealistic to describe this accident as a variant of the perils from splashing. The cause of the accident, to quote Lord Reid's words, was 'the intrusion of a new and unexpected factor.' There was an eruption due to chemical changes underneath the surface of the liquid as opposed to a splash caused by displacement from bodies falling on to its surface. In my judgment, the reasoning in Hughes v. Lord Advocate cannot be extended far enough to cover this case.

Diplock LJ: In Hughes v. Lord Advocate the breach of duty by the defendant which was relied upon was his omission to guard a dangerous allurement to children which was liable to cause them injury (inter alia) by burning. The infant plaintiff, to whom the duty was owed, was allured and was injured by burning, although the particular concatenation of circumstances which resulted in his burns being more serious than they would have been expected to be could not reasonably have been foreseen. But they were the direct consequence of the defendant's breach of duty and of the same kind as could reasonably have been foreseen, although of unforeseen gravity. But in the present case the defendants' duty owed to the plaintiff in relation to the only foreseeable risk, that is of splashing, was to take reasonable care to avoid knocking the cover into the liquid or allowing it to slip in in such a way as to cause a splash which would injure the plaintiff. Failure to avoid knocking it into the liquid, or allowing it to slip in, was of itself no breach of duty to the plaintiff. It is not clear on the evidence whether the dropping of the cover on to the liquid caused any splash at all…However that may be, it is incontrovertible that, even if there was some slight splash when the cover fell on to the liquid, the plaintiff was untouched by it and it caused him no injury. There was thus, in the circumstances of this case, no breach of duty to the plaintiff involved in inadvertently knocking the cover into the liquid or inadvertently allowing it to slip in.

On the whole, courts now tend to follow the less restrictive approach in *Hughes v Lord Advocate* [1963] AC 837. In *Page v Smith* [1996] AC 155, for instance, the House of Lords held that psychiatric injury and physical injury should be treated as the same type of injury (for which their Lordships used the umbrella term 'personal injury') for the purposes of foreseeability.

A more recent example which built on that decision is *Corr v IBC Vehicles* [2006] EWCA Civ 331, where an employee suffered post-traumatic stress disorder following an accident at work. He eventually committed suicide by jumping from a building. The Court of Appeal found that, since physical injury had been foreseeable, psychological harm was foreseeable under the principle established in *Page v Smith* [1996] AC 155. Suicide should not be treated as a separate type of damage from psychological illness in general. Therefore, the employer was liable for the death. The Court of Appeal also found that the employee's act of jumping from the building did not break the chain of causation.

However, defendants are not necessarily liable for all the consequences of a psychiatric injury to the claimant. In *Meah v McCreamer* [1986] 1 All ER 943, a man suffered a head injury in a car accident. The injury changed his personality, and he went on to attack several women. He went to prison, and some of the women he had attacked successfully sued him for damages. The court held that he could recover compensation from the driver who had caused the accident, but only for his own injuries and the consequences of his imprisonment, not for the damages which he had to pay to the women. This was a different type of loss which was too remote to impose on a careless driver.

Extent of damage

The Court of Appeal confirmed in *Vacwell Engineering Ltd v BDH Chemicals Ltd* [1971] 1 QB 111 that if the type of damage is foreseeable, it does not matter if the extent of the damage is not (in other words if the damage is on a larger scale than might be expected). In that case, a chemical exploded on contact with water, causing one death and extensive property damage. A minor explosion was foreseeable, but not one on this scale. The defendant, who had supplied the chemical without an adequate safety warning, was found liable.

Damage caused by people in the control of the defendant

In *Carmarthenshire County Council v Lewis* [1955] AC 549, a child was left unattended in a nursery and ran out of the playground into the road, where a driver swerved to avoid the child, crashed into a telegraph post and was killed. The House of Lords found that the education authority, as occupier of premises adjoining the highway, had a duty to prevent children escaping from the premises onto the highway. Their Lordships then had to decide whether the accident was too remote. They decided that it was not, because it was foreseeable that an unsupervised child might run into the road and that a driver would then swerve to avoid the child.

Damage due to the claimant's carelessness

Damage may be too remote if the claimant has not taken proper care for his or her own safety, presumably because a reasonable defendant would foresee that people will take reasonable steps to protect themselves. For instance, in *McKew v Holland & Hannen & Cubitts (Scotland) Ltd* [1969] 3 All ER 1621, the plaintiff suffered an injury at work which meant that his left leg sometimes gave way under him. A few days after the accident, he and his family were viewing a flat, which was up a steep staircase. He could have asked his wife to help him on the stairs, but failed to do so. While walking down the stairs, the plaintiff felt his leg give way. He reacted by throwing himself down the stairs, apparently in the belief that this would reduce the risk of landing on his head. He suffered a severe fracture of the ankle. He sued his employers for damages. The House of Lords held that his behaviour, both in failing to ask for help and in throwing himself down the stairs, was unreasonable and could not have been foreseen by the employers. They were therefore only liable for the effects of the original injury—the damage to the ankle was too remote.

cross reference

McKew v Holland & Hannen & Cubitts (Scotland) Ltd [1969] 3 AER 1621 was discussed previously in section 4.3.

This case contrasts with *Wieland v Cyril Lord Carpets* [1969] 3 All ER 1006, where a woman was injured in a bus accident. She was fitted with a neck collar. When she left the hospital, she felt dizzy, so she went to her son's office to ask him to take her home. While he was helping her down the stairs from his office, she fell and, again, injured her ankle. The reason for the fall was that the neck collar prevented her from using her bifocals properly, and she had misjudged where the step was. The court found that she had taken reasonable care in the circumstances, and therefore the damage to her ankle was not too remote. It could be regarded as a foreseeable consequence of the original bus accident. In both these two cases, the courts made the point that defendants must expect their victims to suffer some difficulties in ordinary life as a result of an accident and must expect to have to pay compensation for any damage that this causes.

Changes due to increased knowledge

What is considered too remote may change over time, as we can see from two cases involving Weil's disease. This is a disease which is spread by contact with rat urine, usually through contaminated water. In *Tremain v Pike* [1969] 3 All ER 1303, the plaintiff was working on a dairy farm and used to wash his hands in a trough in the milking parlour. He also handled hay. Either the hay or the water was contaminated with rat urine, and he became ill with Weil's disease. The court heard evidence that at that time, Weil's disease was rare in Britain, and only a few public officials were aware of it. The court concluded that Weil's disease was not foreseeable by the farmer and therefore too remote. However, by the time of *Campbell v Percy Bilton*, The Guardian, 17 February 1988, Weil's disease had become more common in Britain, and a wider range of employers were aware of it. The plaintiff in this case came into contact with contaminated water while working on a building site. The court held that in these circumstances, Weil's disease was not too remote for the employers to foresee.

4.4.3 Claimants with special circumstances

Sometimes, claimants suffer more damage than a defendant would normally foresee because they are in some way unusually vulnerable to the effects of the defendant's negligence. The rule which the courts use to decide such cases is known as the 'eggshell skull rule', after a famous observation made by Kennedy J in *Dulieu v White* [1901] 2 KB 669:

> If a man is negligently run over or otherwise negligently injured in his body, it is no answer to the sufferer's claim for damages that he would have suffered less injury, or no injury at all, if he had not had an unusually thin skull or an unusually weak heart.

This rule is often expressed by saying that defendants must take their victims as they find them. *Dulieu v White* [1901] 2 KB 669 concerned a pregnant woman who was working in a pub when a horse-drawn van burst through the doors, having been negligently driven by an employee of the defendant. The woman became seriously ill from the shock and went into labour. Her baby was born prematurely and had learning difficulties. The defendant argued that the pregnancy was unforeseeable and that the injury to the woman and her baby were too remote. However, the court disagreed and awarded her damages for her illness and the premature birth. (She did not seek damages for the child's learning difficulties, so the court did not decide that point. Today, social understanding of disability has changed considerably, and it is quite likely that a mother in a similar position would claim for all the child's difficulties, both physical and mental.)

Other well-known examples where the egg-shell skull rule was applied include *Smith v Leech Brain & Co L* [1962] 2 QB 405, where an employee had a pre-cancerous condition which turned into actual cancer after he was burned at work, and *Robinson v The Post Office* [1974] 2 All ER 737, where an employee needed a tetanus vaccination after an injury at work, but turned out to be allergic to the vaccine. In both cases, the employees were able to recover full damages even though their unusually sensitive conditions made the injuries much more extensive than would normally be the case.

The courts have yet to decide whether the egg-shell skull rule can apply when the damage is to property rather to a person. There is also some doubt as to whether the rule should apply where the damage is increased because the claimant does not have the funds to tackle it properly. This is often known as the problem of 'impecunious claimants'. The cases on this are somewhat complex. However, we can broadly categorize them as follows:

- First, if the claimant's lack of funds is unconnected to the defendant's tort, and the tort involves the loss of a profit-making asset, then the increased loss caused by the lack of funds will be too remote. The classic case on this is *The Liesbosch* (also known as *The Edison*) [1933] All ER 144. In this case a tanker collided with a dredger, which then sank. The owners of the dredger needed to continue work to avoid penalty payments under their contract. The cheapest way of doing this would have been to buy a new dredger, but they could not raise a sufficient lump sum to do so. Instead, they hired a dredger, which was considerably more expensive. The House of Lords held that this was too remote and that the plaintiffs were only entitled to the damages they would have got if they had been able to buy a new dredger in the market.

- Second, if the claimant's lack of funds is unconnected to the tort and does not involve a profit-making chattel, the additional loss will not be too remote. In *Alcoa Minerals of Jamaica Inc v Broderick* [2001] EWCA Civ 1142, an appeal from Jamaica, the Privy Council dealt with a case where the defendant had damaged the claimant's roof and the claimant had been unable to repair it due to lack of funds. By the time of the judgment, the repairs had become much more expensive due to rapid inflation in Jamaica. The Privy Council held that this was not too remote, distinguishing *The Liesbosch* [1933] All ER 144 on the basis that the roof was not a profit-making asset, and awarded damages to the claimant.

- Third, if the claimant's lack of funds is itself a result of the defendant's tort, the increased loss caused by the lack of funds will also not be too remote. An example of this is *Jarvis v T Richards & Co* 124 SJ 793. There, Mrs Jarvis engaged a firm of solicitors to represent her in divorce proceedings. After some negotiation, Mr Jarvis agreed to transfer various assets to Mrs Jarvis, including the flat in which they had lived together. In order to do so, Mr Jarvis first needed to pay off a mortgage on the property. However, due to delays by the solicitors, this never actually happened and Mr Jarvis never signed the agreement. Eventually his financial position changed so that he was unable to pay off the mortgage. Mrs Jarvis sued for compensation, including a sufficient sum to buy a similar flat. Mrs Jarvis did not have enough funds to buy a flat before receiving a judgment award. Meanwhile, the housing market had gone up. The solicitors argued that the additional cost due to the market rises was too remote.

The Court of Appeal disagreed, saying that Mrs Jarvis would have had sufficient funds if it had not been for the solicitors' negligence, and they could not rely on their own wrongdoing to avoid paying the higher amount.

- Fourth, if the claimant's loss is a result of the defendant's tort, but depends on some unusual feature of an employment relationship, it will be too remote. In *Malcolm v Broadhurst* [1970] 3 All ER, a husband and wife were injured in a car accident. Before the accident, the wife worked for her husband as a part-time secretary, but her husband had to give up working following the accident, leaving her unemployed as well. The court said that the egg-shell skull rule did not extend to 'infirmities of employment' and that the driver was not liable for her loss of earnings.

- Fifth, if the claimant has sufficient funds, but incurs increased loss due to an attempt to manage its cashflow prudently, the additional loss is unlikely to be too remote. In *Dodd Properties (Kent) Ltd v Canterbury City Council* [1980] 1 All ER 928, the Court of Appeal held that it was reasonable for a plaintiff to await a judgment against the defendant before carrying out repairs, even though high inflation was making those repairs more expensive as time went on. In *Mattocks v Mann* [1993] RTR 13, awaiting payment from insurers was also held to be a sufficient reason to delay action.

EXAM TIP Causation and remoteness are not just important in negligence—they are required elements in all torts except those which are 'actionable per se', i.e., those where the claimant does not need to have suffered any damage. Remember to consider these elements whenever you are analysing a tort that requires damage.

 For more revision tips, including self-test questions and suggestions for further reading, see the Online Resource Centre at www.oxfordtextbooks.co.uk/orc/strong_complete/.

revision tasks

By now you may be able to think of your own tasks to help you revise this chapter. Here are some ideas to get you started.

- List the problems that can be associated with proving causation.

- Make a table setting out the different types of 'multiple cause' and 'long-term cause' cases and how the courts deal with each type. Include case references in your table.

- Review the cases on remoteness that are cited in this chapter and ask yourself which of them would have been decided differently if the test in *Re Polemis and Furness, Withy & Co Ltd* [1921] All ER 40 had been applied.

- Write a few paragraphs explaining how the requirements of causation and remoteness provide safeguards for defendants. Consider whether these requirements put claimants at an unfair disadvantage.

5 Negligence: Defences

 5.1 ## Introduction

We have now considered each of the four elements of negligence, namely:

- That the defendant owed the claimant a duty;
- That the defendant breached the duty;
- That the breach caused damage to the claimant; and
- That the damage was not too remote from the breach.

This chapter looks at negligence from the defendant's point of view and examines the possible defences that the defendant may be able to rely on in order to avoid (or, in some cases, minimize) liability to the claimant. Whereas the claimant has the burden of proving the elements of negligence, as with any other tort the claimant may be alleging, the defendant has the burden of proving, on the balance of probabilities, that a defence applies. Most of the defences we will consider are complete defences. If the defendant can establish one of these, then the defendant will not be liable to the claimant, even if all four elements of negligence are present. However, we will also look at contributory negligence, which is a partial defence. A partial defence is one which (in most cases) reduces the defendant's liability rather than getting rid of it altogether.

NOTE The defences which are available in negligence cases are also available in most other torts. Other torts may also have their own specific defences, as indicated in the relevant chapters later in this book.

This chapter covers the following defences:

- Consent;
- Illegality;
- Exclusion of liability;
- Limitation periods; and
- Contributory negligence.

5.2 Consent

The basic idea behind the **defence of consent** is that people should not be able to recover damages for something they have agreed to do or allow to be done to them. In order to establish this defence, the defendant needs to prove two things:

- That the claimant knew that there was a risk of being harmed by the defendant; and
- That the claimant willingly accepted that risk.

VOCABULARY

This defence is also known as 'voluntary assumption of risk' or *volenti non fit injuria*, which is Latin for 'no injury is done to a person who consents'.

These tests were laid down by Denning LJ in *Nettleship v Weston* [1971] 2 QB 691 and confirmed in *Morris v Murray* [1991] 2 QB 6, which we will consider shortly. *Nettleship v Weston* [1971] 2 QB 691 was also covered in chapter 3 in the section concerning the standard of care of learner drivers. The case appears both there and here because some of the judgments treat consent as a defence, while others suggest that it changes the scope of the defendant's duty. Both approaches are quite common in the case law. The courts appear to be more inclined to adopt the 'defence' approach in cases that involve accidents at work, drunk drivers (or pilots and the like), or intrinsically dangerous activities such as high-risk sports. In other contexts, the courts generally seem to be more inclined to adopt the 'breach of duty' approach. However, there are no hard and fast rules on this.

This chapter deals only with consent as a defence to negligence. To use consent as a defence to other torts, the defendant will usually need to show that the claimant consented to the specific action which the defendant took, rather than just to a risk of harm.

Morris v Murray [1991] 2 QB 6 addressed several questions about the defence of consent that had been uncertain up to that point. These were:

- Whether the defence is available in cases of negligence, and if so, on what conditions;
- Whether the degree of risk the claimant is taking makes a difference to whether or not the defence is available; and
- Whether the two tests are objective (that is, based on whether a hypothetical reasonable person would think that the claimant had consented) or subjective (that is, based on whether the claimant was conscious of having consented).

NOTE *Morris v Murray* [1991] 2 QB 6 also deals with the relationship between consent and another defence, contributory negligence. We will consider this issue later in this chapter.

Morris v Murray [1991] 2 QB 6 involved a plaintiff who had been out drinking alcohol with a friend for the whole of the afternoon before deciding to go on a flight in the friend's light aircraft. The plaintiff drove his friend to the airfield and helped him to start and refuel the aircraft (this detail was important in the resulting lawsuit). Shortly after take-off, the aircraft crashed, killing the plaintiff's friend, who was acting as pilot, and severely injuring the plaintiff. The court at first instance held that the pilot's estate had proven contributory negligence (which is considered in a later section of this chapter), but not consent. The defendant appealed.

● *Morris v Murray* [1991] 2 QB 6

Fox LJ: The present case is, however, far removed on its facts from Dann v Hamilton. In that case the plaintiff was engaged in a quite ordinary social outing to London and back, with a driver who was not drunk when the drive started and, indeed, who was not drunk until quite a late stage when it was not very easy for the plaintiff to extricate herself without giving offence. The whole situation seems to me to bear little resemblance to the drunken escapade, heavily fraught with danger from the first, upon which the plaintiff and Mr. Murray embarked in this case.

Asquith J...held that the plaintiff by embarking in the car, or re-entering it, with the knowledge that through drink the driver had materially reduced his capacity for driving safely, did not implicitly consent to or absolve the driver from liability for any subsequent negligence on his part whereby she might suffer harm. Having reached that conclusion, Asquith J., however, continued, at p. 518:

'There may be cases in which the drunkenness of the driver at the material time is so extreme and so glaring that to accept a lift from him is like engaging in an intrinsically and obviously dangerous occupation, intermeddling with an unexploded bomb or walking on the edge of an unfenced cliff. It is not necessary to decide whether in such a case the maxim 'volenti non fit injuria' would apply, for in the present case I find as a fact that the driver's degree of intoxication fell short of this degree.'

The question before us, I think, is whether, as a matter of law, there are such cases as Asquith J. refers to and, if so, whether this present case is one of them. As to the first of these questions there is a fundamental issue whether the volenti doctrine applies to the tort of negligence at all. In Wooldridge v Sumner [1963] 2 Q.B. 43, 69 Diplock L.J. said: 'In my view, the maxim in the absence of expressed contract has no application to negligence simpliciter where the duty of care is based solely upon proximity or "neighbourship" in the Atkinian sense.'

In general, I think that the volenti doctrine can apply to the tort of negligence, though it must depend upon the extent of the risk, the passenger's knowledge of it and what can be inferred as to his acceptance of it. The passenger cannot be volens (in the absence of some form of express disclaimer) in respect of acts of negligence which he had no reason to anticipate and he must be free from compulsion.

If the plaintiff had himself been sober on the afternoon of the flight it seems to me that, by agreeing to be flown by Mr. Murray, he must be taken to have accepted fully the risk of serious injury. The danger was both obvious and great. He could not possibly have supposed that Mr. Murray, who had been drinking all the afternoon, was capable of discharging a normal duty of care. But as he himself had been drinking, can it be assumed that he was capable of appreciating the risks? The matter was not very deeply examined at the trial, but he was certainly not 'blind drunk'. In cross-examination, he agreed with the description 'merry'. He was capable of driving a car from the Blue Boar to the airfield; and he did so for the purpose of going on a flight with Mr. Murray. He helped to start the aircraft and fuel it. Immediately before take off he asked Mr. Murray whether he should not 'radio in'—a sensible inquiry. None of this suggests that his faculties were so muddled that he was incapable of appreciating obvious risks. Moreover, he gave no specific evidence to the effect, 'I was really too drunk to know what I was doing'. Nor did anyone else give such evidence about him.

NOTE The use of consent as a defence in cases where a passenger sues a driver has now been ruled out by section 149 of the Road Traffic Act 1988.

The flight served no useful purpose at all; there was no need or compulsion to join it. It was just entertainment. The plaintiff co-operated fully in the joint activity and did what he could to assist it. He agreed in evidence that he was anxious to start the engine and to fly. A clearer source of great danger could hardly be imagined. The sort of errors of judgment which an intoxicated pilot may make are likely to have a disastrous result...The situation seems to me to come exactly within Asquith J.'s example...The result, in my view, is that the maxim volenti non fit injuria does apply in this case.

Stocker LJ: [W]hether the volenti maxim applies depends upon the facts of each case. In particular, it is relevant to consider the degree of intoxication and the nature of the act to be performed by the driver...[I]n my view to pilot an aircraft requires a far higher standard of skill and care than driving a motor car and the effect of intoxication becomes all the more important. It seems to me from the authorities cited that this is the approach which the courts ought to apply to this problem: how intoxicated was the driver? How obvious was this to the plaintiff, the extent of the potential risk if he voluntarily accepted the offer of carriage?...

Thus, on the basis that the plaintiff himself was capable of appreciating the full nature and extent of the risk and voluntarily accepted it, I would have no doubt whatever that this maxim would have applied to defeat his claim. If this was not a case of volenti non fit injuria I find it very difficult to envisage circumstances in which that can ever be the case. However, the position is that the plaintiff himself must have consumed an amount of drink not dissimilar to that consumed by Mr. Murray and, therefore, the question falls to be considered whether or not his own condition was such as to render him incapable of fully appreciating the nature and extent of the risk and of voluntarily accepting it.

This matter does not seem to have been canvassed to any great extent in evidence and was not argued in any great detail before this court...It was submitted to this court that the proper test of this, that is to say, the plaintiff's appreciation of the risk and his consent to it, was an objective one....I do not, for my part, go so far as to say that the test is an objective one (though if it is not, a paradoxical situation arises that the plaintiff's claim could be defeated by the application of the maxim if he was sober, but he could recover damages if he was drunk), but unless there is specific evidence either from the plaintiff himself or from some other source that the plaintiff was in fact so intoxicated that he was incapable of appreciating the nature and extent of the risk and did not in fact appreciate it, and thus did not consent to it, it seems to me that the court is bound to judge the matter in the light of the evidence which is put before it for consideration...

In my view, therefore, there was no evidence before the judge, even if the matter had been fully canvassed, which could have justified the proposition that the plaintiff's own condition was such as to render him incapable of appreciating the nature of the risk and its extent or indeed that he did in fact fail to appreciate the nature and extent of such risk. My conclusion, therefore, is that this case does fall within the exceptional circumstances stated by Asquith J. ...For these reasons, in my judgment the judge ought to have found that the plaintiff's claim should be rejected on the basis of the application of the maxim volenti non fit injuria.

You should have seen from these extracts that the case decided the first two questions, but did not definitively decide whether the tests are objective or subjective. This issue, identified above, remains to be decided in a future case. The rest of this section looks at knowledge of the risk and consent to the risk in more detail.

5.2.1 Knowledge of the risk

VOCABULARY

Many cases and textbooks refer to this principle using the phrase '*sciens* is not *volens*', which means 'knowing is not willing'.

The claimant's knowledge must include not only the fact that there is a risk, but also its nature and extent. As *Morris v Murray* [1991] 2 QB 6 demonstrates, the greater the risk, the more likely it is that the defence of consent will apply. The risk that is relevant here is the risk that the defendant will behave negligently, not just the general risk that is involved in a particular situation. So, for instance, in that case the question was whether or not the plaintiff had consented to the risk that the pilot's drunkenness would lead to him making a mistake, not whether the plaintiff had consented to the general risks involved in being a passenger in a plane.

5.2.2 Willing acceptance

Consent to a risk can be written, oral or implied by conduct. However, as *Morris v Murray* [1991] 2 QB 6 also makes clear, the fact that the claimant knew about the risk is not sufficient to imply consent. In that case, Fox LJ cited the following comment made in *Nettleship v Weston* [1971] 2 QB 691 by Lord Denning MR:

cross reference

Nettleship v Weston [1971] 2 QB 691 involved learner drivers and was discussed in chapter 3.

> Knowledge of the risk of injury is not enough. Nor is a willingness to take the risk of injury. Nothing will suffice short of an agreement to waive any claim for negligence. The plaintiff must agree, expressly or impliedly, to waive any claim for any injury that may befall him due to the lack of reasonable care by the defendant: or more accurately, due to the failure of the defendant to measure up to the standard of care that the law requires of him.

Another important principle is that consent which is given under duress is not valid and does not create a defence. For instance, if the defendant threatened the claimant in order to get consent, the defendant could not rely on that consent as a defence. The duress need not go as far as that, however. For example, the courts have tended to recognize that it is difficult for employees to refuse to give consent to their employers. This means that employers will not normally be allowed to use consent as a defence. This has been established since *Smith v Baker* [1891] AC 325, where the plaintiff was injured while working in an area where he knew he might be struck by stones falling from a crane. The House of Lords held that carrying out an order that the plaintiff knew was dangerous did not amount to consent, provided the job for which he was employed was not intrinsically dangerous. A professional stuntman, for instance, would be deemed to have consented to the dangers of that job. Claimants who are not themselves employers may also be affected by this rule. For instance, in *Burnett v British Waterways Board* [1972] 2 All ER 1353 the plaintiff was working on his employer's barge, which was queuing to get into a dock run by British Waterways. Some British Waterways employees attached the barge to a rope, which was so worn that it broke and injured the plaintiff. British Waterways tried to rely on the defence of consent but were unsuccessful because the court held that the plaintiff had to carry out his employer's instructions and had no real choice as to whether or not to use the dock.

think point

Why is this kind of case not covered by the principle that people who take an intrinsically dangerous job cannot sue their employers?

An employer may, however, be able to use the defence of consent if the employee was hurt as a result of ignoring a direct instruction. For instance, in *ICI v Shatwell* [1965] AC 656, three employees were placing explosives in a quarry. All of the explosives were connected by electric wiring, which the employees had to test before the explosives were set off. For safety reasons, the employers had instructed the employees to carry out the test from inside a shed. They also knew that this was a statutory requirement. However, they did not have a cable with them that was long enough to carry out the test from the shed. One of the employees went to get a longer cable, but while he was away, the other two went ahead with the test in the open and were injured. The House of Lords found that the defence of consent was available in these circumstances.

Peer pressure may also be sufficient to prevent consent being valid. For instance, you may recall that in the excerpt from *Morris v Murray* [1991] 2 QB 6, Fox LJ explained the different result in *Dann v Hamilton* [1939] 1 KB 509 by noting that the plaintiff could not have left the car without giving offence.

The defence of consent cannot be used against rescuers, whether they are members of the general public or professionals for whom the rescue is part of their job, such as police officers or fire-fighters. The rescuers can therefore sue the person who created the danger that led to the need for rescue. For instance, in *Chadwick v British Railways Board* [1967] 1 WLR 912 a man suffered psychiatric injuries after spending several hours helping the victims of a train crash which had happened near his home. The Railways Board said that it was his choice to help and that they should therefore be entitled to rely on the defence of consent. However, the Court of Appeal rejected the argument, as it usually does in such cases, because the courts assume that rescuers feel a duty to act and do not exercise a real choice. There may also be public policy considerations in favour of altruistic volunteerism involved. However, the rescue attempt must have been reasonably necessary. This can be illustrated by comparing two cases involving runaway horses. In *Haynes v Harwood* [1935] 1 KB 146, two horses bolted in a busy street, and a police officer ran after them and stopped them. One of the horses fell on him and injured him. He sued the owner of the horses. The court held that the owner could not use consent as a defence. In *Cutler v United Dairies (London) Ltd* [1933] 2 KB 297, on the other hand, the horses bolted into a nearby field. A bystander went to try to recapture them and was hurt in the process. The court found that consent was a defence in these circumstances because the horses did not pose any danger where they were, and so it was not reasonably necessary for the bystander to attempt a rescue.

Chapter 3 showed that people who are injured during sporting events may find it difficult to prove negligence because the standard of care is lower in those circumstances than it normally is. Defendants in such cases have also tried to use consent as a defence. A well-known example is *Smoldon v Whitworth and Nolan* [1997] PIQR P133, which concerned a rugby match in which a player broke his neck. The player sued the referee on the basis that the referee did not properly enforce the safety rules concerning scrums. A scrum is a manoeuvre in which players from each team form three rows with arms around each others' shoulders, facing the other team, and the front rows for each team close up in such a way that their heads interlock. They then compete for the ball in this formation. Because of the pressure from behind, players in the front row of the scrum are at high risk of falling and injuring their necks. The referee accepted that he had a duty of care to the players. The main issues in the case were whether or not the referee had met the required standard of care (as discussed in chapter 3) and whether or not, by agreeing to be in the front row of the scrum, the player had consented to the risk of being injured. The Court of Appeal rejected the contention that the player had agreed to accept the risk of harm. In order for consent to be a defence, the player would have had to consent to the referee breaching the rules which were designed to protect the players, and that was not the case.

Similar issues have come before the courts in cases of rough play between young people outside the context of a recognized sport. The courts have generally applied the same rules to these cases as to the sports cases. For instance, in *Blake v Galloway* [2004] EWCA Civ 814, some 15-year-old boys were throwing pieces of bark at each other during a break in a music rehearsal. One of the boys was hit in the eye and badly injured. The boy who had thrown the bark relied on consent as a defence. The Court of Appeal held that the plaintiff 'must be taken to have impliedly consented to the risk of a blow on any part of his body, provided that the offending missile was thrown more or less in accordance with the tacit understandings or conventions of the game'. These conventions were held to be that:

> the objects that were being thrown were restricted to twigs, pieces of bark and other similar relatively harmless material that happened to be lying around on the ground; they were being thrown in the general direction of the participants in a somewhat random fashion, and not being aimed at any particular parts of their bodies; and they were being thrown in a good-natured way, without any intention of causing harm.

cross reference

Reeves v Metropolitan Police Commissioner [2000] 1 AC 360 is discussed more fully in chapter 4.

cross reference

Corr v IBC Vehicles Ltd [2006] EWCA Civ 331 was also discussed in chapter 4.

Finally, the defendant cannot use consent as a defence if the thing the claimant consented to was something the defendant had a duty to prevent. In *Reeves v Metropolitan Police Commissioner* [2000] 1 AC 360, the police were unable to use the defence of consent for exactly this reason. If their duty was to be meaningful, then the suicide could neither break the chain of causation nor constitute consent. Indeed, it seems that suicide will rarely give rise to the defence of consent, even if there is no specific duty to prevent the suicide. For example, in *Corr v IBC Vehicles Ltd* [2006] EWCA Civ 331, a widow sued her husband's employers after he committed suicide following an accident at work which caused him to become severely depressed. The Court of Appeal held in that case that consent was not available as a defence.

5.3 Illegality

If the claimant was doing something illegal when the damage occurred, the defendant may be able to rely on that as a defence. The defence is also known as *ex turpi causa non oritur actio*, which is Latin for 'no action will be heard which arises out of a disgraceful situation'. It exists for public policy purposes, the main ones being to discourage people from breaking the law and to avoid rewarding those who do so. There is not a great deal of case law on this defence, partly because the courts have often preferred to say that there was no duty of care between parties who were engaged in illegal activity rather than say that the illegal activity was a defence. For instance, in *Ashton v Turner* [1981] QB 137, the court found that the driver of a get-away car did not owe a duty of care to a fellow burglar who was a passenger in the car. In *Vellino v Chief Constable of Greater Manchester* [2001] EWCA Civ 1249, the Court of Appeal said that it did not matter which of these two approaches was used, because they would both lead to the same outcome. However, not all illegal acts will give rise to the defence, as the case of *Pitts v Hunt* [1991] 1 QB 24 shows. This case considers how closely the negligence and the illegality have to be connected in order for the defence to apply, and also illustrates both possible approaches. Here, the plaintiff was riding on a motorcycle driven by the first defendant. The motorcycle collided with a vehicle driven by the second defendant, resulting in the death of the first defendant and seriously injuring the plaintiff. Both the plaintiff and the first defendant had been drinking before the accident. The plaintiff knew that the first defendant did not hold a driving licence and was uninsured. Furthermore, at the time of the collision, the plaintiff was encouraging the first defendant to drive in a reckless and dangerous manner.

....

● ***Pitts v Hunt*** [1991] 1 QB 24

Balcombe LJ: In a case of this kind I find the ritual incantation of the maxim ex turpi causa non oritur actio more likely to confuse than to illuminate. I prefer to adopt the approach of the majority of the High Court of Australia in the most recent of the several Australian cases to which we were referred—*Jackson v Harrison*, 138 C.L.R. 438. That is to consider what would have been the cause of action had there been no joint illegal enterprise—that is, the tort of negligence based on the breach of a duty of care owed by the deceased to the plaintiff—and then to consider whether the circumstances of the particular case are such as to preclude the existence of that cause of action. This approach seems to me to enable the court to differentiate between those joint enterprises which, although involving a contravention of the criminal law and hence illegal—e.g., the use of a car by an unlicensed and disqualified driver as in *Jackson v Harrison* 138 C.L.R. 438—are not such as to disable the court from determining the standard of care to be observed, and those, such as the use of a getaway car as in *Ashton v Turner* [1981] Q.B. 137, where it is impossible to determine the appropriate standard of care.

Mr. Peppitt submitted that, however reprehensible the plaintiff's conduct may have been, his culpability involved neither dishonesty nor violence nor any moral turpitude such as is inherent in crimes of dishonesty or violence. Although an assessment of the degree of moral turpitude becomes unnecessary if one adopts, as I do, the approach of the majority of the High Court of Australia in *Jackson v Harrison*, I would not wish it to be thought that I accept this submission. It was only by good fortune that no innocent third party was injured by this disgraceful piece of motor cycle riding, in which the judge found on the facts that the plaintiff was an active participant. If moral turpitude were relevant, here was moral turpitude of a high degree.

However, I prefer to found my judgment on the simple basis that the circumstances of this particular case were such as to preclude the court from finding that the deceased owed a duty of care to the plaintiff.

Dillon LJ: It is clear for a start that the fact that a plaintiff was engaged in an illegal activity which brought about his injury does not automatically bring it about that his claim for damages for personal injury as a result of the negligence of the defendant must be dismissed. See also the judgment of Latham C.J. in *Henwood v Municipal Tramways Trust (South Australia)* (1938) 60 C.L.R. 438. In that case a passenger on a tram, feeling ill, lent out of a window of the tram to be sick, and was killed because his head was struck in succession by two steel standards erected by the tram company to carry the overhead cables which supplied the current for the trams. It was an offence punishable by a fine under a byelaw having statutory force for any passenger in a tram to lean out of the window. But it was nonetheless held that the parents of the deceased could bring an action for negligence in respect of his death, and seemingly he himself could have brought the action if he had merely been injured and survived, on the grounds that the tram company had failed to take sufficient steps to protect passengers against a foreseeable, and indeed known, danger.

So much is common ground between the parties, but it raises questions which have been the subject of discussion in English and Australian judgments as to whether a line can be drawn between different grades of illegality, and whether there is a distinction, and if so, on what ground, between the ordinary case of negligence, albeit involving a criminal act, such as the two last cited, and cases where a passenger sues the driver for injuries sustained by reckless driving at the time of the accident when they were both engaged in a joint criminal enterprise of which the reckless driving was an inherent part.

Mr. Peppitt for the plaintiff founds on certain recent authorities in this country which he relied on as establishing a 'conscience test' to be applied in cases of illegality... That test was put as follows, at p. 687:

> 'That test, [counsel] suggested, involved the court looking at the quality of the illegality relied on by the defendant and all the surrounding circumstances, without fine distinctions, and seeking to answer two questions: first, whether there had been illegality of which the court should take notice and, second, whether in all the circumstances it would be an affront to the public conscience if by affording him the relief sought the court was seen to be indirectly assisting or encouraging the plaintiff in his criminal act.'

The context in which that submission was put forward in *Thackwell v Barclays Bank Plc.* seems to have been one of the proximity of the illegality to the matters of which complaint was made in the action... The suggestion seems to have been in *Thackwell v Barclays Bank Plc* that it would be an affront to the public conscience to allow one thief to maintain an action because a second of the thieves had stolen the first's share in the course of the division of the swag.

The conscience test was approved by this court in *Saunders v Edwards* [1987] 1 W.L.R. 1116. That was again a case of the proximity, or relevance, of the illegality to the matters of which the plaintiff was complaining. The plaintiff claimed damages for fraudulent misrepresentation which had induced him to purchase a flat from the defendant. The defendant sought unsuccessfully to defend himself by asserting that the contract for the sale of the flat, and presumably also the **conveyance**, were tainted with illegality in that in the apportionment of the purchase price in the contract between chattels and the flat itself the amount attributable to the chattels had been fraudulently inflated, and the amount attributable to the flat had been correspondingly reduced, in order to reduce the stamp

VOCABULARY

'Conveyance' is an old word for the document which passes legal title in a property from one person to another at completion of a real estate transaction.

duty payable to the revenue. This court applied Hutchison J.'s test, to which Nicholls L.J., at p. 1132, added at the end of the formulation the words 'or encouraging others in similar criminal acts.'

Saunders v Edwards was, it seems to me, a case where the alleged illegality over the stamp duty apportionment was independent of, or unrelated to, the wrong in the way of fraudulent misrepresentation for which the plaintiff was suing...Bingham L.J. used rather different language where he said, at p. 1134:

'I think that on the whole the courts have tended to adopt a pragmatic approach to these problems, seeking where possible to see that genuine wrongs are righted so long as the court does not thereby promote or countenance a nefarious object or bargain which it is bound to condemn. Where the plaintiff's action in truth arises directly ex turpi causa, he is likely to fail. Where the plaintiff has suffered a genuine wrong, to which allegedly unlawful conduct is incidental, he is likely to succeed.'

I find a test that depends on what would or would not be an affront to the public conscience very difficult to apply, since the public conscience may well be affected by factors of an emotional nature, e.g., that these boys by their reckless and criminal behaviour happened to do no harm to anyone but themselves. Moreover if the public conscience happened to think that the plaintiff should be compensated for his injuries it might equally think that the deceased driver of the motor cycle, had he survived and merely been injured, ought to be compensated, and that leads into the much-debated question whether there ought to be a universal scheme for compensation for the victims of accidents without regard to fault.

Beyond that, appeal to the public conscience would be likely to lead to a graph of illegalities according to moral turpitude, and I am impressed by the comments of Mason J. in *Jackson v Harrison*, 138 C.L.R. 438, 455: 'there arises the difficulty, which I regard as insoluble, of formulating a criterion which would separate cases of serious illegality from those which are not serious.'

Bingham L.J.'s dichotomy in *Saunders v Edwards* [1987] 1 W.L.R. 1116 between cases where the plaintiff's action in truth arises directly ex turpi causa and cases where the plaintiff has suffered a genuine wrong to which allegedly unlawful conduct is incidental avoids this difficulty, in that it does not involve grading illegalities according to moral turpitude.

That a defence of illegality can be pleaded to a case founded in tort is, in my judgment, clear...On the facts of *Progress and Properties Ltd. v Craft*, 135 C.L.R. 651 it became clear that merely to say that if the parties were engaging in a joint illegal act neither would owe any duty of care to the other was to put the proposition too widely...For relief to be denied on the ground of the illegality, the circumstances of the joint illegal venture in the course of which the accident which caused the plaintiff's injuries occurred must be such as to negate, as between the two of them, any ordinary standard of care. Thus Mason J. said in *Jackson v Harrison*, at p. 456: 'A plaintiff will fail when the joint illegal enterprise in which he and the defendant are engaged is such that the court cannot determine the particular standard of care to be observed.'

...and Jacobs J. said in *Progress and Properties Ltd. v Craft*, 135 C.L.R. 651, 668: 'Where there is a joint illegal activity the actual act of which the plaintiff in a civil action may be complaining as done without care may itself be a criminal act of a kind in respect of which a court is not prepared to hear evidence for the purpose of establishing the standard of care which was reasonable in the circumstances.'

compare
A no-fault compensation scheme has, in fact, been adopted in New Zealand.

This formulation would clearly cover the instances given in the authorities of the careless smuggler or safebreaker, or the reckless driving, to escape capture, of the getaway car after a robbery, as in the English case of *Ashton v Turner* [1981] Q.B. 137. It was regarded in *Jackson v Harrison* as also covering...an agreement to drive the stolen car recklessly for the purpose of racing on the highway...Jacobs J. said in *Jackson v Harrison*, 138 C.L.R. 438, 460: 'It was a jaunt, an escapade, a joyride even though of a most serious kind from the beginning to the end. How could a standard of care be determined for such a course of criminal activity?'

I feel unable to draw any valid distinction between the reckless riding of the motor cycle in the present case by the deceased boy Hunt and the plaintiff under the influence of drink, and the reckless driving of the cars, albeit stolen, in *Smith v Jenkins* and *Bondarenko v Sommers*. The words of Barwick C.J. in *Smith v Jenkins*, 44 A.L.J.R. 78: 'The driving of the car by the appellant, the manner of which is the basis of the respondent's complaint, was in the circumstances as much a use of the car by the respondent as it was a use by the appellant. That use was their joint enterprise of the moment.'

...apply with equal force to the riding of the motor cycle in the present case. This is a case in which, in Bingham L.J.'s words in *Saunders v Edwards* [1987] 1 W.L.R. 1116, 1134, the plaintiff's action in truth arises directly ex turpi causa.

We saw in the section on consent that a statute, such as the Road Traffic Act 1988, can prevent a defence from operating in certain situations. The Occupiers' Liability Act 1984 has the same effect on the defence of illegality where the victim is a trespasser. This is because under the 1984 Act, the occupiers of premises have a limited duty of care to people who are on their land unlawfully. This duty would be meaningless if occupiers could use the defence of illegality in such cases. In *Revill v Newbery* [1996] QB 567, which involved a landowner who shot a burglar who was trespassing, the Court of Appeal decided that, for reasons of consistency, the defence is unavailable in cases where a trespasser sues for breach of the statutory duty under the 1984 Act or in negligence. Millett LJ also suggested in this case that someone who has inflicted disproportionate force on the criminal cannot use the defence of illegality.

cross reference

The Occupiers Liability Act 1987 is discussed at more length in chapter 7, along with cases such as Revill v Newbery [1996] QB 567.

Illegality can be used as a defence even if the claimant's illegal act was one that the defendant had a duty to prevent. In *Clunis v Camden and Islington Health Authority* [1998] QB 978, a man suffering from mental illness was supposed to be under the supervision of the health authority when he killed an innocent bystander. He was convicted of manslaughter and detained indefinitely in a secure hospital. He sued the health authority, but the Court of Appeal held that the defence of illegality applied. Beldam LJ there said:

NOTE You will study the criminal defences of insanity and diminished responsibility on your criminal law course.

In the present case the plaintiff has been convicted of a serious criminal offence. In such a case public policy would in our judgment preclude the court from entertaining the plaintiff's claim unless it could be said that he did not know the nature and quality of his act or that what he was doing was wrong. The offence of murder was reduced to one of manslaughter by reason of the plaintiff's mental disorder but his mental state did not justify a verdict of not guilty by reason of insanity. Consequently, though his responsibility for killing Mr. Zito is diminished, he must be taken to have known what he was doing and that it was wrong.

In *Meah v McCreamer* [1985] 1 All ER 367, which was discussed in chapter 4, a plaintiff who was injured in an accident recovered damages from the driver after he was imprisoned for attacking two women. Although a crime was involved (criminal assault), the defendant in that case did not raise illegality as a defence, so the court did not consider it there as it did in *Clunis v Camden and Islington Health Authority* [1998] QB 978.

The court in *Gray v Thames Trains Ltd* [2007] EWHC 1558 (QB) also gave weight to a conviction for manslaughter on the grounds of diminished responsibility. In this case, the claimant was a victim of a notorious train crash at Ladbroke Grove in London. He suffered from severe post-traumatic stress disorder, which caused a personality change and led him to stab a stranger to death. Like Mr Zito, he was not acquitted on the grounds of insanity, but was convicted of manslaughter instead of murder because of his diminished responsibility. His tort claim against the train operator included damages for loss of earnings that he suffered following his conviction. The court said that the law still regarded him as responsible and must assume that he knew what he was doing. The court would appear to condone his conduct if it allowed him to recover the losses which his crime had caused him, thus he could not therefore recover his loss of earnings.

(5.4) Exclusion of liability

Businesses (and occasionally individuals) operating in fields that are likely to lead to lawsuits in negligence or some other kind of fault sometimes try to exclude or limit their liability in writing, either by way of a contract or by publishing a disclaimer. For example, a contract may say something like 'the supplier shall not be liable for any loss or injury to the customer'. Another approach is for the contract to limit liability to a certain amount or to certain kinds of loss or to make it more difficult for a customer to make a claim by requiring him or her to make the claim within a very short timescale. In this section, we will refer to all of these types of clause as 'exclusion clauses'. Disclaimers, on the other hand, are notices that are posted publicly rather than being part of a contract.

In order for a disclaimer to be valid at common law, the party who wants to rely on it must have taken reasonable steps to draw it to the claimant's attention before the tort took place. The court will take into account factors such as where the notice was placed, how obvious it was, how easy it was to see and read, and so on. It must have been clearly worded and not ambiguous. If the exclusion is part of a contract, there may be issues of contract law that the court has to consider in order to decide whether or not the exclusion is effective. These issues may include whether the exclusion has been properly incorporated into the contract, whether it is sufficiently clear, whether one of the parties to the contract has misled the other party as to what the clause means, whether the breach of duty which has occurred is the same kind that the clause tries to exclude, and so on. You will learn about these issues on your contract law course. The only contract-related issue which we will consider here is whether or not the exclusion is made void by the Unfair Contract Terms Act 1977 (usually known as 'UCTA', pronounced uck-ta) or by the Unfair Terms in Consumer Contracts Regulations 1999 (the '1999 Regulations'). The

think point

As a matter of public policy, should all types of businesses be able to avoid negligence through a contract or disclaimer?

think point

Signs in restaurants and car parks often include disclaimers. What other disclaimers have you seen in your daily life?

1999 Regulations generally only apply to contracts where at least one party is a business and at least one other party is a consumer (i.e. someone not acting for the purposes of a trade, business, or profession). UCTA applies whether any party is a consumer or not, although in some cases the effects on contracts with consumers may be different from the effects on contracts with businesses. These provisions should be dealt with in more detail on your contract course, but they are summarized here because they can have a very significant effect on negligence claims. Firstly, section 2(3) of UCTA provides:

> Where a contract term or notice purports to exclude or restrict liability for negligence a person's agreement to or awareness of it is not of itself to be taken as indicating his voluntary acceptance of any risk.

NOTE Because exclusion of liability involves an agreement by the claimant to accept the risk of a loss, it could also have been considered in the same section as consent.

This section indicates that the defence of consent does not apply simply because someone has made a contract that has an exclusion clause in it.

Second, UCTA imposes restrictions on the types of damage for which a business can exclude liability and the extent to which it can do so. The general principle is that a business cannot exclude liability for death or personal injury. It can exclude liability for other types of loss, provided the exclusion is reasonable. If it is not reasonable, the attempted exclusion will be void. This is known as the 'reasonableness test' under UCTA. To decide whether or not an exclusion is reasonable, the court must, as per section 11 of UCTA, consider all the circumstances which were 'known to or in the contemplation of the parties when the contract was made' or which 'obtain[ed]' when the liability arose or (but for the notice) would have arisen'. The court must also, under section 11, consider what resources the defendant could expect to have available to meet any liability and whether or not the defendant could have insured against the liability instead of excluding it.

Schedule 2 to UCTA adds some further detail to the factors that the court should consider when it applies the reasonableness test, namely:

- The relative strength of the parties' bargaining positions;
- Whether or not the customer received something extra in return for agreeing to the exclusion clause;
- Whether or not the customer could have avoided the exclusion clause by going elsewhere;
- Whether or not the customer knew or should reasonably have known that the exclusion clause was part of the contract;
- If the exclusion clause imposes some condition on the customer, whether or not it was reasonable at the time of the contract to expect the customer to be able to comply with that condition; and
- Whether or not the customer is buying goods that were manufactured, processed or adapted to that customer's special order.

The burden of proving that the clause is reasonable is on the party that wants to rely on the clause.

The 1999 Regulations implement the European Council Directive on Unfair Terms in Consumer Contracts 93/13/EEC. Under Regulation 8 of the 1999 Regulations, unfair contract terms are not binding on consumers. Regulation 5(1) indicates that terms are unfair if they were not individually negotiated between the parties and lead to a significant imbalance in the parties' rights and obligations which is to the disadvantage of the consumer. When deciding this issue, the court must take into account the nature of the goods or services which are being provided, the other terms of the contract and all the circumstances in which the contract was made. Schedule 2 to the 1999 Regulations gives examples of clauses that will be considered unfair, but the 1999 Regulations do not contain any other specific guidelines that the court must apply. This means that, in practice, courts are likely to consider the same factors that they are accustomed to taking into account under UCTA.

5.5 Limitation periods

A limitation period is a period of time set by statute indicating the maximum period a claimant has to issue the claim form that initiates a lawsuit. If the claimant issues the claim form after that time has expired, the defendant can plead the defence of limitation. This defence did not exist at common law, but has been created by a series of statutes, beginning in 1623. The purpose of limitation periods is to limit the difficulties that can be caused by documents being lost, witnesses' memories deteriorating over time, and so on. It also enables potential defendants (particularly businesses) to plan their affairs with greater certainty. For instance, many businesses take limitation periods into account when deciding how long their documents should be kept in an archive. The archiving process is an expensive one, and businesses benefit from being able to assess when it is safe to destroy documents rather than continuing to pay an archiving company. One of the most common legal claims against solicitors involves a solicitor's failure to issue a claim on time, usually because he or she forgot to consider limitation issues or because he or she did not calculate the period correctly. It is worth taking the time to understand this topic!

cross reference
Nuisance and the intentional torts are covered in later chapters of this text.

The current statute dealing with limitation is the Limitation Act 1980. Under section 14A of this statute, the normal limitation period for tort claims is six years. If the claim involves personal injuries, then the period is reduced to three years, according to section 11(1), provided the claim is for 'negligence, nuisance or breach of duty'. The House of Lords ruled in *Stubbings v Webb* [1993] AC 498 that section 11's reference to 'breach of duty' is to 'breach of a duty of care', which effectively rules out torts are committed intentionally, such as trespass to land or assault. The usual six-year limitation period therefore applies to these claims.

In order to calculate when a limitation period expires, you need to know not only how long the period is, but also when it starts. The limitation period begins when the claimant's cause of action accrues, which means when all the elements of the tort are in place. In negligence, damage will usually be the last element to occur, and so the limitation period will typically run from the date of the damage. This can cause problems if potential claimants are not aware of the damage straight away or are unable to control their own affairs because they are under 18 years of age or are mentally ill. The 1980 Act refers to being mentally ill or under 18 as being 'under a disability', but this has nothing to do with the more common use of the word to refer to a physical limitation. Instead, it refers to a legal disability which disallows an individual from bringing a claim in his or her own name, without a guardian or other protective device to assist. Some textbooks use the word 'incapacity' instead. In the context of the 1980 Act, any potential claimant who is under a disability has extra time in which to file a claim, since the limitation period only starts to run when the disability comes to an end.

Latent damage

Another condition that might delay the onset of a limitation period is the existence of some kind of **latent** damage. For example, a building might be badly designed and develop cracks that are too small to be detected at first or that exist in a place where they would not normally be seen. Similarly, a worker who inhales asbestos dust may develop scarring in the lungs long before any obvious symptoms appear. If the limitation period runs from the date of either the first cracks or the earliest scarring, it may have run out before the potential claimants realize that they may have a claim. For personal injury claims that fall within section 11(1) of the 1980 Act, this problem is resolved by section 11(4), which provides that the limitation period does not start to run until the potential claimant has the requisite 'knowledge'. 'Knowledge' in turn is defined in section 14.

● **Limitation Act 1980**

14 Definition of date of knowledge for purposes of sections 11 and 12

(1) ...In sections 11 and 12 of this Act references to a person's date of knowledge are references to the date on which he first had knowledge of the following facts—
   (a) that the injury in question was significant; and
   (b) that the injury was attributable in whole or in part to the act or omission which is alleged to constitute negligence, nuisance or breach of duty; and
   (c) the identity of the defendant; and
   (d) if it is alleged that the act or omission was that of a person other than the defendant, the identity of that person and the additional facts supporting the bringing of an action against the defendant;
   and knowledge that any acts or omissions did or did not, as a matter of law, involve negligence, nuisance or breach of duty is irrelevant...

(2) For the purposes of this section an injury is significant if the person whose date of knowledge is in question would reasonably have considered it sufficiently serious to justify his instituting proceedings for damages against a defendant who did not dispute liability and was able to satisfy a judgment.

(3) For the purposes of this section a person's knowledge includes knowledge which he might reasonably have been expected to acquire—
   (a) from facts observable or ascertainable by him; or
   (b) from facts ascertainable by him with the help of medical or other appropriate expert advice which it is reasonable for him to seek;

(4) but a person shall not be fixed under this subsection with knowledge of a fact ascertainable only with the help of expert advice so long as he has taken all reasonable steps to obtain (and, where appropriate, to act on) that advice.

The last clause in section 14(1) means that it does not matter whether or not the potential claimant has a correct understanding of the legal impact of what has happened. For instance, if a claimant is wrongly advised by a solicitor that there is no claim, that will not stop the limitation period from running. The courts take the view that the fact that the claimant had enough knowledge to consult lawyers in the first place shows that the claimant had sufficient knowledge to satisfy section 14. For example, in *Spargo v North Essex District Health Authority* [1997] 37 BMLR 99, where a woman was wrongfully kept in a psychiatric institution for six years following a mistaken diagnosis, the Court of Appeal provided guidelines to assist judges in determining whether or not a claimant has 'knowledge' in this sense.

● *Spargo v North Essex District Health Authority* [1997] 37 BMLR 99

Brooke LJ: (1) the knowledge required to satisfy s 14(1)(b) is a broad knowledge of the essence of the causally relevant act or omission to which the injury is attributable;

(2) 'attributable' in this context means 'capable of being attributed to', in the sense of being a real possibility;

(3) a plaintiff has the requisite knowledge when she knows enough to make it reasonable for her to begin to investigate whether or not she has a case against the defendant. Another way of putting this is to say that she will have such knowledge if she so firmly believes that her condition is capable of being attributed to an act or omission which she can identify (in broad terms) that she goes to a solicitor to seek advice about making a claim for compensation;

(4) on the other hand, she will not have the requisite knowledge if she thinks she knows the acts or omissions she should investigate but in fact is barking up the wrong tree: or if her knowledge of what the defendant did or did not do is so vague or general that she cannot fairly be expected to know what she should investigate; or if her state of mind is such that she thinks her condition is capable of being attributed to the act or omission alleged to constitute negligence, but she is not sure about this, and would need to check with an expert before she could be properly said to know that it was.

In addition to section 14, claimants who have suffered personal injuries can rely on section 33(1) of the 1980 Act, which gives courts a wide discretion to override the three-year limitation period. Section 33(1) requires the court to weigh the prejudice that would be caused to the claimant by insisting on the time limit against the prejudice to the defendant if the limit is not upheld. In doing so, section 33(3) requires the court to take into account all the circumstances of the case, particularly the following factors:

• How long the claimant delayed before bringing the proceedings, and why;

• To what extent the delay has caused evidential problems;

• The defendant's conduct, especially in response to any requests by the claimant for information;

• Whether the claimant was 'under a disability' (in the sense we have explained earlier in this section) at any time while the limitation period was running;

• Whether the claimant acted promptly and reasonably after realizing that he or she might have a claim against the defendant; and

- What steps the claimant took to obtain medical, legal or other expert advice and the nature of any advice received.

You saw earlier that the special rules on limitation periods for personal injury cases only apply if the claimant's injuries were caused by a non-intentional tort. Thus, section 33 also does not apply to intentional torts. *Sniezek v Bundy (Letchworth) Ltd* [2000] All ER (D) 942 illustrates the interplay between section 14 and section 33 of the 1980 Act and further clarifies the common law gloss on the statute. That case involved a claimant who was responsible for cleaning an enclosed area that was exposed to polymer powder. He was given special clothing and a filtered mask to protect him from the dust. After taking on the job, he became aware of a burning sensation on his lips and in his throat, but did not think he was suffering from anything more than a sore throat due to irritation from the dust. He visited his doctor in 1984 and was referred to an ENT (ears, nose and throat) clinic but never followed through. He was dismissed in 1989 and was again referred for an ENT opinion, but the consultant found nothing unusual. In 1990 he was again given a clean bill of health. In the same year he went to his union solicitors, who requested a report from a consultant physician. The report said that the claimant had no discernible physical disability. In December 1992 the claimant consulted another set of solicitors who instructed another expert. That expert report found that the continued exposure to polymer powder could have resulted in the claimant's condition. However, it was not until June 1997 that counsel discovered from the defendants that the powder the claimant was exposed to contained a chemical called trimetallic anhydride (TMA). In January 1998 the consultant concluded that there might be a link between the claimant's symptoms and the exposure to TMA. In June 1998 counsel advised there was a reasonable case against the defendants, leading to the issuance of proceedings on 14 September 1998.

· ·

● **Sniezek v Bundy (Letchworth) Ltd** [2000] All ER (D) 942

Bell LJ: [F]or the purposes of the present case the vital effect of... O'Driscoll is to distinguish between a claimant who has a firm belief that he has a significant injury, attributable to his working conditions, especially one which takes him to a solicitor for advice about a claim, a belief which he retains whatever contrary advice he receives, and a claimant who believes that he may have, or even probably has, a significant injury which is attributable to his working conditions, but is not sure and feels it necessary to have expert advice on those questions. The former has knowledge of significant injury and attribution for the purposes of section 14; the latter does not. In my view, Mr Sniezek fell into the former category before the date of knowledge chosen by the judge.

Although the cases to which I have referred related to the question of knowledge of attributability with its low threshold of a real possibility, only, of causation, I believe that the essential principle must be the same so far as knowledge of significant injury is concerned, while interpreting 'significant' injury in accordance with section 14(2)...

I do not consider that the judge's decision on the date of knowledge can be sustained. It was not sufficient, to postpone knowledge, that the claimant recognized the need to get both medical and legal advice, and that the advice was adverse until January 1994... Whatever may be said about difficulties of attribution, a claimant such as Mr Sniezek either feels a sore throat, and burning lips, and has difficulties swallowing, as Mr Sniezek claimed from

> an early stage, or he does not...It may seem hard that time should run for the purposes of the Limitation Act when a claimant has taken reasonable steps to obtain medical or other expert advice to confirm his own belief in an injury, or its attribution, and the advice obtained has proved negative until he is well outside the primary period of limitation; but the three year period will be sufficient in most cases to obtain the necessary positive advice if a claim is good, and in hard cases where a claim is in fact good, and a claimant acts reasonably, but for one reason or another the advice is negative, the remedy lies in section 33 of the Act.

The court made a direction under section 33 that the limitation period should be overridden so that the claim could go ahead. People bringing negligence claims for any damage other than personal injuries are protected by sections 14A and 14B of the 1980 Act rather than by section 33. These provisions were inserted into the Limitation Act by the Latent Damage Act 1986. The main (or 'primary') limitation period for damages other than personal injury resulting from negligence remains at six years, but in cases where the claimant did not have the necessary knowledge (defined in the same way as for personal injuries), sections 14A and 14B allow the claimant to bring a claim within a 'secondary' limitation period of three years after acquiring that knowledge. There is, however, a 'long-stop' date of 15 years after the negligence occurred. After the 'long stop' date, claimants cannot sue, regardless of when they had the necessary knowledge. Note that:

- This provision only applies to negligence, not to other torts which may cause similar damage; and

- Courts have no discretion to override these limits (unlike the limits for personal injury claims).

Concealment

If the defendant deliberately conceals facts that are essential to the claimant's case, then section 28 of the 1980 Act states that the limitation period will run from the date when the claimant discovers the concealment or could have discovered it with reasonable diligence. According to section 32(3) of the 1980 Act, concealment for these purposes includes deliberately committing a breach of duty in circumstances where the claimant will not discover it for some time.

The time limit for an action based on fraud also runs from the date when the claimant could reasonably have discovered the fraud. In tort law, this is probably only relevant to the tort of deceit, which is beyond the scope of this text.

Continuing wrongs

cross reference

Negligent omissions are discussed in chapter 2.

If there is an ongoing breach of duty by the defendant, the claimant can sue for any damage which occurs during the six years (or three years in the case of personal injuries) immediately prior to issuing proceedings. In the context of negligence, a continuing wrong is probably most likely to take the form of an omission.

Proposals for reform

think point

Do you think the recommendations in the Law Commission Report are fair? Why or why not? What policy rationales are at work?

In 2001, the Law Commission proposed some reforms to the limitation regime in its report Limitation of Actions, Law Com 270 (2001). The general gist of the recommendations were that the core limitation period should be reduced to three years for almost all causes of action, including tort, but that this period should run from the claimant's date of knowledge rather than the date when the cause of action arose. A long-stop date of ten years would apply to all cases except those involving physical injury, fraud or concealment. In physical injury cases, the court would have a discretion to override the limitation period.

5.6 Contributory negligence

Contributory negligence is the only partial defence in English law. A defendant who successfully uses this defence will usually still have some liability to the claimant, but the amount the defendant has to pay will be reduced by a percentage proportional to the extent to which the claimant was at fault for the injury. The defence is designed to deal with situations where both the claimant and the defendant are at fault and have contributed to causing the claimant's loss. Some typical examples of contributory negligence include:

think point

We have already seen one example of contributory negligence in Barrett v Ministry of Defence [1995] 1 WLR 1217, discussed in chapter 2.

- Not following safety instructions;
- Not wearing a seatbelt;
- Not wearing a crash helmet when riding a motorcycle; or
- Accepting a lift from a drunk driver.

The defence is defined in the Law Reform (Contributory Negligence) Act 1945.

● **Law Reform (Contributory Negligence) Act 1945**

> **1 Apportionment of liability in case of contributory negligence**
>
> (1) Where any person suffers damage as the result partly of his own fault and partly of the fault of any other person or persons, a claim in respect of that damage shall not be defeated by reason of the fault of the person suffering the damage, but the damages recoverable in respect thereof shall be reduced to such extent as the court thinks just and equitable having regard to the claimant's share in the responsibility for the damage...
>
> **4 Interpretation**
>
> The following expressions have the meanings hereby respectively assigned to them, that is to say—
>
> ...

'damage' includes loss of life and personal injury;

'fault' means negligence, breach of statutory duty or other act or omission which gives rise to a liability in tort or would, apart from this Act, give rise to the defence of contributory negligence.

The definition of 'damage' in the 1945 Act is not exhaustive. In practice, courts will also apply the defence in cases of property damage and economic loss. Note also that the claimant does not have to be suing in negligence for the defence to be available. It can apply in any tort claim. The basic premise of contributory negligence is that claimants should not be able to recover full damages if they have not taken sufficient care for their own safety and wellbeing. This means that the claimant does not have to owe the defendant any duty of care. The other elements of negligence do have to be present, though: the same standard of care is applied, the claimant's carelessness must have contributed to causing the loss, and the harm must have been foreseeable. The courts have established the following rules for the standard of care in contributory negligence:

Recall

What standard of care applied to claimants who were children, disabled, or rescuers in chapter 4? These same standards apply in situations involving contributory negligence.

- Children are only guilty of contributory negligence if an ordinary child of the same age would have taken more care in the circumstances.

- If a claimant breaches a duty to someone else (e.g. the duty to drive carefully) because of a disability, no allowance is made for the disability when considering the defence of contributory negligence. However, if there is no breach of duty to a third party involved, then allowances are made.

- Rescuers are only guilty of contributory negligence if they show a wholly unreasonable disregard for their own safety. The courts are reluctant to make such a finding. Similarly, if the defendant puts the claimant in a dangerous situation, the claimant is entitled to take risks in order to escape the danger, and this is not treated as contributory negligence. This was decided in *Jones v Boyce* (1816) 1 Start 493, where a passenger jumped from a moving coach after the driver lost control of one of the horses.

- Employees who are injured at work can be guilty of contributory negligence, but the court may take into account their working conditions and the effect these may have on their perception of risk.

Furthermore, contributory negligence must be the claimant's own negligence and not the negligence of someone who was responsible for the claimant's behaviour. For instance, a child's damages are not reduced simply because the child's parent was negligent in allowing the child to do something, and a passenger's damages are not reduced because the driver drove negligently.

cross reference

Froom v Butcher [1975] 3 All ER 520 is discussed more fully in chapter 11.

If the court finds that there has been contributory negligence, it must decide how much that negligence contributed to the loss and how blameworthy the claimant was. The court expresses this as a percentage, which is then deducted from the claimant's damages. In cases where the contributory negligence consists of failing to wear a seatbelt or a motorcycle crash helmet, the court follows guidelines which were laid down in *Froom v Butcher* [1975] 3 All ER 520. That case indicated a 25 per cent reduction if the claimant could have avoided injury altogether by wearing the seatbelt, a 15 per cent reduction if the claimant could only have reduced the severity of the injuries, and no reduction if wearing the seatbelt would have made no difference. If the facts are more complex, the court will use these percentages for guidance, but may make different reductions. For instance, in *Capps v Miller* [1989] 1 WLR 839 the plaintiff was knocked off a moped. He was wearing a crash helmet with the chin-strap unfastened, and it came off during the accident. The plaintiff suffered severe brain damage when his head hit the road, and the Court of Appeal reduced his damages by 10 per cent. Interestingly, the position for bicycle helmets seems to be different than for motorcycle helmets. In the case of *Re A v Shorrock* (2001) 10 CL 386, a child riding a bicycle was injured in a traffic accident. The child was not wearing a cycle helmet. The court held that her damages should not be reduced because the medical evidence on the effectiveness of cycle helmets was too complex to allow a deduction.

In other cases, courts have to use their discretion, although they will take account of previous case law when doing so. In very rare cases, the use of discretion may result in a reduction of 100 per cent, which means that the claimant will receive no damages at all. The first example of this was the case of *Jayes v IMI (Kynoch) Ltd* [1985] ICR 155, which involved a very experienced factory supervisor who was working with two fitters to repair a machine. They had removed a safety guard in order to be able to lubricate the machine and started the machine up to test it. The supervisor put his hand into the moving machine to remove some excess lubricant and lost part of his finger. The supervisor himself admitted that this was 'a crazy thing to do', and the court found that he should be held wholly responsible for it even though the machine had not been fenced off by the employer (which was a breach of a statutory duty).

NOTE In some textbooks, you will see references to an old defence known as 'inevitable accident'. This defence originated in the nineteenth century, when the tort of negligence had not yet fully developed. Nowadays, inevitable accidents should result in a finding that there has been no breach of duty, so the defence no longer appears to be needed.

 For more revision tips, including self-test questions and suggestions for further reading, see the Online Resource Centre at www.oxfordtextbooks.co.uk/orc/strong_complete/.

revision tasks

Here are some ideas to get you started on your revision of this chapter:

- Re-read the section on consent. Can you identify any other defences that could have been used in the cases cited?

- Make a mind map showing the special rules that apply to sporting events, both regarding the standard of care and regarding defences.

- Make a list of the special rules that apply to rescuers as regards the duty of care, the standard of care, and defences.

- Make a chart summarising the current rules on limitation, distinguishing between personal injury claims and other claims.

Part 3

Breach of Statutory Duty

6

Breach of statutory duty

6.1 ## Introduction

So far, we have focused on what happens when someone breaches a common law duty of care and causes damage to someone else. In this chapter, we look at what happens when the duty is not found in the common law but in a statute. In these instances, the courts have to look very closely at the statute to decide whether the person who has suffered damage can claim compensation for it from the person who breached the duty. The ability to recover turns on what effect the courts think Parliament intended the statute to have. Some statutes make the task easy for the courts by specifying that individuals either can or cannot bring claims for any breach of the duties described in the legislation. Most statutes, however, do not address the issue one way or the other and leave it to the courts to work out what was intended.

The situations in which people may claim for breach of statutory duty are often the same as those in which they can claim for negligence. For instance, claims against employers for failing to take proper health and safety precautions are common examples of both kinds of action. In fact, claimants will often sue for both negligence and breach of statutory duty in the same proceedings (though of course they will still only receive one set of damages for each type of injury, even if they prevail on both claims). As with negligence, the elements of the tort of breach of statutory duty can be summarized as involving a duty, a breach of that duty and damage that was caused by that breach. However, the factors that have to be considered for each of these elements are not exactly the same as in negligence, so we will look at each element in detail. This chapter proceeds as follows:

* Elements of the tort of breach of statutory duty;

* Defences to a claim for breach of statutory duty; and

* Criticism of the tort of breach of statutory duty.

think point
Why might Parliament leave such an important issue to the courts to decide? Why could it be better for Parliament to decide these issues?

TIP If you have already studied statutory interpretation in other courses, you may find it useful to revise that topic before reading on.

Elements of the tort of breach of statutory duty

6.2.1 Duty

In order for individuals to be able to claim for a breach of statutory duty, the statute must impose on the defendant a positive duty to act, and the duty must be intended to protect the class of individuals to which the claimant belongs. The rest of this section explains this rule in more detail.

Positive duty

> **VOCABULARY**
> A prohibition can be termed a negative duty to act, since it requires someone not to do something. A positive duty requires someone to go out and affirmatively do something.

To permit individuals to claim for a breach of statutory duty, the duty which the statute imposes must be a positive duty to act. A **prohibition** is not enough, nor is a power to act which is not accompanied by a duty to do so. For instance, in *Lonrho Ltd v Shell Petroleum Co Ltd (No 2)* [1982] AC 173, Lonrho was supplying oil to Rhodesia (now Zimbabwe) through a pipeline. Following a coup in Rhodesia, Parliament passed a statute prohibiting British nationals from supplying oil to that country. Lonrho stopped supplying oil through the pipeline, but Shell and some other companies continued to supply oil in breach of the new statute. Lonrho sued for damages on the basis that the breach prolonged the survival of the illegal government in Rhodesia and therefore increased Lonrho's losses. The House of Lords held that Lonrho could not claim damages because a prohibition on trading with Rhodesia was not sufficient to give rise to an action for breach of statutory duty.

Imposed on the defendant

> **think point**
> *What policy reasons support the decision not to allow defendants to delegate their duty to comply with statutory duties? Are there any reasons to support the ability to delegate?*

The claimant also has to satisfy the court that the statute imposes the duty on the defendant and not on a third party. For instance, in a case about a workplace accident, the court may have to decide whether a particular safety duty is imposed on the employers or on a manager or fellow employee of the claimant. In *Harrison v National Coal Board* [1951] AC 639, for example, the House of Lords decided that some general duties in the regulations made under the Coal Mines Act 1911 were imposed on the mine owner, whereas specific duties relating to explosives were imposed on an explosives expert appointed by the manager of the mine. The plaintiff could only sue the National Coal Board, as the owner of the mine, for breach of the general duties.

If the statute does impose a duty on the defendant, then he or she cannot avoid liability by delegating the task to someone else. This was decided in *Groves v Wimborne* [1989] 2 QB 402, where the employer had a duty to put up and maintain a fence around a dangerous machine. He delegated the task to a foreman, who did put up the fence, but later took it down again. The plaintiff's arm became trapped in the machine and had to be amputated. The court recognized that the employer's factory was too large to expect him to know personally that the fence had been taken down, but still held him liable for the breach of the statute.

Intended to protect a class of individuals

NOTE The European Court of Human Rights subsequently found in *Z v UK* [2001] FLR 612 that the children's human rights had been violated; nowadays, the children would be able to enforce these rights in the British courts under the Human Rights Act 1998. This is a separate issue from breach of statutory duty.

The courts distinguish between statutes which are designed to protect the general public and those which are intended to protect specific classes of people individually. If the statute protects the general public, then individuals will not normally be able to sue for any breach. For instance, in *X v Bedfordshire County Council* [1995] 2 AC 633, the court held that child protection legislation was for the benefit of the public at large, and so individual children could not sue the local authority for breach of that legislation. Likewise, in *Atkinson v Newcastle and Gateshead Waterworks* (1871) LR 6 Exch 404, the Court of Appeal held that a house owner could not sue a public water company for failing to maintain water pressure at the statutory minimum, since that duty was owed to the public at large. You may have noticed that both of these cases involved public bodies as defendants. Part of the rationale for the distinction between statutes that protect the general public and those that protect a specific class is that the defendants in the former cases are often public authorities, and the courts do not like to interfere with their operational decisions. The fact that a mechanism exists for challenging the decisions of public authorities, in the form of judicial review, adds to this reluctance, as we will see below.

The courts are less likely to hold that a statute protects individuals if it expressly creates a remedy which can be used by public authorities to cure the activity or state of affairs that caused the harm. In *Keating v Elvan Reinforced Concrete Co Ltd* [1968] 2 All ER 139, a pedestrian fell into a trench that had been dug by the local authority's contractors. A third party had maliciously removed the fence the contractors had put around the trench, which left the contractors inadvertently in breach of the Public Utilities Street Works Act 1950. The Court of Appeal held that the pedestrian could not sue the contractors because the statute created a mechanism for the local authority to enforce the contractors' duties.

think point
Do you recall other kinds of cases where the courts preferred not to intervene in a public authority's decisions? If not, you may want to revise chapter 2.

An example of a case where the Court of Appeal did decide that a statute protected individuals was *Ex parte Island Records Ltd* [1978] Ch 12. In that case, the Court held that the Dramatic and Musical Performers' Protection Act 1958 was intended to protect the individual rights of musicians to prevent others from using their performances without permission (in this case, by making unauthorized recordings). Thus, the musicians whose rights had been infringed upon had the ability to sue for breach of statutory duty. In general, however, it appears to be the case that legislation on health and safety in the workplace is more likely to be interpreted as creating a private remedy than legislation on other topics. Indeed, in *Lonrho Ltd v Shell Petroleum Co Ltd (No 2)* [1982] AC 173, Lord Diplock took legislation on health and safety in factories as a classic example of statutes protecting a specific class.

If a statute does protect a class of individuals, then members of that class may be able to sue for breach of statutory duty, while members of the public who are not part of that class may not. For example, in *Cutler v Wandsworth Stadium Ltd* [1949] AC 398, the occupier of a dog-racing track breached a statutory duty by refusing entry to a bookmaker. The House of Lords held that the statute was for the protection of the race-going public rather than bookmakers, so this particular bookmaker—being outside the protected class—could not recover damages. In *Knapp v Railway Executive* [1949] 2 All ER 508, the railway authority breached a statutory duty to maintain the gates at level crossings. One of the gates swung back unexpectedly and hit a train driver. He was unable to claim compensation for breach of the statute because the statute was intended to protect road users rather than train drivers.

Even if the courts decide that the statute in question protects a class of individuals to which the claimant belongs, the courts may still refuse to find that it creates a remedy for those individuals. For instance, if a statute imposes a criminal penalty for breach of the duties described, the courts may decide that Parliament did not intend them to add a civil penalty as well. For example, in *Atkinson v Newcastle* (1876–77) LR 2 Ex D 441, the court took the fact that the statute imposed a fine of £10—a more significant sum of money in 1877 than it is now—as a sign that Parliament did not intend there to be a civil remedy for individuals as well. Similarly, in *Todd v Adam* [2002] EWCA EWCA Civ 509, four fishermen drowned when their boat sank. Their relatives sued the owner of the boat for breaches of the Fishing Vessel (Safety Provisions) Rules 1975, but the court held that Parliament did not intend owners to pay damages in addition to a fine. The existence of a fine or other criminal penalty is not conclusive, though; in *Groves v Lord Wimborne* [1898] 2 QB 402, a fine of up to £100 could be imposed for breaches of the statute, but the court still awarded compensation to an individual plaintiff, partly because the court felt that £100 was not proportionate to the seriousness of the injury in that case, which had resulted in the plaintiff's arm being amputated. Similarly, in *Monk v Warbey* [1935] 1 KB 75, a car owner committed an offence by allowing an uninsured driver to drive his car. The Court of Appeal held that, because the purpose of the legislation was to ensure that victims of car accidents would be compensated by insurers, it was fair to impose civil liability on owners who prevented this by allowing someone to drive their car uninsured.

NOTE Today, victims of uninsured drivers are usually compensated by the Motor Insurers' Bureau, which did not exist at the time.

The varying weight that courts have attached to the existence of criminal penalties is probably due to fluctuations in the social and political climate over the years. Thus, different cases may appear to lay down different rules. To begin to get a handle on how courts will decide the issue, it is useful to read a variety of cases. For example, *Olotu v Home Office* [1997] 1 All ER 385 involved a plaintiff who was arrested and charged with various criminal offences and held in custody awaiting trial. The plaintiff was released 81 days after the expiry of her custody time limit as prescribed by certain statutes and regulations, so she brought proceedings against the Home Office, as the department with oversight of the prison governor in whose custody she had been. She claimed damages for false imprisonment and for breach of the prison's statutory duty to bring her case before the court before the expiry of the custody time limit so that she could apply for bail.

● *Olotu v Home Office* [1997] 1 All ER 385

Mummery LJ: There is no dispute that regulation 6 imposed specific statutory duties on the CPS [Crown Prosecution Service], that it failed to perform them and that the plaintiff remained in custody 81 days longer than the custody time limit . . . In those circumstances, the only question for this court is whether, assuming the facts pleaded in the statement of claim to be true, the plaintiff has a reasonably arguable claim in law for damages for breach of statutory duty. There is no allegation of malice, of misfeasance in a public office, or of negligence, on the part of the CPS. The claim is starkly pleaded as one of strict liability for damages for breach of a duty imposed by statute.

It is a question of available remedies. The plaintiff was undoubtedly entitled to remedies in the criminal proceedings (bail) and in judicial review proceedings. The issue is whether she is entitled to an additional remedy against the CPS by way of a civil law claim for damages. It is common ground that it is not enough for the plaintiff simply to show that she has suffered damage in consequence of a breach of duty imposed by statute. The court must be satisfied that, on the true construction of the relevant statutory provisions, a right of action for damages has been created by Parliament. This question is answered by the application of well established principles stated by the Lord Chief Justice.

As this case concerns the liberty of the subject, it requires the fullest and most anxious consideration. I am, however, unable to accept Mr Blake's submission that a claim in damages lies against the CPS for breach of statutory duty. The statute and the regulations are silent on damages. There are strong indicators against the implied creation of a statutory tort of strict liability in a case such as this: the availability to the plaintiff of other remedies both in the criminal proceedings (bail) and in public law proceedings (habeas corpus and mandamus); the absence of any indication in section 22 of the Prosecution of Offences Act 1985 that the Secretary of State had power to make regulations conferring a private right of action on accused persons; and considerations of the kind relied on by the Court of Appeal in Elguzouli-Daf v Commissioner of Police Metropolis [1995] Q.B. 335 in concluding that, in the absence of voluntary assumption of responsibility to a particular defendant in criminal proceedings, there is no general duty of care owed by the CPS at common law in the conduct of its prosecution of a defendant and that the CPS is immune from actions for negligence.

Thus, the plaintiff could not obtain damages in tort for the injury she suffered. *Richardson v Pitt-Stanley* [1995] QB 123 had a similar outcome. That case involved a plaintiff who injured his hand during the course of his employment with a company. He claimed damages for personal injuries due to negligence and breach of statutory duty and obtained a **default judgment** against the company, with damages to be assessed later. However, the company went into liquidation with no assets to satisfy the judgment; neither did it have insurance against liability for injury sustained by its employees in the course of their employment as required by the Employers' Liability (Compulsory Insurance) Act 1969. The plaintiff then decided to bring an action against the company's directors and secretary, claiming that they had committed an offence under section 5 of the 1969 Act by consenting to the failure to insure, resulting in economic loss to the plaintiff equivalent to the sum he would have recovered had the company been properly insured.

VOCABULARY

A default judgment occurs when a defendant is properly served with notice of a civil action but does not appear in court to defend itself.

● *Richardson v Pitt-Stanley* [1995] QB 123

Russell LJ: Duties are owed by the employer both at common law and by statute whereby the employee is protected against the negligence or breach of statutory duty of the employer. If such a duty is breached and it causes personal injury to the employee he has the right to claim damages against the employer. The breach of statutory duty owed to the employee may also involve the employer in criminal proceedings, for example, under the Factory Acts, but the converse does not apply unless it can be shown that the particular statute creating the criminal offence, either by virtue of its express provisions or by necessary implication, creates civil liability...In my judgment the Employers' Liability (Compulsory Insurance) Act 1969 is and was intended to be a statute within the confines of our criminal law...The plaintiff's remedy against the company subsisted at common law and under the Factories Act 1961. The failure to insure did not deprive the plaintiff of his remedy as such, but rather the enforcement of that remedy by way of the recovery of damages...In my judgment there are a number of distinguishing features between Monk v. Warbey [1935] 1 K.B. 75 and the instant case. The owner of the motor vehicle, unlike the employer, has no direct liability to the injured party in a road traffic accident occasioned by the negligence of the driver to whom the vehicle has been lent. Secondly the wording of section 143 of the Act of 1972 is different to the wording of the Act of 1969. In the former the words used are 'it shall not be lawful' whereas those words do not appear in the Act of 1969. Thirdly, the position of anyone other than the owner of the vehicle is not dealt with by the Act of 1972, and if a director of a company which owns a vehicle has been involved in the failure to insure the Act of 1972 does not create direct criminal responsibility on the part of the director.

In other cases, non-tort remedies such as appeals and judicial review have been considered sufficient to exclude a claim for breach of statutory duty. Furthermore, if there are other remedies available to the claimant, either under the common law or under another statute, then, again, the courts may decide there is no claim for breach of statutory duty under a particular piece of legislation.

The courts are also influenced by the degree of detail with which the statute defines the duty. If the duty is rather vague and general, the court is less likely to decide that it gives individuals a right of action than if the duty is described in great detail. For instance, in *X v Bedfordshire City Council* [1995] 2 AC 633 the Council had a very general duty to protect the welfare of children and a wide discretion as to how to do so. Thus, no individual tort claim was allowed. Finally, the courts may be more reluctant to impose a civil remedy where the statute provides for strict liability, since this could make the remedy very draconian.

cross reference

X v Bedfordshire County Council [1995] 2 AC 633 was discussed in detail in chapter 2.

Author Alex Ruck Keene has examined the relationship between statute, breach of statutory duty and negligence, focusing on the leading case of *Gorringe v Calderdale MBC* [2004] UKHL 15. In this case, the claimant had an accident on a country road and sued the local authority for failing to provide signs indicating that she was coming to a dangerous part of the road. She argued that this was a breach of the authority's statutory duties to maintain the highway and to promote road safety. The House of Lords found that neither of these statutory duties created a private remedy for the claimant.

● Alex Ruck Keene, *'Negligence claims against public bodies'*, 155 New Law Journal 86

Their [Lordships'] conclusions can be summarised in the form of two specific questions that practitioners should ask themselves in respect of each claim that appears on its face to be a negligence claim against a public body:

(i) On a proper analysis, is the claim founded on breach of statutory duty or in negligence?

(ii) On a proper analysis, is the claim that the public body omitted to act or is it, rather, that the public body has been negligent in its actions?

The distinction between claims brought in breach of statutory duty and in negligence is often blurred. However, as Lord Steyn emphasised at para 3 of his speech in Gorringe, this can be highly misleading.

If a claim is founded on breach of statutory duty, the central question is whether from the provisions and structure of the statute the intention can be gathered to create a private law remedy. In construing the statute, key factors identified by Lord Hutton . . . were: (i) whether the statutory duty was imposed for the protection of a limited class of the public; and (ii) whether Parliament intended to confer on members of that class a private right of action for breach of that duty.

In contrast to the position, for instance, as regards claims against employers, the case law makes it clear that it will often be difficult to establish a right of action against public bodies for breach of statutory duty: see, for instance, X (no cause of action for breach of the Children and Young Persons Act 1969, the Children Care Act 1980 and the Children Act 1989) . . .

By contrast to the position in respect of claims in breach of statutory duty, if the claim is brought in negligence against a backdrop of a statutory duty or power, the first question that the court must ask itself is whether the statute in question excludes a private law remedy.

Only if it is satisfied that it does not can it then go on to consider whether a common law duty of care can co-exist with the statutory duty or power. Importantly, however, although statutory duties and powers may constitute part of the relevant factual background, the existence of those duties and powers cannot reinforce parasitically the existence of a common law duty of care owed by the public authority . . .

In deciding whether a common law duty of care exists, . . . the court must first be satisfied that the matter is justiciable, before applying the standard tests of a common law duty of care laid down in Caparo Industries plc v Dickman [1990] 2 AC 605 and Henderson v Merrett Syndicates [1995] 2 AC 145. 'Justiciability' is a slippery concept, but one assistance can be found in Lord Hutton's speech in Barrett [Barrett v Enfield LBC [2001] 2 AC 550] (at 583): a case is justiciable if it does not involve the weighing of competing public interests and is not dictated by considerations which the courts are not fitted to assess . . .

cross reference

Caparo Industries plc v Dickman [1990] 2 AC 605 and Henderson v Merrett Syndicates [1995] 2 AC 145 are discussed in chapter 13.

6.2.2 Breach

Having established that the statutory duty is one which an individual can enforce, the courts next have to decide whether the defendant has breached that duty. This exercise is similar to determining whether there has been a breach in the tort of negligence. The court must consider exactly what the statute requires the defendant to do and what standard of care applies.

What the statute requires the defendant to do

Determining what acts are required by statute can be difficult. For example, in *R v East Sussex County Council, ex parte Tandy* [1998] AC 714 the local authority reduced a

NOTE This case involved judicial review proceedings rather than a claim for compensation for breach of statutory duty, but the principles of statutory interpretation are the same.

sick child's home tuition because it decided it could no longer afford the additional costs. The House of Lords found that the authority was in breach of its statutory duty under section 298 of the Education Act 1993 to provide 'suitable education'. Other sections in the statute expressly allowed the local authority to take financial resources into account when providing services, but this section did not, so the House of Lords held that Parliament must have intended to require the authority to make its decision on educational grounds alone. Sometimes the courts must infer the purpose of the legislation. For example, in *Close v Steel Company of Wales* [1962] AC 367, the House of Lords held that the statutory duty to fence machines meant that employers had to fence the machines sufficiently to prevent employees from getting close enough to be trapped in the machine; they did not have to provide fences which would also catch any parts that broke off the machine. Therefore, an employee who was struck by a piece flying off the machine could not sue for breach of this statutory duty.

Courts also must decide which statute applies. For example, in *Shine v London Borough of Tower Hamlets* [2006] EWCA Civ 852, a boy hurt himself trying to leapfrog a bollard which turned out to be loose. The court found that he could not claim compensation from the council for breach of its statutory duty to maintain the highway because the bollard was not part of the highway—it was an article placed on the highway for safety purposes, which meant it fell under a different statutory provision that did not impose a duty.

Because of the need to look closely at what the defendant is required to do, it is possible for the defendant to be liable in negligence without also being liable for breach of statutory duty. For instance, in *Bux v Slough Metals* [2006] EWCA Civ 852, the employers had a statutory duty to provide safety goggles and a common law duty to take reasonable steps to provide a safe system of work. The employers did provide goggles, but because these misted up easily, the employees gave up wearing them. The Court of Appeal decided that the employers were not in breach of the statute, but they were negligent, because they had failed to supervise the employees effectively so as to ensure that they wore the goggles.

Standard of care

VOCABULARY The term 'strict liability' in tort means that the defendant need not have acted intentionally, maliciously, recklessly, or even negligently. No sort of fault need exist.

The standard of care depends on the statute which is alleged to have been breached. Some statutes, including many health and safety statutes, impose **strict liability**. For instance, in *John Summers & Sons Ltd v Frost* [1955] AC 740, an employer was held strictly liable for failing to fence a machine, even though doing so would have rendered it unusable. Other statutes may only require reasonable care (in which case the standard of care is the same as it is in the tort of negligence) or demand that the defendant takes reasonably practicable steps to avoid the harm. It may not always be obvious what standard a statute imposes, since statutes do not generally use phrases such as 'strict liability'. The court has to construe the statute to decide what Parliament intended. For instance, the courts have found that the words 'shall be maintained' impose strict liability, whereas 'reasonably practicable' has been interpreted in different ways in different statutes. The term can be interpreted in the same way as the standard of care in negligence, but it can also have its own special definition. For example, *Larner v British Steel plc* [1993] 4 All ER 102 involved a plaintiff who was an experienced mechanical fitter employed by the defendants. He was instructed to remove a part from a heavy piece of machinery. He was informed that one end of the structure's supporting framework was cracked, but, because of an undetected crack in the other end, the structure fell on him and injured his right leg severely in the course of removing the part. The plaintiff claimed that the defendants were negligent and were in breach of statutory duty. In this case, the Court of Appeal said that foreseeability of danger—a critical element of the tort of negligence—was not relevant to a requirement to take reasonably practicable steps to make a workplace safe.

Furthermore, in assessing what is practicable, the court will take into account the state of scientific knowledge at the relevant time. For instance, in *Adsett v K & L Steelfounders & Engineers Ltd* [1953] 1 WLR 773, the Court of Appeal found that it was not practicable in 1940 for the plaintiff's employers to install a dust extractor that would have stopped him getting the lung disease pneumoconiosis. The employers installed the machine in 1942, shortly after inventing it. The Court said that the employers could not be made liable for failing to invent it sooner. The onus of proving that a particular step was not practicable is on the defendant, which can sometimes be a reason for the claimant to sue for breach of statutory duty rather than for negligence.

6.2.3 **Damage**

think point
Could the court in Gorris v Scott (1874) LR 9 Ex 125 have reached the same result through different analytical means?

The rules on causation in the tort of breach of statutory duty are the same as in negligence, but the test of remoteness is somewhat different in breach of statutory duty. In statutory duty cases, the courts do not consider whether the damage was of a foreseeable type, as is the case with negligence. Instead, the courts look at whether the damage that occurred was the type of damage the statute was designed to prevent. For instance, in the leading case of *Gorris v Scott* (1874) LR 9 Ex 125, the plaintiff's sheep were being transported on the defendant's ship. Because the ship did not have pens in which to keep the animals, the sheep were kept on the decks and were lost overboard during a storm. There was a statute which required the use of pens, but it was designed to prevent the spread of disease rather than the loss of the animals from the deck of the ship. As a result, the plaintiff could not recover compensation for breach of the duty, since the damage was not of the type the statute was meant to prevent.

However, if the type of injury is of the type contemplated by the statute, it does not matter if the way that injury comes about is different than the statute seems to anticipate. For example, in *Donaghey v Boulton and Paul Ltd* [1968] AC 1, the statute at issue required employers to provide ladders or boards to support employees who were working on a fragile roof. The statute was clearly designed to ensure that employees did not fall through fragile roofing materials. In fact, the plaintiff fell through a pre-existing hole in the roof. He was still able to recover because the type of damage he suffered—personal injury—was within the scope of the statute.

Defences to a claim for breach of statutory duty

The defences to breach of statutory duty are similar to those to negligence. Four, in particular, apply to this tort:

• Contributory negligence;

• Illegality;

• Consent; and

• Limitation.

6.3.1 Contributory negligence

Contributory negligence is available as a defence to breach of statutory duty in broadly the same circumstances as in negligence cases. However, the defence is not available where employees are careless about their own safety because of the effects of the job itself, e.g. where the employee becomes over-familiar with the job or where the noise or stress of the job interfere with the employee's ability to pay attention. This is because health and safety legislation is partly designed to protect employees against those risks. For example, the plaintiff in *Staveley Iron and Chemical Co Ltd v Jones* [1956] AC 627 was moving heavy cores by means of a crane and suffered personal injuries. He brought an action against his employers for damages in respect of the negligence of the crane driver. It was held by the House of Lords that the crane driver had been guilty of negligence and the employers were responsible for the acts of their servant done in the course of the employment; and that, even though the accident arose in part from his own error, the injured workman was not guilty of contributory negligence and was accordingly entitled to damages.

6.3.2 Illegality

The defence of illegality is available in cases of breach of statutory duty in the same way as in negligence cases, as confirmed in *Hewison v Meridian Shipping Services PTE Ltd* [2002] EWCA Civ 1812. In this case, the claimant was seriously injured following an epileptic seizure while working as a crane operator on a cable-laying ship. He sued his employer and the owner and charterer (hirer) of the ship for negligence and breach of statutory duty. Part of the claim was for loss of earnings. However, it turned out that when he applied for the job, he had lied to the employer by saying that he had never had a seizure, when in fact he knew he had epilepsy. This amounts to the criminal offence of obtaining a pecuniary advantage by deception, and the Court of Appeal thus held that he could not recover for loss of earnings.

6.3.3 **Consent**

cross reference
Imperial Chemical Industries Ltd. v Shatwell [1965] AC 656 was discussed in detail in chapter 5.

Consent is available as a defence to claims for breach of statutory duty, but only in certain types of claim. *Imperial Chemical Industries Ltd. v Shatwell* [1965] AC 656, which involved two workers in a rock quarry who agreed between themselves to set off a detonation in violation of statutory regulations regarding test explosions, sets forth the necessary rules.

• *Imperial Chemical Industries Ltd v Shatwell* [1965] AC 656

> Lord Pearce: Where Parliament has laid down that certain precautions shall be taken by the master to protect his workmen, a master is not and should not be entitled to neglect those precautions and then rely on an express or implied agreement between himself and the workman that the latter, if injured as a result of the neglect, will bear the loss alone...In my opinion, the rule which the courts have rightly created disallowing the defence where the employer is in breach of statutory duty should not apply to a case such as the present. The defence should be available where the employer was not himself in breach of statutory duty and was not vicariously in breach of any statutory duty through the neglect of some person who was of superior rank to the plaintiff and whose commands the plaintiff was bound to obey (or who had some special and different duty of care...), and where the plaintiff himself assented to and took part in the breaking of the statutory duty in question. If one does not allow some such exception one is plainly shutting out a defence which, when applied in the right circumstances, is fair and sensible.

cross reference
You will learn more in chapter 16 about when employers can be liable for the torts of their employees.

This case establishes the following principles:

- Consent is not a defence when an employee sues the employer for breaching the employer's statutory duty.
- Consent is a potential defence when an employee sues the employer for a fellow employee's breach of statutory duty.
- Consent is also a potential defence in any claim for breach of statutory duty when parties are not employee and employer.

In situations where consent is available as a potential defence, the principles are the same as in negligence.

6.3.4 **Limitation**

The Limitation Act 1980 applies to claims for breach of statutory duty in the same way as it does to claims for negligence.

6.4 Criticism

The law on breach of statutory duty is often criticized because it is difficult for courts to determine whether or not Parliament intended to allow a civil remedy. This issue could be avoided if Parliament expressly said in each statute what its intentions were. However, most statutes still do not do this. Amongst those that do specify a civil remedy are the

cross reference

Two of these statutes are discussed in later chapters. See chapter 7 for more on the Occupiers Liability Act 1984 and chapter 15 for the Consumer Protection Act 1987.

Nuclear Installations Act 1965, the Sex Discrimination Act 1975, the Race Relations Act 1976, the Occupiers' Liability Act 1984, the Consumer Protection Act 1987, and the Protection from Harassment Act 1997. The failure to state whether a civil remedy is available may be due, at least in part, to political concerns, since politicians may not want to draw attention to the fact that they are not creating a remedy for individual victims.

Interestingly, the Law Commission recommended in 1969 that there should be a statutory presumption in favour of allowing a claim, unless the statute specifically rules it out. However, this recommendation has never been implemented, and no such presumption exists.

For more revision tips, including self-test questions and suggestions for further reading, see the Online Resource Centre at www.oxfordtextbooks.co.uk/orc/strong_complete/.

revision tasks

Here are some ideas to try when you revise this chapter:

- Make an outline showing what the claimant has to prove to recover compensation for breach of statutory duty.

- Make a table comparing the tort of negligence with breach of statutory duty. What are the main differences? Which tort is more favourable to a claimant?

- Consider the policy issues supporting and opposing the rules creating an ability to establish a private remedy for breach of statutory duty. Identify where the risk of loss falls and why.

Part 4

Torts Involving Land

7 Occupiers' liability

7.1 Introduction

So far, we have looked at liability arising out of actions that could be taken virtually anywhere. The next several chapters investigate liability associated with ownership or occupation of land. Some of the torts are primarily statutory and some are entirely born out of the common law. All, however, have direction connections with the ownership, occupation or use of land.

The first and most important land-based tort, and the one that is the subject of this chapter, is known as occupiers' liability. There are two possible types of defendants: (1) those who actually occupy or use the land and (2) those who may not be in physical possession of the land but still retain some responsibility over its condition. The second category of potential defendants includes landlords, builders and other construction professionals, such as architects.

Occupiers' liability is primarily statutory, so this chapter focuses on the various statutes relevant to occupiers' liability, thought it still discusses the case law construing those statutes, since those decisions give an important gloss to the Parliamentary language. We then turn to the law regarding the liability of non-occupiers of land for torts associated with land. This chapter proceeds as follows:

- Pre-1957 common law;
- Liability to visitors under the Occupiers' Liability Act 1957;
- Liability to non-visitors under the Occupiers' Liability Act 1984; and
- Liability of non-occupiers under relevant statutory and case law.

7.2 Pre-1957 common law

Although occupiers' liability is now governed almost entirely by statute, the old common law still has some relevance because the applicability of the two major pieces of legislation in this area of law—the Occupiers' Liability Act 1957 (1957 Act) and the Occupiers' Liability Act 1984 (1984 Act)—varies according to the status of the claimant. The status of a claimant is defined by old common law categories.

NOTE Although Parliament has eliminated the distinction between invitees, licensees, and trespassers, you still need to be aware of the status of the entrant to the land.

Prior to the enactment of the 1957 Act, occupiers of land owed different duties to different types of entrants onto the land. The highest standard of care was owed to those who had come onto the land pursuant to contract—for example, a guest in a hotel. Slightly less care was due to an invitee, meaning a person invited by the landowner to enter the land, often in pursuit of mutual business—for example, a customer in a shop. Even less care was due to a licensee, which was defined as a person permitted to come onto the land but not specifically invited to do so. Finally, the common law held that occupiers owed only a minimal duty of care to a trespasser who came onto the land without any sort of permission.

Although the 1957 Act and the 1984 Act replaced the common law in many ways, the old common law still retains some importance. For example, the 1957 Act applies to 'visitors' who turn out to be the same as invitees and licensees at common law. In contrast, the 1984 Act applies to 'non-visitors' who turn out to be the same as trespassers at common law. The distinction will become clearer as the discussion progresses.

7.3 Liability to visitors—Occupiers' Liability Act 1957

When dealing with a statute, consider the original language of the legislation, since every word matters. This section goes through the relevant aspects of the legislation in detail, since the statute often tells you all you need to know to decide an issue of law.

7.3.1 Scope of the 1957 Act

Section 1 of the Occupiers' Liability Act 1957 describes the interplay between the 1957 Act and the pre-1957 common law. Notice how the common law remains relevant, despite the explicit renunciation of the existing case law in section 1(1).

● **Occupiers' Liability Act 1957**

1 Preliminary

(1) The rules enacted by the next two sections shall have effect, in place of the rules of the common law, to regulate the duty which an occupier of premises owes to his visitors in respect of dangers due to the state of the premises or to things done or omitted to be done on them.

Thus, the 1957 Act applies to invitees and licensees, as defined by the pre-Act common law.

· ·

● **Occupiers' Liability Act 1957**

1 Preliminary

(2) The rules so enacted shall regulate the nature of the duty imposed by law in consequence of a person's occupation or control of premises and of any invitation or permission he gives (or is to be treated as giving) to another to enter or use the premises, but they shall not alter the rules of the common law as to the persons on whom a duty is so imposed or to whom it is owed; and accordingly for the purpose of the rules so enacted the persons who are to be treated as an occupier and as his visitors are the same (subject to subsection (4) of this section) as the persons who would at common law be treated as an occupier and as his invitees or licensees.

Now the common law appears to return, at least for purposes of identifying on whom the duty of care is imposed and to whom it is owed.

· ·

● **Occupiers' Liability Act 1957**

1 Preliminary

(3) The rules so enacted in relation to an occupier of premises and his visitors shall also apply, in like manner and to the like extent as the principles applicable at common law to an occupier of premises and his invitees or licensees would apply, to regulate—
   (a) the obligations of a person occupying or having control over any fixed or moveable structure, including any vessel, vehicle or aircraft; and
   (b) the obligations of a person occupying or having control over any premises or structure in respect of damage to property, including the property of persons who are not themselves his visitors.

Subsection 1(3) thus describes what property is involved. As we will see later in this chapter, 'premises' can be more than a house or a shop—'premises' can include movable items like ships and automobiles. This subsection also indicates that the occupier may be liable for property that is owned by someone other than the person on the property. For example, if you are wearing your sister's shoes and ruin them because of a defect on the premises, the occupier may have to replace the shoes, even though they're not yours and your sister was never invited onto the premises.

Although section 1(2) the 1957 Act discusses both invitees and licensees at common law, courts do not distinguish between the duties owed to these two categories of entrants. The key thing to remember is that permission to enter cannot be implied. Instead, '[t]here must be evidence either of express permission or that the land-owner has so conducted himself that he cannot be heard to say that he did not give it', as indicated by Lord Goddard in *Edwards v Railway Executive* [1952] AC 737, which involved a nine-year-old boy who was injured after having gone onto a railway line. Although trespassers, including children, had habitually gone onto the land, the railway did not need to do more than it did, which was keep and maintain a fence around the premises.

Another important common law definition is that of 'occupier'. Nowhere in the 1957 Act is an occupier defined. Instead, section 1(2) of the Act refers the reader back to the common law. However, in 1966, the House of Lords definitively defined an occupier in *Wheat v E Lacon & Co Ltd* [1966] 2 AC 552.

● ***Wheat v E Lacon & Co Ltd*** [1966] 2 AC 552

Lord Morris of Borth-y-Gest: My Lords, the tragic death of the appellant's husband set a perplexing problem of deciding how it came about... He purposed to go to the lower part of the premises and he proceeded to use the back staircase. In some way... he fell...

[T]he Occupiers' Liability Act, 1957, regulates the duty of an occupier but does not alter the rules of the common law which determine the question as to who is an occupier. When someone is an occupier then the rules laid down in the Act (in sections 2 and 3) take the place of the rules of the common law. For the purpose of those rules the persons 'who are to be treated as an occupier and as his visitors' are (subject to one qualification) the same as the persons who would at common law 'be treated as an occupier and as his invitees or licensees.'

The statutorily regulated duty of the occupier to his visitors (unless the occupier is free to and does make variation by agreement or otherwise) is the common duty of care. He must take such care as in all the circumstances of the case is reasonable to see that the visitor will be reasonably safe in using the premises for the purposes for which he is invited or permitted by the occupier to be there.

Who, then, for this purpose is an occupier?... Section 1 (1) of the Act speaks of 'an occupier of premises.' Section 1 (2) refers to 'a person's occupation or control of premises': it goes on to refer to 'any invitation or permission he gives (or is to be treated as giving) to another to enter or use the premises.' This I think shows that exclusive occupation is not necessary to constitute a person an occupier...

[T]here may [also] be someone who would ordinarily be regarded as the occupier of premises while at the same time there may be another occupier who has 'control so far as material.' Lord Wright gave the illustration of an occupier of a theatre permitting an independent company to give performances: and the further illustration of a person holding a fair who grants concessions to others to hold side shows...

[T]he conception of 'occupation' is not necessarily and in all circumstances confined to the actual personal occupation of the person termed the occupier himself and that in certain contexts and for certain purposes it extends to vicarious occupation by a caretaker or other servant or by an agent.

This brings me to the question whether Lacons were in occupation or control... Much turns upon the facts and also upon the effect of the agreement of April 3, 1951. That was a service agreement. Lacons were called the employers.' Mr. Richardson was being employed as 'the manager' of the public-house called the 'Golfers' Arms.' He was being employed upon the terms and conditions of the agreement...

As a privilege (which could be withdrawn) Lacons allowed their managers to take visitors for reward during the summer... It was as a result of this privilege that Mrs. Richardson agreed to accommodate Mr. Wheat and his party for a period of about a week which covered the early days of September, 1958.

> The general result of the agreement and of the arrangements to which I have referred was that Lacons through their servant were in occupation of the whole premises. Their servant was required to be there...Lacons would see to the condition of the premises and would effect any necessary repairs...
>
> The conclusion I reach is that as regards the premises as a whole both Lacons and the manager were occupiers, but that by mutual arrangement Lacons would not (subject to certain overriding considerations) exercise control over some parts. They gave freedom to their manager to live in his home in privacy...I think it follows that both Lacons and the Richardsons were 'occupiers' vis-a-vis Mr. Wheat and his party. Both Lacons and the Richardsons owed Mr. Wheat and his party a duty. The duty was the common duty of care. The measure and the content of that duty were not, however, necessarily the same in the case of Lacons and in the case of the Richardsons. The duty was to take such care as in all the circumstances of the case was reasonable to see that Mr. Wheat and his party would be reasonably safe in using the premises as guests for reward. Lacons did not know that Mr. Wheat and his party were to arrive but they had given permission to their manager to take guests, and the result was that Mr. Wheat and his party were on the premises with Lacons' permission...
>
> It may, therefore, often be that the extent of the particular control which is exercised within the sphere of joint occupation will become a pointer as to the nature and extent of the duty which reasonably devolves upon a particular occupier.

TIP Examiners love to write problem questions with more than one occupier. Look out for this type of fact pattern in your essays and exams!

In this case, the House of Lords held that there could be two or more occupiers of the same space at the same time. If there is more than one occupier, then there is no need for either party to have exclusive control over the property. Instead, the test is whether a defendant has some degree of control associated with the premises and arising out of either the use of or activities in the property. The House of Lords also indicated that if there is more than one occupier, then the degree of care owed by each occupier to the claimant is proportional to the degree of control that occupier exercises over the property.

Remember, 'premises' does not always mean real property. As section 1(3)(a) of the 1957 Act indicates, the duty of care extends to those who occupy or have control over 'any fixed or moveable structure, including any vessel, vehicle or aircraft'. Thus, a contractor engaged in converting a ship into a troopship can be considered an occupier while that ship is in dry dock, as seen in *Hartwell v Grayson Rollo and Clover Docks Ltd* [1947] KB 901.

Although a 'movable structure' is easily defined, the meaning of a 'fixed structure' is slightly more confusing. The term cannot mean the same thing as 'premises,' which is used both in section 1(1) and 1(3). The consensus is that 'premises' means 'land' and any buildings permanently constructed on land. A 'fixed structure' constitutes something that is non-movable (i.e. not a vessel or vehicle) that is built on the premises, i.e. the land. For example, the scaffolding around a building would constitute a 'fixed structure', since it is not movable, yet is also not permanent. Be careful here. How a particular item is categorized may affect the liability of the defendant, since different duties may arise depending on whether something is part of the premises or simply a fixed structure. For example, if the defendant provides a ladder to an independent contractor to use while

NOTE The 1984 Act covers not only those persons who would be considered trespassers under the common law, but other people as well, including someone who involuntarily entered land without authority.

completing a task on the premises, the defendant may no longer be an 'occupier' of the ladder, because it is now under the contractor's exclusive control. Alternatively, as shown in *Wheeler v Copas* [1981] 3 All ER 405, the plaintiff could argue that the defendant should still be liable as a bailor of the ladder or as an occupier of premises who intends to allow the claimant to use the defendant's equipment on the land.

Wheat v E Lacon & Co Ltd [1966] 1 AC 552 demonstrated that there can be more than one occupier of premises. However, must the relationship between the various occupiers and the entrant always be the same? Is it possible that a person can be a visitor under the 1957 Act as to one occupier but a non-visitor (i.e. a trespasser) as to the other?

The House of Lords addressed this issue in *Ferguson v Welsh* [1987] 1 WLR 1553, which involved a local council which put out invitations to tender for the demolition of a building on council land. Despite an express condition that the work not be sub-contracted without the council's authority, the winning contractor arranged for certain sub-contractors to carry out the actual demolition. The sub-contractors caused a wall to collapse on one of their workers, who brought an action against the sub-contractors, the contractors and the council.

. . . .

● *Ferguson v Welsh* [1987] 1 WLR 1553

Lord Goff of Chieveley: I, for myself, can see no difficulty in law in reaching a conclusion that Mr. Ferguson may have been a lawful visitor in relation to Mr. Spence but a trespasser in relation to the council. Once it is accepted that two persons may be in occupation of the same land, it seems to me inevitable that on certain facts such a conclusion may have to be reached. If it be the case that one only of such occupiers authorises a third person to come onto the land, then plainly the third person is, vis-a-vis that occupier, a lawful visitor. But he may not be a lawful visitor vis-a-vis the other occupier. Whether he is so or not must, in my opinion, depend on the question whether the occupier who authorised him to enter had authority, actual (express or implied) or ostensible, from the other occupier to allow the third party onto the land. If he had, then the third party will be, vis-a-vis that other occupier, a lawful visitor. If he had not, then the third party will be, vis-a-vis that other occupier, a trespasser. No doubt, in the ordinary circumstances of life, the occupier who allows the third party to come onto the land will frequently have implied or ostensible authority so to do on behalf of the other occupier . . . But this may not always be so, as for example where the third party is aware that [one occupier] has expressly forbidden the [other occupier] to allow him on the site. These problems have, as I see it, to be solved by the application of the ordinary principles of agency law.

compare

Remember, some torts require physical harm to the victim before allowing recovery to property.

Another issue relating to the scope of the 1957 Act involves injury to property. Section 1(3)(b) allows recovery not only for personal injury, but also for injury to property, including 'the property of persons who are not themselves [the occupier's] visitors'. Therefore, if Brian is a visitor on Shima's property and steps into a hole and injures himself, he can recover for his injuries. If he injures himself and tears his trousers, he can recover for his injuries and the damaged trousers. Furthermore, if he only tears his trousers, he can recover for them, even if he has not suffered physical harm to himself. However, Brian's recovery does not stop there. If Brian is carrying a Ming vase owned by the British Museum when he trips, Shima is also liable for any damages to the vase. The outcome may seem surprising, since Shima has no connection to the British Museum and didn't invite the British Museum—in the form of the vase—to come onto her property, but this approach actually makes sense, because the British Museum cannot proceed directly against Shima to recover the amount of any damage to the vase. If the 1957 Act did not give Brian the right to recover against Shima, he would himself be liable to the British Museum. However, public policy considerations dictate that he should not have to bear the loss caused by Shima, since he is the victim of Shima's improper use of her property.

NOTE The British Museum, as a non-visitor to Shima's property, has no ability to assert a claim under the 1957 Act.

Oddly enough, the 1957 Act does not cover loss of property, even though it covers damages to property. There is no remedy at common law, either. *Tinsley v Dudley* [1951] 2 KB 18 involved a publican who was not liable to the owner of a motorcycle that was stolen from the yard of the pub. Thus, neither the 1957 Act nor the common law provides recovery for property that is destroyed or otherwise lost. In the case of Brian and Shima, Shima would not be liable under the 1957 Act if Brian left the Ming vase unguarded and allowed some unknown third party to walk off with it.

7.3.2 Common duty of care

Once the claimant has established that the 1957 Act applies and a duty exists, the claimant must establish that the duty was breached by the defendant. However, the claimant does not need to establish what the standard of care is, as would be true in a negligence case. Instead, the standard of care is set by statute.

● **Occupiers' Liability Act 1957**

> **2 Extent of occupiers' ordinary duty**
>
> (1) An occupier of premises owes the same duty, the 'common duty of care', to all his visitors, except in so far as he is free to and does extend, restrict, modify or exclude his duty to any visitor or visitors by agreement or otherwise.
>
> (2) The common duty of care is a duty to take such care as in all the circumstances of the case is reasonable to see that the visitor will be reasonably safe in using the premises for the purposes for which he is invited or permitted by the occupier to be there.
>
> (3) The circumstances relevant for the present purpose include the degree of care, and of want of care, which would ordinarily be looked for in such a visitor, so that (for example) in proper cases—
>   (a) an occupier must be prepared for children to be less careful than adults; and
>   (b) an occupier may expect that a person, in the exercise of his calling, will appreciate and guard against any special risks ordinarily incident to it, so far as the occupier leaves him free to do so.

Recall
Chapter 6 shows how the courts interpret statutes to glean Parliamentary intent regarding the standard and duty of care for a civil remedy. The 1957 Act is explicit on both counts.

Sections 1 to 3 of the 1957 Act describe the existence of the common duty of care and what the standard of care is. Some of these principles are similar to those of other torts, such as negligence, but in this area of law you do not need to cull through numerous cases to identify the relevant concepts. Parliament has already decided what factors you should consider. The statute then goes on to identify how the duty can be discharged and the circumstances in which the duty is not triggered.

● **Occupiers' Liability Act 1957**

2 Extent of occupiers' ordinary duty

(4) In determining whether the occupier of premises has discharged the common duty of care to a visitor, regard is to be had to all the circumstances, so that (for example)—

    (a) where damage is caused to a visitor by a danger of which he had been warned by the occupier, the warning is not to be treated without more as absolving the occupier from liability, unless in all the circumstances it was enough to enable the visitor to be reasonably safe; and

    (b) where damage is caused to a visitor by a danger due to the faulty execution of any work of construction, maintenance or repair by an independent contractor employed by the occupier, the occupier is not to be treated without more as answerable for the danger if in all the circumstances he had acted reasonably in entrusting the work to an independent contractor and had taken such steps (if any) as he reasonably ought in order to satisfy himself that the contractor was competent and that the work had been properly done.

(5) The common duty of care does not impose on an occupier any obligation to a visitor in respect of risks willingly accepted as his by the visitor (the question whether a risk was so accepted to be decided on the same principles as in other cases in which one person owes a duty of care to another).

(6) For the purposes of this section, persons who enter premises for any purpose in the exercise of a right conferred by law are to be treated as permitted by the occupier to be there for that purpose, whether they in fact have his permission or not.

As seen in section 2(2), the common duty of care is limited to those uses and purposes that are associated with the reason for the visitor's entry onto the premises. If the visitor does not use the premises in accordance with the agreed-upon purpose, then he or she is a non-visitor and must rely on the 1984 Act for any remedy. Scrutton LJ described the limitations on the duty under the 1957 Act when he said in *The Carlgarth* [1927] P 93 that '[w]hen you invite a person into your house to use the stairs, you do not invite him to slide down the bannisters'. Therefore, an occupier may legitimately limit the type of activities a person may undertake on the premises. A plumber, for example, may be able to recover for any injuries suffered from an exploding toilet he or she has been asked to inspect, but will not be able to recover for injuries experienced while climbing on the toilet to see the view out of an upper window. Similarly, an occupier may limit the places to which a visitor may go—if the occupier tells a visitor to stay in the front yard, for example, no liability will exist if the visitor falls into a trench while wandering around in the back yard.

Interestingly, an occupier who wants to limit its own liability may contract certain duties out to an independent contractor who carries the necessary insurance. For example, in *Gwilliam v West Hertfordshire Hospitals NHS Trust* [2002] EWCA Civ 1041, a hospital holding a fair for fund-raising purposes hired an independent contractor to provide a 'splat wall', wherein people bounced from a trampoline onto a wall covered in Velcro. The hospital specifically enquired about the independent contractor's insurance coverage. When injury occurred, it came out that the insurance policy had expired four days before the fair. In holding that the hospital was not liable to the claimant, the Court of Appeal noted that, to discharge the common duty of care under the 1957 Act, the hospital need not ask to see the contractor's insurance policy; it was enough that it had taken reasonable steps to ensure proper insurance coverage for any potential injuries. The Court of Appeal upheld this line of reasoning in *Maguire v Sefton Metropolitan Borough Council* [2006] EWCA Civ 316, wherein the claimant was injured on the defendant's exercise equipment. The defendant had hired an independent contractor to perform inspection and maintenance of the equipment. In so doing, the defendant borough council fulfilled the common duty of care by relying on the expert advice and qualifications of the contractor, and thus would not be liable even though the contractor did not fulfil its duties properly.

Sometimes entrants are not specifically invited onto the premises by the occupier, but still have a right to be there. Since, according to section 2(6) of the 1957 Act, any person 'who enter[s] the premises for any purpose in the exercise of a right conferred by law are to be treated as permitted by the occupier to be there for that purpose, whether they in fact have his permission or not', postal carriers generally have a right to walk up to the front door to deliver the post. Thus, if the postal carrier trips on a flagstone, the occupier will not be heard to say that he or she did not authorize the postal carrier to come onto the land.

Whether the common duty of care has been met in any particular situation is a question of fact. However, some limitations exist as a matter of law, including remoteness of damage. Section 2(3) of the 1957 Act also indicates the factors that the court must consider when deciding whether the standard of care has been met. For example, subsection 2(3)(a) states 'an occupier must be prepared for children to be less careful than adults'. In making special accommodations for children, Parliament was carrying on a tradition that had been long established at common law. Pre-1957 decisions often speak of allurements when considering cases involving children. In interpreting the 1957 Act, foreseeability of harm is an important issue, just as it is in negligence. For example, the House of Lords in *Jolley v Sutton London Borough Council* [2000] 3 All ER 409, addressed the issue of the foreseeability of injury in a case involving a boy who was injured after he had jacked up an old, rotting boat on the defendant's land, intending to repair the boat. There, the Lords concluded that the injury was recoverable because the injury was caused in a foreseeable fashion.

One of the seminal cases involving an occupier's liability to a child is *Glasgow Corp v Taylor* [1922] 1 AC 44, wherein the House of Lords held that shiny red berries that looked like cherries or blackcurrants but were in fact highly poisonous could constitute a dangerous allurement to children, even if an adult would not be similarly attracted to them.

● ***Glasgow Corp v Taylor*** [1922] 1 AC 44

Lord Atkinson: The child in the present case was of right in the gardens...The defendants planted and maintained in the garden, near the playground, which children, like the deceased, frequented, a shrub bearing, to their knowledge, berries in appearance alluring and tempting to children, apparently harmless, but deadly poisonous. The deceased child

think point

What public policy considerations are playing out in these two decisions? Does it matter that the defendants in both cases are public entities?

161

yielded to the temptation which was presented to him. The defenders…knew of the nature, character, and strength of the temptation, and the dangerous, possibly deadly, result of yielding to it. The deceased child did not know, and could not reasonably have discovered, this latter fact…

The liability of defendants in cases of this kind rests, I think, in the last resort upon their knowledge that by their action they may bring children of tender years, unable to take care of themselves, yet inquisitive and easily tempted, into contact, in a place in which they, the children, have a right to be, with things alluring or tempting to them, and possibly in appearance harmless, but which, unknown to them and well known to the defendants, are hurtful or dangerous if meddled with. I am quite unable to see any difference in principle between placing amongst children a dangerous but tempting machine, of whose parts and action they are ignorant, and growing in the vicinity of their playground a shrub whose fruit is harmless in appearance and alluring, but, in fact, most poisonous. I think, in the latter case, as in the former, the defendant would be bound, by notice or warning or some other adequate means, to protect the children from injury. In this case the averments are that the appellants did nothing of the kind. If that be true, they were, in my view, guilty of negligence, giving the pursuer a right of action.

Still, an occupier wishing to avoid liability need not do away with every allurement on his or her premises. It may be enough to post a notice warning trespassers that they enter at their own risk or requiring children to be accompanied by a responsible adult.

Children are not the only people who get special treatment under the 1957 Act. Section 2(6) of the 1957 Act also provides a different standard of care for those who enter pursuant to their calling and who must face special risks. Therefore, a plumber who is injured by an exploding toilet cannot pursue a claim against the occupier, if an exploding toilet is the type of risk ordinarily incident to the plumbing business. However, if the plumber attempted to guard against that type of risk before exposing him or herself to it—for example, by checking to see if there were potentially explosive gases in the region—and the occupier prohibited the plumber from doing so, then the occupier might be liable to the plumber for injuries associated with the incident.

cross reference
Chapter 5 discussed notices and disclaimers in detail.

Warnings at common law discharged occupiers of any liability to the extent that the warning gave the visitor full knowledge of the type and extent of the danger. The rule was changed under the 1957 Act. Now, section 2(4)(a) indicates that a warning is not enough to discharge liability unless the warning 'was enough to enable the visitor to be reasonably safe'. To some extent, the adequacy of the notice may depend on whether any safer alternatives exist. In *Roles v Nathan* [1963] 2 All ER 908, Lord Denning stated that simply warning visitors about the danger of a footbridge crossing a stream is not enough to allow the occupier to escape liability for any injuries that may arise from the use of that bridge, if the bridge is the only means of entering the premises. However, if there were two bridges, one of which was safe and one which was not, then a warning as to the unsafe bridge would suffice. Furthermore, an occupier of land is not required to provide a notice to warn of a danger which is reasonably obvious. For example, in *Darby v National Trust* [2001] PIQR 27, the Court of Appeal indicated that a swimmer who drowned in a dark, murky pond knew the risk of swimming in open water, and a 'Danger—No Swimming' sign would have told the claimant 'no more than he already knew'. Furthermore, the fact that the occupier had failed to post the necessary notices warning against Weil's disease was not enough to result in liability, since, as May LJ stated, 'The risks are of an intrinsically different kind and so are any dependent duties'.

What if a warning is given but the claimant ignores it? Under section 2(5), an occupier has no obligation towards any visitor who willingly accepts a risk. The standard for assumption of the risk is the same as it is in negligence. At first it appeared as if assumption of the risk was merely one of the factors to consider when deciding liability under the 1957 Act, but more recent cases have held that a visitor's knowledge of **patent** dangers relieves the occupier from any liability under the Act. For example, in *Cotton v Derbyshire Dales District Council*, The Times, 20 June 1994, the Court of Appeal held that a landowner had no duty to warn visitors about the danger of a cliff that ran along the side of a footpath.

Furthermore, a claimant cannot act carelessly and then claim the entirety of his or her damages from the occupier. Courts agree that section 2(3) of the Law Reform (Contributory Negligence) Act 1945 apply to actions under the 1957 Act to the same extent that it applies to negligence actions.

7.3.3 Liability in contract

Before the enactment of the 1957 Act, the common law imposed certain implied terms about the safety of an occupier's premises into any contract between the occupier and a user of the premises. However, as indicated below, section 5 of the 1957 Act replaces the common-law duty of care with the common duty of care under the Act.

● **Occupiers' Liability Act 1957**

> **5 Implied term in contracts**
>
> (1) Where persons enter or use, or bring or send goods to, any premises in exercise of a right conferred by contract with a person occupying or having control of the premises, the duty he owes them in respect of dangers due to the state of the premises or to things done or omitted to be done on them, in so far as the duty depends on a term to be implied in the contract by reason of its conferring that right, shall be the **common duty of care**.
>
> (2) The foregoing subsection shall apply to fixed and moveable structures as it applies to premises.
>
> (3) This section does not affect the obligations imposed on a person by or by virtue of any contract for the hire of, or for the carriage for reward of persons or goods in, any vehicle, vessel, aircraft or other means of transport, or by or by virtue of any contract of bailment.

Importantly, by indicating that the common duty of care exists only 'in so far as the duty depends on a term to be implied in the contract', the 1957 Act allows the parties to create a higher or lower standard of care if they so desire. All the parties need to do is make that higher or lower standard of care explicit in the contract. If the parties have explicitly

---

cross reference
Assumption of the risk was discussed previously in chapter 5.

VOCABULARY
A 'patent' danger is one that can easily be seen. A 'latent' danger is one that is hidden. Think of the phrase 'patently obvious' to help distinguish them.

cross reference
For more on the defence of contributory negligence, see chapter 5.

VOCABULARY
Be careful of terms here. The 'common duty of care' is the duty imposed under and defined by section 2 of the 1957 Act, not the old common-law duty.

Recall

As you have learned—or will learn—in your contract course, an explicit contractual duty typically overrides an implied contractual duty.

....

VOCABULARY

A notice excludes or restricts liability while a warning alerts people to the existence of a particular danger on the premises.

....

stated that the duty of care will be less than the common duty of care in their contract, then another section of the 1957 Act applies, as discussed below.

One question is whether a claimant must proceed in contract, relying on the implied term discussed in section 5 of the 1957 Act, whenever the parties have entered into a contract, or whether the claimant may also proceed (or alternatively proceed) with a cause of action in tort. In *Sole v W J Hall Ltd* [1973] 1 All ER 1032, Swanick J held that those who entered the premises pursuant to a contract could proceed in contract under section 5(1) or in tort under section 2(1).

Under section 5 of the 1957 Act, the parties to a contract may alter the duty of care owed by the occupier of the premises to the visitor. However, another section of the 1957 Act—section 2(1)—also discusses the alteration of the common duty of care under the Act. That section indicates that an occupier owes the common duty of care to all visitors 'except in so far as he is free to and does extend, restrict, modify or exclude his duty to any visitor or visitors by agreement or otherwise'. That language has been interpreted as allowing an occupier to modify the common duty of care either by (1) contract—for example, by not allowing someone onto the premises without first getting a signed contract that lays out the occupier's obligations—or (2) clear and unequivocal **notice** about the scope of the occupier's duty.

Notice can be made in many different ways. For example, an occupier could affix a sign at the point of entry to the land. Alternatively, the occupier could put a notice into a programme or ticket giving access to the land, although the notice must be given before the entrant comes onto the land. According to the courts, the key is not whether the visitor has actually read the conditions but whether proper steps have been taken to draw the visitor's attention to them.

Whenever an occupier puts a limitation clause into a contract, that clause will be read in connection with section 3 of the 1957 Act. That section states:

....

● **Occupiers' Liability Act 1957**

3 Effect of contract on occupier's liability to third party

(1) Where an occupier of premises is bound by contract to permit persons who are strangers to the contract to enter or use the premises, the duty of care which he owes to them as his visitors cannot be restricted or excluded by that contract, but (subject to any provision of the contract to the contrary) shall include the duty to perform his obligations under the contract, whether undertaken for their protection or not, in so far as those obligations go beyond the obligations otherwise involved in that duty.

(2) A contract shall not by virtue of this section have the effect, unless it expressly so provides, of making an occupier who has taken all reasonable care answerable to strangers to the contract for dangers due to the faulty execution of any work of construction, maintenance or repair or other like operation by persons other than himself, his servants and persons acting under his direction and control.

(3) In this section 'stranger to the contract' means a person not for the time being entitled to the benefit of the contract as a party to it or as the successor by assignment or

> otherwise of a party to it or as the successor by assignment or otherwise of a party to it, and accordingly includes a party to the contract who has ceased to be so entitled.
>
> (4) Where by the terms or conditions governing any tenancy (including a statutory tenancy which does not in law amount to a tenancy) either the landlord or the tenant is bound, though not by contract, to permit persons to enter or use premises of which he is the occupier, this section shall apply as if the tenancy were a contract between the landlord and the tenant.

Under section 3(1), the occupier may not limit or restrict the duty of care owed to a stranger to the contract who is nevertheless on the premises by virtue of that contract. However, the occupier may be liable to that stranger for any heightened duty that is included in the contract (and whether the heightened duty is to be extended to the stranger is a question to be considered at trial). This, obviously, provides the highest degree of protection for the entrant, which is what Parliament intended.

NOTE The Unfair Contract Terms Act 1977 applies to both contracts and notices, and is discussed in more detail in chapter 5.

Critically, contracts or notices made to alter liability under the 1957 Act must be read in conjunction with the Unfair Contract Terms Act 1977. For example, section 2(1) of the Unfair Contract Terms Act 1977 limits the ability of a person to exclude or restrict liability.

TIP This is one of the areas where contract law and tort law overlap and is thus often the subject of examinations. Know how the Unfair Contract Terms Act 1977 applies to occupiers' liability under the 1957 Act. In particular, be familiar with section 1(1)(c) of the Unfair Contract Terms Act 1977, which mentions the 1957 Act. Remember also that the Unfair Contract Terms Act 1977 only refers to the Occupiers' Liability Act 1957, not the Occupiers' Liability Act 1984.

● **Unfair Contract Terms Act 1977**

> **2 Negligence liability**
>
> (1) A person cannot by reference to any contract term or to a notice given to persons generally or to particular persons exclude or restrict his liability for death or personal injury resulting from negligence.
>
> (2) In the case of other loss or damage, a person cannot so exclude or restrict his liability for negligence except in so far as the term or notice satisfies the requirement of reasonableness.
>
> (3) Where a contract term or notice purports to exclude or restrict liability for negligence a person's agreement to or awareness of it is not of itself to be taken as indicating his voluntary acceptance of any risk.

Simply agreeing or knowing about a contractual term or notice does not, by itself, mean that the visitor has assumed the risk of injury, according to section 2(3) of the 1977 Act. Therefore, a defendant cannot automatically assert the defence of *volenti non fit injuria* every time there is a contract term or notice altering the scope of liability.

Section 3(2) provides some relief from liability for an occupier with respect to work done by someone other than the occupier or the occupier's agents. However, you must apply the provision carefully, since it only relates to 'the faulty execution of any work of construction, maintenance or repair or other like operation.' Dangers not falling under that category of activities are not covered by section 3(2).

Section 1 of the Unfair Contract Terms Act 1977 defines the scope of Part I of that Act, and, in so doing, refers to the Occupiers' Liability Act 1957.

. . . .

● **Unfair Contract Terms Act 1977**

1 Scope of Part I

(1) For the purposes of this Part of this Act, 'negligence' means the breach—
  (a) of any obligation, arising from the express or implied terms of a contract, to take reasonable care or exercise reasonable skill in the performance of the contract;
  (b) of any common law duty to take reasonable care or exercise reasonable skill (but not any stricter duty);
  (c) of the common duty of care imposed by the Occupiers' Liability Act 1957 or the Occupiers' Liability Act (Northern Ireland) 1957.

(2) This Part of this Act is subject to Part III; and in relation to contracts, the operation of sections 2 to 4 and 7 is subject to the exceptions made by Schedule 1.

(3) In the case of both contract and tort, sections 2 to 7 apply (except where the contrary is stated in section 6(4)) only to business liability, that is liability for breach of obligations or duties arising—
  (a) from things done or to be done by a person in the course of a business (whether his own business or another's); or
  (b) from the occupation of premises used for business purposes of the occupier; and references to liability are to be read accordingly but liability of an occupier of premises for breach of an obligation or duty towards a person obtaining access to the premises for recreational or educational purposes, being liability for loss or damage suffered by reason of the dangerous state of the premises, is not a business liability of the occupier unless granting that person such access for the purposes concerned falls within the business purposes of the occupier.

(4) In relation to any breach of duty or obligation, it is immaterial for any purpose of this Part of this Act whether the breach was inadvertent or intentional, or whether liability for it arises directly or vicariously.

The only attempt to clarify the meaning of 'business purposes' is found in section 1(3)(b) of the 1977 Act, which states, 'liability of an occupier of premises for breach of an obligation or duty towards a person obtaining access to the premises for recreational or educational purposes, being liability for loss or damage suffered by reason of the dangerous state of the premises, is not a business liability of the occupier unless granting that person such access for the purposes concerned falls within the business purposes of the occupier'.

When other types of loss or damage are at issue, any attempt to restrict or exclude liability by contract is subject to the rule of reasonableness found in section 2(2) of the Unfair

Contract Terms Act 1977, quoted above. As you know (or will learn) from your contract course, 'reasonableness' under the Unfair Contract Terms Act 1977 is a somewhat difficult term to define. With reference to a contract term, 'reasonableness' is defined in section 11(1), quoted below. However, with reference to a notice, 'reasonableness' is defined in section 11(3). Of the two tests, the requirements regarding contract terms is probably easier for the claimant to meet, since the language concerning 'all the circumstances' in section 11(3) brings in events and facts that both include and extend beyond the circumstances contemplated by the parties. In both cases, however, sections 11(4) and 11(5) apply. These provisions identify the factors to be taken into account in determining reasonableness and indicate that the burden of proving reasonableness falls on the party claiming that it exists.

● **Unfair Contract Terms Act 1977**

> **11 The 'reasonableness' test**
>
> (1) In relation to a contract term, the requirement of reasonableness for the purposes of this Part of this Act, section 3 of the Misrepresentation Act 1967 and section 3 of the Misrepresentation Act (Northern Ireland) 1967 is that the term shall have been a fair and reasonable one to be included having regard to the circumstances which were, or ought reasonably to have been, known to or in the contemplation of the parties when the contract was made...
>
> (3) In relation to a notice (not being a notice having contractual effect), the requirement of reasonableness under this Act is that it should be fair and reasonable to allow reliance on it, having regard to all the circumstances obtaining when the liability arose or (but for the notice) would have arisen.
>
> (4) Where by reference to a contract term or notice a person seeks to restrict liability to a specified sum of money, and the question arises (under this or any other Act) whether the term or notice satisfies the requirement of reasonableness, regard shall be had in particular (but without prejudice to subsection (2) above in the case of contract terms) to—
>
>   (a) the resources which he could expect to be available to him for the purpose of meeting the liability should it arise; and
>
>   (b) how far it was open to him to cover himself by insurance.
>
> (5) It is for those claiming that a contract term or notice satisfies the requirement of reasonableness to show that it does.

Liability to non-visitors— Occupiers' Liability Act 1984

7.4.1 Pre-1984 common law

Obviously, not all who enter another person's premises do so with implicit or explicit permission. As discussed above, there are those whom the common law would call trespassers. Prior to 1984, the common law imposed a duty of care on an occupier akin to that in ordinary negligence. The occupier was not to use the property in such a way as to put others, including trespassers, in danger.

Upon the enactment of the Occupiers' Liability Act 1984 (1984 Act), the common law ceased to have any real relevance to liability to non-visitors for physical injury. As you will recall, the Occupiers' Liability Act 1957 made specific reference to the pre-1957 common law and incorporated many of its principles through that reference. The 1984 Act does not incorporate the common law in the same way and indeed indicates that it is to replace the common law altogether. Thus it is doubtful that any of the pre-1984 common law survives for these types of injuries.

However, the 1984 Act does not address damages to property. Therefore, the common law probably still retains some relevance to those sorts of damages.

7.4.2 Scope of liability

Section 1 of the 1984 Act sets forth an occupier's liability to uninvited entrants, including those called trespassers at the common law.

. . . .

● **Occupiers' Liability Act 1984**

1 Duty of occupier to persons other than his visitors

(1) The rules enacted by this section shall have effect, in place of the rules of the common law, to determine—

(a) whether any duty is owed by a person as occupier of premises to persons other than his visitors in respect of any risk of their suffering injury on the premises by reason of any danger due to the state of the premises or to things done or omitted to be done on them; and

(b) if so, what that duty is.

(2) For the purposes of this section, the persons who are to be treated respectively as an occupier of any premises (which, for those purposes, include any fixed or movable structure) and as his visitors are—

(a) any person who owes in relation to the premises the duty referred to in section 2 of the Occupiers' Liability Act 1957 (the common duty of care), and

(b) those who are his visitors for the purposes of that duty.

(3) An occupier of premises owes a duty to another (not being his visitor) in respect of any such risk as is referred to in subsection (1) above if—

(a) he is aware of the danger or has reasonable grounds to believe that it exists;

(b) he knows or has reasonable grounds to believe that the other is in the vicinity of the danger concerned or that he may come into the vicinity of the danger (in either case, whether the other has lawful authority for being in that vicinity or not); and

(c) the risk is one against which, in all the circumstances of the case, he may reasonably be expected to offer the other some protection.

. . .

(7) No duty is owed by virtue of this section to persons using the highway, and this section does not affect any duty owed to such persons.

(8) When a person owes a duty by virtue of this section, he does not, by reason of any breach of the duty, incur any liability in respect of any loss of or damage to property.

(9) In this section—

'highway' means any part of a highway other than a ferry or waterway;

'injury' means anything resulting in death or personal injury, including any disease and any impairment of physical or mental condition; and

'movable structure' includes any vessel, vehicle or aircraft.

Although this section appears relatively wide ranging at first, there are three fact scenarios that fall outside the Act. First, section 1(8) indicates that an occupier shall only be liable for personal injuries. Injuries to property are—unlike the 1957 Act—not covered. Therefore the pre-1984 common law position regarding damage to property still applies.

Second, under section 1(7), an occupier does not owe any duty to persons using a highway. Because this is a situation outside the scope of the 1984 Act, the common law, again, applies. The most important case discussing the duty owed to users of public ways is *British Railways Board v Herrington* [1972] AC 877, wherein a child who was on National Trust property passed through a gap in a fence and was injured on the railway tracks. In setting out the duty towards trespassers, Lord Morris of Borth-Y-Gest cited the duty of 'common humanity'.

● ***British Railways Board v Herrington*** [1972] AC 877

Lord Morris of Borth-y-Gest: By taking ordinary thought and exercising 'common sense and ordinary intelligence'—even apart from the guidance of common humanity—I think that the railways board would see that in the circumstances of this case there was a likelihood that some child might pass over the broken down fence and get on to the track with its live rail and be in peril of serious injury. Even though the child would be a trespasser ought it not to be their 'plain duty' to repair the fence? That would be a relatively simple operation not involving any unreasonable demands of time or labour or expense.

Finally, acts of the occupier that do not relate to the occupation of the premises fall outside the 1984 Act. In those situations, general principles of the common law will apply. Therefore, you would look to general principles of negligence, unless you had some other way of establishing a duty flowing from the defendant to the claimant, such as, for example, through breach of statutory duty.

According to the 1984 Act, three conditions must exist before an occupier may be found liable to a non-visitor. These three conditions are found in section 1(3) of the 1984 Act. Interestingly, these three conditions require courts to consider both objective and subjective elements. Subsections 1(3)(a) and 1(3)(b) are subjective, in that they focus on the individual occupier's state of mind. In some ways, this would appear to be an anomaly. For example, if Calvin occupies a particular piece of property but never takes a look around to see if there are any obvious dangers, Calvin—who has no actual knowledge and no way to reasonably foresee such dangers—will not meet the first two prongs of section 1(3). On the other hand, Donielle, another occupier, will fall under the first two elements of section 1(3) if she simply notices some dangers in passing but does nothing about them. At first glance, the 1984 Act almost seems to be rewarding unsafe practices by occupiers.

However, the third element of the test offsets these potential problems of public policy. On its face, section 1(3)(c) appears entirely objective, in that it brings the considerations of a 'reasonable' occupier into the analysis. However, section 1(3)(c) also focuses on all the circumstances of the case, which will permit the court to consider how and why the entrant came to be on the property. As it turns out, burglars and thieves are given little or no protection under the 1984 Act if their injury results from the dangerous nature of the premises. However, if their injury occurs as a result of the negligence of the occupier, then the burglar or trespasser may have a remedy, albeit outside the 1984 Act. For example, in *Revill v Newbery* [1996] 1 All ER 291, a burglar was injured when the defendant occupier negligently shot him during the burglary. The burglar was still able to sue in negligence, even though the 1984 Act did not apply.

7.4.3 Substance of the duty

Once you have evaluated whether the occupier owes a duty to a particular non-visitor, you must consider what the occupier must do to discharge his or her duty. The 1984 Act describes the occupier's duty in section 1(4).

NOTE The 1984 Act, like the 1957 Act, emphasizes the concept of reasonableness when defining the duty to the claimant. Look to the common law to help define that term.

● **Occupiers' Liability Act 1984**

> **1 Duty of occupier to persons other than his visitors**
>
> (4) Where, by virtue of this section, an occupier of premises owes a duty to another in respect of such a risk, the duty is to take such care as is reasonable in all the circumstances of the case to see that he does not suffer injury on the premises by reason of the danger concerned.

However, the 1984 Act—unlike the 1957 Act—gives an occupier the opportunity to discharge his or her duty by giving a warning, as indicated in section 1(5).

● **Occupiers' Liability Act 1984**

> **1 Duty of occupier to persons other than his visitors**
>
> (5) Any duty owed by virtue of this section in respect of a risk may, in an appropriate case, be discharged by taking such steps as are reasonable in all the circumstances of the case to give warning of the danger concerned or to discourage persons from incurring the risk.

Recall

The Unfair Contract Terms Act 1977 does not apply in cases involving the Occupiers' Liability Act 1984.

Warnings and notices thus operate very differently. A notice that states, 'Danger! Do not enter! Concealed mine shaft' may be sufficient to discharge a duty to an uninvited adult entrant under section 1(5) of the 1984 Act but might not be enough to avoid liability to a visitor under the 1957 Act. Furthermore, courts must consider whether merely reading and ignoring a notice such as this constitutes an assumption of the risk of injury. *Tichener v British Railways Board* [1983] 3 All ER 770, a case that pre-dates the 1984 Act, held that reading and ignoring a warning does not, by itself, allow a defence of *volenti non fit injuria*. However, section 1(6) of the 1984 Act suggests such a defence might exist, under the proper circumstances. The recent House of Lords case of *Tomlinson v Congleton Borough Council* [2003] UKHL 47 also suggests that an occupier—in this case, the occupier of a country park with a lake on it—can avoid liability for injuries resulting from dangers that are patently obvious. In that case, a man was paralysed after diving into shallow water despite the 'Dangerous Water—No Swimming' signs. The Lords held that there was no duty to make the property safe (as by fencing in all open water) for those who would willingly disregard the posted notices.

think point

Would a notice be sufficient to discharge a duty to a child or other person who could not read? Furthermore, if there are allurements on the property, might not a court classify a child as a visitor and thus avoid the application of section 1(5) of the 1984 Act altogether?

● **Occupiers' Liability Act 1984**

1 Duty of occupier to persons other than his visitors

(6) No duty is owed by virtue of this section to any person in respect of risks willingly accepted as his by that person (the question whether a risk was so accepted to be decided on the same principles as in other cases in which one person owes a duty of care to another).

NOTE Although the 1984 Act does not explicitly incorporate the common law to the same extent as the 1957 Act, this section of the 1984 Act does explicitly reply on reported case law. Even more importantly, this section of the 1984 Act does not limit itself to cases involving occupiers' liability—any case that discussed the acceptance of risk is potentially relevant. See chapter 5 for a further discussion of the defence of acceptance of the risk.

A related issue under the 1984 Act arose in *Keown v Coventry Healthcare NHS Trust* [2006] EWCA Civ 39. There, the Court of Appeal considered a claim from an 11-year-old child who fell after playing on a fire escape. The Court of Appeal held that recovery was not permitted, because a fire escape was not inherently dangerous. The injury was caused as a result of the claimant's own actions in choosing to climb over the railing in the way that he did. Since the injury did not arise as a result of the state of the defendant's property, liability could not result. In so deciding, Longmore LJ noted that the age of the claimant could be relevant, since 'premises which are not dangerous from the point of view of an adult can be dangerous for a child but it must be a question of fact and degree'. However, in this case the claimant knew and appreciated the danger. Since the case fell outside the provisions of section 1(1), (3), and (4) of the 1984 Act, the Court of Appeal did not have to explicitly reach the defence of *volenti non fit injuria*.

Finally, section 1(8) of the 1984 Act specifically states that non-visitors may not sue for the recovery of damages to property. Recall Brian, the clumsy carrier of the Ming vase in the example above. If he were a non-visitor on Shima's land, he would not only have to cover the cost of his ripped trousers himself but would also have to pay the British Museum for the damage to the Ming vase.

This outcome makes sense if one thinks about policy considerations such as allocation of risk and the ability to insure against harm. Brian or the British Museum is in the best position to know the value of the Ming vase and any potential dangers arising out of its transportation. They could easily take out insurance to cover any possible damage and therefore should be the one to shoulder the risk of harm. If Brian were particularly attached to his trousers, he could do the same. Shima—who cannot know that a Ming-carrying person will be wandering over her property—is not in a good position to insure against the possibility of this kind of astronomical financial risk. On the other hand, any landowner should be aware that uninvited entrants may come onto their premises and suffer minor (or possibly major) personal injury. Landowners typically insure against such risks, often for minimal cost.

. . . .

● **Occupiers' Liability Act 1984**

1 Duty of occupier to persons other than his visitors

(8) Where a person owes a duty by virtue of this section, he does not, by reason of any breach of the duty, incur any liability in respect of any loss of or damage to property.

7.5 Liability to persons outside the premises

Up until this point, we have been discussing occupiers' liability for injuries occurring on the premises. However, some aspect of the property may pose a danger to persons off the premises. A slate could fall off a rooftop and smash into a car parked on the street nearby. A conker could rap some by passer on the head or lurk underfoot, ready to cause someone to slip and fall on a public pavement.

There are several special causes of action for injuries caused elsewhere as a result of activities or characteristics of the defendant's land, including nuisance and *Rylands v Fletcher*. However, occupiers are also under a general common law duty to take reasonable care to prevent dangers on the premises from injuring persons or property off the premises. The danger can arise many different ways: disrepair of the premises (such as a ramshackle wall that falls down onto the neighbouring property), a man-made hazard (such as medieval enthusiast who builds a mock catapult on his property) or a natural hazard

cross reference
See chapter 8 for more on nuisance and chapter 9 for more on liability under Rylands v Fletcher.

(such as flooding resulting from too much rain overfilling a pond). Owners of neighbouring land are also entitled to mutual structural support, so that activities on one piece of property do not cause subsistence or collapse of buildings next door. Although some or all of these activities might support a claim in nuisance or *Rylands v Fletcher*—and, indeed, that is usually the best course of action, as will be described in later chapters—a claimant has the right to pursue any cause of action he or she wishes, or even to pursue all possible claims in the alternative.

There are two problem areas to consider, however. First, what happens when a tenant sues a landlord for damage that arose as a result of defective repairs on premises over which the landlord has retained control? The case law is unsettled. On the one hand, some courts have held that the landlord should be liable. For example, in *Cunard v Antifyre Ltd* [1933] 1 KB 551:

> Some defective roofing and guttering, which formed part of the premises retained by the defendant landlord, fell into a part of the premises let by him to the plaintiff tenant. As a result, his wife was injured and his goods were damaged. Damages in general negligence were awarded to both the tenant and his wife.

However, a different result arose in *Cheater v Cater* [1918] 1 KB 247, an earlier case which was not cited in *Cunard v Antifyre Ltd* [1933] 1 KB 551. There, the Court of Appeal held that a landlord was not liable to a tenant whose horse died after eating poisonous leaves from a yew tree that was on the landlord's premises and that had been there when the tenant took over the lease.

It appears as if *Cunard v Antifyre Ltd* [1933] 1 KB 551 is the more persuasive precedent, based on later cases such as *Taylor v Liverpool Corpn* [1939] 3 All ER 329, wherein one of the tenant's children was injured by the fall of a chimney stack into the yard adjoining the premises. The defendant landlords had negligently maintained the chimney, which was under their control. Stable J granted recovery to the plaintiff in negligence, distinguishing *Cheater v Cater* [1918] 1 KB 247 on the grounds that the danger involved—the yew tree—had been in existence at the time the tenant took over the lease. Certainly the outcome in *Cunard v Antifyre Ltd* [1933] 1 KB 551 and *Taylor v Liverpool Corpn* [1939] 3 All ER 329 seems preferable, since it encourages landlords to make retained property—including common property shared by several tenants, such as foyers and stairwells—safe.

The other difficult question involves injuries to adjoining premises caused by a third person who is on the occupiers' premises. Not surprisingly, courts have been hesitant to impose liability in these situations, absent extraordinary circumstances. In particular, the House of Lords held in *Smith v Littlewoods Organisation Ltd* [1987] AC 241 that there is no duty when the actions of vandals or burglars result in injury to adjoining property, even when the occupier has contributed to the injury by allowing the premises to fall into disrepair or by failing to keep the premises secure from unauthorized intruders. If no special relationship exists between the third party and the occupier, liability will likely not result.

think point
What policy considerations indicate that only dwellings should receive additional protections?

7.6 Liability of non-occupiers

For the most part, liability for premises is limited to occupiers, meaning those with either exclusive or, in the case of multiple occupiers, sufficient control over the premises. However, the law has recognized that, in some limited circumstances, non-occupiers can and should be held liable for injuries to others.

7.6.1 Defective Premises Act 1972—Scope

Section 1 of the Defective Premises Act 1972 (1972 Act) imposes strict liability on any 'person taking on work for or in connection with the provision of a dwelling' to ensure that any work is completed in 'a workmanlike, or as the case may be professional manner, with proper materials and so that as regards that work the dwelling will be fit for habitation when completed'. Case law has established that section 1 of the 1972 Act applies to omissions as well as to affirmative acts. Notably, the 1972 Act speaks of 'dwellings', and thus is not applicable to commercial properties.

On one hand, the protections offered by the 1972 Act appear quite broad, since section 1(3) of the Act indicates that it applies to anyone involved in building new homes, including builders, contractors, architects, developers and local authorities. However, the strict liability under section 1 is limited by its short statute of limitations, which begins to run immediately upon the completion of the dwelling. This can cause problems, however, when damages may not arise or be known to exist for some time.

Because of these and other perceived limitations, the 1972 Act fell into disrepute very soon after it was passed. Instead, the courts imposed a common law duty of care on builders, local authorities and other construction industry professionals whenever it appeared reasonably foreseeable that their negligence would cause loss or injury. The case that brought about this revolution, *Anns v Merton London Borough Council* [1978] AC 728, became the centre of controversy, since the duty was extended not just to initial purchasers of the property, but also to subsequent purchasers or visitors to the property. This broad extension of the 'neighbour principle' of *Donoghue v Stevenson* was intended to provide protections to consumers that the 1972 Act failed to give, but the principle drew criticism from the House of Lords and was finally extinguished in 1991, in the seminal case of *Murphy v Brentwood District Council* [1991] 1 AC 398. There, a local authority had, in accordance with its statutory duty, passed on plans for construction of a new home. The house was built with a defective foundation that caused damage to walls and pipes. The plaintiff suffered economic loss as a result of the diminished value of the house as built, as compared to the value of a properly built home.

NOTE This case also discusses recovery for economic loss and the differences between recovery in contract and recovery in tort. See chapter 13 for a further discussion of those points.

● *Murphy v Brentwood District Council* [1991] 1 AC 398

> Lord Keith of Kinkel: The present problem is concerned with the scope of the duty. The question is whether the appellant council owed the respondent a duty to take reasonable care to safeguard him against the particular kind of damage which he has in fact suffered,

which was not injury to person or health nor damage to anything other than the defective house itself...

[A]n essential feature of the species of liability in negligence established by Donoghue v. Stevenson was that the carelessly manufactured product should be intended to reach the injured consumer in the same state as that in which it was put up with no reasonable prospect of intermediate examination... It is the latency of the defect which constitutes the mischief. There may be room for disputation as to whether the likelihood of intermediate examination and consequent actual discovery of the defect has the effect of negativing a duty of care or of breaking the chain of causation... But there can be no doubt that, whatever the rationale, a person who is injured through consuming or using a product of the defective nature of which he is well aware has no remedy against the manufacturer. In the case of a building, it is right to accept that a careless builder is liable, on the principle of Donoghue v. Stevenson, where a latent defect results in physical injury to anyone, whether owner, occupier, visitor or passer-by, or to the property of any such person. But that principle is not apt to bring home liability towards an occupier who knows the full extent of the defect yet continues to occupy the building. The Dorset Yacht case was concerned with the circumstances under which one person might come under a duty to another to take reasonable care to prevent a third party from committing a tort against that other. So the case had affinities with Anns where a local authority was held to be under a duty to take reasonable care to prevent a builder from causing damage through carelessness to subsequent occupiers of houses built by him. In Dorset Yacht, however, the damage caused was physical damage to property, and... the prison officers in charge of the Borstal boys had created a potential situation of danger for the owners of yachts moored in the vicinity of the encampment by bringing the boys into that locality. No such feature was present in Anns...

The jump which is here made from liability under the Donoghue v. Stevenson principle for damage to person or property caused by a latent defect in a carelessly manufactured article to liability for the cost of rectifying a defect in such an article which is ex hypothesi no longer latent is difficult to accept... there is no liability in tort upon a manufacturer towards the purchaser from a retailer of an article which turns out to be useless or valueless through defects due to careless manufacture. The loss is economic. It is difficult to draw a distinction in principle between an article which is useless or valueless and one which suffers from a defect which would render it dangerous in use but which is discovered by the purchaser in time to avert any possibility of injury. The purchaser may incur expense in putting right the defect, or, more probably, discard the article. In either case the loss is purely economic... in the case of a house the builder would not be liable to a purchaser where the defect was discovered in time to prevent injury but that a local authority which had failed to discover the defect by careful inspection during the course of construction was so liable...

Consideration of the nature of the loss suffered in this category of cases is closely tied up with the question of when the cause of action arises. Lord Wilberforce in Anns [1978] A.C. 728, 760 regarded it as arising when the state of the building was such that there was present an imminent danger to the health or safety of persons occupying it. That state of affairs may exist when there is no actual physical damage to the building itself... On that view there would be no cause of action where the building had suffered no damage (or possibly... only very slight damage) but a structural survey had revealed an underlying defect, presenting imminent danger. Such a discovery would inevitably cause a fall in the value of the building, resulting in economic loss to the owner. That such is the nature of the loss is made clear in cases where the owner abandons the building as incapable of being put in a safe condition…or where he choses [sic] to sell it at the lower value rather than undertake remedial works…

In my opinion it must now be recognised that, although the damage in Anns was characterised as physical damage by Lord Wilberforce, it was **purely economic loss**…In Anns v. Merton London Borough Council [1978] A.C. 728, it was held by the House of Lords that a local government authority owed a relevant duty of care, in respect of inspection of the foundations of a building, to persons who subsequently became long term lessees (either as original lessees or as assignees) of parts of the building. Lord Wilberforce, at p. 759, in a speech with which three of the other four members of the House of Lords agreed, expressed the conclusion that the appropriate classification of damage sustained by the lessees by reason of the inadequacy of the foundations of the completed building was 'material, physical damage, and what is recoverable is the amount of expenditure necessary to restore the dwelling to a condition in which it is no longer a danger to the health or safety of persons occupying and possibly (depending on the circumstances) expenses arising from necessary displacement.' While, in a case where a subsequent purchaser or long term tenant reasonably elects to retain the premises and to reinforce the foundations, one possible measure of the damages involved in the actual inadequacy would (if such damages were recoverable) be that suggested by his Lordship, I respectfully disagree with the classification of the loss sustained in such circumstances as 'material, physical damage.' Whatever may be the position with respect to consequential damage to the fabric of the building or to other property caused by subsequent collapse or subsidence, the loss or injury involved in the actual inadequacy of the foundations cannot, in the case of a person who purchased or leased the property after the inadequacy existed but before it was known or manifest, properly be seen as ordinary physical or material damage. The only property which could be said to have been damaged in such a case is the building. The building itself could not be said to have been subjected to 'material, physical damage' by reason merely of the inadequacy of its foundations since the building never existed otherwise than with its foundations in that state. Moreover, even if the inadequacy of the foundations could be seen as material, physical damage to the building, it would be damage to property in which a future purchaser or tenant had no interest at all at the time when it occurred. Loss or injury could only be sustained by such a purchaser or tenant on or after the acquisition of the freehold or leasehold estate without knowledge of the faulty foundations. It is arguable that any such loss or injury should be seen as being sustained at the time of acquisition when, because of ignorance of the inadequacy of the foundations, a higher price is paid (or a higher rent is agreed to be paid) than is warranted by the intrinsic worth of the freehold or leasehold estate that is being acquired. Militating against that approach is the consideration that, for so long as the inadequacy of the foundations is neither known nor manifest, no identifiable loss has come home: if the purchaser or tenant sells the freehold or leasehold estate within that time, he or she will sustain no loss by reason of the inadequacy of the foundations. The alternative, and in my view preferable, approach is that any loss or injury involved in the actual inadequacy of the foundations is sustained only at the time when that inadequacy is first known or manifest. It is only then that the actual diminution in the market value of the premises occurs. On either approach, however, any loss involved in the actual inadequacy of the foundations by a person who acquires an interest in the premises after the building has been completed is merely economic in its nature.'…

It being recognised that the nature of the loss held to be recoverable in Anns was pure economic loss, the next point for examination is whether the avoidance of loss of that nature fell within the scope of any duty of care owed to the plaintiffs by the local authority. On the basis of the law as it stood at the time of the decision the answer to that question must be in the negative. The right to recover for pure economic loss, not flowing from physical injury, did not then extend beyond the situation where the loss had been sustained through reliance on negligent mis-statements, as in Hedley Byrne....Upon analysis, the nature of the duty held by Anns to be incumbent upon the local authority went very much further than a duty to take reasonable care to prevent injury to safety or health. The duty held to exist may be formulated as one to take reasonable care to avoid putting a future inhabitant owner of a house in a position in which he is threatened, by reason of a defect in the house, with avoidable physical injury to person or health and is obliged, in order to continue to occupy the house without suffering such injury, to expend money for the purpose of rectifying the defect.

The existence of a duty of that nature should not, in my opinion, be affirmed without a careful examination of the implications of such affirmation. To start with, if such a duty is incumbent upon the local authority, a similar duty must necessarily be incumbent also upon the builder of the house. If the builder of the house is to be so subject, there can be no grounds in logic or in principle for not extending liability upon like grounds to the manufacturer of a chattel. That would open up an exceedingly wide field of claims...

In my opinion it is clear that Anns did not proceed upon any basis of established principle, but introduced a new species of liability governed by a principle indeterminate in character but having the potentiality of covering a wide range of situations, involving chattels as well as real property, in which it had never hitherto been thought that the law of negligence had any proper place...

In my opinion there can be no doubt that Anns has for long been widely regarded as an unsatisfactory decision...I think it must now be recognised that it did not proceed on any basis of principle at all, but constituted a remarkable example of judicial legislation. It has engendered a vast spate of litigation, and each of the cases in the field which have reached this House has been distinguished...There can be no doubt that to depart from the decision would re-establish a degree of certainty in this field of law which it has done a remarkable amount to upset...

It is also material that Anns has the effect of imposing upon builders generally a liability going far beyond that which Parliament thought fit to impose upon house builders alone by the Defective Premises Act 1972, a statute very material to the policy of the decision but not adverted to in it...

My Lords, I would hold that Anns was wrongly decided as regards the scope of any private law duty of care resting upon local authorities in relation to their function of taking steps to secure compliance with building byelaws or regulations and should be departed from. It follows that Dutton v. Bognor Regis Urban District Council [1972] 1 Q.B. 373 should be overruled, as should all cases subsequent to Anns which were decided in reliance on it.

Since *Murphy v Brentwood District Council* [1991] 1 AC 398, the 1972 Act has regained its position as the primary mechanism by which liability is to be imposed on non-occupiers. As this case demonstrates, the common law still has a role to play, primarily in situations where a defect is latent, as occurred in *Donoghue v Stevenson* [1932] AC 562, and the damage experienced is either personal injury or damage to property other than the building itself. When a patent defect is at issue, a builder is not generally liable for the cost of removing or fixing that defect, although the builder may be liable if personal injuries or damages to other property occur and if it is considered unreasonable both for the occupier to have removed the damage and for the claimant to have run the risk of injury due to the defect.

Although section 1 of the 1972 Act has its limitations, other aspects of the 1972 Act play a vital role in protecting landowners and others from harm, as described below.

7.6.2 Defective Premises Act 1972—Builders

Now that the 1972 Act has regained a position of respect under the law, it is more likely to be applied, thus creating a real risk of liability of non-occupiers for injuries arising out of residential property. Section 3 of the 1972 Act describes the liability of builders.

● **Defective Premises Act 1972**

> **3 Duty of care with respect to work done on premises not abated by disposal of premises**
>
> (1) Where work of construction, repair, maintenance or demolition or any other work is done on or in relation to premises, any duty of care owed, because of the doing of the work, to persons who might reasonably be expected to be affected by defects in the state of the premises created by the doing of the work shall not be abated by the subsequent disposal of the premises by the person who owed the duty.

Thus, the 1972 Act can result in liability to those who simply visit the premises, even though the builder has no direct contractual relationship with those persons, so long as those visitors 'might reasonably be expected to be affected by defects in the state of the premises created by the doing of the work'. Furthermore, the builder's liability under the Act does not cease when the property is sold, but continues on to the purchaser and the purchaser's visitors. Thus, for example, if Carl improperly repaired Clara's wonky front step, he is liable not only to Clara and her visitors, but to Denise (who purchased the house from Clara) and her visitors.

Section 3 of the 1972 Act does not cover all contingencies, however. Omissions do not seem to be included under the Act, meaning someone who suffers as a result of an omission will have to rely on the pre-existing common law. Under those cases, liability for negligent construction or repair could extend not only to the person who occupied the premises at the time the repairs were made and his or her visitors, but also to subsequent occupiers and their visitors.

The question of economic loss relating to negligent repairs and construction has been a thorny one. At one point, case law—particularly *Anns v Merton London Borough Council* [1978] AC 728—suggested that a party could recover for that type of loss. Since then, the House of Lords has set the record straight in *Murphy v Brentwood District Council* [1991] 1 AC 398, as indicated in the excerpt above.

7.6.3 Defective Premises Act 1972—other non-occupiers

Builders are not the only non-occupiers who may become liable to occupiers and visitors to a property. Architects and designers are in a position similar to that of builders. First, architects and designers are included in the strict liability regime provided for under section 1 of the 1972 Act. Second, architects and designers owe a duty of care to occupiers and their visitors, including subsequent occupiers and their visitors, under *Murphy v Brentwood District Council* [1991] 1 AC 398.

A local authority can also become liable to occupiers and visitors by virtue of the local authority's acting as a builder and/or contractor. For example, in *Rimmer v Liverpool County Council* [1985] QB 1, a local council was liable when an occupier of a council flat injured himself when he fell against a glass panel that was too thin to be safe. However, a local authority must act directly (such as by acting as a builder or contractor) for liability to ensue. Local authorities who simply inspect and approve premises for habitation under the local authorities' general oversight capacity will not be liable to an occupier or visitor for any injury to person or property caused by defects in the construction of the building. Although some might consider such an outcome illogical, since the purpose behind the local authority's inspection is to make buildings safe, to hold otherwise would cause the local authority to act as an insurer for all buildings constructed in its geographic region. Economically speaking, that could be disastrous and would provide no incentive for private persons—either those involved in the design and construction of a building or those involved in purchasing a building—to take proper precautionary measures, including the acquisition of insurance.

Finally, landlords can become liable in tort even if they are not in occupation of the premises. For example, if a landlord is responsible for the construction or repair of property, the landlord may be liable under the common law. *Rimmer v Liverpool City Council* [1985] QB 1. Furthermore, section 4 of the 1972 Act creates important statutory duties for landlords who are under an obligation to repair or maintain the premises or who are permitted to carry out repairs.

· ·

● **Defective Premises Act 1972**

> **4 Landlord's duty of care in virtue of obligation or right to repair premises demised**
>
> (1) Where premises are let under a tenancy which puts on the landlord an obligation to the tenant for the maintenance or repair of the premises, the landlord owes to all persons who might reasonably be expected to be affected by defects in the state of the premises a duty to take such care as is reasonable in all the circumstances to see that they are reasonably safe from personal injury or from damage to their property caused by a relevant defect.
>
> (2) The said duty is owed if the landlord knows (whether as the result of being notified by the tenant or otherwise) or if he ought in all the circumstances to have known of the relevant defect.

(3) In this section 'relevant defect' means a defect in the state of the premises existing at or after the material time and arising from, or continuing because of, an act or omission by the landlord which constitutes or would if he had had notice of the defect, have constituted a failure by him to carry out his obligation to the tenant for the maintenance or repair of the premises....

Therefore, the landlord must comply with the rule of reasonableness in repairing or maintaining property that is under his or her control.

For more revision tips, including self-test questions and suggestions for further reading, see the Online Resource Centre at www.oxfordtextbooks.co.uk/orc/strong_complete/.

revision tasks

Occupiers' liability is perhaps the most heavily statutory aspect of tort law. To understand this area of law, you must know the precise language of the 1957 Act and the 1984 Act. Some of the following tasks will help you organize your materials into a workable outline.

- Identify the similarities and differences between the 1957 Act and the 1984 Act.

- Be aware how the Unfair Contract Terms Act 1977 affects attempts to limit or eliminate liability for occupiers.

- Understand the liability of non-occupiers under the Defective Premises Act 1972 and be aware of how the common law first expanded and then narrowed the liability of builders, contractors, designers and other non-occupiers for defects associated with premises.

8 Nuisance

8.1 Introduction

The previous chapter discussed liability resulting when injuries occur on an occupier's premises. However, owning or occupying land can also result in liability to third parties who never even set foot on the property. This liability arises through the law of nuisance, which is discussed in this chapter, and *Rylands v Fletcher* liability, which discussed in the next chapter, and/or general principles of negligence.

Two types of nuisance exist—private nuisance, where the harm is done to one particular person, and public nuisance, where the harm is done to the public at large, although, as shall be seen, an individual cause of action may exist if there is heightened injury to the claimant. Private nuisance is the more common of the two torts and will thus be given much more attention.

This chapter will proceed as follows:

- Elements of private nuisance;
- Possible claimants;
- Possible defendants;
- Nuisance and other torts;
- Remedies;
- Defences; and
- Elements of public nuisance.

8.2 Elements of private nuisance

To state a cause of action in private nuisance, a claimant must show an activity or state of affairs on the defendant's land that causes a substantial and unreasonable interference with the claimant's land or with the claimant's use or enjoyment of that land. Interestingly, the law does not focus on the act of the defendant so much as it is on the effect on the claimant. For example, the tort does not require that the *defendant* act unreasonably; it simply requires an unreasonable (and significant) interference with the *claimant's* protected interests. This emphasis is the opposite of other torts, such as negligence, which focus on the reasonableness of the defendant's actions. Nuisance is also different than other torts that require an objective, context-neutral analysis, since what may be an 'unreasonable' or 'significant' interference with another's property under one set of circumstances (for example, a neighbour who blasts loud music at 2 am in a quiet, residential setting) may not be unreasonable or significant under another set of circumstances (if, for example, the music was played at the same time and at the same volume level, but in a commercial district next to a noisy motorway).

The reasonableness at issue in nuisance is the reasonableness of the *effect* of the defendant's action, not the reasonableness of the conduct itself. Don't confuse this sort of reasonableness with the 'reasonable person' test in negligence, which emphasizes the desire to avoid harm to others altogether. Nuisance focuses on the reasonableness of a harm that does, in fact, arise, even if the defendant has taken every possible—or every reasonable—step to avoid that harm.

Thus, there are two elements to evaluate when considering whether nuisance exists. First, was there a substantial interference with the claimant's land? Second, was that interference unreasonable?

8.2.1 Substantial interference

Some torts—most notably, negligence—require the claimant to have suffered an injury before the court can even consider making an award. Other torts, such as libel, do not require the claimant to demonstrate that he or she has suffered any harm whatsoever. Nuisance falls into the first category of torts and requires some sort of harmful effect on the claimant before a cause of action may be initiated.

However, the effect on the claimant need not be tangible. Certainly the law allows recovery for physical damage to the claimant's property, but the law also permits a claimant to sue for damage to the use or enjoyment of his or her property. **Use and enjoyment** cases often arise when the claimant is offended by certain smells or sounds. For example, a claimant may be able to recover for the odour emanating from a nearby factory, even if nothing from the factory ever lands on the claimant's property and even if many people like the smell (for example, of biscuits baking).

Both tangible and intangible interference with property are actionable, but courts analyse them differently. Because courts consider interference with the use or enjoyment of another's property to be less serious than interference with the property itself, the law requires the claimant to put up with some types of activities, even if they technically interfere with the use or enjoyment of the land. As Lord Wright said in *Sedleigh-Denfield v O'Callaghan* [1940] AC 880, a 'balance has to be maintained between the right of the occupier to do what he likes with his own [land], and the right of his neighbour not to be interfered with'.

Nuisance may be experienced in many different ways, which makes it difficult for courts to formulate a specific legal test. However, courts have, on occasion, attempted to describe the necessary requirements. One of the first tests for nuisance was enunciated in *Walter v Selfe* (1851) 4 De G & Sm 315, where the court had to consider air pollution stemming from the manufacture of bricks.

● *Walter v Selfe* [1851] 4 De G & Sm 315

> Knight Bruce VC: [T]his inconvenience [is] to be considered in fact as more than fanciful, more than one of mere delicacy or fastidiousness, as an inconvenience materially interfering with the ordinary comfort physically of human existence, not merely according to elegant or dainty modes and habits of living, but according to plain and simple notions among the English people.

If this sort of interference exists, then so, too, may nuisance. However, the test in *Walter v Selfe* (1851) 4 De G & Sm 315 is still relatively vague, and courts have traditionally tended to focus on at least two factors when trying to decide whether a particular interference is substantial. First, the court looks to see if the claimant is abnormally sensitive to the defendant's activity. Usually this abnormal sensitivity relates to the claimant's business. For example, *Robinson v Kilvert* (1889) 41 Ch D 88 involved a landlord who allowed the hot air from the cellar (over which he retained control) to escape to the tenant's premises above. The Court of Appeal held that the landlord was not liable in nuisance, even though the hot air ruined the paper that the tenant was storing on the premises. The court reasoned that the landlord should not be required to alter his behaviour simply because the tenant's business was abnormally sensitive to heat. If the transfer of heat would not have injured anyone other than this tenant, a cause of action in nuisance could not succeed, and the court refused to **enjoin** the landlord from carrying on his normal business.

VOCABULARY
When a court 'enjoins' someone, it enters an injunction or an injunctive order requiring that person to do or, more frequently, not to do something.

compare

In chapter 4 in negligence, we discussed the 'egg shell skull' claimant and concluded that a defendant takes a claimant as he or she finds that person. Thus, the claimant's special characteristics are, for the most part, irrelevant in determining whether a cause of action in negligence exists. In those cases, the defendant was liable for the damage caused, even if the claimant was unusually sensitive. However, as seen here, nuisance law takes a different approach.

A similar outcome was handed down in *Bridlington Relay Ltd v Yorkshire Electricity Board* [1965] Ch 436. There, the defendants owned and operated a power line that interfered with the plaintiff's business, which involved the relaying of radio and television signals to individual subscribers. The court said that no nuisance existed because interference with television viewing was not a substantial interference. The House of Lords also considered television reception in 1997, in *Hunter v Canary Wharf Ltd* [1997] AC 655. There, the plaintiffs' new building interfered with television reception in a neighbouring building.

The House of Lords stated that, although interference with television reception 'might in appropriate circumstances be protected', 'more is required than the mere presence of a neighbouring building to give rise to an actionable private nuisance'. The rationale was that, since the law does not prohibit a landowner from constructing a building that interferes with the light or air that passes to a neighbour's property, constructing a building that interferes with television reception is equally permissible. Thus, claimants cannot do anything they wish on their property; some give-and-take with the outside world is required.

Once a claimant proves nuisance, he or is able to recover the full scope of damages, no matter whether those damages are far greater than that would have been experienced by an 'ordinary' claimant. For example, in *McKinnon Industries Ltd v Walker* [1951] 3 DLR 577, the Privy Council held that the owner of a factory had to pay a significant amount of damages to a nearby commercial orchid-grower whose plants had been damaged by sulphur dioxide gas coming from the factory. In that case, even a non-sensitive land-owner would have found the use or enjoyment of the premises diminished by the presence of the gas, so it was immaterial that the defendant had to pay an unexpectedly high amount.

The other factor that the courts focus on when determining whether an injury is substantial involves the location of the premises in question. Conduct that may be absolutely appropriate in a commercial context may constitute a nuisance in a residential setting.

In *Sturges v Bridgman* (1879) 11 Ch D 852, a physician had complained about the noise coming from a nearby confectioner, whose pestle and mortar were disturbing the physician's business. Thesiger LJ noted that the neighbourhood was made up primarily of medical specialists who expected and required a certain degree of peaceful quiet to conduct their business. Thus, when considered in context, the confectioner's actions constituted a nuisance.

. . . .

● *Sturges v Bridgman* (1879) 11 Ch D 852

> Thesiger LJ: Whether anything is a nuisance or not is a question to be determined, not merely by an abstract consideration of the thing itself, but in reference to its circumstances; what would be a nuisance in Belgrave Square would not necessarily be so in Bermondsey; and where a locality is devoted to a particular trade . . . [the court] would be justified in finding, and may be trusted to find, that the trade . . . is not an actionable wrong.

As important as locality is, it is not the only factor that is important. Furthermore, the predominant use of a neighbourhood may change over time. Courts may also consider whether there has been any planning permission that changes the use of the neighbourhood. For example, in *Gillingham Borough Council v Medway (Chatham) Dock Co Ltd* [1993] QB 343, the local council had given planning permission to change the use of a naval dockyard to a commercial dockyard. As a result, the area became very noisy at night. Buckley J stated that the change in use should have been taken into account, since, 'where planning of permission is given . . . the question of nuisance will thereafter fall to be decided by reference to a neighbourhood with...[the new] development or use and not as it was previously'. However, planning permission alone will not justify activities that would otherwise constitute a nuisance.

The discussion above focuses on amenity nuisance, which involves an injury to the use and enjoyment of premises. Nuisance can also involve physical injury to the land, although locality is not a major factor when the nuisance involves physical damage. The leading case of *St Helen's Smelting Co v Tipping* (1865) 11 HL Cas 642 involved physical damage to plaintiff's shrubbery caused by noxious fumes emitted by the defendants' copper-smelting plant. In his opinion, Lord Westbury clearly distinguished between amenity damages—which 'depend greatly on the circumstances of the place where the thing complained of actually occurs'—and physical damages. However, physical damages—just like amenity damages—must be substantial to be recoverable.

Not everyone agrees that the courts have drawn a defensible distinction between different types of damage.

● Conor Gearty, *'The Place of Private Nuisance in a Modern Law of Torts'*,
   [1989] Cambridge Law Journal 215

As things stand at present, no clear distinction is drawn between physical and non-physical damage to the land of a neighbour: both may be, and usually are, described as private nuisances. The textbook writers, taking their cue from the judges, have rarely probed this divide. There are important differences between them. The latter head, non-physical damage, epitomises the classic nuisance action: smell, noise, smoke etc. interfering with the enjoyment of our land but not destroying, uprooting or otherwise tangibly affecting it. The majority of straightforward cases in nuisance are concerned with this head. The first head, however, (D doing something on his land which causes P's house to burn down or his crops to be destroyed, for example) more closely resembles negligence as we understand that tort today. It involves analysis of the conduct of the defendant to see whether he knew or ought to have known what was happening. There are examples in the law reports of its being treated solely as a negligence question. Where nuisance is invoked, it is usually in the form of an odd version of that tort with special rules and novel departures clearly indicating a drift away from the main stream. Nuisance may be the theoretical basis of liability, but negligence is its driving force.

The argument here will be that this occasional categorisation of physical harm as private nuisance is anomalous. The breadth of negligence was not fully understood in the nineteenth century or even in the first half of the twentieth, and nuisance provided a superficially attractive receptacle for cases that were otherwise hard to classify. This has done serious damage to nuisance by introducing an emphasis on the conduct of the defendant which is foreign to the action and subversive of its doctrines. In this paper, our task is to establish that indirectly causing physical damage to land once properly belonged to the tort of negligence (albeit then a very junior creature indeed). We will argue that the bits and pieces of this part of negligence should now be returned to their proper home...

This strategic surrender will enable nuisance to turn its undivided attention to what it does best, protecting occupiers against non-physical interference with the enjoyment of their land.

8.2.2 Unreasonable interference

Although some torts, such as negligence, focus on the reasonableness of the defendant's actions, nuisance focuses on the reasonableness of the effect of the defendant's action on the claimant. When deciding whether the effect on the claimant is unreasonable, courts weigh the seriousness of the interference against the reasonableness of the defendant's behaviour. Although courts do not take the reasonableness of the defendant's behaviour into effect directly (as is the case in other torts, such as negligence), the reasonableness of the defendant's use of his or her land comes in through the back door, when the court considers whether the interference with the claimant's land was unreasonable.

The courts agree that every person must put up with some degree of inference from one's neighbours. For example, one cannot complain about the happy sounds of a table-tennis game coming from the garden next door every sunny afternoon, no matter how annoying it may be when one is trying to revise for exams. Similarly, one cannot complain about the smells from a summer cook-out, even if one is a vegetarian and finds the odour of roasting meat repulsive and ethically abhorrent. However, sounds and smells (and other types of interference) can become a nuisance if they become strong enough or are experienced often enough so that they interfere significantly with others' use or enjoyment of their premises. As has been famously said by Lord Wensleydale, 'the law does not regard trifling and small inconveniences, but only regards sensible inconveniences which sensibly diminish the comfort...of the property which is affected'. *St Helen's Smelting Co v Tipping* (1865) 11 HL Cas 642. Since nuisance is entirely context-dependent, the courts cannot set a bright line standard (such as the number of decibels of sound that must exist before a noise becomes a nuisance) that define when nuisance begins. Instead, the common law has considered four different factors as relevant to the issue of how serious an interference is: (1) how long the interference lasts; (2) the degree of harm of the interference; (3) the type of the interference; and (4) the social value of the use interfered with. As one would guess, the longer an interference lasts and the more harm it causes, the more likely it is to be termed a nuisance. Similarly, interference of a permanent (as opposed to temporary) nature to an activity with high social value is more likely to be considered a nuisance than a one-time only affair that infringes on an activity that provides little benefit to society at large. However, since it is difficult to consider these issues in the abstract, we will discuss each factor separately and in more detail.

Perhaps the easiest of the factors to consider is the duration of the interference. Quite simply, people living in modern society must be expected to put up with temporary interferences with their land or the use or enjoyment of their land. If a landowner could sue every time an unpleasant smell wafted in the window, the courts would be jammed with tort actions. Thus, nuisance generally only results when there has been continuous interference over a period of time. However, the interference need not be permanent in nature, as shown in *De Keyser's Royal Hotel v Spicer Bros Ltd* (1914) 30 TLR 257. There, noise from pile driving at night was held to be a private nuisance, even though the building works were only temporary.

Even more transitory actions can constitute a nuisance, if the circumstances are right. In most cases where the offending activity is very brief, a cause of action in nuisance will lie only if the damage resulted from a dangerous state of affairs. For example, *Spicer v Smee* [1946] 1 All ER 489 allowed recovery when defective wiring in the defendant's premises resulted in a fire that destroyed the plaintiff's structure. Similarly, *Midwood & Co Ltd v Manchester Corp* [1905] 2 All ER 1252 allowed recovery when an explosion resulting from accumulated gas set fire to the plaintiff's premises. *Crown River Cruises Ltd v Kimbolton Fireworks Ltd* [1996] 2 Lloyds Rep 533, also involved a one-off event (another fire, this one following a fireworks display). There, the judge stated that '[w]here an activity creates a state of affairs which gives rise to risk of escape of physically dangerous or damaging material...then the law of nuisance is...available to give a remedy for that state of affairs, albeit brief in duration'.

NOTE We will be discussing the escape of dangerous things in chapter 9, when we address *Rylands v Fletcher* liability.

Determining the extent of the interference is also a matter of degree, but again the courts take a common sense approach. A nasty odour, such as from a compost pile, is more likely to be a nuisance than a pleasant smell, such as from a bakery, even if the smell from the bakery is very strong. However, even a pleasant smell can constitute a nuisance, just as loud, but very well played, music can constitute a nuisance. The focus must always be on the subjective perception of the action as an unreasonable interference with the land, or the use and enjoyment of the land, of the claimant. One can reasonably assume that a noxious smell will bother the claimant more than a pleasant smell, but the law realizes that not everyone agrees about what is 'pleasant' and thus will not become an arbiter of taste.

The third factor involves the type of interference. There are three kinds to consider: (1) physical interference with the premises; (2) amenity interference to the use of the premises; and (3) amenity interference to the enjoyment of the premises. Physical interference is the most readily actionable. Courts can evaluate the effect of physical damage relatively easily and can quantify that damage with some precision. Amenity damage— either to the use or enjoyment of the premises—is more difficult to prove, just as it is more difficult to define. However, as Lord Lloyd of Berwick stated in *Hunter v Canary Wharf* [1997] AC 655, the mere fact that '[d]amages for loss of amenity value cannot be assessed mathematically...does not mean that such damages cannot be awarded'.

Finally, courts look at whether the defendant's actions have interfered with a socially valuable activity. If the claimant's land is being used in a way that benefits society, then the court is more likely to find that the harm to that activity is serious. Nevertheless, just because some social benefit results from the nuisance-making behaviour does not mean that the court will allow it. For example, a smelly fried fish shop was closed in *Adams v Ursell* [1913] 1 Ch 269, even though its closing caused hardship to the owner and his customers.

VOCABULARY

The term 'user' is a legal term of art describing the purpose to which land is being put. It does not describe the person using the land.

Once the court has considered whether the interference is serious, it will move on to consider the reasonableness of the defendant's use of the defendant's land. As Lord Goff said in one of the leading cases on nuisance, *Cambridge Water Co Ltd v Eastern Counties Leather plc* [1994] 1 AC 264, discussed in detail further below, 'if the **user** is reasonable the defendant will not be liable for consequent harm to his neighbour's enjoyment of his land'. However, you need to be careful here. It is true that, if a party engages in unreasonable behaviour, the interference with the claimant's premises will be unreasonable. However, the interference may not be actionable as nuisance if it is not also significant. Both heads of the test must be met before an action in nuisance will lie.

Again, it is difficult to define the reasonableness of any particular use of land in the abstract, so courts have had to identify a series of factors that are relevant to the reasonableness analysis. First, courts always look at whether the defendant could have taken any reasonable steps to avoid interfering with the claimant, while still achieving the defendant's own goals. Thus, as stated in *Andreae v Selfridge & Co Ltd* [1938] Ch 1, a case wherein a hotelier was inconvenienced by demolition and building going on nearby, parties are under a duty:

> to take proper precautions, and to see that the nuisance is reduced to a minimum. It is no answer for them to say: 'But this would mean that we should have to do the work more slowly than we would like to do it, or it would involve putting us to some extra expense.'

If one can reasonably avoid harming one's neighbour, one should do so. No man—or woman, or corporation—is an island.

While a major expenditure would not be deemed necessary, courts will require defendants to undertake—or at least to investigate—options that would require a proportional outlay of money. The courts will also take into account the resources that are available to the defendant. Indeed, '[t]he extent of the defendant's duty [to avoid or minimize interference with its neighbours], and the question of whether he has or has not fulfilled that duty, may... depend on the defendant's financial resources', as noted in *Leakey v National Trust* [1980] QB 485, concerning a landslip from one property to another.

The courts also look at the purpose of the defendant's activity when deciding whether the user is reasonable. Illegal and/or highly dangerous objectives—such as the storing of explosive materials for use in terrorist bombs—are never reasonable. However, socially useful objectives, such as the construction of a public motorway, will tend to be reasonable. Just because someone does or may derive a profit from the activity does not lessen its social worth. For example, in *Bradford Corp v Pickles* [1895] AC 587, the plaintiff claimed that the defendant was wrongfully preventing clean water from making its way to the plaintiff's reservoir. The plaintiff claimed that the defendant—who said that he was simply excavating flagstone, as was his right to do—was acting out of a profit-based motive, attempting to force the plaintiff to pay a higher price to purchase the defendant's land. Lord Macnaghten dismissed the plaintiff's case, holding that:

> It is the act, not the motive for the act, that must be regarded. If the act, apart from motive gives rise merely to damages without legal injury, the motive, however reprehensible it may be, will not supply that element.

In many ways, *Bradford Corp v Pickles* [1895] AC 587 appears to contradict other cases concerning motive. For example, in *Hollywood Silver Fox Farm Ltd v Emmett* [1936] 2 KB 468, the court held that an action for nuisance would lie where the defendant continually fired guns out of spite in order to frighten the plaintiff's silver foxes and prevent them from breeding. Other cases, including *Christie v Davey* [1893] 1 Ch 316, concerning a neighbour who banged pots and pans to retaliate for music played by his neighbours, have also held that actions taken 'deliberately and maliciously for the purpose of annoying the plaintiffs' constituted a nuisance, based primarily on the motive of the defendant. However, the recent case of *Cambridge Water Co Ltd v Eastern Counties Leather plc* [1994] 2 AC 264 would seem to put the debate about motivation to rest. That case involved the release by a leather manufacturer of certain chemicals into the ground, contaminating the subterranean water supply used by the claimants 1.3 miles away. There, Lord Goff stated that nuisance is a strict liability tort, suggesting that motive is irrelevant.

compare

Think about other strict liability torts. Is motive relevant in those cases, or does the court simply consider whether this particular defendant took the particular action that caused the injury?

● **Cambridge Water Co Ltd v Eastern Counties Leather plc** [1994] 2 AC 264

> Lord Goff: [T]he fact that the defendant has taken all reasonable care will not of itself exonerate him...But it by no means follows that the defendant should be held liable for damage of a type which he could not reasonably foresee; and the development of the law of negligence in the past 60 years points strongly toward a requirement that such foreseeability be a prerequisite of liability in damages for nuisance, as it is of liability in negligence.

However, despite the holding in *Cambridge Water Co Ltd v Eastern Counties Leather plc* [1994] 2 AC 264, the issue of motive was not put to rest. Three years after that decision was handed down, Lord Cooke claimed (*obiter*) in *Hunter v Canary Wharf Ltd* [1997] AC 655, the case about television reception, that a defendant who acts out of malice may be liable for nuisance in situations where another defendant, acting innocently, would not.

● **Hunter v Canary Wharf Ltd** [1997] AC 655

> Lord Cooke: In the light of the versatility of human malevolence and ingenuity, it is as well to add a second qualification. The malicious erection of a structure for the purpose of interfering with television reception should be actionable in nuisance on the principle of such well-known cases as Christie v. Davey [1893] 1 Ch. 316 and Hollywood Silver Fox Farm Ltd. v. Emmett [1936] 2 K.B. 468. Obviously this has no bearing on the present case or on the vast majority of cases. All the same it is not inconceivable. In his book, Canadian Tort Law, Allen Linden cites Attorney-General of Manitoba v. Campbell (1983) 26 C.C.L.T. 168 where a farmer was found to have put up a 74-foot steel tower of no practical use in his farming, directly in line with the runway of an adjoining airport, with no purpose other than as part of a maliciously conceived plan to prevent the upgrading of the airport. This he did just before the effective date of a planning order covering the height and locality of adjacent structures. A mandatory injunction to dismantle the tower was granted and obeyed and not appealed from. Even so the defendant did appeal successfully against an award of solicitor-and-client costs, and two of the three members of the Court of Appeal thought that he would have had a good chance of success in an appeal against the injunction: see [1985] 4 W.W.R. 334. I do not think, however, that the view that malice is irrelevant in nuisance would have wide acceptance today.

Thus, the debate rages on at the highest levels, leaving litigants in something of a state of limbo.

Finally, the court will consider where the defendant's premises are located. Remember, cases involving amenity nuisance looked at where the claimant was located when evaluating whether a 'substantial' interference existed, but this inquiry involves the reasonableness of the defendant's action. Thus, if the area is zoned for commercial activity, most commercial activity will be reasonable. If the area is zoned for residences only, then commercial activity might not be reasonable if it interfered with the normal expectations of residential life.

8.3 Possible claimants

Because nuisance grew out of the need to redress an injury to the land, traditionally only the owners of the land could bring suit. This led to odd results, such as in *Malone v Laskey* [1907] 2 KB 141, which was brought after the vibrations caused by the defendant resulted in a lavatory cistern falling off the wall and onto the plaintiff's head. Because the plaintiff was the wife of the landowner, she did not have the requisite proprietary interest in the land and thus could not recover in nuisance.

think point

The proprietary interests required in nuisance sound very similar to the proprietary interests required in occupiers' liability.

In the early 1990s, it appeared as if the law would shift to allow a person who did not have exclusive control over the premises to sue in nuisance when the Court of Appeal allowed an injunction in *Khorasandjian v Bush* [1993] WLR 476. In that case, a woman was subjected to harassing telephone calls while she lived at her parents' residence. A few years later, however, the House of Lords made it clear that one needs to be the owner of the premises (or have some other form of exclusive possession) to have an action in nuisance. In *Hunter v Canary Wharf Ltd* [1997] 2 AC 655, Lord Goff stated that:

> an action in private nuisance will only lie at the suit of a person who has a right to the land affected. Ordinarily such a person can only sue if he has the right to exclusive possession of the land, such as a freeholder or tenant in possession . . .

If the estate in land is split between a future interest and a present interest, the reversioner (i.e. the person who will eventually hold full title to the land) may only sue if the damage to the property will be permanent. The courts seem to take a common sense approach to this issue, describing a permanent interference as one that 'will continue indefinitely unless something is done to remove it', as indicated in *Jones v Llanrwst UDC* [1911] 1 Ch 393, which involved whether damages for pollution by an upstream user was recoverable by a downstream user. Thus, reversioners will have a cause of action in nuisance if a neighbour constructs a building that overlaps the property line. However, they will not be able to sue if the neighbour is merely noisy or creates unpleasant odours, since those activities can be stopped at any time before the reversioner takes hold of the property.

Once you know who can assert a cause of action in nuisance, you need to consider what injuries are recoverable. For example, although the wife of the landowner in *Malone v Laskey* [1907] 2 KB 141 would now be able to assert a cause of action in nuisance because of her own proprietary interest in the land, she would still have problems quantifying her claim because personal injuries are not strictly recoverable in nuisance. In *Hunter v Canary Wharf Ltd* [1997] AC 655, Lord Lloyd noted that an action will only lie when the injury to land 'consists in the fact that persons on it are liable to suffer inconvenience, annoyance or illness'. Therefore, any personal injury must be defined in terms of an injury to the ability to enjoy the premises in question. Injury to personal property, on the other hand, is clearly recoverable.

compare
As shall be seen later in this chapter, there are no difficulties in recovering damages for personal injuries in public nuisance cases.

8.4 Possible defendants

Earlier, we stated that nuisance is a strict liability tort and that 'fault' is therefore not really at issue. Nevertheless, the defendant must have some degree of personal responsibility if he or she is to be held liable to the claimant.

There are several classes of persons who may find themselves defending an action in nuisance. First, a landlord will be responsible for certain defects existing at the time the premises were let, including those that are known or should have been known through reasonable inspection. The only way to avoid this liability is for the landlord to obtain a **covenant** from the tenant, whereby the tenant takes responsibility for repair. Under those circumstances, the tenant is liable for any nuisance. A landlord will also be responsible for defects arising from the failure to repair the premises during the tenancy, if the landlord has agreed to take on the duty of repair through an explicit covenant, or if the landlord has reserved the right to enter and repair.

VOCABULARY
'Covenant' is another word for 'legally binding promise'.

compare
Consider how the liability in nuisance tracks liability under the two Occupier's Liability Acts.

Second, occupiers may also be liable in nuisance. For example, if a dangerous condition exists on the property, the occupier must take reasonable steps to cure it. However, the courts again consider the issue in context, taking into account the financial resources of the occupier and how the dangerous condition came about. For instance, if the dangerous condition was created by the previous occupier and the defendant knew or ought to know about its existence, then the defendant will likely be liable for nuisance. This makes sense if one thinks about putting the risk of loss (and the cost of repair) on the party who is best equipped to know about a dangerous condition in advance.

Similarly, if the dangerous state of affairs is created by a trespasser, the occupier may be held liable if he or she knew or should have known about it. In *Sedleigh-Denfield v O'Callaghan* [1940] AC 880, a trespasser interfered with the drainage system on the defendant's land. The condition existed for three years before causing water to flood onto the plaintiff's land. Because the occupier had undertaken the responsibility of cleaning the draining system and ought to have noticed the risk of flooding, the occupier was held liable in nuisance. In its decision, the House of Lords stressed the importance of actual or constructive knowledge of the risk.

● **Sedleigh-Denfield v O'Callaghan** [1940] AC 880

Lord Wright: [A]n occupier is not prima facie responsible for a nuisance created without his knowledge and consent. If he is to be liable a further condition is necessary, namely, that he had knowledge or means of knowledge, that he knew or should have known, of the nuisance in time to correct it and obviate its mischievous effects. The liability for a nuisance is not, at least in modern law, a strict or absolute liability. If the defendant by himself or those for whom he is responsible has created what constitutes a nuisance and if it causes damage, the difficulty now being considered does not arise. But he may have taken over the nuisance, readymade as it were, when he acquired the property, or the nuisance may be due to a latent defect or to the act of a trespasser, or stranger. Then he is not liable unless he continued or adopted the nuisance, or, more accurately, did not without undue delay remedy it when he became aware if it, or with ordinary and reasonable care should have become aware of it. This rule seems to be in accordance with good sense and convenience. The responsibility which attaches to the occupier because he has possession and control of the property cannot logically be limited to the mere creation of the nuisance. It should extend to his conduct if, with knowledge, he leaves the nuisance on his land. The same is true if the nuisance was such that with ordinary care in the management of his property he should have realised the risk of its existence.

The need for actual or constructive knowledge is underscored in the more recent case of *Smith v Littlewoods Organisation Ltd* [1987] AC 241, where some trespassers broke into the defendants' disused cinema and caused a fire which spread to the plaintiff's property.

● **Smith v Littlewoods Organisation Ltd** [1987] AC 241

Lord Goff: [I]f a duty of care is imposed to guard against deliberate wrongdoing by others, it can hardly be said that the harmful effects of such wrongdoing are not caused by such breach of duty. We are therefore thrown back to the duty of care. But one thing is clear, and that is that liability in negligence for harm caused by the deliberate wrongdoing of others cannot be founded simply upon foreseeability that the pursuer will suffer loss or damage by reason of such wrongdoing. There is no such general principle. We have therefore to identify the circumstances in which such liability may be imposed.

[After identifying several special circumstances, Lord Goff recognized that there was] . . . a more general circumstance in which a defender may be held liable in negligence to the pursuer, although the immediate cause of the damage suffered by the pursuer is the deliberate wrongdoing of another. This may occur where the defender negligently causes or permits to be created a source of danger, and it is reasonably foreseeable that third parties may interfere with it and, sparking off the danger, thereby cause damage to persons in the position of the pursuer.

compare

The liability of independent contractors (as opposed to employers) is discussed in chapter 16, relating to liability for the torts of others.

An occupier may also attract liability in nuisance for the actions of another type of third party, namely an independent contractor. Occupiers often call in an independent contractors such as plumbers, electricians, construction workers, etc to fix or create something on their property. Normally, parties are not liable for the actions of an independent contractor, but an occupier can be held liable if the independent contractor undertakes an act which carries the risk of the nuisance that results. For example, in *Matania v*

National Provincial Bank and Elevenist Syndicate Ltd [1936] 2 All ER 633, the occupier of a multi-floor building was held liable to the upstairs neighbours when the dust and noise from the contractors hired by the occupier to renovate the premises created a nuisance. Indeed, as Cockburn CJ stated in *Bower v Peate* (1876) 1 QBD 321, which involved the collapse of the plaintiff's house after the defendant hired a contractor to demolish the house, excavate the foundation and rebuild a new structure:

> a man who orders a work to be executed, from which, in the natural course of things, injurious consequences to his neighbour must be expected to arise...is bound to see to the doing of that which is necessary to prevent the mischief, and cannot relieve himself of his responsibility by employing someone else.

Again, the rationale makes sense: the occupier is the one most likely to be able to anticipate and control the behaviour causing the nuisance. Therefore, the occupier should not be permitted to escape liability simply by contracting another to do the dirty work (literally and figuratively).

The third and perhaps most important group of persons who may become liable in tort are the creators of the nuisance. If someone exercises control over the property which causes the nuisance, he or she is liable for the damage that results, even if that person is not an 'occupier' of the land in the technical sense. Notice the lack of parallelism in the risk of liability versus the possibility of recovery—to recover in nuisance, one (typically) must have some sort of proprietary interest in the land, broadly defined. To be liable in nuisance, however, one does not have to have any proprietary interest in land.

think point

If the creator of the nuisance is liable for any damages resulting from acts or conditions over which he or she has control, why does the law also consider the liability of occupiers and landlords? Might it have something to do with the possibility that not all creators of nuisances can be found by the claimant or can cover the cost of the damage, economically speaking? What public policies does the law support by allowing recovery from several different categories of defendants?

The key to creator liability is the right to control the premises at the time the nuisance arose. The creator need not be the occupier so long as the creator was given the authority to act as he or she did. As Devlin J said in *Esso Petroleum Co Ltd v Southport Corporation* [1956] AC 218, 'I can see no reason why...if the defendant as a licensee or trespasser misuses someone else's land, he should not be liable for a nuisance in the same way as an adjoining occupier would be'. In that case, the defendant was the owner of an oil tanker that had discharged 400 tons of oil in her cargo after becoming stranded in a river estuary. The owners of the foreshore upon which the oil landed brought suit in negligence, nuisance and trespass to land, but ultimately failed to prove their case.

Recall

In chapter 16, we discuss liability for the torts of others and how one who authorizes another to act tortiously will also be liable for any tort that results. The same principle is true here: anyone who authorizes a nuisance is also liable to the claimant. For example, in Tetley v Chitty [1986] 1 All ER 663, a local authority authorized go-kart racing on council land and was held liable in nuisance for the resulting noise, since that sort of nuisance was the inevitable result of go-kart racing.

As we have discussed, sometimes a tort arises from an action that is not problematic in itself but that eventually leads to a nuisance. In those cases, the courts look to the foreseeability of harm. For example, the defendant in *Butler v Standard Telephones and Cables Ltd* [1940] 1 KB 399 planted trees whose roots eventually grew under neighbouring property and caused a nuisance. Because the harm was foreseeable, the defendant was liable. However, if the harm is not foreseeable, then liability will not attach, as in *Ilford UDC v Beal* [1925] 1 KB 671, where a defendant built a retaining wall by a river. Because the defendant built the wall badly, it moved forward and pressed against the plaintiff's sewer. Because the defendant did not know about the presence of the sewer and could not be said to ought to have known about it, the damage was unforeseeable and the defendant was not liable.

The most cogent discussion of foreseeability of harm in nuisance cases arises in *Cambridge Water Co Ltd v Eastern Counties Leather plc* [1994] 2 AC 264, which is the case mentioned above involving the discharge of chemicals into the groundwater by a leather manufacturer. Nuisance was not strictly at issue in the case argued in the House of Lords, since that cause of action had not been appealed from the Court of Appeal, but the discussion is still instructive.

. . . .

● **Cambridge Water Co Ltd v Eastern Counties Leather plc** [1994] 2 AC 264

Lord Goff: It is, of course, axiomatic that in this field we must be on our guard, when considering liability for damages in nuisance, not to draw inapposite conclusions from cases concerned only with a claim for an injunction. This is because, where an injunction is claimed, its purpose is to restrain further action by the defendant which may interfere with the plaintiff's enjoyment of his land, and ex hypothesi the defendant must be aware, if and when an injunction is granted, that such interference may be caused by the act which he is restrained from committing. It follows that these cases provide no guidance on the question whether foreseeability of harm of the relevant type is a prerequisite of the recovery of damages for causing such harm to the plaintiff. In the present case, we are not concerned with liability in damages in respect of a nuisance which has arisen through natural causes, or by the act of a person for whose actions the defendant is not responsible, in which cases the applicable principles in nuisance have become closely associated with those applicable in negligence ... We are concerned with the liability of a person where a nuisance has been created by one for whose actions he is responsible. Here, as I have said, it is still the law that the fact that the defendant has taken all reasonable care will not of itself exonerate him from liability, the relevant control mechanism being found within the principle of reasonable user. But it by no means follows that the defendant should be held liable for damage of a type which he could not reasonably foresee; and the development of the law of negligence in the past 60 years points strongly towards a requirement that such foreseeability should be a prerequisite of liability in damages for nuisance, as it is of liability in negligence. For if a plaintiff is in ordinary circumstances only able to claim damages in respect of personal injuries where he can prove such foreseeability on the part of the defendant, it is difficult to see why, in common justice, he should be in a stronger position to claim damages for interference with the enjoyment of his land where the defendant was unable to foresee such damage. Moreover, this appears to have been the conclusion of the Privy Council in Overseas Tankship (U.K.) Ltd. v. Miller Steamship Co. Pty. (The Wagon Mound (No. 2)) [1967] 1 A.C. 617. The facts of the case are too well known to require repetition, but they gave rise to a claim for damages arising from a public nuisance caused by a spillage of oil in Sydney Harbour. Lord Reid, who delivered the advice of the Privy Council, considered that, in the class of nuisance which included the case before the Board, foreseeability is an essential element in determining liability. He then continued . . .

> 'It could not be right to discriminate between different cases of nuisance so as to make foreseeability a necessary element in determining damages in those cases where it is a necessary element in determining liability, but not in others. So the choice is between it being a necessary element in all cases of nuisance or in none. In their Lordships' judgment the similarities between nuisance and other forms of tort to which The Wagon Mound (No. 1) applies far outweigh any differences, and they must therefore hold that the judgment appealed from is wrong on this branch of the case. It is not sufficient that the injury suffered by the respondents' vessels was the direct result of the nuisance if that injury was in the relevant sense unforeseeable.'

Since this case was handed down, it has been understood that foreseeability forms a necessary part of the law of nuisance.

Although *Cambridge Water Co Ltd v Eastern Counties Leather plc* [1994] 1 AC 264 involved a man-made hazard, there may be times when a dangerous condition is created by a natural act, such as a fire or a rainstorm. The leading case of *Goldman v Hargrave* [1967] 1 AC 645 involved a decision of the Privy Council wherein the defendant was found liable in nuisance after a fire spread to a neighbour's land. The fire was caused when a tree on the defendant's land was hit by lightning. The defendant felled the tree and cut it into sections, thinking the fire was out, but weather conditions changed, causing the fire to reignite and spread. The Privy Council held that the defendant owed a duty to the neighbour to abate the nuisance which the defendant knew, or should have know, could arise from the natural state of affairs on the defendant's land.

The English precedent is *Leakey v National Trust* [1980] QB 485, wherein the defendants owned a hill that everyone knew was at risk of slippage. When the hill eventually did slip and damage the plaintiffs' homes at the foot of the hill, the court found the defendants liable in nuisance, since they had known about the danger for more than eight years and yet had done nothing to eliminate or minimize the risk of harm. Megaw J stated that the defendant there had a duty to minimize the nuisance, and 'the duty is a duty to do that which is reasonable in the circumstances . . . to prevent or minimise the known risk of damage or injury to one's neighbour or his property'.

Holbeck Hall Hotel Ltd v Scarborough Borough Council [2000] 2 All ER 705 involved a similar risk of land collapse, and there Stuart-Smith LJ emphasised the court must establish foreseeability, proximity and the need for fairness, justice and reasonableness before imposing liability. He went on to say that 'I do not think it is just and reasonable in a case like the present to impose liability for damage which is greater in extent than anything that was foreseen or foreseeable'.

8.5 Nuisance and other torts

Nuisance bears a very close relationship to two other torts: *Rylands v Fletcher* liability involving the escape from land of things (discussed in the next chapter) and negligence. *Cambridge Water Co Ltd v Eastern Counties Leather plc* [1994] 2 AC 264 contains an excellent discussion of the relationship between negligence, nuisance and *Rylands v Fletcher* liability, and will be considered at length in the next chapter.

One also should consider how nuisance relates to trespass to land, another tort that will be discussed in a later chapter. Because (as you will learn) trespass is a per se violation of another's land that does not require the claimant to prove damages, trespass will provide a remedy in situations where there is no nuisance. For example, *Kelsen v Imperial Tobacco Co (of Great Britain and Ireland) Ltd* [1957] QB 334 considered whether a sign that was hung so that it protruded into the space above the plaintiff's shop was actionable. There it was held that there was a trespass—because the plaintiff owned the airspace above the shop and the defendant had infringed on that space—but no nuisance, since the sign did not interfere with the plaintiff's use or enjoyment of the airspace.

However, the one thing that really distinguishes nuisance from other torts is the remedy that is typically sought. Nuisance is one of those torts that allows a claimant to obtain injunctive relief, as opposed to only recovering money damages. Therefore, a claimant whose land or whose use or enjoyment of the land has been injured may wish to assert a claim in negligence (so that he or she can recover money damages for a wider variety of injuries than are available in nuisance) as well as a claim in nuisance (so that he or she can enjoin the defendant from carrying on with the activity in the future). The types of remedies that are available in nuisance are discussed in the next section.

NOTE In examination situations, always consider nuisance, negligence, *Rylands v Fletcher* liability and trespass to land together. You may not be able to prove all of the elements of all of the different torts, but you need to think about whether it's possible to prove more than one. Remember, a claimant may assert a number of different claims in the alternative, even if he or she may not obtain double recovery for the same wrong.

8.6 Remedies

Courts are not always clear about what recovery is possible in nuisance. Certainly, a claimant is entitled to full recovery of loss to land, with the damages calculated as the difference between the value of the property before the damaging event and the value of the property after the event. Consequential damages to a business may also be recoverable, whether it be through loss of inventory or a loss of custom. The method of calculating the percentage of business lost due to nuisance can be quite complex, as suggested by *Marquis of Granby v Bakewell UDC* (1923) 87 JP 105, where the court had to decide the losses associated with the death of fish following the pollution of a stream, but it is still possible.

The damages awarded for nuisance increase the longer the nuisance continues. Interestingly, courts do not calculate a long-term nuisance as a continuation of one initial nuisance. Instead, courts evaluate the situation as a series of newly created nuisances, as indicated by *Maberley v Peabody & Co of London Ltd* [1946] 2 All ER 192, where a wall was falling down as a result of the defendant's action. The court there said that 'a fresh cause of action arises as each brick topples down, and that there is a continuing cause of action until the root of the trouble is eradicated'.

A continuing nuisance was at issue in *Delaware Mansions Ltd v Westminster City Council* [2001] UKHL 55, [2001] 3 WLR 1007, where tree roots caused a neighbouring building to sustain structural damage. The question for the House of Lords was whether the defendant was liable for the damage and when the duty to abate the nuisance arose.

● ***Delaware Mansions Ltd v Westminster City Council*** [2001] UKHL/55, [2001] 3 WLR 1007

> Lord Cooke of Thorndon: I think that the answer to the issue falls to be found by applying the concepts of reasonableness between neighbours (real or figurative) and reasonable foreseeability which underlie much modern tort law and, more particularly, the law of nuisance. The great cases in nuisance decided in our time have these concepts at their heart. In Sedleigh-Denfield v O'Callaghan [1940] AC 880, the House of Lords held that an occupier of land 'continues' a nuisance if, with knowledge or presumed knowledge of its existence (in that case a defective grating giving rise to flood damage), he fails to take reasonable means to bring it to an end when he has reasonable time to do so. In Overseas Tankship (UK) Ltd v Miller Steamship Co Pty [1967] 1 AC 617, the second Wagon Mound case, the Privy Council, approaching the case under the rubrics of both nuisance and negligence, said, at p 644 per Lord Reid: 'If it is clear that the reasonable man would have realised or foreseen and prevented the risk, then it must follow that the appellant is liable in damages.'
>
> Once more, in Goldman v Hargrave [1967] 1 AC 645, the Privy Council per Lord Wilberforce, as to an occupier's duty to take reasonable steps to prevent the spreading of a fire caused by lightning striking a tree, said, at p 663, and likewise not discriminating between nuisance and negligence (see pp 656–657):
>
> > 'So far it has been possible to consider the existence of a duty, in general terms. But the matter cannot be left there without some definition of the scope of his duty. How far does it go? What is the standard of the effort required? What is the position as regards expenditure? It is not enough to say merely that these must be "reasonable",

since what is reasonable to one man may be very unreasonable, and indeed ruinous, to another: the law must take account of the fact that the occupier on whom the duty is cast has, ex hypothesi, had this hazard thrust upon him through no seeking or fault of his own. His interest, and his resources, whether physical or material, may be of a very modest character either in relation to the magnitude of the hazard, or as compared with those of his threatened neighbour. A rule which required of him in such unsought circumstances in his neighbour's interest a physical effort of which he is not capable, or an excessive expenditure of money, would be unenforceable or unjust. One may say in general terms that the existence of a duty must be based upon knowledge of the hazard, ability to foresee the consequences of not checking or removing it, and the ability to abate it....'

...

Damage consisting of impairment of the load-bearing qualities of residential land is, in my view, itself a nuisance...Cracking in the building was consequential. Having regard to the proximity of the plane tree to Delaware Mansions, a real risk of damage to the land and the foundations was foreseeable on the part of Westminster...It is arguable that the cost of repairs to the cracking could have been recovered as soon as it became manifest. That point need not be decided, although I am disposed to think that a reasonable landowner would notify the controlling local authority or neighbour as soon as tree root damage was suspected.

As discussed above, at one time it appeared as if courts would allow claimants in nuisance to recover for personal injuries. However, in 1997, the House of Lords stated (*obiter*) in *Hunter v Canary Wharf Ltd* [1997] AC 655 that personal injuries were only recoverable in negligence, not nuisance. However, since claimants may assert several causes of action at the same time, the Lords' decision may not have much practical effect.

> **VOCABULARY**
> An injunction is an order of the court requiring the party to abstain from certain activities, and imposing fines or other penalties until the order is complied with.

Sometimes, a claimant is given money damages even though he or she requests an **injunction**, thus effectively permitting the defendant to carry on with committing the nuisance. Courts must consider various factors when deciding whether to allow money damages instead of an injunction. In *Shelfer v City of London Electric Lighting Co* [1895] 1 Ch 287, Smith LJ stated that the court may give damages instead of an injunction when the plaintiff's injury is small, when it is easily quantifiable and capable of being compensated in money, and when granting an injunction would be oppressive to the defendant. Thus, for example, if a homeowner could smell manure from a fertilizer factory every time the wind blew west (which only happened rarely), the court might give money damages rather than shut down the factory's operations altogether. The damage to the claimant is small, the damages are quantifiable (for example, the diminution in property values since the factory was built) and compensable, and granting an injunction would be oppressive to the defendant.

NOTE What we are talking about here is money damages in lieu of an injunction for future injuries. A claimant may—and often does—demand money damages for past injuries while also asking for an injunction to cure injuries on a going-forward basis. This makes sense because an injunction will do nothing to cure injuries that have already occurred.

Typically, however, claimants seek and obtain injunctions when nuisance is proven. Once the claimant has proven that a nuisance exists as a matter of law, the defendant is allowed to show any special circumstances that might allow it to pay monetary damages instead of being required to submit to an injunction. When deciding whether to grant an injunction, the court typically looks at all of the factors at issue, although two—the degree of interference with the claimant's premises and any interest the public may have in the outcome—are weighed more heavily than the others. For example, if the interference only occurs occasionally, the court may not think it necessary to enjoin the activity.

The public interest at stake can take a variety of different forms. In *Wheeler v JJ Saunders Ltd* [1995] 2 All ER 697, for instance, it took the form of a pig farm. There, Peter Gibson LJ concluded that the public interest demanded the continued operation of the pig farm and therefore awarded the claimant damages instead of an injunction. Similarly, in *Miller v Jackson* [1977] QB 966, the Court of Appeal held that nuisance existed when cricket balls fell continuously into the yards of people living in a new housing estate that had been built next to the cricket ground. Although Lord Denning dissented in that opinion, finding that the private interest of the homeowners should prevail over the public interest in cricket, the majority held that the activity should be allowed to continue, even if it constituted a nuisance, and therefore allowed the owners of the cricket grounds to simply pay damages to the homeowners.

8.7   Defences

Some of the defences in nuisance are similar to those in other torts, whereas some defences are unique to this particular tort. The easiest defence to prove and comprehend is statutory authority. If Parliament has permitted either a public or private actor to undertake the activity, then no claim of nuisance will lie. However, potential defendants must be very careful that the statute or statutory instrument explicitly provides for the behaviour in question. If the statutory authority is merely permissive in nature, then the defendant must behave in such a way as to not interfere with private rights.

Thus, when the defendant is a public authority, you must look at whether the authority granted is a discretionary statutory power. If the behaviour falls within the scope of a discretionary power, no liability will typically arise. However, if the policy chosen is negligently carried out, then the public body may be liable.

As Lord Wilberforce said in *Allen v Gulf Oil Refining Ltd* [1981] AC 1001, 'where Parliament by express direction or by necessary implication has authorised [an activity], that carries with it an authority to do what is authorised with immunity from any action based on nuisance'. There, the defendant oil company had built a refinery in accordance with a private Act of Parliament. The plaintiff, who lived nearby, brought suit in nuisance based on the noxious fumes that were emitted by the refinery as well as concerns about the safety of the plant. The House of Lords held that the grant of the right to construct and operate a refinery also gave the oil company immunity from any case in nuisance that might constitute the inevitable result of constructing such a refinery. However, the Lords held that the defendant's activities were limited in scope to what is authorized by statute, and the defendant would be liable to the extent it exceeds the powers described. Thus, the defendants in *Tate & Lyle Industries Ltd v Greater London Council* [1983] 2 AC 509 were liable when they did not exercise reasonable care in the design and construction of new ferry terminals. Although the construction was authorized by statute, the failure to exercise that power reasonably resulted in a public nuisance. The case did include one quirk: the facts adduced at trial showed that reasonable design and construction of the terminals would still have resulted in some nuisance to the public. While this did not eliminate liability, it did reduce the damages award so that the plaintiffs received only that portion of their damages—in this case, 75 per cent—that was attributable to the improper behaviour of the defendant.

cross reference

For more on breach of statutory duty, see chapter 6.

Statutory language can vary considerably. Some statutes explicitly state that a civil cause of action will not lie against anyone carrying out the permitted activity. Other statutes set forth a scheme for remedying or addressing any claims while not expressly prohibiting a civil cause of action. It appears that in the latter cases, the only remedy is through the statutory scheme. As Lord Nicholls stated in *Marcic v Thames Water Utilities Ltd* [2003] UKHL 66, which involved habitual flooding of the claimant's land from an overloaded public sewer system, the common law can 'not impose on Thames Water obligations inconsistent with the statutory scheme'.

compare

When you study property law, you will learn about how other sorts of easements by prescription arise.

Another possible defence arises when the defendant has committed the offending act for so long that the claimant loses the right to bring a suit in nuisance. In such cases, the defendant is said to have acquired an easement by prescription. Typically, an easement by prescription arises after 20 years' open and undisturbed activity. The defendant must act openly and notoriously so that the claimant can see the activity and bring a cause of action to stop it. If the defendant acts secretly, then no easement arises. Furthermore, the offending activity must be relatively consistent, though it does not have to exist every minute of every day. Too much variation, though, and the activity is not considered continuous enough to give rise to a prescriptive easement.

compare

See chapter 5 for a general discussion of the defences of consent, assumption of the risk and contributory negligence.

Other sorts of tort defences are available to actions in nuisance. For example, a defendant may claim that consent or assumption of risk exists. If the claimant has contributed to the injury, the defendant may argue that contributory negligence will reduce any eventual award. Furthermore, a claimant will be required to mitigate his or her damages, as in other sorts of tort.

Many times the law is logical, but there is one seemingly logical defence that does not actually exist. Sometimes a defendant tries to argue that the activity cannot be a nuisance because the offending elements had existed for years before the claimant even moved to the neighbourhood. The defendant then claims that the claimant 'moved to the nuisance' and cannot now be heard to complaint in tort. In fact, no such defence as 'moving to the nuisance' exists. Once someone has purchased or acquired another sort of interest in the land, he or she can sue for nuisance, even if the neighbour has been engaging in the offensive activity for years.

8.8 Elements of public nuisance

The preceding discussion has focused on private nuisance, which occurs when a defendant—be it a private citizen or a public body—does something to a private person or legal entity. However, the law of tort also recognizes that there are times when an activity offends more than one person. Instead, it offends the public at large. The tort of public nuisance is not as well defined as private nuisance, but it tends to address any acts or omissions which endanger life, health, property or morals or which diminish the public's ability to exercise and enjoy its rights.

NOTE Public nuisance can also result in a criminal charge, but that sort of action is beyond the scope of this text.

Two sorts of civil actions that can be brought in public nuisance. First, a private citizen may bring a relator action in the name of the Attorney-General, seeking an injunction to stop the activity. This sort of action can be brought when some behaviour results in damage to a large number of private citizens, all of whom are affected in similar ways and to a similar degree. To prevail, the person bringing the action must establish the elements of the crime of public nuisance. In fact, this sort of action is very seldom brought or made out.

Second, a private citizen may bring a tort action, alleging that he or she has suffered **special damages** above and beyond what other members of the public have experienced. There is still the need to prove widespread harm, since that is what makes this sort of action public, rather than private, nuisance. Interestingly, the tort of public nuisance can take one of two forms. First, the case can arise in exactly the same way as a private cause of action, but with a much wider number of people affected. This sort of situation has been described by Denning LJ in *A-G v PYA Quarries Ltd* [1957] 2 QB 169, a case involving the dust and vibrations emitted from a quarry, thus disturbing the owners of several nearby houses, thusly:

VOCABULARY

'Special damage' in public nuisance is not the same as 'special damages', which are specific damages that must be pleaded and proved in negligence or defamation actions.

> A nuisance which is so widespread in its range or so indiscriminate in its effect that it would not be reasonable to expect one person to take proceedings on his own responsibility to put a stop to it, but that it should be taken on the responsibility of the community at large.

Second, the cause of action of public nuisance can arise even though the claimant's land—or the use or enjoyment of the claimant's land—is not affected. Often this sort of case will involve some sort of danger on the highway, though the danger must be unreasonable. For example, in *Trevett v Lee* [1955] 1 All ER 406, a plaintiff tripped over a pipe laid across the highway by the defendant. There, no nuisance existed because the defendant was acting reasonably, since he had no water mains connection to his land, but the case demonstrates how the public can be affected by a private action. Similarly, in *Noble v Harrison* [1926] 2 KB 332, the defendant was not liable in nuisance when a tree branch fell from his property onto the plaintiff's vehicle, which was on the road adjacent to the defendant's property. There, the court held that the plaintiff could have reasonably seen the danger from the tree branch when he parked his car. Nevertheless, the case shows how an action in public nuisance might be framed.

To prevail in a tort action for public nuisance, the claimant must demonstrate that he or she has suffered or will suffer some kind of 'special damage' or 'particular damage'. Although no single definition of 'special damage' exists, there are several types of harm for which courts have typically allowed recovery, including pecuniary loss, personal injury and property damage. For example, the claimant may suffer pecuniary loss from injury to his or her business. The damage has to be 'substantial' rather than 'fleeting or evanescent', but such damages were found to exist in *Benjamin v Storr* (1847) LR 9 CP 400, when a defendant parked his horse-drawn carts outside the plaintiff's coffee shop, leading to both increased costs in the coffee house when the owner had to run gas lamps to overcome the lack of light caused by the carts' blocking the light and decreased income when customers had trouble getting into the shop and were disinclined to stay because of the smell of the horses. Furthermore, it is important to prove that the claimant's loss is of a different type than that suffered by other members of the public. It is not enough that the claimant has simply suffered a higher degree of harm than others have.

think point

As you recall, claimants in private nuisance may not recover for personal injury. What sorts of public policies support a wider range of recovery in public nuisance than private nuisance?

Although most of the defences available in matters involving private nuisance are available in cases involving public nuisance, easement by prescription is not one of them. This makes sense as a matter of public policy, since one does not want to allow public rights to be eliminated by private action.

The remedies in public nuisance are also similar to those in private nuisance. Injunctions are available both to those individuals who are proceeding via a relator action and to those who are pursuing a tort action. Those claimants who are able to prove special damage may also receive compensation, although exemplary damages will never be available in a public nuisance case.

Finally, nuisance is one of those areas of law that is particularly affected by the Human Rights Act 1998. There are times when an activity cannot give rise to liability under the common law but will still be actionable under the Human Rights Act 1998. For example, in *Hatton v United Kingdom* (2003) 37 EHRR 28, the claimants argued that night flights into and out of Heathrow Airport violated their rights. Because the Civil Aviation Act 1982 barred common law claims in nuisance for this particular activity, the claimants proceeded under the Human Rights Act 1998, claiming a violation of Article 8's protection of 'private and family life'. In the end, the European Court of Human Rights held that a proper balance had been struck between state and private interests, but the case demonstrates how an alternative basis for a nuisance-type claim might be found in the Human Rights Act 1998. Indeed, in *Dennis v Ministry of Defence* [2003] EWHC 793 (QB) claimants were given compensation for the reduced value of their land based on violations of Article 8 after the Ministry of Defence was found to have caused a nuisance by using its land as a training base for Harrier Jump Jets, thus causing a great deal of noise and disturbing the neighbours.

 For more revision tips, including self-test questions and suggestions for further reading, see the Online Resource Centre at www.oxfordtextbooks.co.uk/orc/strong_complete/.

revision tasks

Nuisance law can be confusing if you do not differentiate between tangible and non-tangible injury to the enjoyment of land and between public and private nuisance. Some of the following tasks will help you organize your materials into a workable outline.

- List the types of public nuisance cases and what facts must exist before an action can be taken.

- Identify the elements of the two types of private nuisance—physical injury to land and intangible injury to the use or enjoyment of land.

- Understand how nuisance overlaps with (or fails to overlap with) other land-based torts, particularly negligence and *Rylands v Fletcher* liability.

9 *Rylands v Fletcher* liability

9.1 Introduction

The previous chapter discussed liability in nuisance, which results when activities on one person's land affects another person's ability to use or enjoy his or her land. However, the law of nuisance overlaps quite significantly with another form of land-based liability that developed out of a famous case from the nineteenth century known as *Rylands v Fletcher*. If the respondent can prove the necessary elements, he or she can recover even if the defendant was non-negligent and took all reasonable—and even all unreasonable—steps to avoid harming the respondent. Thus, *Rylands v Fletcher* is a strict liability tort, meaning that all the claimant needs to prove is that the defendant is the one who caused the harm. The claimant does not need to prove the defendant was negligent or acting intentionally.

Although *Rylands v Fletcher* liability can be traced back to a single revolutionary case, subsequent decisions have altered the scope of recovery. This chapter will therefore proceed as follows:

- Original interpretation of *Rylands v Fletcher*;
- Possible defendants;
- Possible claimants;
- Activities giving rise to liability;
- Foreseeability;
- Defences; and
- *Rylands v Fletcher* and other torts.

Original interpretation of *Rylands v Fletcher*

The original decision in *Rylands v Fletcher* is useful to know, although later opinions have modified the rule in certain important ways.

● **Rylands v Fletcher** (1868) LR 3 HL 330

Lord Cairns LC: My Lords, in this case the Plaintiff...is the occupier of a mine and works under a close of land. The Defendants are the owners of a mill in his neighbourhood, and they proposed to make a reservoir for the purpose of keeping and storing water to be used about their mill..., which...may be taken as being adjoining to the close of the Plaintiff...Underneath the...reservoir there were certain old and disused mining passages and works...[I]t does not appear that any person was aware of [their] existence...In the course of the working by the Plaintiff of his mine, he had...come into contact with the old and disused works underneath the close of the Defendants.

In that state of things the reservoir of the Defendants was constructed...As regards the engineer and the contractor, we must take it from the case that they did not exercise...that reasonable care and caution which they might have exercised...[W]hen the reservoir was constructed, ...the weight of the water bearing upon the disused and imperfectly filled-up vertical shafts, broke through those shafts. The water passed down them and...passed on into the workings under the close of the Plaintiff, and flooded his mine, causing considerable damage, for which this action was brought...

My Lords, the principles on which this case must be determined appear to me to be extremely simple. The Defendants, treating them as the owners or occupiers of the close on which the reservoir was constructed, might lawfully have used that close for any purpose for which it might in the ordinary course of the enjoyment of land be used; and if, in what I may term the natural user of that land, there had been any accumulation of water, either on the surface or underground, and if, by the operation of the laws of nature, that accumulation of water had passed off into the close occupied by the Plaintiff, the Plaintiff could not have complained that that result had taken place. If he had desired to guard himself against it, it would have lain upon him to have done so, by leaving, or by interposing, some barrier between his close and the close of the Defendants in order to have prevented that operation of the laws of nature...

On the other hand if the Defendants, not stopping at the natural use of their close, had desired to use it for any purpose which I may term a non-natural use, for the purpose of introducing into the close that which in its natural condition was not in or upon it, for the purpose of introducing water either above or below ground in quantities and in a manner not the result of any work or operation on or under the land, and if in consequence of their doing so, or in consequence of any imperfection in the mode of their doing so, the water came to escape and to pass off into the close of the Plaintiff, then it appears to me that that which the Defendants were doing they were doing at their own peril; and, if in the course of their doing it, the evil arose to which I have referred, the evil, namely, of the escape of the water and its passing away to the close of the Plaintiff and injuring the Plaintiff, then for the consequence of that, in my opinion, the Defendants would be liable...

The same result is arrived at on the principles referred to by Mr. Justice Blackburn in his judgment, in the Court of Exchequer Chamber, where he states the opinion of that Court as to the law in these words:

'We think that the true rule of law is, that the person who, for his own purposes, brings on his land and collects and keeps there anything likely to do mischief if it escapes, must keep it in at his peril; and if he does not do so, is prima facie answerable for all the damage which is the natural consequence of its escape. He can excuse himself by shewing that the escape was owing to the Plaintiff's default; or, perhaps, that the escape was the consequence of vis major, or the act of God; but as nothing of this sort exists here, it is unnecessary to inquire what excuse would be sufficient. The general rule, as above stated, seems on principle just. The person whose grass or corn is eaten down by the escaping cattle of his neighbour, or whose mine is flooded by the water from his neighbour's reservoir, or whose cellar is invaded by the filth of his neighbour's privy, or whose habitation is made unhealthy by the fumes and noisome vapours of his neighbour's alkali works, is damnified without any fault of his own; and it seems but reasonable and just that the neighbour who has brought something on his own property (which was not naturally there), harmless to others so long as it is confined to his own property, but which he knows will be mischievous if it gets on his neighbour's, should be obliged to make good the damage which ensues if he does not succeed in confining it to his own property. But for his act in bringing it there no mischief could have accrued, and it seems but just that he should at his peril keep it there, so that no mischief may accrue, or answer for the natural and anticipated consequence. And upon authority this we think is established to be the law, whether the things so brought be beasts, or water, or filth, or stenches.'

Thus, the rule of *Rylands v Fletcher* was created. Justice Blackburn's formulation—quoted by Lord Cairn—is the most succinct summation of liability under this rule and the one that is most often referred to by subsequent courts. Thus, traditionally, the claimant need only prove that:

- The defendant brought something onto the defendant's land;

- The defendant made a 'non-natural use' of the defendant's land;

- The thing was something likely to do mischief if it escaped; and

- The thing did escape and cause damage to the claimant.

cross reference
Cambridge Water Co Ltd v Eastern Counties Leather plc [1994] 2 AC 264 is discussed in more detail below.

However, the important case of *Cambridge Water Co Ltd v Eastern Counties Leather plc* [1994] 2 AC 264 altered the rule in the mid-1990s, adding a new element to be proven. Contemporary claimants cannot pursue an action in *Rylands v Fletcher* without taking this new factor into account.

 9.3 # Possible defendants

According to Blackburn J, those who, for their own purposes, bring the thing in question onto the land and keep it there are liable to those who are injured as a result of that action. When identifying possible defendants, therefore, the court looks to see whether anyone affirmatively acted to bring and keep the harmful items on the land. In

Rylands v Fletcher itself, the defendants accumulated the damage-causing agent—the water—by constructing a reservoir. Had the defendants not collected the water, but instead only redirected it—as through the construction of a levee or seawall—onto their neighbours' property, then they would have been liable in nuisance (since they either injured their neighbours' property itself and/or injured their neighbours' use and enjoyment of the property) or perhaps in trespass to land (discussed in the next chapter). However, because they gathered the water first, they increased the likelihood and magnitude of danger and created a whole new head of tort liability.

NOTE Nuisance can also result from the 'escape' of a non-physical thing, such as noise or odours. These cases typically fall under the heading of amenity nuisances.

Simply allowing something that exists naturally on the land to accumulate does not seem to result in liability. For example, in *Giles v Walker* (1890) 24 QBD 656, the defendant ploughed up some land, which resulted in a large number of thistles growing there. When the thistles took seed and blew onto some neighbouring land, the plaintiff sued but could not recover, because the thistles were 'the natural growth of the soil'. However, one can see how escaping seeds could result in liability under *Rylands v Fletcher*. For example, if a farmer planted a crop of genetically modified plants and allowed pollen from those crops to escape to neighbouring fields, he or she could be liable in *Rylands v Fletcher*. Similarly, an estate owner might not be liable if a wild wolf escaped from forests on the estate and killed a neighbouring farmer's sheep, since one might say that the wolf—like the thistles—had not been brought or accumulated on the land. If that same estate owner's pet tiger went on a rampage, liability under *Rylands v Fletcher* would be much more likely to result.

Must a defendant own the property in question before liability can arise? Not necessarily. For example, in *Rainham Chemical Works Ltd v Bellvedere Fish Guano Co.* [1921] 2 AC 465, the House of Lords considered a limited company that manufactured explosives on land owned by two other persons. When the explosives—predictably—exploded, causing damage to neighbouring landowners, the limited company was sued along with the landowners.

NOTE In *Rainham Chemical Works Ltd v Bellvedere Fish Guano Co.* [1921] 2 AC 465, the limited company was a licensee of the landowners. Since the common law distinctions between various types of entrants to land have been, for the most part, eliminated in tort law (see chapter 7), a modern court would most likely look at the degree of control that the non-owning entity had over the thing that escaped to see whether liability should result.

What about the landowner who allows another to bring or accumulate the escaped things onto the land? Should the landowner also be liable in *Rylands v Fletcher*? The answer may depend on the degree of control retained by the landowner over the land. Lord Sumner in *Rainham Chemical Works Ltd v Bellvedere Fish Guano Co.* [1921] 2 AC 465 stated, *obiter*, that if landowners 'simply suffered others to manufacture upon the site which they nevertheless continued to occupy', then they should be liable in tort. However, Eve J in *Whitmores (Edenbridge) Ltd v Stanford* [1909] 1 Ch 427 stated (*obiter*) that if someone other than the owner had a prescriptive right to undertake a certain act—such as to accumulate water—for his or her own purposes, then the landowner would not be liable for any resulting damages. That case involved the historic rights of both a tanner and a downstream mill owner who both drew water from the same channel but who now contested who, if anyone, had the right to stop the flow of the millstream.

9.4 Possible claimants

In *Rylands v Fletcher* itself, the plaintiff owned the land that suffered injury. However, that injury need not be to real property. In *Jones v Festiniog Rly Co* (1868) LRD 1 Exch 265, sparks from a railway set a haystack of fire. In that case, recovery was possible, thus demonstrating that injury to personal property is also covered by *Rylands v Fletcher*.

cross reference

See chapter 8 for a further discussion of Hunter v Canary Wharf Ltd [1997] AC 655.

Personal injury is another matter altogether. In *Read v J Lyons & Co Ltd* [1947] AC 156, a munitions inspector was injured when an explosion occurred during a visit to a munitions manufacturer. The inspector was unable to recover for several reasons, one of which was that, as Lord Macmillan stated, *Rylands v Fletcher* 'derives from a conception of the mutual duties of adjoining or neighbouring landowners'. Since the munitions inspector did not suffer an injury to property, recovery was not possible. This view is supported by *Hunter v Canary Wharf Ltd* [1997] AC 655, when the House of Lords confirmed that nuisance is a tort against land, meaning that any injuries not associated with the land are not recoverable. Since the leading case of *Cambridge Water Co Ltd v Eastern Counties Leather plc* [1994] 2 AC 264 confirmed that *Rylands v Fletcher* is a special form of nuisance, it follows that *Rylands v Fletcher* can, like nuisance, only address injuries to real or personal property, not injuries to the person.

compare

Cambridge Water Co Ltd v Eastern Counties Leather plc [1994] 2 AC 264 is discussed further below.

9.5 Activities giving rise to liability

9.5.1 No need for a ultra-hazardous activity

As originally enunciated by Blackburn J, liability in *Rylands v Fletcher* results when someone collects and keeps 'anything likely to do mischief if it escapes'. A common mistake is to assume that the things that are collected must be inherently dangerous or even ultra-hazardous in nature. Lord Goff negated that supposition in *Cambridge Water Co Ltd v Eastern Counties Leather plc* [1994] 2 AC 264, stating that:

> [T]here is much to be said for the view that the courts should not be proceeding down the path of developing such a theory . . . I incline to the view that . . . it is more appropriate for strict liability in respect of operations of high risk to be imposed by Parliament, than by the courts.

Instead, the thing need only be likely to cause damage should an escape take place. Thus, almost anything can result in liability under *Rylands v Fletcher* if it escapes and causes mischief. Water was the culprit in both *Rylands v Fletcher* and *Cambridge Water Co Ltd v Eastern Counties Leather plc* [1994] 2 AC 264, but courts have also imposed liability for the escape of:

- Fire caused by a wire breakage in one building that spread to the adjoining premises, as in *LMS International Ltd v Styrene Packaging and Insulation* [2005] EWHC 2065.
- Electricity stored in high voltage cables that electrocuted some cows, as in *Hillier v Air Ministry* (1962) CLY 2084.
- A chair from a carnival ride that flew loose, injuring the adjoining stall-holder, as in *Hale v Jennings Bros* [1938] 1 All ER 579.
- Yew trees that grew across a boundary line, where they poisoned animals in the adjoining field, as in *Crowhurst v Amersham Burial Board* (1879) 4 Ex D 5.

Perhaps the strangest case falling under *Rylands v Fletcher* was *A-G v Corke* [1933] Ch 89, wherein a landowner was found liable to his neighbours when certain caravan dwellers who were allowed to live on his property 'escaped' and caused mischief.

9.5.2 Escape

When considering *Rylands v Fletcher* liability, the claimant must demonstrate that something escaped from the defendant's property. According to Viscount Simon LC in *Read v J Lyons & Co Ltd* [1947] AC 156, escape 'means from a place which the defendant has occupation of, or control over, to a place which is outside his occupation or control.' In that case, there had been an explosion at a munitions factory and an inspector—who was on the factory premises—was injured. Although there had been escape of a thing—the munitions—from one place to another, the escape had not crossed any property lines and the claim in *Rylands v Fletcher* failed.

However, the thing that escapes need not be the thing that is contained on the property itself. For example, in *Miles v Forest Rock Granite Co (Leicestershire) Ltd* (1918) 34 TLR 500, another explosion caused damage, this time by rocks falling onto adjoining property. However, the thing that was kept—explosives—was not the thing that escaped. The court still found that an escape existed.

9.5.3 Non-natural user

When one considers that the thing that escapes need not be inherently dangerous but only likely to cause damage if it escapes, the potential for liability looks very broad. However, one of the quirks about *Rylands v Fletcher* is its traditional requirement that the defendant is only liable if the thing brought onto the land constitutes a 'non-natural use' of the land. This terminology has created a great deal of confusion. Blackburn J only said that liability ensued when a thing 'which was not naturally there' escaped and caused mischief. Subsequent decisions have failed to provide any firm guidance on this point, however. For example, Lord Porter said in *Read v J Lyons & Co Ltd* [1947] AC 156, the munitions case, that the court should consider 'all the circumstances of time and practice of mankind . . . so that what may be regarded as dangerous or non-natural may vary according to the circumstances.' Lord Goff, in his minority opinion in *Cambridge Water Co Ltd v Eastern Counties Leather plc* [1994] 2 AC 264, took exception to the traditional view that 'non-natural use' could be equated with 'some special use bringing with it increased danger to others'. Previous cases had also said that non-natural use 'must not merely be the ordinary use of the land or such a use as is proper for the benefit of the community'. Lord Goff believed that this test would extend the concept of natural use beyond 'reasonable bounds'.

The traditional view has met with more approval recently, when the House of Lords considered *Transco plc v Stockport Metropolitan Council* [2003] UKHL/61. In this case, the House of Lords was asked to provide recompense for damage following the escape of water from a pipe in a multi-story block of flats built by the defendants. The escaping water caused an embankment under the claimants' gas mains to collapse, and the claimants took the necessary repairs to avoid any leakage of gas. Afterwards, they sought to recover the cost of the repairs from the defendants, based on *Rylands v Fletcher*, since there had been no negligence.

In his opinion, Lord Bingham stated that 'I think it clear that ordinary user is a preferable test to natural user, making it clear that the rule in *Rylands v Fletcher* is engaged only where the defendant's use is shown to be extraordinary and unusual'. Many believed that *Transco plc v Stockport Metropolitan Council* [2003] UKHL 61 would sound the death knell for *Rylands*, based on the narrowness of Lord Bingham's definition of 'non-natural user'.

However, the even-more recent case of *LMS International Ltd v Styrene Packaging and Insulation* [2005] EWHC 2065 (TCC) has shown that *Rylands v Fletcher* is still alive and well. In that case, the judge found that, for a cause of action to exist, the defendant must have brought onto his land things which were likely to cause and/or catch fire and keep them in such a way that, if a fire began, it would be likely to spread to another's land. Furthermore, the defendant's actions had to arise from a non-natural use of the defendant's land. The court relied on Lord Porter's opinion in *Read v J Lyons & Co Ltd* [1947] AC 156 to construe 'non-natural use' by reference to contemporary standards. Certainly there was precedent for that stance. For example, in *British Gas Plc v Stockport Metropolitan Borough Council* [2001] Env. L. R. 44, the Court of Appeal held that the escape of gas or water from domestic gas or water pipes or electricity from electrical wires was not considered a 'non-natural user', at least to the extent that such use was for ordinary, reasonable purposes. In that case, it was reasonable to store water in a pipe used to service a tower block of flats.

9.5.4 Foreseeability

Up until the mid-1990s, *Rylands v Fletcher* liability did not seem to carry any requirement of foreseeability. Instead, liability truly was strict, in the sense that even the unlikeliest of escapes could result in liability. However, *Cambridge Water Co Ltd v Eastern Counties Leather plc* [1994] 2 AC 264 changed all of that.

● **Cambridge Water Co Ltd v Eastern Counties Leather plc** [1994] 2 AC 264

Lord Goff of Chieveley: My Lords, this appeal is concerned with the question whether the appellant company, Eastern Counties Leather Plc. (E.C.L.), is liable to the respondent company, Cambridge Water Co. (C.W.C.), in damages in respect of damage suffered by reason of the contamination of water available for abstraction at C.W.C.'s borehole at Sawston Mill near Cambridge. The contamination was caused by a solvent known as perchloroethene (P.C.E.), used by E.C.L. in the process of degreasing pelts at its tanning works in Sawston, about 1.3 miles away from C.W.C.'s borehole, the P.C.E. having seeped into the ground beneath E.C.L.'s works and thence having been conveyed in percolating water in the direction of the borehole. C.W.C.'s claim against E.C.L. was based on three alternative grounds, viz. negligence, nuisance and the rule in Rylands v. Fletcher (1868) L.R. 3 H.L. 330...

[A] reasonable supervisor at E.C.L. would not have foreseen, in or before 1976, that such repeated spillages of small quantities of solvent would lead to any environmental hazard or damage—i.e., that the solvent would enter the aquifer or that, having done so, detectable quantities would be found down-catchment. Even if he had foreseen that solvent might enter the aquifer, he would not have foreseen that such quantities would produce any sensible effect upon water taken down-catchment, or would otherwise be material or deserve the description of pollution...The only harm that could have been foreseen from a spillage was that somebody might have been overcome by fumes from a spillage of a significant quantity...

Nuisance and the rule in Rylands v. Fletcher

...

In order to consider the question in the present case in its proper legal context, it is desirable to look at the nature of liability in a case such as the present in relation both to the law of nuisance and the rule in Rylands v. Fletcher, and for that purpose to consider the relationship between the two heads of liability.

I begin with the law of nuisance. Our modern understanding of the nature and scope of the law of nuisance was much enhanced by Professor Newark's seminal article on 'The Boundaries of Nuisance' (1949) 65 L.Q.R. 480...In Professor Newark's opinion (p. 487),...liability which should have arisen only under the law of negligence was allowed under the law of nuisance which historically was a tort of strict liability; and that there was a tendency for 'cross-infection to take place, and notions of negligence began to make an appearance in the realm of nuisance proper.' But in addition, Professor Newark considered, at pp. 487-488, it contributed to a misappreciation of the decision in Rylands v. Fletcher:

'This case is generally regarded as an important landmark—indeed, a turning point—in the law of tort; but an examination of the judgments shows that those who decided it were quite unconscious of any revolutionary or reactionary principles implicit in the decision. They thought of it as calling for no more than a restatement of settled principles, and Lord Cairns went so far as to describe those principles as "extremely simple" and in fact the main principle involved was extremely simple, being no more than the principle that negligence is not an element in the tort of nuisance. It is true that Blackburn J. in his great judgment in the Exchequer Chamber never once used the word "nuisance," but three times he cited the case of fumes escaping from an alkali works—a clear case of nuisance—as an instance of liability under the rule which he was laying down. Equally it is true that in 1866 there were a number of cases in the reports suggesting that persons who controlled dangerous things were under a strict duty to take care, but as none of these cases had anything to do with nuisance Blackburn J. did not refer to them'.

'But the profession as a whole, whose conceptions of the boundaries of nuisance were now becoming fogged, failed to see in Rylands v. Fletcher a simple case of nuisance. They regarded it as an exceptional case—and the Rule in Rylands v. Fletcher as a generalisation of exceptional cases, where liability was to be strict on account of "the magnitude of danger, coupled with the difficulty of proving negligence," [Pollock, Law of Torts, 14th ed. (1939), p. 386] rather than on account of the nature of the plaintiff's interest which was invaded. They therefore jumped rashly to two conclusions: firstly, that the Rule in Rylands v. Fletcher could be extended beyond the case of neighbouring occupiers; and secondly, that the Rule could be used to afford a remedy in cases of personal injury. Both these conclusions were stoutly denied by Lord Macmillan in Read v. Lyons [1947] A.C. 156, but it remains to be seen whether the House of Lords will support his opinion when the precise point comes up for decision.'

compare

Chapter 8 discusses nuisance in detail and includes an excerpt of Lord Goff's opinion to the extent it discusses nuisance.

We are not concerned in the present case with the problem of personal injuries, but we are concerned with the scope of liability in nuisance and in Rylands v. Fletcher. In my opinion it is right to take as our starting point the fact that, as Professor Newark considered, Rylands v. Fletcher was indeed not regarded by Blackburn J. as a revolutionary decision: see, e.g., his observations in Ross v. Fedden (1872) 26 L.T. 966, 968. He believed himself not to be creating new law, but to be stating existing law, on the basis of existing authority; and, as is apparent from his judgment, he was concerned in particular with the situation where the defendant collects things upon his land which are likely to do mischief if they escape, in which event the defendant will be strictly liable for damage resulting from any such escape. It follows that the essential basis of liability was the collection by the defendant of such things upon his land; and the consequence was a strict liability in the event of damage caused by their escape, even if the escape was an isolated event. Seen in its context, there is no reason to suppose that Blackburn J. intended to create a liability any more strict than that created by the law of nuisance; but even so he must have intended that, in the circumstances specified by him, there should be liability for damage resulting from an isolated escape.

Of course, although liability for nuisance has generally been regarded as strict, at least in the case of a defendant who has been responsible for the creation of a nuisance, even so that liability has been kept under control by the principle of reasonable user—the principle of give and take as between neighbouring occupiers of land, under which 'those acts necessary for the common and ordinary use and occupation of land and houses may be done, if conveniently done, without subjecting those who do them to an action:' see Bamford v. Turnley (1862) 3 B. & S. 62, 83, per Bramwell B. The effect is that, if the user is reasonable, the defendant will not be liable for consequent harm to his neighbour's enjoyment of his land; but if the user is not reasonable, the defendant will be liable, even though he may have exercised reasonable care and skill to avoid it. Strikingly, a comparable principle has developed which limits liability under the rule in Rylands v. Fletcher. This is the principle of natural use of the land. I shall have to consider the principle at a later stage in this judgment. The most authoritative statement of the principle is now to be found in the advice of the Privy Council delivered by Lord Moulton in Rickards v. Lothian [1913] A.C. 263, 280, when he said of the rule in Rylands v. Fletcher:

'It is not every use to which land is put that brings into play that principle. It must be some special use bringing with it increased danger to others, and must not merely be the ordinary use of the land or such a use as is proper for the general benefit of the community.'

It is not necessary for me to identify precise differences which may be drawn between this principle, and the principle of reasonable user as applied in the law of nuisance. It is enough for present purposes that I should draw attention to a similarity of function. The effect of this principle is that, where it applies, there will be no liability under the rule in Rylands v. Fletcher; but that where it does not apply, i.e. where there is a non-natural use, the defendant will be liable for harm caused to the plaintiff by the escape, notwithstanding that he has exercised all reasonable care and skill to prevent the escape from occurring.

Foreseeability of damage in nuisance

It is against this background that it is necessary to consider the question whether foreseeability of harm of the relevant type is an essential element of liability either in nuisance or under the rule in Rylands v. Fletcher. I shall take first the case of nuisance...

Foreseeability of damage under the rule in Rylands v. Fletcher

It is against this background that I turn to the submission advanced by E.C.L. before your Lordships that there is a similar prerequisite of recovery of damages under the rule in Rylands v. Fletcher.

I start with the judgment of Blackburn J. in Fletcher v. Rylands (1866) L.R. 1 Ex. 265 itself...

Blackburn J. spoke of 'anything likely to do mischief if it escapes;' and later he spoke of something 'which he knows to be mischievous if it gets on his neighbour's [property],' and the liability to 'answer for the natural and anticipated consequences.' Furthermore, time and again he spoke of the strict liability imposed upon the defendant as being that he must keep the thing in at his peril; and, when referring to liability in actions for damage occasioned by animals, he referred, at p. 282, to the established principle that 'it is quite immaterial whether the escape is by negligence or not.' The general tenor of his statement of principle is therefore that knowledge, or at least foreseeability of the risk, is a prerequisite of the recovery of damages under the principle; but that the principle is one of strict liability in the sense that the defendant may be held liable notwithstanding that he has exercised all due care to prevent the escape from occurring.

There are however early authorities in which foreseeability of damage does not appear to have been regarded as necessary... I feel bound to say that these... cases provide a very fragile base for any firm conclusion that foreseeability of damage has been authoritatively rejected as a prerequisite of the recovery of damages under the rule in Rylands v. Fletcher... In my opinion, the matter is open for consideration by your Lordships in the present case...

The point is one on which academic opinion appears to be divided... However, ...the historical connection with the law of nuisance must now be regarded as pointing towards the conclusion that foreseeability of damage is a prerequisite of the recovery of damages under the rule...

Even so, the question cannot be considered solely as a matter of history. It can be argued that the rule in Rylands v. Fletcher should not be regarded simply as an extension of the law of nuisance, but should rather be treated as a developing principle of strict liability from which can be derived a general rule of strict liability for damage caused by ultra-hazardous

compare

Again, see chapter 8 for Lord Goff's opinion concerning foreseeability in nuisance. That discussion also bears on the need to demonstrate foreseeability in Rylands v Fletcher.

operations, on the basis of which persons conducting such operations may properly be held strictly liable for the extraordinary risk to others involved in such operations...[T]his would lead to the practical result that the cost of damage resulting from such operations would have to be absorbed as part of the overheads of the relevant business rather than be borne (where there is no negligence) by the injured person or his insurers, or even by the community at large...

I have to say, however, that there are serious obstacles in the way of the development of the rule in Rylands v. Fletcher in this way...I incline to the opinion that, as a general rule, it is more appropriate for strict liability in respect of operations of high risk to be imposed by Parliament, than by the courts...Having regard to these considerations,...it appears to me to be appropriate now to take the view that foreseeability of damage of the relevant type should be regarded as a prerequisite of liability in damages under the rule. Such a conclusion can, as I have already stated, be derived from Blackburn J.'s original statement of the law; and I can see no good reason why this prerequisite should not be recognised under the rule, as it has been in the case of private nuisance...It would moreover lead to a more coherent body of common law principles if the rule were to be regarded essentially as an extension of the law of nuisance to cases of isolated escapes from land, even though the rule as established is not limited to escapes which are in fact isolated...

The facts of the present case

Turning to the facts of the present case, it is plain that, at the time when the P.C.E. was brought onto E.C.L.'s land, and indeed when it was used in the tanning process there, nobody at E.C.L. could reasonably have foreseen the resultant damage which occurred at C.W.C.'s borehole at Sawston...

[S]ince those responsible at E.C.L. could not at the relevant time reasonably have foreseen that the damage in question might occur, the claim of C.W.C. for damages under the rule in Rylands v. Fletcher must fail.

Natural use of land

I turn to the question whether the use by E.C.L. of its land in the present case constituted a natural use, with the result that E.C.L. cannot be held liable under the rule in Rylands v. Fletcher. In view of my conclusion on the issue of foreseeability, I can deal with this point shortly...

It is a commonplace that this particular exception to liability under the rule has developed and changed over the years. It seems clear that, in Fletcher v. Rylands, L.R. 1 Ex. 265 itself, Blackburn J.'s statement of the law was limited to things which are brought by the defendant onto his land, and so did not apply to things that were naturally upon the land. Furthermore, it is doubtful whether in the House of Lords in the same case Lord Cairns, to whom we owe the expression 'non-natural use' of the land, was intending to expand the concept of natural use beyond that envisaged by Blackburn J. Even so, the law has long since departed from any such simple idea...; and,...natural use has been extended to embrace the ordinary use of land. I ask to be forgiven if I again quote Lord Moulton's statement...

'It is not every use to which land is put that brings into play at that principle. It must be some special use bringing with it increased danger to others, and must not merely be the ordinary use of the land or such a use as is proper for the general benefit of the community.'

...

It is obvious that the expression 'ordinary use of the land' in Lord Moulton's statement of the law is one which is lacking in precision...Fortunately, I do not think it is necessary for the purposes of the present case to attempt any redefinition of the concept of natural or ordinary use. This is because I am satisfied that the storage of chemicals in substantial quantities, and their use in the manner employed at E.C.L.'s premises, cannot fall within the exception...The mere fact that the use is common in the tanning industry cannot, in my opinion, be enough to bring the use within the exception, nor the fact that Sawston contains a small industrial community which is worthy of encouragement or support. Indeed I feel bound to say that the storage of substantial quantities of chemicals on industrial premises should be regarded as an almost classic case of non-natural use; and I find it very difficult to think that it should be thought objectionable to impose strict liability for damage caused in the event of their escape. It may well be that, now that it is recognised that foreseeability of harm of the relevant type is a prerequisite of liability in damages under the rule, the courts may feel less pressure to extend the concept of natural use to circumstances such as those in the present case; and in due course it may become easier to control this exception, and to ensure that it has a more recognisable basis of principle. For these reasons, I would not hold that E.C.L. should be exempt from liability on the basis of the exception of natural use.

However, for the reasons I have already given, I would allow E.C.L.'s appeal with costs before your Lordships' House and in the courts below.

It is not clear from Lord Goff's opinion whether the resulting damage has to be foreseeable in terms of the kind of harm by itself or whether the resulting damage has to be foreseeable both in terms of the likelihood of escape as well as the harm that occurs. However, Lord Bingham made it clear in *Transco plc v Stockport Metropolitan Council* [2003] UKHL 61 that it is the first type, which is very similar to the principles of foreseeability found in negligence. Lord Bingham phrased the test thusly:

> It must be shown that the defendant has done something which he recognised, or judged by the standards appropriate at the relevant place and time, he ought reasonably to have recognised, as giving rise to an exceptionally high risk of danger or mischief if there should be an escape, however unlikely an escape may have been thought to be.

Therefore, foreseeability is a necessary part of the *Rylands v Fletcher* analysis, even if the tort is considered to be one of strict liability.

9.6 Defences

compare
For the defences of consent and contributory negligence, see chapter 5.

Many of the defences available in other torts, including negligence, are available in *Rylands v Fletcher* cases. For example, if the claimant has given the defendant either implicit or explicit consent to accumulate the thing that escapes and causes damage, the defendant has a good defence. Similarly, if the claimant's actions helped bring about the escape of the thing that causes mischief, the defendant can claim that the award should be reduced because of contributory negligence. Furthermore, if the defendant has a statutory duty to perform the activity, then the defendant will not be liable in tort.

NOTE As is often the case, the defence of statutory duty only exists of the defendant is under a duty to act. If the statute simply gives the defendant a statutory power, then liability will result. Furthermore, a defence of statutory authority will only apply to actions argued under *Rylands v Fletcher*. If a claimant pursues a negligence claim as well, the defence will not apply to that cause of action.

Two defences in *Rylands v Fletcher* rely on outside forces to negate responsibility and require slightly more discussion. First, a defendant could claim that the escape happened as a result of the acts of the third party. *Rylands v Fletcher* itself demonstrates that this defence is not good when the escape results from the acts of the defendant's independent contractor. While that case could be attributed to an unusual sort of vicarious liability, more recent cases suggest that foreseeability might be the key. For example, in *Hale v Jennings Bros* [1938] 1 All ER 579, the Court of Appeal held that the owner of a fun fair ride was liable when part of it (in this case, a chair from a chair-o-plane) 'escaped' to a neighbouring stall, even though the accident occurred as a result of a passenger's tampering with the chair. Similarly, the owner of a flag pole was held responsible in *Shiffman v Grand Priority in British Realm of Venerable Order of the Hospital of St John of Jerusalem* [1936] 1 All ER 557 after the pole fell and injured the plaintiff, even though the fall occurred as a result of some children's meddling with the pole. In these cases, as well as others, the courts' rulings seem to be based on the principle that the defendant should be liable for escapes, even those caused by others, if the defendant ought to have reasonably foreseen the act of the third party and had sufficient control over the premises to be able to prevent an escape.

compare

Normally, a defendant is not liable for the acts of an independent contractor, unless there was negligence in the hiring or the independent contract was undertaking acts that were inherently dangerous. See chapter 16 for a further discussion of vicarious liability.

However, there are certain acts that apparently do not need to be foreseen. For example, in *Rickards v Lothian* [1913] AC 263, the defendant was not liable for damage caused by flooding after an unknown third party maliciously blocked up a lavatory basin in the defendant's basement and turned on a water tap. While some courts, including Parker LJ in *Perry v Kendricks Transport Ltd* [1956] 1 All ER 161, have taken the view that the actions of a stranger cause a defendant to 'avoid liability, unless the plaintiff can go on to show that the act which caused the escape was an act of the kind which the owner could reasonably have contemplated and guarded against', others have disagreed with this analysis, concluding that cases such as *Rickards* are really about negligence, rather than *Rylands v Fletcher*. This position is based on the fact that *Rylands v Fletcher* is a strict liability tort, and neither motive, fault nor breach of a duty of care has any role in the determination of liability.

Lord Goff appears to make this point clearly in *Cambridge Water Co Ltd v Eastern Counties Leather plc* [1994] 2 AC 264, when he states that 'the defendant will be liable for harm caused to the plaintiff by the escape, notwithstanding that he has exercised all reasonable care and skill to prevent the escape from occurring'. Thus, the extent to which the defendant has guarded against the escape—be it reasonable or not—is irrelevant in determining liability under *Rylands v Fletcher*. Lord Goff's analysis is supported by the House of Lords' decision in *Smith v Littlewoods Organisation Ltd* [1987] 1 All ER 710, in which the Lords held that the failure to control the reasonable foreseeable acts of a third party could constitute negligence. That case involved vandals who set a disused building on fire, causing harm to the building next door. While this may sound similar to *Rylands v Fletcher* liability, since the fire could be said to have 'escaped', the case was decided in negligence.

However, at least one recent Court of Appeal case—*Ribee v Norrie* [2001] PIQR 8—has suggested that the act of a stranger—meaning someone who has acted outside the scope of the activities permitted by the occupier of the premises—will relieve an occupier of liability under *Rylands v Fletcher*. In this instance, a fire began in the common area of a house, and the smoke escaped next door, causing harm to the claimant. Because the owner of the house that caught fire was an occupier of the common area where the fire began (even though he had let the individual rooms as bed-sit accommodations), he was liable for the escaper of the smoke under *Rylands v Fletcher*. The defendant could have limited liability by indicating that smoking in the common area was not allowed, but he had not done so. Thus the tenant in the common area whose act caused the fire was not a 'stranger' to the defendant.

Not every act of a third party is committed unintentionally. Sometimes a person will come onto another's land and purposefully undertake the action that results in the discharge of injury-causing materials onto another's property. Some of these cases can proceed under trespass to land, which is discussed in the next chapter. However, since *Rylands v Fletcher* is a strict liability tort, the defendant cannot defend him or herself on the grounds that due care was taken to avoid the third party from injuring the claimant's property.

The second defence under *Rylands v Fletcher* that relies on the work of outside forces is known as the 'act of God' defence. Lord Hobhouse in *Transco plc v Stockport MBC* [2003] UKHL 61 held that an act of God occurs when the event involves no human agency, but is instead due directly and exclusively to natural causes. Furthermore, an act of God cannot be realistically guarded against or prevented by any amount of foresight or care. In *Transco plc v Stockport MBC* [2003] UKHL 61, the House of Lords was considering damages caused to the claimants' gas pipes after the escape of water from pipes maintained by a local authority. Because the damage was something the defendants could insure against, the act of God defence failed in this case.

Water damage was also at issue at two famous, albeit conflicting, opinions discussing *Rylands v Fletcher* liability. *Nichols v Marsland* (1876) 2 Exc D 1, for example, involved the damage caused when an artificial lake overflowed after excessive rainfall. There, the court held that the defendant could not reasonably have anticipated that four bridges

cross reference

Transco plc v Stockport Metropolitan Council [2003] UKHL 61 was discussed above.

would be washed away and thus could not be held liable for the damage caused by an act of nature. The opposite conclusion was reached by the House of Lords in *Greenock Corpn v Caledonian Rly Co* [1917] AC 556, where the defendants again collected water, this time by creating an artificial paddling pool. Again, there was an unusually strong rainstorm that caused the pool to overflow, damaging the plaintiffs' property. In this case, the rainfall was held not to be an act of God, allowing the plaintiffs to recover. There does not seem to be a great deal to distinguish the cases, other that the jury found that no reasonable person could foresee the type of rainfall in *Nichols v Marsland* (1876) 2 Exc D 1.

compare

Cambridge Water Co Ltd v Eastern Counties Leather plc [1994] 2 AC 264 is discussed in more detail above.

The problem with the formulation of the act of God defence, both traditionally and as recently enunciated by the House of Lords in *Transco plc v Stockport Metropolitan Council* [2003] UKHL 61, is that it relies on the reasonable foreseeability of the act of nature that causes the damage. Since *Rylands v Fletcher* has traditionally been viewed as a strict liability tort, the introduction of reasonable foreseeability would seem anomalous. However, such a development seems more logical in the wake of *Cambridge Water Co Ltd v Eastern Counties Leather plc* [1994] 2 AC 264. While the act of God defence was not at issue in that case, Lord Goff indicated foreseeability is always important in a *Rylands v Fletcher* case.

9.7 *Rylands v Fletcher* and other torts

Rylands v Fletcher is just one of many torts that arise from ownership or use of property. How do they all fit together? First, there is no need for a claimant to choose which tort is most suitable under the circumstances. As of *Cambridge Water Co Ltd v Eastern Counties Leather plc* [1994] 2 AC 264 shows, a claimant may seek recovery under alternate heads of liability—in that case, for nuisance, negligence and *Rylands v Fletcher*. It may be that the facts will support one claim but not another. However, because the claimant cannot know how the finder of fact will rule on any one point, the claimant is best served by proceeding on multiple counts. Second, a claimant may need to pursue different theories of recovery because no one tort will provide the claimant with full recompense for his or her injuries. For example, a claimant may have suffered personal injury as well as property damage. Alternatively, a claimant may wish to seek an injunction to avoid future harm in addition to damages for past injuries.

Of all the land-based torts, *Rylands v Fletcher* most resembles nuisance, particularly physical nuisance. Both have to do with the movement of a thing from one person's property to another's, and, since the decision in *Cambridge Water Co Ltd v Eastern Counties Leather plc* [1994] 2 AC 264 and *Transco plc v Stockport Metropolitan Council* [2003] UKHL 61, both torts require a foreseeability analysis. However, the thing in *Rylands v Fletcher* that escapes must be likely to cause mischief, whereas no such requirement exists in nuisance. Furthermore, liability in *Rylands v Fletcher* includes acts undertaken by independent contractors, whereas defendants under nuisance law may not be liable for the acts of these sorts of third parties. Finally, the concept of 'non-natural user' under *Rylands v Fletcher* is not, according to Lord Goff in *Cambridge Water Co Ltd v Eastern Counties Leather plc* [1994] 2 AC 264, precisely the same as the concept of 'unreasonable user' that one sees in nuisance, although they carry out similar functions.

Finally, when distinguishing the two torts, one must also consider the qualities of the claimant. For example, in nuisance, one must have a proprietary interest in the property affected by the nuisance, whereas there does not appear to be a similar requirement under *Rylands v Fletcher*.

As shall be seen in the next chapter, trespass to land is similar to *Rylands v Fletcher* in that it also requires the invasion of another's property, but in those cases, the thing or person that crosses the boundary line does not need to come from a particular piece of property. In other words, the liability results from the act of invasion rather than the ownership of property, as with *Rylands v Fletcher*.

 For more revision tips, including self-test questions and suggestions for further reading, see the Online Resource Centre at www.oxfordtextbooks.co.uk/orc/strong_complete/.

revision tasks

Some of the following tasks will help you organize your materials into a workable outline.

- Define the various terms of art under *Rylands v Fletcher*. Know what was originally meant by 'non-natural user', 'escape', and 'thing likely to cause mischief' and compare each phrase to its current meaning.

- Create an outline setting forth the ways in which *Rylands v Fletcher* differs from similar torts. Pay special attention to issues involving foreseeability.

- Become familiar with the limited ways in which a defendant can escape liability based on the acts of third parties or an act of God.

10 Trespass to land

10.1 Introduction

We have now come to the final land-related tort, trespass to land. The previous chapters have dealt primarily with liability that arises from activities or the state of affairs on one's own property. Whether the injury was caused to the claimant personally or to the claimant's land does not matter as much as the fact that the action emanated from the defendant's land. Trespass to land, however, does not require the defendant to be an owner or occupier of land. Instead, it focuses on damage to the claimant's propriety interest in land through unauthorized entry onto the land. The property need not drop in value or become unsuitable for use or enjoyment—the mere fact of ownership is what is at issue here.

The elements of the tort are relatively straightforward and include:

- The defendant's mental state;
- The defendant's physical acts;
- Issues involving the claimant;
- Damages and other remedies; and
- Defences.

10.2 The defendant's mental state

Unlike the other land-related torts, trespass to land is an intentional tort, requiring the defendant to have consciously undertaken the act in question. Be careful: the defendant need not have intended to injure the claimant in any way or even know that he or she is doing so. For example, the defendant could (mistakenly) believe that he or she owns the land or that he or she has permission to enter. That mistake would not matter so long as the defendant intended to enter onto the land. Similarly, if the defendant does a negligent act that could foreseeably result in an entry on another's land—for example,

NOTE As will be discussed below, mistake is not a defence to trespass to land.

leaving the brake off a vehicle, which then rolls onto another person's property—trespass will result. As Lord Bramwell stated in *Holmes v Mather* (1874–85) LR 10 Ex 261 (which actually involved trespass to the person after a runaway horse and carriage ran down a bystander, but which is equally applicable to the intent necessary for trespass to land):

> If the act that does the injury is an act of direct force, *vi et armis*, trespass is the proper remedy (if there is any remedy), where the act is wrongful either as being wilful or as being the result of negligence. Where the act is not wrongful for either of these reasons no action is maintainable, though trespass would be proper form of action if it were wrongful.

Thus, in *League Against Cruel Sports Ltd v Scott* [1986] QB 240, no action in trespass could be maintained after a pack of hunting dogs went onto land maintained as a deer preserve unless the master of the hounds could be shown to have either intentionally encouraged the dogs to go onto the property or negligently failed to keep the dogs from doing so.

10.3 The defendant's physical acts

Recall

See chapter 4 for a further discussion of the distinction between legal causation (forseeability) and factual ('but for') causation.

Before an act can constitute trespass, it must be shown to be a direct result of the defendant's action. Here, again, we come across the concept of legal foreseeability rather than factual causation. For example, a person may build a spout on his roof to drain water away from his house which results in water being dripped on his neighbour's land, as was the case in *Reynolds v Clarke* (1795) 2 Ld Raym 1399. However, the encroachment of the water on the plaintiff's land, while causally direct, was not considered to be a trespass (whether it would be considered legally foreseeable, and thus negligent, in a modern legal context is unknown; those criteria were not fully developed at the time the decision was made).

Later cases demonstrate that potential defendants should consider the foreseeable impact of natural forces. For example, in *Gregory v Piper* (1829) 9 B & C 591, trespass occurred when the defendant placed some rubbish near the plaintiff's land. When the rubbish dried up, it rolled onto the plaintiff's property as a result of natural forces. Even though the defendant did not intend the entry of the rubbish onto the plaintiff's land, the defendant did intend to place it near the property line. Thus, the defendant's acts were sufficiently intentional, since the outcome was foreseeable. However, Lord Denning in *Southport Corpn v Esso Petroleum Co Ltd* [1954] 2 QB 182 seemed to take the opposite view, claiming that the defendant was not liable in trespass when the tide carried some oil discharged by a ship onto the plaintiff's land, since the act was a consequential, rather than a direct, result of the defendant's action. Thus the question may be somewhat open when the final act of trespass is carried out by a foreseeable force of nature.

Notably, the defendant does not need to intrude personally onto the claimant's land for trespass to occur. It is sufficient if the defendant simply causes another object, person or animal to go onto another's property. For example, discharging a gun onto another's land, allowing one's animals (such as dogs, cats, pigs or sheep) to enter onto another's property or pushing another person onto the claimant's land can constitute trespass. Omissions—such as the failure to restrain an animal—can result in negligence to the same extent as affirmative acts.

Sometimes a trespasser may enter onto another's property as a matter of right. For example, someone may be invited to come onto the land for a limited purpose—such as to repair a leaky faucet—or may have a limited legal right to enter, such as to go up to the front walk to deliver post. However, if the person remains after that the right to enter has expired or exceeds the scope of the right (such as by straying from the front path into a shed in the back yard), that person may be liable in a special type of trespass, called 'continuing trespass'. Similarly, if a person places an object on another's land and allows that object to remain, there is a continuing trespass so long as the item stays on the claimant's property. Again, the damage is to the landowner's proprietary rights rather than to the land. The trespasser may not injure anything on the property by remaining on the land or exceeding the scope of the invitation, but the law protects the landowner's right to control who or what comes onto the property.

For instance, the law gives people the presumptive right to walk up a stranger's path to the front door. 'When a householder lives in a dwelling-house to which there is a garden in front and does not lock the gate of the garden, it gives an implied licence to any member of the public who has lawful reason for doing so to proceed form the gate to the front door or back door, and to inquire whether he may be admitted and to conduct is lawful business', as noted in *Robson v Hallett* [1967] 2 QB 939. If permission to remain is denied, the person has a reasonable time in which to leave the premises before being considered a continuing trespass.

Trespass to land need not involve the touching of soil or structures. As you will learn in your property course, a possessor of land has the exclusive right not only to the surface of the property, but also to the land below (including any minerals or water found there) and the air above. Therefore, drilling beneath someone else's property can result in an action for trespass. Similarly, trespass may occur if someone infringes on another's airspace through the construction of a building that overhangs the property line or the release of a projectile, even if the object does not fall on the claimant's land. However, a possessor's exclusive right to the air above is limited to that amount of air which would normally be used for the purposes associated with the land, such as the construction of buildings upon the land. Aircraft may fly a reasonable height over another's property without incurring liability, as per the Civil Aviation Act 1982. A person in an aircraft may even take photographs of another's land without risking an action in trespass. However, if anything falls from the aircraft onto the land, then a case in trespass may be brought.

10.4 Issues involving the claimant

cross reference

Future interests in land are considered in detail in property courses, but a brief discussion can also be found in chapter 8.

To be a claimant in trespass, one must have a legal estate in the land in question (a freehold, leasehold, license, etc) and exclusive possession. Thus, if there is a tenant on the land when a trespass occurs, the tenant is the proper person to bring a cause of action, rather than the landlord, since the landlord has no immediate right to possession. Similarly, someone with a reversionary or other type of future interest in land has no immediate right to sue in trespass. However, the holder of a future right may have an action against the current possessor, either in contract (as in the case of a landlord-tenant arrangement) or in property law (such as for waste). Furthermore, if a person has a right to immediate possession of land but has not yet entered upon it, that person can sue for trespasses that occurred between the time the claimant's right to possession arose and the time the claimant eventually did enter onto the property. This action is called trespass by relation, since it 'relates back' to a previous time. Your property course will give you more details regarding the types of legal interests in land. For the purposes of tort law, it is sufficient to know that a claimant in trespass must have some legal right to use or possess the land, either because the claimant owns the land or has the right to occupy or use the land.

One case has suggested that the right in land need not be permanent or even a formal occupation of the land. In *Monsanto v Tilly* [2000] Env LR 313, the Court of Appeal held that Monsanto plc—a biochemical company engaging in research and development—had a sufficient interest in certain genetically modified crops that were being grown on other people's land across the country to support a claim for trespass to land against certain protestors who came onto the land to destroy the crops. Because the crops were not 'goods' until they were severed from the land, the Court of Appeal considered Monsanto's interest in the crops to be an interest in the land.

compare

See chapter 5 for a further discussion of contributory negligence and ex turpi causa non oritur actio.

Any wrongful acts taken by the claimant at the time of the trespass may affect any eventual award. Therefore, when considering whether a cause of action exists in trespass, consider whether defences such as contributory negligence or *ex turpi causa non oritur actio* would apply.

10.5 Damages and other remedies

Often, people who sue in trespass are not interested in obtaining monetary damages. Instead, claimants in trespass often bring the case as a way to establish who is the rightful owner of land. Since only one with a legal estate and exclusive possession can pursue an action in trespass, bringing a case is often the proper way to establish ownership as a matter of law. Once title to land has been established, a claimant in trespass can obtain an injunction to throw the wrongful occupant off the land.

Since the tort of trespass is actionable *per se*, there is no need to establish any injury to the claimant or the land as part of the *prima facie* case. However, if injury has occurred, claimants are entitled to full restitution for their losses. For example, if the land or the buildings upon it have been damaged, the claimant can recover the cost of repairs or replacement. If the only injury has been wrongful occupancy, the rate of recovery is calculated by the reasonable rental value of the land during the time of occupancy. It is not necessary for the claimant to prove that he or she could have or would have rented the property during that time period; the rate is still calculated by the rental value during that time.

If the trespasser has taken goods from the land—such as minerals, lumber or water—then the measure of damages is calculated either by reference to the value of the goods taken less the cost incurred in removing the goods from the land (in cases where the act is 'innocent', meaning without wilful knowledge of the wrongdoing) or by reference to the value of the thing taken (in cases where the act is wilful). The difference is that innocent trespassers can subtract the cost of removing the goods from the damage award; wilful trespassers must absorb the cost of their own wrongdoing.

10.6 Defences

A person may use reasonable force to defend his or her land from a potential trespasser, though the person doing so must have the requisite possessory interest in land to allow a case in trespass to be brought. Thus, for example, the cricket captain in *Holmes v Bagge* (1853) 1 E & B 782 who removed an alleged trespasser from the pitch could not claim defence of property since the captain was not in possession of the field. However, if a person has possession of property and asks someone to leave who then remains (thus committing a continuing trespass), the proper possessor of the land may eject the person.

In all cases, the amount of force used to eject a trespasser or prohibit the trespasser's entry must be reasonable under the circumstances. Thus, *Tullay v Reed* (1823) 1 C & P 6, which dealt with assault and battery, held:

> [i]f a person enters another's house with force and violence, the owner of the house may justify turning him out (using no more force than is necessary),without a previous request to depart; but if the person enters quietly, the other party cannot justify turning him out, without a previous request to depart.

Simply breaking into a building may not be sufficient to justify extreme force, as shown by *Revill v Newbery* [1996] QB 567, when a defendant was found to have wrongfully shot a trespasser who broke into a garden shed but who showed no intention of committing violence on a person. However, the plaintiff there was found contributorily negligent, diminishing his damages award by two thirds.

As a matter of law, setting a dangerous mechanical device—such as a spring gun—to defend property alone is unreasonable, although if the intent is to protect persons as well, then a defence may exist, depending on the circumstances. Fixed and visible deterrents—such as razor wire or spiked rails—are a reasonable defence of property, even if a trespasser is injured by them. However, no matter how reasonable the amount of force used, the defence will not be available if a defendant is mistaken in his or her belief that the claimant is a trespasser. Therefore, a defendant bears the risk of error when repelling a potential trespasser by force.

Arguments relating to the defence of property are often confused with the defence of necessity. Necessity involves an act that is lawfully taken to protect people or property from a threatened harm, even if an innocent person suffers a loss as a result. The defence requires an actual (or what would appear to a reasonable person to be an actual) and immediate danger, and the steps taken in response must also be reasonable, in light of all the circumstances. For example, the possessor of land may act to protect the land from flooding, even if the waters are thereby diverted to a neighbour's land. Under those circumstances, the actor will not be liable for any damages resulting from the diverted waters. Similarly, a person may break into an empty house for protection during a violent storm and will not be liable in trespass. However, the defence of necessity requires there to be an urgent threat of immediate harm, so that a perennially homeless person may not take up customary residence in a deserted warehouse and claim necessity as a defence against a claim of trespass.

When an individual acts on his or her own behalf, it is termed private necessity. However, a defendant may also claim the defence of public necessity to protect against fire or other public threats.

In all cases, the acts taken must be reasonable, both in the short and long term. Thus the police were liable for a fire that resulted after they shot a CS gas canister into a shop to expel a dangerous psychopath in *Rigby v Chief Constable of Northampton* [1985] 2 All ER 985. The judge held that while the initial act was defensible as a public necessity, the police were negligent by not having sufficient fire-fighting equipment available to control the resulting fire.

For more revision tips, including self-test questions and suggestions for further reading, see the Online Resource Centre at www.oxfordtextbooks.co.uk/orc/strong_complete/.

revision tasks

Some of the following tasks will help you organize your materials into a workable outline.

- Consider how trespass to land is similar to trespass to the person, which is discussed in chapter 9.

- Create a chart outlining the different elements of land-based torts. Know which torts address which types of injuries, offer which types of remedies and require which types of acts or mental elements.

- Know how the different land-based torts can assist in interpreting similar torts. For example, consider how the common law relating to occupiers' liability can help establish the necessary possessory interest for an action in trespass.

Part 5
Damages and Other Remedies

Damages and other remedies

Introduction

Once a claimant proves that a tort has been committed, there is yet more to do, since the court must then turn to the remedy that is to be awarded. Although the preceding chapters have shown that courts will sometimes provide for injunctive relief that requires a party either to do or refrain from doing some act, injunctions are seldom granted outside a few well-defined areas, and torts are primarily remedies by money damages.

At one time, the law followed well-defined rules setting a particular monetary value on various body parts. Loss of a hand might be worth X pounds, whereas loss of a leg might be worth Y pounds. At best, this approach gave very rough justice, since the calculations did not take into account individual circumstances; for example, the loss of a leg might have a very different impact on the life and future income of a manual labourer as compared to a writer. Similarly, a keen amateur musician might find his or her quality of life greatly diminished by an injury causing deafness, whereas an avocational painter might not suffer as much.

This chapter describes the various types of remedies available in tort, with a particular emphasis on how to calculate damages for personal injuries and death. The chapter proceeds as follows:

- Mitigation of damage;
- Sharing of damages;
- Types of damages;
  - Contemptuous;
  - Nominal;
  - General versus special;
  - Aggravated and exemplary;
  - Multiple causes of action;
  - Personal injury and death;
  - Property damage; and
- Inunctions and other relief.

11.2 Mitigation of damage

compare

Contract law also requires claimants to mitigate damages, as you will learn on your contract course.

Tort law requires claimants to mitigate—or minimize—damage as much as possible. This principle may be linked, to a certain extent, to the concept of contributory negligence. For example, if a landowner sees that property is being flooded because a sewage pipe on a neighbour's land has broken, the landowner cannot just do nothing and let the water flow for several hours or several days. The landowner must take appropriate steps to minimize the damage, either by calling someone, such as the neighbour or the fire department, or taking appropriate steps, such as placing sandbags in the path of the water, to lessen the damage that will occur. Note that failing to take steps such as these does not mean that the defendant is absolved of liability. The tort has still occurred—it is just a question of how much the claimant will be awarded in damages.

The issue is similar to that of contributory negligence in that the claimant is not contributing to the initial act that causes the harm, but is contributing to the scope of the harm by not taking steps to minimize the damage. Interestingly, under the Law Reform (Contributory Negligence) Act 1945, an act taken by a claimant before the tort occurs may constitute a failure to mitigate damages if the act increases the magnitude of the damage that will (and does) result if a tort occurs. Thus, in *Froom v Butcher* [1976] QB 286, a passenger's failure to wear a seatbelt resulted in a reduction in damages, even though the decision not to wear the seatbelt took place before the road accident that constituted a tort occurred.

think point

What policy principle underpins the decision to award full damages in situations where the claimant's attempt to mitigate result in increased injury?

All that a claimant need do to mitigate damages is act reasonably. There is no requirement that the claimant's actions actually result in a lessening of the injury. In fact, if the claimant takes reasonable actions that in fact increase the scope of the injury, the claimant will still be able to recover the entire costs.

11.3 Sharing of damages

cross reference

Contributory negligence is discussed in detail in chapter 5.

There are instances where damages can be shared proportionally between several people. Contributory negligence is by far the most important sharing mechanism and the one that arises most frequently. Remember, contributory negligence applies in virtually any circumstance where the claimant's own negligent behaviour contributed to the injury suffered. Whenever contributory negligence is pled and proven, the amount that the defendant must pay is reduced by a sum proportional to the fault of the claimant.

cross reference

Concurrent and sequential causes of harm are discussed in detail in chapter 4.

In some cases, however, it is some third party—not the claimant—who bears the blame for part of the injury suffered by the claimant. Sometimes the injury suffered by the claimant was concurrently caused by several parties, and sometimes it was suffered sequentially. Whenever multiple defendants are identified—even when they do not actively or intentionally work together—the claimant may choose the one that he or she wishes to pursue. That defendant will be responsible for the entire amount of damages. However, the defendant can claim back some of the money paid to the claimant by seeking contribution from the other defendant(s). The court will allocate fault proportionally among the defendants and require the defendants to pay sums reflecting the proportion of fault through the Civil Liability (Contribution) Act 1978.

cross reference

Contribution under the Civil Liability (Contribution) Act 1978 is discussed in chapter 16.

Although the concept of allocation of damages between different parties (either including or excluding the claimant) is relatively simple, students often confuse contribution with contributory negligence. Just remember that an action for recovery of a portion of a damage award under the Civil Liability (Contribution) Act 1978 is between two parties who could (or were) made defendants to a cause of action brought by the person who was originally injured in tort. A claim to reduce damages based on the contributory negligence of the original claimant in tort (i.e. the person who was originally harmed) is brought under the Law Reform (Contributory Negligence) Act 1945 and is a means by which one (or more) defendants to a tort action reduce their damages based on the behaviour of the claimant.

11.4 Types of damages

11.4.1 Contemptuous damages

Contemptuous damages are often the smallest award that a claimant can obtain. These sorts of damages would be awarded where a tort technically occurred, but where the court considered the suit to be frivolous or the claimant's behaviour to be entirely lacking in merit. Thus the court signals its contempt for the claimant by providing for a very small sum—one pound sterling, for example.

11.4.2 Nominal damages

....
VOCABULARY

'Nominal' means 'in name only'. How does that help you remember what nominal damages address?
....

Nominal damages may be awarded where a tort has technically occurred but no real injury occurred. As previous chapters have demonstrated, some torts do not require the claimant to prove that any harm occurred as a result of the defendant's actions. These types of torts are, as you recall, considered actionable *per se* and are the only types of torts that can result in an award of nominal damages. However, the purpose behind tort law is to provide compensation for injuries suffered. If a claimant has suffered a tort, technically speaking, but has not suffered any, or any significant, hardship as a result of that tort, the court may award a minimal cash award. These minimal awards—or nominal damages—provide the proper amount of recompense, since they allow the court to enter a judgment in favour of the claimant without behaving punitively toward the defendant, since a larger amount would not reflect the actual injury suffered by the claimant.

Don't confuse nominal damages with small awards. If the court rules that the damages, in fact, have been small and grants a sum commensurate with that determination, then it has not issued a nominal award.

11.4.3 General versus special damages

think point

Which torts require claimants to prove up 'special damages'?

Throughout this text, you have heard mention of the need, in certain circumstances, to prove up 'special damages.' These are damages that the law does not presume to have occurred as a result of the defendant's actions. Instead, the claimant must plead and prove them separately. These detailed damages—which can include property damage, medical treatment in personal injury cases, and any other easily quantifiable costs and expenses—are termed special damages, whereas those damages that cannot be individually assessed—emotional distress, for example, or pain and suffering—are general damages. Remember, in torts that are not actionable *per se*, the law will not presume that a loss has arisen as a result of the actions taken by the defendant, so special damages must be proven in these cases.

11.4.4 Aggravated and exemplary damages

think point

Why might a court want to take additional steps to restrict behaviour intended to cause outrage?

The purpose of tort law is to provide compensation for the claimant. As a policy matter, Parliament and the courts have decided that claimants should not profit from the events resulting in the tort, although neither should they suffer a detriment. The loss should fall squarely on the shoulders of the defendant. However, sometimes the defendant's actions are so blameworthy as to justify the imposition of additional damages. For example, if the defendant has acted malevolently or spitefully, the court may provide for aggravated damages, which are said to compensate for torts that were intended to and did outrage the claimant. For example, a libel might be spread only to those persons who would be most likely and able to act on it to the claimant's harm. Similarly, a trespass to land might occur at a time (such as a wedding or funeral) that would cause maximum embarrassment, grief or anger. While compensatory damages in tort do, to some extent, take these sorts of circumstances into account, Lord Woolf MR said in *Thompson v Metropolitan Police Commissioner* [1998] QB 498 that aggravating damages 'can be awarded where there are aggravating features about the case which would result in the [claimant] not receiving sufficient compensation for the injury suffered...Aggravating features can include humiliating circumstances...or any conduct of those responsible...which shows that they had behaved in a high-handed, insulting, malicious or oppressive manner'. In that case, the claimant had been arrested by the police in circumstances leading to a claim of malicious prosecution, false imprisonment, and assault and battery, due to the nature in which the arrest was made.

However, aggravated damages are not available for all torts. For example, the Court of Appeal held in *AB v South West Water Services Ltd* [1993] QB 507 that aggravated damages were not available for cases involving personal injuries resulting from negligence. The court was of the view that any emotional distress or anxiety should be addressed as part of the normal compensatory damages scheme, and that any emotional harm that was 'magnified or exacerbated' by the defendants' behaviour should and would be included in the initial award. Any further compensation would be punitive in nature.

compare

Other jurisdictions, most notably the United States, allow punitive damages, whose purpose is to punish tortfeasors and decrease the likelihood that a tortfeasor will merely factor anticipated compensatory damages awards into the cost of doing business. The use of punitive damages increased dramatically in the 1980s, after consumer advocates discovered that a major automobile manufacturer continued to market a defective car on the assumption that profits from sales would offset the amounts that the manufacturer would have to pay to future plaintiffs for actual injuries. In what became known as the 'Ford Pinto Memo', named after the vehicle that was believed to explode on rear impact, the Ford Motor Company stated that it would not redesign the car for a minimal cost, since it anticipated any future tort cases would only cost the company $11 per vehicle. Soon afterward, in Grimshaw v Ford Motor Company, 119 Cal App 3d 757 (4th Dist. 1981), a California state court awarded $2.5 million in compensatory damages and $3.5 million in punitive damages (down from $125 million awarded at trial) to two plaintiffs injured in a fiery explosion. In recent years, commentators in the US have criticized the prevalence of punitive damages—which can rise to millions or billions of dollars—but proponents of the system say that there is no other way to control large corporations who prefer profit to principles. The most recent example of corporate greed has involved the tobacco industry, which was recently shown, in a document similar to the Ford Pinto Memo, to have hidden the addictive and poisonous nature of cigarette smoking. Punitive damages in those cases (some of which are individual and some of which are class actions, an American form of group litigation) commonly fall in the millions, with some awards exceeding several billion dollars.

The reason why courts must be careful to restrict their damages awards is that tort law may not use damages awards to punish a wrongdoer in the United Kingdom. To do so would blur the line between civil law (which is compensatory in nature) and criminal law (which is punitive). However, British law does permit courts to award exemplary damages in certain limited circumstances. Exemplary damages—which are intended to punish tortfeasors and deter future wrongdoing—are awarded for conduct which outrages the court (as opposed to aggravated damages, which are awarded for conduct which outrages the claimant). Exemplary damages are said to be permissible because tort law is not solely about compensation, but also—like criminal law—carries an element of deterrence. For example, in the recent case of *Rowlands v Chief Constable of Merseyside Police* [2006] EWCA Civ 1773, the Court of Appeal held that the jury should have been able to consider giving exemplary damages following a case against the police for assault, false imprisonment and malicious prosecution. The Court of Appeal's decision was made despite the fact that the named defendant was merely vicariously liable for the acts of others. However, Moore-Bick LJ noted that the case was brought against the police force and would have a deterrent effect on future abuses of the police power. Moore-Bick LJ cited the arguments for and against the imposition of exemplary damages in cases involving vicarious liability, as outlined in the Report of the Law Commission on Aggravated, Exemplary and Restitutionary Damages (1997) (Law Com No 247), but eventually decided to allow the issue to go to the jury in this instance.

As a practical matter, however, courts find it difficult to decide when and how to allow exemplary damages. In *Rookes v Barnard* [1964] AC 1129, which involved the plaintiff's refusal to join a union in order to work in a closed shop and subsequent threats by the union of unlawful strikes, the House of Lords attempted to identify precisely those cases where exemplary damages were proper. Lord Devlin stated that such an award could only be made in three categories of cases:

- 'Where the plaintiff has been the victim of oppressive, arbitrary or unconstitutional action by servants of government'.
- 'Where the defendant's conduct has been calculated by him to make a profit for himself which may well exceed the compensation payable to the plaintiff'.
- 'Where authorised by statute'.

Even after Lord Devlin defined his three categories of cases, it was unclear whether exemplary damages were still limited to the types of cases where exemplary damages had previously been considered proper. In 1997, the Law Commission issued its Report on Aggravated, Exemplary and Restitutional Damages (Law Com No 247), which stated that exemplary damages should extend to all torts, regardless of whether those categories existed prior to Lord Devlin's 1964 formulation. The House of Lords considered the issue in 2002 in *Kuddus v Chief Constable of Leicestershire* [2001] UKHL 29, which involved wrongdoing on the part of a police officer. The officer, who had been called in by the claimant to investigate a burglary, later forged the claimant's signature on a report withdrawing the complaint of theft. The House of Lords held that the police officer's actions could result in an award of exemplary damages. In coming to that conclusion, the Lords noted the findings of the Law Commission report and concluded that it was not necessary to consider whether cause of action was of the type that had been subject to exemplary damages prior to 1964. Instead, all that was necessary was whether the factual situation was covered by one of Lord Devlin's formulations in *Rookes v Barnard* [1964] AC 1129.

11.4.5 Multiple causes of action

Whenever a claimant brings a tort action, he or she should consider bringing multiple causes of action. Thus, for example, when faced with a encroachment on land, the claimant should consider bringing claims in nuisance, negligence, trespass to land and *Rylands v Fletcher*. Sometimes all the elements will exist for all four causes of action and sometimes they will not; however, as a tactical matter, clever claimants try as many claims as is feasible, since different torts very often address different injuries and/or carry different remedies. For example, it is easier to obtain an injunction in nuisance than it is in negligence. Conversely, it is easier to claim certain types of damages in negligence than it is in nuisance.

A claimant will not be able to obtain damages in respect of the exact same type of injury under two different causes of action, since that would constitute double recovery. Thus, a person whose house is damaged by flooding from a neighbouring reservoir cannot receive compensation for that house both in negligence and nuisance and *Rylands v*

TIP Make a list of which damages are allowed under which torts by discussing the possible heads of recovery (including injunctive relief) and then charting the associated torts which must be proven.

Fletcher. However, a claimant can obtain different remedies, including damages for different aspects of harm, for different causes of action arising out of the same fact pattern. Thus, a claimant could receive damages from the flood based in negligence and an injunction (but not damages) based in nuisance.

However, if two different causes of action exist, they may be pled at different times, and even in different courts. For example, *Brunsden v Humphrey* (1884) 14 QBD 141 involved a collision between a cab and a van. The plaintiff recovered for property damage in county court then brought another action for personal injuries in the High Court. This was held to be permissible, since the interests protected were different—one involved property and the other involved personal integrity. The interests protected must be different for such a strategy to prevail—if the two torts protect the same interest (property interest, for example), then they must be brought at the same time.

Similarly, claimants may not come back to court to gain additional damages if the injury turns out to be more extensive than originally anticipated. One exception exists under section 32A of the Supreme Court Act 1981, which indicates that when personal injuries are at stake, a provisional award may be made, thus allowing alterations to be made to the damages award if circumstances change in the future. Another potential solution is the creation of a structured settlement, as outlined in section 5 of the Damages Act 1996. There, a structured **settlement** is defined as a means of settling a claim for personal injuries in cases where '(a) the damages are to consist wholly or partly of periodical payments; and (b) the person to whom the payments are to be is to receive them as the annuitant under [an annuities policy] purchased for him by the person against whom the claim is brought . . . or his insurer.' However, a court cannot order structured settlements, nor does the Damages Act 1996 contain any means for assessing any deterioration in the claimant's health.

VOCABULARY
A 'settlement' occurs when parties to a lawsuit privately agree to accept a certain disposition of the dispute. What public policy considerations support structured settlements when agreed between parties?

11.4.6 Personal injury and death

Claims for damages incurred following personal injuries constitute a high proportion of civil actions that are started in the courts in the United Kingdom. When considering how to calculate these sorts of damages, one needs to consider (1) who can sue and (2) what a claimant can recover. The answers to these questions differ slightly depending on whether death or simply personal injury occurred.

EXAM TIP Because awards in respect of personal injury and death are so common, you can expect your examiners to test you on this. Be prepared!

Damages recoverable after death

When death occurs as a result of a tortious action, two different claimants may exist: (1) the decedent in his or her own right (represented by the decedent's estate) and (2) the surviving dependants of the decedent in their own right.

The decedent's own causes of action

The Law Reform (Miscellaneous Provisions) Act 1934 states that a decedent, through his or her estate, retains the right to pursue any cause of action that has vested in him or her at the time of death. However, the 1934 Act contains three exceptions to the general rule about survival of causes of action:

cross reference

The tort of defamation is discussed in chapter 14.

- Actions based in defamation do not survive the death of the claimant.
- Actions for bereavement under the Fatal Accidents Act 1976 (discussed below) do not survive the death of the claimant.
- Claims for exemplary damages do not survive the death of the claimant.

Notably, the Law Reform (Miscellaneous Provisions) Act 1934 does not actually require the decedent to have made a decision to pursue a cause of action before death. Instead, the relevant causes of action survive for the benefit of the decedent's estate, which means that the executor of the estate makes the decisions on whether and how to pursue a claim.

think point

What policy considerations support the courts' not taking these other payments into account when calculating damages? What policy considerations can be raised in opposition?

Thus, when the decedent dies as a result of a tortious action, the estate may pursue a cause of action in tort and claim damages for the time period between the act or omission and the time of death. The various heads of recovery are the same as those described for damages in personal injury below, although the various types of damages—pain and suffering, lost wages, etc—are only for a limited amount of time. The 1934 Act also states that damages awarded to a decedent's estate should not take into account any other monies given to or taken from the estate as a result of the death. For example, any insurance monies payable to the estate upon the death of the decedent will not be considered when calculating damages.

In cases involving personal injury alone, damages payable to the claimant are calculated into the future, even though no one knows how long the claimant will live. In cases involving death, damages payable to the decedent's estate are calculated from the time of the tort to the time of death—no extra sum is added for future expectations, even if the decedent is quite young. However, the decedent's family might be able to recover for some or all of those future expectations, as discussed below.

Sometimes death occurs immediately upon the commission of the tort, thus eliminating any need to calculate lost wages, pain and suffering, etc., under the 1934 Act. However, whether death is instantaneous or not, the Administration of Justice Act 1982 indicates that the estate may still make a claim for funeral expenses under the 1934 Act, with one minor exception. If a dependant of the decedent has already paid for funeral expenses, the dependant may not make a claim against the estate; the proper mode of recovery is against the estate under the Fatal Accidents Act 1976, discussed below.

The estate may recover damages even when the death resulting from the tort occurs long after the event or even after the conclusion of litigation. According to section 3 of the Damages Act 1996, if a claimant was awarded provisional damages under section 32A of the Supreme Court Act 1981 and then subsequently dies as a result of the injuries suffered in the tort, the estate can claim any losses that were not covered by the initial damages award. This is perhaps the only exception to the general rule that a claimant may not go back to court later and demand additional damages. However, it is permitted only in cases where the first award was provisional, rather than final, in nature.

Dependants' causes of action

VOCABULARY

A 'dependant' is someone financially dependent on the decedent and linked by legal or familial ties—a child, a parent, a spouse, etc.

For many years, the common law did not allow dependants to bring an action against a tortfeasor for losses the **dependants** suffered as a result of the death of the victim of the tortious act. An exception was made by statute, however, when Parliament decided in 1846 to allow the families of victims of railway accidents to recover for certain losses. The initial legislation was gradually expanded over the years, eventually eliminating the common law rule and allowing recovery in all types of misconduct resulting in death. The current statute, known as the Fatal Accidents Act 1976, begins by identifying the proper category of defendants, stating that:

> If death is caused by any wrongful act, neglect or default which is such as would (if death had not ensued) have entitled the person injured to maintain an action and recover damages in respect thereof, the person who would have been liable if death had not ensued shall be liable to an action for damages, notwithstanding the death of the person injured.

If the decedent was partially responsible for the act that resulted in death, the damages award will be reduced proportionally, as per the Law Reform (Contributory Negligence) Act 1945. If one of the dependants who is to receive damages under the Fatal Accidents Act 1976 was partially responsible for the act that resulted in death, then that person will receive a reduced damages award, though other dependants' awards will remain unaffected.

The 1976 Act then goes on to define who may act as a proper claimant. The list is not as wide as it could be and only affects certain categories of dependants of the decedent. Although the executor or administrator of the estate is the named claimant, the action is brought on behalf of one or all of the following persons:

- Spouses (current or past);
- Children or grandchildren;
- Parents or grandparents;
- Siblings;
- Aunts and uncles; and/or
- Cousins.

In all cases, the 1976 Act provides for step-relations, adopted relations and illegitimate relations. Furthermore, the Administration of Justice Act 1982 recognizes a protectable interest in any person who was living in the same household as the decedent as the decedent's wife or husband for at least two years before death. Although these types of co-habitants are entitled to some damages, the fact that they never married the decedent will be taken into account, since the failure to marry means that there is no legally enforceable right to financial support.

NOTE Typically, the only people who can recover under the Fatal Accidents Act 1976 are the decedent's immediate family. Other third parties—even those who may have suffered emotional or economic loss as a result of the death—have no claim against a tortfeasor. Therefore, be on the lookout in an exam situation for bereaved fiancées, bankrupt employees and inconsolable third cousins. These people will almost assuredly have no claim under the Fatal Accidents Act 1976.

However, the Fatal Accidents Act 1976 does not allow every relative on the face of the planet to bring a claim through the estate's executor or administrator. Only those dependants who have suffered a pecuniary loss may receive damages. One of the leading cases on this subject is the House of Lords decision in *Davies v Taylor* [1974] AC 207.

● *Davies v Taylor* [1974] AC 207

Viscount Dilhorne: My Lords, on August 14, 1968, Mr. Davies, the appellant's husband, was killed in a motor accident. He and the appellant married in 1955. They had no children. She went to work and at work met a Mr. Evans with whom she committed adultery after an office party. Thereafter they committed adultery about once a month. The appellant said that last took place in February 1968. In May 1968, she left her place of employment and on July 9, 1968, she left her husband and the matrimonial home and went to live with her parents...She took all her personal belongings with her.

They met on two other occasions before the end of July. On each occasion she says he begged her to go back to him and gave her money...Then on July 31, 1968, he came to the door of the house where she was and begged and pleaded with her to return to him...She said that the only other occasion on which she spoke to her husband was on the day he died. They met in the street. He told her that he had been to a solicitor; that he had named Philip Evans but that he did not want to drag her name through the courts; that he wanted her back, and that she could go back at any time during the five months (presumably the time it was expected would elapse before a divorce petition would be heard) and everything would be forgotten.

She said that in reply she asked if he would give her time, that she would think about it and 'given time would go back to him.'...Having learnt of her adultery on July 31, 1968, her husband on August 2, 1968, instructed solicitors and made a statement...

The appellant after the death of her husband claimed damages from the driver of the other car who admitted that his negligence caused the death of her husband. She claimed under the Law Reform (Miscellaneous Provisions) Act 1934 and under the Fatal Accidents Acts. Bridge J. held that she was entitled to damages under the former Act but dismissed her claim under the Fatal Accidents Acts. She appealed against this dismissal to the Court of Appeal and her appeal was dismissed by a majority. For the appellant to succeed in her claim she had to show that she had a reasonable expectation of pecuniary benefit from her husband of which she had been deprived by his death: *Taff Vale Railway Co. v. Jenkins* [1913] A.C. 1. In that case Lord Atkinson said, at p. 7: 'It is quite true that the existence of this expectation is an inference of fact—there must be a basis of fact from which the inference can reasonably be drawn.' In some cases, e.g. *Barnett v. Cohen* [1921] 2 K.B. 461, it is said that there has to be a reasonable probability of pecuniary benefit. I do not think that it makes the slightest difference whether one speaks of a 'reasonable expectation' or a 'reasonable probability.'

In this case whether the appellant had been deprived by the death of her husband of a reasonable expectation or a reasonable probability of pecuniary benefit depended on determining whether or not there was a reasonable expectation or probability of a reconciliation.

That there was a possibility that if Mr. Davies had lived there would have been one, cannot be denied. She might have changed her mind and her husband might not have changed his and have continued, despite the institution of proceedings for divorce, to have wanted her to return. A possibility of something happening is very different from an expectation that it will happen or it being probable that it will happen.

In this case in the light of the evidence to which I have referred and in view of Bridge J.'s rejection of her evidence that she had told her husband that all she wanted was time, I see no basis of fact from which an inference can reasonably be drawn that there was an expectation of a reconciliation.

...

I agree with Megaw L.J. that there was a speculative possibility of reconciliation but not a reasonable expectation of one and I would therefore dismiss the appeal.

Furthermore, it is not only wives who are dependent on their husbands. Husbands may also claim for damages arising from the loss of their wives, particularly when both spouses work. Spouses and children are not the only ones who can be dependent on another; elderly parents can also be dependent on their adult children. *Kandalla v British Airways Board* [1981] QB 158 concerns two parents who intended to come live with their adult children in the United Kingdom.

● *Kandalla v British Airways Board* [1981] QB 158

Griffiths J: My conclusion is that the plaintiff and his wife were intending to leave Iraq and live with their daughters but that they were hoping to be able to make arrangements to get part of their fortune out with them. If however that had not proved possible, I believe they would nevertheless have left Iraq to live in their old age as dependants of their daughters. The departure from Iraq was I think precipitated by the death of the daughters but not caused by it. I believe the probabilities are that the plaintiff would have been unable to bring out any substantial part of his funds. I see no reason to suppose it would be more likely that he would be successful in getting out funds, if his daughters had not been killed, than has in fact proved to be the case since their death. I cannot accept the submission of the defendants that but for this accident he would in all probability have continued living in Baghdad...

I turn now to consider the question of valuing the dependency for the purpose of the Fatal Accidents Acts and this presents formidable difficulties. As I have already pointed out, there is no firm evidence as to the income that the two daughters were earning at the date of their death; it is really a matter of conjecture based upon the assumption that it was probably more than they could have been earning in the National Health Service as junior hospital doctors. They were, however, both undoubtedly competent and well trained doctors with the advantage of speaking several languages and I have come to the conclusion that their earning capacity must be taken to be at least equal to that of the average general practitioner. If they had chosen to enter general practice, no doubt it would have taken a year or so to work up to the national average but that they were capable of doing so I have no doubt. I have by agreement been provided with figures showing the national average earnings of general practitioners in this country from 1972 to the present date. These figures show that the net earnings, after deduction of tax, for an unmarried doctor with the advantage of a dependant's allowance has risen from £4,071.50 for the year 1972–73 to the sum of £9,084.50 for the year 1979–80. But the question remains, how much of this money would the two daughters have been able to or prepared to make available for the support of their parents?...

The next question is how much of their income would have been needed for the support of their parents? This would depend upon how much of their fortune the parents could have removed from Iraq and what, if any, earning capacity might have been left to the plaintiff after his arrival in this country...

What I suppose would have happened if the parents had come to this country would have been that they would have lived with either one or both their daughters and would thus have been provided with a home, food, clothing and such reasonable comforts as their daughters' available incomes could provide. I can only approach the matter broadly. The plaintiff suggests that I should allocate two-fifths of the daughters' income to the support of their parents, but with the many imponderables I think this is too high a percentage. I propose to assume that the two daughters would have been prepared to spend up to a quarter of their available net income for the support of their parents and to make the further assumption that this dependency would have commenced in the year 1973–74. In considering the question of the proportion of the income to be applied I have not, of course, overlooked the fact that the girls might have married and thus have had less of their income available for their parents' support because of their own immediate families' needs. However, as I propose to ignore the possibility of marriage and dependants for the purpose of assessing the Law Reform Act claims as will appear later, I have not given any great weight to this factor in valuing the Fatal Accidents Acts claim.

Taking this then as my starting point the total net available income from both daughters from the tax year 1973–74 to the end of the tax year 1979–80 was, to the nearest round figure, £72,000; thus I allow as a loss of dependency a quarter of this figure, namely £18,000, to take one up to the end of the current tax year, i.e., April 1980, which I apportion equally between the plaintiff and his wife. The plaintiff is now 74 with a life expectation, according to the life expectation tables, of 8.59 years; his wife is 68 with a life expectation of 14.97 years. I shall quantify the plaintiff's continuing dependency at five years' purchase and the wife's at nine years' purchase. The current net income of the two daughters would be approximately £19,000, a quarter of which is £4,750. Accordingly, I shall allow five years' purchase at £4,750, which I shall round up to the sum of £24,000, which again I apportion equally between the plaintiff and his wife. Finally, I shall allow a further four years' purchase on the wife's claim at the rate of £3,000 per annum. I allow rather more than half the joint dependency to the wife because in fact it costs proportionately more to provide support for one person than it does for two people living together. This then is a further £12,000; thus the total dependency before considering any deductions that have to be made because the parents have inherited their daughters' estates comes to a total sum of £54,000 apportioned as to £21,000 to the plaintiff and £33,000 to his wife.

Again, however, the claim to support must have some measurable parameters; entirely speculative claims will not be enforced. For example, in *Taff Vale Rly Co v Jenkins* [1913] AC 1, the House of Lords held that a parent was allowed to recover the future wages

NOTE Always consider the extent to which social context plays into these decisions. How much did the social reality of 1913 factor into this decision?

of a 16-year-old dressmaker's apprentice who was just about to start earning income. However, in *Barnett v Cohen* [1921] 2 KB 461, the parents of a three-year-old were not allowed to pursue a claim for pecuniary loss. The future earnings there were too speculative to support an award.

Although a legal right to financial aid will obviously strengthen a claim, gratuitous services can also form the basis of a legal claim. For example, in *Stimpson v Wood & Son* (1888) 57 LHQB 484, a wife who had committed adultery—thus losing her legal right to be maintained financially by her husband—was still able to pursue a claim for pecuniary loss. Similarly, a husband could cover the value added to the household as a result of his wife's work as a homemaker.

. . . .

● *Berry v Humm Co* [1915] 1 KB 627

Scrutton J: [The plaintiff] had been married four years and had one child of three years of age. He had kept no servant, but his wife did all the work of the house and looked after the child. Since the death of his wife he was obliged to employ a housekeeper…He further said that his late wife had herself made the bread and did everything in the house, and that before the war began he found that the house as managed by a housekeeper instead of his wife was costing him 3s. a week more…I directed the jury to assess the pecuniary damage the husband had sustained by the death of his wife, omitting all compensation for wounded feelings or funeral expenses, and considering the cost of the wife's maintenance, clothing, and pocket money which the husband was saved by her death, the chance of the husband marrying again, and of his or the child's death…

Counsel for the defendants then argued that this sum was not recoverable in that damages by loss of services by death were not recoverable in tort, even under Lord Campbell's Act, where, as here, the deceased was killed on the spot; and that the only damages recoverable were pecuniary loss where the deceased had made pecuniary contributions in the past, or there was a reasonable probability that he would do so in the future…

It is clear that at common law, in the present state of the authorities, the death of a human being could not be complained of as an injury…But this common law rule in tort has been interfered with by Lord Campbell's Act, which allows the executor of the deceased to bring an action for the benefit of the wife, husband, parent or child of the deceased, in which the jury may award them damages proportioned to the injury resulting to them from the death. While the cause of action fails if the deceased, if alive, could not have recovered damages for the negligence, the measure of damages is quite different. It excludes compensation for injury to the deceased, or for the wounded feelings of his relatives, and is based solely on compensation for a pecuniary loss to the relatives, assessed either on the loss of such contribution in the past, or on the loss of a reasonable expectation of pecuniary benefit in the future…I can see no reason in principle why such pecuniary loss should be limited to the value of money lost, or the money value of things lost, as contributions of food or clothing, and why I should be bound to exclude the monetary loss incurred by replacing services rendered gratuitously by a relative, if there was a reasonable prospect of their being rendered freely in the future but for the death.

Not every form of support will allow damages to be paid. If, for example, the income stemmed from an illegal act, the dependants may not pursue a cause of action, even if they meet all the other qualifications.

However, the Fatal Accidents Act 1976 does allow the spouse of the deceased to bring a claim for bereavement, regardless of whether the decedent's business was legal or illegal and regardless of whether the surviving spouse relied financially on the deceased's financial support. The proper sum for bereavement is set by statutory instrument and is currently £7,500. Only currently married spouses are entitled to an award for bereavement; co-habitants and former spouses do not get similar treatment under the law. The only other persons who can make a claim to damages for bereavement are parents of a deceased minor (i.e. under the age of 18) child who has never married. If both parents are living, the £7,500 is split evenly among them. If the child is illegitimate, the mother receives the entire amount.

For claims other than bereavement, the amount of damages allowed depends on the amount and type of support given to the dependants during the life of the decedent. In *Davies v Powell Duffryn Associated Collieries Ltd* [1942] AC 601, which involved two colliers who were killed by an explosion in the respondents' coal mine. Lord Wright described the traditional means of assessing damages as follows:

> The starting point is the amount of wages which the deceased was earning, the ascertainment of which to some extent may depend on the regularity of his employment. Then there is an estimate of who much was required or expended for his own personal and living expenses. The balance will give a datum or basic figure which will generally be turned into a lump sum by taking certain number of years' purchase. That sum, however, has to be taxed down by having due regard to uncertainties.

The House of Lords defined these criteria in even more detail in 1971, in a case dealing with the need to ascertain the future earnings of an architect following his death in a car accident caused by the defendant.

● *Taylor v O'Connor* [1971] AC 115

Lord Guest: Section 2 of the Fatal Accidents Act, 1846, lays down the measure of damages in a death claim thus: 'The jury may give such damages as they may think proportioned to the injury resulting from the death.' It is thus a jury question to be arrived at on broad lines. The two important matters to be considered are the extent of the dependency or, as I would prefer to put it, the amount of the loss of support occasioned to the widow by the death of her husband. And, secondly, the method by which this sum is to be converted into a lump sum which would constitute the award.

So far as the first figure is concerned the judge has calculated that the deceased had a spendable income of £6,000 per annum at the date of his death. And upon this basis he has concluded that the widow has lost the chance of support at two-thirds of that sum, namely, £4,000.

There was very little material for the judge to go on, but, in my view, this was a generous estimate having regard to the figures which would appear to produce a sum in the region of £3,000 as being spent on the family apart from the deceased. But justification can be found for the figure of £4,000 in allowing for possible future increase in salary and the effects of inflation. The judge made a deduction of £250 in respect of the acceleration of the widow's interest in the deceased's estate. This seems not unreasonable. So that so

NOTE Juries are no longer used in most civil cases, so the question would be answered by the judge, as the finder of fact.

far as the starting figure of £3,750 is concerned I can detect no error of principle in the judge's calculation.

The next question is what has been conveniently described as 'the multiplier' which will convert the loss of support into a lump sum of damages. The judge applied a multiplier of 12 to the figure of £3,750 resulting in a total of £45,000 under this head. It has been suggested that a more precise method of arriving at the extent of the loss would be to obtain actuarial figures as to what sum would be required, based on the widow's expectancy of life, to purchase an annuity of the extent of the loss. This method has been disapproved in the past and never adopted except as a very rough guide. Its adoption would depend on current rates of interest and would not allow for inflation. If it were adopted it would have to be discounted in respect that it provides certainty and does not allow for contingencies. I would not be in favour of its adoption for this or any similar type of case. This method would require actuarial evidence which would increase the length and expense of trials and would unduly complicate matters which might have to be considered by juries.

It was suggested that where incomes in the present bracket are in question, allowance should be made for taxation by grossing up the basic figure to provide such a sum as would, after allowing for income tax and possibly surtax at the appropriate rate, provide a net sum equal to the loss. It may be that where appropriate figures are produced it will be necessary to make some adjustment of the figure in order to make provision for income tax and surtax. I have not seen any sufficiently accurate figures in the present case which would enable me to make any suitable adjustment to the figures. Any such adjustment would be in the nature of a wild speculation. I would prefer to leave the question until it arises in a concrete form with appropriate evidence and figures, when the implications can properly be studied.

I return then to the 'multiplier.' The aim of this exercise is to provide a figure which is proportionate to the injury resulting from the death. It is not to provide such a sum as would at current rates of interest leave the widow with the income she has lost. This would put her into a better position than she would have been apart from the death because at the end of the day she would still have the capital sum left. It is anticipated that the capital will be gradually reduced over the years to provide for her support. In my opinion, the multiplier is intended to provide in a rough measure adequate compensation for the loss sustained. No precise method can be expected. It is well hallowed in practice and depends in some measure on the expertise of judges accustomed to try these cases. The judge would have applied a multiplier of ten but he increased it to 12 to take account of future inflation. In my opinion, this was not a good ground for increasing the multiplier. As I have already said, this should have been reflected in the amount of the dependency. But I think a multiplier of 12 can be justified in this case to take account of other matters such as the uncertainty of the incidence of income tax and surtax.

EXAM TIP Whenever your examiner gives you a question regarding damages accruing as a result of death or personal injury, be sure to calculate the amount in pounds sterling, if at all possible. If that is not possible, then at least indicate what multipliers would be used, using what factors. Damages questions such as these tend to focus on your maths skills—not your policy analysis.

In *Cookson v Knowles* [1979] AC 556, the House of Lords put another spin on the subject of calculation of damages for injury resulting in death.

● *Cookson v Knowles* [1979] AC 556

Lord Diplock: The instant case is a typical fatal accident case... The deceased, the husband of the plaintiff, was killed in a motor accident in December 1973. He was then aged 49 and was in steady work as a woodwork machinist. Had he lived it would have been 16 years before he reached the age of 65 when he would have qualified for a retirement pension and, in the ordinary course, might have been expected to cease working. The plaintiff was aged 45 and it was held by the Court of Appeal and is now common ground that her dependency at the date of death can be taken as £1,614 a year and that by the date of the trial in June 1976 the dependency as it would have been by then can be taken as £1,980 a year, owing to increases in wages during the two and a half years that had elapsed since December 1973.

...

[T]he Court of Appeal... held that for the purpose of awarding interest on damages the damages should be divided into two parts, one assessed by reference to the assumed dependency during the period between the date of death and the date of trial, and the other by reference to the assumed future dependency from the date of trial onwards. On the former part, interest should be awarded at half the short term investment rate, but on the latter part in respect of future dependency no interest should be allowed.

...

My Lords, in general I agree with the judgment of the Court of Appeal in the instant case.... Two separate though related questions are involved in the appeal to your Lordships' House [, including]... whether in such actions, where there are no unusual circumstances, interest should be awarded on the whole or part of that capital sum and, if the latter, on what part.

...

I turn then to the question of interest on the two components in the award of damages; the loss of the dependency sustained by the widow up to the date of trial, and the future loss of the dependency after that date... Once it has been decided to split the damages into two components which are calculated separately, the starting point for the second component, the future loss... is the present value not as at the date of death but at the date of the trial of an annuity equal to the dependency starting then and continuing for the remainder of the period for which it is assumed the dependency would have enured to the benefit of the widow if the deceased had not been killed. To calculate what would have been the present value of that annuity at the date of death, its value at the date of trial would have to be discounted at current interest rates for the 2½ years which had elapsed between the death and trial. From the juristic standpoint it is that discounted amount and no more to which the widow became entitled at the date of her husband's death. Interest on that discounted figure to the date of trial would bring it back up to the higher figure actually awarded. To give in addition interest on that higher figure would be not only to give interest twice but also to give interest on interest.

On the other hand the first component of the total damages, the loss of dependency up to the date of trial, is in respect of losses that have already been sustained over a period of 2½ years before the award is made. Had her husband lived the widow would have received the benefit of the dependency in successive instalments throughout that period. A rough and ready method of compensating her for the additional loss she has sustained by the delay in payment of each instalment (which ranges from 2½ years to none) is that adopted by the Court of Appeal, viz., to give interest for the whole of the period but at half the short term investment rate upon the mean annual amount which represents the assumed dependency during that period. Looked at from the juristic standpoint the justification for giving interest at only half the current rate is that the amount that the widow became entitled to at the date of her husband's death in respect of the instalments of the dependency which would have enured to her benefit up to the date of trial, would be the present value of each successive instalment as *at the date of death*. To calculate that value the nominal amount of the first instalment after the death would not need to be discounted at all, that of the median instalment would need to be discounted at current interest rates, but for half the period only between date of death and trial while that of the last instalment would need to be discounted at current interest rates for the whole of the period. The discounted figure for the sum of the instalments which represents their present value as at the date of death would thus be less than the sum actually awarded by an amount which represents the discount at current rates of interest on the nominal amount of each instalment for a period which over all the instalments averages approximately half the period between the date of death and trial. So, in effect, interest for half the period had already been included in an award of the sum of the nominal amounts of the instalments due up to the date of trial. To give interest on the sum of the instalments for the whole of that period instead of only half would be to give interest twice. This may be avoided either by halving the period for which interest is given at current rates or by giving interest for the whole period at half the current rates, as suggested by the Court of Appeal.

To summarise: for the reasons I have given, which follow largely upon the arithmetical basis for the assessment of damages which is called for by the provisions of the Fatal Accidents Act 1976 I consider that:

1. In the normal fatal accident case, the damages ought, as a general rule, to be split into two parts: (a) the pecuniary loss which it is estimated the dependants have already sustained from the date of death up to the date of trial ('the pre-trial loss'), and (b) the pecuniary loss which it is estimated they will sustain from the trial onwards ('the future loss).

2. Interest on the pre-trial loss should be awarded for a period between the date of death and the date of trial at half the short term interest rates current during that period.

3. For the purpose of calculating the future loss, the 'dependency' used as the multiplicand should be the figure to which it is estimated the annual dependency would have amounted by the date of trial.

4. No interest should be awarded on the future loss.

5. No other allowance should be made for the prospective continuing inflation after the date of trial.

Typically, damages awards for future earnings of a decedent are reduced to take income taxes into account. However, the Fatal Accidents Act 1976 specifically states that a damages award shall not consider the remarriage of a widow (or, presumably, a widower) or any prospect of remarriage. Furthermore, the Act requires the court to disregard the existence of any insurance or other benefits accruing to the estate as a result of the death.

Calculation of damages are relatively straightforward when the decedent earns money outside the home, but courts have struggled to find the best way to put an economic value on work done inside the home. Courts agree that the remaining spouse and children are entitled to recover the amount that they will now have to pay to replace the services to the household. Typically, the court will look at the cost of hiring a nanny or housekeeper, at least where the children are still in school. Additionally, some recompense should be made for parental services beyond cooking and cleaning—namely, the moral guidance and care given by a parent. If the family reasonably decides to have another relative tend to the children and that relative gives up paid employment, the courts tend to provide compensation based on that relative's loss of earnings rather than on the hypothetical cost of a nanny.

Most of the early law on compensation for in-home family care involved mothers, but in the 1990s, the common law had to deal with the reality that fathers were also providing parental care. Two diametrically opposed cases are *Hayden v Hayden* [1992] 4 All ER 681 and *Stanley v Saddique* [1992] QB 1. However, *Hayden v Hayden* [1992] 4 All ER 681, as the latter of the two cases, appears to prevail.

● *Hayden v Hayden* [1992] 4 All ER 681

Parker LJ: It was long ago established that a dependant child could recover under the Fatal Accidents Act damages for the loss of the gratuitous services of a deceased mother who had been killed due to the negligence of a tortfeasor. In such cases, even without complications, the court is faced with the task of quantifying in money that which cannot in reality be so quantified...

The essential facts are that the infant plaintiff (Danielle) who was aged four at the time of the accident lost her mother's services, that in order himself to replace such services, her father whose negligence had caused her mother's death gave up his employment to look after her and that his remuneration from his former employment had been £15,000 per annum.

For the defendant it is submitted that the value of his services should be taken into account, i.e. set against the value of the mother's lost services in arriving at her loss and for the plaintiff that the father's services must be wholly disregarded by reason of the provisions of section 4 of the Fatal Accidents Act 1976 as amended by section 3(1) of the Administration of Justice Act 1982. That section provides:

'In assessing damages in respect of a person's death in an action under this Act, benefits which have accrued or will or may accrue to any person from his estate or otherwise as a result of his death shall be disregarded.'

For the defendant it is pointed out that if his services are to be disregarded he will in effect be paying damages three times over. First he will be providing replacement services free of charge, secondly, he will be paying for the services which he has so provided, and thirdly he will have lost his employment in order to provide such services. This is true and on the face of it appears not to be in accordance with justice. Furthermore in cases in which it is shown that the services of the father are in every respect as good as, or even better than the services previously provided by the mother it is, again on the face of it, difficult to see that the child has suffered a recoverable loss. He will or she will of course have been deprived of the mother's love and affection but it is not and could not be suggested that this loss sounds in damages.

In order to determine whether the defendant's contention is well founded it is, I fear, necessary to embark on an examination of the authorities. It is convenient to start with the decision of this court in Hay v. Hughes [1975] Q.B. 790. In that case both the parents of two children aged 4 1/2 and 2 1/2 were killed in a motor accident.... After the death the children's grandmother took them into her home and cared for them as an unpaid mother substitute. The judge assessed the value of the mother's services which had been lost at £1,000 p.a. and declined to make a deduction in respect of the substitute services provided by the grandmother. This court held that he had been correct in so doing. It is important to note that at that time there was no equivalent to Section 4 of the Act of 1976. To justify a deduction required that the services of the grandmother resulted from the death of the mother. This court held that the services of the grandmother did not so result.

...

By the time Hay v. Hughes was decided there had already been statutory exceptions to the so-called rule that benefits resulting from death could be taken into account but except where covered by such exceptions the rule still applied.

...

In Stanley v. Saddique (Mohammed) [1992] Q.B. 1 this court had to consider a case in which Section 4 of the Act of 1976 was in question and in which the facts were that the deceased's mother's services, had she lived, would have been of indifferent quality and lacking in continuity, but that, by contrast, the motherly services provided (after an interval) by her stepmother were excellent and of a higher standard than could reasonably be expected of the deceased...

In his judgment Purchas LJ said at p.13:

'The problem is to decide whether in construing the new Section 4 there is any justification for construing the words "benefits which have accrued or will or may accrue to any person from his estate or otherwise as a result of his death shall be disregarded" as in any way being restricted or whether they should be given the full ambit of the word "otherwise.". . .[N]one of the pre-existing statutory exemptions from the deductions of benefits from Fatal Accidents Acts damage survived unless it is through the medium of the word "otherwise." It seems inconceivable that Parliament would have effected a wholesale repeal of all the long-standing previous statutory exceptions from the deduction of benefits by a sidewind of this sort with the exception of the exclusion of the prospects of remarriage on the part of the widow (semble but not the widower). In my judgment, the preferable construction is that advanced by Mr. Ashworth, namely that Section 3(3) was left in as being a particularly significant question of policy, but that by Section 4 Parliament intended to further the departure from ordinary common law assessment of damages for personal injuries by the artificial concept which has for many decades been the basis of damages recoverable under the Fatal Accidents Acts.'

It is thus clear that he regarded the services of the stepmother as being a benefit resulting from the death of the deceased, which is directly contrary to the decision in Hay v. Hughes [1975] Q.B. 790.

...

With conflicting decisions on the point whether the gratuitous services of a relative do or do not result from the death of the mother I for my part have no hesitation in following Hay v. Hughes [1975] Q.B.790 rather than Stanley v. Saddique (Mohammed) [1992] Q.B. 1 and if this is right Section 4 does not apply. This however does not dispose of the matter because in Hay v. Hughes [1975] Q.B.790 the benefit of such gratuitous services was excluded, quite apart from any relevant statutory exclusion, on the grounds that they did not result from the death...

In my judgment...it must first be established what injury has been suffered by the child. What it has prima facie lost is the services provided by the mother but the fact that they were provided by the mother is irrelevant. If *in fact* those services were replaced without interval of time up-to-date of trial by as good or better services it is in my view at least open to a judge or jury to conclude that the child has lost nothing up to that date. But if the replacement services can be discontinued it is of course exposed to the risk that such services may be discontinued and that risk must be quantified...

What then has the judge done in this case? He had before him a figure of £48,000 as being the full cost of a nanny until the plaintiff was 11 and half such cost from 11 to 15. He then, without giving specific reasons concluded that an appropriate figure would be £20,000, apportioned £15,000 to date of trial and £5,000 thereafter. I do not consider that we have before us material to enable us to interfere with this award, which if I am right as to the approach, appears to me to be an entirely reasonable award and to do justice between the parties I would, therefore, like Sir David Croom-Johnson, dismiss both appeal and cross-appeal.

I would add by way of postscript that, where the provider of the replacement services is the tortfeasor, arguments successfully advanced in earlier cases that it would be unjust if the tortfeasor were to benefit from the generosity of a third party cannot apply.

Even more unusual, perhaps, was the decision in *Watson v Willmott* [1991] 1 QB 140, which held that a child who lost both his parents in an accident and was subsequently adopted by his aunt was only entitled to compensation for financial losses, not for any loss of parental services. The court's rationale was that, having officially adopted the child, the aunt was legally required to provide those parental services and the child had thus suffered no loss. This case was distinguished on the grounds that adoption in *H v S* [2002] EWCA Civ 792, in which children who were living exclusively with their mother had to move to their father's home following their mother's death. The Court of Appeal held that the support now provided by the father and stepmother would not be taken into account to reduce the damages award, relying heavily on the fact that the children were not living with the father at the time of the accident (as was the case in *Hayden v Hayden* [1992] 4 All ER 681) and he had previously been liable for only a small child support payment.

Claimants under the 1976 Act also need to be careful to bring the action in the proper amount of time, which is three years from the date of death or from the date when the person is to benefit from the action knows about the death. If there are several claimants, time will run separately as to each. Furthermore, the Limitation Act 1980 states that no claim under the Fatal Accidents Act 1976 can be brought if the decedent's time to bring a claim had elapsed at the time of death (typically, a tort claim must be brought within three years of the time of the tortious act). Therefore, even if someone dies as a result of a tortious event, a claim by a dependant may be barred if the death occurs too long after the accident.

Damages recoverable after personal injury

The preceding section addresses the claims that can be made if the victim of a tortious act dies as a result of the accident. However, most cases of personal injury do not involve death. Instead, they relate to varying degrees of discomfort and/or disability. Courts tend to break down the analysis into two separate categories:

- Pecuniary losses (typically involving lost earnings and cost of further care, perhaps through hospital or other medical expenses); and
- Non-pecuniary losses (generally encompassing pain and suffering, loss of amenities and the like).

'Pecuniary' means 'monetary'. Thus, pecuniary damages are injuries suffered to money or its equivalent. Non-pecuniary damages are losses associated with items or experiences that cannot be easily measured by money. For example, what is the price of a sunset? Time spent with a loved one? The ability to walk down the street? Because a price tag cannot easily be put on these experiences, they fall into the category of non-pecuniary interests.

NOTE You need to consider damages relating to personal injury even in cases involving death, since you may need to calculate damages relating between the time of the injury and the time of death.

Pecuniary losses

If someone is injured by a tortious act, he or she may have to take time off work temporarily or permanently, thus losing income. When courts calculate a claimant's lost earnings, they consider the issue from two different perspectives. First, the court considers the actual income lost between the time of the accident and the time that the damages award is issued. Although the loss constitutes a special damage that must be specifically pled by the claimant, the method of calculation is relatively straightforward, since it involves actual losses, which can be tallied up by multiplying the hourly wage times the number of hours lost or dividing the annual salary by the number of days spent on disability leave. Courts will also include sums for the loss of business profits and other perquisites such as company cars, private health insurance, etc. Allowances are made for income tax that would have been paid, thus reducing the award somewhat.

cross reference
Special damages are discussed above.

Second, the court makes an award for earnings that will be lost in the future. As indicated above, the judicial system has no way to revisit a damages award once made, other than possibly through a structured settlement agreement. Therefore, the court must make an award about the claimant's future prospects based on the best information available at the time of trial. Prospective earnings are calculated by considering the claimant's future employment prospects (including likely promotions), the length and duration of the claimant's disability and the number of years the claimant was likely to be employed. The sum is then reduced to take into account possible unemployment and illness. Even more importantly, the amount is reduced to reflect the time value of money. The rate and method of reduction was discussed in *Wells v Wells* [1999] 1 AC 345 and has now become standard, particularly the 3% rate of return for a conservative investment and the use of the actuarial indicators known as the Ogden Tables, which is now recognized by section 10 of the Civil Evidence Act 1995 as a suitable predictor of life expectancy. Furthermore, according to the Court of Appeal in *Cooke v United Bristol Healthcare NHS Trust* [2003] EWCA Civ 1370 , no evidence may be presented that the costs in an individual situation—in this case, health care costs—would exceed the general inflation rate. Thus, there can be no adjustment to the discounted rate set by the Lord Chancellor under section 1(1) of the Damages Act 1996.

It is important to understand why courts used discounted awards. Basically, an undiscounted lump sum distribution of all past, present and future damages would over-compensate the claimant, since, by simply investing the money, the claimant would, over time, end up with more money than he or she was entitled to receive. Therefore, courts take into account the 'time value of money', reversing out of any damages award the amount of money the claimant would receive by behaving as a reasonably prudent investor. Notably, courts only make this reduction for future injuries such as lost prospective earning; past losses are paid for in full, and may even be subject to taxation for interest, since the claimant not only lost the item itself (be it pecuniary or non-pecuniary), but also lost the value of the money over time in the past, since the claimant could have invested the money for some gain.

. . . .

● **Wells v Wells** [1999] 1 AC 345

Lord Lloyd of Berwick: In 1981 the government introduced index-linked government securities [ILGS] which are tied to the retail price index and hence protected against inflation. In 1982 these forms of financial instrument became freely available to individuals. Since that date a market in such instruments has developed and expanded. This has radically altered the investment scene. It is now practicable for a plaintiff to protect himself against inflation by investing in index-linked government securities. This form of investment guarantees that the sums invested will retain their real value. It is tailor-made for investors who want a safe investment...It is in practical terms a virtually risk-free investment guaranteeing a return based on the market's view of inflationary trends. In its reports published in 1984 and 1994 the working party chaired by Sir Michael Ogden Q.C. recommended that in future the discount rate should be based on availability of an investment in index-linked government stock. The working party observed that whereas in the past a plaintiff had to speculate by investing in equities, or in a basket of equities and gilts or a selection of unit trusts, he need speculate no longer if he buys index-linked government stock. After in-depth research the Law Commission took a similar view...

While acknowledging an element of arbitrariness in any figure, I am content to adopt about 3 per cent as the best present net figure. For my part I would derive that rate from the net average return of index-linked government securities over the past three years. While this figure of about 3 per cent should not be regarded as immutable, I would suggest that only a marked change in economic circumstances should entitle any party to reopen the debate in advance of a decision by the Lord Chancellor. The effect of the decision of the House on the discount rate, together with the availability of the Ogden Tables, should be to eliminate the need in future to call actuaries, accountants and economists in such cases...

My conclusion is that the judges in these three cases were right to assume for the purpose of their calculations that the plaintiffs would invest their damages in I.L.G.S. for the following reasons.

(1) Investment in I.L.G.S. is the most accurate way of calculating the present value of the loss which the plaintiffs will actually suffer in real terms.

(2) Although this will result in a heavier burden on these defendants, and, if the principle is applied across the board, on the insurance industry in general, I can see nothing unjust. It is true that insurance premiums may have been fixed on the basis of the 4 to 5 per cent. discount rate indicated in Cookson v. Knowles [1979] A.C. 556 and the earlier authorities. But this was only because there was then no better way of allowing for future inflation. The objective was always the same. No doubt insurance premiums will have to increase in order to take account of the new lower rate of discount. Whether this is something which the country can afford is not a subject on which your Lordships were addressed. So we are not in a position to form any view as to the wider consequences.

(3) The search for a prudent investment will always depend on the circumstances of the particular investor. Some are able to take a measure of risk, others are not. For a plaintiff who is not in a position to take risks, and who wishes to protect himself against inflation in the short term of up to 10 years, it is clearly prudent to invest in ILGS. It cannot therefore be assumed that he will invest in equities and gilts. Still less is it his duty to invest in equities and gilts in order to mitigate his loss.

(4) Logically the same applies to a plaintiff investing for the long term. In any event it is desirable to have a single rate applying across the board, in order to facilitate settlements and to save the expense of expert evidence at the trial. I take this view even though it is open to the Lord Chancellor under Section 1(3) of the Act of 1996 to prescribe different rates of return for different classes of case. Mr. Leighton Williams conceded that it is not desirable in practice to distinguish between different classes of plaintiff when assessing the multiplier.

(5) How the plaintiff, or the majority of plaintiffs, in fact invest their money is irrelevant. The research carried out by the Law Commission does not suggest that the majority of plaintiffs in fact invest in equities and gilts but rather in a building society or a bank deposit.

(6) There was no agreement between the parties as to how much greater, if at all, the return on equities is likely to be in the short or long term. But it is at least clear that an investment in ILGS will save up to 1 per cent. per annum by obviating the need for continuing investment advice.

(7) The practice of the Court of Protection when investing for the long term affords little guidance. In any event the policy may change when lump sums are calculated at a lower rate of return.

(8) The views of the Ogden Working Party, the Law Commission and the author of *Kemp & Kemp 'The Quantum of Damages'* in favour of an investment in ILGS are entitled to great weight.

(9) There is nothing in the previous decisions of the House which inhibits a new approach. It is therefore unnecessary to have resort to the Practice Statement (Judicial Precedent) [1966] 1 W.L.R. 1234.

Consequences

Once it is accepted that the lump sum should be calculated on the basis of the rate of return available on ILGS, then an assessment of the average rate of return at the relevant date presents no problem. The rates are published daily in the 'Financial Times'. A table of average rates for the period June 1990 to December 1994 ('Gross Return on Index-Linked Government Securities') is included in Kemp & Kemp 'The Quantum of Damages' vol. 1, para. 8–068. No doubt the table will be brought up to date from time to time. The average gross redemption yield in June 1995 when Mr. Prevett gave his evidence was 3.4378%. If one takes the average over the previous six months it was 3.438%, and if over the previous 12 months it was 3.4383 per cent. The equivalent figures for November and December 1995 when Collins J and Dyson J. gave judgment were marginally lower at 3.4353 per cent and 3.4352 per cent. There must then be a deduction for tax on income. In his valuable appendix to the judgment below [1997] 1 W.L.R. 652, 380, 382, Thorpe L.J. scorns the assumption of a 25 per cent flat rate of tax as 'crude, unrealistic, and favourable to plaintiffs'. I agree. In the first place it ignores the impact of allowances and tax bands. Secondly, it assumes a constant rate of income throughout the period to be covered, whereas in reality the income element in the annual draw-down will reduce and the tax-free capital element will increase as time goes by. The Duxbury Tables (Duxbury v. Duxbury [1992] Fam 62; 'At a Glance,' Family Law Bar Association (1991 and annually)) attempt a much more accurate calculation of the incidence of tax. Figures put before us show that on a fund of £1m. invested to produce 3 per cent over 20 years the actual incidence of tax would be no more that 15.4337 per cent.

It is not altogether clear how Judge Wilcox arrived at his 2.5 per cent as the appropriate discount on an average gross return of 3·8 per cent. If he deducted tax at 25 per cent, he would have arrived at 2.8 per cent net, not 2.5 per cent. But for reasons already mentioned 25 per cent is certainly too high, quite apart from the fact that it is no longer the standard rate of tax. Judge Wilcox's figure of 2.5 per cent cannot stand.

In its place I would substitute 3 per cent, which is the net discount rate adopted by Collins J. and Dyson J., representing a deduction of 14 per cent for the impact of taxation on a gross return of 3.5 per cent. This sounds about right. I appreciate that such an approach is less precise than what is available by using the Duxbury Tables, which was Thorpe L.J.'s preferred approach. On the other hand it is important to keep the calculations simple as well as accurate, as Thorpe L.J. was the first to recognise. So far as the three appeals currently before the House are concerned I would regard 3% as the appropriate net return. It follows that the award in Wells v. Wells will have to be recalculated on that basis.

Typically, future inflation is not taken into account, since the House of Lords in Lim Poh Choo v Camden and Islington Area Health Authority [1980] AC 174 considered such information too speculative to be useful in calculating damages. In that case, the court was faced with assessing damages after an operation went awry, causing the patient—a senior psychiatric registrar with the NHS—to suffer irreparable brain damage.

For a while, the courts struggled with the question of how to deal with claimants who were still living but who were expected to die early as a result of their injuries. For example, a claimant could have been negligently exposed to asbestos through his or her work and thus be at high risk for dying early from asbestosis or mesothelioma. Alternatively, a claimant could have been in an automobile accident that injured his or her internal organs so severely that it seemed likely that one or more will give out, causing an early death. According to *Pickett v British Rail Engineering Ltd* [1980] AC 136 (and overruling an earlier case), a claimant can recover the income for these 'lost years', although a deduction for the claimant's living expenses will have to be made.

....

● ***Pickett v British Rail Engineering Ltd*** [1980] AC 136

Lord Wilberforce: The Fatal Accidents Acts under which proceedings may be brought for the benefit of dependants to recover the loss caused to those dependants by the death of the breadwinner. The amount of this loss is related to the probable future earnings which would have been made by the deceased during 'lost years'. This creates a difficulty. It is assumed in the present case, and the assumption is supported by authority, that if an action for damages is brought by the victim during his lifetime, and either proceeds to judgment or is settled, further proceedings cannot be brought after his death under the Fatal Accidents Acts. If this assumption is correct, it provides a basis, in logic and justice, for allowing the victim to recover for earnings lost during his lost years. This assumption is based upon the wording of section 1 of the Act of 1846 (now section 1 of the Act of 1976) and is not supported by any decision of this House. It cannot however be challenged in this appeal, since there is before us no claim under the Fatal Accidents Acts. I think, therefore, that we must for present purposes act upon the basis that it is well founded, and that if the present claim, in respect of earnings during the lost years, fails, it will not be possible for a fresh action to be brought by the deceased's dependants in relation to them . . .

[A]n important ingredient, which I would accept, namely that the amount to be recovered in respect of earnings in the 'lost' years should be after deduction of an estimated sum to represent the victim's probable living expenses during those years. I think that this is right because the basis, in principle, for recovery lies in the interest which he has in making provision for dependants and others, and this he would do out of his surplus.

cross reference
See the discussion above regarding claims by the estate after the death of a victim of a tort.

Although the claimant will likely not be around to enjoy the benefits of the award, the point is that the claimant's family will not suffer as a result of the accident. Indeed, under section 3 of the Damages Act 1996, the estate of a claimant can claim for wages associated with lost years when a provisional award has been made and the victim eventually dies as a result of the tortious act.

The courts have addressed not only actual future earnings, but future earning capacity as well. Therefore, if a person is not currently employed but can be reasonably expected to undertake employment, he or she can enter a claim for prospective lost wages. Typical scenarios might include a stay-at-home parent who anticipates returning to the workforce or a young person who has not yet entered the work force. *Croke v Wiseman* [1981] 3 All ER 852 suggests that very young children are unlikely to receive large sums to compensate for prospective lost earnings. In that case, a child under the age of two was permanently incapacitated, but was only awarded a multiplicand of £5,000 per year for a five-year period, even though he was expected to live until he was 40. Furthermore, he was not awarded anything for his 'lost years', even though the medical evidence indicated that his life would likely be shortened as a result of the accident.

Lost wages are not the only pecuniary damage that a claimant can face. The victim of a tortious act can also request special damages relating to any out-of-pocket medical expenses which have been reasonably incurred or which will be reasonably incurred in the future. If a person chooses to use private health care instead of the National Health Service, the court will not take that decision into account. However, the court will not provide a claimant with a windfall by providing damages at the private health care level if the claimant simply might have chosen to take that route. If the claimant uses the NHS for medical care, then the amount saved will be deducted from the final award.

Other types of pecuniary damages may include necessary alterations to dwellings to take into account a claimant's changed physical circumstances, the purchase of special equipment (such as modified vans, telephones or computers) for safety or lifestyle reasons, and the like. In general, the rate of recovery is limited by the principle of reasonableness. For example, a person who will be temporarily confined to a wheelchair will not be allowed to remodel completely his or her home to make it wheelchair-accessible if less expensive alterations are possible. However, if the disability is permanent, a wholesale refitting of the claimant's home may be appropriate.

Claimants can recover any type of reasonably necessary health care: medical costs, nursing costs and hospital costs are all treated the same way. If a friend or relative provides the necessary care, the injured claimant may still recover back the cost of the treatment, calculated at commercial rates. However, if the claimant fails to pay the caregiver, the caregiver has no direct claim against the tortfeasor; all recovery flows solely to the victim of the tort.

Once the loss has been calculated, the court must consider whether to deduct any amounts to take into account any benefits received. There are several types of benefits that might accrue to the victim of a tort. For example, some would say that any state benefits payable upon proof of disability should be deducted from the damages award, since to allow them would result in double recovery for the same injury. Parliament dealt with this particular issue in the Social Security (Recovery of Benefits) Act 1997, which states that any damages award for non-pecuniary losses such as pain and suffering or loss of amenity (defined further below) cannot be offset against any social security benefits paid out by the state. Instead, the 1997 Act only allows the state to recoup those damages that represent pecuniary losses such as lost wages and the cost of caring for the claimant. The 1997 Act operates to provide an immediate pass-through of any damages award from the defendant to the claimant for pecuniary losses that can be recouped under the Act; instead of being liable to the claimant, the defendant is now directly liable to the state. For non-pecuniary losses, however, the defendant remains liable to the claimant. Furthermore, the Court of Appeal held in *Crofton v National Health Service Litigation Authority* [2007] EWCA Civ 71 that when a local authority takes responsibility for certain care costs (outside the 1997 Act), there is no reason to reduce the amount of damages payable by the defendant, since that would improperly shift the burden of paying for tortious behaviour from the individual tortfeasor to the public. In that case, the claimant had suffered serious brain damage following negligent medical treatment and was eligible for welfare payments after a means-testing analysis.

An injured claimant might receive other benefits as a result of a personal injury. For example, a charity might step in and provide emergency funds, or the claimant might be entitled to an insurance payout. For the most part, courts will not take these sorts of benefits into account when calculating damages awards for at least two reasons. First, courts want to encourage charitable giving as a matter of policy and thus will not offset any money or that is gratuitously given to the victim of a tort. Second, courts want to encourage people to buy insurance (whether as a **third party** or as a **first party**) and so will not penalize that decision by offsetting any damages. In either situation, allowing an offset would benefit the defendant while also possibly further harming the claimant, particularly if the claimant had paid for insurance cover out of his or her own pocket.

VOCABULARY

An example of third party insurance cover would be an employer who purchased disability insurance on behalf of its employees. The purchaser of the insurance does so to benefit another person (i.e., a third party). An example of first party insurance would be someone who purchased insurance on his or her own behalf.

Non-pecuniary losses

Though the various heads of non-pecuniary losses are relatively well defined, such losses are inherently difficult to prove and quantify. The two major types of non-pecuniary loss are (1) pain and suffering and (2) loss of amenity. Pain and suffering can relate to both physical and emotional harm. Awards can be made for both actual pain and suffering (up to and including the time of trial) and prospective pain and suffering. The law only requires that there be some nexus with the original tortious act. Therefore, even if the pain comes in the future (for example, from an operation that is necessary because of the initial accident), it is a legitimate basis for recovery, so long as there is a link to the tort in question.

Awards for physical pain appear straightforward, but what kinds of emotional or psychic pain are recognized by the law? In *Kralj v McGrath* [1986] 1 All ER 54, a plaintiff was allowed to recover for the anxiety she felt concerning a future pregnancy following a nightmarish—and tortious—childbirth experience. Under the Administration of Justice Act 1982, a claimant can recover for mental pain and suffering associated with the realization that one's life will be cut short as a result of a tort. However, as *Wise v Kaye* [1962] 1 QB 638 shows, a permanently unconscious claimant has no cause of action for this sort of pain and suffering, since the mental anguish must be experienced to count as a loss.

● **Wise v Kaye** [1962] 1 QB 638

Upjohn LJ: As a result of the accident the plaintiff received very serious injuries to her brain and she has ever since been, so far as the doctors can tell, and is now, in a state of unconsciousness. The chances of making an even limited improvement are extremely slender and for all practical purposes the present situation is likely to be a permanent one....As has been said in the case, her life is a living death.

Damages, being proved and properly assessed, when paid become the absolute property of the plaintiff. If a plaintiff has sustained the most serious injuries so that he is permanently bedridden and is maintained at the expense of the State, damages in a sense cannot be applied for his needs, but provided he remains sui juris he can enjoy the money in many ways. He can spend it well or stupidly; he can enjoy it by gambling or giving it away; he can invest it and accumulate the income and give it by will to his relations or to a charity; it is under his entire dominion in every way and he can deal with it as he pleases and it must be wrong in principle to deny damages to a plaintiff because his personal needs are nil... I do not see why the plaintiff should be in any different position merely because she is not sui juris unless, indeed, ignorance of her loss is relevant, a point I deal with later.

It seems to me upon the principle that once the loss is proved and quantified at the proper figure that sum of money becomes the absolute property of the plaintiff, and it matters not that the plaintiff is incapable of personal enjoyment of the money in the very vague and, as I think, indefinable sense of spending it on herself. That has never been the test and I think it would be a mistake to introduce it now. Indeed, it would, I think, be inconsistent with cases such as *Benham v. Gambling*. In that case,...the short answer would have been: The plaintiff is dead; he cannot enjoy the money personally, it will only go to his creditors, his legatees or his next-of-kin, therefore he has suffered no loss. On the contrary, it was held in those cases that damages for loss of expectation of life passed to the deceased's estate...

Under our law a dead man's estate can only claim for loss of expectation of life or loss of happiness...

Damages suffered by a living plaintiff are assessed upon entirely different principles. He may claim under many heads in appropriate cases, loss of amenities, loss of earnings, expenses for maintenance, pain and suffering, loss of expectation of life, and so on. These are real losses for which he is entitled to claim damages; and for my part I am unable to see why the plaintiff while living is prevented from so claiming merely because she is wholly ignorant of the grave loss she has suffered and her chances of recovery are negligible. The injury to her has been done; the damage has been suffered. Her ignorance of either is immaterial.

If a plaintiff suffers personal injuries from the wrong-doing of another his cause of action accrues though he may be ignorant of the fact that he has been damaged...It is difficult to see why, in general, damages for such injury should be affected by ignorance unless the ignorance prevents the head of damage arising as in the case of pain and suffering...

In my judgment it would be a misdirection by a judge to tell the jury that, apart from loss of earnings and so on, they ought to assess damages for loss of amenity by reference to a living plaintiff's loss of happiness. Damages are assessed not merely for the loss of the good or bright things of life, but for the disability which prevents the full living of life, including not only the good things but all that goes to make up a full life without that disability.

Life is worth living even when it involves hard and sometimes unrewarding work, when it entails anxiety and unhappiness, fears and difficulties. These are the experiences of life, on the whole worth while, of which the plaintiff has been deprived. This plaintiff is surely entitled to point on the one side to the active and normal life, with its ups and downs, both valuable, she had every hope of leading, and on the other to the living death which she will lead for the rest of her life.

Similar circumstances and principles of law were considered in *Lim Poh Choo v Camden and Islington Health Authorities* [1980] AC 174.

. . . .

● **Lim Poh Choo v Camden and Islington Health Authorities** [1980] AC 174

Lord Scarman: Dr. Lim Poh Choo, a senior psychiatric registrar employed in the National Health Service, was admitted to a National Health Service hospital for a minor operation, which was carried out the next morning. When, following upon the operation, she was in the recovery room, she suffered a cardiac arrest. It was the result of the negligence of some person for whom the area health authority is vicariously responsible... She is now the wreck of a human being, suffering from extensive and irremediable brain damage, which has left her only intermittently, and then barely, sentient and totally dependent upon others...

The course of the litigation illustrates, with devastating clarity, the insuperable problems implicit in a system of compensation for personal injuries which (unless the parties agree otherwise) can yield only a lump sum assessed by the court at the time of judgment. Sooner or later—and too often later rather than sooner—if the parties do not settle, a court (once liability is admitted or proved) has to make an award of damages. The award, which covers past, present, and future injury and loss, must, under our law, be of a lump sum assessed at the conclusion of the legal process. The award is final; it is not susceptible to review as the future unfolds, substituting fact for estimate. Knowledge of the future being denied to mankind, so much of the award as is to be attributed to future loss and suffering—in many cases the major part of the award—will almost surely be wrong. There is really only one certainty: the future will prove the award to be either too high or too low...

My Lords, I think it would be wrong now to reverse by judicial decision the two rules which were laid down by the majority of the House in *H. West & Son Ltd. v. Shephard*, namely: (1) that the fact of unconsciousness does not eliminate the actuality of the deprivation of the ordinary experiences and amenities of life (see the formulation used by Lord Morris of Borth-y-Gest, at p. 349); (2) that, if damages are awarded upon a correct basis, it is of no concern to the court to consider any question as to the use that will thereafter be made of the money awarded. The effect of the two cases *(Wise v. Kaye* being specifically approved in *H. West & Son Ltd. v. Shephard)* is two-fold. First, they draw a clear distinction between damages for pain and suffering and damages for loss of amenities. The former depend upon the plaintiff's personal awareness of pain, her capacity for suffering. But the latter are awarded for the fact of deprivation—a substantial loss, whether the plaintiff is aware of it or not. Secondly, they establish that the award... is not to be compared with, and has no application to, damages to be awarded to a living plaintiff for loss of amenities.

Loss of amenities is the other major head of non-pecuniary damages. Unconscious claimants will still be able to recover for this loss, even if they are no longer in any condition to enjoy the amenities in question.

....

VOCABULARY

As discussed in chapter 8, which covered 'amenity nuisance', an amenity is defined as something pleasant or attractive—the positive aspects of being alive. Therefore, loss of amenity, in a tort context, includes the loss of all good things associated with being alive. It can include physical pleasures, such as the ability to hear music, to walk or to eat. It also can include emotional pleasures, such as the ability to enjoy a particular person's company or to see a beautiful sunset. Loss of amenity is the most nebulous of all tort damages, since, at its core, it attempts to sum up and define the benefits of being human.

....

Courts struggle with finding a reasonable and reasonably predictable way of assessing non-pecuniary damages. The only way to provide some consistency is for courts to look at previous case law and try to fall within the same general parameters as had been used before. This led, at one point, to the creation of a tariff system for different injuries—X amount for loss of a hand, Y amount for loss of a leg, etc. Of course, because individual awards have to take into account the particular circumstances of the case, the courts still had to use their discretion. The loss of a hand in a surgeon or keen amateur piano player is a much more serious matter than it is to a professional footballer who plays any position other than goal tender, and the courts will take those differences into account when calculating the damages award. The continuing changes in the value of money (£1 does not go as far as it did in 1900 or even 1970) also requires a continued re-evaluation of the tariffs for personal injury matters.

NOTE Typically, practitioners in this area consult specialized reporters and periodicals that contain recent decisions regarding the different heads of personal injury awards. That way, both counsel and the court have roughly similar ideas of what any particular injury is worth.

When an event has caused the risk of the claimant developing a particular disease or condition later in life, the Administration of Justice Act 1982, along with the Supreme Court Act 1981, allows courts to assess the claimant's situation as it currently stands (i.e., without the onset of the disease or condition) and award damages accordingly, while still giving the claimant the right to come back later and claim additional damages if the disease or condition should arise. These sorts of provisional awards were supposed to provide for more useful damages awards than the approach which had been used until that time, wherein the court simply calculated the probability of the future deterioration in the claimant's physical condition and then reduced the damages award by that amount. The concern was that the old system either provided a windfall to the claimant (if the disease or condition did not arise) or provided an insufficient amount to cover the actual injury (since the award had been discounted based on probability rates). However, the provisional award system still has its flaws, primarily in deciding when such an award should be provided. For example, in *Wilson v Ministry of Defence*

[1991] 1 All ER 638, the court held that the probability that the plaintiff would suffer continuing deterioration of an existing injury was not proper grounds for a provisional award. Instead, the claimant should be awarded a single lump sum now, taking into account the fact that deterioration was likely.

Interest is typically payable on damages awards, including those for pecuniary or non-pecuniary losses for personal injury or death. Interest is payable from the time the tortious act occurred through the time the damages award is made.

11.4.7 Property damage

Victims of torts often experience damage to property. Claimants can recover these amounts in addition to any damages awarded for personal injury or death. For the most part, damage to property is assessed at the replacement cost. Therefore, if a car is written off in an accident, the claimant can recover the cost of getting a similar (though not necessarily identical) car. If the claimant decides to upgrade to a better car, the defendant will not be required to pay for the improvements. However, if a slightly better car is all that is available, the defendant will not be heard to complain about the additional cost; there is no requirement that the claimant search high and low to find the identical item that was destroyed as a result of the defendant's actions.

If the property in question was merely damaged, the defendant is liable for the cost of repair. Claimants can also obtain damages for loss of use and for the cost of temporarily replacing the damaged goods, as through the hiring of a rental car while the damaged car is being repaired. As with all torts, the guiding principles are reasonableness and the avoidance of loss to the claimant.

11.5 Injunctions and other relief

Although injunctions are most commonly associated with the tort of nuisance, an injunction may be issued whenever there is a risk a tort may be repeated and/or when damages alone are insufficient to compensate the victim. There are two kinds of injunctions: (1) prohibitive and (2) mandatory. Prohibitive injunctions—which order a defendant not to do something—are the more common for several reasons. First, as a matter of civil liberties, courts are more comfortable with restraining certain offensive behaviour than they are with requiring other sorts of behaviour, since that smacks of involuntary servitude. Second, enforcing a prohibitive injunction is relatively easy, since the court does not need to monitor a situation continually and indefinitely, nor does the court need to decide what constitutes full and adequate performance of a task.

Mandatory injunctions—which require a defendant to undertake a specific, affirmative act—are far less common. Not only do they run afoul of policy concerns about civil liberties, they also can require ongoing supervision that the court is both unwilling and ill-equipped to handle. For example, it is much easier for a court to oversee an order requiring a tortfeasor to refrain entirely from walking along a easement along a neigh-bour's lawn than it is to oversee an order requiring a tortfeasor to walk on that lawn, every day, at a prescribed time and in a prescribed manner.

An injunction may be temporary and put in place only until a hearing and/or full trial can be had on the matter. Alternatively, an injunction may become perpetual after the action has been heard. In either case, issuing the injunction is firmly within the discretion of the court.

Two forms of injunction are particularly useful. One is the injunction for search and seizure, formerly (and perhaps still colloquially) known as an Anton Piller order. This injunction requires a defendant to allow the claimant to enter the defendant's premises to look for property in which the claimant has an interest or for documents relevant to the claimant's cause of action. Such injunctions can be critical in cases where it appears likely that a party will destroy or otherwise abscond with valuable or important goods or evidence.

The second injunction is a freezing injunction, formerly (and again, still colloquially) known as a Mareva injunction. Here, the claimant asks the court to freeze the defend-ant's assets, for example, by advising any banks where the defendant has an account that they must not allow the funds to be withdrawn or moved lest the banks themselves be held in contempt of court. This injunction protects valuable property so that the claimant will have sufficient assets from which to collect a damages award. Both the freezing order and the search and seizure order are highly intrusive, and thus courts require claimants to demonstrate why such measures are necessary before the orders will be issued. Claimants also must given an undertaking to return any property taken and compensate defendants for any damages should the claimants' suit fail.

 For more revision tips, including self-test questions and suggestions for further reading, see the Online Resource Centre at www.oxfordtextbooks.co.uk/orc/strong_complete/.

revision tasks

Damages is an area that is often included on an examination, simply because it requires a different type of thinking than other areas of law. Damages calculations must be logical, complete and as precise as possible, taking into account both statutory and case law. Despite the numerous special terms, the concepts are quite straightforward, allowing you to do well with a minimum of revision. Some tasks that will help you prepare for your examination include:

- Working through the relevant statutes (the Fatal Accidents Act 1976, the Damages Act 1996, etc) and charting out the situations to which those statutes apply.

- Creating a vocabulary list including all the various types of damages and the circum-stances which must exist for a proper claim to be made.

- Identifying all the different types of recovery for a person who has suffered personal injury and then dies several months after the fact. Consider all possible claimants.

Part 6
Special Kinds of Harm

12 Psychiatric damage

12.1 Introduction

think point
Why might recovery for psychiatric injuries cause difficulties for the legal system either as a matter of fact or a matter of policy?

In chapters 12 to 14, we look at types of damage which give rise to special difficulties. This chapter deals with psychiatric damage, while chapters 13 and 14 consider financial loss and damage to a person's reputation. This chapter proceeds as follows:

• Psychiatric damage;

• The scope of the duty not to cause psychiatric damage;

• Negligent communication;

• The remoteness test in psychiatric damage cases; and

• Proposals for reform.

We will consider each issue in turn.

12.2 Psychiatric damage

TIP In exams and other assignments, you should use the newer phrase 'psychiatric damage'.

Psychiatric damage is often referred to in the cases as 'nervous shock', which is an older expression for the same kind of damage. Psychiatric damage only causes difficulties if it is the sole type of injury that the claimant suffers. Claimants who have received physical injuries can also recover damages for emotional distress and mental anguish under the head of damage known as 'pain and suffering', including damages for any psychiatric illness that they suffer as a result of physical injuries. However, courts have been slow to allow claims for psychiatric damage that is not accompanied by some sort of physical injury. In fact, until the turn of the twentieth century, such claims were not allowed at all. *Wilkinson v Downton* [1897] 2 QB 57 was the first case in which a claim for purely psychiatric damage was successful. As you read the following extract, try to identify what factor led the judge to allow the claim.

● **Wilkinson v Downton** [1897] 2 QB 57

cross reference

The aspects of Wilkinson v Downton [1897] 2 QB 57 relating to intentional torts are discussed in chapter 17.

VOCABULARY

As you can probably guess, *injuria* is Latin for 'injury' or 'damage'.

Wright J: In this case the defendant, in the execution of what he seems to have regarded as a practical joke, represented to the plaintiff that he was charged by her husband with a message to her to the effect that her husband was smashed up in an accident, and was lying at The Elms at Leytonstone with both legs broken, and that she was to go at once in a cab with two pillows to fetch him home. All this was false. The effect of the statement on the plaintiff was a violent shock to her nervous system, producing vomiting and other more serious and permanent physical consequences at one time threatening her reason, and entailing weeks of suffering and incapacity to her as well as expense to her husband for medical attendance. These consequences were not in any way the result of previous ill-health or weakness of constitution; nor was there any evidence of predisposition to nervous shock or any other idiosyncrasy...

It was argued for her that she is entitled to recover this as being damage caused by fraud...I am not sure that this would not be an extension of that doctrine, the real ground of which appears to be that a person who makes a false statement intended to be acted on must make good the damage naturally resulting from its being acted on. Here there is no **injuria** of that kind. I think, however, that the verdict may be supported upon another ground. The defendant has, as I assume for the moment, wilfully done an act calculated to cause physical harm to the plaintiff—that is to say, to infringe her legal right to personal safety, and has in fact thereby caused physical harm to her. That proposition without more appears to me to state a good cause of action, there being no justification alleged for the act. This wilful injuria is in law malicious, although no malicious purpose to cause the harm which was caused nor any motive of spite is imputed to the defendant.

It remains to consider whether the assumptions involved in the proposition are made out. One question is whether the defendant's act was so plainly calculated to produce some effect of the kind which was produced that an intention to produce it ought to be imputed to the defendant, regard being had to the fact that the effect was produced on a person proved to be in an ordinary state of health and mind. I think that it was. It is difficult to imagine that such a statement, made suddenly and with apparent seriousness, could fail to produce grave effects under the circumstances upon any but an exceptionally indifferent person, and therefore an intention to produce such an effect must be imputed, and it is no answer in law to say that more harm was done than was anticipated, for that is commonly the case with all wrongs. The other question is whether the effect was, to use the ordinary phrase, too remote to be in law regarded as a consequence for which the defendant is answerable. Apart from authority, I should give the same answer and on the same ground as the last question, and say that it was not too remote...It is, however, necessary to consider two authorities which are supposed to have laid down that illness through mental shock is a too remote or unnatural consequence of an injuria to entitle the plaintiff to recover in a case where damage is a necessary part of the cause of action. One is the case of *Victorian Railways Commissioners v Coultas*, where it was held in the Privy Council that illness which was the effect of shock caused by fright was too remote a consequence of a negligent act which caused the fright, there being no physical harm immediately caused. That decision was treated in the Court of Appeal in *Pugh v London, Brighton and South Coast Ry. Co.* as open to question...Nor is it altogether in point, for there was not in that case any element of wilful wrong; nor perhaps was the illness so direct and natural a consequence of the defendant's conduct as in this case. On these grounds it seems to me that the case of *Victorian Railways Commissioners v Coultas* is not an authority on which this case ought to be decided...There must be judgment for the plaintiff.

cross reference

Dulieu v White & Sons [1901] 2 KB 669 is explained more fully in chapter 4.

The effect of this case was that a claimant could recover damages for psychiatric damage if the defendant had acted intentionally, but not if the defendant had only been negligent. Claims for intentional psychiatric damage are brought under a separate tort known as 'intentional harm', rather than in negligence. However, negligence claims for psychiatric damage began to be allowed shortly after *Wilkinson v Downton* [1897] 2 QB 57. The first such case was *Dulieu v White & Sons* [1901] 2 KB 669, where the plaintiff feared for her own safety when a pair-horse van was driven into her husband's public house. This resulted in the plaintiff giving birth prematurely, which caused the child to be disabled. The plaintiff herself also suffered psychiatric illness. In *Hambrook v Stokes Brothers* [1925] 1 KB 141, the court also allowed the plaintiff to recover damages for psychiatric damage caused by her fear for the safety of others, after she saw an out-of-control lorry heading towards the spot where her children had been walking and was afraid that they would be injured.

Nonetheless, the courts are still cautious when dealing with psychiatric damage. This is partly due to a desire to avoid 'opening the floodgates' to excessive claims (a concept you will encounter in more detail in chapter 13), and partly because of a related concern that it may be difficult to distinguish genuine psychiatric damage claims from opportunistic ones. Causation can also be difficult to prove in such cases, and it is often difficult to put a figure on the damages that should be awarded. In *Bourhill v Young* [1943] AC 92, a motorcyclist, while negligently driving at an excessive speed, collided with a car and was killed. The plaintiff, standing nearby, heard the noise, although she did not see the accident, and suffered fright resulting in severe nervous shock. This disabled her from working for some time. She also miscarried as a result of the injuries sustained by her. Lord Macmillan commented in this case that:

> It is no longer necessary to consider whether the infliction of what is called mental shock may constitute an actionable wrong. The crude view that the law should take cognizance only of physical injury resulting from actual impact has been discarded, and it is now well recognized that an action will lie for injury by shock sustained through the medium of the eye or the ear without direct contact. The distinction between mental shock and bodily injury was never a scientific one, for mental shock is presumably in all cases the result of, or at least accompanied by, some physical disturbance in the sufferer's system. And a mental shock may have consequences more serious than those resulting from physical impact. But in the case of mental shock there are elements of greater subtlety than in the case of an ordinary physical injury and these elements may give rise to debate as to the precise scope of legal liability. The courts therefore impose special conditions on claims of this type, much as they do in cases of pure economic loss.

It is important to keep in mind that claims for negligent psychiatric damage need to have the same elements of duty, breach, and damage as any other negligence claim, though there are special rules for some of these elements. We will now look at some of these special rules, beginning with damage. We will then consider the special rules that restrict the duty not to cause psychiatric damage, before coming back to other aspects of damage and remoteness.

12.2.1 The types of damage that will be compensated

Because of concerns about the vast number of potential claims for psychiatric damage, courts have imposed several rules to limit recovery. One such rule requires claimants to suffer from a recognized medical condition. Thus, to establish the claim in court, claimants must present expert medical evidence to confirm that they have indeed suffered such a condition and that the condition was probably caused by the defendant's actions. Sometimes this is a purely psychiatric condition; sometimes it is a physical condition brought on by mental distress. For example, the plaintiff in *Dulieu v White & Sons* [1901] 2 KB 669 gave birth prematurely as a result of emotional trauma, and, due to the premature birth, the child was mentally disabled. Both types of case are treated in the same way by the law.

The case of *McLoughlin v O'Brian* [1983] 1 AC 410 took the law in this area forward significantly, as it allowed a plaintiff who was some distance away from the accident to claim for psychiatric damage. Here, the plaintiff was at home, two miles away, when her husband and three children were involved in a road accident. When she reached the hospital about two hours later, she heard that her daughter had been killed and saw the extent of her son's injuries. The shock which she suffered resulted in psychiatric illness. The House of Lords held that the plaintiff could recover damages, since it was reasonably foreseeable that she would suffer nervous shock as a result of injuries to her family.

In *Page v Smith* [1996] AC 155, a later case, the plaintiff was involved in a collision with a car driven by the defendant. The plaintiff had suffered from a condition variously described as myalgic encephalomyelitis, chronic fatigue syndrome, or post-viral fatigue syndrome for the last 20 years. Three hours after the accident, the plaintiff felt exhausted, and the exhaustion continued. However, he sustained no physical injury. The plaintiff sued for damages for personal injuries caused by the defendant's negligence, in that as a result of the accident his condition had become chronic and permanent and that it was unlikely that he would be able to take full-time employment again. Here, the egg-shell skull rule came into play.

● *Page v Smith* [1996] AC 155

Lord Lloyd of Berwick: The approach in all cases should be the same, namely, whether the defendant can reasonably foresee that his conduct will expose the claimant to the risk of personal injury, whether physical or psychiatric. If the answer is yes, then the duty of care is established, even though physical injury does not, in fact, occur. There is no justification for regarding physical and psychiatric injury as different 'kinds of damage'. A defendant who is under a duty of care to the plaintiff, whether as primary or secondary victim, is not liable for damages for nervous shock unless the shock results in some recognised psychiatric illness. It is no answer that the plaintiff was predisposed to psychiatric illness. Nor is it relevant that the illness takes a rare form or is of unusual severity. The defendant must take his victim as he finds him.

Finally, in *Leach v Chief Constable of Gloucestershire* [1999] 1 All ER 215, the police planned to interview W, whom they considered to be mentally disordered, about several murders that had been committed in particularly harrowing and traumatic circumstances.

In accordance with existing procedural requirements, they asked the plaintiff, a voluntary worker, to attend the police station to act as an appropriate adult during the police interview. The plaintiff sat in on interviews and accompanied W to scenes of the murders. On numerous occasions, she was left alone with him in a locked cell. Subsequently, the plaintiff alleged that she had suffered post-traumatic stress and psychological injury as well as a stroke by reason of her involvement in the matter, and she brought an action for damages for negligence against the police. She further claimed that she should have been offered counselling during or within a reasonably short time of her exposure to the trauma. The Court of Appeal held that the law imposed no duty of care on the police towards an appropriate adult appointed under the procedural requirements to take care to protect that adult from mental or psychological harm. The whole essence of the relationship between the appropriate adult and the police was that they did not assume responsibility towards her in relation to her duties. An appropriate adult was there at the police station to help the suspect, and if the police were under a concurrent legal duty to protect her psychological well-being, the police might not be able to do their job of interviewing the suspect effectively. The court noted that the plaintiff could have stopped at any time and was under no obligation to continue her voluntary work. However, the existence of a duty to provide counselling would not interfere with interviews, and, accordingly, the issue of the police's failure to provide counselling services to the plaintiff was allowed to proceed to trial.

These three cases show the outer parameters of claims in this area. Typically, however, injured parties want to seek compensation for normal anxiety, stress, grief or sorrow. For the most part, these injuries are non-recoverable. However, if a particular claimant's grief goes beyond a normal reaction to the point where it can be considered an illness, then a claim is possible. This was the case in *Vernon v Bosley (No 1)* [1997] 1 All ER 577, where the plaintiff developed a pathological form of grief after he witnessed his children drowning. Post-traumatic stress disorder (PTSD) is probably the most common form of psychiatric damage to reach the courts. Claimants who have suffered distress that cannot be compensated in negligence may be able to bring some other cause of action instead, such as breach of contract (in narrowly-defined cases), deceit, or a statutory action under the Protection from Harassment Act 1997. Grief is compensable in a few circumstances, as described in chapter 11.

12.2.2 **The event that causes the damage**

Another condition the courts have imposed to limit recovery is that the damage must have been caused by a sudden event rather than an ongoing state of affairs. For instance, the court in *Alcock v Chief Constable of South Yorkshire* [1992] 1 AC 310 said that someone who developed a psychiatric illness as a result of caring for a disabled spouse would not be able to claim. Similarly, in *Sion v Hampstead Health Authority* [1994] 5 Med LR 170 a father could not recover damages for a psychiatric illness caused by watching his son die slowly in intensive care. The exact limits of this principle are not yet clear. In *W v Essex County Council* [2000] 2 AC 592, foster parents sued for the shock they suffered when they discovered that a foster child that they had taken in had a history of abusing

cross reference
Alcock v Chief Constable of South Yorkshire [1992] 1 AC 310 is discussed in more detail below.

other children. The local authority asked the court to strike out the claim on the basis that the shock was not sudden, but the court refused to do so, stating that although the claimants did not meet the usual criteria, the categories of potential claimants for psychiatric damage should not yet be regarded as closed. It therefore seems that there is room for further development in this area of the law.

12.3 The scope of the duty not to cause psychiatric damage

12.3.1 Introduction

Most of the restrictions which the courts have imposed on psychiatric damage claims work by restricting the duty of care. In particular, there are significant restrictions on the categories of people to whom a defendant will owe a duty to prevent psychiatric damage. *Alcock v Chief Constable of South Yorkshire* [1992] 1 AC 310 and *White v Chief Constable of South Yorkshire* [1999] 1 All ER 1 are the leading cases in this area. These were amongst several cases which followed the so-called 'Hillsborough disaster' in 1989. In this tragic incident, the Hillsborough football stadium became overcrowded and 95 people were crushed to death when they became trapped against the high security fences which separated the fans from the pitch. Another 400 people were physically injured. Many others developed mental illnesses as a result of the events they witnessed, either in person or on television. In *Alcock v Chief Constable of South Yorkshire* [1992] 1 AC 310, a number of spectators whose relatives had been killed or injured sued the police for psychiatric damage, on the basis that the police had been negligent in allowing such a large crowd into the stadium. In *White v Chief Constable of South Yorkshire* [1999] 1 All ER 1, the plaintiffs were police officers who had been on duty in the stadium. They were not themselves involved in the decision to allow an excessively large crowd. Some of them had given first aid to the injured and dying; others had been involved in recovering bodies and taking them to a temporary morgue. The plaintiffs were ultimately unsuccessful in both actions. We will touch on these cases at several points in this section.

12.3.2 Potential claimants

The case law categorizes claimants into primary victims and secondary victims. Both types of victim can potentially bring a claim for psychiatric damage, but more restrictions apply to secondary victims. *Page v Smith* [1996] AC 155 defined the two categories in the context of a discussion about a psychiatric injury, in the form of chronic onset of chronic fatigue syndrome, which occurred three hours after a car accident.

● *Page v Smith* [1996] AC 155

> Lord Keith of Kinkel: As was observed by Lord Oliver in *Alcock v Chief Constable of the South Yorkshire Police* [1992] 1 AC 310 at 407, the cases divide broadly into two categories, those in which the plaintiff was involved as a participant in the incident which gave rise to the action, and those in which the plaintiff was a witness to injury caused to others, or to the immediate aftermath of an accident to others. The first category includes *Dulieu v White & Sons* [1901] 2 KB 669…where the plaintiff was terrified by a cart and horses bursting into the public house where she was employed, and *Schneider v Eisovitch*[1960] 2 QB 430…where the plaintiff was herself injured in the accident which resulted in the death of her husband. Cases in the second category include, *Hambrook v Stokes Bros* [1925] 1 KB 141…where a mother was terrified by the prospect of injury to her children from a runaway lorry, and *McLoughlin v O'Brian*…[1983] 1 AC 410, where the plaintiff shortly after a road accident saw her husband and children badly injured in hospital. Liability for negligence depends upon proof both that it was reasonably foreseeable that injury would result from the act or omission called in question and that a relationship of proximity existed between plaintiff and defendant. Where the plaintiff is personally involved in a terrifying incident proof of proximity presents no problem. Where, however, the plaintiff is what may be described as a secondary victim proximity may be very difficult to establish.

Primary victims

There are several reasons why it is important to know the difference between primary and secondary victims, but perhaps it is most important in that primary victims are subject to a less demanding version of the remoteness test than secondary victims are.

As the preceding excerpt makes clear, the basic distinction between primary and secondary victims is that primary victims are people who were themselves in physical danger during the dangerous event, whereas secondary victims were not. Although this distinction may seem simple, it can sometimes be difficult to know where to draw the dividing line. It is clear that claimants will not be primary victims if they had no reasonable grounds for believing that they were in danger. For instance, in *McFarlane v Wilkinson* [1997] 2 Lloyd's Rep 259 the plaintiff was in a boat near an oil rig when the oil rig exploded. The Court of Appeal held that the plaintiff's boat was not in any danger during the accident and therefore he could not be a primary victim. It is less clear whether claimants are to be categorized as primary or secondary victims if they were not in fact in danger, if it was still reasonable for them to believe that they were.

The courts have also blurred the line between primary and secondary victims by treating certain people as primary victims even though they do not strictly fit the definition. For instance, in *Butchart v Home Office* [2006] EWCA Civ 239, the claimant was a prisoner who suffered from depression. He was placed with a cellmate who was also mentally ill, and this prisoner subsequently committed suicide while the claimant was present. The effects of witnessing the suicide made the claimant's depression worse. The claimant did not meet the usual definition of a primary victim because he had neither been in danger himself nor believed that he was. However, if the claimant were treated as a secondary victim, he would not be able to recover damages, because (as you will see in the next section) secondary victims need to show that they had close ties of affection with the victim, and there were no such ties between the two prisoners. The Court of Appeal nonetheless allowed the claimant to recover damages, effectively treating him as a primary victim.

Prior to 1999, rescuers who suffered psychiatric injuries were often treated as primary victims even if they were never in physical danger. One example of this was *Chadwick v British Railways Board* [1967] 1 WLR 912, which involved a man who voluntarily assisted at the scene of a railway accident and later developed a psychiatric injury. In this case, the fact that the risk run by the rescuer was not of the same kind as that run by the persons being rescued did not deprive the rescuer of his remedy. However, the House of Lords decided in *White v Chief Constable of South Yorkshire* [1999] 1 All ER 1 that if the rescuers were not themselves in danger, they should be treated as secondary victims, regardless of whether they were professional rescuers, such as fire-fighters, paramedics, and police officers, or volunteers, such as Mr Chadwick. The Lords made this rule to avoid requiring the courts to make difficult decisions about how much help a person had to give to count as a rescuer. The Lords also thought it was unfair to treat rescuers more favourably than bereaved relatives. Nonetheless, a rescuer who has been in physical danger can still be considered a primary victim. For instance, in *Cullin v London Fire and Civil Defence Authority* [1999] PIQR P 314, a fire-fighter tried to rescue two of his colleagues from a burning building, but was unable to do so and later saw their bodies being carried out. He was able to claim for psychiatric damage because the Court of Appeal considered that he himself had been in danger during the rescue.

Special rules may apply to people who suffer psychiatric harm as a result of the belief that they have harmed someone else, even if they did not, in fact, cause any injury. The classic example of this type of scenario is *Dooley v Cammell Laird* [1951] 1 Lloyd's Rep 271, where a faulty crane dropped its load, causing the crane operator (who was not at fault himself) to believe—wrongfully, as it turned out—that he might have injured or killed one of his workmates. Nevertheless, the crane operator received damages for psychiatric injuries. The later case of *Hunter v British Coal* [1999] 1 QB 140 also appears to assume that such claims are possible, though it seems to treat them as claims by secondary victims. In this case, a driver accidentally hit a water hydrant. While the driver was away from the scene looking for the valve to turn off the water supply, the hydrant exploded and killed one of his colleagues. The driver irrationally believed that the accident was his fault, whereas in fact, his employer was in breach of statutory duty by positioning the hydrant so that it protruded onto the road on which the plaintiff was driving. The claim failed because there was insufficient proximity in time and space between the plaintiff and the accident. The need for proximity is one of the requirements for secondary victims, which supports the position that those who suffer psychiatric harm due to an incorrect belief that they have injured others will be classified as secondary victims.

Secondary victims

As you recall, the claim in *Alcock v Chief Constable of the South Yorkshire Police* [1992] 1 AC 310 involved secondary victims who were not themselves in the part of the stadium where the crush occurred. As indicated below, the House of Lords said that three factors have to be present to give rise to a duty in these circumstances.

cross reference

Chadwick v British Railways Board [1967] 1 WLR 912 was discussed in chapter 5.

● ***Alcock v Chief Constable of the South Yorkshire Police*** [1992] 1 AC 310

> Lord Ackner: Because 'shock' in its nature is capable of affecting such a wide range of persons, Lord Wilberforce in *McLoughlin v. O'Brian* [1983] 1 A.C. 410, 422, concluded that there was a real need for the law to place some limitation upon the extent of admissible claims and in this context he considered that there were three elements inherent in any claim. It is common ground that such elements do exist and are required to be considered in connection with all these claims. The fundamental difference in approach is that on behalf of the plaintiffs it is contended that the consideration of these three elements is merely part of the process of deciding whether, as a matter of fact, the reasonable fore-seeability test has been satisfied. On behalf of the defendant it is contended that these elements operate as a control or limitation on the mere application of the reasonable foreseeability test. They introduce the requirement of 'proximity' as conditioning the duty of care.
>
> The three elements are (1) the class of persons whose claims should be recognised; (2) the proximity of such persons to the accident—in time and space; (3) the means by which the shock has been caused.

Thus, in order to bring a claim for psychiatric damage, a secondary victim must satisfy three tests, which operate as controls to restrict the scope of such claims:

- First, it must have been reasonably foreseeable to the defendant that a person of normal fortitude might suffer psychiatric illness in the claimant's position.

- Second, there must have been proximity in time and space between the claimant and the event which caused the psychiatric damage.

- Third, the damage must have been caused by seeing or hearing the event or its immediate aftermath.

We will consider each of these tests in turn. Remember, rescuers are considered secondary victims and must therefore pass these tests. Similarly, people who suffer psychiatric damage because they wrongly believe they have killed or injured someone else may also be in this category.

First, in order for psychiatric damage to be foreseeable, the secondary victim must have a close relationship of love and affection with someone who was killed or injured. This will be presumed if the parties were married or engaged (and presumably now if they are in a civil partnership), or were parent and child. Even then, the defendant can try to rebut the presumption if there is evidence that the claimant and the injured or deceased party were not in fact close. If the parties were not married, engaged, or in a parent-child relationship, the secondary victim will have to prove that they had a close relationship. In *Alcock v Chief Constable of the South Yorkshire Police* [1992] 1 AC 310, for instance, the brother of one of the victims was unable to recover because he was unable to prove that the two had been close. In that case, Lord Ackner commented *obiter* that psychiatric damage might be foreseeable if the secondary victim witnessed a particularly horrific incident, such as a petrol tanker crashing into a school and bursting into flames. If this is correct, then even an unrelated bystander would be able to recover in such circumstances, but it is not entirely clear how such 'horrific incidents' could be identified or why the petrol tanker crash should be considered more horrific than the Hillsborough tragedy.

Second, the claimant must show proximity to the event in time and space. This means that the claimant must have been present at the event itself or during its immediate aftermath. The difficulty is in determining what counts as the immediate aftermath. For example, in *McLoughlin v O'Brian* [1982] 2 All ER 298, the plaintiff's daughter was killed in a car accident, while her husband and two other children were badly injured. The plaintiff did not see the accident, but was told about it by a friend, who drove her to the hospital. She arrived about an hour after the accident and found her family still covered in dirt and oil and her son screaming. The House of Lords held that this was sufficiently proximate to the immediate aftermath. It is important to understand that the plaintiff in this case recovered damages from the person who caused the accident for the distress caused by what she saw at the hospital, not for the distress caused by hearing about the accident from her friend. The claimant must directly hear or see the accident or its aftermath; being told about it is not enough. *French v Chief Constable of Sussex Police* [2006] EWCA Civ 312 was an example of a case where the claimants were not sufficiently proximate to the aftermath. They were police officers who were involved in preparations for an armed raid, but did not attend the raid itself. During the raid, a suspect was shot and killed. The Police Complaints Authority thought the killing was the result of systemic failures in the preparation of the raid, and the claimants were suspended, served with disciplinary notices and charged with misfeasance in public office. All charges against them were dropped, and they sued for psychiatric losses caused by the stress of this chain of events. The Court of Appeal found that the claimants could be categorized as secondary victims, but that the criminal and disciplinary proceedings were not part of the immediate aftermath of the shooting. Therefore, the psychiatric damage was too remote, and the claimants could not recover for it.

Proximity is discussed in detail by Lord Keith of Kinkel in the extract below.

● *Alcock v Chief Constable of South Yorkshire* [1992] 1 AC 310

> Lord Keith of Kinkel: The first [factor] is proximity of the plaintiff to the accident in time and space. For this purpose the accident is to be taken to include its immediate aftermath, which in *McLoughlin's* case was held to cover the scene at the hospital which was experienced by the plaintiff some two hours after the accident. In [the Australian case of] *Jaensch v. Coffey* (1984) 155 CLR. 549, the plaintiff saw her injured husband at the hospital to which he had been taken in severe pain before and between his undergoing a series of emergency operations, and the next day stayed with him in the intensive care unit and thought he was going to die. She was held entitled to recover damages for the psychiatric illness she suffered as a result. Deane J. said, at p. 608:
>
> > 'the aftermath of the accident extended to the hospital to which the injured person was taken and persisted for so long as he remained in the state produced by the accident up to and including immediate post-accident treatment. Her psychiatric injuries were the result of the impact upon her of the facts of the accident itself and its aftermath while she was present at the aftermath of the accident at the hospital.'

NOTE The person who communicates bad news may be liable in some circumstances, but this is a different situation from those where the claimant sues the person responsible for the accident.

As regards the means by which the shock is suffered, Lord Wilberforce said in *McLoughlin v. O'Brian* [1983] 1 A.C. 410, 423 that it must come through sight or hearing of the event on or of its immediate aftermath . . .

[Three of the plaintiffs] watched scenes from Hillsborough on television, but none of these depicted suffering of recognizable individuals, such being excluded by the broadcasting code of ethics, a position known to the defendant. In my opinion the viewing of these scenes cannot be **equiparated**, nor can the scenes reasonably be regarded as giving rise to shock, in the sense of a sudden assault on the nervous system. They were capable of giving rise to anxiety for the safety of relatives known or believed to be present in the area affected by the crush, and undoubtedly did so, but that is very different from seeing the fate of the relative or his condition shortly after the event. The viewing of the television scenes did not create the necessary degree of proximity.

In some circumstances, secondary victims can also claim where they witness property damage rather than an injury to another person. In *Attia v British Gas plc* [1988] 1 QB 304, the plaintiff came home to find her house on fire. She had invested a great deal of money and effort in her house over many years and was very emotionally attached to it. The Court of Appeal allowed her claim for psychiatric damage.

We have now considered the first two of the tests—foreseeability and proximity. The third test relates to the means by which the event is communicated to the claimant. As discussed above, this must be through first-hand sight or hearing. The House of Lords said in *Alcock v Chief Constable of the South Yorkshire Police* [1992] 1 AC 310 that hearing or seeing a television broadcast is not normally sufficient, because the defendant could normally expect that broadcasters would not show the suffering of identifiable individuals. If the broadcasters actually did do so, that would break the chain of causation, since it would be unforeseeable. However, the House of Lords did leave open the possibility that the shock of seeing an event on television could, in some circumstances, be greater than that of seeing it in person. In such a case, a claimant might be able to recover compensation for psychiatric damage, but it is difficult to imagine in what circumstances this would apply, if it did not apply to Hillsborough, and it is not clear why the chain of causation would not be broken. The example that is given in the judgments is of a televised balloon ride for children in which the balloon suddenly bursts into flames, but this is not strikingly different from Hillsborough and does not seem very convincing.

Even if secondary victims can satisfy the three tests laid down in *Alcock v Chief Constable of the South Yorkshire Police* [1992] 1 AC 310, there may be some further restrictions which were not relevant in that case and were therefore not considered by the judges. For instance, a secondary victim cannot sue a primary victim, as shown by *Greatorex v Greatorex* [2000] 1 WLR 1970. In that case, the claimant was a fire-fighter who was called to the scene of a road accident, where he discovered that the victim was his own son. The claimant suffered psychiatric injury and sued his son (on the basis that the Motor Insurance Bureau, which compensates people who are injured by uninsured drivers, would pay any damages). He was unsuccessful because the court felt it would be excessively restrictive to impose a duty on individuals to take care of themselves in order to prevent psychiatric harm to others.

VOCABULARY
'Equiparated' is a word derived from Latin and means 'compared with'.

NOTE The idea of a chain of causation is discussed in chapter 4.

---

think point
The requirement that the claimant sees or hears the event directly can also be analysed as part of the requirement of proximity. Which is the stronger method?

12.4 Negligent communication

Generally, a secondary victim must have seen or heard the event that caused the psychiatric injury, and it is not enough simply to have heard about it from a third party. However, in some circumstances, third parties may be independently liable for negligently communicating bad news. In such cases, the person receiving the bad news is arguably a primary victim. For example, in *Allin v City and Hackney Health Authority* (1996) 7 Med LR 167, the plaintiff was wrongly told that her baby had been stillborn and was able to recover from the person who passed on the incorrect information. Similarly, in *Farrell v Avon Health Authority* [2001] All ER (D) 17, a father was negligently told that his baby had died and was given the body of someone else's dead child to hold, believing that it was his own. He, too, was able to recover compensation for psychiatric damage. The fact that the health authorities in these cases had a general duty to give correct information to parents about their child's condition may well be significant; it is much less likely that friends or relatives passing on information would incur liability, provided they did not act maliciously. Such an act might give rise to an action for intentional harm, as suggested near the beginning of the chapter in the discussion of *Wilkinson v Downton* [1897] 2 QB 57. It also appears that there is no claim if the information is correct, even if it is communicated in an insensitive manner. For example, a cause of action failed in *AB v Tameside & Glossop Health Authority*, The Times, 27 November 1996, where a health authority told patients by letter rather than in person that they might have been infected with HIV by one of the authority's staff.

12.5 The remoteness test in psychiatric damage cases

Chapter 4 set forth the usual remoteness test in negligence claims, based on the principles discussed in *Overseas Tankship (UK) Ltd v Morts Dock and Engineering Co Ltd, The Wagon Mound* [1961] AC 388. *Page v Smith* [1995] 2 All ER 736 explained how remoteness works in the case of psychiatric damage claims. According to that case, primary victims only have to demonstrate that the defendant could have foreseen that the primary victim would suffer physical injury. It does not matter if the psychiatric damage which the claimant actually suffers is greater in extent than an average claimant might suffer, so long as this will not usually be difficult, since primary victims have by definition been in physical danger. Secondary victims, on the other hand, are required by *Page v Smith* [1995] 2 All ER 736 to show that the defendant could have foreseen that a person of 'reasonable fortitude' in the claimant's position would suffer psychiatric illness. This can be considerably more difficult to prove.

Psychiatric damage cases also have their own version of the egg-shell skull rule, which is a special rule of remoteness. The psychiatric injury version of the egg-shell rule applies if it is foreseeable that the claimant would suffer physical injury (in the case of primary victims) or psychiatric injury (in the case of secondary victims). For instance, in *Brice v Brown*

[1984] 1 All ER 608, a woman had a pre-existing psychiatric illness which was largely controlled by medication and did not disrupt her daily life. After being involved in a car accident with her daughter, she developed a severe personality disorder—treated by the courts as another type of mental illness, although from the point of view of psychiatry it is in a slightly different category—which left her unable to take care of herself. The medical experts at the trial agreed that the case was unique in its severity and could not have been foreseen by the defendants. Nevertheless, the plaintiff was entitled to recover, since it was foreseeable that a physical injury would result from the accident (remember, she was a primary victim), so the severity of the psychiatric harm was irrelevant. As Lane J said in an often-quoted passage in his judgment in *Malcolm v Broadhurst* [1970] 3 All ER 608, which involved a man who was in a car accident that resulted in his personality changing from an easygoing one to a violent and irritable one: 'there is no difference in principle between an egg-shell skull and an egg-shell personality'.

(12.6) Proposals for reform

The decision in *Alcock v Chief Constable of the South Yorkshire Police* [1992] 1 AC 310 that the relatives of Hillsborough victims could not in most cases recover compensation attracted considerable public criticism. As a result, this area of law was reviewed by the Law Commission, which published a lengthy report in March 1998 entitled 'Liability for Psychiatric Injury'. The Law Commission Report has not been acted upon, but provides much fodder for discussion.

 For more revision tips, including self-test questions and suggestions for further reading, see the Online Resource Centre at www.oxfordtextbooks.co.uk/orc/strong_complete/.

revision tasks

Here are some ideas to try when you revise this chapter:

- Summarize the current law regarding:
  - Rescuers;
  - People who wrongly believe they have killed someone;
  - People who see a traumatic event on television; and
  - People who witness the death of a stranger.
- Imagine you are a civil servant briefing the government on law reform proposals. Write a short memo summarizing the Law Commission's proposals on psychiatric damage and making a recommendation as to whether the government should support these proposals.
- Summarize the differences between the remoteness rules in general negligence claims and those in claims for psychiatric damage. Do you think these differences are fair? Why or why not?
- Make a list of aspects of the current law on psychiatric damage that you think are unsatisfactory (if any).

13 Economic loss

13.1 Introduction

VOCABULARY

Financial loss is usually known in the case law as 'economic loss'.

Chapter 4 looked at the types of damage the law recognizes with respect to negligence actions and noted briefly that certain types of damage, particularly financial loss and psychiatric damage, give rise to some special difficulties. This chapter explores in more detail the rules that apply to a claimant who wants to recover financial loss, usually known in the case law as **economic loss** or pure economic loss. This chapter proceeds as follows:

- Types of economic loss;

- The current law on economic loss;

- Key cases in the historical development of the law on economic loss; and

- Problems with the current law.

We will cover each subject in turn.

13.2 Types of economic loss

Some kinds of economic loss arise out of a personal injury to the claimant. For example, medical expenses would quality as an out-of-pocket economic loss. Other types of financial loss arise out of damage to the claimant's property. For example, if someone breaks a vase in a shop display, the shop will lose the profit on that vase. Losses such as these, which are directly due to physical damage or injury, do not cause any special legal problems. The difficulties relate to 'pure' economic loss, which is not caused by any injury to the claimant or any physical damage to the claimant's property. There are several possible ways in which pure economic loss can arise. For example:

- Loss may be caused by damage to someone else's property. For instance, a road maintenance worker may accidentally drill through a cable belonging to the local electricity company. Nearby shops and other local businesses may have to close temporarily and may lose profits as a result, but it is not their property which has been damaged. The loss of profit is pure economic loss.

- Loss may be caused by incorrect advice. For example, an art expert may advise a gallery to buy a painting for £1 million because it was done by an Old Master. The painting may then turn out to be a fake which is only worth £100. The difference in value (£9,999,900) is pure economic loss.

- Loss may be caused by some other form of incorrect statement. For instance, a newspaper may say in its business pages that a particular company is in serious financial trouble. Readers of the paper may start selling their shares, which will cause the share price to fall. If it later turns out that the company was not in trouble when the article was printed, the readers who sold their shares at the lower share price will have suffered pure economic loss.

- Loss may be in the form of property that was defective when the claimant acquired it. If someone buys a watch that doesn't work, the loss is the amount the person paid for the watch. The courts treat this as pure economic loss, because the property was already in a defective condition before it was sold, so there is no damage to the purchaser's existing property.

A person may suffer several different kinds of loss arising out of the same incident. For instance, in the example of the cut power cable, a shop may have to throw away frozen foods which have defrosted. If the shopkeeper sues, the wholesale price of the food is treated as physical damage, which is readily recoverable. However, the loss of profit on the frozen food is treated as economic loss caused by physical damage to the food. Furthermore, the loss of profit on fresh foods that could not be sold while the shop was shut is treated as pure economic loss, because it is caused by the physical damage to the electricity company's cable rather than the physical damage to the food itself, as was the case with the frozen food.

The courts have been reluctant to allow people to sue in negligence for pure economic loss, especially if the loss was caused by relying on the words of others rather than by those people's actions. There are three main reasons for this hesitance to allow a claim.

- First, courts took the view that people who were concerned about economic loss could and should protect themselves from such loss by entering into a contract—either a commercial contract with an identified party such as a contractor or an insurance contract to cover damage that might be caused by strangers. As you will learn on your contract law course, it is much easier to sue for economic loss in contract than in tort.

- Second, the law recognizes certain specific torts that provide a remedy against defendants who deliberately make false statements. The most important of these is the tort of deceit. A claimant who sues successfully in deceit can recover pure economic loss. There was a feeling amongst judges that allowing claimants to sue for pure economic loss in negligence would undermine the existing case law on deceit.

- Finally and most importantly, courts have been swayed by what is known as the 'floodgates' argument. This means that courts tend to worry that widening the scope of negligence (or any other cause of action) will lead to a flood of claims that will

think point
Can you think of any reasons why judges might think this kind of loss is more problematic than loss caused by injury or physical damage to the claimant's property?

think point
Of course, the electricity company may also sue. What kind of loss is the cost of repairing the power cable? What if the company has to give refunds to customers?

NOTE The tort of deceit is not covered in this text.

overwhelm the courts' resources. Usually, the number of people who suffer injury or physical damage in a given incident will be relatively small and predictable. The number of people who suffer pure economic loss in the same incident is often far greater and less predictable. For instance, in the cut cable example, the physical damage may be confined to the electricity company and a few shopkeepers who were selling frozen foods. The pure economic loss may extend to hundreds of local businesses selling non-perishable goods and services. *Weller & Co v Foot and Mouth Disease Research Institute* [1966] 1 QB 569 is a case where the 'floodgates' argument was raised. In that case, the defendants conducted experimental work relating to foot and mouth disease. Cattle near the defendants' premises became infected with the disease, leading the Minister of Agriculture, Fisheries and Food to give an order closing two markets in the area. It was thought that the outbreak was caused by the escape of a virus that the defendants had imported for study. The plaintiffs were auctioneers who were unable to auction cattle at those markets during the closure. They brought a case against the defendants for damages related to their loss of business. They sought to establish that the defendants owed them a duty to take reasonable care to ensure that the virus did not escape.

● **Weller & Co v Foot and Mouth Disease Research Institute** [1966] 1 QB 569

> Widgery J: There are probably a dozen other cases which could be cited . . . but I am invited to consider those cases in the light of the more recent decision of the House of Lords in Hedley Byrne & Co. Ltd. v. Heller & Partners Ltd. That was a case in which an action was brought against a bank for having negligently given a reference as to the standing of one of its customers upon which reference the plaintiffs were alleged to have acted to their detriment. No contract existed between the plaintiffs and the defendants and the claim was based on negligence at common law, the injury to the plaintiffs being the foreseeable consequence of the defendants' failure to take care. The giving of the reference was not an act which could conceivably do direct injury to the person or property of anyone, and the claim was of a kind sometimes described as an action for negligent words rather than for negligent acts, and of a kind which had not previously been recognised in the absence of a contractual or fiduciary relationship between the parties. It is now submitted that the plaintiffs' ultimate success in the House of Lords in Hedley Byrne & Co. Ltd. v Heller & Partners Ltd. has swept away any existing notion that direct injury to the person or property of the plaintiff is necessary to support an action in negligence and that the door is now open for the plaintiffs in the present action to recover the indirect or consequential loss which they have suffered.
>
> I think it important to remember at the outset that in the cases to which I have referred, the act or omission relied upon as constituting a breach of the duty to take care was an act or omission which might foreseeably have caused direct injury to the person or property of another. The world of commerce would come to a halt and ordinary life would become intolerable if the law imposed a duty on all persons at all times to refrain from any conduct which might foreseeably cause detriment to another, but where an absence of reasonable care may foreseeably cause direct injury to the person or property of another, a duty to take such care exists.

In this case, the judge limited the 'floodgates' of massive claims by using the concept of proximity and duty. In so doing, he was guided by the seminal case of *Hedley Byrne & Co v Heller* [1964] AC 465, which involved an allegedly negligent financial reference when a bank which carelessly gave a good reference on the financial stability of one of its customers. Relying on the reference, an advertising agency extended credit to the customer and lost money as a result. The damage to the bank was thus pure economic loss. In reaching its opinion, the House of Lords was very concerned about how far and easily a written statement could travel and how many people could, logically, rely on such a statement.

cross reference

Hedley Byrne & Co v Heller [1964] AC 465 is a critical case for a variety of reasons and is discussed in more detail below.

● ***Hedley Byrne & Co v Heller*** [1964] AC 465

> Pearce LJ: The reason for some divergence between the law of negligence in word and that of negligence in act is clear. Negligence in word creates problems different from those of negligence in act. Words are more volatile than deeds. They travel fast and far afield. They are used without being expended and take effect in combination with innumerable facts and other words. Yet they are dangerous and can cause vast financial damage. How far they are relied on unchecked . . . must in many cases be a matter of doubt and difficulty. If the mere hearing or reading of words were held to create proximity, there might be no limit to the persons to whom the speaker or writer could be liable. Damage by negligent acts to persons or property on the other hand is more visible and obvious; its limits are more easily defined.

Simpson & Co v Thomson (1877) 3 App Cas 279 illustrates the concern of judges that allowing people to claim for pure economic loss might lead to an excessive number of claims being brought. There, two ships, owned by the same person, collided, and the underwriters who had insured the ships sought to collect from each other for their losses.

● ***Simpson & Co v Thomson*** (1877) 3 App Cas 279

> Lord Penzance: The principle involved seems to me to be this—that where damage is done by a wrongdoer to a chattel not only the owner of that chattel, but all those who by contract with the owner have bound themselves to obligations which are rendered more onerous, or have secured to themselves advantages which are rendered less beneficial by the damage done to the chattel, have a right of action against the wrongdoer . . . This, I say, is the principle involved in the respondents' contention. If it be a sound one, it would seem to follow that if, by the negligence of a wrongdoer, goods are destroyed which the owner of them had bound himself by contract to supply to a third person, this person as well as the owner has a right of action for any loss inflicted on him by their destruction. But if this be true as to injuries done to chattels, it would seem to be equally so as to injuries to the person. An individual injured by a negligently driven carriage has an action against the owner of it. Would a doctor, it may be asked, who had contracted to attend him and provide medicines for a fixed sum by the year, also have a right of action in respect of the additional cost of attendance and medicine cast upon him by that accident? And yet it cannot be denied that the doctor had an interest in his patient's safety. In like manner an actor or singer bound for a term to a manager of a theatre is disabled by the wrongful act

of a third person to the serious loss of the manager. Can the manager recover damages for that loss from the wrongdoer? Such instances might be indefinitely multiplied, giving rise to rights of action which in modern communities, where every complexity of mutual relation is daily created by contract, might be both numerous and novel.

The United States case of *Ultramares Corp v Touche, Niven & Co* 255 NY 170 (1931) is very often cited in English judgments on the importance of limiting claims for economic loss (and indeed other cases where new categories of negligence are being considered). The case involved misrepresentations through negligence and fraud by the defendants. The defendants had been employed by a third party to prepare and certify a balance sheet showing the condition of the business. They were aware that the certificate of audit would be used to obtain credit for the business. Capital and surplus were certified to be intact, when in fact the business was insolvent. On the faith of the defendants' certificate, the plaintiff had made several loans. It was held that if, in certifying information, defendants made a statement as true to their knowledge when they had no knowledge on the subject, liability for fraud could ensue.

· ·

● ***Ultramares Corp v Touche, Niven & Co*** 255 NY 170 (1931)

> **Cardozo J**: The defendants owed to their employer a duty imposed by law to make their certificate without fraud, and a duty growing out of contract to make it with the care and caution proper to their calling. Fraud includes the pretense of knowledge when knowledge there is none. To creditors and investors to whom the employer exhibited the certificate, the defendants owed a like duty to make it without fraud, since there was notice in the circumstances of its making that the employer did not intend to keep it to himself . . . A different question develops when we ask whether they owed a duty to these to make it without negligence. If liability for negligence exists, a thoughtless slip or blunder, the failure to detect a theft or forgery beneath the cover of deceptive entries, may expose accountants to a liability in an indeterminate amount for an indeterminate time to an indeterminate class. The hazards of a business conducted on these terms are so extreme as to enkindle doubt whether a flaw may not exist in the implication of a duty that exposes [sic] to these consequences.

TIP Some electronic databases allow you to see at a glance whether a case has been approved or overruled. Your law librarian can show you how to use these.

In the rest of this chapter, we will first examine the current state of the law on pure economic loss, followed by a look at some of the key cases in the history of this area of law. You need to be able to recognize these older decisions because they are still often cited in court and referred to in judgments, since they are still important landmarks in the history of the law. It has taken several decades for the current rules on pure economic loss cases to evolve, and there have been many twists and turns along the way. Because of this, it is particularly important in this area of law that you do not rely on old editions of textbooks or on individual cases taken out of context.

The current law on economic loss

13.3.1 The cause of the loss

Damage to third party property

In order to restrict negligence claims for pure economic loss and avoid opening the floodgates to large numbers of claims, the courts either disallow such claims altogether or apply stricter rules of construction than are used in other negligence claims, depending on how the particular loss was caused. Before we look at these principles in detail, it is important to understand how they fit into the wider scheme of negligence claims. Chapter 2 showed how negligence consists of three elements which the claimant must prove: duty, breach, and damage. If the courts want to restrict a particular kind of claim, one way of doing so is to impose special rules for one of these elements. In cases involving pure economic loss, the courts have generally focused on duty as the best means of limiting claims. Where the claimant suffers loss because of damage to the property of a third party, the courts have held that the claimant cannot recover because there is no duty to prevent this type of loss. Often the courts base this conclusion on the lack of sufficient proximity. This was confirmed in *Londonwaste v AMEC Civil Engineering* (1997) 83 BLR 136, where a contractor cut through a power cable, shutting down a power station. The owners of the power station suffered several kinds of loss, including physical damage to the power station, loss of profit on the electricity they would normally have generated, and some transportation costs relating to rubbish which would normally have been burned in the power station but had to be thrown away instead. The High Court ruled that the owners could only claim for the physical damage to the power station, not for the other kinds of loss, because there was insufficient proximity between the contractor and the owners of the power station to hold the contractor liable for economic loss.

This restrictive interpretation of duty can produce odd results. In *Leigh and Sullivan v Aliakmon Shipping Co Ltd (The Aliakmon)* [1986] AC 785, the plaintiffs made a contract to buy some steel coils, but they were unable to complete the purchase because they could not raise the necessary money. The sellers agreed to allow the plaintiffs to hold the coils as the sellers' agents while the plaintiffs continued to try to raise the funds. The coils were shipped to the plaintiffs but were damaged in transit because the ship-owners had stowed them incorrectly. However, the plaintiffs remained bound under the contract to complete their purchase. Eventually, they were able to raise the funds to do so, and the purchase was completed. The plaintiffs then tried to sue the ship-owners for the difference in value between the coils as ordered and the damaged coils they actually received. However, because the plaintiffs were not the owners of the coils at the time the damage took place, their loss was caused by damage to the property of a third party rather than by damage to their own property. The Court of Appeal held that the plaintiffs could still recover, using a concept of 'transferred loss' (which is explained in the opinion of Lord Justice Goff below), but this was overruled by the House of Lords, as indicated in the excerpt from Lord Brandon.

● *Leigh & Sullivan Ltd v Aliakmon Shipping Co Ltd (The Aliakmon)* [1986] AC 785 (in the Court of Appeal, subsequently overruled)

Goff LJ: In my judgment, there is no good reason in principle or in policy, why the ... buyer should not have such a direct cause of action. The factors which I have already listed point strongly towards liability. I am particularly influenced by the fact that the loss in question is of a character which will ordinarily fall on the goods owner who will have a good claim against the shipowner, but in a case such as the present the loss may, in practical terms, fall on the buyer. It seems to me that the policy reasons pointing towards a direct right of action by the buyer against the shipowner in a case of this kind outweigh the policy reasons which generally preclude recovery for purely economic loss. There is here no question of any wide or indeterminate liability being imposed upon wrongdoers; on the contrary, the shipowner is simply held liable to the buyer in damages for loss for which he would ordinarily be liable to the goods owner. There is a recognisable principle underlying the imposition of liability, which can be called the principle of transferred loss. Furthermore, that principle can be formulated. For the purposes of the present case, I would formulate it in the following deliberately narrow terms, while recognizing that it may require modification in the light of experience. Where A owes a duty of care in tort not to cause physical damage to B's property, and commits a breach of that duty in circumstances in which the loss of or physical damage to the property will ordinarily fall on B but (as is reasonably foreseeable by A) such loss or damage, by reason of a contractual relationship between B and C, falls upon C, then C will be entitled, subject to the terms of any contract restricting A's liability to B, to bring an action in tort against A in respect of such loss or damage to the extent that it falls on him, C.

● *Leigh & Sullivan Ltd v Aliakmon Shipping Co Ltd (The Aliakmon)* [1986] AC 785 (in the House of Lords)

Lord Brandon of Oakbrook: My Lords, there is a long line of authority for a principle of law that, in order to enable a person to claim in negligence for loss caused to him by reason of loss of or damage to property, he must have had either the legal ownership of or a possessory title to the property concerned at the time when the loss or damage occurred, and it is not enough for him to have only had contractual rights in relation to such property which have been adversely affected by the loss of or damage to it ...

[Counsel] said, rightly in my view, that the policy reason for excluding a duty of care ... was to avoid the opening of the floodgates so as to expose a person guilty of want of care to unlimited liability to an indefinite number of other persons whose contractual rights have been adversely affected by such want of care. [Counsel] went on to argue that recognition by the law of a duty of care owed by shipowners to a ... buyer, to whom the risk but not yet the property in the goods carried in such shipowners' ship has passed, would not of itself open any floodgates of the kind described. It would, he said, only create a strictly limited exception to the general rule, based on the circumstance that the considerations of policy on which that general rule was founded did not apply to that particular case. I do not accept that argument. If an exception to the general rule were to be made in the field of carriage by sea, it would no doubt have to be extended to the field of carriage by land, and I do not think that it is possible to say that no undue increase in the scope of a person's liability for want of care would follow. In any event, where a general rule, which is simple to understand and easy to apply, has been established by a long line of authority over many years, I do not think that the law should allow special pleading in a particular case within the general rule to detract from its application. If such detraction were to be permitted in one particular case, it would lead to attempts to have it permitted in a variety of other particular cases, and the result would be that the certainty, which the application of the general rule presently provides, would be seriously undermined. Yet certainty of the law is of the utmost importance, especially but by no means only, in commercial matters. I therefore think that the general rule . . . ought to apply to a case like the present one . . . The buyers, when they agreed to the variation of the original contract of sale, did not take the steps to protect themselves which, if properly advised, they should have done . . .

With the greatest possible respect to Lord Goff the principle of transferred loss which he there enunciated, however useful in dealing with special factual situations it may be in theory, is not only not supported by authority, but is on the contrary inconsistent with it. Even if it were necessary to introduce such a principle in order to fill a genuine lacuna in the law, I should myself, perhaps because I am more faint-hearted than Lord Goff, be reluctant to do so. As I have tried to show earlier, however, there is in truth no such lacuna in the law which requires to be filled.

cross reference

The issue of already defective goods is also addressed in chapter 15 on product liability.

This decision illustrates that, when the claimant acquires goods or property which are already defective, the claimant cannot recover the loss.

Non-damaging interference with the claimant's property

The recent case of *Transco plc v United Utilities Water plc* [2005] EWHC 2784 (QB) provides an interesting contrast with *Londonwaste v AMEC Civil Engineering* (1997) 83 BLR 136, where a contractor cut through a power cable, shutting down a power station. That case held that the loss of income from sale of electricity, following the severance of electrical cables belonging to a third party, could not be recovered, since the loss of income had not been caused by damage to any property belonging to the electricity suppliers. *Transco plc v United Utilities Water plc* [2005] EWHC 2784 (QB), on the other hand, appears to suggest that there is a right to recover economic loss that is caused by interference with one's own property (as opposed to the property of a third party), even if the interference did not cause any physical damage. This could considerably expand the type and numbers of claims brought for economic loss.

. . . .

● ***Transco plc v United Utilities Water plc*** [2005] EWHC 2784 (QB)

Butterfield J: The factual matrix within which I am to consider the preliminary issue is wholly agreed. I summarise the position in the following way. The Claimants, Transco, are responsible for the operation of the gas transmission and distribution network throughout the United Kingdom. The Defendants operate water and waste water networks in the United Kingdom. On or around 29 November 2002, a network controller of the Defendants closed off a valve on Transco's gas network in the Rope Lane and Grestry Road area of Shavington in Crewe. It is accepted on behalf of the Defendants that the work then being carried out by and on behalf of the Defendants, was 'street works'. It is quite obvious that a hole had been excavated to enable the Defendants to carry out some work of repair or renewal or inspection of their utility, in the course of which the valve was turned off of the Claimants' utility.

As a result of the closure of the valve, about 2,600 of Transco's customers in the Shavington area of Crewe had their gas supply cut off. Once alerted to the interruption of the gas supply, Transco took steps to investigate the interruption and to restore the gas supply. In consequence they incurred, it is said, costs and expenses, including contractor's costs, engineering staff overtime costs and non-engineering staff over-time costs, amounting in broad terms, to a little less than £100,000.

Furthermore, Transco was obligated to pay compensation payments of about £74,000 to affected customers, and also incurred a small amount of costs in relation to the supply of appliances which had presumably been damaged in consequence of the interruption of supply.

The Claimants, by their particulars of claim, allege that the Defendants were negligent in various specific respects, including failing to liaise with Transco to request any plans showing the location of gas valves and pipes in the relevant area and failing to operate any, or any adequate monitoring of the effect of the work performed . . .

On behalf of the Defendants, it is admitted that the network controller was negligent in shutting off the gas valve rather than the water valve. It is further admitted that as a result of the gas supply being shut off, a number of the Claimants' customers were affected, the exact number of which not being within the Defendants' knowledge. It is further admitted that the Claimants employed its own staff and other contractors in order safely to re-establish the supply of gas to the customers, and that there were inevitable cost consequences as a result thereof.

The Defendants, however, submit that the losses claimed are pure economic loss and therefore not recoverable in law. There is no evidence, it is said, that there was any physical damage to any item belonging to the Claimants or any customer as a result of the interruption in the supply of gas.

Against that factual background, I turn to consider the competing submissions of law. First I consider the issue of negligence. [Counsel] submits that there is here a clear duty owed by the Defendants to the Claimants, that there has been a breach of that duty, and that, accordingly, it is reasonable just and fair that there should be liability to compensate for the damage sustained. On behalf of the Defendants, it is submitted that, whilst the foreseeability of damage is satisfied here, the proximity of the relationship between the two utility companies is not such as to satisfy the threefold test referred to in *Caparo Industries v Dickman* [1990] 2 AC 605, [1990] 1 All ER 568, nor is it reasonable to impose a duty. There was, it is submitted, no special relationship here between Defendants and Claimants. True it is that the Defendants owned water pipes in the same area as the Claimants owned gas pipes, but there was no special fiduciary or other relationship of exceptional particular proximity from the mere fact that the pipes happened to be in physical proximity.

In my judgment, however, there is such a special proximity in this relationship. It is not sensible, in my judgment, to conclude that two public utilities, both using the sub-strata area under the same street in which to convey their respective commodities, do not have a close relationship, the one with the other. They must be aware, in my judgment, that their actions or omissions may affect the installations of other providers of utilities which, in broad terms, are likely to be using precisely the same sub-strata underneath the streets . . . It is well known that such is the position and, in my judgment, that sort of situation, is capable of, and in this case does, provide a special relationship, the one with the other.

Is it reasonable to impose a duty to take reasonable care not to harm another utility's installation? For reasons already sufficiently expressed, in my judgment it plainly is. I therefore hold that it is both reasonable and proportionate to impose a duty of care in considering the conduct of the two utilities in this case, one, I should say, with the other. Just as the Defendants owed that duty of care to the Claimants, so do the Claimants owe such a duty to the Defendants, and indeed so would any other utility provider using the same general area.

But, says Mr Field, this is pure economic loss. Mr Field QC accepts that, if the Defendants' employee had damaged the valve when turning off the gas supply, thereby causing gas to cease to flow through the pipe, there could be no argument that he could advance properly to dissuade the court from finding that the Claimants should succeed in recovering whatever damages flowed from that event. But, said Mr Field, because the wrongful act resulting in that consequence did not cause physical damage to the pipe or valve, the Defendants are not liable for the extensive damage their negligent act plainly caused.

He puts this matter this way (these, I have to say are my words not his, but I hope they accurately encapsulate the basis of his submission). There is, he says, clear authority that pure economic loss is not, in general terms, recoverable where it arises as a result of tortious negligence, not consequent on physical damage. The courts, he submits, must be astute to ring-fence the outer limits of liability for negligence giving rise to economic loss. There must ultimately be an outer edge of liability, and in this case the cost of the washer damaged in turning off the value, if such had occurred (and it did not) provides the perimeter fence for the liability of the Defendants in such circumstances as this. Outwith any such damage they are not liable. That is, said Mr Field, because that is the public policy of the courts and it should be upheld, however apparently unfair it may, at first glance, appear to be.

As I have already observed, the term 'pure economic loss' is well known in the realm of tortious negligence where it refers to economic loss that is not consequent on physical damage. What then is physical damage? Physical damage must most obviously comprise personal injury or property damage, but its 'spirit', to adopt the expression used by Professor Andrew Burry in the current edition of Remedies for Torts in Breach of Contract, also, in my judgment, includes (amongst other things) damage to reputation and wrongful interference with goods or land, quite apart from property damage.

[Counsel] refers me, helpfully, to the decision of *Spartan Steel v Martin & Co* [1973] 1 QB 27, [1972] 3 All ER 557. That was a case in which the Defendants' employees were digging up a road when they negligently damaged an electric cable which the Defendants knew was the direct supply from the Electricity Board's power station to the plaintiff's factory. The plaintiffs were without electricity until the Board was able to repair the cable. The owners of the factory brought proceedings seeking compensation first for the physical damage to their factory, secondly for consequential economic loss arising from that physical damage and thirdly pure economic loss, described by counsel in submissions as 'parasitic damages', a phrase which Lord Denning MR disliked ... Lawton LJ, giving a concurring judgment observed at page 46H:

> 'In my judgment the answer to this question is that such financial damage cannot be recovered save when it is the immediate consequence of a breach of duty to safeguard the plaintiff from that kind of loss. Negligent interference with such services is one of the facts of life and can cause a lot of damage, both physical and financial. Water conduits have been with us for centuries; gas mains for nearly a century and a half; electricity supply cables for about three-quarters of a century; but there is not a single case in the English law reports which is an authority for the proposition that mere financial loss resulting from negligent interruption of such services is recoverable. Why?'

NOTE *Spartan Steel* is a case similar to *Londonwaste v AMEC* and *Transco plc v United Utilities* that is often cited in this area of law.

> That citation, it seems to me, is not strictly to the point. This is a case in which the Defendants negligently directly interfered with property owned by the Claimants and loss was sustained in consequence. It is not consequential loss flowing from the interruption of supply that is sought to be recovered by the Claimants, but the cost of rectifying the damage that the Defendants negligently caused. That, to my mind, is a different proposition altogether.
>
> In my judgment, there is sufficient proximity between the Defendants and the Claimants.

compare

Traditionally, psychiatric damage was only considered foreseeable if it was caused by some physical danger. Compare the developments in the law on pure economic loss and psychiatric damage.

As this discussion shows, pure economic loss can now be recovered even if there is no physical damage, provided that there is some sort of interference with property and sufficient proximity between the parties. It remains to be seen whether the courts will need to limit this principle in any way.

Negligent statements or advice

Sometimes loss arises as a result of negligent statements or advice. In these sorts of circumstances, the courts have set a higher standard for imposing a duty than they have in other cases. A claimant cannot recover pure economic loss caused by negligent statements or advice unless there is a special relationship between the claimant and the defendant. In the next section, we will consider what the claimant needs to prove in order to establish a special relationship, but it is useful first to understand how this relates to the usual criteria for establishing a duty of care. In chapter 2, we saw that the test laid down in *Caparo Industries plc v Dickman* [1990] 2 AC 605 for establishing a duty of care requires three factors: proximity, foreseeability of loss, and the conclusion that it is just and reasonable to impose a duty of care on the defendant. In cases of pure economic loss caused by negligent statements or advice, the courts have chosen to set higher standards for demonstrating proximity. In other words, the claimant in a pure economic loss case must show a much closer relationship between claimant and defendant than in other cases.

NOTE Once the claimant has established that the defendant had a duty to prevent pure economic loss, breach and damage (including causation and remoteness) still have to be established in the usual way. Don't forget to deal with these factors in assignments and exams.

13.3.2 Special relationships

Hedley Byrne & Co v Heller & Partners Ltd [1964] AC 465 is the key case on the special relationship which is required in a claim for pure economic loss caused by negligent statements or advice. The standards described in this decision have also been applied in other cases of pure economic loss. The case involved a bank which carelessly gave a good reference on the financial stability of one of its customers. Relying on the reference, an ad agency extended credit to the customer and lost money as a result. The damage to the bank was thus pure economic loss. The House of Lords held that the bank was not liable because it had used a disclaimer when providing the reference. However,

TIP Disclaimers were discussed at length in chapter 5.

the House of Lords also made it quite clear that if there had not been a disclaimer, the claim would have succeeded. Strictly, this was *obiter* commentary, but it has been widely followed and can now be treated as binding. Their Lordships indicated that the reason they would have allowed the claim in the absence of a disclaimer was that the bank would have impliedly assumed responsibility for the advertising agency's decision to extend credit.

● ***Hedley Byrne & Co v Heller & Partners Ltd*** [1964] AC 465

compare

Lord Reid is talking about damage resulting from negligent statements. When you read chapter 14 on defamation, you will consider another type of tort involving damage resulting from words.

Lord Reid: The appellants' first argument was based on *Donoghue v Stevenson*. That is a very important decision, but I do not think that it has any direct bearing on this case. That decision may encourage us to develop existing lines of authority, but it cannot entitle us to disregard them. Apart altogether from authority, I would think that the law must treat negligent words differently from negligent acts. The law ought so far as possible to reflect the standards of the reasonable man, and that is what *Donoghue v. Stevenson* sets out to do. The most obvious difference between negligent words and negligent acts is this. Quite careful people often express definite opinions on social or informal occasions even when they see that others are likely to be influenced by them; and they often do that without taking that care which they would take if asked for their opinion professionally or in a business connection. The appellant agrees that there can be no duty of care on such occasions, and we were referred to American and South African authorities where that is recognised, although their law appears to have gone much further than ours has yet done. But it is at least unusual casually to put into circulation negligently made articles which are dangerous. A man might give a friend a negligently-prepared bottle of homemade wine and his friend's guests might drink it with dire results. But it is by no means clear that those guests would have no action against the negligent manufacturer.

Another obvious difference is that a negligently made article will only cause one accident, and so it is not very difficult to find the necessary degree of proximity or neighbourhood between the negligent manufacturer and the person injured. But words can be broadcast with or without the consent or the foresight of the speaker or writer. It would be one thing to say that the speaker owes a duty to a limited class, but it would be going very far to say that he owes a duty to every ultimate 'consumer' who acts on those words to his detriment. It would be no use to say that a speaker or writer owes a duty but can disclaim responsibility if he wants to. He, like the manufacturer, could make it part of a contract that he is not to be liable for his negligence: but that contract would not protect him in a question with a third party, at least if the third party was unaware of it.

So it seems to me that there is good sense behind our present law that in general an innocent but negligent misrepresentation gives no cause of action. There must be something more than the mere misstatement. I therefore turn to the authorities to see what more is required. The most natural requirement would be that expressly or by implication from the circumstances the speaker or writer has undertaken some responsibility, and that appears to me not to conflict with any authority which is binding on this House...[In a previous case,] Lord Haldane did not think that a duty to take care must be limited to cases of fiduciary relationship in the narrow sense of relationships which had been recognised by the Court of Chancery as being of a fiduciary character. He speaks of other special relationships, and I can see no logical stopping place short of all those relationships where it is plain that the party seeking information or advice was trusting the other to exercise such a degree of care as the circumstances required, where it was reasonable for him to do that, and where the other gave the information or advice when he knew or ought to have known that the inquirer was relying on him. I say 'ought to have known' because in questions of negligence we now apply the objective standard of what the reasonable man would have done.

A reasonable man, knowing that he was being trusted or that his skill and judgment were being relied on, would, I think, have three courses open to him. He could keep silent or decline to give the information or advice sought: or he could give an answer with a clear qualification that he accepted no responsibility for it or that it was given without that reflection or inquiry which a careful answer would require: or he could simply answer without any such qualification. If he chooses to adopt the last course he must, I think, be held to have accepted some responsibility for his answer being given carefully, or to have accepted a relationship with the inquirer which requires him to exercise such care as the circumstances require.

Lord Morris of Borth-y-Gest: My Lords, it seems to me that if A assumes a responsibility to B to tender him deliberate advice, there could be a liability if the advice is negligently given. I say 'could be' because the ordinary courtesies and exchanges of life would become impossible if it were sought to attach legal obligation to every kindly and friendly act. But the principle of the matter would not appear to be in doubt. If A employs B (who might. [sic] for example, be a professional man such as an accountant or a solicitor or a doctor) for reward to give advice and if the advice is negligently given there could be a liability in B to pay damages. The fact that the advice is given in words would not, in my view, prevent liability from arising. Quite apart, however, from employment or contract there may be circumstances in which a duty to exercise care will arise if a service is voluntarily undertaken. A medical man may unexpectedly come across an unconscious man, who is a complete stranger to him, and who is in urgent need of skilled attention: if the medical man, following the fine traditions of his profession, proceeds to treat the unconscious man he must exercise reasonable skill and care in doing so...I can see no difference of principle in the case of a banker. If someone who was not a customer of a bank made a formal approach to the bank with a definite request that the bank would give him deliberate advice as to certain financial matters of a nature with which the bank ordinarily dealt the bank would be under no obligation to accede to the request: if, however, they undertook, though gratuitously, to give deliberate advice (I exclude what I might call casual and perfunctory conversations) they would be under a duty to exercise reasonable care in giving it. They would be liable if they were negligent although, there being no consideration, no enforceable contractual relationship was created...

My Lords, I consider that it follows and that it should now be regarded as settled that if someone possessed of a special skill undertakes, quite irrespective of contract, to apply that skill for the assistance of another person who relies upon such skill, a duty of care will arise. The fact that the service is to be given by means of or by the instrumentality of words can make no difference. Furthermore, if in a sphere in which a person is so placed that others could reasonably rely upon his judgment or his skill or upon his ability to make careful inquiry, a person takes it upon himself to give information or advice to, or allows his information or advice to be passed on to, another person who, as he knows or should know, will place reliance upon it, then a duty of care will arise.

These extracts suggest that one way of proving the necessary special relationship is to demonstrate that the defendant has voluntarily assumed responsibility to the claimant.

The importance of this concept of voluntary assumption of responsibility in pure economic loss cases has been controversial because courts have not always taken a consistent stance on it. Some cases have tended to suggest that voluntary assumption of responsibility is required in every case of pure economic loss, while others hold that it is simply one test amongst several. In the recent case of *Customs and Excise Commissioners v Barclays Bank plc* [2006] UKHL 28, the House of Lords clarified the issue. Here, the commissioners obtained court orders to assist them in recovering outstanding taxes from two taxpayers who were customers of Barclays. The orders required Barclays to freeze the customers' accounts, but Barclays mistakenly allowed the customers to withdraw money after the orders had been made. The commissioners sued Barclays for damages in negligence associated with allowing the withdrawals to take place. Amongst other arguments, the commissioners alleged that Barclays had assumed responsibility to them. Both parties' counsel made representations about the importance of voluntary assumption of responsibility as a test for whether or not there was a duty on the part of Barclays to prevent economic loss on the part of the commissioners. All the judgments in the House of Lords stressed that assumption of responsibility is not the only test for the existence of a duty to prevent pure economic loss. Lord Bingham of Cornhill made the following comment:

> I think it is correct to regard an assumption of responsibility as a sufficient but not a necessary condition of liability, a first test which, if answered positively, may obviate the need for further inquiry. If answered negatively, further consideration is called for.

In other words, if the defendant freely takes on a responsibility to the claimant to prevent economic loss, then the court will enforce that responsibility. If the defendant does not take on such responsibility voluntarily, the court has to consider other factors which may point to a duty. In *Customs and Excise Commissioners v Barclays Bank plc* [2006] UKHL 28, the court decided that because Barclays had received a court order, any responsibility they had was not voluntary, and therefore the court had to go on to investigate other factors. These factors are principally those set out in *Caparo Industries plc v Dickman* [1990] 2 AC 605. In *Customs and Excise Commissioners v Barclays Bank plc* [2006] UKHL 28, the court ultimately decided that it was not fair and reasonable to impose a duty on the bank to protect the commissioners from economic loss because the bank already faced possible proceedings for contempt of court if it did not comply with the order.

Chapter 2 discussed the effect of *Caparo Industries plc v Dickman* [1990] 2 AC 605 on general principles of negligence, but the case also gives specific guidance on pure economic loss cases. Caparo was a company which held shares in another public company, F. The public accounts of F suggested that it was very profitable. Relying on these accounts, Caparo bought more shares in F. It later turned out that the directors of F were involved in a fraud and that F was actually making a loss. Caparo successfully sued F's auditors for negligence in auditing the accounts, since a non-negligently conducted audit would have revealed the fraud. The judgment sets out three elements that, if present, will create a duty to prevent pure economic loss in the context of giving statements or advice.

● **Caparo Industries plc v Dickman** [1990] 2 AC 605

Lord Bridge of Harwich: The salient feature of all these cases [where defendants have been held liable for negligent statements] is that the defendant giving advice or information was fully aware of the nature of the transaction which the plaintiff had in contemplation, knew that the advice or information would be communicated to him directly or indirectly and knew that it was very likely that the plaintiff would rely on that advice or information in deciding whether or not to engage in the transaction in contemplation. In these circumstances the defendant could clearly be expected, subject always to the effect of any disclaimer of responsibility, specifically to anticipate that the plaintiff would rely on the advice or information given by the defendant for the very purpose for which he did in the event rely on it. So also the plaintiff, subject again to the effect of any disclaimer, would in that situation reasonably suppose that he was entitled to rely on the advice or information communicated to him for the very purpose for which he required it. The situation is entirely different where a statement is put into more or less general circulation and may foreseeably be relied on by strangers to the maker of the statement for any one of a variety of different purposes which the maker of the statement has no specific reason to anticipate. To hold the maker of the statement to be under a duty of care in respect of the accuracy of the statement to all and sundry for any purpose for which they may choose to rely on it is not only to subject him, in the classic words of Cardozo C.J. to 'liability in an indeterminate amount for an indeterminate time to an indeterminate class': see *Ultramares Corporation v Touche* (1931) 174 N.E. 441, 444; it is also to confer on the world at large a quite unwarranted entitlement to appropriate for their own purposes the benefit of the expert knowledge or professional expertise attributed to the maker of the statement. Hence, looking only at the circumstances of these decided cases where a duty of care in respect of negligent statements has been held to exist, I should expect to find that the 'limit or control mechanism imposed upon the liability of a wrongdoer towards those who have suffered economic damage in consequence of his negligence' rested in the necessity to prove, in this category of the tort of negligence, as an essential ingredient of the 'proximity' between the plaintiff and the defendant, that the defendant knew that his statement would be communicated to the plaintiff, either as an individual or as a member of an identifiable class, specifically in connection with a particular transaction or transactions of a particular kind (e.g. in a prospectus inviting investment) and that the plaintiff would be very likely to rely on it for the purpose of deciding whether or not to enter upon that transaction or upon a transaction of that kind.

Lord Oliver of Aylmerton: What can be deduced from the *Hedley Byrne case*, therefore, is that the necessary relationship between the maker of a statement or giver of advice ('the adviser') and the recipient who acts in reliance upon it ('the advisee') may typically be held to exist where (1) the advice is required for a purpose, whether particularly specified or generally described, which is made known, either actually or inferentially, to the adviser at the time when the advice is given; (2) the adviser knows, either actually or inferentially, that his advice will be communicated to the advisee, either specifically or as a member of an ascertainable class, in order that it should be used by the advisee for that purpose; (3) it is known either actually or inferentially, that the advice so communicated is likely to be acted upon by the advisee for that purpose without independent inquiry, and (4) it is so acted upon by the advisee to his detriment. That is not, of course, to suggest that these conditions are either conclusive or exclusive, but merely that the actual decision in the case does not warrant any broader propositions...As I have already mentioned, it is almost always foreseeable that someone, somewhere and in some circumstances, may choose to alter his position upon the faith of the accuracy of a statement or report which comes to his attention and it is always foreseeable that a report—even a confidential report—may come to be communicated to persons other than the original or intended recipient. To apply as a test of liability only the foreseeability of possible damage without some further control would be to create a liability wholly indefinite in area, duration and amount and would open up a limitless vista of uninsurable risk for the professional man.

These judgments have been very influential, giving rise to the so-called 'Caparo test', which consists of the following three elements:

- The defendant must have known, either actually or by inference:
  - that the statement or advice would be communicated to the claimant (either as an individual or as a member of a class);
  - the purpose of communicating the statement or advice to the claimant; and
  - that the claimant was likely to act on the statement or advice without making independent inquiries.
- The claimant must have acted on the statement or advice.
- The claimant must have suffered some detriment as a result.

All three elements must exist for liability for pure economic loss to result. The last two bullet points are often treated as a single element, known as 'detrimental reliance', but you may find it helpful to think of them separately so that you are not tempted to leave either of them out when you are analysing a set of facts. Although Oliver LJ identifies these points as part of the proximity test, they can also be considered as simply restating the 'but for' test on causation, which was discussed in chapter 4.

The test in *Caparo Industries plc v Dickman* [1990] 2 AC 605 does not really change the test laid down in *Hedley Byrne & Co v Heller & Partners Ltd* [1964] AC 465, but rather clarifies it by providing more detail. Both tests emphasize the need for the claimant to have relied on the defendant's statement or advice. Both require that the defendant either realized, or ought to have realized, that the claimant was likely to rely on the defendant's statement or advice. *Caparo Industries plc v Dickman* [1990] 2 AC 605 is just a little more detailed about this requirement than *Hedley Byrne & Co v Heller & Partners Ltd* [1964] AC 465 is, splitting that element into three constituent parts. The only real difference seems to be the requirement in *Hedley Byrne & Co v Heller & Partners Ltd* [1964] AC 465 that it must have been reasonable for the claimant to rely on the advice. This has no obvious equivalent in the *Caparo* test, though it is arguably included in the requirement that the defendant should have known that the claimant was likely to rely on the advice. It will be difficult to establish this if the reliance was unreasonable, so, in reality, the tests are not very different—just differently expressed. However, in practice, the test in *Hedley Byrne & Co v Heller & Partners Ltd* [1964] AC 465 can be applied quite easily to situations which do not involve incorrect statements or advice, whereas the *Caparo* test does not lend itself so easily to other contexts, as discussed further below.

13.3.3 Applying the proximity test

As in many areas of the law, legal principles concerning pure economic loss must be discussed in context if they are to be fully understood and defined. This section sets out examples of situations where the courts have found that there is enough proximity to create a duty to prevent pure economic loss and situations where there is not enough proximity. Most of the cases relate to negligent statements or advice, but you will see that liability has been extended by analogy to other situations in some instances.

Purpose of communication

Machin v Adams (1997) 59 Con LR 14 is an example of a case where no proximity existed because the defendant did not sufficiently understand the purpose of communicating his advice to the plaintiff. Here, Mrs Machin ran care homes for the elderly and was purchasing a property from Mr and Mrs Adams for that purpose. Mr Adams was an experienced builder who, as part of the sale, agreed to convert the property for use as a care home. He hired an architect to provide a certificate for Mrs Machin certifying that the works were complete and satisfactory. About two weeks before the certificate was due, the architect wrote to Mrs Adams to say that the works were nearly complete, that they were satisfactory, and that it would cost about £25,000 to finish them. Mrs Adams passed this letter on to Mrs Machin. It was agreed that Mrs Machin would go ahead with the sale before the works were completed, in return for a reduction of £25,000. Mrs Machin said that she had relied on the architect's letter in agreeing to this. It later emerged that some of the works were defective. Mrs Machin claimed that it cost £35,000 to put these errors right and that she had lost £100,000 in profits as a result of the delay. Both constituted pure economic loss because the property was already defective when it was first acquired by Mrs Machin. The Court of Appeal did not accept that Mrs Machin had relied on the architect's letter, because it turned out that her solicitor had realized before she bought the property that the estimate of £25,000 to complete the works was incorrect.

The Court of Appeal also held that the architect never owed Mrs Machin a duty in the first place. The court thought that the architect must have realized that Mrs Adams was going to pass his letter on to Mrs Machin—otherwise she could just have asked her husband how the building work was going—but the court did not think the architect would have realized that the purpose of passing this information on was to renegotiate the contract. The architect expected to be asked back to the property in the next two weeks to give his final certificate, so he would have expected any final contract negotiations to await that certificate and not be based on an interim letter. Thus, Mrs Machin could not recover her losses.

It is possible for a claimant to be entitled to rely on a communication for one purpose, but not for others. For instance, in *Al-Nakib Investments (Jersey) Ltd v Longcroft* [1990] 3 All ER 321, directors issued a prospectus to shareholders encouraging them to take part in an issue of new shares. The plaintiffs invested money in that share issue and six months later bought additional shares on the stock market. When the plaintiffs lost money on the transaction and sued, the court held that the directors owed no duty of

think point

Do you think this case could have been analysed under any of the other elements of the proximity test, such as likelihood of reliance?

care to the shareholders relating to the additional shares, because the directors did not know that the shareholders would rely on the prospectus for that purpose. Similarly, in *Reeman v Department of Transport* [1997] 2 Lloyd's Rep 648, the Department of Transport gave a certificate of seaworthiness to the owner of a boat. The boat was later sold to the plaintiff, who relied on the certificate. It turned out that the boat was not seaworthy after all, and the plaintiff was left with a worthless boat. The Court of Appeal held that the purpose of the certificate was to ensure public safety, not to protect people from the economic consequences of transactions. The Department of Transport would not have been able to identify the class of people who might rely on the certificate for such purposes at the time it issued the certificate and thus owed them no duty.

Reasonable reliance and likelihood of reliance

The case law has established that it must have been reasonable for the claimant to rely on the defendant without making independent enquiries. In order for reliance on a defendant's statement to be reasonable, the claimant must have known who made the statement at the time of relying on it. For instance, in *Abbott v Strong* [1998] 2 BCLC 420, the directors of a hotel company were planning to issue new shares in the company to the existing shareholders. In order to provide the shareholders with enough informa-tion to decide whether or not to buy the new shares, the directors were obliged to put out a prospectus. In the prospectus, the directors made remarks about the profitability of the company, based on a forecast they had obtained from the company's account-ants. The company turned out to be less profitable than expected because of a fraud, and the shareholders sued the accountants. The court held that the shareholders could not have relied on the accountants because the shareholders would not have known when they bought the shares that the prospectus was based on the accountants' profit forecast.

The reverse was true in *Andrew v Kounnis Freeman* [1999] All ER (D) 553. Here, the Civil Aviation Authority was considering refusing to renew a tour operator's licence because of its poor financial position. The tour operator's auditors faxed a letter to the Civil Aviation Authority expressing an opinion on the financial position of the company. The letter enclosed the tour operator's latest accounts, which the auditors had approved. The auditors knew that the Authority was considering refusing a licence and that the existing licence was due to expire on the day of the fax. There was an error in the accounts, and the Authority sued the auditors. The auditors claimed that they had not known that the Authority would rely on the accounts as well as on the letter. The Court of Appeal did not accept this, holding that the auditors must have realized that the Authority would rely on the accounts, given that the auditors knew why the Authority was considering refusing to issue a new licence and given that there was no time for the Authority to obtain independent advice after receiving the fax. Thus, the auditors were liable in tort.

Law Society v KPMG Peat Marwick [2000] 4 All ER 540 was a similar case. Solicitors' firms at that time had a duty to send an accountants' report to the Law Society every year. The report had to say whether or not the firm had complied with Law Society regulations on the handling of clients' money. The Law Society used the reports to spot potential cases of dishonesty. In this instance, the accountants failed to notice irregularities on the part of a firm which, it later emerged, had been involved in a fraud amounting to about £8.4 million. The lost monies had to be repaid to the firm's clients out of a compensation fund run by the Law Society. The Law Society sued the accountants, who argued that they had no duty of care to the Law Society. The Court of Appeal found that there was sufficient proximity between the accountants and the Law Society, since all the elements of the *Caparo* test were present. Thus, the accountants were liable for the damages.

In the Privy Council case of *Yuen Kun Yeu v Attorney-General for Hong Kong* [1988] AC 175, investors sued the governmental commissioner who was responsible for regulating the company in which they had invested. They claimed that, by allowing the company to be registered, the commissioner had impliedly represented that the company was a fit and proper body to receive funds. The Privy Council found that, even if there was such a representation, it would have been unreasonable for the investors to have relied on it, because the commissioner did not have sufficient control over the company. The Privy Council also held that the commissioner could not have been expected to know of their reliance. This case, which was discussed in chapter 2, used to be considered a decisive move away from the previous theory that the key to pure economic loss cases was whether or not there was a 'voluntary assumption of responsibility' by the defendant. *Customs and Excise Commissioners v Barclays Bank plc* [2006] UKHL 28 shows that this is not in fact correct.

As the preceding discussion shows, most of the cases involving reliance on statements have come about in a financial services context. Exceptions do exist, however. In *Goodwill v British Pregnancy Advisory Service* [1996] 2 All ER 161, a woman sued a pregnancy advisory service for telling her partner that he would not need to use contraception following his vasectomy. She claimed that she had relied on that statement when deciding not to use contraception in their relationship, which did not begin until several years after the vasectomy. She had become pregnant and wanted compensation for the costs of raising the child. The Court of Appeal held that the pregnancy advisory service could not have been expected to realize that the patient would communicate the advice to future partners or that those partners would rely on it. Also, on the particular facts of this case, the woman had not in fact relied on the advice in any case: she had also consulted her GP, who had correctly told her that there was a small risk that she would become pregnant.

Reliance in formal and informal settings

cross reference
Hedley Byrne & Co v Heller & Partners Ltd [1964] AC 465 is discussed above.

As the judgments in *Hedley Byrne & Co v Heller & Partners Ltd* [1964] AC 465 stated, advice given in social settings does not create a duty of care. For instance, lawyers—and even law students!—are often asked at parties to comment on legal problems that other guests may be having. The giver of advice normally has no duty of care in this situation. The same applies to other professionals, such as doctors, psychologists, accountants, social workers, and so on. The refusal to recognize a duty is clearly related to the 'reasonableness' element of *Hedley Byrne & Co v Heller & Partners Ltd* [1964] AC 465 and is well-established. However, applying the principle can be difficult in borderline situations. The case of *Chaudhry v Prabhakar* [1988] 3 All ER 718 focused on the boundary between social and professional settings, with surprising results. In this case, a young woman had just passed her driving test and did not know much about cars. She asked a friend to find a car for her to buy, which he did. He told her that she did not need to have it checked by a mechanic and that the seller was a friend of his. This was untrue. The young woman bought the car that her friend had recommended, but it turned out to be unroadworthy because of a previous accident. The court at first instance found that the friend was acting as her agent in looking for the car, even though he was unpaid, and that this agency relationship was so similar to a professional arrangement that it created sufficient proximity to give rise to a duty. The court also found that the friend had breached that duty. He appealed, but only on the issue of breach, so the Court of Appeal did not have to review whether there was a duty in the first place. Nevertheless, Stocker LJ and Stuart-Smith LJ made *obiter* comments agreeing with the decision not to appeal on that issue, whereas May LJ expressed doubts. Subsequent decisions have followed this case in other cases of unpaid agency, but these have all been in a clearly professional setting. It is possible that this case would not be followed if similar facts arose again.

In addition to considering whether statements made in social situations give rise to duties of care, the courts have been called upon to decide cases in which there was a business relationship between the parties, but one of them argued that this was not enough to create a duty of care. For instance, *Mutual Life and Citizens' Assurance v Evatt* [1971] AC 793—an Australian case which was appealed to the Privy Council—involved an insurance policy held by Mr Evatt with Mutual Life. One of Mutual Life's representatives gave Mr Evatt some information about an associated company in which he was considering investing. The Privy Council held that Mutual Life did not owe Mr Evatt a duty of care to give accurate information because Mutual Life was not in the business of giving investment advice and did not claim to have any skill in that area.

Similar principles seem to apply to public authorities. In *Tidman v Reading Borough Council* [1994] 3 PLR 72, a council employee gave informal advice over the telephone to a man who was trying to sell his house. The court held that there was no duty of care because the call was informal and the council employee who gave the advice had very little information about the caller's situation. In these circumstances, the caller could reasonably be expected to seek independent advice before going ahead with the sale. An important factor was that the court did not want to deter councils from giving informal assistance to residents in future.

Relying on the defendant to give advice

As shown by *Machin v Adams* (1997) 59 Con LR 14, the case discussed above involving the care home and the architect's certificate, a claimant must actually rely on the statement for a claim to prevail. Sometimes, the reverse issue arises, and claimants sue a defendant for failing to make a statement, e.g. for failing to advise on a particular issue when there was a duty to do so. In this type of case, the claimant needs to show that he or she relied on the defendant to give this type of advice. For example, in *Van Oppen v Clerk to the Bedford Trustees* [1999] 3 All ER 889, a school boy had an accident whilst playing rugby and claimed damages against the defendants for, amongst other things, negligently failing to advise his father of the risk of serious injury inherent in the game of rugby or of the consequent need for personal accident insurance. The Court of Appeal decided that the father had not relied on the school for advice in connection with personal accident insurance for his son, and thus there was no detrimental reliance. Accordingly, the claim was dismissed.

Cases where reliance is not required

Detrimental reliance is an essential ingredient in establishing proximity, albeit with a few exceptions. In rare cases, the courts have held that, despite the decisions in *Caparo Industries v Dickman* [1990] 2 AC 605 and *Hedley Byrne & Co v Heller & Partners Ltd* [1964] AC 465, reliance on the negligent statement is not required. Almost all of these cases have related to wills, though a few have concerned gifts and other transactions between living people. The first such case was *Ross v Caunters* [1980] Ch 297. Here, a firm of solicitors drafted a will for a client and sent it to the client for signature. Signatures to a will have to be witnessed, and the solicitors failed to explain that the witness should not be someone whose spouse is going to benefit under the will. The client had the will witnessed by the wife of one of the beneficiaries. He then sent the will back to the solicitors for safe-keeping, but the solicitors still did not notice what had happened. As a result, the beneficiary was unable to inherit. The solicitors argued that they had no duty to prevent pure economic loss to the beneficiary, because the beneficiary did not know that the will contained a gift to him and therefore did not rely on the solicitors to ensure that it was executed correctly. The court held that it would be inappropriate to distinguish between beneficiaries who did or did not know the contents of the will and allowed the claim. The decision was followed by the House of Lords in *White v Jones* [1995] 2 AC 207, which was not strictly a case about a negligent statement, but about negligent delay in carrying out the testator's instructions to amend a will. Again, the solicitor was found to have a duty to beneficiaries under the will, even though they were not his clients.

The decision in *Ross v Caunters* [1980] Ch 297 has also been followed in circumstances where the will was drafted by another professional rather than a solicitor, as in *Esterhuizen v Allied Dunbar Assurance plc* [1998] Fam Law 527. Recovery has also been allowed in *Gorham v BT Telecommunications plc* [2000] 4 All ER 867, when a professional gave an employee incorrect advice about his pension arrangements, leading to loss on the part of the employee's wife and children. Despite the breadth of these cases, however, there are some limitations to the ability of beneficiaries to sue. For example, solicitors do not owe a duty to beneficiaries on transactions which are not designed to benefit the beneficiaries. In *Clarke v Bruce Lance & Co* [1988] 1 All ER 364, the will included the gift of a service station. The testator later let the service station on a lease which was not commercially sound, using the same solicitor to draw up the lease as had drafted the will. After the testator's death, the beneficiary sued the solicitor for failing to point out that the transaction was uncommercial. The Court of Appeal held that there was no duty to the plaintiff because the lease was not intended to benefit the plaintiff.

In situations involving gifts between living people rather than by will, a solicitor is not liable to a beneficiary unless the donor is not in a position to put right the solicitor's mistake. In *Hemmens v Wilson Browne* [1995] Ch 223, Mr Wilson Browne promised to give his mistress, Mrs Hemmens, £110,000 to buy a house. He signed a document to that effect which was prepared by his solicitor. However, the document was not enforceable as a matter of contract law, for reasons you will learn about on your contract course. By the time Mrs Hemmens had found a house to purchase, Mr Wilson Browne was no longer willing to pay. The court found that the solicitor had no liability to Mrs Hemmens, since it would not be just and reasonable to impose such a duty on the solicitor when Mr Wilson Browne was in a position to put matters right for Mrs Hemmens if he wished. Similarly, if the beneficiary is able to apply to have the will rectified or obtain compensation from the estate, he or she must attempt to do so before suing the solicitor, provided there is a reasonable prospect of succeeding. The circumstances in which wills can be rectified or compensation paid out of the estate are beyond the scope of this textbook, as it is unlikely that examiners will expect you to know them for a tort exam.

References and other employment issues

Just as giving a reference for a business can give rise to liability, as it did in *Hedley Byrne & Co v Heller* [1964] AC 465, so, too, can giving a reference to a employee or a contractor. The person giving the reference can be liable to the subject of the reference (the person the reference is about) as well as to the recipient, as decided in *Spring v Guardian Assurance plc* [1995] 2 AC 296. In this case, Guardian was an insurance company which also sold investment products. Mr Spring was the sales director and office manager of one of Guardian's subsidiary companies. He was dismissed from those positions and applied to another company, Scottish Amicable, which asked Guardian for a reference. Guardian's compliance officer prepared the reference, based on information she received from the chief executive of the subsidiary company that Mr Spring had worked for. This reference was highly unfavourable, saying (amongst other things) that Mr Spring was a person of 'little or no integrity', that he 'could not be regarded as honest' and that he had given 'bad advice' on a number of occasions. Unsurprisingly, Scottish Amicable refused to hire him. Mr Spring sued Guardian, and the judge at first instance found that the reference was incorrect; in his view, Mr Spring had been incompetent, but not dishonest. The court then had to decide whether or not Guardian owed Mr Spring a duty of care in negligence. His loss was of course entirely financial and therefore fell under the category of pure economic loss. The judge at first instance thought that there was a duty, but the Court of Appeal and one of the judges in the House of Lords took the view that there should be no duty on public policy grounds, because there was a public interest in encouraging employers to be frank about any suspicions they had when giving references. However, the majority in the House of Lords found that there was sufficient proximity to give rise to a duty, because of the employer's special knowledge of the employee and because the job market works in a way which makes employees highly dependent on getting a good reference from their employers. Employees rely on the care and skill of the employer in preparing that reference. The majority in the House of Lords also considered that protecting employees was more important than the public policy of encouraging frankness. The plaintiff thus prevailed as a matter of law, and the case was sent back to the Court of Appeal for an assessment of damages, though it seems to have settled before a decision was given.

Lennon v Metropolitan Police Commissioner [2004] EWCA Civ 130 raised similar issues, though it did not involve a reference. Mr Lennon was a police officer with the Metropolitan Police in London. He successfully applied for a transfer to the Royal Ulster Constabulary (as it was then known). A personnel officer with the Metropolitan Police made the arrangements for him and told him to 'leave everything to her'. She arranged things in such a way that there was a gap of three weeks between Mr Lennon's leaving the Metropolitan Police and starting his duties with the RUC. Because of this lack of continuity, he lost his entitlement to a housing allowance. The Court of Appeal held that the Metropolitan Police Commissioner, as the equivalent of an employer to Mr Lennon, owed him a duty relating to the transfer arrangements because he was dependent on the skill and knowledge of the personnel officer.

A related issue is whether a professional who is engaged by an employer to give an opinion on an applicant has a duty of care to that applicant in providing the opinion. This was the situation in *Kapfunde v Abbey National plc* [1999] ICR 1, where Abbey had engaged an occupational health expert to interpret some medical information provided by Ms Kapfunde with her job application. The expert had never met Ms Kapfunde and had never done anything to suggest that she was accepting any liability. The expert had only been engaged to advise Abbey, and Ms Kapfunde had never seen a copy of the advice. In these circumstances, the court found that there was no proximity between Abbey and Ms Kapfunde because there was no doctor-patient relationship between the Ms Kapfunde and the expert. This does not mean that occupational health experts never owe a duty to people on whom they give opinions for employers. For example, in *Hartman v South Essex Mental Health and Community Care NHS Trust* [2005] EWCA Civ 6, where the expert did meet with the patient and the patient was an existing employee of the Trust, the Court of Appeal acknowledged that there could be a duty to take steps for the patient's welfare. While it is true that this was not an economic loss case, it is possible that the duty may extend to preventing pure economic loss.

Personal liability of individuals acting for their employers

If a claimant relies on statements or advice by a firm or a company, the court may have to decide whether the individual employee who spoke or wrote to the claimant also had the necessary proximity to owe the claimant a duty of care. The best-known case on this is probably *Williams v Natural Life Health Foods* [1998] 2 All ER 577, which reached the House of Lords. Natural Life was a health food franchise, and Mr Williams and his business partner were considering becoming franchisees. Natural Life sent them brochures and financial projections emphasizing how profitable the business was. The brochure said that the success of the business was due to the expertise of its managing director, who had also been involved in preparing the financial projections. Mr Williams and his partner took the franchise, but stopped trading after 18 months because the turnover was much less than expected. They sued Natural Life for negligence in preparing the financial projections, but they also sued the managing director, even though they had never dealt with him directly. The House of Lords held that in the absence of personal dealings with the managing director, it was not reasonable for them to rely on him.

This contrasts with the case of *Merrett v Babb* [2001] QB 1174, where mortgage borrowers relied on a valuation obtained by their bank from a firm of surveyors. The court found that the borrowers had relied on the skill of the individual surveyor who prepared the valuation, even though they had never met him and did not even know his name. The court appears to have thought that the position of a company director was different from that of a professional in an unincorporated firm, but the reasons for making such a distinction are not clear in the judgment.

Parallel claims in tort and contract

A court is less likely to find that there was a duty of care in negligence if the parties also had a contract which does not provide for liability. In these circumstances, the court may take the view that since the parties had the opportunity to make that provision and chose not to do so, the court should not interfere with the parties' decision. An example of this is *Greater Nottingham Co-operative Society v Cementation Piling and Foundations Ltd* [1989] QB 71, where some building contractors carelessly operated their drilling equipment in a way which caused damage to an adjoining restaurant. The owners of the building site paid damages to the restaurant owners, which meant that the site owners had suffered pure economic loss. The contract between the site owners and the contractors excluded any liability for pure economic loss, so the site owners sued in negligence rather than breach of contract. The court found that they could not circumvent the contractual exclusion in this way.

This case contrasts with *Smith v Bush* [1990] 1 AC 831, where a surveyor was appointed by a building society to give an opinion on a property that was going to be mortgaged. The plaintiff was the borrower, who relied on the surveyor's opinion when she decided to go ahead with the purchase. She also paid the surveyor's fee, as borrowers are usually required to do. However, she had been told to get her own professional advice, and the mortgage application form and the survey report both made it clear that the surveyor did not accept liability to her. One of the chimneys later collapsed, and the borrower sued the surveyor. The court found that the exclusion of liability was unreasonable and did not prevent the surveyor from having a duty to the borrower. However, the court may have been influenced in this case by the fact that the plaintiff in this case was a private individual.

There are also instances where the contract does not exclude liability, but for some other reason (such as different limitation periods in tort and contract or the different measures of damages), the claimant prefers to sue in tort. In those cases, the courts are generally willing to allow the tort claim. For instance, in *Esso Petroleum Co. Ltd v Mardon* [1976] QB 801, Mr Mardon entered into a tenancy agreement with Esso for one of Esso's petrol stations. He based his decision on a turnover estimate which Esso had provided to him. Actual turnover was much less than expected, and he made heavy losses. This was pure economic loss, because he had effectively bought something which was worth less than he expected. The court found that the turnover estimate was both a term of the tenancy agreement and a negligent misrepresentation, and that Mr Mardon could recover either in tort or in contract. On this particular occasion, the court also found that the damages would be the same in either case. These principles are not unique to pure economic loss cases. The courts take a similar approach to parallel claims in tort and contract involving other kinds of losses.

A case that turned on whether the claim was brought in contract or tort was *Henderson v Merrett Syndicates Ltd* [1995] 2 AC 145. Merrett was an agent for individuals investing in Lloyd's, an insurance market based in London. Individual Lloyd's investors are known as 'Names' and effectively provide capital to fund claims on certain Lloyd's insurance contracts. They also guarantee to meet claims out of their own pockets if the up-front capital proves insufficient. In return, they receive the right to any profits on the insurance contracts. Lloyd's had made large profits for many years, so becoming a Name was considered a good investment, despite the potential for Names to have to pay insurance claims out of their own pockets if the contracts turned out to be unprofitable. Merrett, as an agent for the Names, took care of various administrative matters for them and employed another agent, Henderson, to decide on behalf of the Names which insurance contracts they should enter into. This decision-making process is known as 'underwriting'. Unfortunately, the whole insurance industry suffered unprecedented losses in the 1990s, and Lloyd's was badly affected. Merrett had a potential contractual claim against Henderson, but the contractual limitation period had expired, so Merrett sued in negligence instead. The House of Lords held that the existence of the contract did not prevent a claim in tort, because there was nothing in the contract which would be incompatible with tortious liability.

NOTE As a result of the crisis caused by the losses of the 1990s, Lloyd's no longer accepts applications from individuals to become Names. Except for those Names who have been investors since before this period, Lloyd's is now entirely funded by companies.

13.4 Key cases in the historical development of the law on economic loss

We have now covered the key features of the current law on economic loss. However, as mentioned at the beginning of the chapter, there are a few other cases which are important for historical reasons.

The first historically-relevant case is *Derry v Peek* (1889) 14 App Cas 337, which involved a tram company whose directors issued a prospectus to potential investors. The prospectus stated that the company had legal authority to use steam as well as horses to power their trams. The directors genuinely believed this to be true, but in fact the company could only use steam with the consent of the Board of Trade, and it never succeeded in getting that consent. The plaintiff was an investor who had relied on the prospectus when he bought shares in the company and had lost money as a result. The House of Lords held that negligence was not sufficient to recover pure economic loss. Instead, there had to be fraud for the plaintiff to recover. This continued to be the position until *Hedley Byrne & Heller* [1964] AC 465 was decided in 1963.

The second historically-important decision is *Candler v Crane, Christmas & Co* [1951] 2 KB 164. In this case, an investor contributed £2,000 to a Cornish tin mine company which later became insolvent. The chairman of the company had arranged for the company's accountants to show the investor the draft accounts of the company before the investment was finalized. It turned out that the accounts grossly overstated the company's assets, because several of the assets actually belonged to the chairman in his personal capacity and the accountants had failed to check the title deeds. The investor sued the accountants. As this case preceded *Hedley Byrne & Heller* [1964] AC 465, the majority of the Court of Appeal followed the line of cases based on *Derry v Peek* (1889) 14 App Cas 337, and so the investor was unsuccessful. Although the outcome was predictable, the case is significant for the dissent of Lord Justice Denning, which was rather prescient in the principles it set out. Lord Denning thought that the plaintiff should succeed because the accountants knew the investor would be relying on their work, and consequently the plaintiff had a right to rely on them to use proper care. Lord Denning also doubted whether there should be a distinction between physical and economic loss, provided there was sufficient proximity. Lord Denning's opinion laid down the following conditions for establishing a duty:

think point
What are the similarities and differences between Lord Denning's views and the law as it stands today?

- Defendants should be in the business of examining accounts or other things and making reports on them;

- Defendants' profession or occupation should be one which requires special care and skill;

- Reports should be relied on by third parties in the ordinary course of business;

- Defendants will only be liable to a third party if they knew that the party was going to rely on their work;

- Defendants will not be liable for casual remarks or remarks not made in a professional capacity;

- Defendants will not be liable if it is reasonable to expect that an 'intermediate person' will be 'interposed' between the claimant and defendant—for instance, if the claimant hires another professional to review the defendants' report; and

- The duty only extends to transactions which the defendants had in mind when handing over their report.

The last historically-relevant case you should know is *James McNaughton Paper Group Ltd v Hicks Anderson & Co* [1991] 2 QB 113. This was a case which took place after *Hedley Byrne & Heller* [1964] AC 465 on facts that were somewhat similar to those in *Candler v Crane* [1951] 2 KB 164. Lord Denning's dissent was cited, but ultimately distinguished on the facts. The plaintiff here was a company which had recently taken over a smaller group of companies. The plaintiff said it had relied on accounts prepared by the defendants (the smaller group's accountants) in the transaction. The accountants had met with the plaintiff to go through the accounts. However, the Court of Appeal concluded that, on these facts, the accountants were entitled to expect the plaintiff to get further advice from its own accountants before going ahead with the takeover. The court may have been influenced by the fact that the accountants were dealing with a large company rather than with an individual investor.

13.5 Problems with the current law

A number of criticisms have been made of the current law on pure economic loss. For example, many people argue that the distinction between economic loss and other kinds of loss is arbitrary and difficult to justify. It may be unfair to claimants to distinguish between their different losses, especially if the various kinds of loss are caused by the same negligence on the part of the defendant and are equally foreseeable. A related point is that because the distinction is somewhat arbitrary, judges sometimes create a lack of clarity in their efforts to provide a just result for the parties before them. The cases where courts have allowed recovery of economic loss in the absence of reliance are sometimes cited as examples of decisions that are difficult to reconcile in a logical fashion with the rest of the case law in this area. These anomalies create uncertainty which make it more difficult for lawyers to advise their clients and for clients to regulate their affairs in a way that minimizes their exposure to liability.

Others take a different view and question whether economic loss should be recoverable at all. Often, the so-called 'loss' is really a failure to make an expected profit, and some people feel that defendants should not be responsible for this. In thinking about this issue, courts and commentators have often focused on whether the defendant received a payment or other reward for offering a service. Some people also feel that economic loss should only be recoverable in contract and that allowing negligence claims for economic loss makes it too easy to avoid the contractual limitation period.

For more revision tips, including self-test questions and suggestions for further reading, see the Online Resource Centre at www.oxfordtextbooks.co.uk/orc/strong_complete/.

revision tasks

Here are some ideas to try when you revise this chapter:

- Make a timeline setting out the most important cases on pure economic loss in chronological order, with a one-line summary of each case.
- Add the principles of economic loss to the negligence checklist you worked on in chapter 5.
- Create a chart showing the different kinds of economic loss and whether or not claimants can recover these kinds of loss.

Defamation

 Introduction

We now turn to a tort that has received a lot of publicity in recent years. Defamation protects against harm to a person's reputation and is often used by celebrities who disagree with what has been said or written about them in the media. Although there is a wealth of reported decisions concerning defamation, very often the court's decision turns on elements of procedure. As you read through the cases, be sure that you differentiate between the substantive law and the procedural law. Unlike in other areas of tort, you may be responsible on your exams for some aspects of procedural law. Follow your lecturer's guidance in this regard.

TIP This chapter will not discuss procedural law at length, but you can review sections 8 to 10 of the Defamation Act 1996 if you want to know more.

This chapter will focus on the constituent elements of defamation and then compare defamation to the developing law of privacy, the tort is not limited to celebrity claimants and media defendants. At this point, many aspects of defamation are regulated by statute, but the common law is very important in construing the relevant statutory provisions. After the discussion of the claimant's affirmative case, we will turn to the various defences that are available. This chapter will proceed as follows:

- Elements of defamation;
- Differences between slander and libel;
- Differences between defamation and invasion of privacy; and
- Defences to defamation.

Elements of defamation

14.2.1 Defamatory statement

Neither of the two statutes on defamation—the Defamation Act 1996 and the Defamation Act 1952—define what constitutes a defamatory statement, so a claimant must rely on the pre-existing common law to know what is defamatory. Traditionally, a defamatory statement is one 'which is calculated to injure the reputation of another, by exposing him to hatred, contempt or ridicule,' as set forth by Parke B in *Parmiter v Coupland* (1840) 6 M & W 105, which involved the alleged defamation of a public figure. There, Parke B noted that even a public figure, who often must endure more public comment than a private figure, still may sue for libel concerning words that charged him with 'wicked or corrupt motives'. Lord Atkin provided another well-known definition, which asks whether 'the words tend to lower the plaintiff in the estimation of right-thinking members of society generally'. In that case, *Sim v Stretch* [1936] 2 All ER 1237, Lord Atkin was dealing with a telegram containing a statement that suggested that a man had borrowed money from his housemaid. Lord Atkin's test improves on the previous one by focusing on an insult to the claimant's reputation, as defined by the opinions of others, but the reference to 'right-thinking members of society' presupposes (a) that such members of society can be easily identified and (b) that those individuals can reach a consensus on the harmfulness of the statement. In the case in question, Lord Atkin did not see how the fact that a person has borrowed money from an employee could be considered defamatory, leading for a denial of the claim.

NOTE Even the statutes do not define defamation, though section 16(1) of the Defamation Act 1952 states that '[a]ny reference in this Act to words shall be construed as including a reference to pictures, visual images, gestures and other methods of signifying meaning'. Therefore, think expansively when considering what constitutes a defamatory statement.

cross reference

Byrne v Deane [1937] 1 KB 818 is also discussed below in the section regarding defamation by omission.

Furthermore, it is unclear what kind of statement 'lowers' a claimant in the estimation of others. Certainly the standard depends very much on the context and time in which the statement was made. Sometimes a statement can lower a claimant in the eyes of his or her peers, but still not result in recovery for defamation simply because the act in question should not be deemed to be defamatory. For example, *Byrne v Deane* [1937] 1 KB 818 involved an anonymous report to the police about several illegal gambling machines kept on the premises of a private golf club. The plaintiff claimed that a notice had been posted suggesting that he had been the one to inform the police about the machines. The plaintiff sued the proprietors and secretary of the club, claiming that they had a duty to remove the notice, which was in a public place and had remained up for several days, even if they had not been the ones to place it there originally.

● *Byrne v Deane* [1937] 1 KB 818

Greene LJ: [T]he matter resolves itself into this: Are words capable of a defamatory meaning which say of the plaintiff that he reported to the police that on the club premises of which he was a member a criminal offence was being habitually committed? Now, it is said that the ordinary sense of society would say of a man who had done that in the case of this particular criminal offence that he had behaved in a disloyal and underhand fashion. It is said that this particular offence is one which can be looked at with an indulgent eye, and that there is something dishonourable in setting in motion the constitutional machinery provided in this country for the suppression of crime. I myself find it embarrassing to take into consideration questions of the way in which members of clubs might regard such an action. It seems to me that no distinction can be drawn between various categories of crime. I suggested in the course of the argument the case where members of a club were habitually engaged in having cock-fights conducted on the club premises, and I asked the question whether to say of a man that he had reported that to the police would be defamatory, and the answer that I got was not to my mind a satisfactory one . . . It seems to me that if the argument is to be accepted it would involve the Court in this position: that it would have to differentiate between different kinds of crime and put in one category crimes which are of so bad a character as to call for universal reprobation even among the more easy-minded, and in another category crimes which many people think are stupid and ought never to have been made crimes at all . . .

In my opinion, therefore, the words in question are not capable of a defamatory meaning, and on that ground I consider that the appeal should be allowed.

The courts have not been helpful in applying Lord Atkin's test to define a defamatory statement more precisely, nor have they come up with something better. However, commentators have considered the matter at length:

. . . .

● Thomas Gibbons, **'*Defamation Reconsidered*'**, 16 Oxford Journal of Legal Studies 587 (1996) (citations omitted)

Defamation has been defined as, ' . . . the publication of a statement which tends to lower a person in the estimation of right-thinking members of society generally, or which tends to make them shun or avoid that person'. To establish liability, however, the law requires nothing more than the intangible. First, members of the audience are not real but hypothetical. The effect is to invoke an objectified standard of values for assessing the impact of the statement, if it were true. Secondly, it is only the 'tendency' for the statement to affect the judgment of others that must be shown.

The objective standard for judgment is that of reasonable persons and what the law regards them as capable of considering to be defamatory. As 'right-thinking members of society generally', they are neither cynical or lax, nor censorious. Being representative of society generally, they do not embody a limited section of the public, for example, a club or the criminal fraternity. Thus, a person cannot be defamed by a statement that she has reported criminal acts to the police: although her criminal friends might think less of her, that would not be the attitude of the 'ordinary good and worthy subject of the King'. As Gatley critically observes, 'The rule . . . [requiring an objective standard] seems to be based on the theory that a consensus of moral opinion exists in England', but that is hardly plausible in a pluralistic society. Furthermore, even the standards of right-thinkers may change over time and the catalogues of expressions which have been found capable of being defamatory are no guide to contemporary views . . .

The requirement to show only a tendency for a statement to have a defamatory effect means that the actual reactions of the audience are irrelevant (as is the way that they actually understand the statement). Thus, a plaintiff does not have to prove that his or her esteem was actually diminished in the eyes of those to whom the defamatory statement was published. Indeed, even if the audience knows it to be untrue, liability will not be escaped for that reason. As for the nature of the defamatory effect, this has evolved to

think point

The changing mores of society affect all definitions involving the reasonable person. What other torts are subject to these kinds of evolutionary shifts?

include a wide range of social reactions which might result from a statement. One element is the traditional notion of bringing a person into 'hatred, contempt or ridicule'. Another is the more recent, generalized test: 'would the words tend to lower the plaintiff in the estimation of right-thinking members of society generally?' This recognizes that a person's reputation may be affected without any feelings of hatred or the like being felt by the audience, for example, if there is an imputation of bankruptcy or a clever fraud. Yet another factor is the acceptance that a statement may be defamatory even if it does not impute immoral conduct, for example, if it refers to the person's trade or calling, or to their mental state, or to their social acceptance generally, and results in their being shunned or avoided. Since a jury's verdict on such matters is no more than speculation about the likely effect of the statement, however, and is not confined to its moral dimension, it is a somewhat artificial process for protecting the plaintiff's reputation. Rather, the law is imposing an ideal standard of response (and to a refined set of facts), albeit without any firm prescription for the defendant's future behaviour. Even if there were justification for seeking to protect reputation as such, the law's present design does not achieve that aim.

Once it is ascertained that the offending statement has a defamatory tendency, the next step is to determine what harm it may have caused. Again, the actual effect of the statement is not taken into account. Instead, it is presumed that damage has occurred, because it is presumed that the plaintiff enjoys a good reputation...

Various suggestions have been offered to explain the law's position on this issue...For Post, however, consistent with his view of the dignity interest in reputation, the presumption of damage allows juries the space to place a value on the plaintiff's reputation in awarding compensation. The issue is not empirical, therefore, but normative, allowing the jury to grade the social worth of the plaintiff's personal image. Certainly, this approach is reflected in those descriptions of damages as contemptuous, nominal, compensatory or exemplary. But the actual experience of jury awards demonstrates that it is a haphazard process, despite changes in judicial attitudes to providing guidance, and hardly provides a sensitive method for making fine social distinctions.

So far, we have been focusing on whether a statement is defamatory, meaning whether those words are likely to lower the reputation of the claimant in the eyes of the community. However, that is only part of the analysis. Sometimes, the court not only has to consider whether the words can support a defamatory meaning, but must also determine what the intended meaning was in the first place. Typically, decisions will refer to the 'innuendo', which is a legal term of art concerning the meaning of the words used by the defendant. When considering the meaning of a particular word, phrase or image, a claimant has three choices. The claimant can focus on the plain meaning of the statement or can choose to assert either true innuendo or false innuendo.

When considering whether a statement is defamatory, the court first looks to see whether the claimant has asserted any type of innuendo. If the claimant has not and instead relies on the plain meaning of the statement itself, the court construes the words according to their ordinary and natural sense. In so doing, the court must look at the entirety of the statement, not just the part that the claimant argues is defamatory, since the context of a statement may offset any potentially defamatory interpretation. For example, in *Charleston v News Group Newspapers* [1995] 2 AC 665, two soap opera stars sued after the newspaper published photos of the actors' faces above near-naked torsos. While the pictures, on their own, might have been defamatory, the House of Lords held that the plaintiffs could not recover for defamation because the article that was printed underneath the doctored photographs came out against the makers of a pornographic computer game. Taken as a whole, the pictures plus the article did not constitute a defamatory statement.

VOCABULARY

'Extrinsic' means 'outside of', so here extrinsic facts means facts existing outside the statement itself.

There are other times when the words or images, on their face, do not appear to be defamatory. However, if the reader or listener knows certain other **extrinsic** facts that will allow a defamatory interpretation, that is called 'true innuendo.' For example, a published article might state that 'Nancy Sheridan took up a six-week stay at 123 North Clanton Street, London'. There is nothing defamatory about that particular statement. If, however, a famous substance abuse centre, known for six-week in-patient treatments for drug and alcohol addiction, was located at 123 North Clanton Street, London, then Nancy Sheridan might have an action in defamation if she did not actually visit that centre. Critically, a claimant must specifically plead and prove those extrinsic facts to prevail.

compare

With true innuendos, the statement plus the extrinsic facts together result in defamation. This is different than the statement 'Nancy Sheridan is a drug addict', which is defamatory by itself.

For a while, courts struggled with the question of whether a person who claims to have been defamed through true innuendo must prove that the statement was made to someone who knew the particular extrinsic facts and interpreted the statement in a defamatory manner. The issue was addressed by the Court of Appeal in *Hough v London Express Newspaper Ltd* [1940] 2 KB 507, where the wife of a famous boxer claimed she was defamed when a newspaper ran an article and photograph referring to the 'curly-headed wife' of the boxer. The plaintiff produced witnesses who said that they interpreted the statement to mean that the plaintiff was not the wife of the boxer, but none of the witnesses said that they believed the statement to be true. To the contrary, all of the witnesses testified that they were not misled by the statement into thinking that the plaintiff was not the wife of the boxer. The Court of Appeal held for the plaintiff, concluding that a plaintiff only need demonstrate that there are people who might interpret the statement in a defamatory manner. There was no need to produce evidence showing that some person actually interpreted it in that way.

NOTE In defamation proceedings, judges determine whether the words or images are capable of having a defamatory meaning. Juries decide whether the words or images were actually defamatory.

The trickiest type of defamation case involves 'false innuendo'. Here, there are no extrinsic facts that must be established, as in true innuendo. Instead, the defamatory meaning must be inferred from the statement itself, even though the statement on its face is not defamatory. For example, if someone said, 'Nancy Sheridan's in the strawberry fields', that wouldn't seem problematic on its face. If, however, the claimant demonstrates that 'strawberry fields' can refer to LSD, that might constitute a false innuendo, inferring that Nancy Sheridan takes drugs. Thus, in *Allsop v Church of England Newspaper Ltd* [1872] 2 QB 151, the Court of Appeal held that the plaintiff, a well-known news reader, had to identify the potentially defamatory meaning of the word 'bent', which was allegedly used by the defendant in reference to the plaintiff. Just as with true innuendo, a claimant must specifically plead and prove false innuendo. One of the best discussions of innuendo and intent is found in *Cassidy v Daily Mirror Newspapers Ltd* [1929] 2 KB 331.

Russell LJ: The relevant facts in this appeal are few, and may be briefly stated. The defendants, in the issue of the Daily Mirror for February 21, 1928, published a photograph of a man and a young woman with the following words beneath it: 'Mr. M. Corrigan, the racehorse owner, and Miss' X, 'whose engagement has been announced.' The man shown in the photograph was the lawful husband of the plaintiff, to whom he had been married in 1916. The plaintiff sued the defendants for damages for libel, alleging that the photograph and words bore a meaning defamatory of the plaintiff—namely, that the plaintiff was not lawfully married to her husband, but had lived with him as his mistress, pretending to her friends to be a respectable married woman. The judge, being of opinion that the photograph and words were capable of bearing a meaning defamatory of the plaintiff, left it to the jury to decide whether they were in fact defamatory of the plaintiff. The jury returned a verdict for the plaintiff for 500l. The defendants appeal...

The defendants contend that the published matter is not, on the face of it, defamatory at all either of the plaintiff or of any one else. That must I think be conceded. Nevertheless words may be published with reference to such circumstances, and to such persons knowing the circumstances, as to convey a meaning which would not be attributable to them in different circumstances... So too, I think, words may be published with reference to such circumstances, and to such persons, knowing the circumstances, as to suggest an inference in regard to some one not in terms mentioned in the statement, which would not be involved by the publication of the same words either in different circumstances or to persons ignorant of the particular circumstances which occasion the inference.

The first thing to consider in this case is this question: Can the published matter be reasonably construed as a statement that Mr. Corrigan is an unmarried man? For myself I would answer that the published matter may not only reasonably be so construed, but must necessarily be so construed. I discard as too far fetched the suggestion that it might refer to the announcement of an engagement made by a married man either in anticipation of a divorce or with a view to seduction. If then the published matter is a statement that A.B. is an unmarried man, can A.B.'s wife successfully complain of that as a statement defamatory of her? This must depend upon (1.) whether the statement that A.B. is an unmarried man is capable of being defamatory of A.B.'s wife, and (2.) whether the statement is in fact defamatory of A.B.'s wife... The Lord Chancellor in E. Hulton & Co. v. Jones used the following language, which seems appropriate to the present case: 'Libel... consists in using language which others, knowing the circumstances, would reasonably think to be defamatory of the person complaining of and injured by it. A person charged with libel cannot defend himself by showing that he intended in his own breast not to defame, or that he intended not to defame the plaintiff, if in fact he did both.' Applying those words to a statement (which for this purpose must be false) that A.B. is an unmarried man, is it a reasonable view that people who have known a lady who has called and is calling herself the wife of A.B. might think the statement to be defamatory of the lady? In my opinion the view is an eminently reasonable one. Whether, being capable of a defamatory meaning, the statement was in the circumstances of the particular case defamatory of the plaintiff, is another question. That is a question of fact for the jury to answer according to their view of the evidence adduced.

It was argued by the appellants that no liability attaches to the publisher of a statement which is not on the face of it defamatory, but which only becomes defamatory in the light of outside facts, unless those facts are known both to the person who publishes the statement and to the persons to whom it is published . . . So far as concerns knowledge on the part of the persons to whom the statement is published, no difficulty presents itself. If the defamatory meaning only arises from a knowledge of outside facts, and the persons to whom the statement is published are ignorant of those facts, those persons could not reasonably attach a defamatory meaning to the statement.

So far as concerns knowledge on the part of the person by whom the statement is published, I feel difficulty in supporting the proposition . . . Liability for libel does not depend on the intention of the defamer; but on the fact of defamation. If you once reach the conclusion that the published matter in the present case amounts to or involves a statement that Mr. Corrigan is an unmarried man, then in my opinion those persons who knew the circumstances might reasonably consider the statement defamatory of the plaintiff. The statement being capable of a meaning defamatory to the plaintiff, it was for the jury upon the evidence adduced to decide whether the plaintiff had been libelled or not.

Thus, according to Russell LJ, a person may be liable for defamation without having any intent to defame anyone.

14.2.2 Referring to the claimant

To prevail, the claimant must show the defamatory words concern him or her. The claimant does not need to be mentioned by name, so long as an ordinary person with sufficient knowledge of the facts might reasonably believe that the statement referred to the claimant. Some categories of persons cannot act as a claimant in defamation. For example, a dead person may not be defamed, nor may a public body or governmental entity. However, an individual government official, such as a council member, an MP or even the Prime Minister, may still pursue an action in defamation for any comments made about the official's public or private life. Interestingly, defamation is not limited to individual people. A corporate entity may also sue to protect its reputation, although a defamatory statement in the commercial context must focus on the way the corporation or company conducts its affairs, essentially claiming fraud or mismanagement of some aspect of its financial position. For example, the House of Lords held in *Jameel (Mohammed) v Wall Street Journal Europe Sprl* [2006] UKHL 44 that a trading company could bring an action for defamation, even though it did no business itself. Because there still could be possible damage to the trading company's reputation and thus its way of business, a cause of action existed.

An entire category of persons can be defamed at the same time in a class libel. The test is the same as that for an individual, but the claimants must show that the class is small enough so that a reasonable person would believe that the statement referred to every person within the class. For example, the Court of Appeal said in *Aspro Travel v Owners Abroad Group plc* [1995] 4 All ER 728 that all the directors of a small family-owned company could sue in defamation on behalf of the company itself when the company's primary competitor stated that the company was going to be bankrupt in a matter of days. However, the Court of Appeal declined to say whether directors of large or publicly-traded companies could obtain the same type of relief.

NOTE Thus, blanket statements are typically not actionable because it is not reasonable to believe that the statement refers to each member of such a broad class.

Even if a class is too large for reasonable person to believe that the statement referred to every person in it, an individual may still bring an action if he or she can show that the statement was targeted at him or her in particular. To do so, the claimant will probably need to plead and prove some sort of innuendo. For example, in *Knupffer v London Express Newspaper Ltd* [1944] AC 115 the defendant newspaper referred to certain activities undertaken by the Young Russian party. Since there were only 24 British members of the Young Russian party at the time, one might think that the class was small enough to be actionable. However, the article referred only to activities undertaken in France and the United States. Since the worldwide membership of the group measured in the thousands, the class was deemed too large to allow an action by any individual member, even though the class of potential plaintiffs in Britain was quite small.

Interestingly, an unwary defendant can make a statement that is non-defamatory as to one person but defamatory as to someone else. For example, in *Newstead v London Express Newspaper Ltd* [1940] 1 KB 377 the Court of Appeal considered whether a newspaper which had written an article covering a trial for bigamy could be held liable for defamation when the newspaper correctly noted that the trial involved 'Harold Newstead, thirty-year-old Camberwell man' but failed to realize that there was more than one Harold Newstead in that age range in Camberwell. The court held that it was no defence that the words were true or that they referred to another person. Instead, the jury was justified in finding that the words referred to the plaintiff.

. . . .

● ***Newstead v London Express Newspaper Ltd*** [1940] 1 KB 377

> Sir Wilfrid Greene MR: Persons who make statements of this character may not unreasonably be expected, when describing the person of whom they are made, to identify that person so closely as to make it very unlikely that a judge would hold them to be reasonably capable of referring to someone else, or that a jury would hold that they did so refer. This is particularly so in the case of statements which purport to deal with actual facts. If there is a risk of coincidence it ought, I think, in reason to be borne not by the innocent party to whom the words are held to refer, but by the party who puts them into circulation.

14.2.3 Publication—malicious or otherwise

To establish an action in defamation, the claimant need only prove that a defamatory statement referring to the claimant was published a third party. There is no need to prove malice or any other intention. Indeed, as discussed above, a defendant can defame someone by mistake. Nevertheless, many cases refer to malice as part of the claimant's affirmative case, which can be confusing. In these instances, the court and the claimant are actually anticipating the defences of fair comment and qualified privilege, which are defeated when malice exists. These defences will be discussed later in this chapter, but it is enough to say now that the claimant need not prove malice as part of the affirmative case, but will often do so as a procedural matter just to save time.

The term 'publication' means to make the defamatory information known to someone other than the person about whom it refers. The tort requires third-party involvement because defamation protects a person's reputation in the community, not the person's opinion of him or herself. Publication need not involve the media or any sort of mass distribution. Instead, publication can be as small-scale as dictating a letter to a typist or sending a postcard or telegram, since that constitutes publication to Royal Post employees. However, the defamatory message must be understood as such by the recipient, so dictating a letter in Russian to a non-Russian-speaking typist, for example, would not be actionable.

Publication can occur both intentionally—such as when speaking in front of witnesses or handing out multiple copies of a written document—and unintentionally, so long as the distribution of the statement was foreseeable. Thus, for example, the author of a defamatory letter will not be held liable for his actions when a butler wrongfully opens a letter directed to his mistress, as seen by *Huth v Huth* [1915] 3 KB 32. There, the Court of Appeal held that the act of opening the letter:

> was a publication, but the question is whether it was a publication by the defendant, or one for which he was responsible. It appears quite clearly from the butler's evidence that he knew perfectly well that although the envelope was addressed to 'Miss Edith Greaves,' it was intended for his mistress, Mrs. Huth. Also there was nothing which entitled him, in the ordinary course of his duty, to open the envelope. He admitted that he did so from curiosity. There can be no doubt, in those circumstances, that the opening of the envelope, and the reading of its contents, was a wrongful act by the butler. In my opinion it is quite clear that, in the absence of some special circumstances, a defendant cannot be responsible for a publication which was the wrongful act of a third person. He cannot be said, except in special circumstances, to have contemplated it. It was not the natural consequence of his sending the letter, or writing, in the way in which he did.

Similarly, if a third party overhears the defendant make a statement to the claimant, no liability for **defamation** will lie if the defendant could not have suspected that the third party would hear the statement.

VOCABULARY

In defamation, the 'sting' is the part of a statement that is allegedly defamatory.

Another common publication problem involves statements that have been passed along from one person to another. Can the original speaker be held responsible for those later statements? It depends. Normally, people are not liable for the acts of third parties, so the originator of a defamatory statement will not be held responsible for subsequent republication by others. However, if Mark asks Kendra to republish the information, then Mark—who, you will note, is acting as a principal, while Kendra is acting as an agent—will be held responsible for the defamatory statement. It's not even necessary that Mark make an explicit request that Kendra republish the information, though such a request can be inferred. For example, if Mark makes a defamatory statement, knowing that reporters are in the room, he will not be responsible if the information is published by the press unless he speaks with the intent that the information will be republished. Republication is discussed in detail in *Slipper v BBC* [1991] 1 QB 283, which involved the broadcast of a defamatory film to the press and the subsequent repetition of the defamatory 'sting' in reviews published the next day.

● *Slipper v BBC* [1991] 1 QB 283

Slade J: The decision in Ward v. Weeks, 7 Bing. 211, may, in my judgment, be regarded as good authority for the general proposition stated in Gatley on Libel and Slander, 8th ed., p. 119, para. 266:

'One who utters a slander, or writes and publishes a libel, is prima facie not liable for damage caused by its voluntary and unauthorized repetition or republication by the person to whom he published it. Such republication is not the necessary, natural, or probable consequence of the original publication.'

Prima facie, the court will treat the unauthorized repetition of a libel as a novus actus interveniens breaking the chain of causation between the original publication and the damage suffered by the injured party through the repetition or republication. Nevertheless, Tindal C.J., in saying in Ward v. Weeks, at p. 215, that 'such spontaneous and unauthorized communication cannot be considered as the necessary consequence of the original uttering of the words' was not, in my judgment, purporting to lay down a universal rule applicable to all cases of unauthorized repetition or republication. He was referring to 'such spontaneous and unauthorized communication' as had occurred on the facts of that case.

Mr. Gray, in the course of argument, himself recognized that there are at least three exceptions to the general rule, which include the cases where either the original publisher authorized or requested the person to whom he published the defamatory matter to repeat or republish it to some third party, or the original publisher intended that such person should repeat or republish it, or where such person was under a moral duty so to repeat or republish it. Thus, it is common ground that a judge, in directing a jury as to the assessment of general damages, would be entitled to direct it to take into account, inter alia, damage suffered by the plaintiff by reason of republication or repetition in circumstances such as are mentioned in (a), (b) or (c) above.

A more recent case on republication suggests that mere foreseeability that the statement will be passed along is not enough. In *McManus v Beckham* [2002] EWCA Civ 939, [2002] 1 WLR 2982, a shop owner specializing in sports memorabilia sued Victoria Beckham for casting aspersions on the legitimacy of items bearing David Beckham's signature. Her statements, which were originally made to customers in the shop in question, were subsequently reported in the press.

● *McManus v Beckham* [2002] EWCA Civ 939, [2002] 1 WLR 2982

Waller LJ: What the law is striving to achieve in this area is a just and reasonable result by reference to the position of a reasonable person in the position of the defendant. If a defendant is actually aware (1) that what she says or does is likely to be reported, and (2) that if she slanders someone that slander is likely to be repeated in whole or in part, there is no injustice in her being held responsible for the damage that the slander causes via that publication. I would suggest further that if a jury were to conclude that a reasonable person in the position of the defendant should have appreciated that there was a significant risk that what she said would be repeated in whole or in part in the press and that that would increase the damage caused by the slander, it is not unjust that the defendant should be liable for it. Thus I would suggest a direction along the above lines rather than by reference to 'foreseeability'.

Defamation need not be an affirmative act. It is also possible to defame someone by omission. For example, in *Byrne v Deane* [1937] 1 KB 818 the plaintiff sued the proprietors and secretary of a golf club for failing to remove an offensive sign that had been tacked up on the wall of the club. The Court of Appeal agreed that those who have the authorization and ability to remove defamatory material must do so or face the consequences.

14.2.4 **Damages and other remedies**

Some torts, such as negligence, require a claimant to prove damages as part of the prima facie case. If no damages can be proven, no liability exists. Other torts do not require a claimant to prove a particular injury, since damages are presumed.

Defamation falls into both categories. Two types of defamation claims—libel and slander per se—do not require the claimant to demonstrate any damages. Libel is a defamatory statement that exists in permanent form by being written, painted, photographer or recorded on DVD, CD, or other recordable means. Slander is non-permanent defamation. The classic example is the spoken word, not recorded in any way. As discussed further below, slander per se consists of particularly inflammatory language regarding the claimant. In libel and slander per se, the court assumes that the claimant's reputation has been harmed by the defendant's actions. Slander that is not actionable per se is different. There, the defamatory statement is not in a permanent form and does not involve any particularly reprehensible topics, so the court requires the claimant to demonstrate damages as part of the case in chief. Otherwise the claimant proves damages only as a means of increasing his or her award.

When reckoning the quantum of damages, the jury—for it is the jury that sets the amount of the award in defamation—considers the extent to which the claimant has lost the esteem and respect of others. This, along with loss of goodwill and association, constitutes 'general damages' recoverable in libel and slander per se. However, a claimant in either of these torts may also recover any consequential pecuniary loss, such as the loss of trade. The difficult thing about damages in defamation is that neither the judge nor counsel is allowed to give the jury any guidelines as to what might constitute a proper award. Nevertheless, defamation awards have escalated rapidly in recent years, which is difficult to understand given that exemplary damages are generally not available unless the defendant has made a conscious choice that the profits he or she would make as a result of the defamatory statement will exceed any damages recoverable at trial and knows that making a defamatory statement is illegal (or proceeds recklessly as to its illegality).

When a claimant pursues an action in slander that is not actionable per se, he or she must prove special damages representing some sort of actual material loss. Loss of employment, for example, would fall under this heading, since lost wages constitute a tangible loss to the claimant. The claimant must actually have experienced the loss; a mere threat of loss is not enough. Furthermore, the loss must be more than simply mental distress or any physical illness that arose as a result of that mental distress, though such losses can be added on once special damages are proved. Therefore, special damages must relate to the type of harm that the tort of defamation is designed to protect, namely damage to reputation and any resulting social injury. Since the tort was not intended to protect against harm to one's body, those sorts of injuries may only constitute additional damages after the tort itself, including special damages, has been proven.

As with any tort, courts must consider causation in defamation suits. Ordinary principles of remoteness apply in defamation, with the question being one of strict foreseeability—could the defendant have reasonably foreseen the consequences of his or her act? Thus, the originator of a defamatory statement may be held liable for the actions of others, as long as those actions were reasonably foreseeable. While an entirely independent and unforeseeable action might break the chain of causation, each case must be decided on its own facts.

A defendant may reduce the damages it must pay by demonstrating that the claimant already had a bad reputation, since a bad reputation is of less value than an untarnished one, as shown by *Turner v News Group Newspapers Ltd* [2006] EWCA Civ 540. There the fact that the claimant was involved in a 'swinging' lifestyle, involving wife-swapping, was considered proper background to the case. However, one need only show what the claimant's reputation in the community is rather than the claimant's true character, since defamation only protects a person's reputation. As Lord Devlin said in *Dingle v Associated Newspapers Ltd* [1961] 2 QB 162, aff'd [1964] AC 371, a case involving defamatory material published in a newspaper concerning the purchase of a cemetery and the allegation that a criminal investigation had been conducted in connection with that purchase:

● ***Dingle v Associated Newspapers Ltd*** [1961] 2 QB 162, aff'd [1964] AC 371

Lord Devlin: In a libel action the plaintiff is seeking to recover compensation for loss of reputation; and it is well established and in accordance with the general principle applicable to all torts that it is open to the defendant to show that, at the time when he inflicted his injury on the plaintiff's reputation, it was already damaged...In cases of defamation evidence of previous bad reputation is usually considered as evidence in mitigation of damage, whereas in cases of bodily injury the same effect is obtained simply by measuring the consequences of the second injury. But, as Mr. Faulks submits, the principle in both cases is the same. In each case you have to take, as you find it at the time when the second injury was done, the state of the plaintiff's bodily fitness or the state of his reputation, as the case may be....

The rule is therefore that evidence of character in mitigation of damage for defamation must be evidence of general reputation only. But in the application of this rule it is necessary to consider just what is meant by 'character' in the sense of reputation...I desire to adopt a definition or description of 'character' which was given by Mr. Erskine...: 'Character is the slow-spreading influence of opinion, arising from the deportment of a man in society; as a man's deportment, good or bad, necessarily produces one circle without another, and so extends itself till it unites in one general opinion, that general opinion is allowed to be given in evidence.'

In my opinion it is only a settled bad character of this sort that ought to be taken into account in mitigation of damage. Where it exists, it shows that the permanent injury to a

NOTE Lord Devlin here indicates that the 'egg shell skull' claimant exists in defamation law. For more on egg shell skull claimants, see chapter 4.

man's character done by a libel upon him is less grave than it would otherwise have been. There are other elements besides permanent injury to character to be taken into account in the assessment of damages for defamation. There is mental distress, the pain caused by those who doubt, even if they hold final judgment in suspense, and maybe financial loss also if they hold business in suspense as well. There is the malice of the defendant if it is proved; the presence or absence of an apology and his conduct and that of his counsel before and during the trial.

Furthermore, when deciding the quantum of damages, a jury must look how far the defamatory statement has travelled. As Lord Devlin said elsewhere in *Dingle v Associated Newspapers Ltd* [1961] 2 QB 162, aff'd [1964] AC 371:

> the damage done by the publication of a libel must be measured, albeit roughly, in accordance with the number of people to whom the publication is made. A man's reputation is in the keeping of others and it is by words uttered to those others that it is injured; the larger the number to whom the publication is made the greater the injury. If the libel is spread from mouth to mouth by a series of utterances, the damage done by each must be separately assessed; if the publication consists of only one utterance to a large number, there can be only one assessment but it must be made in accordance with size.

cross reference

Injunctions are discussed in more detail in chapter 11.

Damages are not the only remedy available in defamation actions. Claimants may also pursue injunctive relief to stop publication of a potentially defamatory statement. When considering whether to grant an injunction, courts weigh the potential damage to the claimant against other interests, such as the freedom of the press. If the defendant objects to an injunction, the court looks at whether the defendant would be likely to raise and establish a good defence at trial.

14.3 Differences between slander and libel

Defamation always involves the communication of a defamatory statement to a third party. However, the law places no restriction on the method of communication. A person may be defamed through spoken words, written words, pictures, gestures, music, photography, video, statuary, topiary, textiles, stained glass windows—virtually anything. The only time that the method of communication matters is when the court is differentiating between libel and slander. As with many areas of the law, there are some easy answers and some difficult ones. For example:

- If the defamatory material exists in permanent form and can be seen, it constitutes libel. Books, newspaper articles and letters routinely fall into this category.

- If the defamatory material exists in temporary form and can only be heard, it constitutes slander. The quintessential example for slander is the spoken word.

- What about something that exists in permanent form but can only be heard? Those types of items—CDs, audio files, etc.—seem to split the difference between libel and slander.

- Similarly, what about something that exists in permanent form and can be seen but can also be heard? Movies, television recordings and amateur videotapes fall into this category.

Youssoupoff v Metro-Goldwyn-Mayer Pictures Ltd (1934) 50 TLR 581 suggested that permanency is an important issue, though not necessarily the only or determinative one. In that case, the Court of Appeal was asked to consider whether defamatory material contained in a film (a novelty at that time) constituted a libel or a slander. Slesser LJ stated in that case that:

> There can be no doubt that, so far as the photographic part of the exhibition is concerned, that is a *permanent matter to be seen by the eye*, and is the proper subject of an action for libel, if defamatory. I regard the speech which is synchronized with the photographic reproduction and forms part of one complex, common exhibition as an ancillary circumstances, part of the surroundings explaining that which is to be seen.

No known case to date has decided the issue regarding permanency definitively. However, it is an important element to consider when attempting to differentiate between libel and slander. When doing so, be sure to distinguish between the form in which the material exists and the manner in which it is communicated. For example, one might think that a letter that is published to a third party by being read out loud is slander, since the method of publication is not permanent, but at least one case, *Forrester v Tyrrell* (1839) 57 JP 532, has held the act to be libel, since the defamatory material exists in a permanent form, visible to the eye. In that instance, a defendant received an anonymous letter while at his lodge meeting and read it aloud, by leave of the chair, to the entire meeting, which included the plaintiff. Some of the grey areas have been addressed by statute, however. For example, section 166 of the Broadcasting Act 1990 indicates that defamatory words contained in television or radio broadcasts shall be treated as if they were published in a permanent form. Similarly, the Theatres Act 1968 indicates that defamatory material published during the performance of a play shall also be treated as being published in a permanent form.

One reason to know the difference between slander and libel is to decide whether damages must be proven as an affirmative part of the claimant's case. In libel, damages are presumed, so a claimant need not prove an actual injury as a result of the defendant's actions. In slander, damages are only presumed when the slander is 'actionable per se', which is a legal term of art referring to certain categories of slander that are so outrageous and damaging that damages are presumed, just as they are in libel. All other slander—meaning any slander that is not actionable per se—must result in special damages. If special damages don't exist, the tort has not been proven and there is no recovery.

Slander per se consists of one of several well-defined categories of speech:

- Imputation of a crime;

- Imputation of certain types of diseases, primarily venereal disease;

- Disparagement of office, profession, calling, trade or business; or

- Imputation of unchastity of a woman.

While each of these categories has its roots in the common law, most are now defined by statute. Any slander outside these subjects is not slander per se and therefore must be accompanied by special damages to be actionable.

14.3.1 Imputation of a crime

Not every crime supports a claim of slander per se. Only those crimes that carry a prison term will be actionable.

EXAM TIP On your tort examination, you will not be required to know which criminal offences lead to a fine and which lead to imprisonment. Just know that only allegations concerning the latter can support an action in slander per se.

Furthermore, the trier of fact must look at the statement as a whole. If the speaker merely conveys a suspicion that the claimant committed a crime—for example, if the speaker says, 'I think John killed Mary'—that does not constitute slander per se. Furthermore, the statement may be accompanied by words that offset the purportedly slanderous allegation. For example, in *Thompson v Bernard* (1807) 1 Camp 48, the court held that:

> The words 'T is a damned thief, and so was his father before him; and I can prove it' seem clear enough, but because they were followed in this case by the statement, 'T received the earnings of the ship, and ought to pay the wages', the court directed a non-suit, because only breach of contract was in fact imputed.

Therefore, for an imputation of crime to be actionable, the words must be clear and unambiguous. While the court may have to make some difficult decisions about whether the crime that was alleged would be punishable by imprisonment, the statement itself must be straightforward.

14.3.2 Imputation of certain diseases

Claiming that someone has a venereal disease is clearly slander per se under the common law. It has been suggested that other communicable diseases, such as leprosy, scarlet fever and tuberculosis, would also give rise to a claim for slander per se, but there are no cases that are definitively on point. Similarly, no decisions have yet determined whether AIDS falls into this category. In deciding whether these other types of diseases can support a claim of slander per se, the court must consider whether they include any moral condemnation or social loathing. In Victorian times, venereal disease was considered as much of a moral failing as a biological one. Now that the social stigma associated with sexually transmitted diseases has been eliminated or at least minimized, it is an open question whether charging someone with having any of these diseases can form the basis for an action in slander per se.

14.3.3 Disparagement of office, profession, calling, trade or business

Although the common law traditionally protected persons from any disparagement of their professional or business skills or traits, Parliament codified this area of law in the early 1950s. Section 2 of the Defamation Act 1952 states that:

> In an action for slander in respect of words calculated to disparage the plaintiff in an office, profession, calling, trade or business held or carried on by him at the time of the publication, it shall not be necessary to allege or prove special damage, whether or not the words are spoken of the plaintiff in the way of his office, profession, calling, trade or business.

However, the Defamation Act 1952 does more than protect the reputation of a person or business. It also protects the reputation of certain objects. Section 3 of the Act states:

> (1) In an action for slander of title, slander of goods or other malicious falsehood, it shall not be necessary to allege or prove special damage—
>
> (a) if the words upon which the action is founded are calculated to cause pecuniary damage to the plaintiff and are published in writing or other permanent form; or
>
> (b) if the said words are calculated to cause pecuniary damage to the plaintiff in respect of any office, profession, calling, trade or business held or carried on by him at the time of the publication.

Therefore a claimant need not prove that his or her own reputation was tarnished; it is sufficient, under section 3(1), that the speaker slandered (or libelled) the claimant's goods by, for example, claiming that they were stolen (slander of title) or of poor quality (slander of goods). This can be useful for the owner of those objects, particularly in a commercial context.

14.3.4 Imputation of unchastity of a woman

The Slander of Women Act 1891 indicates that 'words spoken and published which impute unchastity or adultery to any woman or girl shall not require special damage to render them actionable'. Presumably, only the woman has the right to recover under this statute, not her alleged partner.

think point

Would this sort of slander would still be actionable in today's culture if it weren't already embodied in existing legislation? How does this particular law perpetuate any particular social myths or mores by the mere fact of remaining on the statute books?

14.4 Differences between defamation and invasion of privacy

The so-called right to privacy has received a great deal of attention in recent years, even though the common law did not protect any such interest. For example, in *Kaye v Robertson* [1991] FSR 62, Gordon Kaye, an actor from *'Allo! 'Allo!* who was in a serious automobile accident, was photographed in his private room in hospital. The journalist and photographer ignored signs indicating that they were not allowed to be there and took pictures of Kaye while he was in no fit state to conduct an interview or give consent to the photographs. The difficulty in *Kaye v Robertson* [1991] FSR 62 was identifying a proper cause of action. In that case, Glidewell LJ specifically stated that:

> It is well-known that in English law there is no right to privacy, and accordingly there is no right of action for breach of a person's privacy. The facts of the present case are a graphic illustration of the desirability of Parliament considering whether and in what circumstances statutory provision can be made to protect the privacy of individuals.

In the absence of such a right, the plaintiff's advisers have sought to base their claim to injunctions upon other well-established rights of action. These are:

- Libel;

- Malicious falsehood;

- Trespass to the person; and

- Passing off.

The court went on to consider each of these various causes of action. The judge below had granted an interim injunction based, in part, on the likelihood of the photograph and article's being defamatory, relying on the case of *Tolley v J.S. Fry & Sons Ltd* [1931] AC 333. That case involved a well-known amateur golfer who sued when a chocolate company used his likeness to promote its product without his consent. Tolley argued that the advertisement suggested that he had been paid for the endorsement, which would damage his reputation as an amateur. The House of Lords in that case ruled that the advertisement was capable of being viewed in a defamatory light. When considering Gordon Kaye's claims, the Court of Appeal in *Kaye v Robertson* [1991] FSR 62 hesitated to rely on *Tolley v J.S. Fry & Sons Ltd* [1931] AC 333, given that Gordon Kaye was seeking an injunction to prohibit publication—thus implicating the right to freedom of the press—rather than damages after the fact. In the end, the Court of Appeal decided not to allow recovery for invasion of privacy (because there was no such right) or libel, although it did uphold the claim in malicious falsehood.

NOTE This is a good example of Parliamentary supremacy. The outcome might be different in a country like the United States, where courts arguably have more freedom to create a remedy.

NOTE This text does not cover the tort of malicious falsehood, although your lecturer may do so. According to Glidewell LJ in *Kaye v Robertson* [1991] FSR 62, '[t]he essentials of this tort are that the defendant has published about the plaintiff words which are false, that they were published maliciously, and that special damage as followed as the direct and natural result of their publication'. However, for malicious falsehood, the claimant need not prove injury to reputation. Instead, the tort addresses other kinds of harm, such as loss of income. For example a defendant might say 'Alice's shop ran out of eggs. Buy mine instead'.

Although there is no well-established right to privacy in the United Kingdom, other common law jurisdictions, particularly the United States, have well-developed jurisprudence in this area. For example, Samuel Warren and future US Supreme Court Justice Louis D. Brandeis wrote a famous article describing principles that are as relevant today as they were when the article was first written.

● Samuel D. Warren & Louis D. Brandeis, *'The Right to Privacy'*, 4 Harvard Law Review 193 (1890)

That the individual shall have full protection in person and in property is a principle as old as the common law; but it has been found necessary from time to time to define anew the exact nature and extent of such protection. Political, social, and economic changes entail the recognition of new rights, and the common law, in its eternal youth, grows to meet the demands of society. Thus, in very early times, the law gave a remedy only for physical interference with life and property…the 'right to life' served only to protect the subject from battery in its various forms; liberty meant freedom from actual restraint; and the right to property secured to the individual his lands and his cattle. Later, there came a recognition of man's spiritual nature, of his feelings and his intellect. Gradually the scope of these legal rights broadened; and now the right to life has come to mean the right to enjoy life—the right to be let alone, the right to liberty secures the exercise of extensive civil privileges; and the term 'property' has grown to comprise every form of possession—intangible, as well as tangible…

Recent inventions and business methods call attention to the next step which must be taken for the protection of the person, and for securing to the individual what Judge Cooley calls the right 'to be let alone.' Instantaneous photographs and newspaper enterprise have invaded the sacred precincts of private and domestic life; and numerous mechanical devices threaten to make good the prediction that 'what is whispered in the closet shall be proclaimed from the house-tops.'…

Of the desirability—indeed of the necessity—of some such protection, there can, it is believed, be no doubt. The press is overstepping in every direction the obvious bounds of propriety and of decency. Gossip is no longer the resource of the idle and of the vicious, but has become a trade, which is pursued with industry as well as effrontery. To satisfy a prurient taste the details of sexual relations are spread broadcast in the columns of the daily papers…

It is our purpose to consider whether the existing law affords a principle which can properly be invoked to protect the privacy of the individual; and, if it does, what the nature and extent of such protection is.

Owing to the nature of the instruments by which privacy is invaded, the injury inflicted bears a superficial resemblance to the wrongs dealt with by the law of slander and of libel, while a legal remedy for such injury seems to involve the treatment of mere wounded feelings, as a substantive cause of action. The principle on which the law of defamation rests, covers, however, a radically different class of effects from those for which attention is now asked. It deals only with damage to reputation, with the injury done to the individual in his external relations to the community, by lowering him in the estimation of his fellows. The matter published of him, however widely circulated, and however unsuited to publicity, must, in order to be actionable, have a direct tendency to injure him in his intercourse with others, and even if in writing or in print, must subject him to the hatred, ridicule, or contempt of his fellow men . . . In short, the wrongs and correlative rights recognized by the law of slander and libel are in their nature material rather than spiritual . . . On the other hand, our law recognizes no principle upon which compensation can be granted for mere injury to the feelings . . .

The common law secures to each individual the right of determining, ordinarily, to what extent his thoughts, sentiments, and emotions shall be communicated to others. Under our system of government, he can never be compelled to express them (except when upon the witness stand); and even if he has chosen to give them expression, he generally retains the power to fix the limits of the publicity which shall be given them . . . In every such case the individual is entitled to decide whether that which is his shall be given to the public . . . It is entirely independent of the copyright laws, and their extension into the domain of art. The aim of those statutes is to secure to the author, composer, or artist the entire profits arising from publication; but the common-law protection enables him to control absolutely the act of publication, and in the exercise of his own discretion, to decide whether there shall be any publication at all . . .

[T]he protection afforded to thoughts, sentiments, and emotions, expressed through the medium of writing or of the arts, so far as it consists in preventing publication, is merely an instance of the enforcement of the more general right of the individual to be let alone. It is like the right not to be assaulted or beaten, the right not to be imprisoned, the right not to be maliciously prosecuted, the right not to be defamed. In each of these rights, as indeed in all other rights recognized by the law, there inheres the quality of being owned or possessed—and . . . there may be some propriety in speaking of those rights as property. But, obviously, they bear little resemblance to what is ordinarily comprehended under that term. The principle which protects personal writings and all other personal productions, not against theft and physical appropriation, but against publication in any form, is in reality not the principle of private property, but that of an inviolate personality . . .

We must therefore conclude that . . . [t]he principle which protects personal writings and any other productions of the intellect or of the emotions, is the right to privacy . . .

The right of one who has remained a private individual, to prevent his public portraiture, presents the simplest case for such extension; the right to protect one's self from pen portraiture, from a discussion by the press of one's private affairs, would be a more important and far-reaching one . . .

It remains to consider what are the limitations of this right to privacy, and what remedies may be granted for the enforcement of the right . . .

First. The right to privacy does not prohibit any publication of matter which is of public or general interest . . .

In general, then, the matters of which the publication should be repressed may be described as those which concern the private life, habits, acts, and relations of an individual, and have no legitimate connection with his fitness for a public office which he seeks or for which he is suggested, or for any public quasi-public position which he seeks or for which he is suggested, and have no legitimate relation to or bearing upon any act done by him in a public or quasi-public capacity... Some things all men alike are entitled to keep from popular curiosity, whether in public life or not, while others are only private because the persons concerned have not assumed a position which makes their doings legitimate matters of public investigation.

Second. The right to privacy does not prohibit the communication of any matter, though in its nature private, when the publication is made under circumstances which would render it a privileged communication according to the law of slander and libel...

Third. The law would probably not grant any redress for the invasion of privacy by oral publication in the absence of special damage...

Fourth. The right to privacy ceases upon the publication of the facts by the individual, or with his consent...

Fifth. The truth of the matter published does not afford a defense...

Sixth. The absence of 'malice' in the publisher does not afford a defense.

Personal ill-will is not an ingredient of the offense, any more than in an ordinary case of trespass to person or to property. Such malice is never necessary to be shown in an actions for libel or slander at common law, except in rebuttal of some defense, *e.g.*, that the occasion rendered the communication privileged, or, under the statutes in this state and elsewhere, that the statement complained of was true.

Although neither Parliament nor the courts have addressed the issue of a right to privacy in any comprehensive manner, some protections have trickled into British law via the Human Rights Act 1998, which gave the European Convention on Human Rights domestic applicability. Article 8(1) of the European Convention states that '[e]veryone shall have the right to respect for his private and family life, his home and his correspondence', suggesting there is now some right to privacy in the United Kingdom. In 2001, the Court of Appeal handed down the ground-breaking decision in *Douglas v Hello! Ltd* [2001] 2 QB 967, in which the actors Michael Douglas and Catherine Zeta Jones sued *Hello!* magazine for publishing unauthorized pictures of their wedding when the exclusive right to cover the wedding had been sold to *OK!* magazine. The *Douglas v Hello! Ltd* litigation spawned numerous reported decisions at all levels. The excerpt noted here is one of the leading judgments in this area of law. For an overview of the law of privacy as it developed after this judgment was issued (as well as description of the soap-opera saga relating to the litigation itself), see the Court of Appeal's later decision in *Douglas v Hello! Ltd* [2005] EWCA Civ 595.

● ***Douglas v Hello! Ltd*** [2001] QB 967

Sedley LJ: Lawyers in this country have learned to accept that English law recognizes no right of privacy...

What a concept of privacy does...is accord recognition to the fact that the law has to protect not only those people whose trust has been abused but those who simply find themselves subjected to an unwanted intrusion into their personal lives...

The convention right in question is the right to freedom of expression contained in art 10:

'1. Everyone has the right to freedom of expression. This right shall include freedom to hold opinions and to receive and impart information and ideas without interference by public authority and regardless of frontiers'.

The exercise of these freedoms, since it carries with it duties and responsibilities, may be subject to such formalities, conditions, restrictions or penalties as are prescribed by law and are necessary in a democratic society . . . for the protection of the reputation or rights of others, for preventing the disclosure of information received in confidence, or for maintaining the authority and impartiality of the judiciary.' . . .

You cannot have particular regard to art 10 without having equally particular regard at the very least to art 8:

'Right to respect for private and family life

1. Everyone has the right to respect for his private and family life, his home and his correspondence.

2. There shall be no interference by a public authority with the exercise of this right except such as is in accordance with the law and is necessary in a democratic society in the interests of national security, public safety or the economic well-being of the country, for the prevention of disorder or crime, for the protection of health or morals, or for the protection of the rights and freedoms of others.' . . .

For reasons I have given, Mr Douglas and Ms Zeta-Jones have a powerful prima facie claim to redress for invasion of their privacy as a qualified right recognized and protected by English law. The case being one which affects the convention right of freedom of expression, s 12 of the Human Rights Act requires the court to have regard to art 10 of the convention (as, in its absence, would s 6 of that Act) . . . What it does is require the court to consider art 10(2) along with art 10(1), and by doing so to bring into the frame the conflicting right to respect for privacy. This right, contained in art 8 and reflected in English law, is in turn qualified in both contexts by the right of others to free expression. The outcome, which self-evidently has to be the same under both articles, is determined principally by considerations of proportionality . . .

It is also as information, however, that the photographs invade the privacy of Mr Douglas and Ms Zeta-Jones: they tell the world things about the wedding and the couple which the claimants have not consented to. On the present evidence, whoever took the photographs probably had no right to be there; if they were lawfully there, they had no right to photograph anyone; and in either case they had no right to publicize the product of their intrusion. If it stopped there, this would have been an unanswerable case for a temporary injunction and no doubt in due course for a permanent one; perhaps the more unanswerable, not the less, for the celebrity of the two principal victims. Article 8 of the convention, whether introduced indirectly through s 12 or directly by virtue of s 6 of the Human Rights Act, will of course require the court to consider 'the rights and freedoms of others', including the art 10(1) right of Hello!. And art 10, by virtue of ss 6 and 12, will require the court, if the common law did not already do so, to have full regard to Hello!'s right to freedom of expression. But the circumstances in which the photographs must have been obtained would have robbed those rights and freedoms of substance for reasons which should by now be plain.

> The facts, however, do not stop here. The first two claimants had sold most of the privacy they now seek to protect to the third claimant for a handsome sum. If all that had happened were that Hello! had got hold of OK!'s photographs, OK! would have proprietary rights and remedies at law, but Mr Douglas and Ms Zeta-Jones would not, I think, have any claim for breach of the privacy with which they had already parted. The present case is not so stark, because they were careful by their contract to retain a right of veto over publication of OK!'s photographs in order to maintain the kind of image which is professionally and no doubt also personally important to them. This element of privacy remained theirs and Hello!'s photographs violated it.

Thus the right of privacy has come into domestic law via the Human Rights Act 1998. However, the application of the right will depend heavily on the facts of the case and whether there are any countervailing interests. Here, the defendant had a protectible right under Article 10 of the European Convention, but that right was overcome by virtue of the manner in which the photographs were obtained and the claimants' privacy and contract rights.

Subsequent cases suggest that there will be little further development of the law of privacy outside, perhaps, the facts reflected in *Douglas v Hello!* [2001] 2 QB 967. In *Wainwright v Home Office* [2003] UKHL 53, [2004] 2 AC 406, the House of Lords considered a claim for invasion of privacy after several guards failed to follow proper procedure when strip-searching visitors to a prison. Unlike the argument in *Douglas v Hello!* [2001] 2 QB 967, the interest here was not in one's image or reputation; it was in one's physical person. Lord Hoffmann reviewed decisions concerning privacy interests, both before and after the passing of the Human Rights Act 1998, and concluded that British courts had, time and again, held that the creation of any overarching right to privacy must be done at the behest of Parliament, rather than the courts. Furthermore, he indicated that compliance with the European Convention on Human Rights did not require the recognition of an overarching right to privacy, and thus limited *Douglas v Hello!* [2001] 2 QB 967 to its facts.

● **Wainwright v Home Office** [2003] UKHL 53, [2004] 2 AC 406

> Lord Hoffmann: [I]n relation to the publication of personal information obtained by intrusion, the common law of breach of confidence has reached the point at which a confidential relationship has become unnecessary. As the underlying value protected is privacy, the action might as well be renamed invasion of privacy. 'To say this' said Sedley LJ [in *Douglas v Hello! Ltd* [2001] QB 967] at p 1001, para 125, 'is in my belief to say little, save by way of a label, that our courts have not said already over the years.'
>
> I do not understand Sedley LJ to have been advocating the creation of a high-level principle of invasion of privacy. His observations are in my opinion no more (although certainly no less) than a plea for the extension and possibly renaming of the old action for breach of confidence.

The House of Lords again confirmed in *Campbell v MGN Ltd* [2004] UKHL 22 that 'there is no over-arching, all-embracing cause of action for invasion of privacy' in the United Kingdom, but recognized that 'protection of various aspects of privacy is a fast developing area of law'. In that case, the international model, Naomi Campbell, brought a cause of action after true facts were printed regarding her drug dependency and treatment. Her claim was that there had been a wrongful disclosure of private information, known also as a breach of confidence, although there is no longer any need for a confidential relationship between the parties. The Lords considered not only the common law basis for this cause of action, but also the values enshrined in articles 8 and 10 of the European Convention on Human Rights and the Strasbourg (European) jurisprudence to conclude that any test regarding the competing interests of privacy and freedom of expression should focus on whether the situation is one 'where a person can reasonably expect his privacy to be respected'. In this case, a majority of the Lords held that a case for privacy was made out.

 ## 14.5   Defences to defamation

Many of the defences available in other torts are also available to defeat a claim in defamation. For example, *Slipper v BBC* [1991] 1QB 283, discussed above, demonstrated how a break in the chain of causation can act as a defence to an action for defamation.

There are a few quirks, however. Courts apply the defences of consent and assumption of the risk slightly differently in defamation cases, and there are a number of defences that are particular to this area of law. Therefore, we will consider each of the following in turn:

- Consent and assumption of the risk;
- Justification;
- Statutory defences;
- Absolute privilege;
- Qualified privilege; and
- Fair comment.

14.5.1   Consent and assumption of the risk

Douglas v Hello! [2001] QB 967 showed how consent can eliminate a claim in tort. In that case, the claimants had contracted away their right to privacy, at least regarding approved photos to be published in *OK!* magazine. The same is true in defamation. A party who consents, implicitly or explicitly, to the publication of defamatory material will not be heard to complain. However, the courts will look closely at the type of consent and will allow recovery for any improper act that exceeds the boundaries of the consent. For example, *Cook v Ward* (1830) 6 Bing 409 held that a person who tells a false story about him or herself in one location—for example, a parish vestry meeting—will still be able to sue if a newspaper reprints the story, since the speaker did not consent to publication to those additional people in that manner. Therefore, consent is very fact-specific.

However, consent in one context could lead a court to conclude that the claimant had assumed the risk of further publication. For example, in *Chapman v Ellesmere* [1932] 2 KB 431 the plaintiff was a trainer whose race horse had been found to have been drugged before a race. The plaintiff was brought before the track stewards and had his license revoked. The Racing Times reported the revocation, but because it was permitted and indeed was required to publish information regarding the licensing of trainers, no action was brought against it. When the general newspapers published the information, the plaintiff sued for libel.

. . . .

● ***Chapman v Ellesmere*** [1932] 2 KB 431

Slesser LJ: I propose to deal with this case of the publication in the Racing Calendar first, as it presents certain peculiar features which do not apply in the case of the other publications with regard to the assent of the plaintiff to the publication. This defence is based upon the doctrine volenti non fit injuria. In the words of Salmond on Torts, 7th ed., p. 58: 'No act is actionable as a tort at the suit of any person who has expressly or impliedly assented to it: Volenti non fit injuria. No man can enforce a right which he has voluntarily waived or abandoned' . . . The argument of Sir Patrick Hastings for the plaintiff to avoid the consequence of the apparent consent to publication in the Racing Calendar is as follows: he says that the plaintiff has only consented to the publication of the decision of the stewards, which I have quoted but repeat, that they 'considered the plaintiff as trainer directly responsible for the care of the horse'; that is to say, to a finding that he was under a duty to see that the horse was not drugged, which duty he failed to perform. Sir Patrick points out that the jury, having found that the statement in the Racing Calendar meant that the plaintiff was a party to the actual drugging of 'Don Pat,' it is a statement, as the jury have construed it, which is not the publication of the decision of the stewards, in that the stewards, to put it briefly, held that the plaintiff was negligent in not preventing the drugging of the horse, whereas the publication alleged that he had actually drugged it. On this matter, the conclusion at which I have already arrived, that the finding of the jury is directed to an innuendo and is not a finding as to the actual meaning of the words, becomes so material, for if the plaintiff assented to a report of the decision of the stewards, and they used words which were not a report of that decision, Sir Patrick Hastings' argument would have great weight; but if, on the other hand, in fact, they did report the actual decision, but in such a way that the jury say that it was to be understood to mean something other than the actual decision, that is a risk which the plaintiff, by agreeing to a report of the decision, has elected to run.

The matter is not free from authority. In the case of Cookson v. Harewood, . . . a very similar rule to the one here under consideration provided that . . . 'If you get a true statement and an authority to publish the true statement, it does not matter in the least what people will understand what it means. The plaintiff has submitted to the jurisdiction.' . . . Sir Patrick Hastings scarcely disputes that if the defamatory matter here can only be sustained by innuendo, the plaintiff has assented to the publication. His case is that the words in their natural meaning are defamatory and so not a true report of the decision; but . . . I think the case can only be based on innuendo, and, applying the doctrine of volenti non fit injuria, I hold that the plaintiff must fail in respect of the publication in the Racing Calendar by reason of his assent thereto.

Slesser LJ suggested that if the statement is true and the plaintiff has consented to its publication, then the plaintiff cannot bring an action based on any possible additional meanings (innuendoes) given to the statement. However, the court did allow the plaintiff's action against other newspapers to proceed, not because the plain meaning of the words—which were substantially the same as in the Racing Calendar—were defamatory, but because the innuendo associated with those words were defamatory and no consent had been given to the publishers of those papers.

14.5.2 Justification

You may have heard the phrase 'truth is an absolute defence', but you may not have known that it describes the defence of justification. In a claim for defamation, there is no need to prove the allegedly defamatory statement is untrue, since that could be difficult, if not impossible, in some cases and would put a heavy burden on the claimant. However, if the defendant can prove that the statement was true, then he or she has a complete defence. At that point, it doesn't matter if the defendant acted maliciously or not—the truth will protect the speaker.

As noted above, a statement may itself be defamatory or may carry an additional meaning (an innuendo) that is defamatory. Sometimes the statement and the innuendo are both defamatory. The rule is that whatever has been claimed to be defamatory—the statement, the innuendo (and there may be more than one innuendo) or both—must be justified. That means that the defendant may have to show that several different facts are true. The defendant need not prove that every minor detail is true, so long as the statement can be proven to be true on the whole. For example, the defendants in *Alexander v North Eastern Rly Co* (1865) 6 B & S 340 had said that the plaintiff had been fined £1 a week, with an alternative punishment of three weeks' imprisonment. In fact, the term had only been two weeks' imprisonment, but the court held that the statement was substantially true and therefore upheld the defence of justification.

If the defendant has made several statements, he or she does not need to prove that every element is true. Instead, the defendant only needs to prove the truth of the 'sting' of the defamatory statement, meaning the part that injured the claimant's reputation. For example, when the defamatory statement in *Clarke v Taylor* (1836) 1 Bing NC 654 involved an alleged 'grand swindling concern at Manchester' and also claimed that the plaintiff had been at Leeds a few days prior to arriving in Manchester, the defendant only needed to prove that swindling went on in Manchester. Since the fact of being in Leeds was not defamatory, that part of the statement did not need to be justified by the defendant.

The common law required the defendant to justify every material element of a defamatory statement. That requirement has been changed by statute, however. According to section 5 of the Defamation Act 1952:

> In an action for libel or slander in respect of words containing two or more distinct charges against the plaintiff, a defence of justification shall not fail by reason only that the truth of every charge is not proved if the words not proved to be true do not materially injure the plaintiff's reputation having regard to the truth of the remaining charges.

Thus, under the statute, a defendant does not need to justify each and every element of a defamatory statement. Each case will be looked at individually to see whether the sting of the statement has been sufficiently removed so as to allow the defence of justification to stand.

14.5.3 Statutory defences

Earlier in this chapter, we learned that a speaker can be held responsible when a third party republishes a defamatory statement. The previous discussion did not consider whether the third party would also be liable for that later republication. The Defamation Act 1996 addresses that issue as well as several others.

Technically, anyone who publishes defamatory material is liable to the person about whom the statement was made. For example, if a defamatory statement is contained in a book, the following people could be sued: the author, the editor of the book who passes the book along to the printer, the printer who makes copies of the book, the marketing executive who distributes excerpts containing the 'sting' of the defamation to news agencies to publicize the book, the news agencies who run advertisements or articles containing the sting, the printers who print the newspapers carrying those advertisements, and so on, right down to the newsagent on the High Street who sells the newspaper containing the advertisement. Purchasers of the book or newspaper could even be named as defendants if they gave their copies to a friend—there is no need for a commercial transaction to take place.

Morally, it seems wrong to hold many of these people—who may not have even known about the defamatory statement when they passed the printed material along the chain of distribution—as culpable as the original speaker. Furthermore, those in certain professions, such as newsagents or printers, would suffer real hardship, since they would continually be subject to actions in defamation. In order to alleviate this burden, the common law created a defence specifically designed for innocent dissemination, though that defence has since been superseded by the statutory defence known as the distributors' defence. Set forth in section 1 of the Defamation Act 1996, the distributors' defence states:

● **Defamation Act 1996**

1 Responsibility for publication

(1) In defamation proceedings a person has a defense if he shows that—
   (a) he was not the author, editor or publisher of the statement complained of,
   (b) he took reasonable care in relation to its publication, and
   (c) he did not know, and had no reason to believe, that what he did caused or contributed to the publication of a defamatory statement.

Sections 1(2), 1(3) and 1(4) of the 1996 Act further define those who may claim the defence.

1 Responsibility for publication

(2) For this purpose 'author', 'editor' and 'publisher' have the following meanings, which are further explained in subsection (3)—

'author' means the originator of the statement, but does not include a person who did not intend that his statement be published at all; 'editor' means a person having editorial or equivalent responsibility for the content of the statement or the decision to publish it; and

'publisher' means a commercial publisher, that is, a person whose business is issuing material to the public, or a section of the public, who issues material containing the statement in the course of that business.

(3) A person shall not be considered the author, editor or publisher of a statement if he is only involved—
   (a) in printing, producing, distributing or selling printed material containing the statement;
   (b) in processing, making copies of, distributing, exhibiting or selling a film or sound recording (as defined in Part I of the Copyright, Designs and Patents Act 1988) containing the statement;
   (c) in processing, making copies of, distributing or selling any electronic medium in or on which the statement is recorded, or in operating or providing any equipment, system or service by means of which the statement is retrieved, copied, distributed or made available in electronic form;
   (d) as the broadcaster of a live programme containing the statement in circumstances in which he has no effective control over the maker of the statement;
   (e) as the operator of or provider of access to a communications system by means of which the statement is transmitted, or made available, by a person over whom he has no effective control.

In a case not within paragraphs (a) to (e) the court may have regard to those provisions by way of analogy in deciding whether a person is to be considered the author, editor or publisher of a statement.

(4) Employees or agents of an author, editor or publisher are in the same position as their employer or principal to the extent that they are responsible for the content of the statement or the decision to publish it.

In addition to defining the people who can claim the distributors' defence, the 1996 Act describes what constitutes reasonable care in section 1(5), which elaborates on section 1(1)(b) and (c).

1 Responsibility for publication

(5) In determining for the purposes of this section whether a person took reasonable care, or had reason to believe that what he did caused or contributed to the publication of a defamatory statement, regard shall be had to—
   (a) the extent of his responsibility for the content of the statement or the decision to publish it,

(b) the nature or circumstances of the publication, and

(c) the previous conduct or character of the author, editor or publisher.

think point

Does the term 'reasonable care' in section 1(5) have any correlation to how that term is used in other areas of tort law, particularly negligence? Is there any mention of foreseeability? Be careful of false friends—your case law on 'reasonable care' in other contexts will not be applicable here.

The 1996 Act also allows those who do not have a complete defence as to distribution to eliminate or at least lessen their liability through an offer to make amends. This defence is described in sections 2 to 4 of the Defamation Act 1996. Section 2 describes the offer itself.

● **Defamation Act 1996**

2 Offer to make amends

(1) A person who has published a statement alleged to be defamatory of another may offer to make amends under this section.

(2) The offer may be in relation to the statement generally or in relation to a specific defamatory meaning which the person making the offer accepts that the statement conveys ('a qualified offer').

(3) An offer to make amends—

(a) must be in writing,

(b) must be expressed to be an offer to make amends under section 2 of the Defamation Act 1996, and

(c) must state whether it is a qualified offer and, if so, set out the defamatory meaning in relation to which it is made.

(4) An offer to make amends under this section is an offer—

(a) to make a suitable correction of the statement complained of and a sufficient apology to the aggrieved party,

(b) to publish the correction and apology in a manner that is reasonable and practicable in the circumstances, and

(c) to pay to the aggrieved party such compensation (if any), and such costs, as may be agreed or determined to be payable.

The fact that the offer is accompanied by an offer to take specific steps does not affect the fact that an offer to make amends under this section is an offer to do all the things mentioned in section 4(a) to (c).

2 Offer to make amends

(5) An offer to make amends under this section may not be made by a person after serving a defense in defamation proceedings brought against him by the aggrieved party in respect of the publication in question.

(6) An offer to make amends under this section may be withdrawn before it is accepted; and a renewal of an offer which has been withdrawn shall be treated as a new offer.

Section 3 describes how an offer may be accepted. Generally speaking, the 1996 Act gives the court the power to uphold any agreement between the parties and to decide certain terms that may remain unsettled, such as the amount of damages or costs. Most importantly, section 3(2) indicates that '[t]he party accepting the offer may not bring or continue defamation proceedings in respect of the publication concerned against the person making the offer, but he is entitled to enforce the offer to make amends'.

Section 4 is critical, in that it gives a defendant the means by which to either defend against a claim in defamation or mitigate any damages that may be awarded at trial. Section 4 also limits any defendant who chooses to rely on the offer to make amends to this defence only; although defendants may plead other defences in the alternative, this particular defence stands alone.

4 Failure to accept offer to make amends

(1) If an offer to make amends under section 2, duly made and not withdrawn, is not accepted by the aggrieved party, the following provisions apply.

(2) The fact that the offer was made is a defense (subject to subsection (3)) to defamation proceedings in respect of the publication in question by that party against the person making the offer. A qualified offer is only a defense in respect of the meaning to which the offer related.

(3) There is no such defense if the person by whom the offer was made knew or had reason to believe that the statement complained of—
    (a) referred to the aggrieved party or was likely to be understood as referring to him, and
    (b) was both false and defamatory of that party;
    but it shall be presumed until the contrary is shown that he did not know and had no reason to believe that was the case.

(4) The person who made the offer need not rely on it by way of defense, but if he does he may not rely on any other defense.
    If the offer was a qualified offer, this applies only in respect of the meaning to which the offer related.

(5) The offer may be relied on in mitigation of damages whether or not it was relied on as a defense.

In practice, the statutory defences have drastically decreased the number of defamation cases that reach the courts.

NOTE Section 4(3) of the 1996 Act protects against people maliciously making false statements and recanting them later, after the damage has been done.

14.5.4 **Absolute privilege**

There are certain utterances that are so important, as a matter of public policy, that society grants the speaker an absolute privilege to make the statement. These statements cannot form the basis of an action in defamation, even if they are, in fact, defamatory. Because the grant of protection is so broad, the areas protected are quite narrow. There are only three types of utterances given absolute privilege. They are:

* Parliamentary proceedings. Because the activities of Parliament may not be entered into evidence as per the Parliamentary Papers Act 1840, no statement made in parliamentary proceedings can form the grounds of a claim in defamation or be used to support or rebut a claim or defence relating to a defamatory statement made outside Parliament. However, section 13 of the Defamation Act 1996 allows an MP to waive these protections.

* Executive issues. In *Chatterton v Secretary of State for India* [1895] 2 QB 189, the Court of Appeal held that a letter from the Secretary of State for India to his Parliamentary Under-Secretary concerning parliamentary matters was absolutely privileged, thus laying the groundwork for the protection of communications between other high-ranking civil servants. The privilege is extended not only to those engaged in domestic affairs, but also to officials of other nations and of the European Union through the principle of international **comity**. It is unclear how senior a person must be before he or she may claim the privilege, but generally those at the level of minister and above are protected.

* Judicial proceedings and reports of judicial proceedings. The law protects not only statements made in court, but also those made in a court-like proceedings leading to a determination of truth which is a matter of public concern. Judges, parties, witnesses, barristers and solicitors all may claim the privilege. Furthermore, any document that is prepared as part of the proceeding is privileged, as are reports of the proceedings. Notably the Defamation Act 1996 extends its protections to include international bodies such as the European Court of Justice and international criminal tribunals established by the United Nations.

· ·

VOCABULARY

'Comity' means the respect given by one court to another. In this context, the British courts will give representatives of foreign governments privileges similar to those granted to representatives of the British government in those foreign courts.

· ·

14.5.5 **Qualified privilege**

The most important defence is that of qualified privilege. Here, society has an interest in protecting the speech, as with absolute privilege, but recognizes that there is a high risk of impropriety and abuse. Therefore, the law qualifies how and when the privilege may be invoked.

The general principles concerning the defence of qualified privilege were laid out in *Toogood v Spyring* (1834) 1 Cr M & R 181, a case involving a farmer who alleged that a journeyman that he had employed had both done shoddy work and had become drunk on the farmer's cider. There, the court stated the defendant is liable for a defamatory statement:

> unless it is fairly made by a person in the discharge of some public or private duty, whether legal or moral, or in the conduct of his own affairs, in matters where his interest is concerned. If fairly warranted by any reasonable occasion or exigency, and honestly made, such communications are protected for the common convenience and welfare of society; and the law has not restricted the right to make them within any narrow limits.

In this particular case, the court held that the farmer could claim a qualified privilege when making the statement to the estate carpenter (who oversaw the journeyman's work) on one occasion and to the plaintiff on another, even though the statement to the plaintiff was made in the presence of a third party. However, the farmer could not claim a qualified privilege when he made a similar statement to another employee, even though it was the same employee as was present when the statement was made to the plaintiff's face.

The privilege has also been described in *Adam v Ward* [1917] AC 309, a case dealing with a plaintiff, a member of Parliament, who had made false statements about his former general's command from the floor of the house of Commons. The general obtained the support of the Army Council, who published a letter to British and colonial press vindicating the general and containing defamatory statements about the plaintiff. The House of Lords held that the Council's statements were privileged on the grounds that a privilege exists 'where the person who makes a communication has an interest or a duty, legal, social, or moral, to make it to the person to whom it is made, and the person to whom it is so made has a corresponding interest or duty to receive it', thus intimating an element of reciprocity. There are a multitude of situations that fall within this broad definition, and the courts have recognized that the categories of the common law privilege are not yet closed.

NOTE Legal duties—which would be set out in statutes or cases—are easy to ascertain. Moral and social duties are more difficult to prove.

The law regarding qualified privilege made a quantum leap with the decision in *Reynolds v Times Newspapers* [2001] 2 AC 127. The case involved allegedly defamatory statements contained in an article published in Britain regarding the resignation of the Irish Taoiseach (prime minister), Albert Reynolds, following a political scandal. Although subsequent decisions have suggested that the case should be limited to situations concerning the media, no such limitation appears in the original decision. Instead, *Reynolds v Times Newspapers* [2001] 2 AC 127 supports a case-by-case analysis in any situation involving the defence of qualified privilege. In his opinion, Lord Nicholl set forth ten different elements that one should consider in cases involving qualified privilege.

● ***Reynolds v Times Newspapers*** [2001] 2 AC 127

Lord Nicholls of Birkenhead: As high-lighted by the Court of Appeal judgment in the present case, the common law solution is for the court to have regard to all the circumstances when deciding whether the publication of particular material was privileged because of its value to the public. Its value to the public depends upon its quality as well as its subject-matter. This solution has the merit of elasticity. As observed by the Court of Appeal, this principle can be applied appropriately to the particular circumstances of individual cases in their infinite variety. It can be applied appropriately to all information published by a newspaper, whatever its source or origin . . .

Depending on the circumstances, the matters to be taken into account include the following. The comments are illustrative only.

1. The seriousness of the allegation. The more serious the charge, the more the public is misinformed and the individual harmed, if the allegation is not true.
2. The nature of the information, and the extent to which the subject-matter is a matter of public concern.
3. The source of the information. Some informants have no direct knowledge of the events. Some have their own axes to grind, or are being paid for their stories.
4. The steps taken to verify the information.
5. The status of the information. The allegation may have already been the subject of an investigation which commands respect.
6. The urgency of the matter. News is often a perishable commodity.
7. Whether comment was sought from the plaintiff. He may have information others do not possess or have not disclosed. An approach to the plaintiff will not always be necessary.
8. Whether the article contained the gist of the plaintiff's side of the story.
9. The tone of the article. A newspaper can raise queries or call for an investigation. It need not adopt allegations as statements of fact.
10. The circumstances of the publication, including the timing.

This list is not exhaustive. The weight to be given to these and any other relevant factors will vary from case to case. Any disputes of primary fact will be a matter for the jury, if there is one. The decision on whether . . . the publication was subject to qualified privilege is a matter for the judge.

Reynolds v Times Newspapers [2001] 2 AC 127 caused quite a stir when it was handed down. Soon after, the Court of Appeal discussed its outer boundaries in *Loutchansky v Times Newspapers Ltd (Nos 4 and 5)* [2001] EWCA Civ 1804, [2002] QB 783, which involved published articles accusing the claimant of being involved in international criminal activities.

● *Loutchansky v Times Newspapers Ltd (Nos 4 and 5)*
   [2001] EWCA Civ 1804, [2002] QB 783

Lord Phillips of Worth Matravers MR: *Reynolds* privilege (as we shall call it), although built upon an orthodox foundation, is in reality *sui generis*.

Whereas previously it could truly be said of qualified privilege that it attaches to the occasion of the publication rather than the publication, *Reynolds* privilege attaches, if at all, to the publication itself: it is impossible to conceive of circumstances in which the occasion of publication could be privileged but the article itself not so. Similarly, once *Reynolds* privilege attaches, little scope remains for any subsequent finding of malice. Actual malice in this context has traditionally been recognized to consist either of recklessness i.e. not believing the statement to be true or being indifferent as to its truth, or of making it with the dominant motive of injuring the claimant. But the publisher's conduct in both regards must inevitably be explored when considering Lord Nicholls' ten factors i.e. in deciding whether the publication is covered by qualified privilege in the first place ...

Once the publication of a particular article is held to be in the public interest on the basis of the public's right to know, can the privilege really be lost because the journalist (or editor?) had the dominant motive of injuring the claimant rather than fulfilling his journalistic duty? It is a surprising thought.

According to the Court of Appeal, *Reynolds*-type privilege may, in fact, be distinct from other types of qualified privilege. Therefore, cases outside the context of media statements may still need to consider pre-*Reynolds* case law concerning the duty (legal, moral or social) to communicate information. This test is highly fact-specific. One can take a relatively broad view of a 'duty' and still fall within the privilege. For example, in *Watt v Longsdon* [1930] 1 KB 130, the Court of Appeal held that:

> A company director was held to be privileged in passing on to the chairman a report that an employee was associating with another woman and otherwise misconducting himself during his employment overseas, but he was not protected in informing the wife of the employee, although she had an interest in receiving that information.

In *Watt v Longsdon* [1930] 1 KB 130, the director had a duty to the company as a result of his professional relationship but had no corresponding duty to the wife of the misbehaving man. Notice how reciprocity existed between the company and the defendant— not only did the director have a duty to report the behaviour, but the company had an interest in hearing it.

The question of interest also arises in another category of cases falling under the qualified privilege. These cases involve statements to protect one of several particular interests. First, a person may receive a qualified privilege to speak in the public interest. For example, a person who gives information to the police to aid in a criminal investigation is protected by a qualified privilege. This encourages people to report crimes, since they do not have to worry about mistakenly defaming someone, and thus benefits society. The House of Lords noted in *Jameel (Mohammed) v Wall Street Journal Europe Sprl* [2006] UKHL 44 that a qualified privilege existed when a publication reported on a matter of public interest—in this case, possible terrorist links—and took reasonable steps to verify the truth of the matter reported. In this case, an experienced and specialist reporter had the article—which was written in a neutral, objective manner—approved by senior staff prior to publication. The paper sought a comment from the defendant prior to publication, but did not obtain a recorded comment in time. On these facts, Lord Bingham of Cornhill held that the test of reasonable journalism had been met.

Second, people may speak in their own interest. For example, *Turner v Metro-Goldwyn-Mayer Pictures Ltd* [1950] 1 All ER 449 involved a film critic whose reputation had been impugned when a film studio disagreed with her criticism and wrote a letter asking her employer, the BBC, not to allow her to review any more of its films.

> Lord Oaksey: [T]here is... an analogy between the criminal law of self defense and a man's right to defend himself against written or verbal [sic] attacks. In both cases he is entitled... to defend himself effectively, and he only loses the protection of the law if he goes beyond defense and proceeds to offence. That is to say, the circumstances in which he defends himself, either by acts or by words, negative the malice which the law draws from violent acts or defamatory words. If you are attacked with a deadly weapon you can defend yourself with a deadly weapon or with any other weapon which may protect your life. The law does not concern itself with niceties in such matters. If you are attacked by a prize fighter you are not bound to adhere to the Queensberry rules in your defense. The [film in question] was probably not as far-reaching as the appellant's voice on the B.B.C. wireless, nor could the respondents, so far as the evidence shows, command so pointed a pen as that of the appellant. They had, therefore, to adopt other means of defense, but provided that they were means of defense and not of offence or attack, they are not evidence of malice, but merely the adoption of the most effective method of defense available.

Third, people may speak in the common interest, such as when neither the public interest nor the speaker's interest carries sufficient weight to act as a defence on its own. For example, in *Hunt v Great Northern Rly Co* [1891] 2 QB 189, the Court of Appeal held that a common interest existed between an employer and its employees, thus creating a qualified privilege when the defendant posted a circular in the common view of the employees stating that the plaintiff had been dismissed for neglecting his duty.

A qualified privilege also exists as a matter of statute. Under section 15 of the Defamation Act 1996, various reports are subject to a qualified privilege. These reports can concern court and legislative proceedings, public inquiries, general meetings of public companies, associations and so on. However, section 15(2) states that a subset of those reports will not be subject to the defence of qualified privilege if the claimant asks the defendant to publish a letter of explanation or contradiction and the defendant refuses to do so. Section 15(4)(b) of the 1996 Act also preserves all pre-existing common law privileges.

The 1996 Act specifically states that malice will defeat the statutory defence of qualified privilege. The common law also holds that malice will defeat a qualified privilege. The only possible exception to the rule involves cases falling under *Reynolds v Times Newspapers* [2001] 2 AC 127, for the reasons discussed in *Loutchansky v Times Newspapers Ltd (No 2)* [2001] EWCA 1805, [2002] QB 783 (excerpted above).

Malice in defamation law carries a special meaning and may be proven by several means. First, a claimant can demonstrate malice—and thus negate the defendant's defence of qualified privilege—by showing that the defendant either (1) did not believe in the truth of the statement when it was made or (2) was reckless as to the truth or falsity of the statement when it was made. Therefore, when a defendant deliberately lies in the published statement, as occurred in *Fraser v Mirza*, 1993 SLT 527, when the defendant lied in a letter to the Chief Constable, complaining of the conduct of a constable in there can be no defence of qualified privilege. On the other hand, as long as the defendant believes in the truth of the statement, a defence may exist, even if the defendant's belief was irrational or based on prejudice. This position was supported by the House of Lords in *Horrocks v Lowe* [1975] AC 135, when an alderman on a city council made disparaging personal comments about a fellow councilmember in a council meeting. Lord Diplock defined malice in that case.

● *Horrocks v Lowe* [1975] AC 135

> Lord Diplock: [A]n example of state of mind which constitutes malice: 'A man may believe in the truth of a defamatory statement, and yet when he publishes it be reckless whether his belief be well founded or not'. If 'reckless' here means that the maker of the statement has jumped to conclusions which are irrational, reached without adequate enquiry or based on insufficient evidence, this is not enough to constitute malice if he nevertheless does believe in the truth of the statement itself. The only kind of recklessness which destroys privilege is indifference to its truth or falsity.

In *Horrocks v Lowe* [1975] AC 135, the defendant was held not to be acting with malice, as a matter of law, even though he admitted he held feelings of ill-will and spite towards the plaintiff. In coming to its decision, the House of Lords looked at what was the defendant's primary motive. In that case, the primary motive was not spite, but was instead political discourse at the city council meeting. If the relative weight of the motives were reversed—if, instead, the defendant acted primarily out of ill-will and spite—then the outcome might have been very different.

Finally, when considering malice, the judge and the jury have different roles. The judge determines as a matter of law whether the occasion is privileged and whether there is sufficient evidence of express malice for the issue to be given to the jury—in other words, whether there is any evidence on which a reasonable person could find malice. If so, then the jury decides the issue of fact.

14.5.6 Fair comment

To assert the defence of fair comment, the defendant must speak about a matter of public interest and the statement must constitute a comment upon true or privileged statements of fact. Furthermore, the comment must be made by someone who honestly believed the statements were true and who was not motivated by malice. Malice in the context of fair comment is defined the same way as it is in cases involving qualified privilege.

When saying the statement must touch on a matter of public interest, the defence obviously includes utterances regarding the public conduct of those who are in public offices. However, even public officials are entitled to keep some aspects of their lives private, and therefore the defence of fair comment will not apply to private conduct unless it affects personal characteristics (such as honesty or integrity) that would affect the official's public role.

Second, the statement must be based upon true facts, unless the facts are privileged in some other way. Sometimes it can be difficult to separate facts from opinion.

Nevertheless, courts must distinguish between the two, since the defence of fair comment requires a two step analysis, first regarding the truthfulness or privileged aspects of the facts and second regarding the nature of the opinion.

In the defence of justification, a defendant need not prove that each and every fact contained in the defamatory statement is true, so long as the statement is substantially true and the remaining untrue statements are not material. The same is true in the defence of fair comment, as described in section 6 of the Defamation Act 1952. Furthermore, the defence of fair comment relates only to statements of opinion, whereas the defence of justification relates to statements of both fact and opinion. Defendants who wish to justify a statement of opinion must not only prove that they honestly believed the statement was true, they must also prove that the statement—meaning the opinion itself—was true.

. . . .

● **Defamation Act 1952**

6 Fair comment

A defence of fair comment shall not fail by reason only that the truth of every allegation of fact is not proved if the expression of opinion is fair comment having regard to such of the facts alleged or referred to in the words complained of as are proved.

Just as with justification, a defendant may not assert a defence of fair comment if the statement was motivated by malice. Again, malice in this context does not require ill-will or spite. Instead, a defence of fair comment may only be raised if the defendant makes the statement honestly. As Lord Esher said in *Merivale v Carson* (1887) 20 QBD 275, a case involving the review of a play that contained an innuendo suggesting the play was immoral:

> Every latitude must be given to opinion and to prejudice, and then an ordinary set of men with ordinary judgment must say whether any fair man would have made such a comment on the work . . . Mere exaggeration, or even gross exaggeration, would not make the comment unfair. However wrong the opinion expressed may be in point of truth, or however prejudiced the writer, it may still be within the prescribed limit. The question which the jury must consider is this—would any fair man, however prejudiced he may be, however exaggerated or obstinate his views, have said that which this criticism has said of the work which is criticized?

Interestingly, if the comment is fair, objectively speaking, the defendant does not have to prove that he or she believes it to be fair. However, a defendant's lack of belief in the fairness of a comment may go to whether the defendant acted primarily with malice. Furthermore, even if the defendant truly believed in the statement, no defence will exist if the defendant acted with malice.

Again, judge and jury have different functions in determining whether the defence of fair comment exists. The jury decides what aspect of the statement is comment and what is fact. First, though, the judge must decide whether the words are capable of being a statement of fact or facts.

For more revision tips, including self-test questions and suggestions for further reading, see the Online Resource Centre at **www.oxfordtextbooks.co.uk/orc/strong_complete/**.

revision tasks

Defamation is an area of law where reasonable minds often can, and do, differ. Consider working with some of your classmates on the following revision tasks, since your colleagues' interpretations of various statements may highlight how differently a statement can be read.

- Identify which cases and which statutes apply to which aspects of the torts of defamation. Be sure to cross-reference those cases and those principles (such as malice) that relate to several different areas of the syllabus. Clarify in your mind the differences between the various defences and between the trickier elements of the claimant's affirmative case, such as the difference between true and false innuendo.

- Consider the law of privacy. What interests does it protect that defamation does not? What kind of case can you make for expanding the law of privacy? How would you do so?

- Now consider the role of the ordinary person in defamation. Does it still make sense to use that standard, given the heterogeneity of modern culture? What could the standard be replaced with? Would the jury still have a role in your ideal world?

Part 7

Product Liability

Product liability

15.1 Introduction

In this chapter, we consider when a claimant can recover damages in tort for a product that has a defect. There are two possible causes of action in tort in these circumstances: a common law cause of action in negligence and a statutory cause of action under the Consumer Protection Act 1987. There may also be a cause of action in contract for breach of an express or implied term, though contractual claims are outside the scope of this book.

15.2 Back to *Donoghue v Stevenson*: the 'narrow rule'

Chapter 2 discussed Lord Atkin's judgment in *Donoghue v Stevenson* [1932] AC 562, particularly as it concerned the 'neighbour principle' in negligence. As you recall, that case involved a partially decomposed snail found in a bottle of ginger beer by someone other than the purchaser of the beer. You will now read another extract from the same judgment, this time focusing not on general principles of negligence, but specifically on product liability. Lawyers now refer to Lord Atkin's remarks on this subject as the 'narrow rule in *Donoghue v Stevenson*'.

● ***Donoghue v Stevenson*** [1932] AC 562

NOTE 'Putting up' in this extract means packaging or getting ready for sale.

> Lord Atkin: My Lords, if your Lordships accept the view that this pleading discloses a relevant cause of action you will be affirming the proposition that by Scots and English law alike a manufacturer of products, which he sells in such a form as to show that he intends them to reach the ultimate consumer in the form in which they left him with no reasonable possibility of intermediate examination, and with the knowledge that the absence of reasonable care in the preparation or putting up of the products will result in an injury to the consumer's life or property, owes a duty to the consumer to take that reasonable care.

It is a proposition which I venture to say no-one in Scotland or England who was not a lawyer would for one moment doubt. It will be an advantage to make it clear that the law in this matter, as in most others, is in accordance with sound common sense. I think that this appeal should be allowed.

In order to be able to apply this rule, you need to know how the courts have interpreted its key words. In the next four sections, we will consider the meaning of the terms 'manufacturer', 'product', 'consumer' and 'intermediate examination', all of which are concepts central to an action in negligence relating to product liability.

15.2.1 'Manufacturer'

cross reference

Griffiths v Arch Engineering Co (Newport) Ltd [1968] 3 All ER 217 is discussed fully below.

In *Donoghue v Stevenson* [1932] AC 562, Lord Atkin only considered the liability of defendants who actually manufactured the product. However, case law has extended the narrow rule to other parties whose role in the production and distribution process seems similar in some way to manufacturing. For instance, the defendant may be someone who hired out the product to another user, as in *Griffiths v Arch Engineering Co (Newport) Ltd* [1968] 3 All ER 217. The defendant may also be someone who repaired the product, as in *Stennett v Hancock* [1939] 2 All ER 578. There, the defendant repaired a lorry, but a part flew off one of the wheels and injured a passer-by. The court found the defendant liable in negligence. Similarly, in *Howard v Furness Houlder Argentine Lines* [1936] 2 All ER 781, the defendants, who were repairing a boiler, fitted one of the parts upside down, which caused an explosion. The court held that the defendants were liable to a worker injured by steam that escaped from the boiler. In the rather macabre case of *Brown v Cotterill* (1934) 51 TLR 21, the defendants had been negligent in putting up a tombstone, which fell over and injured a child. Although this process can only loosely be compared to manufacturing, the court found the defendants liable. Finally, *Read v Croydon Corp* [1938] 4 All ER 631 held that water companies are another proper defendant, even though they clearly do not 'manufacture' the water they supply.

Eventually, the courts extended liability from manufacturers and those who act like manufacturers to those who simply supply the defective product. This was not always the case. One of the reasons Mrs Donoghue sued the manufacturer of the ginger beer in the first place was that the café-owner who supplied the ginger beer to her could not be held liable, because he had not created the danger. However, in some circumstances, suppliers can be sued even for dangers they have not created, as indicated in the extract below, which discusses the sale of a defective second-hand car.

● *Andrews v Hopkinson* [1957] 1 QB 229

McNair J: There was before me abundant evidence that in the case of an old car such as this the danger spot is in the steering mechanism and that this particular defect could have been discovered by a competent mechanic if the car had been jacked up. No such examination was in fact carried out, though the defendant, who had taken the car in part exchange, had had the car in his possession for a week or so. Having regard to the extreme peril involved in allowing an old car with a defective steering mechanism to be used on the road, I have no hesitation in holding that the defendant in the circumstances was guilty of negligence in failing to make the necessary examination, or at least in failing to warn the plaintiff that no such examination had been carried out.

Thus, suppliers can be liable under the common law if it would have been reasonable to expect them to inspect or test their products, or if they knew there was a danger and did not warn the buyer. In fact, in some cases the supplier will be liable to the exclusion of the manufacturer. This was true in *Kubach v Hollands* [1937] 3 All ER 907, which involved a packet labelled as a chemical called manganese dioxide. A teacher bought the product to use in a school lab. In fact, the packet contained a mixture of manganese dioxide and another chemical, which were dangerous in combination. The manufacturer had supplied the package to the seller with instructions to test the contents before selling it on, but the seller had not done so. When a pupil used the contents in an experiment, they exploded and injured her. Because the manufacturer had provided the supplier with specific instructions on how to safeguard customers from dangers caused by the product, which instructions the supplier had disregarded, the seller was liable to the pupil, but the manufacturer was not.

15.2.2 'Product'

Similarly, the courts interpret the term 'product' very widely. Anything that a person can buy and that can cause damage is likely to be considered a product. You can see some examples of 'products' in the table below. If any of these items are defective, a person who suffers loss or injury may be able to sue.

Figure 15.1

Some examples of products

Product	Case
Car	*Andrews v Hopkinson* [1957] 1 QB 229
Instructions accompanying a product	*Watson v Buckley, Osborne, Garrett & Co* [1940] 1 All ER 174
Lift	*Vacwell Engineering Co Ltd v BDH Chemicals Ltd* [1971] 1 QB 88
Packaging	*Barnes v Irwell Valley Water Board* [1939] 1 KB 21
Tombstone	*Brown v Cotterill* (1934) 51 TLR 21

The courts rarely have to consider disputes about the meaning of the word 'product', but they have had to consider in contract cases whether computer software is a 'good' or a 'service'. This suggests that similar issues could, at some point, arise in tort cases. In the dispute regarding software, one party argued that it should be classified as a service, because the buyer was purchasing the professional skill of the programmer and because it was installed directly onto the buyer's computer, rather than being supplied on a tangible item such as a disk. The other party argued the software was a 'good'. The outcome would probably have been the same if the question had been whether the software was a 'product', in the tort sense, or a service.

● **St Albans City Council v International Computers Ltd** [1996] 4 All ER 481

> Sir Iain Glidewell: There is no English authority on this question, and indeed we have been referred to none from any common law jurisdiction. The only reference I have found is an article published in 1994 by Dr Jane Stapleton. This is to a decision in *Advent Systems Ltd v Unisys Corp* (1991) 925 F 2d 670 that software is a 'good'; Dr Stapleton notes the decision as being reached 'on the basis of policy arguments'. We were referred, as was Scott Baker J, to a decision of Rogers J in the Supreme Court of New South Wales, *Toby Constructions Products Pty Ltd v Computa Bar (Sales) Pty Ltd* [1983] 2 NSWLR 48. The decision in that case was that the sale of a whole computer system, including both hardware and software, was a sale of 'goods' within the New South Wales legislation, which defines goods in similar terms to those in the English statute. That decision was in my respectful view clearly correct, but it does not answer the present question. Indeed, Rogers J specifically did not answer it. In expressing an opinion I am therefore venturing where others have, no doubt wisely, not trodden.
>
> Suppose I buy an instruction manual on the maintenance and repair of a particular make of car. The instructions are wrong in an important respect. Anybody who follows them is likely to cause serious damage to the engine of his car. In my view, the instructions are an integral part of the manual. The manual including the instructions, whether in a book or a video cassette, would in my opinion be 'goods' within the meaning of the 1979 Act, and the defective instructions would result in a breach of the implied terms in s 14.
>
> If this is correct, I can see no logical reason why it should not also be correct in relation to a computer disk onto which a program designed and intended to instruct or enable a computer to achieve particular functions has been encoded. If the disk is sold or hired by the computer manufacturer, but the program is defective, in my opinion there would prima facie be a breach of the terms as to quality and fitness for purpose implied by the 1979 Act or the 1982 Act.
>
> However, in the present case, it is clear that the defective program 2020 was not sold, and it seems probable that it was not hired. The evidence is that, in relation to many of the program releases, an employee of ICL went to St Albans' premises where the computer was installed taking with him a disk on which the new program was encoded, and himself performed the exercise of transferring the program into the computer.
>
> As I have already said, the program itself is not 'goods' within the statutory definition. Thus a transfer of the program in the way I have described does not, in my view, constitute a transfer of goods.

Thus, it seems that software will be a 'product' if it is bought on a disk, but not if it is installed by the supplier. It is not clear what approach the court would take to downloads from the internet, which were not common when *St Albans City Council v International Computers Ltd* [1996] 4 All ER 481 was decided.

15.2.3 'Consumer'

In order to sue in negligence for losses caused by a defective product, the potential claimant must be a 'consumer'. Obviously, this includes the person who ultimately uses the product, like Mrs Donoghue. However, it can also extend to other people. The test focuses on whether they are within the *Donoghue* definition of 'neighbour'. In other words, claimants must be people whom the defendant should reasonably have in mind as likely to be injured if the defendant was negligent in manufacturing or supplying the product. For instance, if the product is a car, then the term 'consumers' includes passengers and bystanders, as well as the driver and owner. For example, in *Stennett v Hancock* [1939] 2 All ER 578, the plaintiff was a passer-by who was injured after part of a lorry flew off and hit her. Similarly, in *Brown v Cotterill* (1934) 51 TLR 21, the 'consumer' was a child who was visiting a graveyard when a tombstone toppled over. In *Barnett v H and J Packer* [1940] 3 All ER 575, the plaintiff was a shopkeeper who, as he was putting some sweets out on the shelves, injured his finger on a piece of wire that was in one of the sweets. He was able to sue successfully.

15.2.4 'Intermediate examination'

As illustrated by *Kubach v Hollands* [1937] 3 All ER 907, which involved the explosive chemical mix sold to a school, the manufacturer will not be liable for a defective product if there was a reasonable possibility that the supplier, or someone else in the contractual chain of production and distribution, would discover the defect by examining the product before it reached the consumer. Liability can be avoided because the possibility of an intermediate examination makes it less foreseeable that anyone will be injured. In *Donoghue v Stevenson* [1932] AC 562, no such examination was possible because the bottle was made of opaque glass, meaning that the café-owner could not see the snail. Likewise, *Fisher v Harrods* [1966] 1 Lloyd's Rep 500 held that sellers of tinned foods could not be expected to examine the contents, since the sellers could not see inside the tin. To avoid liability, it was sufficient for the sellers to buy from a reputable supplier and store the tins hygienically.

cross reference
Griffiths v Arch Engineering Co (Newport) Ltd [1968] 3 All ER 217 is discussed above.

An example in a different context is *Griffiths v Arch Engineering Co (Newport) Ltd* [1968] 3 All ER 217. In that case, a company hired out a grinding machine to a contractor who was doing some work in a dockyard. The contractor allowed an employee from another company to use the machine, and the employee was injured. It turned out that the injury occurred because the owners had replaced a wheel in the machine with a new one that was the wrong size. The court found that the owners could not have expected the hirer to examine the machine for defects of this kind before allowing the employee to use it, and therefore the owners were liable for the injury.

Provided that the instructions supplied with the product are adequate, the defendant is probably entitled to assume that the consumer will follow them. For instance, in the Australian case of *Regal Pearl Pty Ltd v Stewart* [2002] NSWCA 291, an importer brought some frozen prawns into Australia and sold them on to a wholesaler, who in turn sold them on to a restaurant. After eating the prawns, some customers of the restaurant became ill, and it was discovered that the prawns had been contaminated with a virus. This was only dangerous if the prawns were not properly cooked. The court found the restaurant liable to the customers, so the restaurant in turn sued the wholesaler and the importer. The court decided that the wholesaler was liable in contract. In negligence, however, the court found the importer not liable because it could not have tested the prawns for the virus without destroying them, which meant there was effectively no possibility of intermediate examination by the importer. The importer could also not have foreseen that the prawns would not be cooked correctly.

15.2.5 **Warnings**

The case of *Kubach v Hollands* [1937] 3 All ER 907, which involved chemicals that exploded after being sold to a school, also illustrates that one way for potential defendants to avoid being in breach of their duty of care is to provide adequate warnings to consumers (or, in that case, intermediate sellers) about any features of the product that may be dangerous. In deciding whether a warning is adequate, the court takes into account how explicit the warning was, considering the degree of danger. In *Hurley v Dyke* [1979] RTR 265, for instance, a garage mechanic bought a car that he knew was not safe to drive, but that he thought he could sell for scrap. He sold it with the warning that he was selling it as seen and with all its faults. The buyer drove the car, and the chassis snapped, injuring his passenger. The House of Lords held that the mechanic knew in general terms that the car was not safe to drive without repairs, but did not know specifically that the chassis could snap. In these circumstances, the warning was sufficient, and the mechanic was not liable to the injured passenger. However, if he had known of the specific danger, he would have needed to give a more specific warning.

15.2.6 **Continuing duty**

The duty that manufacturers, suppliers and so on owe under the narrow rule in *Donoghue v Stevenson* [1932] AC 562 is a continuing one. This means the duty does not end when the product leaves the manufacturer or when the consumer buys it. If the manufacturer learns at a later date that the product may be dangerous, the manufacturer has a duty to take all reasonable steps to ensure that consumers are kept safe, even if the reason the product is dangerous is not the fault of the manufacturer. This often means recalling the product. Large manufacturers and distributors usually insure against the cost of such recalls.

15.2.7 **Breach**

Standard of care

The standard of care in product liability cases under the narrow rule in *Donoghue v Stevenson* [1932] AC 562 is the same as in negligence generally. Courts judge manufacturers by the standard of the reasonable manufacturer, suppliers by the standard of the reasonable supplier, and so on. Note that a breach can arise through an omission as well as an affirmative act.

Proving breach

The claimant in a product liability case has the burden of proving that there has been a breach of duty, just as in any other negligence case. However, in product liability cases it can be particularly difficult for the claimant to identify exactly what the defendant did wrong, because doing so can require a detailed knowledge of the manufacturing process. In *Grant v Australian Knitting Mills* [1936] AC 65, the Court of Appeal allowed the plaintiff to recover compensation for a skin rash that was probably caused by excessive sulphides in a pair of underpants. The plaintiff could not prove what level of sulphides was present in the underpants when they left the defendant's factory, but the court was prepared to give judgment for him on the balance of probabilities. Following that principle, a claimant usually proves breach simply by establishing that there is a defect in the product and that, on the balance of probabilities, it was not caused by anything that happened after the product left the defendant. This is sufficient for the courts to draw an inference of negligence based on the principle of *res ipsa loquitur*. For example, in *Mason v Williams & Williams* Ltd [1955] 1 WLR 549, the plaintiff was injured while using a chisel that was harder than it should have been. He was able to show that nothing had happened to make the chisel harder since it left the defendant's factory, so the court was willing to infer that the defendant had been negligent.

cross reference

Grant v Australian Knitting Mills [1936] AC 65 was discussed in chapter 4.

cross reference

Res ipsa loquitur was discussed in detail in chapter 4.

However, the defendant can try to overturn this inference. For instance, in *Daniels v R White and Sons* [1938] 4 All ER 258, a couple became ill after drinking lemonade that was contaminated with carbolic acid. The manufacturer overturned the inference of negligence by providing the court with detailed evidence of its bottling system to show that the acid could not have entered the bottle during that process. Furthermore, the longer the gap between the time the product left the defendant and the time the claimant suffered injury, the less likely it is that the courts will rely on an inference of negligence. For instance, in *Evans v Triplex Safety Glass Co* [1936] 1 All ER 283, the plaintiff's windscreen shattered for no apparent reason. However, because the windscreen was already a year old and because it was possible that the windscreen might have been damaged during installation rather than during the manufacturing process, the court was not prepared to infer that the manufacturer had been negligent.

15.2.8 Causation

The test for causation in product liability cases is the usual 'but for' test discussed in chapter 4. For instance, if the consumer misuses the product, the court may find that the defect was due to the misuse and not to any negligence by the manufacturer. Likewise, if the claimant knows of the defect before using the product, then the chain of causation is broken. Thus, there was no recovery in *Farr v Butters Bros* [1932] 2 KB 606 when a worker was killed while putting up a crane which he knew was defective. However, this principle may not apply if the claimant has no practical alternative to using the product. This supposition is based on an analogy with a case that was not about products, but about the negligent loading of a barge, *Denny v Supplies & Transport* [1932] 2 KB 374. In this case, a company employed the plaintiff to unload barges in the Port of London. On this occasion, the plaintiff noticed that the barge had been loaded in a dangerous way. However, there was no practical way of correcting this, so he went ahead and unloaded it, and was injured. The Court of Appeal found that the company that had loaded the barge was liable for his injuries.

15.2.9 Types of loss

As in any other negligence claim, the claimant in a product liability case must prove some loss in order to assert a claim successfully. It is not enough just to show that a product could cause loss—the product must actively have done so. For instance, in *D & F Estates v Church Commissioners for England* [1989] AC 177 the plaintiffs had leased a building and discovered that it had faulty plasterwork. They repaired the building to prevent any damage from occurring. They sought to recover the cost of the repairs, but the court denied recovery. Courts are generally reluctant to allow claims for pure economic loss, and product liability cases are no exception. The consequence of this in product liability cases is that claimants cannot recover compensation for any damage to the product itself, but instead may only claim for damage that the defective product causes to other property or for injuries that it causes to people. The cost of replacing or repairing the product itself is not recoverable. This means it is important to be able to distinguish what is part of the product and what is 'other property'. This is not always straightforward, as shown by *Aswan Engineering Establishment Co v Lupdine Ltd* [1987] 1 All ER 135, where the plaintiff bought a large quantity of a waterproofing compound. The seller shipped the compound to the plaintiff in large plastic pails. These pails turned out to be unsuitable, and they collapsed, spilling the entire load of waterproofing compound. If the compound and the pails constituted the same property, then the manufacturers of the pails would not be liable for the loss. However, if the compound and the pails counted as different property, the manufacturers would be liable for the loss. As it turned out, two of the three judges in the Court of Appeal thought the pails were different property. Therefore, the current law is that a claimant who buys something that is damaged by a defective container can sue the manufacturer of the container. However, the split decision illustrates how difficult it is to make fine distinctions of this type.

cross reference
Pure economic loss was discussed in chapter 13.

15.2.10 Defences

cross reference
See chapter 5 for more on defences to negligence.

Because a product liability claim under the narrow rule is a form of negligence claim, the same defences that are available in negligence claims generally are available here. Contributory negligence is a particularly common defence, as is consent. Liability can be limited or excluded by contract to the same extent as liability for any other kind of negligence claim.

15.3 Construction cases

Buildings are not normally considered to be 'products' for the purposes of the narrow rule. However, where a building is negligently designed or constructed, the issues concerning damages can be similar to those discussed earlier in this chapter. Pure economic loss can cause particular problems. For this reason, it is convenient to consider construction cases separately.

NOTE Some claim-
ants may also
proceed under the
Defective Premises
Act 1972, which
is discussed in
chapter 7.

The claimants in construction-oriented product liability cases are usually owners or
occupiers of the building. If they are owners, they are usually people who purchased the
building after the negligence had already occurred. Since parties who owned the building at the time when it was designed or constructed will usually sue in contract, issues
of pure economic loss will not arise. The defendants are most commonly either building
contractors or local authorities who are responsible for giving planning permission and
various other approvals for the buildings.

As discussed previously, claimants in product liability cases cannot recover compensation for damage to the product itself because those injuries are considered to be pure
economic loss. Claimants can recover compensation for damage to persons and to other
property, however. For instance, in *AC Billings & Sons v Riden* [1958] AC 240, a couple
hired building contractors to work on the front of their house. The contractors failed to
provide a safe way of getting in and out of the house during the works, and a visitor
was hurt while leaving the house. The court held the builders liable. Similarly, if someone buys a building which collapses because the foundations are unsound, the builders
may be liable for any injuries the purchaser suffers. However, builders do not have a
duty to prevent pure economic loss, so there can be difficulties if the purchaser's only
loss is that the building was not worth the purchase price, as suggested by *D & F Estates
v Church Commissioners for England* [1989] AC 177, which involved some plastering
that had been improperly done on a new block of flats, leading to pure economic loss
on behalf of the lessee, who repaired the faulty plastering. This also goes to the issue
of what constitutes 'the product' and what constitutes 'other property', since, as non-
construction cases show, claimants may only recover for losses to 'other property', not
the product itself.

....

● *D & F Estates v Church Commissioners for England* [1989] AC 177

Lord Bridge of Harwich: If the defect is discovered before any damage is done, the loss sustained by the owner of the structure, who has to repair or demolish it to avoid a potential
source of danger to third parties, would seem to be purely economic. Thus, if I acquire a
property with a dangerously defective garden wall which is attributable to the bad work-
manship of the original builder, it is difficult to see any basis in principle on which I can
sustain an action in tort against the builder for the cost of either repairing or demolishing
the wall. No physical damage has been caused. All that has happened is that the defect in
the wall has been discovered in time to prevent damage occurring . . .

My example of the garden wall, however, is that of a very simple structure. I can see that
more difficult questions may arise in relation to a more complex structure like a dwelling-
house. One view would be that such a structure should be treated in law as a single indivisible unit. On this basis, if the unit becomes a potential source of danger when a hitherto
hidden defect in construction manifests itself, the builder, as in the case of the garden wall,
should not in principle be liable for the cost of remedying the defect.

However, I can see that it may well be arguable that in the case of complex structures, as
indeed possibly in the case of complex chattels, one element of the structure should be
regarded for the purpose of the application of the principles under discussion as distinct
from another element, so that damage to one part of the structure caused by a hidden
defect in another part may qualify to be treated as damage to 'other property,' and

whether the argument should prevail may depend on the circumstances of the case. It would be unwise and it is unnecessary for the purpose of deciding the present appeal to attempt to offer authoritative solutions to these difficult problems in the abstract. I should wish to hear fuller argument before reaching any conclusion as to how far the decision of the New Zealand Court of Appeal in *Bowen v. Paramount Builders (Hamilton) Ltd.* should be followed as a matter of English law. I do not regard *Anns v Merton London Borough Council* as resolving that issue.

In the instant case the only hidden defect was in the plaster. The only item pleaded as damage to other property was 'cost of cleaning carpets and other possessions damaged or dirtied by falling plaster; £50'. Once it appeared that the plaster was loose, any danger of personal injury or of further injury to other property could have been simply avoided by the timely removal of the defective plaster. The only function of plaster on walls and ceilings, unless it is itself elaborately decorative, is to serve as a smooth surface on which to place decorative paper or paint. Whatever case there may be for treating a defect in some part of the structure of a building as causing damage to 'other property' when some other part of the building is injuriously affected, as for example cracking in walls caused by defective foundations, it would seem to me entirely artificial to treat the plaster as distinct from the decorative surface placed upon it.

cross reference

Anns v Merton London Borough Council [1978] AC 728 was discussed at length in chapter 7.

cross reference

Murphy v Brentwood District Council [1990] 2 All ER 908 was also discussed in chapter 7.

The builders here were not liable because the court felt that the damaged part was essentially the same as the part that contained the defect. The question the House of Lords did not decide was whether there could be liability where one part of a building caused damage to another part. The question was answered in *Murphy v Brentwood District Council* [1990] 2 All ER 908, which involved a house that had been built with a faulty foundation, leading to a drop in the value of the house.

● ***Murphy v Brentwood District Council*** [1990] 2 All ER 908

Lord Keith of Kinkel: Counsel for the council did not seek to argue that a local authority owes no duty at all to persons who might suffer injury through a failure to take reasonable care to secure compliance with building byelaws. He was content to accept that such a duty existed but maintained that its scope did not extend beyond injury to person or health and (possibly) damage to property other than the defective building itself. Not having heard argument on the matter, I prefer to reserve my opinion on the question whether any duty at all exists. So far as I am aware, there has not yet been any case of claims against a local authority based on injury to person or health through a failure to secure compliance with building byelaws. If and when such a case arises, that question may require further consideration. The present problem is concerned with the scope of the duty. The question is whether the defendant council owed the plaintiff a duty to take reasonable care to safeguard him against the particular kind of damage which he has in fact suffered, which was not injury to person or health nor damage to anything other than the defective house itself... However, an essential feature of the species of liability in negligence established by *Donoghue v Stevenson* was that the carelessly manufactured product should be intended to reach the injured consumer in the same state as that in which it was put up with no reasonable prospect of intermediate examination... It is the latency of the defect which constitutes the mischief...

The jump which is here made from liability under the *Donoghue v Stevenson* principle for damage to person or partly caused by a latent defect in a carelessly manufactured article to liability for the cost of rectifying a defect in such an article which is ex hypothesi no longer latent is difficult to accept...The loss is economic. It is difficult to draw a distinction in principle between an article which is useless or valueless and one which suffers from a defect which would render it dangerous in use but which is discovered by the purchaser in time to avert any possibility of injury. The purchaser may incur expense in putting right the defect, or, more probably, discard the article. In either case the loss is purely economic...In *D & F Estates Ltd v Church Comrs for England*...Lord Bridge suggested that in the case of a complex structure such as a building one element of the structure might be regarded for *Donoghue v Stevenson* purposes as distinct from another element, so that damage to one part of the structure caused by a hidden defect in another part might qualify to be treated as damage to 'other property'...I think that it would be unrealistic to take this view as regards a building the whole of which had been erected and equipped by the same contractor. In that situation the whole package provided by the contractor would, in my opinion, fall to be regarded as one unit rendered unsound as such by a defect in the particular part. On the other hand, where, for example, the electric wiring had been installed by a sub-contractor and due to a defect caused by lack of care a fire occurred which destroyed the building, it might not be stretching ordinary principles too far to hold the electrical sub-contractor liable for the damage.

Lord Bridge of Harwich: The reality is that the structural elements in any building form a single indivisible unit of which the different parts are essentially interdependent. To the extent that there is any defect in one part of the structure it must to a greater or lesser degree necessarily affect all other parts of the structure. Therefore any defect in the structure is a defect in the quality of the whole and it is quite artificial, in order to impose a legal liability which the law would not otherwise impose, to treat a defect in an integral structure, so far as it weakens the structure, as a dangerous defect liable to cause damage to 'other property'...

Lord Jauncey of Tullichettle: My Lords, I agree with the views of my noble and learned friend Lord Bridge in this appeal that to apply the complex structure theory to a house so that each part of the entire structure is treated as a separate piece of property is quite unrealistic. A builder who builds a house from foundations upwards is creating a single integrated unit of which the individual components are interdependent. To treat the foundations as a piece of property separate from the walls or the floors is a wholly artificial exercise. If the foundations are inadequate the whole house is affected. Furthermore, if the complex structure theory is tenable there is no reason in principle why it should not also be applied to chattels consisting of integrated parts such as a ship or a piece of machinery. The consequences of such an application would be far reaching. It seems to me that the only context for the complex structure theory in the case of a building would be where one integral component of the structure was built by a separate contractor and where a defect in such a component had caused damage to other parts of the structure, eg a steel frame erected by a specialist contractor which failed to give adequate support to floors or walls. Defects in such ancillary equipment as central heating boilers or electrical installations would be subject to the normal *Donoghue v Stevenson* principle if such defects gave rise to damage to other parts of the building.

Based on this decision, it seems that, in construction cases, builders are only liable to later purchasers or occupiers if the defect causes personal injury, damage to property that is not part of the building, or damage to a part of the building that was built or installed by a different contractor. In addition, the defect in the building must have been a **latent** one, i.e. one that could not reasonably have been discovered by inspection. If the defect could reasonably have been discovered, then the builders are not liable. In *Baxall Securities Ltd v Sheard Walshaw Partnership* (2001) TCC 36, the court extended this principle from building contractors to architects. This was a case where an architect negligently designed a drainage system that did not have overflows and therefore could not cope with unusually heavy rainfall or blockages in the main pipes. The Court of Appeal held that this was a defect that the owners of the building could have discovered by inspecting the drains. Therefore, the architect was not liable to the occupiers.

Cases prior to *Murphy v Brentwood District Council* [1990] 2 All ER 908 took a different approach, but the courts now treat those cases as confined to their own facts. Two you should know about are *Anns v Merton London Borough Council* [1978] AC 728 and *Junior Books v Veitchi* [1983] 1 AC 520. In the former, some tenants sued a local council after one of its building inspectors approved some foundations that were, in fact, defective. Because of the defect, the rest of the building—a block of flats—developed cracks. The House of Lords held that the tenants of the flats could recover damages from the council on the basis that the foundations had caused damage to the rest of the building. However, the Lords did not consider the issue of economic loss in any detail, and since the decision in *Murphy v Brentwood District Council* [1990] 2 All ER 908, it is no longer safe to rely on *Anns v Merton London Borough Council* [1978] AC 728.

Junior Books v Veitchi [1983] 1 AC 520 was a Scottish case, but it also had an impact in England because it reached the House of Lords. In this case, a specialist subcontractor laid a floor in a factory. The floor cracked, and the owners of the factory sued the subcontractor for the cost of repairs and various incidental costs such as moving machinery to allow access to the floor, loss of profits while the repairs were done, etc. Although these were purely economic losses, the House of Lords allowed the factory owners to recover them on the basis that there was sufficient proximity between the owners and the subcontractor to create a duty to prevent economic loss. The factory owners had relied on the subcontractor's skill and expertise. This case has never been followed, with courts generally taking the view that it turned on an unusual degree of reliance by the owners on the subcontractor. It is now generally regarded as an anomaly in the history of negligence law, and *Murphy v Brentwood District Council* [1990] 2 All ER 908 should be considered as controlling.

15.4 The Consumer Protection Act 1987

15.4.1 Introduction

Those who have been injured by a defective product need not only rely on common negligence principles. Potential claimants can also look to the Consumer Protection Act 1987, which was enacted to comply with European Council Directive 85/374/EEC of

25 July 1985 on the approximation of the laws, regulations and administrative provisions of the Member States concerning liability for defective products (EC Directive 85/374). Section 1 of the 1987 Act expressly states that '[t]his Part shall have effect for the purpose of making such provision as is necessary in order to comply with the product liability Directive and shall be construed accordingly'. There are very few cases decided under the 1987 Act or EC Directive 85/374, but the key parts of the 1987 Act are considered below. The discussion will clarify the extent to which a statutory claim differs from a common law claim under the narrow rule.

15.4.2 Potential claimants

Potential claimants under the 1987 Act are referred to only as 'the person[s] who suffered the damage'. This means that the range of potential claimants is wider under the statute than under the common law. Under the 1987 Act, anyone can sue who has suffered damage caused by a defect in a product. It does not matter whether or not the defendant should reasonably have had that person in mind, as is true under the narrow rule in *Donoghue v Stevenson* [1932] AC 562.

15.4.3 Potential defendants

Section 2 of the 1987 Act discusses potential defendants.

● **Consumer Protection Act 1987**

2 Liability for defective products

(1) Subject to the following provisions of this Part, where any damage is caused wholly or partly by a defect in a product, every person to whom subsection (2) below applies shall be liable for the damage.

(2) This subsection applies to—
   (a) the producer of the product;
   (b) any person who, by putting his name on the product or using a trade mark or other distinguishing mark in relation to the product, has held himself out to be the producer of the product;
   (c) any person who has imported the product into a member state from a place outside the member States in order, in the course of any business of his, to supply it to another.

(3) Subject as aforesaid, where any damage is caused wholly or partly by a defect in a product, any person who supplied the product (whether to the person who suffered the damage, to the producer of any product in which the product in question is comprised or to any other person) shall be liable for the damage if—
   (a) the person who suffered the damage requests the supplier to identify one or more of the persons (whether still in existence or not) to whom subsection (2) above applies in relation to the product;
   (b) that request is made within a reasonable period after the damage occurs and at a time when it is not reasonably practicable for the person making the request to identify all those persons; and

> (c) the supplier fails, within a reasonable period after receiving the request, either to comply with the request or to identify the person who supplied the product to him.

'Producer' is defined in section 1(2) of the 1987 Act.

. . . .

● **Consumer Protection Act 1987**

1 Purpose and construction of Part I

(2) In this Part, except in so far as the context otherwise requires—... 'producer', in relation to a product, means—

   (a) the person who manufactured it;

   (b) in the case of a substance which has not been manufactured but has been won or abstracted, the person who won or abstracted it;

   (c) in the case of a product which has not been manufactured, won or abstracted but essential characteristics of which are attributable to an industrial or other process having been carried out (for example, in relation to agricultural produce), the person who carried out that process.

The potential defendants set out in section 2 of the 1987 Act are thus the producer (which means the manufacturer); anyone who puts their own brand on the product (usually known as an 'own-brander'); anyone who imports the product into the European Union (usually referred to for convenience as an 'importer'); and a supplier who is unable to identify the others involved in the chain of supply (often called a 'forgetful supplier'). This is a narrower range of potential defendants than under the common law rule.

Note that the following persons are not covered under these definitions and therefore cannot be sued under the 1987 Act:

* Someone who imports a product from one EU member state into another;

* Someone who imports or exports a product from an EU member state to a non-member state; and

* Suppliers who identify one of the parties above them in the chain (even if they cannot identify all of them).

A person who supplies a component part that is integrated into another product can be sued for defects in the component, but not for defects in the wider product. Likewise, according to section 1(3) of the 1987 Act, the person who supplies the wider product can be sued for defects that relate to the whole product—defective design of the way the components fit together, for instance—but cannot be sued for defects in components supplied by someone else.

. . . .

● **Consumer Protection Act 1987**

1 Purpose and construction of Part I

(3) For the purposes of this Part a person who supplies any product in which products are comprised, whether by virtue of being component parts or raw materials or otherwise, shall not be treated by reason only of his supply of that product as supplying any of the products so comprised.

15.4.4 'Damage'

The 'damage' that is recoverable under the 1987 Act is set out in section 5.

● **Consumer Protection Act 1987**

5 Damage giving rise to liability

(1) Subject to the following provisions of this section, in this Part 'damage' means death or personal injury or any loss of or damage to any property (including land).

(2) A person shall not be liable under section 2 above in respect of any defect in a product for the loss of or any damage to the product itself or for the loss of or any damage to the whole or any part of any product which has been supplied with the product in question comprised in it.

(3) A person shall not be liable under section 2 above for any loss of or damage to any property which, at the time it is lost or damaged, is not—
   (a) of a description of property ordinarily intended for private use, occupation or consumption; and
   (b) intended by the person suffering the loss or damage mainly for his own private use, occupation or consumption.

(4) No damages shall be awarded to any person by virtue of this Part in respect of any loss of or damage to any property if the amount which would fall to be so awarded to that person, apart from this subsection and any liability for interest, does not exceed £275.

(5) In determining for the purposes of this Part who has suffered any loss of or damage to property and when any such loss or damage occurred, the loss or damage shall be regarded as having occurred at the earliest time at which a person with an interest in the property had knowledge of the material facts about the loss or damage.

(6) For the purposes of subsection (5) above the material facts about any loss of or damage to any property are such facts about the loss or damage as would lead a reasonable person with an interest in the property to consider the loss or damage sufficiently serious to justify his instituting proceedings for damages against a defendant who did not dispute liability and was able to satisfy a judgment.

(7) For the purposes of subsection (5) above a person's knowledge includes knowledge which he might reasonably have been expected to acquire—
   (a) from facts observable or ascertainable by him; or
   (b) from facts ascertainable by him with the help of appropriate expert advice which it is reasonable for him to seek;
   but a person shall not be taken by virtue of this subsection to have knowledge of a fact ascertainable by him only with the help of expert advice unless he has failed to take all reasonable steps to obtain (and, where appropriate, to act on) that advice.

Thus, 'damage' under the 1987 Act includes personal injury (regardless of value) and property damage, provided the property damage:

• Exceeds £275 (only the excess over this figure is recoverable, so if the damage is £300, the claimant can only recover £25);

- Does not relate to business property (since the 1987 Act is primarily intended to protect consumers); and

- Does not relate to the cost of repairing or replacing the product itself. As under the common law's narrow rule, damage to the product itself is not recoverable under the 1987 Act, since such damage is considered to be pure economic loss. A 'product' for these purposes is the whole item, even if only a component part is defective. In other words, if a component part is defective, but the only damage is to the component and other parts of the item, there is no claim. It is not clear whether a consumer can claim if defective packaging causes damage to the product, since there are no reported cases on the point.

Note that under the narrow rule under *Donoghue v Stevenson* [1932] AC 562, there is no lower limit for the amounts that can be recovered. There is also no distinction between business property and personal property. This means that there is no generally applicable answer as to whether the 1987 Act or the narrow rule is better for claimants. It depends on the circumstances of the individual claim.

15.4.5 'Caused by'

As with the narrow rule, the test for causation is the usual 'but for' test, although this is not actually specified in the 1987 Act.

15.4.6 'Defect'

Section 3 explains when a product has a 'defect' under the 1987 Act.

. . . .

● **Consumer Protection Act 1987**

3 Meaning of 'defect'

(1) Subject to the following provisions of this section, there is a defect in a product for the purposes of this Part if the safety of the product is not such as persons generally are entitled to expect; and for those purposes 'safety', in relation to a product, shall include safety with respect to products comprised in that product and safety in the context of risks of damage to property, as well as in the context of risks of death or personal injury.

(2) In determining for the purposes of subsection (1) above what persons generally are entitled to expect in relation to a product all the circumstances shall be taken into account, including—

    (a) the manner in which, and purposes for which, the product has been marketed, its get-up, the use of any mark in relation to the product and any instructions for, or warnings with respect to, doing or refraining from doing anything with or in relation to the product;

    (b) what might reasonably be expected to be done with or in relation to the product; and

    (c) the time when the product was supplied by its producer to another;

> and nothing in this section shall require a defect to be inferred from the fact alone that the safety of a product which is supplied after that time is greater than the safety of the product in question.

Thus, a 'defect' under section 3 of the statute is something that makes the product less safe than the consumer is entitled to expect. This is a narrower meaning than the word normally has in English, although the effect is probably the same as under the common law rule, since it is difficult to imagine a product causing loss without its being unsafe in some way.

There have been few reported decisions on this point. For example, in *Bogle v McDonald's Restaurants Limited* [2002] EWHC 490 (QB), the court decided that hot drinks served by McDonald's in plastic cups with lids were not defective, because it was clear that consumers wanted their drinks to be served hot and therefore would not reasonably expect them to be served at a lower temperature for safety's sake. The court said that the 1987 Act should not be used to deny consumers a convenience that they wanted. In contrast, *Abouzaid v Mothercare (UK)* [2000] All ER (D) 2436 held in favour of a 12-year-old boy who injured his eye while helping his mother fasten a sleeping-bag to his brother's push-chair. The fastenings were elastic, and one of the hooks snapped back and caught him in the eye. The court found that the sleeping-bag was less safe than consumers would reasonably expect and could have been made safe by supplying instructions advising consumers on how to position themselves so that the fastenings could not catch them in this way.

NOTE The claimants in *Bogle v McDonald's* also sued in negligence, and the court made similar observations regarding the narrow rule in *Donoghue v Stevenson*.

The court also considered the meaning of 'defect' in *A v National Blood Authority* [2001] 3 All ER 289. This case was brought by people who had received blood transfusions using blood that was infected with hepatitis C, a liver disease. At the time of the transfusions, scientists had not yet discovered the virus that causes hepatitis C, and the blood transfusion service had no way of detecting it. The authority said that the court had to consider, in deciding what level of safety could reasonably have been expected, what more could have been done. However, the claimants argued that the 1987 Act is intended to impose liability irrespective of fault and that considering what could have been done by the defendant would 'let fault in by the back door'. The claimants also argued that, where the defect is not present in the 'standard product'—i.e. where the defect is not part of the design—the product should automatically be considered defective. In this case, blood did not normally carry the hepatitis C virus. The court did not agree with either of those suggestions, although it did think that liability was probably more likely in the case of a non-standard product than in the case of a standard one. The court therefore had to go on to consider whether the authority had a defence to the claim, which will be discussed in the section on defences below.

XYZ v Schering Health Care [2002] EWHC 1420 also considered whether a medical product, in this case a new contraceptive pill, was less safe than consumers were entitled to expect and was therefore defective. The concern was that the new pill was more likely to cause dangerous blood clots than similar pills on the market. The parties agreed that the pill would be defective if the risk of such clots from taking the new pill was at least double the risk from taking existing pills. On that definition, and on the specific facts of this case, the court found that the new pill was not defective. However, this case is not necessarily a good guide to how much of an increase in risk there must be before a new product can be considered defective. The risk of a blood clot when taking the existing pills was very small, so asking whether a new pill doubled the risk may well have been a reasonable approach. It might be less reasonable if the risk were much larger to start with. Also, the court might have taken a different approach if the parties had not agreed between themselves that the key to the case was whether the new pill doubled the risk.

Under section 3(2) of the 1987 Act, the factors which the courts must take into account in deciding what a consumer can expect from a product are (1) how the product is presented, (2) the instructions and warnings which are supplied with the product, (3) how the product is expected to be used, and (4) how old the product is. These factors are very similar to those which the courts take into account under the narrow common law rule.

15.4.7 'Product'

'Product' has quite a broad definition under section 1(2) of the 1987 Act.

• **Consumer Protection Act 1987**

> **1 Purpose and construction of Part I**
>
> (2)…
>
> (c)…'product' means any goods or electricity and (subject to subsection (3) below) includes a product which is comprised in another product, whether by virtue of being a component part or raw material or otherwise;

'Goods' is defined in section 45(1) of the statute and includes substances, crops and things attached to land (which probably includes components of a building, but not the building as whole), and all kinds of vehicles, One interesting example of a 'substance' is blood for transfusion, which was treated as a product in *A v National Blood Authority* [2001] 3 All ER 289, the hepatitis C case. There, the parties agreed to that characterization, but there is no indication in the judgment that the court thought otherwise.

An item remains a 'product' even if it is incorporated as a component part into another product; thus, the manufacturer of a component part can still be sued if the part is defective. Information, on the other hand, is probably not a 'product', so a reader could not sue under the 1987 Act if a book contained inaccurate information. Although software technically consists of information, it may be an exception to this principle, especially if it is contained on a disk. As discussed at the beginning of this chapter, software on a disk has been found to be considered 'goods' for the purposes of the Sale of Goods Act 1979, so it would be consistent if the same approach applied under the Consumer Protection Act 1987.

think point
What policy considerations are at stake here?

15.4.8 The nature of liability under the 1987 Act

Unlike the narrow rule under *Donoghue v Stevenson* [1932] AC 562, the 1987 Act does not concern itself with whether or not the manufacturer has been careless. There is no mention of duties of care, negligence, or other such terms in the statute. Liability under the 1987 Act is often referred to as 'strict', which means that it does not matter whether or not the defendant was at fault. The justification for this approach is that it is considered fairer for any risks associated with the product to be borne by the manufacturer, who stands to profit by selling the product, rather than by the consumer.

NOTE There is some debate as to whether the characterization of liability as 'strict' is technically correct in this case.

15.4.9 Defences

A number of defences are provided under section 4 of the 1987 Act.

● **Consumer Protection Act 1987**

4 Defences

(1) In any civil proceedings by virtue of this Part against any person ('the person proceeded against') in respect of a defect in a product it shall be a defence for him to show—

   (a) that the defect is attributable to compliance with any requirement imposed by or under any enactment or with any Community obligation; or

   (b) that the person proceeded against did not at any time supply the product to another; or

   (c) that the following conditions are satisfied, that is to say—

      (i) that the only supply of the product to another by the person proceeded against was otherwise than in the course of a business of that person's; and

      (ii) that section 2(2) above does not apply to that person or applies to him by virtue only of things done otherwise than with a view to profit; or

   (d) that the defect did not exist in the product at the relevant time; or

   (e) that the state of scientific and technical knowledge at the relevant time was not such that a producer of products of the same description as the product in question might be expected to have discovered the defect if it had existed in his products while they were under his control; or

   (f) that the defect—

      (i) constituted a defect in a product ('the subsequent product') in which the product in question had been comprised; and

      (ii) was wholly attributable to the design of the subsequent product or to compliance by the producer of the product in question with instructions given by the producer of the subsequent product.

(2) In this section 'the relevant time', in relation to electricity, means the time at which it was generated, being a time before it was transmitted or distributed, and in relation to any other product, means—

   (a) if the person proceeded against is a person to whom subsection (2) of section 2 above applies in relation to the product, the time when he supplied the product to another;

(b) if that subsection does not apply to that person in relation to the product, the time when the product was last supplied by a person to whom that subsection does apply in relation to the product.

Each of these defences is briefly explained below.

Legal compliance

Under section 4(1)(a) of the 1987 Act, a defendant will not be liable if the defect has been caused as a result of the manufacturer's complying with a legal requirement. For instance, if the law requires manufacturers to add vitamins to a certain food, and the vitamins later turn out to be harmful to some groups of people, the manufacturers will not be liable to any injured parties.

No supply

The defendant is not liable if he or she did not in fact supply the product. For instance, it may have been supplied to the claimant without the defendant's consent—e.g. if the product was stolen from the manufacturer.

Supply not in the course of business

Under section 4(1)(c) of the 1987 Act, the defendant is also not liable if the supply of the product does not take place in a business context—for instance, there might be an exchange between friends, or something might be donated for charity.

No defect at time of supply

If the product was not defective when it left the defendant, then the defendant is not liable, according to section 4(1)(d) of the 1987 Act. For instance, the consumer may have made alterations that left the product unsafe, or the danger may be the result of normal wear and tear. In the first reported case on this defence, *Piper v JRI (Manufacturing)* [2006] EWCA Civ 1344, the cause of the defect was unknown. The product was a replacement hip which had fractured six months after the operation inserting it into the claimant's body. The manufacturer was able to produce enough evidence of its production and inspection processes to convince the court that the defect was not present when the manufacturer supplied the artificial hip to the patient's hospital. The Court of Appeal confirmed that the manufacturer did not have to demonstrate the true cause of the defect in order to rely on the defence.

Component parts

Section 4(1)(f) of the 1987 Act indicates that if a producer manufactures components which are incorporated into another product, the producer can defend itself by showing that its components were not defective and that it is the design of the other parts of the product, or instructions given to the producer of the component by the producer of the larger product, that made the product as a whole unsafe. This is the mirror image of the principle in section 1(3) of the 1987 Act, indicating that the person who supplies the wider product can be sued for defects that relate to the whole product, but not for defects in components supplied by someone else.

Development risks

NOTE *A v National Blood Authority* [2001] 3 All ER 289 was also discussed in connection with the discussion of the definition of terms such as 'product' and 'defect'.

The development risks defence, described in section 4(1)(e) of the 1987 Act, is the most controversial of the defences available under the statute. This defence requires the defendant to prove that the defect was of a kind that a producer in the relevant industry could not have been expected to discover, given the scientific and technical means available at the time the product was supplied. The defence was included in the statute because without it, there was a risk that the 1987 Act would discourage innovation in design and manufacturing. This defence was used in *A v National Blood Authority* [2001] 3 All ER 289, which was brought by people who had received blood transfusions using blood that was infected with hepatitis C, a liver disease. At the time of the transfusions, scientists knew that there was a risk of hepatitis C being transmitted in this way, but there was no way of detecting the hepatitis C virus in any particular blood sample. The National Blood Authority argued that they were therefore entitled to rely on the development risks defence. However, the claimants countered by saying that this defence only applied where the risk itself was unknown, rather than merely the means of detecting it in a particular product, and the court agreed with the claimants.

cross reference

Abouzaid v Mothercare (UK) [2000] All ER (D) 2436 was discussed above in the section on defects.

The development risks defence was also argued unsuccessfully in *Abouzaid v Mothercare (UK)* [2000] All ER (D) 2436, which involved a boy injuring his eye when a sleeping-bag hook snapped back into his face while he was fastening the sleeping-bag to his brother's pushchair. Mothercare argued that, because no similar accident had been reported in the past, the state of technical knowledge at the time did not allow it to take steps to prevent the accident. The court held that previous accident reports were not within the meaning of 'technical knowledge' for the purposes of the statute, and thus Mothercare was liable.

think point

What policy considerations support the producer bearing the risk of loss? What policies suggest the consumers should bear the risk of loss?

As the preceding cases suggest, the development risks defence is rather controversial, partly because of the difficulty of judging when a producer could be expected to discover a defect or cure for a defect and partly because many commentators feel that the producer should bear the risk of any scientific uncertainty. As it currently stands, consumers bear the risk of scientific or technical uncertainties.

Contributory negligence

cross reference

Contributory negligence was discussed in chapter 5.

Section 6 of the 1987 Act addresses the defence of contributory negligence.

● **Consumer Protection Act 1987**

6 Application of certain enactments

(4) Where any damage is caused partly by a defect in a product and partly by the fault of the person suffering the damage, the Law Reform (Contributory Negligence) Act 1945 and section 5 of the Fatal Accidents Act 1976 (contributory negligence) shall have effect as if the defect were the fault of every person liable by virtue of this Part for the damage caused by the defect.

This means that contributory negligence is available as a defence to claims under the 1987 Act in the usual way.

Exclusion of liability

According to section 7, liability under the 1987 Act cannot be limited or excluded. This is consistent with the aim of protecting consumers, since any exclusion or limitation would be to their detriment.

Limitation periods

You will not normally need to know about limitation periods in detail for a tort course, but you should be aware that Schedule 1 of the 1987 Act amended the Limitation Act 1980 by adding a new section. Under this provision (section 11A of the 1980 Act), claims under the 1987 Act must be brought within three years of the time the damage or injury occurred, or within three years of the time the claimant became aware of the key facts that gave rise to the claim, whichever is later. Section 12 of the Limitation Act 1980 gives a detailed definition of the key facts that the claimant must be aware of to start the three-year period. Broadly speaking, the relevant facts are that the injury or damage was significant and that it was caused by the defendant. There is also a ten-year 'long-stop' period after which no claim can be made, even if the claimant does not acquire the knowledge of the key facts until after that time has run. The purpose of a longstop period is to give manufacturers and their insurers some degree of certainty about when possible claims will end. For causes of action under the common law regarding product liability, the same rules apply if the claim is for personal injuries (by virtue of section 11 of the Limitation Act 1980). However, if the claim is for damage to property, section 14A of the 1980 Act indicates the limitation period is six years from the date when the damage occurred, or three years from the date when the claimant knows sufficient facts to justify instituting proceedings, including that the damage was caused by the defendant.

15.4.10 Differences between the 1987 Act and the EC Directive 85/374

Although the 1987 Act was introduced to implement EC Directive 85/374, various commentators have suggested that it did not do so effectively. The European Court of Justice considered the issue in *European Commission v United Kingdom* [1997] All ER (EC) 481. In this case, the Commission argued that section 4(1)(e) of the 1987 Act did not properly implement Article 7(e) of EC Directive 85/374, which stated that a producer should not be liable if 'the state of scientific and technical knowledge at the time when he put the product into circulation was not such as to enable the existence of the defect to be discovered.' When EC Directive 85/374 was adopted, the UK Government stated that this provision should be interpreted to mean that the producer should not be liable if, 'given the state of scientific knowledge at the time the product was put into circulation, no producer of a product of that kind could have been expected to have perceived that it was defective in its design', which is a rather wider statement than that contained in EC Directive 85/374. As it turned out, section 4(e) of the 1987 Act eventually stated was that there is a defence if the producer shows that 'the state of scientific and technical knowledge at the relevant time was not such that a producer of products of the same description as the product in question might be expected to have discovered the defect if it had existed in his products while they were under his control', which again could be seen as a wider defence than the one contemplated by EC Directive 85/374. The European Court concluded in *European Commission v United Kingdom* [1997] All ER (EC) 481 that there was an ambiguity in the 1987 Act, but the European Court was prepared to assume that the United Kingdom did not intend judges to interpret the 1987 Act differently from EC Directive 85/374. The European Court also stated that United Kingdom courts are obliged to interpret the 1987 Act and EC Directive 85/374 consistently. As a result, the court in *A v National Blood Authority* [2001] 3 All ER 289 referred to the decision of the European Court of Justice in its analysis and focused very closely on the wording of EC Directive 85/374when dealing with the issues the parties had raised.

For more revision tips, including self-test questions and suggestions for further reading, see the Online Resource Centre at www.oxfordtextbooks.co.uk/orc/strong_complete/.

revision tasks

Here are some ideas to try when you revise this chapter:

- Write down the two 'rules' in *Donoghue v Stevenson* [1932] AC 562 (that is, the general rule that applies in all negligence cases, and the 'narrow rule' for product liability cases).

- Consider whether the cases discussed in this chapter under the narrow rule in *Donoghue v Stevenson* [1932] AC 562 would have been successful under the Consumer Protection Act 1987.

- Draw a diagram illustrating the rules on component parts under the 1987 Act.

- Remind yourself of the limitation period under the narrow rule and under the 1987 Act. Ask yourself whether it is possible to say which limitation period is more favourable to consumers.

Part 8

Liability for the Torts of Others

16 Liability for the torts of others

16.1 Introduction

Chapter 2 discussed several cases in which employers were held liable for actions taken by their employees. This is known as vicarious liability. This chapter explores this concept in more detail. **Vicarious** liability can arise in several different contexts, but it is most often seen in employment cases. For this reason, it is important to understand when the law will treat someone as an employee rather than, for instance, a contractor or an agent. We will look at this in the next section. It is also important to understand that **vicarious** liability does not cancel out the original tort. If an employee acts tortiously, the employee has what is known as primary liability, even if the employer also has vicarious liability for the same tort. Sometimes, there will also be a separate tort by the employer, so the employer will have primary liability for its own acts as well as vicarious liability for the acts of the employee. As a result, a claimant will often have a choice of whether to sue the employee, the employer, or both. The torts involved are often negligence or breach of statutory duty.

One reason which is often used to justify imposing vicarious liability is that the person who stands to profit from a business endeavour should also be responsible for the risks associated with it. Making employers pay damages for their employees' torts helps to make sure that responsibility falls where it ought. Employers are also generally in a better financial position to pay damages than their employees are, since employers usually have more funds available and they will generally be able to insure against accidents or borrow money more easily than employees can. Knowing that they are likely to have to pay damages may also encourage employers to take more care over their workers' training and equipment, so that accidents are less likely to occur.

This chapter proceeds as follows:

- The difference between employees, independent contractors and agents;
- Liability for employees;
- Liability for independent contractors;
- Liability in hospitals;

> **VOCABULARY**
> 'Vicarious' means 'enjoyed or experienced through another person'. Thus, the phrases 'vicarious thrill', or 'Sue's mum lived vicariously through Sue'.

> **NOTE** Older cases often talk about a master/servant relationship rather than an employment relationship, but they mean the relationship between employers and employees in general, not just the relationship between domestic servants and their employers.

- Liability in the police force;
- Loans with delegation of authority; and
- Relations between defendants.

16.2 The difference between employees, independent contractors and agents

16.2.1 Employees and independent contractors

Typically, employers are liable for the acts of their employees, but not for acts of independent contractors. Agents fall into both categories. Thus, it is important to be able to distinguish between the various types of workers. Broadly speaking, an independent contractor is usually a self-employed individual who is hired by other businesses to work on a particular project. Sometimes an independent contractor can be a firm or company. In this chapter, we are only concerned with self-employed individuals, since firms and companies are not likely to be mistaken for employees.

Distinguishing independent contractors from employees is not always difficult, though there are a few areas that are tricky. For the most part, self-employed people usually have to provide their own equipment and hire any additional help they need, while employees usually have their equipment and co-workers provided by their employer. The person who hires the worker is known as the employer in both cases, regardless of whether the worker is an employee or an independent contractor. The courts have used three main tests to try to distinguish between employees and independent contractors: the control test, the integration test, and the pragmatic test. We will examine each of these in turn.

Control test

The courts have decided that if an employer can not only tell a worker what to do but also how to do it, then the worker is more likely to be an employee than an independent contractor. However, this test does not work very well if the worker has more expertise than the employer. For instance, a hospital manager is not in a position to tell a surgeon how to carry out an operation, but the surgeon may very well be an employee. As the British economy comes to be based more on knowledge and less on manufacturing, the control test is becoming rather outdated, and the courts rely on it less than they used to.

Integration test

The integration test is also known as the organization test. It was suggested by Denning LJ in the case of *Stevenson, Jordan and Harrison Ltd v MacDonald and Evans* [1952] 1 TLR 101 as an alternative to the control test, and it distinguishes between employees and

Exercise

· · · · · · · · · · · · ·

Make a list containing some examples of employees and some examples of independent contractors. For instance, a plumber is usually an independent contractor, but a secretary is usually an employee.

· · · · · · · · · · · · ·

NOTE The cases deciding whether someone is an employee or an independent contractor are not always about vicarious liability. Often, they are about other issues where the worker's status may be decisive, including questions about tax or the employer's duties to the worker under health and safety regulations.

independent contractors based on how closely the worker is integrated into the employer's organization. The worker in this case was an accountant. He wrote a textbook on business management and sent the draft to a firm of publishers, but then left his job. He died before the book was published. His employers claimed that he had written the book as an employee. If this was correct, they would own the copyright under the copyright statute of the time. However, the Court of Appeal held that, although the worker was employed by the firm, writing the textbook was not part of that employment. He had written the book under a separate arrangement, and, under that arrangement, he was an independent contractor. The copyright was therefore part of his estate. Lord Denning described the test in *Stevenson, Jordan and Harrison Ltd v MacDonald and Evans* [1952] 1 TLR 101 as follows: 'One feature which seems to run through the instances is that, under a contract of service, a man is employed as a part of the business; whereas under a contract for services, his work, although done for the business, is not integrated into it, but is only accessory to it'. Here, Lord Denning is referring to a contract for service as synonymous with an employer-employee relationship and a contract for services as synonymous with an independent contractor relationship.

Pragmatic test

Although the integration test may work better than the control test in some cases, it has been criticized for being too vague. In *Ready-Mixed Concrete (South-East) Ltd v Minister of Pensions and National Insurance* [1968] 1 All ER 433, the court suggested a third test, which is known as the pragmatic test. That case involved an individual, L, who used his own vehicle to deliver concrete for a company under a contract which required him to paint the vehicle in the company's colours, abide by its rules, and wear its uniform, among other things. L was nevertheless held by the court to be an independent contractor, because he was found to have sufficient freedom in the performance of his obligations. According to this test, a worker is an employee if:

- The worker has agreed to use his or her own labour and skill to provide a service to the employer and cannot, for instance, hire someone else to provide the service instead;

- The employer has agreed to pay the worker a wage or some other form of regular earnings in return for the service (as opposed to paying the entire amount due on completion of the job);

- The worker has agreed (expressly or impliedly) that the employer can control the manner in which the worker performs the service;

- The other provisions of the contract are consistent with an employment relationship. No single factor is conclusive. For instance, the court in *Ready-Mixed Concrete (South-East) Ltd v Minister of Pensions and National Insurance* [1968] 1 All ER 433 said that it would be inconsistent with an employment relationship if the employer did not provide workers with the tools they needed to do the job or expected them to hire other people to help them. Any expressed intention of the parties may also be taken into account. However, the fact that a contract says the worker is self-employed will not necessarily be enough to stop the worker being an employee. Otherwise, it would be too easy for employers to exploit their workers by avoiding health and safety legislation, much of which applies to employees, but not independent contractors. The

Court of Appeal drew attention to this policy consideration in *Lane v Shire Roofing Co (Oxford) Limited* [1995] IRLR 493. In this case, the plaintiff fell from a ladder while working on a roof. Under health and safety legislation, if he was an employee, the employer should have provided scaffolding rather than a ladder. The plaintiff ran his own roofing business, was described in his contract as self-employed for tax purposes, worked without supervision, and had no guarantee of continuing work with the employer. Nevertheless, he was treated by the Court of Appeal as an employee. The court seems to have been influenced by the fact that the work he was doing was not of a kind which required a specialist, but the real reason may have been a desire on the part of the Court of Appeal to give full effect to legislation intended to protect workers;

• There is some form of mutual obligation under the contract. Workers are not employees if they have no obligation to work regularly, but are simply called up by the employer on an 'as required' basis and have the option of refusing to work on each occasion. Workers who are hired through a temp agency also appear to be independent contractors rather than employees, unless they can show that there is a mutual obligation between them and the agency and that the agency controls their work.

You will probably have noticed that the third bullet-point here is essentially the same as the control test, and the fourth one is arguably just as vague as the integration test. It is therefore questionable whether the pragmatic test is better than either of the other tests. In practice, the courts will take other factors into account as well, such as whether the worker bears any financial risk. This is sometimes expressed as an enquiry into whether the worker 'is in business on his own account', and involves looking at factors such as whether or not the worker has financially invested in the business, has bought tools to use in it, stands to share in its profits, and so on. This approach was adopted by the Privy Council in *Lee Ting Sang v Chung Chi-Keung* [1990] 2 AC 364. In this case, a mason was employed to chisel concrete at a building site. His employer supplied his tools and inspected his work regularly, but did not directly supervise him. At different times, he was paid either a piece-work rate or a daily rate for working from 8 am to 5 pm. If he finished his work early, he assisted the employer by sharpening tools. He sometimes worked for other employers, but he gave priority to any urgent work on the building site and turned down other work in those circumstances. The Privy Council found that he was an employee. However, this approach has not been developed subsequently.

16.2.2 **Agents**

compare
Contract law, unlike tort law, is very interested in determining who is an agent and for what purposes.

Independent contractors and employees are different from an agent who is authorized to represent another person (known as the principal) in dealings with third parties. For instance, lawyers may act as agents of their clients when negotiating contracts. The acts of the agent are treated as if they were the acts of the principal. This raises the possibility of the principal being liable for the torts of the agent. However, in most situations, the law of tort is only concerned with whether someone is an employee or an independent contractor. A person may also be an agent, but tort law generally does not concern itself with the agency relationship itself.

There are some exceptions to this rule. Firstly, if an agent makes a negligent misstatement, the principal will be liable for any resulting harm, provided that the misstatement related to something which was within the scope of the agent's authority from the principal. The scope of the agent's authority is determined in much the same way as is the course of a worker's employment. If a worker is both an agent and an employee, then acting beyond the scope of the agency will automatically take the worker outside the course of employment.

Second, if the agent makes statements which are dishonest, the principal may be liable in the tort of deceit. Again, the statements must have been within the agent's authority to make.

 ## 16.3 Liability for employees

16.3.1 General principles

Three conditions must apply for an employer to be vicariously liable for the acts of another person:

- The worker must be an employee. We looked at how this is determined in the previous section;
- The employee must have committed a wrong (such as a common law tort, a breach of statutory duty, a breach of a statutory prohibition, or an equitable wrong);
- The employee must have been acting in the course of his or her employment.

We will now consider the second and third of these conditions.

The employee must have committed a wrong

Whether or not the employee has committed a wrong is assessed in the normal way, by applying the elements of the wrong to the facts of the case. For example, in a negligence claim, a court would determine whether or not the employee owed the claimant a duty of care, whether the employee had breached that duty, and whether the employee had caused damage to the claimant which was not too remote. Liability can also attach in cases involving breach of statutory duty, and many of the cases considered in chapter 3 would also give rise to vicarious liability on the part of the employer in question. Another example of vicarious liability for breach of a statutory prohibition was *Majrowski v Guy's and St Thomas's NHS Trust* [2006] UKHL 34. Here, an employee of the Trust harassed a colleague, which was contrary to the Protection from Harassment Act 1997. The court found the Trust vicariously liable for the colleague's distress and anxiety. Remember, the employee will incur primary liability for the wrongful act, but without an initial wrong, the employer cannot be held vicariously liable.

In the course of employment

The question of whether or not an employee was acting in the course of his or her employment is the most complex element of vicarious liability. Acts are viewed as being in the course of employment if they were either authorized by the employer or so closely connected with an authorized act that they can be viewed as an unauthorized manner of doing that authorized act. Authorized acts, broadly speaking, are the acts which the employee was employed to do. Even if the employee does these acts carelessly or makes mistakes, the employer will still be liable for any injury that occurs as a result of those acts. For instance, in *Century Insurance Co. Ltd v Northern Ireland Road Transport Board* [1942] AC 509, a driver was employed to deliver petrol. During one delivery, he lit a cigarette and carelessly dropped a match on the floor, causing an explosion. His employer was vicariously liable for the driver's negligence, because he was doing what he was employed to do, even though he did it in a negligent way. In *Bayley v Manchester, Sheffield & Lincolnshire Railway Co* (1873) LR 8 CP 148, a station manager dragged a passenger off a train and put him on the wrong train instead. The railway company was vicariously liable to the passenger because it was part of the station manager's job to make sure that passengers got on the correct trains. Notably, dragging the passenger off the train could also be a criminal assault. We consider below when employers will be liable for criminal acts by their employees.

Given the emphasis on authorized acts, you may expect that an employer would not be vicariously liable if an employee does something which is against the employer's direct instructions. As it turns out, the law is not quite that simple. The following two cases show how nuanced the analysis can become, even on very similar facts. In *London County Council v Cattermoles (Garages) Ltd* [1953] 1 WLR 997, the defendants owned a garage and employed P in a general capacity as a garage hand. One aspect of his job was to move cars in the garage so as to make way for other cars. Because he had no driving licence, he was forbidden to drive vehicles, but instead had to push them by hand. One day, the garage attendant asked P to remove a motor van from in front of the garage's petrol pumps to allow some lorries to get petrol. Instead of pushing the van out of the way, P decided to drive it. Because there was not enough space to drive straight into the garage, he drove onto the road with the intention of turning and coming back to the garage behind the lorries. On the road, P collided with a van belonging to the plaintiffs, who sued the garage owners for damages. The court held that P's duty was to move cars in the garage and that it was impossible to define the scope of his employment as that of pushing them by hand rather than by other means. Even though he was expressly forbidden to drive cars, his action was within the scope of his employment. Granted, it was a wrongful and unauthorized way of performing an act which he was employed to perform, but driving onto the road was 'merely incidental' to moving the van out of the way of the lorries, the work for which he was employed. Thus, the defendants were liable in damages to the plaintiffs for P's negligence.

The outcome in *Iqbal v London Transport Executive* (1973) 16 KIR 329 was slightly different. In this case, the plaintiff was employed as a bus driver. He worked with a conductor, C. One morning, as they were getting ready to set off, they discovered that they could not get their bus out of the garage because another bus was parked in front of it. The plaintiff told C to get someone to move the other bus. Instead, C attempted to move the bus himself, even though he did not know how to drive a bus and knew that his employer had prohibited conductors from doing so. When he started the engine, the bus moved forward suddenly and crushed the plaintiff between it and his own bus. The court held that C had not been acting within the scope of his employment when he had driven the bus and that the defendants were therefore not liable to the plaintiff.

The difference between the two cases is that in *London County Council v Cattermoles* [1953] 1 WLR 997, the employee was employed to move cars; however, he moved them in a manner contrary to his employer's instructions. Similarly, in *Limpus v London General Omnibus* Co [1861–1873] All ER 559, a bus driver raced his bus against other drivers after being told not to, and in *Harrison v Michelin Tyre Co Ltd* [1985] 1 All ER 918, a driver deliberately drove slightly to one side of the designated driveway as a prank and knocked over a fellow employee. In both cases, the employer was vicariously liable for the acts of the drivers, because the employees were employed as drivers and were simply driving in a way that was contrary to instructions. In *Iqbal v London Transport Executive* (1973) 16 KIR 329, on the other hand, the employee was not employed to drive or move buses at all. Employers are vicariously liable if employees breach a rule about the way in which they do their jobs, but they are not liable if the employees breach a rule about the scope of the job itself. However, this can be a difficult distinction to draw. For instance, in *Irving v The Post Office* [1987] IRLR 289, the employee was authorized to write notes on envelopes to ensure that they were correctly delivered. Instead, he wrote racial abuse on a letter intended for his neighbours, with whom he had a long-standing disagreement. The Court of Appeal held that he was only authorized to write on the envelopes for specific purposes and was not acting in the course of his employment when he wrote the abusive remarks. In *General Engineering Services Limited v Kingston and St Andrew Corporation* [1988] 3 All ER 867, fire-fighters who arrived late at a fire because of a 'work to rule' were found to be acting outside the course of their employment, rather than performing an authorized act in an unauthorized manner. A 'work to rule' is a form of industrial action in which employees work exactly as required by their contracts, but refuse to do overtime or anything else which is not in their contracts. It is also sometimes known as 'withdrawing goodwill'.

Another common fact pattern for unauthorized acts concerns situations where a driver gives a lift to an unauthorized passenger. Again, the following cases reach different conclusions despite similar facts. In *Twine v Bean's Express Ltd* (1946) 175 LT 131, the defendants were responsible for providing a commercial van and a driver for the use of a bank. The driver was to remain the employee of the defendants, although the defendants accepted no liability in respect of persons riding in the van who were not employees of the defendants. The defendants forbade the driver from taking any passengers with him, and a notice prohibiting unauthorized people from travelling in the van was posted on the dashboard of the van. One day, the driver allowed an employee of the bank to take a lift in the van, but informed the passenger that he did so at his own risk. An accident occurred due to the driver's negligence, and the passenger was killed.

· ·

● ***Twine v Bean's Express Ltd*** [1946] 175 LT 131

> Lord Greene MR: The appellant, who was plaintiff in the action, can, of course, only succeed if she can show that her husband's unfortunate death was due to a breach of duty owed towards him by these defendants, Bean's Express, Limited. The fact that the driver

think point

Do you think the fact that fire fighting is a socially valuable activity factored into this decision? Might there be a public policy answer in favour of encouraging fire-fighters to work freely whereas other employees might not be subject to the same rule?

of the van owed a duty to her husband cannot help her in these proceedings. In my opinion the case is a perfectly clear one. The deceased man was upon the defendants' van in circumstances in which the judge has found (and I do not see that he could have found otherwise) that he had no right to be there at all and the driver of the van had no right to take him on to the van. Only limited classes of persons with properly authenticated authority were entitled to be carried on this van, and it is as clear as possible that the deceased man was not one of those persons.

[Counsel for the plaintiff] pointed out that certain employees of the Post Office were entitled to ride on vans, and he invited us to say that because the deceased man was an employee of the Post Office he belonged to the class of persons authorised to ride on vans. But that argument really will not bear examination. We are not discussing here the duty owed by these defendants towards a class of persons: we are discussing the duty alleged to be owing to this particular deceased man in the particular circumstances in which he met his death. Unfortunately for the plaintiff, he was on that van, as the judge found, as a trespasser, and I cannot see how any other conclusion of fact could have been come to.

That being so, it seems to me there is an end of the matter, because if the question is asked: Was the driver, Harrison, in giving a lift to the deceased man acting within the scope of his employment? The answer is clearly, No. He was doing something that he had no right whatsoever to do, and **qua** the deceased man he was as much on a frolic of his own as if he had been driving somewhere on some amusement of his own quite unauthorised by his employers. His employers, of course, are Bean's Express, Limited; and part of the confusion that has arisen in the argument is caused by treating the driver of the van as though in some way he was employed by the Post Office. Of course he was not. He was the employee of the independent contractor, and when he ran into the omnibus (which was the cause of the deceased man's death) he was of course acting as a driver of the van in the course of his employment. He was employed to drive the van. That does not mean, as [counsel for the plaintiff] suggested, that because the deceased man was in the van it was within the scope of his employment to be driving the deceased man. He was in fact doing two things at once. He was driving his van from one place to another by a route that he was properly taking when he ran into the omnibus, and as he was driving the van he was acting within the scope of his employment. The other thing that he was doing simultaneously was something totally outside the scope of his employment, namely, giving a lift to a person who had no right whatsoever to be there.

In my opinion, once the facts are understood the case is a perfectly simple one, and there is only one answer to it. The appeal must be dismissed.

The facts in the following case, *Rose v Plenty* [1976] 1 All ER 97, are strikingly similar, but the analysis comes out differently here. In this case, a milkman was employed by a dairy company to drive a milk float to deliver milk to the employer's customers. The employer posted notices at the milk depot expressly prohibiting the milkmen both from employing children to help with their duties and from giving children lifts on the milk float. Nevertheless, the milkman hired a 13-year-old boy to help him on the milk round. The boy was injured when the milkman drove the float negligently and brought a cause of action against both the milkman and his employer.

················

VOCABULARY

'Qua' is a Latin word which usually means 'as', but here Lord Greene uses it to mean 'in so far as... is concerned'.

················

Scarman LJ: I think it important to realise that the principle of vicarious liability is one of public policy. It is not a principle which derives from a critical or refined consideration of other concepts in the common law, for example the concept of trespass or indeed the concept of agency. No doubt in particular cases it may be relevant to consider whether a particular plaintiff was or was not a trespasser. Similarly, when, as I shall indicate, it is important that one should determine the course of employment of the servant, the law of agency may have some marginal relevance. But basically, as I understand it, the employer is made vicariously liable for the tort of his employee not because the plaintiff is an invitee, nor because of the authority possessed by the servant, but because it is a case in which the employer, having put matters into motion, should be liable if the motion that he has originated leads to damage to another. What is the approach which the cases identify as the correct approach in order to determine this question of public policy? First, as Lord Denning MR has already said, one looks to see whether the servant has committed a tort upon the plaintiff. In the present case it is clear that the first defendant, the servant of the dairy company, who are the second defendants, by the negligent driving of the milk float, caused injury to the plaintiff, a boy 13.5 years old, who was on the float at his invitation. There was therefore a tort committed by the servant. The next question, as Lord Denning MR has said, is whether the employer should shoulder the liability for compensating the person injured by the tort. With all respect to the points developed by Lawton LJ, it does appear to me to be clear, since the decision of Limpus v London General Omnibus Co 1 H&C 526 that question has to be answered by directing attention to what the first defendant was employed to do when he committed the tort that has caused damage to the plaintiff. The first defendant was, of course, employed at the time of the accident to do a whole number of operations. He was certainly not employed to give the boy a lift, and if one confines one's analysis of the facts to the incident of injury to the plaintiff, then no doubt one would say that carrying the plaintiff on the float—giving him a lift—was not in the course of the first defendant's employment. But in Ilkiw v Samuels [1963] 1 W.L.R. 991 Diplock LJ indicated that the proper approach to the nature of the servant's employment is a broad one. He said:

'As each of these nouns implies—he is referring to the nouns used to describe course of employment, sphere, scope and so forth—the matter must be looked at broadly, not dissecting the servant's task into its component activities—such as driving, loading, sheeting and the like—by asking: What was the job on which he was engaged for his employer? and answering that question as a jury would.'

Applying those words to the employment of the first defendant, I think it is clear from the evidence that he was employed as a roundsman to drive his float round his round and to deliver milk, to collect empties and to obtain payment. That was his job. He was under an express prohibition—a matter to which I shall refer later—not to enlist the help of anyone doing that work. And he was also under an express prohibition not to give lifts on the float to anyone. How did he choose to carry out the task which I have analysed? He chose to disregard the prohibition and to enlist the assistance of the plaintiff. As a matter of common sense, that does seem to me to be a mode, albeit a prohibited mode, of doing the job with which he was entrusted. Why was the plaintiff being carried on the float when the accident occurred? Because it was necessary to take him from point to point so that he could assist in delivering milk, collecting empties and, on occasions, obtaining payment.

The plaintiff was there because it was necessary that he should be there in order that he could assist, albeit in a way prohibited by the employers, in the job entrusted to the first defendant by his employers

...

It does seem to me that the principle that I have been attempting to describe is to be found in the case law, notably in Limpus v London General Omnibus Co 1 H&C 526, Hilton v Thomas Burton (Rhodes) Ltd [1961] 1 W.L.R. 705 and Ilkiw v Samuels [1963] 1 W.L.R. 991. Yet it is said that the flow of this current of authority must be damned and the stream of the law diverted because of the two decisions to which Lawton LJ has referred: Twine v Bean's Express Ltd., 62 T.L.R. 458 and Conway v George Wimpey & Co Ltd. (No.2) [1951] 2 K.B. 266. Both of those decisions seem to me distinguishable upon their facts. In Twine's case Lord Greene M.R. says, at p.459: 'The other thing that he [that is the servant] was doing simultaneously was something totally outside the scope of his employment—namely, giving a lift to a person who had no right whatsoever to be there.' In that case the conclusion of fact was that the express prohibition on giving lifts was not only a pro-hibition but was also a limiting factor on the scope of the employment; and, of course, once a prohibition is properly to be treated as a defining or limiting factor on the scope of employment certain results follow. In Twine's case the driver was engaged to drive his employers' van, his employers having a contract with the Post Office. When so doing, he gave Mr Twine a lift from A to B. With deep respect, I can well understand why the court reached the conclusion that in the circumstances of that case it was not possible to say that the driver in giving Mr Twine a lift was acting within the scope of his employment or doing improperly that which he was employed to do. Similarly when one looks at Conway's case [1951] 2 K.B. 266, one again sees that on the facts of that case the court considered it right so to define the scope of employment that what was done, namely giving somebody a lift, was outside it and was not a mode of doing that which the servant was employed to do. That also was a case of a lift: the person lifted was not in any way engaged, in the course of the lift or indeed otherwise, in doing the master's business or in assisting the servant to do the master's business; and no doubt it was for that reason that Asquith LJ was able to say that what was done—that is giving somebody else's employee a lift from the airport home—was not a mode of performing an act which the driver was employed to do, but was the performance of an act which he was not employed to perform. In the present case the first defendant, the servant, was employed to deliver milk, to collect empties, to obtain payment from customers. The plaintiff was there on the float in order to assist the first defendant to do those jobs. I would have thought therefore that whereas Conway v George Wimpey & Co Ltd (No.2) [1951] 2 K.B. 266 was absolutely correctly decided on its facts, the facts of the present case lead to a very different conclusion...Appeal allowed.

Here, there was no distinction between the jobs the employees were employed to do. Both of them were employed partly as drivers. However, in *Rose v Plenty* [1976] 1 All ER 97, the passenger helped the driver to do his job. In *Twine v Bean's Express Ltd.* (1946) 175 LT 131, he did not. This seems to have influenced the Court of Appeal in its decision.

Interestingly, employers can sometimes be held liable for injuries resulting from an unauthorized act even if that act is a criminal offence. The courts have considered this in relation to thefts, frauds, and assaults by employees. In *Morris v C.W. Martin & Sons Ltd* [1966] 1 QB 716, the plaintiff sent a fur stole to be cleaned. One of the cleaners' employees stole the coat. The court held that, because the coat had been entrusted to the employee as part of his job, the employer was liable. However, employers are not liable if employees steal articles that were not entrusted to them as part of their jobs. For instance, if a shop assistant steals a purse from a customer's bag, the shop-owner will not be liable, because the customer did not entrust the purse to the assistant. The customer will of course still be able to sue the assistant directly or press criminal charges. Similarly, in *Heasmans v Clarity Cleaning Co* [1987] IRLR 286, a cleaning company was not liable for long-distance phone calls which one of their employees made without permission from a client's premises.

NOTE The act of entrusting someone to hold an item of personal property is called a 'bailment'. There are differing levels of duties depending on whether the bailee (the person entrusted with the item) accepts the item gratuitously or in return for payment from the bailor.

A similar issue arose in *Lister v Hesley Hall Ltd* [2001] 2 All ER 769. There, an employee in a children's home sexually assaulted some of the children for whom he was employed to care. The House of Lords held that there was such a close connection between the abuse of the children entrusted to his care and the job he was employed to do that it was fair and just to hold the employer liable. In *Bracebridge Engineering Ltd v Darby* [1990] IRLR 3 an employer was held vicariously liable after a supervisor used a disciplinary meeting about time-keeping to sexually harass an employee. It was held that, since the supervisor was engaged in his supervisory function when the harassment took place, he was acting in the course of his employment. Likewise, in *Mattis v Pollock* [2003] EWCA Civ 887, a nightclub was vicariously liable for a bouncer who not only removed some guests from the club—which was clearly part of his job—but also went home to fetch a knife, then followed them down the street, and assaulted them several hundred metres away from the club. In *Fennelly v Connex South Eastern Ltd* [2001] IRLR 390, a railway company was vicariously liable for a ticket inspector who, after dealing with a customer whom he mistakenly thought did not have the correct ticket—which was part of his job—then followed the customer down the platform and put him in a headlock. In all of these cases, the employer was held liable for the tortious effects of the employee's crime.

These cases are difficult to reconcile with *Daniels v Whetstone Entertainments Limited* [1962] 2 Lloyd's Rep 1, where a doorman was found to be acting outside the course of his employment when he assaulted the plaintiff. The court held that the assault was an act of personal revenge, even though the assault took place immediately after the doorman had evicted the plaintiff from the dance hall where he was working. These cases also seem contrary to *Warren v Henlys Ltd* [1948] 2 All ER 935, where a garage attendant mistakenly accused a customer of stealing petrol. After paying, the customer called the police and threatened to complain to the attendant's employer. The attendant then assaulted the customer. The employer was not liable for the assault. Preventing customers from leaving without paying for their petrol was part of the attendant's job, but what happened after the customer had paid was no longer part of the job. If the assault had been part of the attempt to prevent the customer stealing, the employer would probably have been liable. This seems to be supported by the case of *Poland v John Parr & Sons* [1927] 1 KB 236, where an employee hit a boy whom he thought was in the act of stealing from his employer's lorry. The employer was liable for the boy's injuries. In *Mattis v Pollock* [2003] EWCA Civ 887, however, the bouncer had clearly completed the act he was employed to do—removing the visitors from the club—some time before the assault. The Court of Appeal appears to have been influenced in that case by the fact that the employer had hired the bouncer even though the bouncer was unlicensed, but if this was the decisive factor, then the claim should have been dealt with as one of primary liability rather than vicarious liability. Likewise, in *Fennelly v Connex South Eastern Ltd* [2001] IRLR 390, the ticket inspector had completed the act of checking the customer's ticket before the assault took place. It may be that over time, the courts are taking a less lenient view towards employers, but this has left the law in a state of some confusion.

A case that centred on fraud rather than assault was *Lloyd v Grace, Smith & Co* [1912] AC 716. There, a solicitor's managing clerk was authorized by the solicitor to carry out conveyancing (i.e. the transfer of land from a seller to a buyer) on the solicitor's behalf. The clerk persuaded a client of the firm to sign a document transferring her property to him. He then disposed of the property for his own ends. The court held that the employers were liable because they had held the clerk out to members of the public as someone who was authorized to do the tasks which he then did fraudulently. The employees had effectively encouraged the plaintiff to trust the clerk. If some other employee had done the same thing without the employers' knowledge and without being held out as authorized, the employers would not have been liable for that act.

Employers are also not liable if the employee's tort involved agreeing not to carry out his or her duties. For instance, in *Makanjuola v Metropolitan Police Commissioner*, The Times, 8 August 1989, a police officer came to the plaintiff's house in search of her former housemate. In the course of the conversation, the police officer realized that the plaintiff was an illegal immigrant. He promised not to arrest her if she would agree to have sexual intercourse with him, which she did. She later sued for assault. The court held that the Metropolitan Police Commissioner was not vicariously liable for the assault because, far from carrying out his duties in an unauthorized way, the police officer had agreed not to carry them out at all.

If the court decides that the employee was not acting in the course of employment, it may say that the employee was engaged in 'a frolic of his own' (or her own). This phrase, which is often used in vicarious liability cases, comes from *Joel v Morison* (1834) 6 C&P 501, where a servant driving his employer's cart had an accident while on an errand of his own. The phrase is thus most often used when a driver takes a detour and causes an accident along the way. The court then has to decide whether the detour took the driver outside the course of employment. Inevitably, these decisions can seem a little arbitrary. For instance, the courts have decided that drivers can take a reasonable detour to get lunch without going beyond the course of employment, but not to get tea (*Harvey v R.G. O'Dell Ltd* [1958] 2 QB 78 and *Hilton v Thomas Burton (Rhodes) Ltd* [1961] 1 WLR 705 respectively). The court considers how far beyond his job the employee has gone, both in terms of physical distance and the scope of the tasks the employee was entrusted to carry out. In *N v Chief Constable of Merseyside Police* [2006] EWHC 3041 (QB), a woman was taken ill in a nightclub after taking an illegal drug and drinking a large quantity of alcohol. The club's first aider helped her outside and recommended that she go to hospital, but she refused. This was overheard by an off-duty police officer who was sitting outside the club in his private car. He was wearing his uniform, but it was hidden by his own jacket, and he was outside his own police area. He identified himself as 'the police' and told the first aider that he would 'sort it'. The first aider then encouraged the woman to get in the car, telling her that the police officer would help her. The woman got into the car, but the police officer drove her to his own home—driving past three police stations on the way—where he raped her. In the subsequent investigation, the police found evidence on the officer's computer suggesting that he had been planning to rape an unconscious woman for some time. The court found that this was a 'frolic of his own' and was not sufficiently closely connected with his employment to make it fair or reasonable to hold his employers vicariously liable.

An employee is not normally acting in the course of employment outside the employee's normal working hours. For instance, an employer is not liable for the acts of an employee who comes into work during his holiday. However, a reasonable time is allowed for incidental tasks such as getting ready to go home, so in *Ruddiman & Co v Smith* (1889) 60 LT 708, when an employee washed his hands before leaving and accidentally left the tap running, the employer was liable for the resulting flooding.

Occasionally it may happen that some of the essential elements of a tort are committed within the course of the employment, but others are outside it. In those instances, the employer is not vicariously liable. However, this is likely to be rare.

16.3.2 Employees 'on loan'

Sometimes, employers send employees to work for another employer on a temporary loan. The original employer is called the 'general employer', and the one who receives the loan is called the 'special employer'. If the employee commits a tort while on loan, it can be difficult to tell which employer should be vicariously liable. In *Mersey Docks & Harbour Board v Coggins & Griffiths Ltd* [1946] 2 All ER 345, the House of Lords said that the general employer has to prove that the liability has passed to the special employer and that this will only be the case in 'quite exceptional circumstances'. The key, once again, is who can control how the employee does the job. The general employer is also more likely to succeed in passing the burden to the special employer if:

- The two employers have agreed between themselves who is to be the employer;
- The special employer is paying the employee's wages;
- The special employer has the power to dismiss the employee;
- The loan is for a long period; or
- The special employer has provided the employee with all the equipment needed to do the job, rather than borrowing the equipment from the general employer.

It used to be thought that the general employer and the special employer could not both be vicariously liable for the same act. However, the courts have now decided that there can be 'dual vicarious liability' in certain circumstances. In *Viasystems Tyneside Ltd v Thermal Transfer (Northern) Ltd* [2005] EWCA Civ 1151, two employees, M and S, were loaned by one employer to another to help install some air-conditioning. M was the more senior of the two. Both were supervised on the job by H, who worked for the special employer. Through S's negligence, the building flooded, and the owner of the factory sued both employers. The court found that both M and H had control of S at the relevant time and would have been entitled to tell him to stop what he was doing. Therefore, both the general and the special employer were vicariously liable for the flood damage.

16.3.3 The employer's indemnity

An employer who has to pay damages because of vicarious liability for an employee's tort can sue the employee to recover the damages. However, employers rarely use this right. This is partly because most employees do not have the funds to repay the damages and partly because employers who make a practice of suing their employees might find it difficult to attract new recruits. For these reasons, employer's liability insurers have made an informal agreement not to force employers to sue their employees, except where there is some evidence that the employee has been involved in deliberate misconduct. The Law Society has also advised solicitors' firms not to sue their employee lawyers unless there has been deliberate misconduct. However, the employer cannot sue the employee if the employer was also at fault, although the employer may also be able to use the Civil Liability (Contribution) Act 1978, as explained below.

16.4 Liability for independent contractors

Contrary to the rule regarding employees, employers are not vicariously liable for the torts of independent contractors because employers generally cannot control what independent contractors do. Employers also may not have the knowledge to appreciate whether or not the contractor is doing something dangerous. Furthermore, it is easier for independent contractors to insure against liability than it is for employees to do so, thus increasing the likelihood a claimant can recover the amount awarded.

Nevertheless, there are some exceptional circumstances in which employers will be liable for the torts of independent contractors. This is a form of primary liability rather than vicarious liability, since the employer itself is treated as doing something wrong. This sort of liability applies where:

- The employer hires the contractor to do something which is unusually hazardous;
- The contractor creates a danger while working on a highway;

- The employer is negligent through:
  - the choice of contractor;
  - the number of contractors who are hired; or
  - the instructions which are given to the contractors;
- The employer authorizes the tort; or
- The employer has a duty which cannot be delegated, such as one which involves strict liability.

We will discuss each in turn.

16.4.1 Hazardous acts

Employers are typically responsible if they hire contractors to carry out unusually hazardous acts. The rationale behind the rule is that the employer has a duty of care to third parties in such circumstances and should not be allowed to delegate it entirely to someone else. An example is *Alcock v Wraith*, The Times 23 December 1991. Here, a couple hired Mr Wraith to re-roof their terraced house. The terrace had slate roof tiles. However, the couple could not afford new slate tiles, so Mr Wraith used concrete tiles instead. A neighbour subsequently found that damp had got into his house through newspaper which Mr Wraith had stuffed into the joint between the old slate tiles and the new concrete ones. The court found that the couple were liable to their neighbour because, according to expert evidence, it was notoriously difficult to make a waterproof joint between slate and concrete tiles. This made the roofing operation sufficiently hazardous that the couple could not delegate their duty of care to their neighbour to Mr Wraith.

16.4.2 Dangers on or near a highway

A similar principle applies where an employer hires a contractor to carry out dangerous operations on or near a highway and it is foreseeable that people using the highway may suffer harm. Thus, in *Holliday v National Telephone Company* [1899] 2 QB 392, a plumber working for the defendant telephone company was laying telephone wires across a street when the petrol lamp he was using exploded, causing molten metal to splash onto a passer-by. The company was held to be under a duty not to let its employees or independent contractors cause a danger to those using the highway.

16.4.3 Collateral negligence

If an employer is liable for actions taken by independent contractors that are inherently hazardous, then one would expect the converse to be true, i.e. that the employer would not be liable in cases where the independent contractor undertakes acts that are not intrinsically dangerous. Indeed, this is the case, even when the independent contractor carries out the act negligently. Negligence of this kind is known as collateral negligence and is not attributable to the employer. For instance, in *Padbury v Holliday & Greenwood Ltd* (1912) 28 TLR 492 a contractor was hired to fit some windows. The contractor put a tool on the windowsill. When the wind blew the window open, the tool fell and injured a passer-by. The employer was not liable because the work was not inherently dangerous. Similarly, in *Wilson v Hodgson's Kingston Brewery Co* (1915) 85 LJKB 270, a contractor was hired to deliver beer to a pub. He used the cellar hatch in the street outside, although in fact the beer could have been delivered through the front door. He carelessly left the hatch open, and, again, a passer-by was injured. The court held that the employer was not liable, because the contractor did not have to use the hatch, and therefore the dangers of doing so were not an intrinsic part of the job he was hired to do.

16.4.4 Torts authorized by the employer

cross reference
Nuisance is covered in chapter 8.

Employers who authorize independent contractors to commit a tort have primary liability for that tort. For instance, in *Ellis v Sheffield Gas Consumers Co* (1853) 2 E&B 767 a gas company hired independent contractors to carry out some roadworks. Since the gas company had no legal right to work on the road, this amounted to the tort of nuisance. Although it was the contractors who actually dug up the road, the gas company was liable because they had authorized the contractors to do the works. Again, imposing liability on employers in these circumstances is consistent with the control test, in that employers are here directing the work of the independent contractors.

(16.5) Liability in hospitals

The issue of whether or not hospitals are liable for their staff was one of the first to expose problems with the control test. Hospitals are generally managed by people who are not themselves medically qualified and who are therefore unable to tell medical staff how to do their work. Nevertheless, in *Cassidy v Ministry of Health* [1951] 1 All ER 574, it was decided that hospitals are vicariously liable for medical professionals who are part of the hospital's permanent staff. Hospitals are not liable for the acts of visiting professionals, such as GPs and some consultants. NHS hospitals, however, have primary liability for the torts of those staff on the basis that the NHS has a non-delegable duty of care towards patients. In practice, the NHS voluntarily accepts vicarious liability for consultants under what is known as the 'NHS Indemnity Scheme'.

(16.6) Liability in the police force

In the case of police officers, section 88(1) of the Police Act 1996 provides that the chief of police for the region is vicariously liable for any torts that individual officers commit in the performance (or purported performance) of their police functions. This is why you will come across cases in which the defendant is the Metropolitan Police Commissioner (the chief of police for the London area) or the Chief Constable for a county. The Chief Constable or Metropolitan Police Commissioner will be liable whenever an ordinary employer in a similar situation would also be liable.

16.7 Loans with delegation of authority

Vicarious liability can also apply when a car-owner asks someone else to use the car to do a favour for the owner. This is also known as 'casual delegation'. The advantage to the claimant is that the owner will usually be insured, whereas the driver may not be. For instance, in *Ormrod v Crosville Motor Services Ltd* [1953] 1 WLR 1120, the owner asked a friend to drive the car to Monte Carlo, where they were going to holiday together. In *Candler v Thomas* [1998] RTR 214, the owner asked a friend to use his van to deliver a package for him. In both cases, the owners were vicariously liable when an accident occurred. These cases contrast with *Morgans v Launchbury* [1973] AC 127, where a woman lent her car to her husband so that he could go to the pub, but asked him to promise that if he got drunk, he would get a friend to drive him home. When the friend was in a car accident, the wife was not vicariously liable for the friend because she did not benefit from the trip to the pub. Thus, there must be a benefit to the lender in order for liability to result.

16.8 Relations between defendants

As we have seen in this chapter, it is possible for several people simultaneously to be liable for the same damage. For instance, an employer and an employee may both be liable to the victim of a tort, either due to vicarious liability or because both have primary liability. People who are liable in tort for the same damage are known as either 'joint tortfeasors' or 'several tortfeasors'. The distinction is not important for the purposes of this book, as most of its practical implications have been abolished by statute. For those interested in the historical distinction, joint tortfeasors were those who acted with a common design and caused an injury. Several tortfeasors each acted independently, but all contributed to the injury.

Where there are joint or several tortfeasors, the claimant can decide whether to sue one of them, all of them, or any combination of them. The claimant will only recover damages once over, however, no matter how many people are sued, even if all of them are shown to be liable to the claimant. If the claimant is successful against more than one potential defendant, those defendants can ask the court to allocate the liability between them. The court will then usually allocate liability in proportion to each defendant's degree of fault, although it has a discretion to allocate liability on some other basis. For instance, if the claimant obtains judgment against both an employer and an employee

cross reference

Chapter 4 discussed how courts allocate liability in relation to multiple causes.

and the employee cannot afford to pay damages, the court may order the employer to pay the full amount. If there are potential defendants who have not been named by the claimant, those defendants who have been named can claim a contribution towards the damages from the other (absent) tortfeasors. They can do this either by suing the others separately or by bringing them into the claimant's proceedings using a procedure known as Part 20 proceedings (because it is dealt with in Part 20 of the Civil Procedure Rules). The ability to claim a contribution is based on the Civil Liability (Contribution) Act 1978, which is excerpted below.

● **Civil Liability (Contribution) Act 1978**

1 Entitlement to contribution

(1) Subject to the following provisions of this section, any person liable in respect of any damage suffered by another person may recover contribution from any other person liable in respect of the same damage (whether jointly with him or otherwise).

(2) A person shall be entitled to recover contribution by virtue of subsection (1) above notwithstanding that he has ceased to be liable in respect of the damage in question since the time when the damage occurred, provided that he was so liable immediately before he made or was ordered or agreed to make the payment in respect of which the contribution is sought.

(3) A person shall be liable to make contribution by virtue of subsection (1) above notwithstanding that he has ceased to be liable in respect of the damage in question since the time when the damage occurred, unless he ceased to be liable by virtue of the expiry of a period of limitation or prescription which extinguished the right on which the claim against him in respect of the damage was based.

(4) A person who has made or agreed to make any payment in bona fide settlement or compromise of any claim made against him in respect of any damage (including a payment into court which has been accepted) shall be entitled to recover contribution in accordance with this section without regard to whether or not he himself is or ever was liable in respect of the damage, provided, however, that he would have been liable assuming that the factual basis of the claim against him could be established.

(5) A judgment given in any action brought in any part of the United Kingdom by or on behalf of the person who suffered the damage in question against any person from whom contribution is sought under this section shall be conclusive in the proceedings for contribution as to any issue determined by that judgment in favour of the person from whom the contribution is sought.

● **Civil Liability (Contribution) Act 1978**

2 Assessment of contribution

(1) Subject to subsection (3) below, in any proceedings for contribution under section 1 above the amount of the contribution recoverable from any person shall be such as may be found by the court to be just and equitable having regard to the extent of that person's responsibility for the damage in question.

(2) Subject to subsection (3) below, the court shall have power in any such proceedings to exempt any person from liability to make contribution, or to direct that the contribution to be recovered from any person shall amount to a complete indemnity.

(3) Where the amount of the damages which have or might have been awarded in respect of the damage in question in any action brought in England and Wales by or on behalf of the person who suffered it against the person from whom the contribution is sought was or would have been subject to—

(a) any limit imposed by or under any enactment or by any agreement made before the damage occurred;

(b) any reduction by virtue of section 1 of the Law Reform (Contributory Negligence) Act 1945 or section 5 of the Fatal Accidents Act 1976; or

(c) any corresponding limit or reduction under the law of a country outside England and Wales;

(4) the person from whom the contribution is sought shall not by virtue of any contribution awarded under section 1 above be required to pay in respect of the damage a greater amount than the amount of those damages as so limited or reduced.

As the above excerpt indicates, the factors the courts take into account in making contribution orders are effectively the same as those that are used to assess contributory negligence.

For more revision tips, including self-test questions and suggestions for further reading, see the Online Resource Centre at www.oxfordtextbooks.co.uk/orc/strong_complete/.

revision tasks

Here are some ideas to try when you revise this chapter:

- Draw a mind-map illustrating how to determine whether someone is an employee or an independent contractor.

- Make a table summarizing the differences between liability for the torts of an employee and the torts of an independent contractor.

- Explain how and when a defendant may be subject to a claim of contribution from another defendant.

Part 9

Torts Against the Person

17 Torts against the person

17.1 Introduction

We come now to our final grouping of torts. These involve intentional—rather than negligent—wrongdoing against another individual and echo certain concepts involved in trespass to land. In fact, older cases often refer to this group of torts as 'trespass against the person'. In addition, you will be reminded of principles discussed in your criminal law course. While there are analogies between crimes and intentional torts, be careful not to confuse the two—civil law is not the same as criminal law.

Torts against the person are amongst the oldest kinds of civil actions. Many of the leading cases date back to the eighteenth and nineteenth century. Don't let the age of these opinions fool you—in this area of law, ancient precedents are still good law. However, the Human Rights Act 1998 has affected torts against the person, providing new claims and bases for relief, and the older precedents may be ripe for reconsideration.

This chapter first identifies four different types of intentional torts and then discusses possible defences. The four intentional torts against the person are:

compare
Although trespass to land is an intentional tort, it was discussed in chapter 10, in connection with other torts involving real property.

• Battery;

• Assault;

• False imprisonment; and

• Liability under *Wilkinson v Downton*.

For each of these torts, we will consider:

• The defendant's mental state;

• The defendant's physical acts;

• Issues involving the claimant; and

• Damages and other remedies.

Finally, we will consider claims for intentional torts against the person under the Human Rights Act 1998. Although these claims do not fall under the traditional headings for intentional torts, the Human Rights Act 1998 may be establishing ways for claimants to recover for behaviour that was previously not remediable at law.

The defences addressed in this chapter include:

• Self-defence;

• Defence of others; and

• *Ex turpi causa non oritur actio*, which involves a claimant who is him or herself a wrongdoer.

Consent may also be considered a defence, but often forms part of the claimant's affirmative case and is therefore discussed in section 17.2.1.

In addition, a defendant to an action for an intentional tort may rely on defences that have been discussed elsewhere in this book, including:

• Contributory negligence; and

• Defence of property and necessity.

We will begin with a discussion of battery, the first of the intentional torts.

cross reference
For more on contributory negligence, see chapter 5. For more on defence of property and necessity, see chapter 10.

17.2 Battery

Battery is defined as the actual and unlawful infliction of force on another person. Notably, battery doesn't have to involve a fist fight—it could involve force transferred by other means, such as a pint of beer thrown into someone else's face. Furthermore, battery doesn't even have to involve violence or a negative intent—battery can just as easily result from a well-intentioned act, such as when a doctor accidentally amputates someone's leg instead of removing an appendix. Although the doctor's act could constitute negligence, it can also involve battery.

As with other torts, a claimant must prove several different elements before he or she can recover damages from the defendant. In particular, the claimant must address:

• The defendant's mental state;

• The defendant's physical acts; and

• Issues involving the claimant.

cross reference
See chapter 11 for a discussion of the various types of damages, including nominal damages.

While claimants do not need to prove damages as part of their initial case, they cannot recover more than a nominal sum if they do not demonstrate the extent of their injury. Therefore, most claimants will include a discussion of the damages they have suffered as a result of the defendant's actions as part of their case in chief.

17.2.1 The defendant's mental state

If battery constitutes an intentional tort, it stands to reason that the defendant must act intentionally. However, what is an intentional act? Must the defendant intend the outcome of his or her behaviour? Is it enough that the result is simply foreseeable? Alternatively, is it enough for the defendant simply to set a course of action accidentally into play?

At this point in your studies, you are well familiar with the principles of negligence. However, as discussed in earlier chapters, the tort of negligence is a relatively recent innovation. For many years, there was no clear distinction between wrongs committed accidentally (in other words, negligently) and those committed intentionally. As a result, early cases failed to identify the extent to which intentional torts, including battery, overlapped with negligence. However, the Court of Appeal set the record straight in 1965 in *Letang v Cooper* [1965] 1 QB 232, which stated explicitly that an act done negligently is negligence, whereas an act done intentionally is trespass to the person, meaning battery. The facts in *Letang v Cooper* [1965] 1 QB 232 are memorable. The plaintiff was sunbathing in a hotel car park when the defendant drove in and accidentally ran over the legs of the plaintiff. Because the limitations period for negligence had expired by the time the plaintiff brought her case, she attempted to frame her cause of action as trespass to the person instead, since the limitations period for trespass was longer. In denying her cause of action, the Court of Appeal ruled that courts should look at the substance of the claim, not the way the plaintiff framed it.

. . . .

● *Letang v Cooper* [1965] 1 QB 323

> Lord Denning: If one man intentionally applies force directly to another, the plaintiff has a cause of action in assault and battery, or, if you so please to describe it, in trespass to the person. 'The least touching of another in anger is a battery,' per Holt CJ in *Cole v Turner* (1704) 6 Mod. 149. If he does not inflict injury intentionally, but only unintentionally, the plaintiff has no cause of action today in trespass. His only cause of action is in negligence, and then only on proof of want of reasonable care. If the plaintiff cannot prove want of reasonable care, he may have no cause of action at all. Thus, it is not enough nowadays for the plaintiff to plead that 'the defendant shot the plaintiff.' He must also allege that he did it intentionally or negligently. If intentional, it is the tort of assault and battery. If negligent and causing damage, it is the tort of negligence.

Thus, *Letang v Cooper* [1965] 1 QB 232 confirmed negligence and trespass to the person as two separate torts, with intent to act comprising an integral part of the latter. As a result of this decision, a claimant alleging battery therefore must prove that the defendant's state of mind is more than negligent. By definition, a battery must be intentional. In torts involving trespass to land, an intentional act can mean many different things. First, an act cannot be considered intentional if the person did not choose to behave in a certain way. For example, a defendant has not committed a trespass if he or she is pushed onto someone else's property. Second, a defendant may intend to undertake a certain action—such as the felling of a tree with a power saw—but may not intend the result that actually occurred—such as the destruction of the house next door when the tree falls the wrong way. That will still be a trespass to land. Similarly, a defendant may intend to undertake a certain action that infringes on the interests of another person—such as walking on neighbouring property to return a ball that has rolled from one yard to another—but may not intend or anticipate that the act will cause offence or harm. Again, the defendant has trespassed.

NOTE Intentional torts raise similar issues, regardless of whether they deal with trespass to the person or trespass to land. Be sure to cross-reference your notes so that you can draw analogies between the different torts.

Similar principles exist for all intentional torts to the person. For example, a person might take an action—such as waving one's arm to scare away an errant wasp—without intending to whack another person standing nearby. Someone else might intend to swat an errant wasp that has landed on another person, but merely intend to kill the wasp rather than injure the person. Does battery exist in either case? These examples raise the question of whether any deliberate, voluntary act is considered 'intentional' such that liability will result if the actor makes contact with someone else.

Unsurprisingly, courts have spent a great deal of time discussing this issue. One common definition of battery used by the Court of Appeal in *Wilson v Pringle* [1987] QB 237 states that the defendant's act must constitute a 'hostile' touching before it can be considered battery. In that case, a 13-year-old boy allegedly jumped on another 13-year-old boy as they were playing, injuring the second boy. The Court of Appeal denied recovery by the plaintiff, finding that the act in question was not hostile.

● *Wilson v Pringle* [1987] QB 237

cross reference

Tuberville v Savage (1669) 1 Mod Rep 3 is discussed below.

Croom-Johnson LJ: In the action for negligence the physical contact (where it takes place at all) is normally though by no means always unintended. In the action for trespass, to constitute a battery, it is deliberate. Even so it is not every intended contact which is tortious. Apart from special justifications (such as acting in self-defence) there are many examples in everyday life where an intended contact or touch is not actionable as a trespass. These are not necessarily those (such as shaking hands) where consent is actual or to be implied. They may amount to one of the instances in mind in *Tuberville v Savage*, 1 Mod. 3 which takes place in innocence. A modern instance is the batsman walking up the pavilion steps at Lord's after making a century. He receives hearty slaps of congratulations on his back. He may not want them. Some of them may be too heavy for comfort. No one seeks his permission, or can assume he would give it if it were asked. But would an action for trespass to the person lie?

Another ingredient in the tort of trespass to the person is that of hostility. The references to anger sufficing to turn a touch into a battery (*Cole v Turner*, 6 Mod. 149) and the lack of an intention to assault which prevents a gesture from being an assault are instances of this. If there is a hostile intent, that will by itself be cogent evidence of hostility. But the hostility may be demonstrated in other ways...

In our view, the authorities lead one to the conclusion that in a battery there must be an intentional touching or contact in one form or another of the plaintiff by the defendant. That touching must be proved to be a hostile touching. That still leaves unanswered the question 'when is a touching to be called hostile?' Hostility cannot be equated with ill-will or malevolence. It cannot be governed by the obvious intention shown in acts like punching, stabbing or shooting. It cannot be solely governed by an expressed intention, although that may be strong evidence. But the element of hostility, in the sense in which it is now to be considered, must be a question of fact for the tribunal of fact. It may

cross reference
Collins v Wilcock [1984] 1 WLR 1172 is discussed below.

be imported from the circumstances. Take the example of the police officer in *Collins v Wilcock* [1984] 1 WLR 1172. She touched the woman deliberately, but without an intention to do more than restrain her temporarily. Nevertheless, she was acting unlawfully and in that way was acting with hostility. She was acting contrary to the woman's legal right not to be physically restrained. We see no more difficulty in establishing what she intended by means of question and answer, or by inference from the surrounding circumstances, than there is in establishing whether an apparently playful blow was struck in anger...[I]n the ordinary give and take of everyday life the tribunal of fact should find no difficulty in answering the question 'was this, or was it not, a battery?' Where the immediate act of touching does not itself demonstrate hostility, the plaintiff should plead the facts which are said to do so.

Although we are all entitled to protection from physical molestation we live in a crowded world in which people must be considered as taking on themselves some risk of injury (where it occurs) from the acts of others which are not in themselves unlawful...

Defences like self-defence, and exercising the right of arrest, are relevant here. Similarly, it may be that allowances must be made, where appropriate, for the idiosyncrasies of individuals or...the irresponsibility of childhood and the degree of care and awareness which is to be expected of children.

Thus, the term 'hostility' does not mean that someone is acting with malice or ill will. Instead, hostility means that the defendant understands that he or she is doing something to which another person will likely object. The test carries elements of objectivity—since the defendant cannot be expected to know, in every circumstance, how the individual claimant will respond—but also carries elements of subjectivity, since the defendant can be charged with anticipating how certain groups of individuals are likely to react. For example, a 13-year-old boy might well believe that another 13-year-old boy would not object to a certain amount of rough horseplay. On the other hand, an adult might find the same behaviour improper and objectionable.

In *Wilson v Pringle* [1987] QB 237, the Court of Appeal decided that rough horseplay between two 13-year-olds, did not, by itself, constitute a hostile touching. Instead, the plaintiff would have to prove that the defendant intended to cause injury or distress before the plaintiff could recover.

Later courts, including the House of Lords in *F v West Berkshire Health Authority* [1989] 1 All ER 545, have questioned the usefulness of the term 'hostile'. In that case, a 36-year-old woman with a mental age of five to six was a voluntary resident of a mental hospital and was thought to have been engaging in sexual relations with another patient. The staff of the hospital came to the court to request that she be sterilized. The House of Lords unanimously agreed, proving an important decision for a number of reasons. First, Lord Goff further explains the definition of battery described in *Wilson v Pringle* [1987] 1 QB 232. For example, Lord Goff recognized that a physician may consider surgery to be the best option for a particular patient and may be motivated by nothing but the best of the intentions in undertaking the surgery. However, sometimes a patient refuses surgery, perhaps because he or she refuses to admit to him or herself the severity of the illness or has an irrational fear of needles or hospitals. What if the patient refuses on religious or economic grounds? According to Lord Goff, any move by the physician to operate on a patient over the patient's objections constitutes battery, no matter how well intentioned the surgeon may be. Thus, the term 'hostile touching' is inappropriate in this context, since the physician intends a positive, rather than a negative, outcome. Lord Goff could have reached his conclusion based on the language in *Wilson v Pringle* [1987] QB 237, since the Court of Appeal's definition of hostility focused on whether the defendant understands that he or she has done something that could be construed as an unlawful intrusion on the plaintiff's rights to physical privacy and personal autonomy.

However, rather than rely on the older definition of battery in that case, Lord Goff decided to define battery as involving (1) the deliberate touching of another person's body which is beyond the bounds of acceptable everyday conduct and (2) the absence of a lawful excuse. As we shall see, in the medical field, a lawful excuse exists when a patient has a permanent or temporary mental incapacity that results in the patient's being unable (as opposed to simply unwilling) to consent to a medical or other necessary procedure. In those instances Lord Goff relied on the principle of necessity as a means of overcoming the need to obtain the patient's consent.

. . . .

● *F v West Berkshire Health Authority* [1989] 2 All ER 545

Lord Goff: I start with the fundamental principle, now long established, that every person's body is inviolate. As to this, I do not wish to depart from what I myself said in the judgment of the Divisional Court in *Collins v Wilcock* [1984] 3 All ER 374, [1984] 1 WLR 1172, and in particular from the statement that the effect of this principle is that everybody is protected not only against physical injury but against any form of physical molestation . . .

Of course, as a general rule physical interference with another person's body is lawful if he consents to it . . . [A] broader exception has been created to allow for the exigencies of everyday life: jostling in a street or some other crowded place, social contact at parties and such like. This exception has been said to be founded on implied consent, since those who go about in public places, or go to parties, may be taken to have impliedly consented to bodily contact of this kind. Today this rationalisation can be regarded as artificial and, in particular, it is difficult to impute consent to those who, by reason of their youth or mental disorder, are unable to give their consent. For this reason, I consider it more appropriate to regard such cases as falling within a general exception embracing all physical contact which is generally acceptable in the ordinary conduct of everyday life.

In the old days it used to be said that, for a touching of another's person to amount to a battery, it had to be a touching 'in anger' (see *Cole v Turner* (1704) Holt KB 108, 90 ER 958 per Holt CJ) and it has recently been said that the touching must be 'hostile' to have that effect (see *Wilson v Pringle* [1986] 2 All ER 440 at 447, [1987] QB 237 and 153). I respectfully doubt whether that is correct . . .

It is against this background that I turn to consider the question whether, and if so when, medical treatment or care of a mentally disordered person who is, by reason of his incapacity, incapable of giving his consent can be regarded as lawful . . . As is recognised in Cardozo J's statement of principle, and elsewhere (see e.g. *Sidaway v Bethlem Royal Hospital Governors* [1985] 1 All ER 643 at 649, [1985] AC 871 at 882 per Lord Scarman), some relaxation of the law is required to accommodate persons of unsound mind. In *Wilson v Pringle* the Court of Appeal considered that treatment or care of such persons may be regarded as lawful, as falling within the exception relating to physical contact which is generally acceptable in the ordinary course of everyday life. Again, I am with respect unable to agree. That exception is concerned with the ordinary events of everyday life, jostling in public places and such like, and affects all persons, whether or not they are capable of giving their consent. Medical treatment, even treatment for minor ailments, does not fall within that category of events. The general rule is that consent is necessary to render such treatment lawful. If such treatment administered without consent is not to be unlawful, it has to be justified on some other principle...

NOTE Notice how Lord Goff analogises between intentional torts to the person (such as battery) and intentional torts to property (such as trespass).

That there exists in the common law a principle of necessity which may justify action which would otherwise be unlawful is not in doubt. But historically the principle has been seen to be restricted to two groups of cases, which have been called cases of public necessity and cases of private necessity. The former occurred when a man interfered with another man's property in the public interest, for example (in the days before we could dial 999 for the fire brigade) the destruction of another man's house to prevent the spread of a catastrophic fire, as indeed occurred in the Great Fire of London in 1666. The latter cases occurred when a man interfered with another's property to save his own person or property from imminent danger, for example when he entered on his neighbour's land without his consent in order to prevent the spread of fire onto his own land.

There is, however, a third group of cases, which is also properly described as founded on the principle of necessity and which is more pertinent to the resolution of the problem in the present case. These cases are concerned with action taken as a matter of necessity to assist another person without his consent. To give a simple example, a man who seizes another and forcibly drags him from the path of an oncoming vehicle, thereby saving him from injury or even death, commits no wrong. But there are many emanations of this principle, to be found scattered through the books. These are concerned not only with the preservation of the life or health of the assisted person, but also with the preservation of his property (sometimes an animal, sometimes an ordinary chattel) and even to certain conduct on his behalf in the administration of his affairs. Where there is a pre-existing relationship between the parties, the intervener is usually said to act as an agent of necessity on behalf of the principal in whose interests he acts, and his action can often, with not too much artificiality, be referred to the pre-existing relationship between them...

We are concerned here with action taken to preserve the life, health or well-being of another who is unable to consent to it. Such action is sometimes said to be justified as arising from an emergency in Prosser and Keeton Torts (5th edn, 1984) p 117 the action is said to be privileged by the emergency. Doubtless, in the case of a person of sound mind, there will ordinarily have to be an emergency before such action taken without consent can be lawful for otherwise there would be an opportunity to communicate with the assisted person and to seek his consent. But this is not always so and indeed the historical origins of the principle of necessity do not point to emergency as such as providing the criterion of lawful intervention without consent...But, when a person is rendered incapable of communication either permanently or over a considerable period of time (through illness or accident or mental disorder), it would be an unusual use of language to describe the case as one of 'permanent emergency', if indeed such a state of affairs can properly be said to exist. In truth, the relevance of an emergency is that it may give rise to a necessity to act in the interests of the assisted person without first obtaining his consent. Emergency is however not the criterion or even a prerequisite it is simply a frequent origin of the necessity which impels intervention. The principle is one of necessity, not of emergency...

[T]he basic requirements, applicable in these cases of necessity, that, to fall within the principle, not only (1) must there be a necessity to act when it is not practicable to communicate with the assisted person, but also (2) the action taken must be such as a reasonable person would in all the circumstances take, acting in the best interests of the assisted person...

But as a general rule, if the above criteria are fulfilled, interference with the assisted person's person or property (as the case may be) will not be unlawful. Take the example of a railway accident, in which injured passengers are trapped in the wreckage. It is this principle which may render lawful the actions of other citizens, railway staff, passengers or outsiders, who rush to give aid and comfort to the victims: the surgeon who amputates the limb of an unconscious passenger to free him from the wreckage the ambulance man who conveys him to hospital the doctors and nurses who treat him and care for him while he is still unconscious. Take the example of an elderly person who suffers a stroke which renders him incapable of speech or movement. It is by virtue of this principle that the doctor who treats him, the nurse who cares for him, even the relative or friend or neighbour who comes in to look after him will commit no wrong when he or she touches his body.

The two examples I have given illustrate, in the one case, an emergency and, in the other, a permanent or semi-permanent state of affairs. Another example of the latter kind is that of a mentally disordered person who is disabled from giving consent. I can see no good reason why the principle of necessity should not be applicable in his case as it is in the case of the victim of a stroke. Furthermore, in the case of a mentally disordered person, as in the case of a stroke victim, the permanent state of affairs calls for a wider range of care than may be requisite in an emergency which arises from accidental injury. When the state of affairs is permanent, or semi-permanent, action properly taken to preserve the life, health or well-being of the assisted person may well transcend such measures as surgical operation or substantial medical treatment and may extend to include such humdrum matters as routine medical or dental treatment, even simple care such as dressing and undressing and putting to bed.

think point
Is Lord Goff's description of consent in emergency situations all that different from implied consent?

think point

What difficulties arise when a court uses societal norms – also known as the view of the 'reasonable man' or the 'man from the Clapham omnibus'—as the legal standard? Does every man on the Clapham omnibus have the same view of others' conduct? Does the view of a woman differ? How about the view of a person on a Liverpool omnibus, an Edinburgh omnibus or a rural omnibus? Does the law adequately take these differing views into account?

Wilson v Pringle [1987] 1 QB 232 is consistent with *F v West Berkshire Health Authority* [1989] 2 All ER 545, but the emphasis is slightly different. Whereas the Court of Appeal focused on whether the behaviour was unwarranted, unwanted and unanticipated, looking at the question from the plaintiff's perspective, Lord Goff focused on whether the behaviour fell outside established societal norms—itself something of a moving target—and without lawful excuse. Lord Goff's test also avoids the unfortunate term 'hostile touching,' which can unnecessarily confuse the issue of mental intent.

One open question in the area of intentional torts involves 'transferred intent'. American courts have decided that if a defendant (A) intends to batter one person (B), but accidentally batters another (C), the intent to batter will be transferred from the first person (B) to the second person (C) and the claimant (C) will have proven the necessary mental element. Courts in the United States have also dealt with the issue of transference of intent between different torts, such as when a defendant intends only to frighten the claimant (which, we shall see, constitutes the tort of assault) but instead unintentionally strikes the claimant. The question there is whether the intent to commit assault transforms itself into an intent to commit battery. British civil courts have not yet addressed the issue, although English criminal courts have held that in the context of criminal battery—which is similar, in many regards, as civil battery—intent can be transferred among different parties so that a defendant (A) who intended to injure one person (B) can be guilty of a crime after accidentally injuring another person (C) instead. Normally you should avoid citing a criminal case in a civil context, since two fields differ in terms of procedure, standards of proof and so on, but an exception exists for cases involving intentional torts, since the elements of the torts are so similar to the elements of the crimes. These criminal cases will be persuasive, rather than binding, authority, similar to cases cited from other jurisdictions. Thus, if you were in an English or Welsh court, you could analogize to cases from Northern Ireland that have held that intent may transfer from one potential victim to an actual victim. For example, in *Livingstone v Ministry of Defence* [1984] NIO 356, a soldier fired a baton round at one rioter but missed and hit the plaintiff instead. The Northern Ireland Court of Appeal held that the soldier's intent to hit one rioter transferred to the plaintiff and that a claim of battery thus could lie.

think point

Which do you think is the better rule, the British position that contact must be directly with the person or the American view that some items that are so intimately involved with the claimant that contact with them should be actionable? Is your decision based on principles (such as your definition of what individuals define as their 'person') or pragmatics (such as the recognition that an expanded definition may lead to more cases that would clog the court system)?

17.2.2 The defendant's physical acts

The essence of battery involves physical contact between the defendant and the claimant. However, that contact must be direct and actionable. A direct action is one that immediately follows from the act of the defendant as a continuation of the defendant's initial conduct. Thus, reaching out and bodily stopping someone constitutes a battery, but so, too, does whipping a horse and causing it to bolt and run down the claimant. In the latter example, the action by the defendant—whipping the horse—led directly to the injury to the plaintiff, thus allowing the judge in *Gibbons v Pepper* (1695) 1 Ld Raym 38 to hold that a battery existed.

cross reference
For more on causation and foreseeability, see chapter 4.

As you know, chains of causation can become rather complex. For example, in *Scott v Shepherd* (1773) 2 Wm Bl 892, person A threw a lighted object into a marketplace, causing it to land on the stall of person B, who threw it away to prevent his stall from burning down, causing it to land on the stall of person C, who also threw it away to prevent his stall from burning down, causing the lighted object to strike a passer-by in the face. De Grey CJ held that a battery existed, since the chain of causation was direct and followed on from the act of the defendant. On the other hand, it was not battery in *Dodwell v Burford* (1669) 1 Mod Rep 24 when one person struck the horse of another, leading the horse to throw its rider and resulting in the rider's being trampled by the horse of a third party. There, the action was not sufficiently direct. Although the cases on battery do not speak of causation and foreseeability in the same way that negligence cases do, particularly when the cases in question are ancient precedent, the analysis is obviously similar.

Furthermore, the contact must be directly with the claimant him or herself, not with some item held by him or her. For example, water thrown onto someone's clothes is not battery unless some force is transmitted to the body of the claimant. This is contrary to the rule in countries such as the United States, where a person may be liable in battery if he or she makes contact with anything connected with another person, including, for example, a car in which the claimant is sitting, an item that the claimant is carrying or any other thing attached to the claimant.

Once the court has decided the contact is sufficiently direct, it must consider how forceful the contact is. Certainly some touching must occur, since it is impossible to batter a person by omission. For example, in *Innes v Wylie* (1844) 1 Car & Kir 257, a police officer blocked the plaintiff's entrance to a meeting place without touching the plaintiff, leading the court to hold that, 'If the policeman was entirely passive like a door or a wall put to prevent the plaintiff from entering the room and simply obstructing the entrance of the plaintiff, no assault has been committed'. However, no matter what level of force is applied, it need not result in any damage or injury to the claimant. Instead, damages in intentional torts are per se, meaning that they arise simply as a result of the defendant's action. Thus, since the bumps and brushing-bys of ordinary life tend not to cause offence in a reasonable person, they tend not to be recoverable. Thus, tapping a stranger on the shoulder to get his or her attention may be an acceptable type of everyday contact, but grabbing a stranger by the arm to force a conversation is not.

17.2.3 Issues involving the claimant

In intentional torts to the person, consent—or the lack thereof—is a critical element. In battery cases, a claimant must prove lack of consent as part of his or her initial case, rather than leaving it to the defendant to claim consent as a defence. For example, *Freeman v Home Office (No 2)* [1984] QB 524 involved a prisoner who claimed that he had been injected with certain drugs against his will. The judge held that it was up to the plaintiff to prove that the injection was non-consensual. This makes sense as a matter of public policy. If, for example, the defendant was required to prove consent, physicians would have to alter their medical routines to obtain explicit—and most likely written—consent for every procedure ranging from a simple ear or throat check to full-fledged surgery. This would quickly become unmanageable and hinder the smooth operation of the medical profession. However, it may make less sense in the context of prison procedure, where policies are needed to protect prisoners.

The claimant must prove lack of consent as part of his or her prima facie case in any of the intentional torts to the person. This is different than the intentional tort of trespass to land, where lack of consent does not form part of the claimant's initial case. In trespass to land, consent constitutes a proper defence to be brought up by the defendant. Furthermore, the need to prove lack of consent in battery is different than the approach used in the tort of negligence, where volenti non fit injuria and assumption of the risk—two consent-like defences—are something to be proven by the defendant.

compare
For more on volenti non fit injuria and assumption of the risk, see chapter 5.

Consent arises in one of two forms: expressly (as through words) or implicitly (as through conduct). Implicit consent arises most often in sport: boxers, rugby players and footballers, for example, all implicitly consent to a certain amount of pummelling from their opponents, as defined by the rules of the game. A boxer may not object to a broken nose resulting from a right jab to the face, if it was given during the bout. He or she may, however, properly object to a broken nose resulting from a kick to the face, even if it was given during the match, since kicking is not permitted under the rules of the sport and is therefore not the type of injury to which the boxer agreed. Similarly, a footballer may have to endure a certain amount of kicking while on the pitch, but will not have to put up with purposeful punching. Some would say that rugby players are required to put up with just about everything, but the rules identify a number of acts as illegal. Therefore, if a rugby tackle is lawful under the rules of the game, it cannot constitute a battery, and a claimant may not recover damages associated with a broken leg that results from such a tackle.

Outside the realm of sport, consent by implication can be difficult to prove. For example, the person must be capable of consent, suggesting that drunken consent is not legal consent. Similarly, the consent must relate to the act at issue. Thus, if a person goes to a hair salon and asks for a permanent, it is a battery to apply a colour rinse, as suggested by *Nash v Sheen* [1955] CLY 3726. Furthermore, consent may not be obtained by duress or by fraud. Therefore, the plaintiff in *R v Clarence* (1888) 22 QBD 23 was unable to recover in battery after her lover infected her with syphilis. The court held that no battery could have occurred since she consented to sexual intercourse, even though she did not know that her lover was infected with a venereal disease.

think point

Would this decision hold up today? Would it make a difference if the woman was infected with HIV rather than with syphilis? Note that at the time of the decision (1888), syphilis was incurable.

Implied consent is also common in the medical context. For example, opening one's mouth in a doctor's surgery and saying 'ahhh' implies consent to a throat examination.

However, physicians often obtain express written consent when they are about to perform an operation or other invasive procedures. The usual consent form indicates that the patient has been told of the 'effect and nature' of the procedure. If the physician does not give an adequate explanation of the planned treatment, at least in broad, general terms, the consent is invalid. However, a physician's failure to explain adequately the risks and possible side-effects of the treatment plan does not normally lead to an action in battery, although it could constitute a breach of the physician's duty of care and thus result in liability for negligence.

What if a patient is unable to consent to a particular procedure or does not provide clear, unequivocal instructions? The Court of Appeal has stated in *Re T (Adult: Refusal of Medical Treatment)* [1994] 4 All ER 649 that when it is unclear whether a patient has rejected life-saving treatment freely and with a full understanding of the consequences of the decision, then a physician who acts to preserve life acts lawfully. In that case, a woman who was not herself a Jehovah's Witness (a religious group that refuses blood transfusions in all circumstances, even to save a person's life) refused to accept medical treatment after some time alone with her mother, who was a Jehovah's Witness. The patient then fell unconscious. The Court of Appeal upheld the legality of a blood transfusion made after the patient became unconscious on the grounds that the patient had not been fully advised of the consequences of her decision. Although the Court of Appeal could be seen as substituting its own views for the views of the patient, Lord Donaldson was careful to note that 'the patient's right of choice exists whether the reasons for making that choice are rational, irrational, unknown or even non-existent. That his [or her] choice is contrary to what is to be expected of the vast majority of adults is only relevant if there are other reasons for doubting his [or her] capacity to decide'.

For the most part, courts are keen to uphold the principles of autonomy and self-determination in law, at least where the patient is adult and competent. Of course, mental competency can be a nebulous concept, particularly since some judges appear inclined to rule that a patient is incompetent if he or she makes a decision that is contrary to majority norms. For example, a lower-level court ruled in *St George's Healthcare NHS Trust v S* [1998] 3 All ER 673 that a pregnant woman might be forced to have a caesarean section if doing so was necessary to protect the interest of her viable foetus, although the Court of Appeal ultimately overruled that decision. What is interesting about the case is how the court at first instance seemed to equate rejection of cultural norms with mental incompetence.

Just because a person suffers from a mental disorder does not mean that he or she lacks capacity to direct or refuse medical treatment. For example, in *Re C (Adult: Refusal of Treatment)* [1994] 1 WLR 290, a mental patient suffering from paranoid schizophrenia developed gangrene in an injured foot and was allowed to obtain an injunction upholding his desire not to have the foot amputated, even if it meant that he would die as a result of his decision. Because the patient understood 'the nature, purpose and effects of the proffered operation', the judge ruled that he was competent to refuse treatment.

Truly incapacitated persons—including those who are unconscious—constitute another problem. Anthony Bland was a patient in a persistent vegetative state who was kept alive through artificial means. His parents and caretakers wished to discontinue artificial feeding, which would inevitably result in his death. In *Airedale NHS Trust v Bland* [1993] 1 All ER 821, the House of Lords looked at whether it was in the patient's best interests that treatment continue and decided unanimously that it was not and thus could be legally withdrawn.

Another key issue involves the right of children to consent to their own medical treatment. Since children are legally capable of asserting claims in tort, including claims in battery, it makes sense to give children the right to provide consent to medical treatment. Indeed, Parliament has specifically done so by statute.

● Family Law Reform Act 1969

8 Consent by persons over 16 to surgical, medical and dental treatment

(1) The consent of a minor who has attained the age of sixteen years to any surgical, medical or dental treatment which, in the absence of consent, would constitute a trespass to his person, shall be as effective as it would be if he were of full age; and where a minor has by virtue of this section given an effective consent to any treatment it shall not be necessary to obtain any consent for it from his parent or guardian.

(2) In this section 'surgical, medical or dental treatment' includes any procedure undertaken for the purposes of diagnosis, and this section applies to any procedure (including, in particular, the administration of an anaesthetic) which is ancillary to any treatment as it applies to that treatment.

(3) Nothing in this section shall be construed as making ineffective any consent which would have been effective if this section had not been enacted.

The Family Law Reform Act 1969 must be read in light of the leading case of *Gillick v West Norfolk and Wisbech Area Health Authority* [1986] AC 388, in which the House of Lords confirmed the standard which minor children must meet before they will be permitted to make their own health care decisions.

● *Gillick v West Norfolk and Wisbech Area Health Authority* [1986] AC 388

Lord Scarman: Victoria Gillick, mother of five daughters under the age of 16, challenges the lawfulness of a memorandum of guidance issued by the Department of Health and Social Security which she says encourages and in certain circumstances recommends health authorities, doctors, and others concerned in operating the department's family planning services to provide contraceptive advice and treatment to girls under the age of 16 without the knowledge or consent of a parent. Mrs. Gillick is a wife and mother living in a united family with her husband and their children. The husband supports the action being taken, as they both see it, to protect their daughters...

Mrs. Gillick began her proceedings by the issue of a writ against two defendants, the health authority for the area in which she lives and the department [of health and social security]. She claims in an ordinary civil action declaratory relief against both defendants that the guidance is unlawful, and against the area health authority alone a declaration that no doctor or other person in its employ may give contraception or abortion advice to Mrs. Gillick's children under the age of 16 without her prior knowledge and consent...

Mrs. Gillick's action is essentially to protect what she alleges to be her rights as a parent under private law...[S]he claims as a parent whose right of custody and guardianship in respect of her children under the age of 16 is (she says) threatened by the guidance given by the department to area health authorities, doctors, and others concerned in the provision by the department of a family health service...

The department's guidance

In 1974 the department assumed statutory responsibility for the provision of family planning services on a national basis...In May 1974 the department circulated a memorandum of guidance HN(80)46...

There can be no doubt that it does permit doctors to prescribe in certain circumstances contraception for girls under 16 without the knowledge and consent of a parent or guardian. (In this opinion I shall use the term 'parent' to include 'guardian'). The text is not, however, clear as to the circumstances (variously described as 'unusual' and 'exceptional') which justify a doctor in so doing...The question to be asked is: what would a doctor understand to be the guidance offered to him, if he should be faced with a girl under 16 seeking contraceptive treatment without the knowledge or consent of her parents?

He would know that it was his duty to seek to persuade the girl to let him bring into consultation her parents (or one of them). If she refused, he (or the counsellor to whom the girl had gone) must ask himself whether the case was one of those exceptional cases in which the guidance permitted a doctor to prescribe contraception without the knowledge or consent of a parent (provided always that in the exercise of his clinical judgment he thought this course to be in the true interest of his patient). In my judgment the guidance clearly implies that in exceptional cases the parental right to make decisions as to the care of their children, which derives from their right of custody, can lawfully be overridden, and that in such cases the doctor may without parental consultation or consent prescribe contraceptive treatment in the exercise of his clinical judgment. And the guidance reminds the doctor that in such cases he owes the duty of confidentiality to his patient, by which is meant that the doctor would be in breach of his duty to her if he did communicate with her parents...

The question, therefore, for the House is—can a doctor in any circumstances lawfully prescribe contraception for a girl under 16 without the knowledge and consent of a parent?

Before discussing the question, I put out of the way the two exceptions which I understand both parties to the appeal accept: namely the order of a competent court, and emergency...

Parental right and the age of consent

Mrs. Gillick relies on both the statute law and the case law to establish her proposition that parental consent is in all other circumstances necessary. The only statutory provision directly in point is section 8 of the Family Law Reform Act 1969. Subsection (1) of the section provides that the consent of a minor who has attained the age of 16 to any surgical, mental, or dental treatment which in the absence of consent would constitute a trespass to his person shall be as effective as if he were of full age and that the consent of his parent or guardian need not be obtained. Subsection (3) of the section provides: 'Nothing in this section shall be construed as making ineffective any consent which would have been effective if this section had not been enacted.'

I cannot accept the submission made on Mrs. Gillick's behalf that subsection (1) necessarily implies that prior to its enactment the consent of a minor to medical treatment could not be effective in law. Subsection (3) leaves open the question whether the consent of a minor under 16 could be an effective consent...I read the section as clarifying the law without conveying any indication as to what the law was before it was enacted. So far as minors under 16 are concerned, the law today is as it was before the enactment of the section...

The law has, therefore, to be found by a search in the judge-made law for the true principle...The House's task, therefore, as the supreme court in a legal system largely based on rules of law evolved over the years by the judicial process, is to search the overfull and cluttered shelves of the law reports for a principle, or set of principles recognised by the judges over the years but stripped of the detail which, however appropriate in their day, would, if applied today, lay the judges open to a justified criticism for failing to keep the law abreast of the society in which they live and work.

It is, of course, a judicial commonplace to proclaim the adaptability and flexibility of the judge-made common law. But this is more frequently proclaimed than acted upon. The mark of the great judge from Coke through Mansfield to our day has been the capacity and the will to search out principle, to discard the detail appropriate (perhaps) to earlier times, and to apply principle in such a way as to satisfy the needs of their own time. If judge-made law is to survive as a living and relevant body of law, we must make the effort, however inadequately, to follow the lead of the great masters of the judicial art.

In this appeal, therefore, there is much in the earlier case law which the House must discard—almost everything I would say but its principle. For example, the horrendous Agar-Ellis decisions, 10 Ch.D. 49; 24 Ch.D. 317 of the late nineteenth century asserting the power of the father over his child were rightly remaindered to the history books by the Court of Appeal in *Hewer v. Bryant* [1970] 1 Q.B. 357, an important case to which I shall return later. Yet the decisions of earlier generations may well afford clues to the true principle of the law: e.g. *Reg. v. Howes* (1860) 3 E. & E. 332, 336, which I also later quote. It is the duty of this House to look at, through, and past the decisions of earlier generations so that it may identify the principle which lies behind them...

Approaching the earlier law in this way, one finds plenty of indications as to the principles governing the law's approach to parental right and the child's right to make his or her own decision. Parental rights clearly do exist, and they do not wholly disappear until the age of majority. Parental rights relate to both the person and the property of the child—custody, care, and control of the person and guardianship of the property of the child. But the common law has never treated such rights as sovereign or beyond review and control. Nor has our law ever treated the child as other than a person with capacities and rights recognised by law. The principle of the law, as I shall endeavour to show, is that parental rights are derived from parental duty and exist only so long as they are needed for the protection of the person and property of the child. The principle has been subjected to certain age limits set by statute for certain purposes: and in some cases the courts have declared an age of discretion at which a child acquires before the age of majority the right to make his (or her) own decision. But these limitations in no way undermine the principle of the law, and should not be allowed to obscure it...

Although statute has intervened in respect of a child's capacity to consent to medical treatment from the age of 16 onwards, neither statute nor the case law has ruled on the extent and duration of parental right in respect of children under the age of 16. More specifically, there is no rule yet applied to contraceptive treatment, which has special problems

NOTE Lord Scarman gives good advice here and in the following paragraphs on how to read ancient and/ or conflicting precedents.

of its own and is a late-comer in medical practice. It is open, therefore, to the House to formulate a rule. The Court of Appeal favoured a fixed age limit of 16, basing themselves on a view of the statute law which I do not share and upon their view of the effect of the older case law which for the reasons already given I cannot accept. They sought to justify the limit by the public interest in the law being certain.

Certainty is always an advantage in the law, and in some branches of the law it is a necessity. But it brings with it an inflexibility and a rigidity which in some branches of the law can obstruct justice, impede the law's development, and stamp upon the law the mark of obsolescence where what is needed is the capacity for development. The law relating to parent and child is concerned with the problems of the growth and maturity of the human personality. If the law should impose upon the process of 'growing up' fixed limits where nature knows only a continuous process, the price would be artificiality and a lack of realism in an area where the law must be sensitive to human development and social change. If certainty be thought desirable, it is better that the rigid demarcations necessary to achieve it should be laid down by legislation after a full consideration of all the relevant factors than by the courts confined as they are by the forensic process to the evidence adduced by the parties and to whatever may properly fall within the judicial notice of judges. Unless and until Parliament should think fit to intervene, the courts should establish a principle flexible enough to enable justice to be achieved by its application to the particular circumstances proved by the evidence placed before them.

The underlying principle of the law was exposed by Blackstone and can be seen to have been acknowledged in the case law. It is that parental right yields to the child's right to make his own decisions when he reaches a sufficient understanding and intelligence to be capable of making up his own mind on the matter requiring decision. Lord Denning M.R. captured the spirit and principle of the law when he said in *Hewer v. Bryant* [1970] 1 Q.B. 357, 369:

'I would get rid of the rule in *In re Agar-Ellis*, 24 Ch.D. 317 and of the suggested exceptions to it. That case was decided in the year 1883. It reflects the attitude of a Victorian parent towards his children. He expected unquestioning obedience to his commands. If a son disobeyed, his father would cut him off with a shilling. If a daughter had an illegitimate child, he would turn her out of the house. His power only ceased when the child became 21. I decline to accept a view so much out of date. The common law can, and should, keep pace with the times. It should declare, in conformity with the recent Report of the Committee on the Age of Majority [Cmnd. 3342, 1967], that the legal right of a parent to the custody of a child ends at the 18th birthday: and even up till then, it is a dwindling right which the courts will hesitate to enforce against the wishes of the child, and the more so the older he is. It starts with a right of control and ends with little more than advice.'...

The modern law governing parental right and a child's capacity to make his own decisions was considered in *Reg. v. D.* [1984] A.C. 778. The House must, in my view, be understood as having in that case accepted that, save where statute otherwise provides, a minor's capacity to make his or her own decision depends upon the minor having sufficient understanding and intelligence to make the decision and is not to be determined by reference to any judicially fixed age limit...

In the light of the foregoing I would hold that as a matter of law the parental right to determine whether or not their minor child below the age of 16 will have medical treatment terminates if and when the child achieves a sufficient understanding and intelligence to enable him or her to understand fully what is proposed. It will be a question of fact whether a child seeking advice has sufficient understanding of what is involved to give a consent valid in law. Until the child achieves the capacity to consent, the parental right to make the decision continues save only in exceptional circumstances. Emergency, parental neglect, abandonment of the child, or inability to find the parent are examples of exceptional situations justifying the doctor proceeding to treat the child without parental knowledge and consent: but there will arise, no doubt, other exceptional situations in which it will be reasonable for the doctor to proceed without the parent's consent.

When applying these conclusions to contraceptive advice and treatment it has to be borne in mind that there is much that has to be understood by a girl under the age of 16 if she is to have legal capacity to consent to such treatment. It is not enough that she should understand the nature of the advice which is being given: she must also have a sufficient maturity to understand what is involved. There are moral and family questions, especially her relationship with her parents; long-term problems associated with the emotional impact of pregnancy and its termination; and there are the risks to health of sexual intercourse at her age, risks which contraception may diminish but cannot eliminate. It follows that a doctor will have to satisfy himself that she is able to appraise these factors before he can safely proceed upon the basis that she has at law capacity to consent to contraceptive treatment. And it further follows that ordinarily the proper course will be for him, as the guidance lays down, first to seek to persuade the girl to bring her parents into consultation, and if she refuses, not to prescribe contraceptive treatment unless he is satisfied that her circumstances are such that he ought to proceed without parental knowledge and consent.

Interestingly, a minor who is competent to request treatment under *Gillick v West Norfolk and Wisbech Area Health Authority* [1986] AC 112 is not necessarily competent to refuse treatment. The Court of Appeal held in *Re W (a minor) (medical treatment)* [1993] Fam 64 that a parent's (or guardian's) power to consent to medical treatment on behalf of a minor child continues even after the minor has become capable of obtaining his or her own treatment plan under either *Gillick v West Norfolk and Wisbech Area Health Authority* [1986] AC 112 or the Family Law Reform Act 1969. In that case, the guardian of a 15-year-old girl suffering from anorexia nervosa sought treatment for her over her objections. The Court of Appeal overrode the girl's wishes in her own best interest, holding that a physician may obtain the necessary consent to treatment from either the parents (or guardians) or the minor.

17.2.4 Damages

Damages are assessed differently in intentional torts than they are in negligence. As you remember, damages in negligence were limited by the principal of foreseeability, as described in *Overseas Tankship (UK) Ltd v Morts Dock and Engineering Co Ltd, The Wagon Mound* [1961] AC 388. If the injury could not be foreseen by the defendant, then damages cannot be awarded, even if the factual chain of causation ('but for' causation) shows that the damage is directly linked to the defendant's negligence.

Torts against the person are different. Here, damage is per se, meaning that the existence and extent of injury need not be proven as part of the claimant's affirmative case. A claimant who proves battery will always be able to recover a nominal sum. In addition, a claimant will recover virtually any sort of damage flowing from the defendant's action, even if it is not foreseeable. For example, in *Williams v Humphrey*, The Times, 20 February 1975, the plaintiff injured his ankle when the defendant pushed him into a swimming pool. That sort of injury would likely not be foreseeable, and the damages associated with it thus would not usually be recoverable in negligence. However, the claimant was able to recovery in battery, since the injury did, in fact, flow from the defendant's actions. Similarly, a party may recover for consequential damages associated with the loss of goods or injury to feelings. When dealing with intentional torts, the chances are the claimant will be able to recover.

erence

...apter 11 for a discussion of the different types of damages recoverable in tort.

17.3 Assault

The preceding discussion focused on battery, which is but one of the intentional torts against a person. Assault is a similar tort, except there is no need for physical contact. Instead, the tort of assault addresses the threat or anticipation of physical contact. All that need be proven is an act which causes the claimant to anticipate the infliction of immediate unlawful force on his or her person.

Analytically, assault can be cast in two different lights. Some assaults can be described as an incomplete battery, brought about when the defendant tried but for some reason failed to come into physical contact with the claimant. The other type of assault results when the defendant never intended to touch the claimant but nevertheless created a reasonable anticipation of physical contact in the mind of the claimant. As was the case with battery, we will discuss each of the constituent elements of the tort, including:

- The defendant's mental state;
- The defendant's physical acts; and
- Issues involving the claimant.

Damages are not an essential part of the tort of assault, but we will discuss them nonetheless.

17.3.1 The defendant's mental state

NOTE To be assaulted, you must know you are being assaulted. Battery, on the other hand, can occur even when you're asleep, unconscious or unaware.

To prove civil assault, the claimant must establish that the defendant had the same type of mental state as in battery—meaning an intention to do the act that led directly to the assault—although the claimant need not prove the intent to cause physical contact. In assault, the claimant need only prove an intent to cause the apprehension of unlawful physical contact.

Often a claimant who suffers a battery will also suffer an assault, since the victim will often see the physical contact coming. However, it is possible to suffer a battery without suffering an assault as well. For example, a patient who is unconscious on the operating table will not be assaulted if a surgeon who was supposed to fix a broken arm also intentionally and non-negligently amputates a leg, since the patient will have had no apprehension of the harm. However, that patient will have a claim for a battery.

As with battery, the claimant must show that the act was intentional rather than merely negligent. In addition, the defendant must have intended either a 'hostile' touching or comply with the requirements set forth by Lord Goff in *F v West Berkshire Health Authority* [1989] All ER 545 by demonstrating the defendant understood that he or she was doing something that could be construed as an unlawful intrusion on the plaintiff's rights to physical privacy and personal autonomy. The intent to cause a 'hostile' touching equates with an unsuccessful battery, whereas the intent to do something that constituted an unlawful intrusion equates with 'pure' assault—there need be no intent to touch the claimant in that scenario. Both intents can form the basis of a modern claim in assault, however.

17.3.2 The defendant's physical acts

In the past, the tort of assault could only exist when someone intended, but for some reason failed, to commit a battery. For example, in *Blake v Barnard* (1840) 9 C & P 626, the defendant pointed an unloaded gun at the plaintiff, although the plaintiff did not know there was no risk of actual harm. The judge there held that there was assault because the defendant could not have intended to batter the plaintiff, since the gun was unloaded. Today, however, the case would be decided differently. Under the modern law, it is only necessary that the act in question raise the reasonable apprehension of immediate physical contact.

Similarly, at one time that words alone could not constitute assault. However, in the criminal case of *R v Ireland* [1998] AC 147, the House of Lords stated that any words that raise a reasonable apprehension of immediate (in other words, within a minute or two) battery can constitute assault. In that case the defendant rang up the victim on the phone but said nothing, only occasionally uttering some heavy breathing. Lord Steyn stated that 'There is no reason why something said should be incapable of causing an apprehension of immediate personal violence'. In the case of the silent caller, the victim may be 'assailed by uncertainty about his intentions. Fear may dominate her emotions'. Even though the case was brought in criminal court, rather than civil court, tort law would come to a similar conclusion if faced with similar facts, since Lord Steyn's view echoes the central premise of civil assault, i.e. the intentional infliction of the fear of unwelcome physical contact.

Traditionally, and under contemporary law, courts have held that words can negate an act that would otherwise constitute assault. For example, putting a hand on one's sword might normally constitute assault (at least in seventeenth century Britain), but the words 'If it were not assize-time, I would not take such language from you' negates the immediacy of the threat and thus changes the nature of the defendant's act, as indicated in *Tuberville v Savage* (1669) 1 Mod Rep 3.

Immediacy is a critical part of the tort of assault. In *Thomas v National Union of Mineworkers (South Wales Area)* [1985] 2 All ER 1, the plaintiff was a miner who was bussed to work during a strike held by the National Union of Mineworkers. As the bus crossed the picket lines, the striking miners made threatening gestures, accompanied by verbal threats. However, the court held that the strikers were not liable for assault, since it was impossible for the striking miners to get to the plaintiff through the line of police protection and the exterior of the bus itself. Therefore, a person who stands on one side of a brick wall and shouts, 'I'm going to beat you to a pulp with my bare hands!' doesn't constitute much of a threat to people standing on the other side. An assault has not occurred, even if the person is an All England rugby player with a penchant for brawling on and off the pitch. The brick wall means that there's no immediate threat of harm. If the short-tempered rugby player were standing on the far side of a chain link fence with an elephant gun, claiming 'I'm going to shoot you', it's a different matter. In that case, an assault likely exists, since the elephant rifle can shoot through in the fence. On the other hand, if the rugby player stands on his side of the chain link fence and says, 'I'm going to get my elephant rifle and shoot you', his actions do not constitute assault, since anyone on the far side of the fence has a sufficient amount of time to escape before the rugby player returns with his rifle.

NOTE The section below on defences discusses whether there is ever any duty to escape or retreat from a dangerous situation, but that deals with a different issue—namely the obligations imposed on a claimant when the assault (or battery) occurs. In the above example, an assault has not occurred because the angry rugby player does not yet have the means (namely, the elephant rifle) of causing the physical contact.

17.3.3 Issues involving the claimant

When considering whether an assault has occurred, one must look at the reasonableness of the claimant's reaction to the alleged assault. The test the courts use is objective, rather than subjective, meaning that they will look at what a reasonable person would think in the same circumstances rather than what this individual claimant thought. A claimant's individual mental characteristics will not be taken into account when deciding whether an assault has occurred, unless the defendant knows about those special characteristics. For example, if Sally has an unreasonable fear that someone will spill hot coffee on her, that fear will not allow Sally to pursue a claim in assault against Joe simply because Joe stands next to her in the Tube, holding an overly full cup of Columbian blend and looking at her threateningly. However, if a reasonable person—the same reasonable person we met in negligence—would fear an intentional spill in that situation, then assault may exist. Remember, the act must be more than negligent and must be beyond the sort of everyday conduct that is expected in modern life.

cross reference
For more on the reasonable person, see chapter 3 on negligence.

17.3.4 Damages

As you recall, damages do not constitute a necessary part of the claimant's prima facie case in battery, and they do not constitute a necessary part of the claimant's case in assault, either. While it is important to prove the extent to which one has been harmed by an assault, since that will affect the amount that can be recovered, the claimant need not show that he or she was injured in any way. Thus the claimant can recover nominal damages simply upon demonstrating that the defendant had the requisite mental state and undertook the requisite act.

 # 17.4 False imprisonment

17.4.1 The defendant's mental state

Like assault and battery, the tort of false imprisonment requires the defendant to act in a direct and intentional manner. In this case, the offending act involves the confinement of the claimant in some way. The person doesn't need to be literally put into prison—although the police may be liable for false imprisonment under the proper circumstances—but merely needs to be intentionally shut inside an area that the defendant identifies. False imprisonment could be combined with assault or battery—for example, if a defendant shoves the claimant into a room or threatens to shove the claimant into a room before locking the door after the claimant is inside—but false imprisonment need not be combined with another intentional tort. Instead, the defendant could lure the person voluntarily into the room and then lock the door after the person is inside. No other tort other than false imprisonment would exist in such a situation.

The focus, as in the other torts, is on whether the defendant intended to do the act that resulted in the false imprisonment. Until recently, it wasn't clear whether negligence could be enough to result in false imprisonment. In *Sayers v Harlow Urban District Council* [1958] 1 WLR 623, a woman was inadvertently locked into a ladies' toilet. Because it was an accident, the court held that she was not falsely imprisoned. This view has changed, however, with the House of Lords' recent decision in *R v Governor of Brockhill Prison, ex parte Evans* [2000] 4 All ER 15. In that case, a woman was initially scheduled to be released from prison on 18 November 1996. After judicial review, it was discovered that her release date should have been 17 September 1996. The House of Lords held that false imprisonment is a strict liability tort and that therefore the claimant could and should be able to recover, despite the fact that the defendant had acted in line with the Home Office guidelines accepted as correct at the relevant time. Therefore, a defendant can become liable for false imprisonment by merely acting in a negligent manner, unlike other torts involving trespass against the person.

17.4.2 The defendant's physical acts

For a confinement to constitute false imprisonment, the claimant must be unable to escape through any reasonable means. Therefore, closing off one door in a shop will not constitute false imprisonment of any customers who remain inside if another door remains open. Similarly, locking all the doors at closing time will not constitute false imprisonment of any customers who remain inside if those customers are allowed to leave upon request. However, if the only escape is unreasonable—say, through a very high, very small window that can only be accessed by ladder—then false imprisonment may exist, even if escape was technically possible. As Lord Denman said, albeit in dissent, in *Bird v Jones* (1845) 7 QB 742:

> As long as I am prevented from doing what I have a right to do, of what importance is it that I am permitted to do something else?...If I am locked in a room, am I not imprisoned because I might effect my escape through a window, or because I might find an exit dangerous or inconvenient to myself, as by wading through water...?

The plaintiff in that case had entered a part of Hammersmith Bridge that had been closed off for seating to view a regatta. The plaintiff, who was prohibited from going through the enclosure and getting out the far side, was not prohibited from leaving the bridge the way he had entered it. The court thus held that false imprisonment did not exist, stating:

> A prison may have its boundary large or narrow, visible and tangible, or, though real, still in the conception only; it may be moveable or fixed: but a boundary it must have; and that boundary the party imprisoned must be prevented from passing.

The place where the claimant has been detained can be of any size and of any character. One can be restrained in one's own home, in a shop or even in a car or on a boat. The important characteristic is that the claimant cannot depart of his or her own free will. It is not even necessary that the barriers be physical. Mere words can be enough, as when, for example, the Commissioner in Lunacy wrongfully dissuaded the plaintiff from leaving the Commissioner's office in *Harnett v Bond* [1925] AC 669. A wrongful arrest by a police officer—meaning one that is not in accord with the Police and Criminal Evidence Act 1984—can lead to a claim of false imprisonment, even when the constable never touched the claimant. If an arrest is proper, however, later changes in circumstances cannot turn that arrest into false imprisonment. This is true even if the arrest was mistaken. Private citizens, including shop detectives, do not have the protection of a reasonable mistake, however, and a wrongful citizen's arrest can lead to a cause of action in tort.

Unlike the torts of assault and battery, which both require some sort of affirmative act, false imprisonment can result from either an affirmative act or an omission, at least if to fail to do a certain act would constitute a breach of some relevant duty. For example, *Herd v Weardale Steel, Coal and Coke Co* [1913] 3 KB 711, aff'd [1915] AC 67, indicates that an action for false imprisonment will not lie when a miner's employers refused to transport him from the mine to the surface before his shift ended. While it may have been false imprisonment to have allowed the miner to remain in the mine after his shift ended, the employers did not breach their contractual duty—or, apparently, any other duty—by refusing to bring the miner to the surface when he requested it, if the shift had not yet ended.

17.4.3 Issues involving the claimant

To recover on a claim of false imprisonment, the claimant need not know at the time of the confinement that he or she could not leave the premises. In *Murray v Ministry of*

Defence [1988] 1 WLR 692, wherein a woman was detained in her own home for 30 minutes before being formally arrested on suspicion of terrorism. The House of Lords held that false imprisonment did not exist in that case, since the arresting officer's reasons for delay were reasonable. The Lords also held that actual knowledge of a confinement is not a necessary element to the tort of false imprisonment. All that a claimant need establish is proof of a total restraint on the claimant's freedom to leave. However, the lack of knowledge of the imprisonment will bear on the damages that the claimant can recover.

17.4.4 Damages

As with the other intentional torts, a claimant need not prove any injury as part of his or her claim for false imprisonment. The loss of liberty alone will result in some form of damages. However, the claimant can also recover for additional losses, such as injury to feelings and loss of reputation. Loss of reputation might arise, for example, if someone saw the claimant being wrongfully detained in a shop detective's office and surmised that the claimant had stolen goods.

cross reference
See chapter 11 for further discussion of the types of damages available in tort.

The quantum of awards for wrongful imprisonment have escalated in recent years, since claimants are able to recover not only for actual (compensatory) damages but also for aggravated and, in some cases, exemplary damages. In *Thompson v Metropolitan Police Commissioner* [1998] QB 498, which dealt with an improper arrest involving all three types of trespass to the person, the Court of Appeal issued guidelines to be used in cases involving false imprisonment and malicious prosecution. Basic damages associated with the loss of liberty itself start at around £500 for the first hour, but diminish thereafter to a total of approximately £3,000 a day, with less per day for subsequent days. Aggravated damages would seldom be under £1,000 a day but would be capped to approximately double the figure for compensatory damages. Exemplary damages would only be allowed in the rarest of cases, as when the sum of the basic and aggravated damages would be insufficient to punish the defendant for oppressive and arbitrary behaviour. The punitive nature of exemplary damages is unusual, since, in most cases, tort damages—including those for false imprisonment—are intended only to compensate the victim. Seldom will more than £25,000 be awarded, and never more than £50,000. In the *Thompson* case, the total award was diminished radically from an initial £200,000 to £15,000, thus demonstrating how disinclined courts in this country are to award massive damages in tort.

17.5 Liability under *Wilkinson v Downton*

Assault and battery both deal with intentional acts aimed directly at the claimant's physical person. False imprisonment also relates to a direct and intentional act against the claimant's physical person, although it does not involve actual or threatened contact with the claimant. One more type of intentional tort exists, this time involving an act or statement that is intended to and does cause physical harm to the claimant, even though the defendant him or herself does not touch the claimant. The tort arises out of a case known as *Wilkinson v Downton* [1897] 2 QB 57, which involved a practical joke gone awry.

. . . .

● ***Wilkinson v Downton*** [1897] 2 QB 57

> Wright J: The defendant, in the execution of what he seems to have regarded as a practical joke, represented to the female plaintiff that he was charged by her husband with a message to her to the effect that the husband had been smashed up in an accident, and was lying at the Elms public-house at Leytonstone with both legs broken, and that she was to go at once in a cab to fetch him home. All this was false. The effect of this statement on the female plaintiff was a violent shock to the nervous system producing vomiting and other more serious and permanent physical consequences, at one time threatening her reason and entailing weeks of suffering and incapacity to her as well as expense to her husband for the medical treatment of her. These consequences were not in any way the result of previous ill-health or weakness of constitution, nor was there any evidence of predisposition to nervous shock or of any other idiosyncrasy...
>
> The defendant has, as I assume for the moment, wilfully done an act calculated to cause physical harm to the female plaintiff, ie, to infringe her legal right to personal safety, and has thereby in fact caused physical harm to her. That proposition, without more, appears to me to state a good cause of action, there being no justification alleged for the act. This wilful injuria is in law malicious, although no malicious purpose to cause the harm which was caused, nor any motive of spite, is imputed to the defendant.
>
> It remains to consider whether the assumptions involved in the propositions are made out. One question is whether the defendant's act was so plainly calculated to produce some effect of the kind which was produced, that an intention to produce it ought to be imputed to the defendant regard being had to the fact that the effect was produced on a person proved to be in an ordinary state of health and mind. I think it was. It is difficult to imagine that such a statement, made suddenly and with apparent seriousness, could fail to produce grave effects under the circumstances upon any but an exceptionally indifferent person, and therefore an intention to produce such an effect must be imputed, and it is no answer in law to say that more harm was done than was anticipated, for that is commonly the case with all wrongs. The other question is whether the effect was, to use the ordinary phrase, too remote to be in law regarded as a consequence for which the defendant is answerable. Apart from authority I should give the same answer, and on the same grounds, as to the last question, and say that it was not too remote. Whether, as the majority of the Lords thought in *Lynch v Knight* (1861) 9 HL Cas 577; 11 ER 854, the criterion is in asking what would be the natural effect on reasonable persons, or whether, as Lord Wensleydale thought, the possible infirmities of human nature ought to be recognised, it seems to me that the connection between the cause and the effect is sufficiently close and complete.

The existence and nature of a cause of action following the principles of *Wilkinson v Downton* was confirmed in *Janvier v Sweeney* [1919] 2 KB 316.

● *Janvier v Sweeney* [1919] 2 KB 316

> Bankes J: The case for the plaintiff was that she was employed by a lady in whose house she resided; that on July 16, 1917, a man called at the house and told her that he was a detective inspector from Scotland Yard representing the military authorities, and that she was the woman they wanted as she had been corresponding with a German spy. Her case was that she was extremely frightened, with the result that she suffered from a severe nervous shock, and she attributed a long period of nervous illness to the shock she received as a result of the language used to her at that time. If she could establish the truth of that story and satisfy the jury that her illness was the direct result of the shock she was entitled to maintain this action…We must take it then that Barker went to this house and deliberately threatened the plaintiff in order to induce or compel her to commit a gross breach of the duty she owed to her employer…
>
> I think there may be cases in which A. owes a duty to B. not to inflict a mental shock on him or her, and that in such a case, if A. does inflict such a shock upon B.—as by terrifying B.—and physical damage thereby ensued, B., may have an action for the physical damage, though the medium through which it has been inflicted is the mind.

The tort fell into disuse through much of the twentieth century and few cases were brought for nearly a century. However, as described further below, the tort was revived in the 1990s, although legislative action may have again limited the need for claimants to proceed under the common law tort.

17.5.1 The defendant's mental state

As with the other intentional torts, the defendant in a *Wilkinson v Downton* case must have undertaken some voluntary act before liability will ensue. The question, as always, is whether the defendant must have intended only the act itself or whether the defendant must also have intended to cause the harm produced. Some commentators have argued that an intentional to do the act alone is sufficient. However, the decision in *Wilkinson v Downton* itself suggests that the defendant's act need only be 'so plainly calculated to produce some effect of the kind which was produced that an intention to produce it ought to be imputed to the defendant'. Since an intent to do something encompasses an intent to cause the natural consequences of the act—for example, throwing a water balloon at someone includes a presumed intent to get that person wet when the balloon lands on or near that person—then a claimant pursing an action under *Wilkinson v Downton* should only need to prove that the defendant undertook an act whose natural consequence was actionable physical harm. The fact that the act was intended to be a joke, as in *Wilkinson v Downton* itself, is irrelevant.

17.5.2 The defendant's physical act

Recent cases involving *Wilkinson v Downton* have focused on the acts taken by the defendant. In *Khorasandijian v Bush* [1993] QB 727, the plaintiff's former boyfriend refused to accept that the relationship was over and began a course of abusive harassment, visiting the plaintiff and her family and calling them continuously on the telephone. *Khorasandjian v Bush* [1993] AC 655 suggested that the plaintiff's recovery was based in nuisance, but the House of Lords overruled that part of the judgment in *Hunter v Canary Wharf Ltd* [1997] AC 655, saying that the defendant's act was tortious harassment, not nuisance. In *Burris v Azadani* [1995] 1 WLR 1372, the defendant also began to harass the plaintiff by telephone after she refused to enter into a romantic relationship with him. In both cases, threats of physical harm existed and in both cases, physical harm in the form of nervous reactions ensued. However, because the threats were made over the telephone, they lacked the immediacy necessary for assault and the actual physical conduct necessary for battery, meaning that the plaintiffs had to find other means of recovery. *Wilkinson v Downton* provided the perfect vehicle. In both cases, the Court of Appeal held that the defendant's actions were tortious and granted the plaintiff injunctive relief in the form of an order to the defendant to cease contacting the plaintiff. Both cases have also been superseded, to some extent, by recent legislation enacted in response to these types of factual scenarios.

● **Protection from Harassment Act 1997**

> **1 Prohibition of harassment**
>
> (1) A person must not pursue a course of conduct—
>   (a) which amounts to harassment of another, and
>   (b) which he knows or ought to know amounts to harassment of the other.
>
> (2) For the purposes of this section, the person whose course of conduct is in question ought to know that it amounts to harassment of another if a reasonable person in possession of the same information would think the course of conduct amounted to harassment of the other.

Section 2 of the Protection from Harassment Act 1997 makes a violation of section 1 a criminal offence, whereas section 3 provides that the victim of the course of conduct described in section one has a civil remedy, with damages being available for '(among other things) any anxiety caused by the harassment and any financial loss resulting from the harassment'. Section 4 of the 1997 Act states that 'A person whose course of conduct causes another to fear, on at least two occasions, that violence will be used against him is guilty of an offence if he knows or ought to know that his course of conduct will cause the other to fear on each of those occasions'. The definition of 'ought to know' is similar to that described in section 1(2).

17.5.3 Issues involving the claimant

cross reference

For more on the developing law of privacy, see chapter 14.

Although the Protection from Harassment Act 1997 may consign *Wilkinson v Downton* claims to the history books, at least with respect to actions arising out of harassment, that need not be the case. The 1997 Act does not provide an all-encompassing definition of harassment, which may leave an opening for the common law to develop. For a while, people thought that the availability of an action under *Wilkinson v Downton* might be useful as the law of privacy developed, at least to the extent that a violation of any interest in privacy were to be accompanied by physical harm. However, the recent decision of the House of Lords in *Wainwright v Home Office* [2003] UKHL 53, [2004] 2 AC 406 may have cut off that line of argument. There, the House of Lords considered a claim for invasion of privacy in addition to a claim under *Wilkinson v Downtown* after several guards failed to follow proper procedure when strip-searching two visitors to a prison. A physical touching occurred in addition to emotional distress and humiliation.

For more on remedies in nuisance, see chapter 8.

● **Wainwright v Home Office** [2003] UKHL 53, [2004] 2 AC 406

> Lord Hoffmann: By the time of Janvier v Sweeney [1919] 2 KB 316, therefore, the law was able comfortably to accommodate the facts of Wilkinson v Downton [1897] 2 QB 57 in the law of nervous shock caused by negligence. It was unnecessary to fashion a tort of intention or to discuss what the requisite intention, actual or imputed, should be…
>
> Commentators and counsel have nevertheless been unwilling to allow Wilkinson v Downton to disappear beneath the surface of the law of negligence. Although, in cases of actual psychiatric injury, there is no point in arguing about whether the injury was in some sense intentional if negligence will do just as well, it has been suggested (as the claimants submit in this case) that damages for distress falling short of psychiatric injury can be recovered if there was an intention to cause it. This submission was squarely put to the Court of Appeal in Wong v Parkside Health NHS Trust [2003] 3 All ER 932 and rejected. Hale LJ said that before the passing of the Protection from Harassment Act 1997 there was no tort of intentional harassment which gave a remedy for anything less than physical or psychiatric injury. That leaves Wilkinson v Downton with no leading role in the modern law…
>
> In my opinion, therefore, the claimants can build nothing on Wilkinson v Downton [1897] 2 QB 57. It does not provide a remedy for distress which does not amount to recognised psychiatric injury and so far as there may be a tort of intention under which such damage is recoverable, the necessary intention was not established [in this case]. I am also in complete agreement with Buxton LJ [2002] QB 1334, 1355–1356, paras 67–72, that Wilkinson v Downton has nothing to do with trespass to the person.

Technically, much of what Lord Hoffmann says about *Wilkinson v Downton* is *obiter*, since the requisite intent on the part of the prison officials was not established. However, the case will be persuasive to later courts struggling to identify the proper role of *Wilkinson v Downton* in modern law.

17.5.4 Damages

cross reference
For more on remedies in nuisance, see chapter 8.

Although it is certainly possible to recover damages for the physical harm suffered by the claimant, the primary remedy sought and obtained by the plaintiff in *Khorasandijian v Bush* [1993] QB 727 and *Burris v Azadani* [1995] 1 WLR 1372 was injunctive relief in the form of an order barring the defendant from having further contact with the plaintiff or the plaintiff's family. This is similar to the remedy typically sought in the tort of nuisance, when a claimant's primary desire is for the noxious behaviour to cease on a going-forward basis. When considering possible damages, one should always consider the availability of injunctive relief, since that may be far more valuable to the claimant than monetary damages for past injuries.

17.6 Human Rights Act 1998

The Human Rights Act 1998 revolutionized the law of the United Kingdom by allowing claims based on the European Convention of Human Rights to be brought in domestic courts. Two cases are of particular interest when considering trespass against the person. *Keenan v United Kingdom* (2002) 33 EHRR 38 involved a prisoner who was known to be mentally ill and who committed suicide while in custody. His suicide was brought about nine days before his release date, when he was given an additional 28 days of detention for assaulting prison officers. His mother argued that the manner in which medical care was given to her son and the delay in his discharge constituted inhuman and degrading punishment in contravention of Article 3 of the European Convention, and the European Court of Human Rights agreed.

In *Price v United Kingdom* (2002) 34 EHRR 53, a disabled woman was arrested after failing to pay a civil debt. At the police station, she was forced to sleep in her wheelchair and was unable to use the toilet. Her condition deteriorated over four hours, yet a doctor was not called. Once she was removed to prison, she was required to allow male officers to assist her when using the toilet. The European Court of Human Rights held that while 'there is no evidence in this case of any positive intention to humiliate or debase the applicant', the treatment of the claimant 'constitutes degrading treatment contrary to Article 3' of the European Convention.

Notably, the detention in both cases was lawful, thus negating any possible claim for false imprisonment. Similarly, the acts in question did not amount to either assault or battery. Instead, it was the propriety and manner of the acts that the European Court found objectionable. Because domestic courts are to take European jurisprudence into account when construing the Human Rights Act 1998, it may be that the Act will provide a remedy for certain types of trespass against the person that the British common law cannot reach.

17.7 Defences

Defendants faced with a claim for an intentional tort have two potential replies. First, they can disprove one of the essential elements of the plaintiff's case. For example, if Alice sues Michael for battery after being hit in the eye by a rock, Michael can defend against the claim by proving that the rock in question wasn't thrown by him but by some third party. Second, they can establish any one of a variety of defences, meaning that they may have committed actions that constitute the tort, but that their actions were excused as a matter of law. Some of these defences have been discussed in the context of other torts, and the principles remain the same in the context of intentional torts. However, some defences are unique to intentional torts and will be discussed here. These include:

cross reference
For more on defences to negligence and trespass to land, see chapters 5 and 10.

- Self-defence;
- Defence of others; and

- The charge that the claimant is a wrongdoer, also known as *ex turpi causa non oritur actio*.

We will address each of these in turn.

17.7.1 Self-defence

When found fighting in the schoolyard, children will often justify their actions to an intervening teacher by saying, 'He (or she) started it', little knowing that they are asserting a legitimate legal defence. Many acts that would otherwise constitute an intentional tort may be excused if the defendant can establish that he or she was acting in response to an attack, either real or perceived, on the part of the claimant. To establish the defence, the defendant must prove both that (1) it was reasonable to defend oneself in these particular circumstances and (2) the force used was reasonable. The question of what is reasonable is a question of fact in each case.

The reasonableness inquiry encompasses numerous factors: whether the claimant could have escaped, whether the use of force was really imminent, whether in responding the claimant used reasonable means, whether the defendant exceeded the force necessary to stop the attack and went on the offensive him or herself, whether the amount of time between the initial attack and the response was reasonable or whether the response constituted an entirely new act, and so on. The first issue—whether the claimant could have escaped—raises the question of whether there is ever any duty to retreat from an attack. The problem arises most often in cases where the defendant has used extreme or deadly force. In *R v Bird* [1985] 1 WLR 816, a criminal case involving a woman who had injured a man in self-defence after he had allegedly slapped and pushed her, the Court of Appeal expressly condemned the notion that there was ever any duty to retreat from harm or the threat of harm. Although criminal cases may not serve as binding precedent for civil cases, they are persuasive analogies for torts involving trespass to the person, and thus it appears that there is no duty to retreat before acting in self-defence as a matter of tort law.

In addition to proving that it was reasonable to act defensively, the defendant must also demonstrate that the amount and type of force used was reasonable. In *Cockcroft v Smith* (1705) 2 Salk 642, a clerk of court had his finger bitten off by a lawyer following a 'scuffle' in court. Although the clerk had initially jabbed his fingers toward the lawyer's eyes, thus endangering the defendant, the act of defence was not reasonable. As Holt CJ stated, 'a man must not in case of a small assault, give a violent or an unreasonable return'. Apparently, biting off an opponent's fingers was considered excessive under the circumstances. At the same time, however, a defendant need not be too punctilious in the face of imminent harm. As Lord Oaksey stated in *Turner v Metro-Goldwyn-Meyer Pictures Ltd* [1950] 1 All ER 449, 'If you are attacked by a prize-fighter you are not bound to adhere to the Queensberry rules in your defence'. In that case, a BBC critic panned a film produced by Metro-Goldwyn-Meyer Pictures Ltd, who wrote the BBC saying that it disagreed with the critique and proposed not to invite that critic to view any more films. Although the case involved the claim of defamation, Lord Oaksey was analogizing to other sorts of assault on a person's body and/or reputation. In an even more recent case, *Ashley v Chief Constable of Sussex Police* [2006] EWCA Civ 1085, involving a police office who shot a suspect, allegedly in self-defence, Sir Anthony Clarke MR said, 'a defendant has a defence of self-defence to a claim for battery if he shows, first that he mistakenly but reasonably thought that it was necessary to defend himself against attack or the risk of imminent attack, and secondly that the force he used was reasonable', taking all the circumstances into account. The burden is on the defendant to prove the elements of the defence.

17.7.2 Defence of others

Sometimes a defendant is not only acting to defend him or herself, but instead intends to protect another person. The first question in cases involving defence of others is whether it is reasonable for the defendant to protect the other person in this manner, under these circumstances. As in cases involving self-defence, the reasonableness inquiry is a fact-specific analysis that takes a variety of factors into account. In addition to the elements described in the preceding section, the court must also inquire into whether it would have been reasonable for the third person to have defended him or herself and the closeness of the relationship between the defendant and third person. While it may not be necessary for any sort of pre-existing relationship to exist, thus allowing a Good Samaritan to protect a total stranger from attack, one can likely use greater force in protecting a close friend or relative than in protecting a casual acquaintance. Certainly the cases demonstrate that individuals may justifiably protect their spouses or other family members or that an employer may protect an employee and vice versa.

17.7.3 Claimant as wrongdoer

There may be times when a claimant has made out a good claim in tort but has also committed some wrongful act that the court believes justifies the denial of a remedy. The classic phrase *ex turpi causa non oritur actio*, meaning 'no action can be based on a disreputable cause', is often used to describe this sort of defence.

The application of *ex turpi causa* can be problematic. The defence started out simply enough, with Lord Mansfield declaring in 1775 in *Holman v Johnson* (1775) 1 Cowp 341 that 'No court will lend its aid to a man who founds his cause of action upon an immoral or illegal act'. There, the plaintiff sought payment for some tea that he had sold to the defendant, knowing that the defendant intended to smuggle the tea illegally into the United Kingdom. The defence in tort is based on the contract law notion laid out in that case that no contract arising out of an illegal transaction may be enforced by the court. If the claimant's tort action relies on an illegal contract, then the action in tort must fail. For example, in *Taylor v Chester* (1869) LR 4 QB 309, the plaintiff deposited £50 with the defendant as security for his agreement to pay rent for use of her brothel in an orgy he had planned. Later, when he wanted to sue for the return of the £50, he found that he could not do so, either in contract or in tort, because to do so he would have to establish and rely upon a contract for illegal and immoral purposes.

cross reference

For more on Pitts v Hunt [1991] 1 QB 24, see chapter 5.

Pitts v Hunt [1991] 1 QB 24, which was discussed earlier in the context of volenti non fit injuria, involved the defence of ex turpi causa in a tort claim. This was the case involving a pillion passenger on a motorcycle who knew that the driver of the motorcycle had been drinking. There, the court had to consider the proper boundaries of the defence.

⬤ ***Pitts v Hunt*** [1991] 1 QB 24

Dillon LJ: It is clear for a start that the fact that a plaintiff was engaged in an illegal activity which brought about his injury does not automatically bring it about that his claim for damages for personal injury as a result of the negligence of the defendant must be dismissed . . .

I find a test that depends on what would or would not be an affront to the public conscience very difficult to apply, since the public conscience may well be affected by factors of an emotional nature, e.g., that these boys by their reckless and criminal behaviour happened to do no harm to anyone but themselves. Moreover if the public conscience happened to think that the plaintiff should be compensated for his injuries it might equally think that the deceased driver of the motor cycle, had he survived and merely been injured, ought to be compensated, and that leads into the much-debated question whether there ought to be a universal scheme for compensation for the victims of accidents without regard to fault.

Beyond that, appeal to the public conscience would be likely to lead to a graph of illegalities according to moral turpitude, and I am impressed by the comments of Mason J. in *Jackson v. Harrison*, 138 C.L.R. 438, 455:

'there arises the difficulty, which I regard as insoluble, of formulating a criterion which would separate cases of serious illegality from those which are not serious. Past distinctions drawn between felonies and misdemeanours, malum in se and malum prohibitum, offences punishable by imprisonment and those which are not, non-statutory and statutory offences offer no acceptable discrimen.' . . .

[However, that] a defence of illegality can be pleaded to a case founded in tort is, in my judgment, clear, whether or not the defence is correctly called ex turpi causa.

Therefore, because the cause of action arose directly from an illegal act, the plaintiff was precluded from recovering damages from the estate of the deceased motorcycle driver.

Two years later, the Court of Appeal upheld a defence of *ex turpi causa* in *Clunis v Camden and Islington Health Authority* [1998] 3 All ER 180. The plaintiff there was a mental patient, who, after being released from in-patient care and missing four appointments for follow-up treatment, attacked a stranger at a Tube station and killed him. After being convicted of manslaughter, Clunis sued the health authority, claiming that their failure to provide him with adequate care had led to the acts that resulted in his conviction. The Court of Appeal upheld the health authority's defence of *ex turpi causa*, on the grounds that Clunis's claim was based on his own criminal act.

Although this case suggests that a claimant's own acts can be used against him or her, the defence is not absolute. Therefore, in *Lane v Holloway* [1968] 1 QB 379, an elderly man who provoked an argument with a man who ended up violently assaulting him was not deemed to have lost his claim as a result of *ex turpi causa*, on the grounds that the defendant acted unreasonably and out of proportion to the provocation.

In the past, illegality was not the only bar to recovery. Immorality also posed a serious threat to those claimants whose lives were not entirely conventional. For example, in *Hegerty v Shine* (1878) 14 Cox CC 145, a woman wished to sue her lover on the grounds that he had infected her with a venereal disease, but the court held that her own immorality in engaging in extra-marital intercourse constituted a bar to any relief she might otherwise be entitled to claim. Nowadays, immorality is more difficult to define as a universal social construct, as suggested by Dillon LJ in *Pitts v Hunt* [1991] 1 QB 24, and is thus less likely to provide a basis for a plea of *ex turpi causa*. For example, suicide, which was considered an immoral act even after it ceased to be illegal, no longer constitutes a bar to recovery in tort. In *Kirkham v Chief Constable of Greater Manchester Police* [1990] 2 WB 283, the defence of *ex turpi causa* failed after the plaintiff's husband committed suicide in prison. There, the police had failed to tell prison officials of the decedent's history of suicide attempts and his currently depressed mental state, which the court may have considered particularly blameworthy behaviour. Nevertheless, any defence based on *ex turpi causa* is subject to changes in social mores and customs, particularly when the defendant alleges immorality, as opposed to illegality.

For more revision tips, including self-test questions and suggestions for further reading, see the Online Resource Centre at www.oxfordtextbooks.co.uk/orc/strong_complete/.

revision tasks

Remember, revision is most effective when you do the work yourself. Here are three tasks to help you organize the materials discussed in this chapter.

- Make a chart demonstrating similarities and differences between the primary case for each of the intentional torts. Know which cases and statutes apply to more than one tort.

- List each of the possible defences to an intentional tort, whether those defences are discussed in this chapter or elsewhere. Identify elements that would eliminate the availability of a defence—for example, recall that excessive use of force negates self-defence, even if it is reasonable to repel an attack with force.

- Consider ways in which the intentional torts work together or with other types of torts. For example, you should always think about whether an assault occurred whenever you believe a battery may exist. Similarly, you should consider whether and in what circumstances it is possible to pursue a claim in negligence at the same time as you pursue a claim for an intentional tort.

Part 10

Revising for a Tort Exam

18 Revising for a tort exam

18.1 Introduction

Excelling on a tort examination requires a combination of skills. First, you must acquire a set of general legal skills which will be useful to you on any course in law. Without these general legal skills, you will be unable to apply your knowledge of tort law in an organized and 'lawyerly' manner. Without these skills, you may also find it difficult to acquire or retain a sufficiently deep understanding of the substantive law that is necessary to do well on an exam. Second, you must attain specialized knowledge of tort law. Without this specialized knowledge, you cannot show your examiners that you know this particular subject. This chapter discusses ways to improve in both areas.

This chapter will proceed as follows:

- General legal skills;
  - Reading, understanding and summarizing legal materials;
  - Elements of a good essay in law; and
  - Using legal materials in an essay.

- Revising for a tort exam;
  - General revision in tort;
  - Negligence;
  - Breach of statutory duty;
  - Torts involving land;
  - Damages and other remedies;
  - Special kinds of harm;
  - Product liability;
  - Liability for the torts of others; and
  - Torts against the person.

While every instructor wants and needs students to acquire general legal skills, very few lecturers focus on these skills in any detail. It is not because instructors de-value these abilities in any way—indeed, a basic proficiency in reading, analysing, and summarizing the law is critical if a person is to understand the substantive law in any real sense. The problem, it seems, relates more to time management. Rather than teach general skills, instructors tend to jump straight into the substantive law for their particular course. Teaching time is limited, and there is always more to cover than can reasonably be done in the number of classes allotted. Instructors may also believe that someone else can, will, or should convey this information, either through a one-off 'legal skills' course at the beginning of term (which is often too brief, too general, and too early in the course to be of much help) or through a general 'legal methods' course, which often deviates from practical skills to a discussion of theoretical or controversial debates.

Despite the lack of focused instruction in this area, students need to acquire general legal skills. Without those skills, students will find it difficult to learn the underlying legal principles that constitute the raw material or building blocks for a sound essay. Furthermore, students lacking competence in reading, analysing, and summarizing the law can find it difficult to pull out the proper information from the instructional materials and convey the necessary information in an exam situation.

The first general legal skill involves learning how to acquire the raw information from the mass of legal material you will be learning on your substantive courses. Doing well in law school involves more than parroting back information to your instructor. You have to manipulate cases and other materials to support your own individual argument. While you must demonstrate an understanding of the fundamental elements of what you have been taught, you must also take the process one step further by putting your own spin on the material. Law—done properly—can involve a great deal of creativity, albeit within a framework for analysis.

Once you know how to do that, you can move on to the second general legal skill, which is conveying that information back to your instructor, accompanied—one hopes—by your own unique analysis. The principles discussed in this section can be used in any substantive area of law—contract law, property law, commercial law, etc—as well as for tort law. This first legal skill involves acquiring the building blocks—i.e. the understanding of the relevant legal authority—of any area of substantive law. Without those building blocks, you cannot create anything worthwhile. You may have a flawless prose style and a logical essay structure, but if you don't have anything substantive to say, then you cannot receive high marks on your work. The best organization and writing style in the world cannot overcome a lack of knowledge. Also, you cannot bluff your way through an examination in law. Although creative thinking is often rewarded, it is like a pudding at the end of a meal—you must make your way through the meat and potatoes of the analysis before you get to the fun, creative part.

Although this first task is framed as a general legal skill, it is actually teaching you how to acquire the specialized knowledge of substantive law in your area of interest—in this case, tort. Detailed knowledge of the substantive law is critical to doing well on a law course. When you don't quite know what points you want to make, you spend a lot of time on vague generalities and common-sense (but not necessarily legal) comments. All of your statements may be true as a matter of law, but they may not be as sophisticated, insightful, detailed, or relevant as your examiners would like them to be. You may also spend a lot of time qualifying your remarks or resorting to 'lawyerly' language to hide your lack of knowledge. Examiners see right through these tactics, and while students often believe that they can fool readers with elaborate, complicated arguments, it is much harder to bluff your way through an examination in law than it is in other subjects. You either know the relevant law or you don't.

NOTE While almost every case or statute provides some 'wiggle room' for interpretation and argument, you cannot hide a complete lack of knowledge. This is particularly true given that a well-written question will not only allow, but will require, you to submit legal authority in support of both sides of an argument and then weigh up the competing interests. You need to know the material well to do so.

Thus, you must acquire the general legal knowledge that will allow you to understand the specialized, substantive law. Learning these skills—like learning the substance of the law itself—takes time and effort. There is no way around it: learning the law is hard work. You must read the texts, attend lectures, and think about the legal concepts on a daily basis. However, simply spending a lot of time on your studies does not guarantee that you will gain a sophisticated understanding of the law. Often, the students with the highest marks are not the ones that put in the most hours. Sometimes the lowest marks come from students who do the most work. Those who fall at the bottom of the class are not necessarily lacking in the ability to understand the material; instead, they may be using their time ineffectively, using revision techniques that are appropriate for other subjects (such as history, literature, or maths) instead of using techniques that reinforce legal learning and analysis. Remember, good lawyers are not born—they are made. Anyone can learn these skills.

18.2.1 Reading, understanding and summarizing legal materials

There are three types of legal materials which you use in the course of your studies: (1) statutes, (2) cases, and (3) legal commentary, which includes treatises and legal articles. You have seen each of these types of works excerpted in this text and know how their language and points of focus differ. To use each of these materials properly in an examination situation, you must know how to read and revise from them. We will take each in turn.

Statutes

The reading and revision method used with 'statutes' (meaning laws enacted by Parliament for domestic application) applies with equal force to legislation (such as regulations and, to a lesser extent, directives) enacted by the European Union. You can use the reading and revision tips in this discussion to refer to international instruments such as treaties or conventions, although none of these will apply to your course on tort.

Students often overlook the importance of legislation, probably because most of their coursework focuses on judicial opinions. In fact, statutes are the first source of law that a lawyer—even a common law lawyer—should consider when faced with a legal problem. This is particularly true in the United Kingdom, since the concept of Parliamentary supremacy means that statutes constitute the supreme law of the land. A lawyer always needs to look to case law, since judicial opinions can put important glosses on legislation, but the common law can never replace or supersede a statute. Thus, you should learn to look first to whether a statute applies to the issue at hand and then identify the extent to which case law can and should apply.

Many textbooks disguise the importance of statutory law by providing summations of the relevant provisions, rather than the provisions themselves. However, this text has given you the precise language of the relevant legislation in an effort to (1) highlight the importance of statutes in legal analysis and (2) help you better grasp the legal issues under discussion, issues that can only really be understood by reading the statutes in the original. While normally you should read every piece of legislation in its entirety to understand its purpose and applicability to a legal question, space limitations have required judicious excerpting in this text. Full-text statutes can be found in Halsbury's Statutes or on various online computer databases, which would allow you at least to skim the section headings of the relevant statutes to see how the legislation works together as a whole.

When reading a statute for the first time, and definitely when revising for an examination, you should pay particular attention to the definitions contained within the legislation, since a word in common usage may be given a different technical definition by the drafters of the statute. Another useful technique is to note the extent to which a defined term differs (if at all) in one statute as compared to another. Also consider how one statute may define a term by reference to a definition in another enactment, such as the way section 1(1)(c) of the Unfair Contract Terms Act 1977 incorporates by reference the common duty of care imposed by the Occupiers' Liability Act 1957 and the Occupiers' Liability Act (Northern Ireland) 1957.

Statutes both help you and require you to pay strict attention to the precise language of the legislation, even more than a judicial opinion does. While judicial opinions can and do use key phrases that must be learned and repeated verbatim, language is especially important in statutory analysis because Parliament has spent a great deal of time debating the language of the statute. Each word counts. Therefore, it's often best to avoid paraphrasing statutes. Instead, use the exact language in your notes, essays, and examination papers. While you may need to paraphrase very long quotations, make sure you understand what you're losing when you do so.

TIP Many students worry about having to memorize lengthy and highly technical statutory provisions. While some examiners will require you to do so (in which case, you must focus on those aspects of the statute that you think are most controversial and thus most likely to appear on an exam), many examiners will allow students to bring an unmarked statute book into the examination room. Ask your instructor early on what his or her policy is. It may affect how you work during the year, since you don't want to mark up your statute book if that means you won't be able to take it into the exam. At the same time, if you know that you will have to memorise legislation, you will need to make a judgment call about what elements are most important.

There are several techniques for revising statutory law. One is to mark up your copy of the statute by highlighting or underlining important passages. This saves you time, since you won't have to rewrite everything into your notes. However, the mere act of marking up your copy of the statute does not mean that you understand (or will remember) why those phrases are highlighted. You need to supplement your mark-ups with notes (in your book or elsewhere) describing (1) why those phrases are important, (2) how they are interpreted or applied by courts, and (3) how they interact with other sections of the statute or with other statutes.

NOTE For the most part, rewriting your notes to make them neater or to cull out unimportant material is not a good use of time. Throughout your course, you should be engaged in eliminating less important material (for example, cases that are raised for illustrative purposes only rather than as leading or controversial opinions) and cross-referencing ideas. While you may worry about missing out on something important, you can always go back and ask your instructor, check a reference book, or discuss the concept with a friend. Furthermore, you are just as likely to miss out an important case or statute if you have so much material to revise that you can't find the leading points. Use your best judgment and move on.

There are two reasons why it is important that you undertake this sort of analysis and cross-referencing. First, simply memorizing the relevant passages will not lead to a deep understanding of the issues involved. At most, you will be able to parrot back what you have heard or read about that particular section of the statute. While that may be helpful if you are asked a question that exactly duplicates the way the legislation was analysed in your text or in your lectures, it is unlikely that your examiner will not throw some new twist into the equation. Mere memorization makes it difficult for you to apply your knowledge in an exam situation, since you don't really understand the importance of that aspect of the statute. Examiners want to see how well you integrate different elements of the statute and relevant case law. They are not as interested in how well you can repeat the language of the statute. Lawyers in practice are not called upon to memorize the entire body of law—they know the law well enough to spot the general issues, but then go to the relevant authorities to pick up the precise language. Although examinations in law do require some memorization (perhaps more elegantly described as 'learning'), instructors definitely value the deeper appreciation and analysis used by practising lawyers and reward it on student exams.

Furthermore, part of the art of exam-taking is the ability to read a question and see what issues and controversies are being raised. Without a deeper understanding of the law, you won't be able to break down the question appropriately and will end up answering a question that wasn't asked (thus guaranteeing a second-class mark, if your examiner follows the marking criteria discussed later in this chapter). Even worse, you might provide the examiner with a pre-prepared treatise on the law regarding subject matter X. According to the marking criteria outlined below, such pre-prepared discussions result in a second class—or in some cases a third class—mark. Don't rely on such mechanical applications. To do well, you must understand and answer the question as asked.

Second, imposing your own organizational structure on the different bits of legislation and case law means that you will remember them better. Researchers who study human memory have found that people remember facts better if those facts are organized into groups of related information. Individual facts (or, in the study of law, individual cases or statutes), standing by themselves, are difficult to remember. While it can be tempting to work from an organizational structure that is given to you—and in some cases, that is to be recommended—the best way of ensuring that you will remember the relevant material is to organize it yourself. Part of the reason why this approach works best is because you are forced to spend a significant amount of time with the material, thinking about how the different elements interact with one another. Furthermore, the process of creating a mnemonic structure ingrains the information into your brain. How you organize the material is up to you and will likely develop out of whatever worked for you when you were in school. Some people prefer traditional outlines, whereas other people cannot work without a 'spider chart' showing how a central idea is surrounded by supplemental points. Anything and everything can work—the key is that you bring your unique perspective to the problem.

NOTE Although creating your own organizational structure is very useful, you can get help from a variety of sources. For example, this text has grouped certain similar subjects together—land-based torts, for example, appear in a single section—with the explicit aim of helping you with your analysis. Often looking at the table of contents of a textbook will show you ways of structuring your outlines or analysis. Lecturers will also give you tips on how to remember and cross-reference material. Use these aids where they help you, but also be confident enough to bring your own thinking to the issue of organization—you will remember the connections better and gain a more complex understanding of the law.

In terms of timing, you should aim to complete these first two steps—i.e. understanding the material fully and organizing it in a way that makes sense to you—as you proceed through your course. If you wait until your revision period, you (1) will probably not remember or understand the material as well as you did the day after you completed your lectures and reading on a certain tort or element of a tort and (2) will likely run out of time, since you have two additional tasks to complete during your revision period. First, you must again cut down the mass of information that you have accumulated during your course into something more manageable. While you should have been discriminating in your note-taking while your course was proceeding, now is the time to be ruthless. You must let go of those elements that are interesting but ultimately not central to your main purpose. When faced with all your textbooks, articles, lecture notes, and outlines, you will recognize that it is impossible for you to remember everything. Therefore, you must focus your attention on those parts of the syllabus that are most important.

Second, you must spend your revision period committing the information to memory. You must be familiar enough with the material that you not only know what each of the statutes (or cases) say, but also how you can apply that material to the questions you will be asked. If you can repeat the language of a statute or the facts and outcome of a case, you have made good progress, but you are only halfway to your goal. You need to know the material well enough to be able to manipulate it for use in novel situations. This is actually what makes the study of law fun, but too many people don't know the rules and principles well enough to reach this point. If you are at all shaky about what the law is, the higher level of analysis will be more difficult in an exam or essay scenario.

NOTE Being able to manipulate the law to support your position (or disprove an opponent's argument) is the ultimate goal of both the study and the practice of law.

It may help your revision to see an example of one way to analyse a statute. While you may not need to get into this amount of detail for all of the statutes that are mentioned in your lectures and texts, you should pay careful attention to any statute that is raised in your materials. It would not be included if it did not have some bearing on the topic you are studying. In our example, we will consider the Unfair Contract Terms Act 1977. The following discussion will show you how to go about identifying important aspects of this or any piece of legislation and how to make your own notes to help you analyse statutory materials.

cross reference
The Unfair Contract Terms Act 1977 is considered in more detail in chapter 5.

The analysis of any statute should focus on:

(1) The applicability of the statute to your coursework;

(2) Any defined terms within the statute;

(3) Any contentious areas within the statute; and

(4) Any case law supplementing or clarifying the statute, as well as any other statutes that may influence the applicability of the legislation in question.

Under this approach, the first step requires you to consider which provisions, if any, of the statute are applicable to your coursework. Although you can assume that any statute introduced in this text or in your lectures is relevant to your studies, you still need to undertake the following three-point analysis. First, you need to see whether the statute contains a section that broadly defines the scope of applicability of the statute. In the case of the Unfair Contract Terms Act 1977, that description is contained in section 1, which is usefully entitled 'Scope of Part I'. However, section 1 notes that the scope of the 1977 Act is further limited or affected by certain other provisions in the Act: for example, Part I is subject to Part III (see section 1(2)) and, in relation to contract, is also subject to the exceptions made by Schedule 1 (although that limitation only applies to sections 2 to 4 and 7 (see section 1(2)). Therefore, you will have to look at each of these different sections and parts to learn the scope of application of the 1977 Act. Section 1(3) makes further qualifications to the scope of applicability in relation to cases arising in contract and tort. You need to work through each of the subsections to identify the circumstances in which the 1977 Act applies. This is a very complex example, but other statutes—for example, section 1 of the Occupiers' Liability Act 1957—are much simpler.

Depending on the intricacy of the statute, you can either highlight the section on scope or make sufficient notes cross-referencing different sections so that you know when the legislation does and does not apply.

Second, you should skim the body of the statute to see if there are further limitations in scope buried within the substantive provisions. In the case of the 1977 Act, you can see that some sections contain their own scope provisions, either limiting the application of the 1977 Act in whole or in part (for example, see section 5(3), nothing the inapplicability of that section of the 1977 Act to contracts in which possession of goods passed) or expanding the application of the 1977 Act in whole or in part (for example, see section 6(4), which notes that the liabilities discussed in that section include not only the business liabilities discussed in section 1(3), the main provision on scope, but also those arising under any contract of sale of goods or hire-purchase agreement). Again, the Unfair Contract Terms Act 1977 is a very complex example, but you will not know how complex your statute is until you look at it. This step may not be as necessary when your textbook provides full excerpts from the statute as this book does, but it still would be helpful for you to find and review a full copy of the most important statutes on the course.

Third, you should skim the headings of the statute to see which sections bear the most substantive applicability to your coursework. This will allow you to bypass sections of the statute which do not relate to you. For example, you may decide not to focus on section 6 of the Unfair Contract Terms Act 1977 because tort does not deal with sale and hire-purchase agreements. However, reading through the section headings at least once does more than indicate which sections are and are not applicable to your work. When reading the section headings, you get a better idea of how the statute is laid out and how it operates. If you only consider a single section of a statute, you may not understand the overall purpose and application of the enactment.

The above three suggestions relate to the first major prong of the statutory analysis—the applicability of the statute to your coursework. The second prong requires you to analyse any defined terms within the statute. Sometimes the definition is contained in the legislation and sometimes it is found in the case law. For example, both section 1 and section 14 of the Unfair Contract Terms Act 1977 contain important definitions. Often legislative drafters place important definitions in the first or last few sections of a statute, so you should check those places first when looking for defined terms. However, sometimes a definition is fitted in amidst the substantive provisions. In a simple statute, it will be enough to highlight the key definitions in your copy of the statute, but in more complex enactments, you will need to list and/or cross-reference any exceptions or further explanations. Again, be careful of copying statutory language directly into your notes—it takes a lot of time and is not necessarily worthwhile. Just make sure you have a roadmap of how the different provisions fit together, if the definitions are complicated.

The third prong of the statutory analysis model requires you to identify the contentious areas within and relating to the statute. Follow the guidance of your instructors and texts in this regard. For example, you will learn from your lecturers and reading materials that the definition of 'reasonableness' has been disputed under the Unfair Contract Terms

Act 1977 with some regularity. You will also identify the content of those substantive disputes, since that is as important as knowing that the disputes exist. Finally, you will identify any cases that discuss or clarify the application or content of the statute, as well as any other enactments that relate to your statute. For example, section 1(1)(c) of the 1977 Act incorporates, by reference, the concept of the common duty of care under the Occupiers' Liability Act 1957. Again, your note taking style will depend on how complex the statute is and the types and quality of the associated cases and statutes.

TIP No matter how simple or complex your statute is, it's always a good idea to create a single list of the cases which discuss your statute and the sections to which they relate. It's amazing how much more easily you can remember a series of cases if you have them all listed in a single place rather than spread out through your notes and other materials.

If you carry out the four steps described above, you will be well on your way towards understanding the important points about any statute. However, in a common law jurisdiction, the majority of your materials will relate to case law, which is discussed in the next section.

Cases

Case law is important to lawyers and law students for three reasons. First, statutes cannot, and are not intended to, cover every possible situation. Instead, they are supplemented by case law that describes how the legislation is to be applied in any particular situation. Second, statutes sometimes retain common law definitions or principles, either explicitly or through implication. Discussing the statute without the attendant case law gives the court—or your examiner—an incomplete, and therefore incorrect, description of the state of the law. Finally, there will be instances where no statute applies. Instead, the common law will reflect all of the relevant principles and rules.

Students often become nervous when faced with the task of reading and taking notes on case law. To some extent, they worry that their understanding of the case is incomplete or inaccurate. Since they know that their revision process will be fatally flawed if it is built on incorrect interpretations of the law, they try to remedy the problem by including more and more information in their notes. Unfortunately, those who worry about their ability to distinguish between relevant and irrelevant information often end up taking notes that are too bulky to be helpful at the revision stage. These people are also less than discriminating when it comes to highlighting their texts and end up with books covered in fluorescent yellow ink. The way around this problem is to understand that the ability to analyse an examination question and construct a strong legal argument is not entirely based on the ability to remember every detail of every case that has been decided since 1066 AD. Good lawyers demonstrate their judgment as much by what they don't say as what they do say. At the end of the day, if you have more information than you can process easily during your revision, you have done yourself no favour.

Because the common law has grown up over centuries, it is inconceivable that there would only be one case on point for any given fact pattern. Even if your universe of available cases is necessarily small, as is the true for law students, your course has been designed to give you a range of judicial opinions to discuss. Such is the nature not only of the common law but of the examination process. Don't fall into the trap of thinking that there is one perfect case for every question—there isn't. Instead, there is a range of suitable cases, and you have the freedom to select those that best support your position.

TIP Note-taking is all about cutting down the material to a manageable size. Be ruthless in what you leave out.

Some students have the opposite problem. Often these people have relied on excellent short-term memories throughout their school careers (which allowed them to cram successfully at the end of every term) or have overestimated their understanding of the materials at the time they are learning it for the first time. People in this category also typically worry about doing too much work before they understand the entirety of the course and want to avoid wasting time on areas that aren't that important. In fact, the process of figuring out what the important points are and why is what learning law is all about.

The students who do the best in exams are those who don't just take notes on automatic. Instead, they engage their brains during each and every step of the learning process. Obviously, the dilemma of note-taking is finding the right balance: neither too much nor too little detail. In the end, the 'right' way of taking notes is whatever works best for you. However you proceed, though, consider the following suggestions on reading and summarizing a case, since they will help you achieve the discretion necessary to do well in your course.

TIP Be very careful if you use a computer to take notes in lecture. Often, your ability to type quickly leads you to take down too much information. A verbatim transcript of a lecture is not the same—and is not as valuable—as carefully considered notes that leave out as much as they put in.

The first obstacle you must overcome is the ability to read case law. Those reading judicial opinions for the first time often conclude that many—if not all—learned members of the bench purposefully intend to make their opinions unclear. Not only does each judge appear to speak in riddles, there are reams of questions associated with cases with multiple judgments. Whose judgment is considered the leading judgment? Which aspect of the leading judgment is most important? Must I read the whole 60-plus page decision? While these questions have been addressed, to some extent, by the use of excerpts in this text, you still may be asked to read certain cases in their entirety for your course.

To learn to read cases, you must first learn the language of the law. As indicated in the very first chapter of this book, lawyers learn special 'terms of art', which refers either to language that is unique to the law or to language that is used in ordinary conversation but which has a special additional meaning when used in legal contexts. While it is often easy to work out a term of art in the context of a judicial opinion, it is equally easy to forget its meaning when you see it out of context. Therefore, you should have a vocabulary list for each subject. Not only will the process of creating the list help solidify your learning, it will allow you to draft essays that are both more concise and more precise, since you will be using language in a lawyerly manner.

When reading a case, you should also be pulling out the important elements. The excerpts in this textbook have give you a very useful starting point, since many of the irrelevant points and conflicting opinions have been excised, but the excerpts can be condensed still more. Identify the various legal rules that are supported by the decision, but also the public policy issues that are raised. Consider any cases that are discussed at length by the judge in the opinion—they may be important for you to know even if they are not independently excerpted in this textbook.

NOTE Some of the excerpts in this text are quite short and are intended only to illustrate a specific point of law. Other excerpts are much longer and are intended not only to provide guidance on a particular point of law, but also to show you (a) the historical development and/or some of the debates in that area of law and (b) how judges use statutes and case law to reach a decision about a particular dispute. In either case, you might want to refer to the original text and compare what has been excerpted with the original opinion, to learn how to identify the most important aspects of the case.

The most important skill that you can learn vis-à-vis the common law is the ability to distinguish and harmonize lines of cases. 'Distinguishing' a case requires you to identify how and why an earlier case differs from the fact scenario presented in your question. You might be able to argue that the facts are sufficiently dissimilar from yours and that the case shouldn't apply for those reasons. That process is called 'distinguishing a case on its facts'. Alternatively—and this is the more sophisticated approach—you can claim that the reasons supporting the legal holding in the earlier case can't or shouldn't apply in the fact pattern you're facing. For example, you might note that the imposition of compulsory insurance in the area of car ownership has made some earlier judgments less than persuasive. This is called 'distinguishing a case on the law' and requires you to know the public policies underlying the law in the earlier case and in the current dispute, as well as any case law that might have arisen in the interim that allows you to argue by analogy for a change in the law. When distinguishing cases, you should always pay attention to the level of the court that handed down the earlier opinion, since later courts will give more deference to opinions from the House of Lords and the Court of Appeal than to courts at the first instance. You should also consider when a case was handed down. Even though ancient precedents are still followed, often a judge can be more easily persuaded by an analogous decision that was handed down more recently.

cross reference

*For example, it is difficult to distinguish Roberts v Ramsbottom [1980] 1 All ER 7,
in which a man who caused an accident while suffering a stroke was held liable in
negligence, and Mansfield v Weetabix Ltd [1998] 1WLR 1263, in which a man who
caused an accident while suffering from a bout of hypoglycaemia was held not liable in
negligence. The cases are discussed further in chapter 3.*

'Harmonizing' a line of cases requires you to identify the direction in which the law is
moving, based on several decisions all discussing similar issues. Harmonization can be
especially difficult when you have seemingly contradictory opinions that have no apparent distinguishing rationale. Note that distinguishing cases often involves two decisions,
whereas harmonization typically requires an analysis of a sequence of cases. Examiners
often pose questions that force you to distinguish and/or harmonize cases, since that
(1) invites you to introduce more than one case into your essay (an invitation that many
people decline to their detriment) and (2) allows you to demonstrate a sophisticated
understanding of the case law. Therefore, when the text or your lecturer indicates a split
in authority on a certain point, make a note of it—you will likely be asked a question
on it.

Once you have read the cases, you need to make notes to ease the revision process,
even if you have the luxury of highlighting important language in the opinion itself.
Remember, you are not going to rewrite the judicial language—you are going to cull it
down and organize it in a helpful manner. A good case summary gives you a snapshot
of the case and why it is important. It also contains enough information to allow you to
look up the reference later in case you need to refresh yourself about a certain point.
Therefore, you should include the following information in your case summary, which
can be done both for cases that are excerpted in this textbook and cases that you read
separately in the original.

- Case name (i.e. *Smith v Jones*);
- Full citation (i.e. [1998] 4 All ER 200) (you could delete this if the case shows in your
  textbook, since you can look the citation up in the index, but it is useful to at least have
  the year of the decision in your case summary);
- Court (i.e. House of Lords);
- Facts (one to two sentences at most);
- Ratio (the legal rationale supporting the outcome; be sure to know what the outcome
  was as well; include precise language if important);
- Relevant *dicta*, if it's important;
- Queries—either questions to ask your instructor or to discuss with your peers or points
  you think worthy of discussion (and thus possible examination questions).

A case summary is a quick, standardized way to help you remember the important
elements of an opinion so that you can apply those elements appropriately in an

NOTE Some cases are important for several different reasons. Be sure to know when a case stands for multiple propositions.

cross reference

Nettleship v Weston [1971] 3 All ER 581 was discussed in chapter 3.

examination situation. A case summary does not include all points of fact or law. Focus on the important bits for your particular course. Include key quotes, if appropriate, but remember, if you don't exclude some points, you diminish the value of the summary. At first this method may seem to slow you down, but in the long run, it will save you time, since you will not have to re-read entire cases and reconstruct your analysis of the relevant issues.

Thus, when considering *Nettleship v Weston* [1971] 3 All ER 581, you might include facts stating, 'Defendant asked friend (plaintiff) to teach her how to drive in her husband's car. Defendant crashed, injuring plaintiff'. The ratio, per Lord Denning, might state, 'Criminal law is objective—skilled, experienced and careful driver. Civil standard of care is (1) (*obiter*) objective toward things/pedestrians outside car; (2) (*obiter*) same to passengers—though contributory negligence may reduce damages; (3) (*ratio*) same standard due to instructors, unless there's an implicit/explicit agreement to waive claim for negligence. Knowledge of risk insufficient (no defence of *volenti non fit injuria*). Holding does not apply to professional instructors'. The query might ask, 'What role did insurance play in this decision?'

This method of summarizing cases is just a suggestion—your notes might emphasize different details and will probably contain your own shorthand and abbreviations. Do whatever works for you. However, if you can briefly jot down judicial language, that will be helpful, since the use of the actual language on an exam will impress your reader.

Once you are past the initial note-taking stage, you must organize your notes and case summaries into a workable format. Again, some people use traditional outlines, whereas others prefer to use other methods. The key is to group individual cases together in some logical manner. In so doing, you can rely on the table of contents in your textbook or on your lecturer's course outline. Don't rewrite the entirety of your notes—keep making your indications shorter and shorter. Break down each major topic (for example, duty in negligence) into several sub-headings (such as the neighbour principle, special groups, etc), then start listing cases and statutes that relate to that subheading. Prioritize your notes by putting statutes and leading cases first, followed by cases that flesh out the parameters of that particular legal issue. The statutes and leading cases give you the general legal rule, whereas the subsequent cases describe how the basic legal principle should be applied in particular circumstances.

NOTE A leading case is either the first in time or the one that sets forth the major general principle of law that is broken down into smaller, constituent pieces by later decisions. *Donoghue v Stevenson* [1932] AC 562 would qualify on both counts in the area of the existence of a duty in negligence.

In your outline, you should pay particular attention to conflicts or shifts in the law, since these are meaty areas for discussion and will therefore likely appear on examinations. If you see an opportunity to distinguish conflicting decisions, you are in luck, since that's an easy way to show off your legal skills. Areas of law that have experienced recent reform or activity are also likely to be the basis of examination questions, so you should make particularly detailed notes of those decisions. Be sure to know not only how the change has played out, but why it came about.

Perhaps the most sophisticated task is indicating to yourself how different areas of law relate to each other. For example, cases regarding the existence of a duty in tort can often also relate to questions about the standard of care, which usually falls under the heading of breach of duty. However, because the duty of care question is a legal issue that parties often bring to the court's attention as a preliminary matter, courts will reframe the dispute to suit their needs. This process also shows you how some cases fall under several different outline headings. Because a case can stand for several different propositions, it is important to indicate why you are citing it, otherwise you may confuse your reader.

For the most part, you should organize your materials in terms of legal issues. However, there are times when grouping information by factual similarities makes sense. For example, you may have a number of cases involving motor accidents. You will want to consider their similarities and differences, since you could confuse them in an exam situation and think every case is applicable to an auto accident simply because the facts are the same.

As the above demonstrates, revision is a time-consuming process, which is why you should not leave it until the last minute. While term time is very busy and stressful, studies on memory have shown that people learn best when they stretch it out over a period of time rather than trying to cram it all in at the last minute. This is particularly true when you are trying to understand deep conceptual issues; sleeping on a problem actually helps. Since you want to develop a deep analytical framework with lots of cross-references, you will want to take the time to build on those skills.

Legal commentary

The final category of materials that lawyers and law students can use in an examination situation is the one that most law students know best—legal commentary, which includes textbooks, articles, and treatises. In fact, these materials are the least important because they are nothing more than persuasive authority; since they have not been passed by a lawmaker (broadly defined as either the legislature or the court), they have no power to bind future decisions.

Revising from a textbook is a simple proposition and a skill that you have been honing at school for years. Textbooks, like lecture notes, provide general information and a structure for organizing other materials. However, neither should be considered the end-all or be-all of your legal studies. During the course of the term, you might also be asked to read an article that appears in a legal journal, rather than one of the excerpts in this book, or you might look up some of the sources listed as 'additional reading' on this book's companion website. Be careful when doing so. First, scholarly articles are written for academic audiences and therefore assume that the reader has a level of knowledge beyond that of the average student. Second, many articles focus on very narrow topics that could mislead a student into overvaluing a certain argument or proposition. Treatises are another form of legal commentary, but in this instance take the form of an entire book of analysis on a certain subject, again written for an academic or practitioner audience. The leading treatise in tort is by Clerk & Lindsell and is excellent, though incredibly detailed. Again, you may find it helpful to refer to a treatise to dig deeper into a particular issue, but the level of detail and analysis is likely much higher than you will need for your studies.

You now have a basic understanding of how to read, understand, and summarize the materials used in legal study. These skills—which are applicable to every area of the law—provide you with a suitable foundation from which to conduct your revision. Having set the stage, we can now move to the skills needed to apply the information you have gained to your essay or examination, either in tort or in another subject.

18.2.2 Elements of a good essay in law

One way to make sure that you are learning and revising properly is to know what will be expected of you on an examination. While the examination guidelines for your subject will always list the elements of the substantive law that could appear on your test, the guidelines seldom say what kind of analysis leads to a high mark. In fact, it is possible to identify the basic parameters that lead to a first class mark, a second class mark, and a third class mark. If your university makes those guidelines available to students, you should read them several times during the course of the term so that you can monitor your learning and focus on those areas that are most important to your examiners. If those standards are not already available to you, ask if you can see them. To do well, you need to know what your examiners want to see.

Although every examiner will have his or her own individual criteria for his or her substantive course, faculties typically have a set standard that everyone has agreed upon to ensure consistency between the different people marking an exam. As an example, however, most instructors would agree that a first-class essay displays the following characteristics:

- Close attention to the question as it is asked (as opposed to how one might wish it to be asked);
- Detailed knowledge of the topic that is the subject of the question, as well as a deeper understanding of the context in which that topic exists;
- Outstanding coverage of the question, in terms of both breadth and accuracy, with no or almost no significant errors or omissions relating to the law at issue;
- Discussion of at least some of the less obvious points of law;
- Exemplary clarity of structure, argument, and writing style;
- Excellent use of supporting authority and ideas;
- Use of more than one possible line of argument; and
- Inclusion of theoretical arguments concerning the subject, significant critical analysis, and thoughtful personal perspective on the issue.

Including all of these characteristics is obviously quite difficult, both in terms of time (since most examiners allow approximately 30 minutes per question in a timed examination) and in terms of knowledge, since it requires both memorization of materials as well as the kind of deeper understanding that lends itself to sophisticated analysis. Nevertheless, first class marks are possible, and it is easier to achieve high marks if you know what types of materials and skills you need to learn and display before you go into the examination room.

As you would expect, a good second-class mark falls slightly below the first-class standard in each of the various regards. Most examiners would agree that an essay earning a good 2:1 demonstrates the following characteristics:

- Attention to the question as it is asked;

- A good and relatively detailed knowledge of the topic that is the subject of the question, as well as a good understanding of the context in which that topic exists;

- Good coverage of the question, in terms of both breadth and accuracy, with few significant errors or omissions relating to the law at issue;

- Strong organization, argument, and writing style;

- Good use of supporting authority and ideas;

- Use of more than one possible line of argument; and

- Some degree of familiarity with theoretical arguments concerning the subject and a significant degree of critical analysis.

A low second-class mark falls slightly below a good second-class mark in some or all of these areas. An essay earning a low 2:1 would therefore include the following characteristics:

- Attention the subject matter that is at issue, but without a precise treatment of the particular question as it is asked;

- Satisfactory knowledge of the topic that is the subject of the question, as well as some understanding of the context in which that topic exists;

- Acceptable coverage of the question, with reasonable breadth and accuracy, though possibly diminished by substantial errors or omissions relating to the law at issue;

- Satisfactory organization, argument, and writing style;

- Acceptable use of supporting authority and ideas, albeit with a weak or insufficient theoretical or critical approach.

Finally, examiners would likely agree about the hallmarks of a third-class essay, which is the lowest passing mark. These submissions contain significant shortcomings in most areas under evaluation and demonstrate the following characteristics:

- Discussion of the subject matter that is at issue, but without sufficient attention to the particular question as it is asked;

- Some knowledge of the topic that is the subject of the question, as well as some understanding of the context in which that topic exists, albeit with lack of accuracy or breadth and possibly diminished by substantial errors or omissions relating to the law at issue;

- Some organization, argument, and ability to express ideas in written form; and

- Some use of supporting authority and ideas, despite a potential lack of clarity or relevance and offering little theoretical or critical analysis.

The more you understand what is required of you, the better you will be able to deliver it in an exam situation. Confer with your instructors to see whether they agree with the marking criteria listed above and ask how they interpret each element. See if they have model answers that illustrate each of these criteria—often it's easier to understand how to write a good essay if you have seen it done.

18.2.3 Using legal materials in an essay

NOTE Everyone—no matter their level of natural ability—must put in the time necessary to learn (and learn how to learn) the law.

The key to doing well in any course in law—including tort—is understanding the materials in the first place. That issue was covered above, and, as you learned, the most difficult thing about law is that it requires revision skills that you have never learned before. Reading, understanding, and summarizing legal materials is a qualitatively different task than any you have been asked to do before. Although some people may seem to catch onto legal analysis naturally, there are certain tricks of the trade that can help everyone improve their ability to understand and analyse legal materials.

However, a law student needs to do more than just learn how to use new and different types of materials. Reading law also requires you to change your way of thinking about the underlying materials and how you incorporate them into your essays. Doing so will, naturally, require you to change your revision habits. This is not to say that you should totally change everything you do. The mere fact that you have made it onto your course proves that you are intelligent and have good revision skills. However, the study of law is qualitatively different from the study of other subjects, and you need to supplement your approach to revision to take that difference into account. Analogies to other subjects you may have studied at school help illustrate these discrepancies, both in how you learn and in how you demonstrate your learning in an exam scenario.

Those people who studied the humanities at school (literature, history, politics, and the like) typically use supporting texts to illustrate the theories that they create in response to a question. Crafting an argument in the humanities often involves finding as much support as possible for the position stated. While contrary arguments can be brought forward, the emphasis is on identifying a position and providing logical support. Those who have studied the humanities know that sometimes it is easy to incorporate the primary texts into essays. For example, the question 'analyse the character of Mr Darcy in *Pride and Prejudice*' requires you to refer to the plot and dialogue of the novel. While you can refer to secondary texts (such as articles written by scholars in the field) to support your argument, the important thing is to base your analysis in the novel itself.

However, some disciplines don't always give such a ready route into primary texts. For example, a question about the causes of the First World War allows you to refer to the commentary of esteemed historians but does not require you to do so. You may earn higher marks by quoting other scholars, but you must also construct an independent theory out of facts that you have gleaned from various sources. While those sources can be named, they need not be, since facts such as date that Archduke Ferdinand was shot exist objectively, regardless of who reports that fact. You can obtain a very good mark even if you refer to only one or two authoritative sources, since your independent analysis of the problem is as important as, if not more important than, your ability to reproduce facts and commentary. Lawyers also must use this sort of creative, independent thinking in their arguments, though they typically rely on the theories of others as well. To win top marks, a student in law must be able to argue by analogy, just as a historian does, drawing fine points from seemingly disparate sources, while also citing to primary text, as a person reading literature does. In this way, the liberal arts provide an excellent shaping ground for those who take up the study of law.

However, those who took the sciences at school have a certain edge over humanities students, based on the different use and conceptualization of supporting authority. Scientists cannot analyse a problem in chemistry or calculus without providing the underlying scientific principles as part of the discussion. For example, one cannot prove an algebraic equation without proceeding step by step through different—but linked—mathematical principles in a logical manner. The source of the information is of minimal to no importance. For example, in a physics question, it is more important to know that $E=mc^2$ than to report that Albert Einstein said it or that it appears in your textbook on physics. Of course, you must know and state the significance of the equation $E=mc^2$ in your answer, while also ensuring that the equation is relevant to the question asked. Producing that particular equation in response to a question about organic chemistry will not win you any marks, even if the equation itself is correct, since the information you produce in your answer must pertain to the question asked. The same is true in law. You must produce correct and relevant statements of law to prove your point. You must also relate those statements in a logical order to persuade your reader that your conclusions are correct.

The above outlines the different ways that students coming to the law think about analysis and argument. To do well in a legal examination, however, you must supplement your existing analytical skills with those that mimic the skill set and approach of a practising lawyer. In particular, you must learn how a practising lawyer uses legal authority.

NOTE Even if you do not intend to practice law after taking your degree, you must learn to think like a lawyer to do well in an examination situation. In particular, you will do best to think like a barrister who must marshal law and facts to bolster a particular argument in court.

In your criminal law course, you either have learned or will learn about the ancient concept of *nulla poena sine lege*, which is Latin for 'no punishment without a law'. The idea is that the state may not punish someone unless it can prove that the defendant acted contrary to an established legal principle. Instead, the principle in question had to (1) exist prior to the time that the act occurred and (2) be well known enough so that the defendant could be said to be on notice that a penalty would arise if he or she acted contrary to that principle of law. The defendant need not have known personally about the specific rule of behaviour; all that is necessary is that the rule could have been discovered. The rationale behind the concept of *nulla poena sine lege* is that is unfair to punish someone for doing something that wasn't outlawed at the time.

The concept of *nulla poena sine lege* can apply to areas other than the criminal law. For example, the law of tort describes the circumstances in which people will be required take care of the wellbeing of others. If someone does not live up to that standard, courts—i.e. the law—will require the defendant to pay damages or provide some other sort of remedy to the injured party. Again, the standard regarding the required behaviour must be known in advance, since it's unfair to require people to pay damages for something that they didn't think was wrongful at the time.

As you have learned on your tort course, 'the law' consists of both judicial opinions and statutes. Both constitute binding legal authority, since courts must follow the rules laid down in those writings. In a case of first impression, where the court is free to act in any way it pleases, it may also consider persuasive authority in the form of judicial opinions from other jurisdictions (which are not binding), commentary from legal scholars, public policy rationales, and legislative papers.

In practice, lawyers use legal authority in ways that mimic the use of authorities in both the humanities and the sciences. Law is similar to the hard sciences in that it is important to state what principles have been proven and accepted by the scientific community as reflecting the true state of scientific understanding at the time of the discussion. Both lawyers and scientists must cite the pre-existing principles (be they theorems, axioms, statutes, or judicial opinions) in an orderly fashion to demonstrate that their conclusions are correct. Both lawyers and scientists must guard against the introduction of irrelevant information—such as $E=mc^2$ in an organic chemistry problem—since such information is extraneous to the problem at hand.

Law is dissimilar to the hard sciences in that there is seldom (if ever) one correct answer or one correct statement of law. As you have learned, law is a matter of nuance and persuasion, and you must look at all the authorities—even conflicting authorities—before you can reach a reasoned conclusion.

Those who have studied the humanities will appreciate the way that the law exists in shades of grey, rather than in black and white. Historians, for example, will know that while one person may argue that World War I was caused by X, another person may argue equally persuasively that World War I was caused by Y. A first-class historian will explicitly consider all possible theories before offering his or her conclusions as to why one particular approach should prevail. A second-class historian will construct a plausible theory which contains sufficient supporting authority for the suggested conclusion but which ignores any conflicting evidence. The same is true in the study of law. First-class students explicitly consider all possible arguments before weighing them up. Second-class students focus on only one way of reading the supporting authorities, either because they don't want to diminish the persuasiveness of their conclusions (which is not the case) or—more worryingly—because they only see one way of interpreting those materials.

NOTE To earn points, you must put your analysis on your paper—your examiner cannot join you in your head, nor can he or she give points for conclusory statements that lack any supporting authority or analysis. Be explicit about *why* you are saying what you are saying.

The study of law differs from the study of history quite radically in one respect. As mentioned above, historians can refer quite easily to objective facts (such as dates of known events) that do not require citation to underlying sources. Lawyers do not have this luxury. They must indicate the source of the law they cite, since a principle alone does not constitute law. The concept of *nulla poena sine lege* requires a principle of law to have been enunciated by a lawmaker prior to the act that is deemed unlawful—thus you must say not only what the principle is but also *who* said it, since the persuasiveness of a legal proposition depends on its source. To do well in law, you must identify where your material comes from.

Often, A-level students are taught to craft their arguments with broad brush strokes, focusing on big ideas and overarching themes. While there are times when law students can and should use broad, sweeping statements—for example, in response to a question designed to flush out public policy concerns or a particular theory of law—it is usually better and more profitable to delve into the details of the materials, sifting carefully through the cases and statutes to identify the important language and controversial issues. This detailed information constitutes the evidence which will support your larger arguments. If you jump straight to the conclusions that you have reached—i.e. the big themes—then you have failed not only to demonstrate your understanding of how legal arguments are constructed and your detailed knowledge about the content of the materials, but you have also failed to persuade your reader that your perspective is correct or at least sound. Thus, avoid saying 'X is true' without saying why X is true—you will do much better to say 'X is true because Y and Z show it to be true', since that gives your reader a basis for understanding your reasoning. In legal essays, the detailed discussion of legal materials that indicates why your conclusion is the best course of action.

NOTE At the end of the day, you don't necessarily have to convince your examiner that your argument is right. All you have to do is demonstrate that it is reasonable. The final conclusion—who wins or loses in a dispute, or which position should prevail as a matter of public policy or theory—is typically not as important as how you get there. To win maximum points, you must show how you arrived at your final answer.

18.3 Revising for a tort exam

18.3.1 General revision in tort

The preceding discussion outlined a number of general revision skills that apply to any substantive area of law: tort, contract, constitutional, property—whatever the subject matter, the skills are the same. There are some general principles that apply to the revision of tort law, however. Before addressing individual causes of action within the tort syllabus, it makes sense to discuss some of these general principles.

First, anyone preparing for an examination in law should pay particular attention to any significant changes in that field—in this case, tort—that have occurred within the last five years. Examiners are more than instructors; they are also legal academics, and they get excited about changes in the law. They also have written and read thousands of examinations over the years, and they are often eager to set a new question. Finally, with textbooks often lagging several years behind new developments in the law, testing on current legal events is often the best way to separate those who attend and pay attention in lecture from those who do not. Therefore, you should be ready for a question in a developing area of law. If you want to do particularly well, do some independent research and look up some scholarly articles on the subject; chances are, they will address the most contentious issue and give you additional insight into the problem. You won't have to do a lot of extra work to impress your examiner: simply by citing an unassigned research article, you set your essay apart from everyone else's. Since the law can change at a moment's notice (and it will take more than six months from the time of writing for this text to get to print), it doesn't make sense to advise you now what the new hot area will be—you have to figure that out for yourself.

TIP Most likely, your law library has a rack of recent legal publications. While you might want to scan some of the scholarly journals, it is even more worth your while to read some of the practitioner journals, especially the Law Society Gazette, which is published by the Law Society (the regulating body for solicitors). It contains brief snippets on recent developments in a variety of areas of law as well as articles about life in practice. Even if you don't intend to become a solicitor, it is useful reading.

You also should be prepared for questions with fact patterns that are based on current events. Examiners believe that students will feel more comfortable with facts that are familiar, but don't worry if you don't know the outcome of the real life case (unless it is a reported decision)—often the examiner is probably just using the issue to set the stage to illustrate common problems in tort, knowing that there is no final resolution of the real-life issue yet.

Second, there are several issues that are so central to tort that you know you will be examined on them in one way or another. Every year, students get these issues wrong, but that's not why examiners continue to test them. Examiners test these areas because they are fundamental to a proper understanding of tort law. Therefore, you should be prepared to answer questions on:

- Causation—*Overseas Tankship (UK) Ltd v Morts Dock and Engineering Co Ltd (The Wagon Mound)* [1961] AC 388 and its progeny are still alive and crying out to be discussed fully and rationally.

- Damages—you will likely get a question either on economic loss, psychiatric harm, or calculation of damages in personal injury and death, but not all three. Damages questions may also meld into causation and foreseeability analyses.

- Legislation—you will get at least one question that requires you to undertake a statutory analysis, though it cannot be said precisely which area it will cover.

NOTE Contrary to popular belief, examiners are not hoping that students will mess up on exams. Instead, readers want to give points to people and hope that every essay is clear, concise, and on point. It pains an instructor to see masses of students making the same mistake, year after year. Be prepared to be one of the few who nail these subjects in your examination.

Third, you will be asked to discuss more than one tort in a single question on at least one occasion. This can arise in one of two ways. In one scenario, you will have to answer a problem question (also known as a fact pattern question) that includes a variety of types of causes of action, either (1) all held by a single claimant who will need to assert all of them simultaneously (such as negligence, nuisance, and liability under *Rylands v Fletcher*) or (2) held by multiple claimants, each of whom will have a different type of action (such as straightforward negligence, negligence with psychiatric injury, and vicarious liability). If you have two claimants or two defendants who look similarly situated, stop—you're missing something. There will be some critical difference between them that you need to discuss. In the second possible scenario, you will be asked to compare and contrast two separate and unrelated torts in an essay question. Be prepared to answer these sorts of questions by considering similarities and differences between different torts rather than compartmentalizing your revision and analysis. There could be some other way that multiple torts arise in a single question, but these are the two most common.

The following sections consider each of the various torts in turn. However, rather than providing a ready-made outline, this chapter will provide guidance to help you create your own outline. Although students often prefer to be given a ready-made revision guide, this text is using this method for several reasons. First, you will learn the material much better if you do the bulk of the work yourself. Although simply memorizing something that you know is 'right' seems easier and less likely to result in error, learning the law is more than learning the names of cases and statutes; it is understanding how they fit together and the reasons why the law works as it does. If you understand those two points, you will find it much easier to remember cases and statutes, because they will all support (or, occasionally, contradict) more general concepts about the way society organizes itself. This deeper understanding will also allow you to manipulate the cases better (a hallmark of a good essay) and draw analogies between apparently disparate areas of law.

Second, each course in tort is different. Yours may not have covered everything in this book or may have included additional items on the syllabus—the law of animals, for example, or trespass to goods (also known as conversion). Similarly, your lecturer almost certainly emphasized different cases or statutes in class, since many different cases can be used to support the same propositions of law. Therefore, any outline that could be offered here would be misleading, since it would perhaps unduly emphasize certain cases that you did not learn about in lecture or miss out on those that your instructor thinks are particularly important. Such an outline would also fail to draw all of the necessary connections and cross-references.

NOTE If your lecturer failed to discuss some of the cases or statutes in this book, that's all right—the materials in this text are still good law, and you can cite them in an examination, if you wish. This book and your instructor will both give you the central, leading cases and statutes for each major point of law, so you will find the materials consistent. The one exception is if there has been a recent change in law; in that case, follow your instructor's lead, even if it contradicts what is in this text, since he or she will have the most up-to-date information.

Third, if this text provided you with an outline, that would encourage you to work independently of others. In fact, law is one of those areas of study where you can benefit from discussions with others, even those who are, as you are, still learning the law. Think of the reasonable person standard—while you may believe that your views are eminently reasonably, others' views may and in fact often do differ. You can learn a lot about alternative reading of cases and statutes by working with study partners. Some people even do their course outlining as a team, giving primary responsibility for outlining a certain section or tort to one person and then coming together later to supplement that person's draft with their own additional thoughts. While you will always know your own section best, working together is one way to make sure that all the work gets done (and often makes it more enjoyable, since sitting alone in a library can be dull at times!). Also, there's something about external deadlines and peer pressure—not to mention the fact that others are relying on you and/or judging your work—that ensures you actually get the work done in the time you set yourself.

As you begin your revision, remember that there is no single 'right' way of doing things. The law allows you to reach the same conclusion through many different means, so don't think there is one knock-out case that will control the issue (it's sometimes true, but very very seldom) or one single technique that will win the day. The truth is, the more work you do, the more you will understand and the better you will do; law is an area where sweat equity pays off.

Now we will address each of the torts considered in this text in turn.

18.3.2 Negligence

As you now know, negligence has developed as something of a catch-all tort, encompassing harms to an individual (both personal injury and death); to real property (meaning land); to personal property (such as cars, clothes, jewellery, or furniture—basically anything that can be owned, other than real property); and even to intangible interests such as economic interests. Because the interests protected are so diverse, so, too, are the ways in which negligence can arise. For the most part, you will need to be able to apply the law of negligence to exam questions that include facts that are legally similar, rather than factually similar, to the cases you have studied. There are some exceptions, of course—questions involving liability of or to children and liability of professionals or experts will, for the most part, require you to rely on cases that are factually similar. However, that is because the cases in this area of law must be factually similar to be legally similar.

Because negligence is such a broad issue, you should break your revision down into separate parts, since any question you will be asked in an examination will likely focus primarily on only one area. Here, your analysis should follow the common elements of the tort: duty, breach, and damage (also known as causation/remoteness). You also need to consider the defences to negligence. When considering duty, you must know the modern parameters of the 'neighbour principle', including not only the categories of people to whom a duty is owed, but also the manner in which a new duty can be established. Both of these issues will require you to consider proximity. Furthermore, you need to know how to handle special cases in negligence—children, professionals, public authorities—as well as special circumstances, such as emergencies. All of these factors bear on whether a duty is owed to an injured person.

When considering whether a breach has occurred, you must focus on the amount and type of care that must be taken in any particular situation (often called the standard of care). You must be comfortable with the 'reasonable man' or 'reasonable person' standard and any deviations from that particular norm for special categories of persons, such as children or professionals. Foreseeability of harm also becomes an issue with breach of duty questions. Furthermore, courts considering these kinds of questions will consider competing interests (for example, the type and severity of harm versus the social merit of the activity causing the harm), so you will need to know what concerns carry weight with the court. Consider any suggestions for reform when revising this material. Finally, you should bear in mind the rules of evidence and civil procedure, particularly as they affect the doctrine of *res ipsa loquitur*, since that provides for an alternate means of proving breach.

The third element that must be proven in an action for negligence is damage, which is often considered in terms of causation. Because negligence law reflects the fluid boundaries of a common law tort, causation—in terms of proximity and foreseeability—also plays a role in the first two elements of negligence (duty and breach of duty). However, you will need to know this subject—particularly the difference between the 'but for' test and the remoteness test very well, since it often forms the basis of an examination question. Thus, you will need to revise the various types of damage and whether they are recoverable in negligence, as well as the question of whether an injury that has been caused by more than one person can support a claim in negligence. When there are multiple causes of injury, you should know the difference between a concurrent cause and series of causes. You also will need to know issues involving long-term causes of harm. You might want to cross-reference this discussion with your notes on calculation of damages, since some long-term causes of harm could be addressed through structured settlements, which is discussed in the chapter on damages. Chains of causation are also an important issue in both negligence and in other torts, so you will want to cross-reference the points made here with points made in other parts of the syllabus. This chapter also introduces the defendant's own negligence (which is covered in more detail in the next chapter) and special characteristics of the defendant (the 'egg-shell skull rule'), which are another set of often-tested subjects.

Finally, you will need to be aware of defences to negligence. This is an area that will require lots of cross-referencing to other torts, since the major discussion of general defences appears in the section on negligence, despite its applicability to other torts. You will need to be familiar with consent, acceptance of the risk of injury, and illegality as means of defending against a claim in tort. Contract-based defences you will need to know include exclusion of liability, either through a notice or disclaimer. For these defences, you will want to discuss the Unfair Contract Terms Act 1977 in some detail. Limitation periods are a defence that operate as a matter of law, meaning that they arise regardless of what the defendant and claimant have done. However, they are seldom tested, since few instructors require students to know the limitations period for individual torts. You will want to be very familiar with the concept of contributory negligence, discussed here in detail, since that is always tested. Also be sure to remember that contributory negligence can be used as a defence in cases other than negligence; don't let the name throw you.

18.3.3 Breach of statutory duty

Although breach of statutory duty obviously deals with statutes, it is not a statute-based tort in the same way that occupiers' liability or defamation is, since there is not a single piece of legislation dealing with a single issue that describes the duties and defences in detail. The tort of breach of statutory duty also bears little resemblance to negligence. Instead, liability here is determined not on what the hypothetical 'reasonable person' would do in any given circumstance, but as a result of a determination by Parliament that certain standards of behaviour must be met. However, Parliament's primary purpose in enacting the legislation in issue was not to define a duty in tort; instead, the purpose is entirely unrelated to tort. For example, the statute in question could deal with issues such as animal health and safety, the provision of public services, or transportation of hazardous goods. Thus, to analyse a question involving breach of statutory duty, you need to know when a private remedy is given for the breach of a civil duty based on a statute existing outside of tort. To do so, you will need to glean Parliamentary intent from a potentially vague piece of legislation. Once a duty is established, you will need to know how to evaluate whether it has been breached and whether the damage is causally linked to the defendant's actions. Remember that the test for remoteness here differs slightly from that used in negligence. Finally, you again need to know which defences are available to this particular tort.

NOTE The one up side to an examination question involving breach of statutory duty is that it is easy to identify it as such, since, to ask the question, your examiner will have to provide a real or imaginary statute (unless it is a question focusing on theory, in which case it will still probably mention the tort by name). While there are a few instructors who will throw a statute into a question as a red herring just to throw you off, most won't. Just be sure to check for the presence of other possible torts, in addition to breach of statutory duty, when answering the question.

18.3.4 Torts involving land

Questions involving land-based torts are easy to recognize on an examination, since someone, somewhere, will own a piece of real property. The potentially difficult part is identifying which of the three (or four, depending on how you count it) land-based torts is at issue. The best way to do that is to cross-reference your revision outlines so that you know which elements are common to the different torts and which are unique. This task should not be too onerous, since the land-based torts are relatively straightforward, either because they are based on well-defined statutes or because they deal with a type of harm (nuisance, trespass) that is limited in scope and familiar to the layperson.

TIP Land-based torts are one of the areas where you are likely to find a claimant in a problem question with multiple causes of action. The claimant may not be able to prevail on all of them, but you should explicitly consider any cause of action that is reasonable to bring.

When revising this area of law, remember that you are dealing with an injury that arises out of the use, ownership, or occupation of land. Therefore, you need to know what constitutes the use of land; ownership of land (though this will not be heavily or deeply tested, since it is more of a question for your property law course); and, most importantly, occupation of land. These questions will pervade each of the four torts in this section, and the law is relatively consistent between the different causes of action. Thus, you can use a case describing ownership or occupation under one of the Occupiers' Liability Acts to address ownership or occupation issues in a trespass or nuisance case. However, you need to be clear that you are drawing analogies across different torts. Also be sure that whatever point you are making does not depend entirely on a quirk of law that is relevant only to one tort—for example, don't draw an analogy from an occupiers' liability case to a nuisance case if the point you're making relies on a provision of the one of the Occupiers' Liability Acts.

To do well in this area of law, you will need to know the Occupiers' Liability Act 1957 and the Occupiers' Liability Act 1984 in detail. This often puts students off, since they think that they must memorize the entire statute. Remember, you may be able to bring a statute book into the examination, so it's not as hard as it seems—just ask your instructor well in advance of your revision what kinds of materials are permissible. Furthermore, this area of law requires an entirely different type of analysis than common law torts do. Again, this can lead people to hesitate about writing on occupiers' liability, since they don't feel as comfortable with the process as they do with common law torts, but that simply means that your essay has more of a chance to stand out. The key is to know the relevant provisions of the two Occupiers' Liability Act 1984 and the Occupiers' Liability Act 1957 very well, in addition to the cases that construe those statutes. You already know where the problematic areas of the statute are—those are the areas that have lots of case law. Furthermore, you need to know what the common duty of care is—that will virtually always form a part of a question concerning occupiers' liability. Be sure to know the cases involving children, which often arise in examinations. Since this is one of the areas where contract law and tort law overlap, be sure to familiarize yourself with the Unfair Contract Terms Act 1977, since it affects the ability of an occupier (or in some cases, a non-occupier) to limit liability. The 'reasonableness test' under the Unfair Contract Terms Act 1977 is a particularly ripe area for examination, since it will require recourse to various judicial opinions.

When it comes to nuisance, private nuisance is by far more important than public nuisance, although you may need to distinguish the two as a secondary matter in one of your answers. Be sure to know how to define 'substantial' and 'unreasonable' in terms of the interference with the claimant's property, and know how the test for amenity nuisance differs from the test for nuisance arising out of a physical interference with the claimant's land. The question of who constitutes a proper claimant is one that is often tested; be sure to know what level of control over the property is necessary for a claimant to be able to recover. Once you know what level of control over the property will open someone up to liability, figure out the extent to which that person (or entity, such as a company or public authority) must have contributed to the situation that caused the injury. Because nuisance carries both special remedies and special defences, you should be prepared to discuss those in any examination question as well as the elements of the tort itself. As for public nuisance—which is a cause of action that is seldom successfully made out and thus seldom tested—it is probably enough to be familiar with the general criteria for who can pursue a case.

For a while, examination questions involving *Rylands v Fletcher* were popular, as instructors tested students' knowledge of the foreseeability element required in that tort and the overlap between *Rylands v Fletcher* and nuisance. That no longer seems to be the case, but it is still possible that you will see a question requiring you to discuss the two causes of action together.

Most torts do not require you to bring a historical perspective to the matter, but *Rylands v Fletcher* may be one of them. Certainly you should know the original decision and how the basic principles have shifted over the years. *Rylands v Fletcher* is also one of the strict liability torts, so you should be aware of what that means in an otherwise fault-based system. When it comes to the elements of the tort, you should know who can constitute a proper defendant and a proper claimant, but it is more important to know the concept of escape, non-natural user and, of course, foreseeability. Foreseeability leads naturally into a discussion of the various defences to an action in *Rylands v Fletcher*, one of which is to claim that the injury was not reasonably foreseeable.

Finally, you will need to know at least the basics of trespass to land. Trespass to land is not one of the trickier or flashier torts that examiners like to address, but it is one of the intentional torts, which are often overlooked because they are considered too simple to form the basis of an interesting examination question. Thus, you might see trespass to land wrapped into another land-based tort question as a secondary matter. It is doubtful that a trespass to land question will stand entirely on its own. To do well, you will need to know the basic legal tests for the defendant's mental state, the defendant's physical acts, and the claimant's connection to the property. When you have a trespass question, there will likely be no physical damage to the property, which will test your knowledge of the tort as one which is per se. Alternatively, the question may suggest that the defendant had no choice but to go onto the land (or injure the land), which raises the defence of necessity. These are interesting questions, but should not take up too much of your revision time.

18.3.5 Damages and other remedies

Damages is a popular examination issue, since, in many cases, a claimant must prove the existence of damage as a required part of the tort. Be sure to know which torts require damage to be present as part of the claimant's affirmative case and which torts do not (also known as torts per se). Damages are also popular with examiners because they require students to show different kinds of skills than other types of questions do. Here, you will need to know lots of different vocabulary (nominal damages, contemptuous damages, special damages, exemplary damages, etc) and must be able to apply both the words and the concepts appropriately. Furthermore, you will need to know which types of damages are recoverable in which torts. For example, some types of actions allow recovery for personal injury unrelated to injury to property and others do not. You need to know what is recoverable in what circumstances.

Damages questions also require you to consider issues such as awards for future damages or speculative damages. This will require you to be familiar with the mathematical calculations needed to quantify those kinds of awards, as well as the availability of structured settlements. You might get a theory question about the propriety of awards for future damages.

Finally, you will need to know the availability of other kinds of remedies, such as injunctions. You will also need to know the manner in which an award of damages can be minimized or shifted to another party, which requires you to understand the concepts of mitigation of damage, contributory negligence, and contribution.

18.3.6 Special kinds of harm

The chapters on negligence suggested the difficulties associated with recovery for special types of harm, and it is likely that you will be tested on either psychiatric damage or economic loss. To answer a question concerning psychiatric harm, you will need to know the kind of psychiatric injuries that are recoverable as well as the type of acts that give rise to a recognizable claim in tort. However, the area most often tested is the difference between primary and secondary victims, since that determination will affect all further analysis. Because recovery for psychiatric harm has come about relatively recently, you might be tempted to undertake a historical analysis, but be careful about doing so unless you are specifically asked that question; there have been enough developments in this area of law for examiners to be more concerned about the current state of affairs than the evolution of the law.

Economic loss is another area where students are tempted to dive into a historical analysis, going back either to the genesis of the action or the cases around the time of *Hedley Byrne & Co v Heller* [1964] AC 465. Again, be very wary of doing so unless specifically invited to do so by your examiner. Instead, focus on the types of damage that are recoverable; the special relationship that must exist; and issues involving causation and proximity. The reliance factor will also be an issue. Examiners are likely as interested in analyses that show why a claimant cannot recover as they are by analyses that show a claimant can recover, so don't assume that you must find for the claimant (or, conversely, against the claimant). If you can focus on applying the cases to the facts in your question, without trying to achieve a certain outcome, you will do better. Finally, this is one of the areas where there is a possible overlap between claims in tort and claims in contract—be sure to know how these two fields of law interact.

The last type of special harm involves defamation, which protects the reputation of the claimant. While you will definitely need to know the elements of the tort, such as what constitutes a statement, defamatory in nature, referring to the claimant and published in the necessary manner, the bulk of any examination question will likely lie with the defences to the tort. Any one of the many defences is fair game, but qualified privilege—as the most complicated of the defences—is the most likely to be the subject of a theoretical or problem question, with fair comment and justification following as the next two most popular examination issues. The statutory distributor's defence also pops up with some regularity. While you should know the difference between libel and slander, the difference between defamation and the developing law of privacy is likely to be a more popular subject for examination. Know all the newest cases in this area, as well as the provisions of the European Convention on Human Rights and the Human Rights Act 1998 that allow such a cause of action to be brought in the British courts. Defamation is a popular area for examination because it involves both a statute—the Defamation Act 1996—and lots of common law quirks, particularly those concerning true and false innuendo.

NOTE Defamation is not covered on every tort syllabus. If you have not covered it, obviously you will not be tested on it.

18.3.7 Product liability

Product liability—as both a statutory claim and a strict liability tort—can be popular on exams. You will need to know the relevant legislation quite well, in addition to the key cases construing that legislation and the common law 'narrow rule'. You should also be prepared to use product liability as an example for any theoretical questions that focus on strict liability issues.

18.3.8 Liability for the torts of others

Vicarious liability, as described in most introductory tort texts, focuses almost entirely on the employer-employee relationship. As such, it is important to know the differences between employees and independent contractors, as well as the impact that that determination has on the liability of the employer. Be sure to create a list of the circumstances in which an employer cannot avoid liability by hiring an independent contractor. Furthermore, be aware of the circumstances that take an employee out of the course of his or her employment, thus releasing the employer from liability.

18.3.9 Torts against the person

Finally, you need to know the law regarding intentional torts against the person—assault, battery, and false imprisonment. These are the oldest actions in the tort syllabus, and you should not feel bad about citing precedent dating back hundreds of years. While you should, of course, cite as many recent cases as you can, the courts are not shy about citing leading cases from the seventeenth or eighteenth century, so you should not be either.

Because the three torts are very similar in the concept of intent—and because both this text and many lecturers use cases on battery to stand in for cases on intent in the other two torts—be sure that you have cross-referenced the decisions so that you have sufficient authority for each of the torts. This is also true for trespass to land—the intent element will be the same as with the three intentional torts against the person, which, as you recall, are also called trespass to the person. Beyond that, you will need to know the difference between the two types of assault and what constitutes 'confinement' for false imprisonment. Because the elements of these torts are relatively straightforward, this is an area where you are likely to be tested as much on the defences to a cause of action as on the tort itself. Therefore, be sure that you know not only the defences that are unique to these torts but also those general defences—such as contributory negligence—that can offset a claimant's liability.

 For more revision tips, including self-test questions and suggestions for further reading, see the Online Resource Centre at www.oxfordtextbooks.co.uk/orc/strong_complete/.

revision tasks

The preceding sections should have given you plenty to do, but if you need more ideas on how to prepare yourself, consider the following:

- Create a vocabulary list, if you have not already.
- Cross-reference as many torts as possible, focusing on:
  - those causes of action that might arise simultaneously out of the same set of facts;
  - instances in which you can borrow cases from one type of case for use in another; and
  - areas of confusion, for example where cases cannot properly be used in any but one line of analysis.
- List which damages are recoverable in which causes of action.
- List which torts are per se.
- List which statutes apply to which causes of action.
- List issues of foreseeability/causation that fall across different torts, as well as their attendant cases.
- List public policy issues that can go on either side of a debate.
- List theoretical debates that you are prepared to discuss in an exam situation, as well as the support on either side of those debates.

Index

Index

461